The objectives of the attacking American foot soldier were relatively simple and always consisted of "take a hill and hold it".

The foot soldier (the grunts) literally fought for every inch of ground, in the most inhospitable climates, seemingly on almost every island in the Pacific.

Dad and Martinson became very good friends during the war. Leonard Martinson from Audubon, MN was killed in Manila while fighting next to Dad.

For several years after the war I was told Dad visited Martinson's widow to keep a promise they both shared while together in the war:

Whoever makes it back will visit the other's widow on their wedding anniversary date. 2 ½ hours NW of Belgrade, Minnesota and one hour east of Fargo, North Dakota. 192 miles one way. This trip was made by Dad and Mom for several years after the war.

They were together through basic training, across the Pacific to the Fiji Islands, New Hebrides, Guadalcanal, New Georgia, Bougainville, and finally, the Philippines. Now, back to the states in spirit only.

TABLE OF CONTENTS

Page

FOREWARD

Initially this was to be a manuscript about my Dad before, during and after World War II. I wrote 118 pages, thinking it was complete. I traced Dad's birthplace in Everett, Washington to his final home in Belgrade, Minnesota and told about some of what he did as a young man. Then I follow his draft date, basic training and eventually arriving on the Fiji Islands. I wrote about only the islands Dad was on while in the Pacific; Fiji, New Hebrides, Guadalcanal, New Georgia, Bougainville and the Philippines. I discussed briefly the skirmishes and added maps and pictures of those islands.

As I was researching data from the many internet resources, I started following Dad's Buckeye Division, and comparing them to his travels from letters and pictures he had sent home. I became more and more interested in strategies, the many different circumstances affecting the war, the many advances in manufacturing and logistics before and during the war, life style changes due to the war, and the overall cohesiveness of a nation coming together in a time of need. I kept writing and re-searching and discovered even more information over and above the dates and lo-cations of battle.

Included are several land, sea and air battles in this book and the success of Opera-tion Cartwheel. I left out many that were just as important towards victory over Japan. Important because of the strategies towards winning the war and the result-ing loss of American lives. Many initiatives took place on the Home Front involving: incarceration, rationing, farming, manufacturing, logistics and medicine.

Guadalcanal, Midway, Bougainville, Philippines, Iwo Jima, Okinawa; These names, and the names of many other battles and campaigns from the Pacific Theater during World War II, serve as a kind of brutal shorthand for scenes of unspeakable car-nage and, at times, unfathomable courage.

But for reasons lost to the decades, countless other pivotal battles in the Pacific have been largely forgotten by most of the world—even as they're remembered and commemorated by those who lost husbands, brothers, fathers, grandfathers and friends to the war. The long, long, three-and-half-year New Guinea Campaign, for example, saw scores of battles as bloody and as strategically vital as any others fought during WWII, but the names and places of many of those battles strike no chord with the general public.

Also forgotten were the many island and atoll skirmishes along with the air and sea battles that were so costly in lives but advanced the push to Japan. Some of the island chains were the Solomon Islands, Admiralty Islands, Russell Islands, Aleutian

Islands, Gilbert Islands, Santa Cruz Islands, Caroline Island s, Marshall Islands, Mariana Islands, Melanesia Islands, Philippine Islands, and Ryukyus Islands.

This book takes you through the pre-war struggles at home and the many battles in the Pacific from north of Australia all the way to Japan. Not in a straight line, but several chronological battles zigzagging northward to the Land of the Rising Sun.

Highly relevant today, World War II has much to teach us, not only about the profession of arms, but also about military preparedness, global strategy, and combined operations in the coalition war against fascism. In addition, how a nation came together in support of a common goal.

The Japanese dominated Asia, crippled the U.S. Navy after the Pearl Harbor attack, and seized most Western colonies in the Pacific.

A war cannot achieve what peace can. The forces of peace can rule over ignorance, illiteracy, immorality, physical suffering, and governmental oppression.

Japanese Battle Flag

"In peace, sons bury their fathers.

In war, fathers bury their sons." Herodotus

I   INTRODUCTION

Thanks to my Aunt Betty Krug (Dad's sister) who told me about fifteen years after Dad's death she tried researching his route during World War II. It was then that I started putting together a timeline from photo albums and letters Dad had sent and brought home from the war. He kept most all of his experiences of the war to himself. There were times I would ask him about the war when I lived at home and he would change the subject. These must have been hurtful memories he did not want to surface.

Now here I am, retired, finally putting dates and locations together during Dad's service in WWII. This book would be incomplete without showing the many influences and decisions before and during the war.   My parents home and where their children were raised:

Belgrade, Minnesota   1940 census = pop. 553   Stearns County west central MN.

Just imagine what your life would be like without the war. My dad in **1941** was the interim publisher, between owners, of the Belgrade Tribune for the months of November and December 1941. He was also the Linotype operator and typesetter. This was during the time of high unemployment. Not a lot of options in Belgrade, Minnesota at that time. He would not have been a veteran eligible to become a federal postal employee. He would not have been a rural mail carrier for thirty plus years. My parents paid most of my way through college and am not sure if I would have attended. I would not have had the experiences of living and working in Iowa, Texas, Georgia and Florida. I would not have the family I have now or my two beautiful granddaughters. I would more than likely be living in Minnesota enjoying a different family with two to three children, a dog, fishing boat, snowmobile and snow blower. What would have happened to my sister and mother if Dad was killed during the war? I would not be here.

Dad never talked about the war while us kids were growing up. He started opening up about the war after he started attending his Army reunion in Chicago which was during the last few years of his life. Dad passed on **March 16, 1990** at the age of 75. He gave us an excerpt from the 2nd Battle of Bougainville with comments written on the side he had received at one of his reunions. He did mention he was wounded in that battle but never mentioned much else that I remember about the war. The excerpt he brought home was a 'boots on the ground' narrative talking specifically of his division and regiment on Bougainville and around Hill 700. He had several factual comments written on the borders of the paper.

Three of the men that were with him in the Pacific and at these reunions attended his funeral and came all the way from Illinois. I so wish I would have taken the opportunity to visit with them. Dad had a military funeral and during the playing of taps a flock of geese flew over in their familiar V pattern honking away during the twenty one gun salute. How appropriate and every time I see and hear that flock of geese fly over I stop, look up, and ponder of all the good times we used to have together.

I have researched the internet and have tried to tie in dates and locations with Dad's pictures and letters he brought and sent home. I can't be sure my Dad was in some of these actual battles and circumstances. However, his division was in them or very close to them.

When I started researching the history of World War II in the Pacific I couldn't stop myself from digging deeper and deeper knowing that this was the environment and conditions that my Dad and others experienced. My research took me to the build-up of Japan's empire, the "homefront" with the trials and tribulations that people at home were incurring.

It is quite fascinating to me of the developments made in the **1930's** that improved battle conditions and shortened the length of both theaters of battle. There were so many firsts in the name of military strength in the Pacific, it was difficult to include all of them.

My research of the war in the Pacific led me to the many islands, chains of islands and atolls that the Allies fought the Japanese and the strategies that both Japanese and American leaders used with the Allies eventual victory.

Put yourself in the shoes of the foot soldier in the Pacific being in those climatic conditions of heat, humidity and monsoon like rains. Or the freezing temperatures of Alaska. Chances of contracting diseases, impenetrable jungles, wading through chest high rivers and swamps, not knowing when you were going to meet the enemy. Hopping from island to island, foxhole to foxhole. Fighting to take over a hill on an island only to find out you had to fight for the same hill the next day. Hoping you get to see another day.

II Before WWII, Seabees and Army Engineers

Grandpa & Grandma Madsen's children in order of age:

Elmer born March 27, 1914 in Everett, WA.
Archie born October 14, 1915 in Holden, Alberta, Canada.
Alice born July 16, 1917 in Denbigh, ND.
Bobby born April 5, 1919 in Aberdeen, SD.
Donny born March 31, 1924 in Aberdeen, SD.
Betty born November 8, 1925 in Aberdeen, SD.
Richard & Russell (twins) born November 12, 1928 in Belgrade, MN.

Christ Madsen was born in Rorvig, Denmark in 1886, son to Laurits Christian and Hanne Rasmussen. He came to America in 1906 at the age of 20. He worked in Iowa, South Dakota and Everett, Washington, where he met and married Christine Westergard in 1913. My research finds my Grandpa Madsen moving to and living in Danish communities throughout his travels. Christine was born in 1891 at Belgrade, Minnesota, the daughter of Christ and Anne Marie Westergard who moved to Belgrade from Denmark in 1889. They were early pioneers in the Belgrade (Crow Lake) area. Christine's parents moved to Everett, Washington around 1907 where they had relatives and her father continued in the construction business.

Dad's parents moved a lot ending up in Belgrade in 1927. Dad lived in four states and Canada by the time he was thirteen. Their final move to Belgrade from Aberdeen, South Dakota was in a 1923 Model T Ford, an all-day drive in those days (190 miles). Grandma, Grandpa and six children ages 13, 12, 10, 8, 3, 2. Their household goods had been shipped by rail to their new home.

For many years they lived on the edge of Belgrade with no houses to the southeast of their house. The property included a barn and pasture where they raised a cow, pigs and chickens. The livestock provided meat and the cow produced milk for the family and cream to be churned into butter. My Uncle Archie told me that dad helped provide food on the table by shooting rabbits.

When I hunted pheasant with Dad he used to tell me you only need to take the shells you need to shoot your limit. The hidden meaning was 'that way you will learn not to miss'. Whether it was ducks or pheasant it was not unusual for Dad to shoot two with one shot.   This was told to me as a youngster and also as a young hunter who personally saw his shooting accuracy. I'm guessing he would have made every shot count in this war.

Everyone owned a radio for news and entertainment. Televisions were not yet part of the rural Minnesota household. Newspapers, radio and word of mouth were the way news was spread to rural Minnesota households. The floor model type radio was still used into the early 1950's as I remember it as a little guy, born in **1950**, when I visited my grandparents.

Golden Age of American radio

American radio industry

WRITTEN BY: **The Editors of Encyclopædia Britannica**

Golden Age of American radio, period lasting roughly from 1930 through the 1940s, when the medium of commercial broadcast radio grew into the fabric of daily life in the United States, providing news and entertainment to a country struggling with economic depression and war.

During American radio's Golden Age, much of the programming heard by listeners was controlled by advertising agencies, which conceived the shows, hired the talent and staff (sometimes drawing performers directly from the old vaudeville theatre circuit), and leased airtime and studio facilities from the radio networks. Programs became fixed in quarter-hour and half-hour blocks and featured a wide variety of formats. Soap operas such as *Ma Perkins* and *The Guiding Light* kept housewives company through the afternoon.

Children listened to the adventure series *Little Orphan Annie* and the science-fiction show *Flash Gordon*. *Amos 'n' Andy*, a situation comedy, was the most popular show ever broadcast, lasting more than 30 years. *The Shadow*, a crime drama, also had a loyal following. "Prestige" anthology shows brought together writers such as Archibald MacLeish and Norman Corwin with actors from the legitimate stage such as Helen Hayes and Orson Welles, and film-based anthology shows such as *The Lux Radio Theatre* and *Academy Award Theater* featured movie stars of the day reading live radio versions of their motion-picture roles. In 1938 Welles's radio adaptation of H.G. Wells' science-fiction tale *The War of the Worlds* created panic when listeners failed to hear the disclaimer and believed Martians actually were invading Earth.

On radio's musical front, the National Broadcasting Company established its own symphony orchestra, led by Italian conductor Arturo Toscanini. On live "band remotes" carried from ballrooms in New York City and Chicago, big bands led by the likes of Artie Shaw, Benny Goodman, and Tommy Dorsey played popular dance music for listeners around the country.

Programming turned political when Pres. Franklin D. Roosevelt used radio to talk directly to Americans in his "fireside chats." News events such as the Lindbergh baby kidnapping and the Hindenburg disaster captured the nation's attention.

In the early 1940s, World War II catalyzed the growth of network news, as local stations depended on the major networks' overseas correspondents. Young reporters such as Edward R. Murrow, William Shirer, and Walter Cronkite covered breaking news at the front, while commentators such as Walter Winchell analyzed events at home. Some radio programming was used for propaganda purposes, while other programs were aimed at keeping up the morale of the public such as Kate Smith performing with studio musicians. The war years clearly raised the profile of radio's role in society.

Fifty million Americans watched newsreels every week in one of 14,000 theatres.

More than 30 government agencies were involved in censorship, but newspaper managing editors were often stricter than the censors.

President Roosevelt set up the Office of Censorship right after Pearl Harbor.

✦ ✦ ✦ ✦

Katharine Phillips while at PBS wrote about the war at home and the following are excerpts of her articles.

"The worst worries we had about the war was just death. We just never knew when we'd lose someone that we loved. Our best friend. The boy that was the brother of your best friend. We lived in constant fear of the telegrams. Each day we would read the list in the newspaper to see if we could identify any of the names that were there."

During World War II most Americans followed the news of the war through three sources: radio broadcasts, newsreels and newspapers. Newsreels preceded the movies at their local theatres and there were more than 11,000 newspapers in the country during that time. These sources played a vital role in connecting the home front with the war front and kept Americans informed about the progress of the fighting overseas as well as its impact on their communities.

War correspondents in World War II spent a good deal of time with the troops, close to and sometimes on the front lines – in planes, aboard ships and on the ground. Their vivid radio broadcasts brought the war into the nation's living rooms as families regularly gathered around to hear about what was happening overseas.

Motion picture newsreels included dramatic footage of combat, uplifting stories about the war effort, and segments featuring politicians and generals explaining the latest developments and strategies.

Government control of the news was comprehensive. All news about the war had to pass through the Office of War Information (OWI) and they suppressed visual material that it feared would threaten domestic unity. A *"Code of Wartime Practices for the American Press"* was issued on **January 15, 1942** giving strict instructions on proper handling of news. The code was voluntarily adopted by all of the major news organizations and implemented by the more than 1,600 members of the press accredited by the armed forces during the war. The government also relied heavily on reporter's patriotism, which ensured that in their dispatches from the front lines, they tended to accentuate the positive.

As the war dragged on, and casualties mounted, citizens scanned the front pages to see if anyone they knew had been wounded, or was missing in action, or killed.

"You started to realize that this isn't just going over there and winning the peace and then coming back. They're not coming back. Some of them aren't," Anne DeVico said. *"you'd pick up the paper and somebody was killed in action. Well, your whole atmosphere, everything changes. Your whole being is feeling for that person and thinking, 'Geez, they're not going to get home. They're not going to get married. They're not going to see their children."*

In the fall of 1943, after almost two years at war, concerns about public complacency led government officials to begin to allow the publication of images that showed the true cost of war. In the **September 20, 1943** issue of LIFE magazine, the editors published a photograph taken on a New Guinea beach in the South Pacific, ten months earlier. It was the first image of dead American servicemen that American civilians were allowed to see in the 21 months since Pearl Harbor.

A few months later, the War Department also produced a film called *"With the Marines at Tarawa"* containing combat footage more brutal than anything ordinary Americans had yet seen. This is a 1944 short propaganda documentary film directed by Louis Hayward. It used authentic footage taken at the Battle of Tarawa to tell the story of the American servicemen from the time they get the news that they are to participate in the invasion to the final taking of the island and raising of the Stars and Stripes. The film shows getting the secret orders from a destroyer shooting a rope across the bow of the ship and attaching the secret orders in a bag to be pulled across the ocean between ships.

Some in Washington argued that its release would damage morale. But President Roosevelt himself ordered that it be shown. He wanted to show Americans a clearer sense of what their men were facing. President Roosevelt consulted the only man who was present at the Battle of Tarawa that he personally knew and trusted, *Time-Life* photographer Robert Sherrod. Quoting Sherrod, *"I tell the President the truth. Our soldiers on the front want people back home to know that they don't knock the hell out of them every day of every battle. They want people* to understand that war is a horrible, nasty business, and to say otherwise is to do a disservice to those who died." Based on Sherrod's prompting, FDR agreed to release the film, uncensored.

"When we saw those first pictures of Tarawa we were overcome, just overcome," Katharine Phillips said. *"It was just devastating to us. Those American boys' bodies floating in the surf. We just sat around and cried and I know that is why they had kept it from the American public for so long."*

Reaction to the film across the country was strong – enlistment went down and bond sales went up. In the coming years even more newsreels and photographs were released showing increasingly graphic images of death and destruction.

✦ ✦ ✦ ✦

The end of World War II in **1945** roughly coincided with the arrival of commercial television, and this new medium—which added the visual element to radios tried-and-true formula of sound and immediacy—soon drew creative talent, listener loyalty, and advertising revenue away from radio. Some stars and programs from the last years of American radio's Golden Age successfully transferred to television—for instance, the comedians George Burns and Gracie Allen, the soap opera *The Guiding Light*, the situation comedy *Father Knows Best*, the police drama *Dragnet*, and the western *Gunsmoke*. Others, however, disappeared from the airwaves. Live big bands, for instance, were scrapped in favor of recorded rock and roll, which was played on local programs by voluble and irreverent disc jockeys. By the mid-1950s American radio had moved beyond its Golden Age to modern formats such as "Top 40," "alternative" FM, talk shows, and public-service programming.

✦ ✦ ✦ ✦

During the 1930's – 1950's the three networks were ABC, CBS and NBC. Many of these programs were in the evening on the radio. The sponsors were the advertising agencies, which conceived the shows, hired the talent, leased airtime and studio facilities from the radio networks. Some of the radio programs transitioned over to television during the 1950's.

Below is an example of the radio programming schedule with the sponsors.

Day	Time	Network	Series	Sponsor	Years
varies	varies	CBS, NBC, ABC	Adventures of Ellery Queen	Bromo Seltzer, Anacin	1939 - 1948
varies	8:00 PM	ABC, CBS, NBC	Adventures of Sam Spade	Wildroot	1946 - 1951
varies	8 or 9 PM	NBC, CBS, Mut, ABC	Adventures of The Thin Man,	Woodbury, Post, Pabst, Heinz	1941 - 1950
Fri or Sun	varies	NBC, CBS	Amos 'n' Andy	Pepsodent, Campbell Soup, Rinso, Rexall	1928 - 1960
varies	varies	CBS, NBC	Bing Crosby	Cremo, Chesterfield, Woodbury, Kraft, Philco, GE,others	1931 - 1956

✦ ✦ ✦ ✦

Dad's father Christ worked on the dray line owned by Herman Gerstenkorn until **1942**. The dray line would deliver coal in the winter and ice in the summer. Coal would be shoveled down a coal shoot into the basement. These were the days of coal and wood burning stoves, and if a customer was lucky enough to be home when the coal was delivered, it would be saturated with water before it was hand shoveled into the coal bin. Otherwise, the fine coal dust would settle throughout the house. Wood and coal produced ashes, and in the spring the drayman would be kept busy hauling away ashes and garbage that had accumulated during the winter months.

Grandpa was known to the children in town as the "Ice Man"; when he made ice deliveries for the ice boxes (pre-cursor to the refrigerator), the children would follow, catching stray bits of ice along the way as he would pick up the ice chunks with large two-handed ice tongs. Christ managed his son Bob's service station while Bob served in the Armed Forces.

Iceboxes had hollow walls that were lined with tin or zinc and packed with various insulating materials such as cork, sawdust, straw or seaweed. A large block of ice was held in a tray or compartment near the top of the box. Cold air circulated down and around storage compartments in the lower section. Some finer models had spigots for draining ice water from a catch pan or holding tank. In cheaper models a drip pan was placed under the box and had to be emptied at least daily. The user had to replenish the melted ice, normally by obtaining new ice from an <u>iceman</u>.

No electric refrigeration existed back home, so almost every home had an ice box that utilized ice for cooling. When the lakes had frozen sufficiently, the dray crew would cut and haul cakes of ice weighing up to 300 #'s to be stored in ice houses. The cakes were piled in rows in the ice house, and each was covered with a heavy layer of sawdust for insulation.

The block of ice was put in the top right door. The left door had shelves and would hold fruits and vegetables, cooked vegetables and other leftovers, uncooked meats, poultry, berries. The right lower door would hold milk, butter, broth, desserts and milk dishes. Variations of the icebox also had the ice chunk loaded at the top.

The use of the Ice Box lasted into the 20's & 30's. The 1940's brought us the refrigerator we recognize today.

✦   ✦   ✦   ✦

Dad started as a typesetter at the age of 15 for the Belgrade Tribune in 1929. From the Belgrade "Tracks through Time" Centennial book the following: "Publisher Ed Vig and Elmer 'Mickey' Madsen taught themselves to run the first linotype with its 'hot lead' slugs, a used machine from Fargo, ND that Ed bought in the early 1930's."

15

Perhaps one of the most notable inventions in the United States print world is the Linotype machine, developed in 1884 by a German watchmaker named Ottmar Mergenthaler. This machine drastically sped up the printing process and helped revolutionize the newspaper industry by its innovative technique of "line casting," which placed entire lines of type for printing, rather than just individual letter typesetting. The name is a derivation from its full name, "Line of Type," which is a literal description of the machine, itself. The tides of technology replaced the Linotype machine in the 1960s and 1970s.

The invention of the Linotype drastically sped up the printing process and allowed letterpress to flourish. Prior to the Linotype, an army of people were needed to set type by hand—one letter at a time. This caused chaos and slowed down the printing process because it would take a lot of time to find letters and assemble them into lines. It proved to be slow, tedious, and labor-intensive work. Many times, typesetters would run out of letters (also known as "sorts"), which is where the phrase **"out of sorts"** originates.

The Linotype created a method for mechanization and drastically cut down on the number of workers needed for typesetting—one person could do the work of six because it was able to set type six times faster than a human.

The linotype machine operator enters text on a 90-character keyboard. The machine assembles *matrices*, which are molds for the letter forms, in a line. The assembled line is then cast as a single piece, called a *slug*, of type metal in a process known as "hot metal" typesetting. The matrices are then returned to the type magazine from which they came, to be reused later.

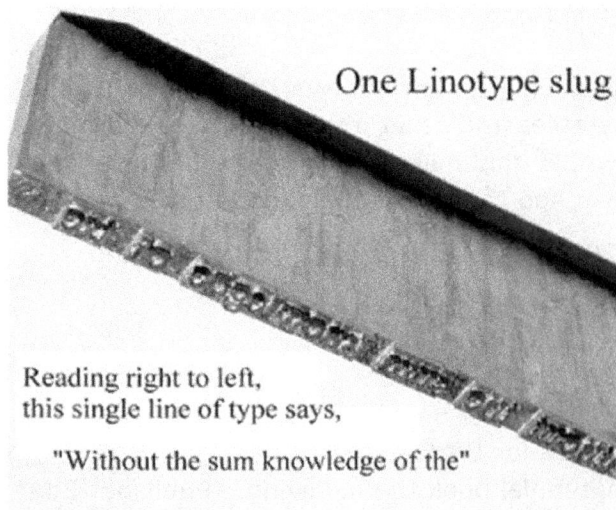

One Linotype slug

Reading right to left,
this single line of type says,

"Without the sum knowledge of the"

Distributor
T
U
A
Matrix Magazine
B
C
E
R
H I
F
Pump
Spaces
Melting pot
M
G
K
J
Mold wheel
Finger Keys
D

The Linotype was very loud, which is why many deaf people were hired to work with them because they were not bothered by the noise level of the machines. They lived with the noise at the Belgrade Tribune.

I was told Dad got his nickname, "Mickey", from a cartoon in the newspaper while working at the paper. I don't have any details or what year this took place but it would have been prior to the war. One possibility would be the "Mickey Finn" comic which was syndicated to newspapers in 1936.

Dad was the interim publisher as well as the typesetter from November through January of 1941 until E.R. Salisbury purchased the paper February 1941. He remained with the paper as a typesetter until he was drafted into the Army on 13 February 1942.

The Belgrade Tribune, dated **December 26, 1940**, lists Elmer Madsen as Publisher along with employees Orvil Medalen and Myrtle Steffensen. Myrtle would become his wife in September of the following year.

✦ ✦ ✦ ✦

Below is the note I found inside the butt end of Dad's Model 12 Winchester shotgun after he had passed away. He would have been fifteen at the time of purchase.

The note read as follows:

Model 12 Winchester I bought new at Lindquist & Linderholm hardware store in fall of 1929 for $35. Paid $5.00 down and $5.00 a month. Included was the leather case. I was working for the Belgrade Tribune for $40.00 per month at the time. Mickey Madsen.

This 12-gauge shotgun had a full choke, 30" full bright bore and was the only shotgun Dad ever used throughout his life while hunting around central Minnesota. He used to tease the other hunters, many who had the Browning Recoil-operated Semi-Automatic 12-gauge shotgun, that he was able to have more hunting success with his old Model 12 than with the shotgun they used. It was said he used to provide meals of rabbit for the family while growing up. He was real proud of that gun. I got this gun after dad's passing and used it for the last time, killing a deer using shotgun slugs, while hunting in southern Iowa with my brother-in-law, Randy Randolph (another adventure). This gun is now packed away in its original knockdown down case and has the original wooden cleaning rod. This gun case was also known as a "leg of mutton" gun case. I have passed this Model 12 to brother Darrel as his boys, Derek and Joey, have continued the Madsen tradition of hunting and fishing.

There is a picture of the 1936 Belgrade baseball team. Dad was 22 years old at the time. I sure wish I would have saved his ball glove. As I remember, its appearance.

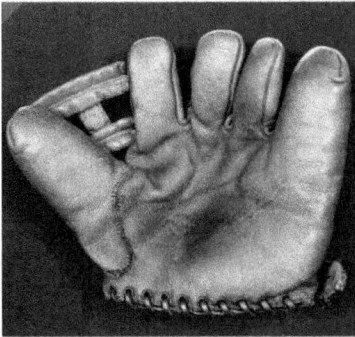

Dad played second base for the Belgrade Town Team before the war. I have been told he was a really good ballplayer. After the war he continued his love of the game playing baseball and then softball on the Men's Town Team while using that same ball glove.

In Town Team Baseball of the 1930's the teams represent either a given city or town, or a commercial enterprise which sponsors the team. Small town Minnesota played against competing towns.

Amateur baseball, also known as town team ball, dates back to the 1800s. In 1924, the first organized tournament was played in Minnesota. Ten years later, a new tournament setup was developed involving eight regional champions from the metro area plus 11 leagues from greater Minnesota.

Although teams and leagues came and went, that format stayed pretty much intact until 1966 when the champions and runners-up from every region were invited to the annual state tournament.

Below: *Information from: The Free Press, http://* www.mankatofreepress.com

"Our high-water mark came in the early 1950s," said Bob Zellmann, who started playing amateur ball in Norwood, Minnesota in 1948 and has been on the state board for 22 years. *"That's when a lot of soldiers had returned from the war and were looking for things to do; baseball was truly the national pastime back then,"* he said.

There were as many as 900 teams and 88 leagues in Minnesota in the 1950s. *"You could drive through almost any town on any night and find the lights of a ballpark illuminating the hub of activity,"* Zellmann said. *"You didn't have things like boating and water skiing and cabins up north drawing people away from the park."*

✦ ✦ ✦ ✦

Depression

The Great Depression lasted from **1929 to 1939** and was the worst economic downturn in the history of the industrialized world. It began after the stock market crash of October 1929, which sent Wall Street into a panic and wiped out millions of investors. Soup kitchens, breadlines, unemployment, poverty.

The greatest hardship was unemployment, so many millions desperate for work and unable to find any, even year after year. The unemployment rate varied from 15-25%. Ashamed husbands abandoned their families, many children left school to work to support the family, women with jobs didn't want to get married because they might be forced to give up their job. The depression was even more harsh on minorities who were already at the bottom and had no reserves to fall back on.

Also, the desperately poor and powerless white and black sharecroppers and tenant farmers in the south of the US were particularly vulnerable. The south was still a plantation system for the most part and poorly educated, indebted landless laborers lived hand to mouth. They were also being replaced by tractors, so many drove westward looking for work.

When President Franklin D. Roosevelt took office in **March 1933**, the United States was in the midst of the Great Depression. Farmers faced the most severe economic situation and lowest agricultural prices since the 1890s. Overproduction and a shrinking international market had driven down agricultural prices.

Agricultural Adjustment Act (AAA) of 1933

The Federal government passed this bill to help the farmers which set limits on the size of the crops and herds farmers could produce. Surplus was the problem; farmers were producing too much and driving down the price. Those farmers that agreed to limit production were paid a subsidy. Most farmers signed up eagerly and soon government checks were flowing into rural mail boxes where the money could help pay bank debts or tax payments.

The Roosevelt Administration was tasked with decreasing agricultural surpluses. Wheat, cotton, field corn, hogs, rice, tobacco, and milk and its products were designated as basic commodities in the original legislation. Subsequent amendments in **1934 and 1935** expanded the list of basic commodities to include rye, flax, barley, grain sorghum, cattle, peanuts, sugar beets, sugar cane, and potatoes. The administration targeted these commodities for the following reasons:

1. Changes in the prices of these commodities had a strong effect on the prices of other important commodities.

2. These commodities were already running a surplus at the time.

3. These items each required some amount of processing before they could be consumed by humans.

In an effort to reduce agricultural surpluses, the government paid farmers to reduce crop production and to sell pregnant sows as well as young pigs. Oranges were being soaked with kerosene to prevent their consumption and corn was being burned as fuel because it was so cheap. There were many people, however, as well as livestock in different places starving to death. Farmers slaughtered livestock because feed prices were rising, and they could not afford to feed their own animals. Under the Agricultural Adjustment Act, "plowing under" of pigs was also common to prevent them reaching a reproductive age, as well as donating pigs to the Red Cross.

Although the Act stimulated American agriculture, it was not without its faults. For example, it disproportionately benefited large farmers and food processors, with lesser benefits to small farmers and sharecroppers. With the spread of cotton-picking machinery after 1945, there was an exodus of small farmers and croppers to the city.

In 1935, the income generated by farms was 50 percent higher than it was in 1932, which was partly due to farm programs such as the Agricultural Adjustment Act.

During the early 30s, sales of farm machinery dropped dramatically. In 1930, there were about 200,000 tractors produced. By 1932, only 19,000 tractors sold. Some manufacturers went out of business or were sold to other companies, but those that remained continued to invent new machines or better parts. By 1935, over 160,000 tractors were being produced again. In some cases, farmers got their first government checks and bought machinery.

Tractors

Rubber Tires

Rubber tires, of course, were used on almost all cars. But it wasn't until orange growers in Florida got fed up with steel lugs damaging the roots of their trees and that farmers began experimenting with rubber tires.

Excerpts from Henry Swanson's book **"Countdown for Agriculture in Orange County, Florida"**: After engineering studies at the University of Florida, Hoyle Pounds eventually became a Ford farm tractor dealer in Winter Garden Florida. In 1919 Pounds sold eight tractors. By 1926 he was selling more than 40 a year. Those tractors moved on metal wheels with metal cleats that grabbed into the soil. Farmers and citrus growers who needed to move their tractors from one piece of property to another had to traverse newly paved roads. The metal cleats chewed up the pavement.

Faced with expensively hacked-up roadways, officials passed laws forbidding the metal wheels from crossing the newly paved highways and tractor owners complained to Hoyle Pounds.

From Oklahoma, pounds ordered some large, hard rubber tires designed for oil-drilling equipment.

After considerable experimentation, Pounds realized that the gear ratio to the drive shaft would have to be changed because the wheels with rubber tires turned at a faster rate than the old metal wheels, moving on top of the soil rather than digging into it.

After all the details had been tested for several months, Pounds applied for and was granted Patent No. 1662208 on **March 13, 1928**, for his rim and lug design for **airless tires**. The rubber wheels were more powerful, gave better gas mileage, kicked up less dust and were more comfortable than steel. The rubber tires not only made tractors faster, they increased mobility. Pounds invention ushered in the use of rubber tires on virtually all movable farm equipment.

Hoyle Pounds' 1928 tractor (below) has a spot of honor in the galleries of the Orange County Regional History Center, Orlando, Florida.

Decal on the nose of the tractor picture above:
Sold and invented by Pounds Motor Company. Winter Haven, Florida. Phone 656-1352.

In 1931, B. F. Goodrich Co. brought out a rubber tire mounted to a common steel rim for tractors. Other companies followed and began demonstrating that rubber tires had just as much traction as steel ones. **By 1933**, tractor companies began offering models with rubber tires already mounted on rims. Blacksmith shops did a growing business retrofitting steel wheels to rubber ones. **By 1940, 95 percent of new tractors rode on rubber wheels.**

Early in **1930**, the Oliver company refined its "Row Crop" tractor with two small drive wheels in front spaced closely together and "tip-toed" in. This design essentially produced a tricycle tractor. The closely spaced front wheels allowed the tractor move easily down the rows of corn or soybeans. A row crop tractor could cultivate a field as well as plow it. Through the 30s, row crop tractors became more and more popular.

The tractor is the main source of power on a farm, and at the beginning of the 1930s tractors were still relatively simple machines. None of the first tractors had a battery in them. You had to crank the Farmall tractor. As the decade continued, tractors went from two-cylinder models to four to six cylinders. In **1936**, the Minneapolis-Moline company began offering an electric starter on some models. By **1939**, Cleveland Tractor Co. outfitted all of their models with electric starters and lights.

Three-Point Hitch

In the 1920s, hooking up an implement, like a plow, to a tractor was a major task. Farmers had hoists and helpers and inventive ways of getting heavy implements hooked up. Each manufacturer had its own ways of hooking implements to their tractors. With most implements, the farmer had to stop at the end of a row, get down off the tractor, raise the plow or cultivator up, make the turn, get down, drop the implement back into the soil and proceed on the next row. All of that changed with the three-point hitch. **Harry Ferguson invented the three-point hitch in the late 20s. His Ferguson Brown Type A was the first tractor to offer the system in 1936. Later, Henry Ford agreed to put it on his new Ford 9N tractor.**

At every step in the process of growing crops, new machines were being developed during the 1930s.

- **Plows**: For the first time in the 30s, plows were mounted directly to the tractor so they could be lifted out at the end of a row.
- **Planters**: Grain drills and corn planters got better at distributing seeds accurately and quickly.

- **Mechanical cultivators**: When the tricycle tractor was invented, it allowed farmers to drive cultivators through closely spaced rows.
- **Harvesters**: **In 1935, the first wheat combine that could be operated by just one man was invented.** The corn and soybean harvesters were not far behind.

All of this innovation changed farming. Humans are adaptable. Machines are not. Humans can cultivate row crops one month, thresh grain in another, and husk corn in another. It usually takes separate machines to do each of these tasks. So, specialized, expensive machines eventually began to force farmers to specialize in one crop and to get bigger.

Harvesting Wheat

Finishing the harvest each season is the reward for a year's hard work. For wheat farmers who could afford it in the 30s, the work of harvest was made a lot easier and cheaper with the development of combines.

On the Plains, wheat had become a popular crop, in part because of another invention – toast. **In 1928, the automatic bread slicer was perfected. Two years later, the automatic toaster was introduced.** *The two inventions helped change the breakfast habits of much of the nation, and wheat farmers moved to cash in.*

At about the same time, combines began to take over the harvest from threshing crews and separate machines. In the 20s, one machine would cut the wheat and then bind the stalks into shocks just big enough for a man or boy to carry. The shocks were gathered and then brought to a centrally located thresher machine. The wheat was fed into the machine. The stalks were beaten and flailed to separate the wheat seeds from the stalks and chaff.

The combine brought all of those functions into one machine pulled by a tractor. And in **1935**, manufacturers figured out a way to allow one man to operate the entire machine. Fifteen years later, the **Farm Equipment Institute** called the development of the one-man combine *"one of those occasional milestones which upset the old pattern completely and changed the very courses of agriculture itself."*

The reason was economic. In **1921**, a farmer who hired a contract threshing crew faced labor costs of between $86 and $116 a day. Even if neighbors worked together to harvest each other's wheat, someone had to keep track of how many days each farmer took. Neighbors paid each other for their labor. One man was a lot cheaper than an entire crew.

In addition, the combine was faster. If a wheat field, for example, averaged 15 bushels per acre, it took over 4.5 man-hours to bind, shock and thresh the wheat. The same field would take only .75 man-hours with a combine. Even if you figured in fuel and repairs, it was estimated that a farmer using a combine could cut an acre of grain for around $1.50. The same acre would cost $4.22 with a binder and thresher. Even with the savings, not every farmer could afford to buy their own combine. Enterprising individuals started doing "custom work" – cutting the wheat of other farmers for a fee. They were the forerunners of today's custom crews who follow the wheat harvest from Texas to Canada.

In some ways farmers were better off than city and town dwellers. Farmers could produce much of their own food while city residents could not. Almost all farm families raised large gardens with vegetables and canned fruit from their orchards. They had milk and cream from their dairy cattle. Chickens supplied meat and eggs. They bought flour and sugar in 50-pound sacks and baked their own bread. In some families the farm wife made clothing out of the cloth from flour and feed sacks. They learned how to get by with very little money. But they had to pay their taxes and debts to the bank in cash. These were tough times on the farms.

City and town dwellers were hit hard during the Great Depression, beginning in 1929 and lasting through most of the 1930's. Out of work, out of money, and standing in food lines. **By early 1933, more than 12 million people, or 25% of eligilble Americans, were unemployed.**

Worst hit were port cities (as world trade fell) and cities that depended on heavy industry, such as steel and automobiles. Service-oriented cities were hurt less severely. Political centers such as Washington, London and Berlin flourished during the Great Depression, as the expanded role of government added many new jobs.

Families had to make do with what clothes they had. Patching and sewing or just wearing ragged and torn items was common. Families joining forces by living under the same roof, sharing expenses.

But in those days, *"doing it yourself"* wasn't a trend; it was a necessity. In those difficult times, if women wanted to provide for their families, they had to get creative — especially when it came to clothing. That's when women noticed that one of their food staples — flour — came in cotton sacks. Innovative and desperate, they often emptied the sacks and used the fabric to make clothing for their children.

But when flour sack manufacturers caught word of the trend, they decided to reinvent the way they packed their flour using different types of sack prints. These sack prints allowed the women to create so-called "designer" outfits.

When factories and stores shut down, many workers lost their jobs. In Dubuque Iowa, for example, 2,200 workers lost their jobs between 1927 and 1934 when their firms closed, while only 13 new businesses opened—employing only 300 workers. That meant a loss of 1,900 jobs. Dubuque Iowa railroads employed 600 workers in 1931; three years later, only 25 jobs remained.

Before the Great Depression, people refused to go on government welfare except as a last resort. The newspapers published the names of all those who received welfare payments, and people thought of welfare as a disgrace. However, in the face of starving families at home, some men signed up for welfare payments. For most it was a very painful experience.

Town families could not produce their own food. Many city dwellers often went hungry. Sometimes there were soup kitchens in larger cities that provided free meals to the poor. Winters were an especially hard time since many families had no money to buy coal to heat their houses.

On **March 4, 1933**, during the bleakest days of the Great Depression, newly elected President Franklin D. Roosevelt delivered his first inaugural address before 100,000 people on Washington's Capitol Plaza.

"First of all," he said, "let me assert my firm belief that the only thing we have to fear is fear itself."

The next day, **March 5**, Roosevelt declared a four-day bank holiday to stop people from withdrawing their money from shaky banks. On **March 9**, Congress passed **Roosevelt's Emergency Banking Act**, which reorganized the banks and closed the ones that were insolvent.

In his first "fireside chat" three days later, **March 12**, the president urged Americans to put their savings back in the banks, and by the end of the month almost three quarters of them had reopened.

✦ ✦ ✦ ✦

NEW DEAL

In what would later be called **"The Hundred Days"**, President Franklin Roosevelt revitalized the faith of the nation by setting motion a "New Deal" for America. One of these New Deal programs was the Civilian Conservation Corps. With this action, he brought together two wasted resources: young men and land. The other program created to put Americans to work was the Works Progress Administration.

The **New Deal** was a series of federal programs, public works projects, and financial reforms and regulations enacted in the United States during the 1930s in response to the Great Depression. These programs included support for farmers, the unemployed, youth, and the elderly, as well as new constraints and safeguards on the banking industry and changes to the monetary system. The programs focused on what historians refer to as the ***"3 Rs", Relief, Recovery, and Reform***: relief for the unemployed and poor, recovery of the economy to normal levels, and reform of the financial system to prevent a repeat depression.

President Roosevelt promised if granted emergency powers he would have 250,000 men in camps (CCC) by the end of July, 1933. The speed with which the plan moved through proposal, authorization, implementation and operation was a miracle of cooperation among all branches and agencies of the federal government. It was a mobilization of men, material and transportation on a scale never before known in time of peace. From FDR's inauguration on March 4, 1933, to the induction of the first enrollee on April 7, only 37 days had elapsed.

Works Progress Administration

The Works Progress Administration (WPA; renamed in **1939** as the Work Projects Administration) was the largest and most ambitious American New Deal agency, employing millions of people (mostly unskilled men) to carry out public works projects including the construction of public buildings and roads. In a much smaller project, Federal Project Number One, the WPA employed musicians, artists, writers, actors and directors in large arts, drama, media, and literacy projects. The Works Progress Administration (WPA) hired many men to work on parks, roads, bridges, swimming pools, public buildings and other projects.

The WPA provided jobs and income to the unemployed during the Great Depression in the United States. At its peak in 1938, it provided paid jobs for three million unemployed men and women, as well as youth in a separate division, the National Youth Administration. Between 1935 and 1943, when the agency was disbanded, the WPA employed 8.5 million people. Most people who needed a job were eligible for employment in some capacity. Hourly wages were typically set to the prevailing wages in each area. Unlike the CCC, the WPA provided work close to where you lived.

Civilian Conservation Corps (CCC)

March 9, 1933 President Franklin D. Roosevelt authorized a program to fight against soil erosion and declining timber resources by utilizing unemployed young men from large urban areas. With this action, he brought together two wasted resources: young men and land. He proposed to recruit thousands of unemployed young men, enroll them in a peacetime army, and send them into battle against destruction and erosion of our natural resources.

Before the CCC ended, over three million young men engaged in a massive salvage operation described as the most popular experiment of the New Deal. Teen age boys were hired by the Civilian Conservation Corps (CCC). They lived in barracks, were given clothing, and provided with free meals. The small salary that they earned was sent back to help their families. The CCC boys planted trees, helped create parks, and did other projects to beautify and preserve natural areas. My Uncle Archie, sometime after graduating high school, worked for the CCC in northern Minnesota.

This young, inexperienced $30-a-month labor battalion had met and exceeded all expectations. The impact of mandatory monthly $25 allotment checks to families boosted the economy across the nation. Allotments of $25 were making life a little easier for the people at home. In communities close to the camps, local purchases of the $5 per worker allotment averaging approximately $5,000 monthly staved off failure of many small businesses. The man on the radio could, for a change, say, *"There's good news tonight"*.

The CCC program peaked in Minnesota in 1935 with 104 active camps. Enrollment nationwide began to decline in the early 1940s as young men joined the military for World War II and as the economy began to rebound. Despite efforts to make the CCC permanent, **funding for the program ended on June 30,1943**. More than seventy-seven thousand Minnesota men found employment with the program. The CCC-ID program assisted more than twenty-five hundred American Indian families in the state. The young men of the CCC credited the program with teaching self-discipline and leadership, instilling confidence and self-respect, and helping them to develop useful career skills.

The 1930s are remembered as hard times for many American families. With the coming of World War II, the government began hiring many men to serve in the army. Factories began receiving orders for military supplies. But the memories of the Depression did not go away. Many Americans worried that when the war ended, hard times would come again.

Drought

The economic depression of the 1930s was longer and harder than any other in American history because it was followed by one of the longest and hardest droughts on record. There are cycles of drought, but this was one of the worst ever recorded. The decade started with dry years in 1930 and 1931 especially in the East. Then, 1934 recorded extremely dry conditions over almost 80 percent of the United States. Extreme drought conditions returned in 1936, 1939 and 1940. Walter Schmitt calls this the "double whammy" of drought and depression.

Dust Bowl

Each year, the process of farming begins with preparing the soil to be seeded. But for years, farmers had plowed the soil too fine, and they contributed to the creation of the Dust Bowl. "In general, the seed bed should be roomy, thoroughly pulverized and compact," according to John Deere's 1935 book, *The Operation, Care and Repair of Farm Machinery.* The goal, according to the book, was to "break up clods and crusted top soil, leaving a fine surface mulch for planting or for plant growth." The suggested method was upon finishing the last narrow strip with a 2-bottom plow, tilt the plow over to the left, drive in the furrow with the right wheels and plow this strip ... Follow up using the cultivator, disc harrows.

The main tool for this job was the plow, an ancient implement that had evolved by the 1930s into several different varieties designed for different soil types. Each design lifted the soil up, broke it up and turned it over. The process pulverized hard dirt into small clods.

In the early 30s, many farmers would come back into a plowed field with a set of disc harrows that would break the clods into fine soil particles. A harrow mounted a series of concave sharpened steel discs close together. These discs were pulled through the field at a slight angle so the soil was cut and then turned over by each disc. This produced what was thought to be the "ideal seed bed... Large air spaces, bunches of field trash and hard lump or clods are undesirable."

The problem with this method is that it leaves fields vulnerable to wind erosion and dust storms. In the 1920s and early 30s, most farmers on the plains plowed their fields right after the previous harvest, leaving the soil open for months until it was time to plant again. And economic pressures in the late 1920s pushed farmers on the Great Plains to plow under more and more native grassland. Farmers had to have more acres of corn and wheat to make ends meet.

During wet years, this didn't cause problems. But when the drought hit, fields that had been covered for centuries by grass had been plowed and disked into fine particles. The soil dried out and began to blow. Dry and light grains of soil were picked up by the incessant winds on the plains. Those particles would hit others, bouncing them into the air, until the entire field was blowing away. The result was the Dust Bowl.

The **Dust Bowl**, also known as the **Dirty Thirties**, was a period of severe dust storms that greatly damaged the ecology and agriculture of the American and Canadian prairies during the 1930s; severe drought and a failure to apply dryland farming methods to prevent wind erosion (the Aeolian processes) caused the phenomenon. **The drought came in three waves, 1934, 1936, and 1939–1940.**

Great Plains is the grassland prairie region of North America, extending from Alberta, Saskatchewan, and Manitoba, in Canada, south through the west-central United States into Texas. The Dust Bowl became the generic term for the drought of the 30's in the Great Plains areas. The drought and erosion of the Dust Bowl affected over 100,000,000 acres that centered on the panhandles of Texas and Oklahoma and extended north into sections of Canada.

The Dust Bowl forced tens of thousands of families to abandon their farms. Many of these families migrated to California and other states to find that the Great Depression had rendered economic conditions there little better than those they had left.

The drought made the Depression worse, especially in the Great Plains. The "Great" Depression was a national and international disaster, but the Plains were hardest hit. **In 1933, the average person living in North Dakota earned only $145 a year. That compared with a national average of $375 a year, over twice as much.**

With no rain, farmers couldn't grow any crops. No crops meant that the wind blew bare soil high in the air creating dust storms. School was canceled because of dust storms, not snowstorms. Some farmers, in trouble because of the bad economy, were forced to give up and move out of the plains looking for work.

The New Deal and Congress recognized the effects of over plowing marginal lands. In 1936, the agency that became the Farm Security Administration (FSA) hired filmmaker Pare Lorenz to produce one of the first documentary films on the problem. It was called "The Plow that Broke the Plains" and drew widespread critical acclaim and audiences in movie theatres across the country.

Around the same time, Congress passed the **Soil Conservation Act** that called for changes in plowing techniques, strip cropping and shelter belts to cut down on wind erosion.

The Soil Conservation and Domestic Allotment Act

(enacted **February 29, 1936**) was a United States federal law that allowed the government to pay farmers to reduce production so as to conserve soil and prevent erosion.

The Act was passed in response to the Supreme Court's declaration that the Agricultural Adjustment Act (AAA) was unconstitutional. These two acts were passed as legislation in an attempt to cut crop and livestock surplus.

Originally, Congress enacted the Soil Conservation Act on April 27, 1935 in an attempt to address farm erosion problems by bringing within its policy and purposes, the improvements and preservation of national soil resources. During the second session of the 74th Congress, the U.S. Congressional session amended the Soil Conservation Act of 1935 by passing and renaming the legislation the Soil Conservation and Domestic Allotment Act with the express purpose of encouraging the use of soil resources in such a manner as to preserve and improve fertility, promote economic use, and diminish the exploitation and unprofitable use of the national soil resources. Franklin D. Roosevelt signed the Act into law on February 29, 1936.

✦ ✦ ✦ ✦

Dad bought a 1930 Chevrolet in 1938. He would have been 24 at the time. It had fender wells on each side. There were two spare tires with yellow wire wheels, one on each side on the fender wells. It had running boards and a trunk behind. This was explained in a letter from Aunt Lillian and Uncle Bob sent to my sister Faye along with a picture likeness of this automobile. It reads as follows:

Hi Faye, Bob thought you would be interested in this picture as your Dad had one like it, a 1930 Chevrolet. It had fender wells on each side, this meant 2 spare tires and wheels. Yellow wire wheels which were considered classy in those days. Also had a trunk on behind. He bought it in 1938, went to the harvest fields in North Dakota in it and later he used it to go to Globe, Arizona, along with three other fellows, to work in the copper mines there. Bob and Lillian.

I never did find out the reason of his travels but researching the 1930's I started to understand you had to go where you thought you could make money. He was 24 in 1938 and would have left his job at the newspaper during this period going to North Dakota to the harvest fields. The work in the copper mines in Globe Arizona was between the winter of 1938 and 1940. Not sure what jobs they did in Arizona or if any money was made. They didn't stay there too long and he went back to the newspaper upon his return to Belgrade.

This is the type of 1930 Chevrolet that Dad drove.

✦ ✦ ✦ ✦

Dad's parents, Christ and Christine, had six sons and two daughters. Three sons, Elmer, Robert and Donald were in the service during WWII. Robert (Army Air Corps) and Donald (Air Corps & Infantry) served in Europe. Archie had a farm deferment. Prior to the war one of the largest contributors to the economy was the farmer. In the early 1940's there was a shortage of farm workers due to enlistment in the war, the increased food demand, and the industrial demand for workers. The twins, Richard & Russell, were too young. They both served when they became old enough after this war.

Each of Christ and Christine's children took their turn delivering the Minneapolis evening paper from 1928 to 1944. The Soo Line railroad went through town and the Winnipeg Flyer came in the late evening and threw off a mail pouch containing mail and newspapers. The newspapers were delivered by Christ's children. Outgoing mail was put in a pouch and with a strap attached to an extended arm and hook, would then be grabbed by the train crew as the Winnipeg Flyer came through as it did not make a stop in Belgrade. A **mail hook** is an installation at a railroad where a catcher pouch can be hung, to be picked up by a passing train without the train having to stop.

Not only did the Soo Line bring freight and mail service to Belgrade, it was the chief mode of transportation in and out of town. During early baseball days, the trains were frequent enough so that ardent fans could hop a train to a competing town and come back the same day. The newspapers would lure local citizens with special offers into taking a train ride to Minneapolis (110 miles) for shopping or special events.

Elmer "Mickey" Madsen married Myrtle Steffensen on **September 14, 1941** and resided in Belgrade, MN. Pearl Harbor was bombed **December 7, 1941**. Dad was drafted in the Army on **February 13, 1942**. Forty- three months later he was discharged as a Staff Sergeant E-6 on **September 6, 1945**. Their first child, Faye, was born **October 9, 1942**. *Faye was three years old before Dad got to see her for the first time.* I bet that was quite the reunion for all of them. He was away from his family for almost four years.

✦ ✦ ✦ ✦

By **1940**, radio had become a mass medium. Almost 80 percent of the households in the U.S. owned a radio. Yet before the war, only seven percent of the airtime was devoted to news. By the end of the war, 25 percent of the airtime was news, and audiences had been transported to the battlefront in live and recorded reports.

When Pearl Harbor was attacked and the U.S. entered the war, only one-third of farms had electricity to run refrigerators or washing machines in

the house or lights and milking machines in the barn. Only 25 percent of farms had telephones.

During the Depression of the 1930s, Americans "did without" because they didn't have jobs to buy food and clothing. During World War II, Americans again "did without," this time because of the war effort. Rationing affected rural America particularly.

The federal government set up a rationing system in 1942 and limited purchases of sugar, coffee, meat, fish, butter, eggs, cheese, shoes, rubber and gasoline. Silk and newly invented nylon was used to produce parachutes, and so women around the world found it hard to get fashion stockings.

Other commodities were in short supply because trade routes were disrupted. Shellac, for instance, was produced in India and was used for building products and music record discs. Because of the war in Asia, trade with India was disrupted, and so new records were hard to come by.

Farm production, however, was vital to the war effort, so farmers got extra rations of gasoline and other staples. Yet, it was hard to get new machinery as factories were retooled to produce tanks rather than tractors.

Throughout the war, rural residents suddenly had new neighbors – military bases and factories. Farmers were sometimes forced to sell land to the government and private companies so that new training bases and military factories could be built. Recruits from the cities were sent to train in isolated rural areas. The new factories provided jobs to farm hands and women.

The war, obviously, affected who lived and died, who married whom, and where people lived. Many men and women married quickly in the early years of the war. Other couples waited. Some soldiers got "Dear John" letters when the woman couldn't wait any longer. Many families made the ultimate sacrifice when their sons, brothers, fathers and husbands were killed during World War II. Others found their loved ones had been forever changed by what they had endured.

✦ ✦ ✦ ✦

The Seabees

Following the Japanese attack on Pearl Harbor and the United States' entry into World War II, the use of civilian labor in war zones became unsafe and impractical. In addition, under international law, civilians were not permitted to engage in enemy warfare. The need for a militarized naval construction force to build advance bases during World War II became self-evident. Therefore, rear Admiral Ben

Moreell, chief of the Navy's Bureau of Yards and Docks, was determined to organize, activate and man Navy construction units.

On **January 5th, 1942**, Moreell received authority from the Bureau of Navigation to recruit men from the civilian construction trades for assignment to a naval construction regiment composed of three naval construction battalions.

The earliest Seabees were placed under the leadership of the Navy's Civil Engineer Corps. Because of an emphasis on experience and skill, rather than physical standards, the average age of Seabees during the early days of the war was 37. In fact, in those initial days, it was not uncommon for skilled men to enlist at upwards of 60 years of age.

The first **Seabees** (from **C**onstruction **B**attalions) were recruited by the United States Navy during World War II. They were skilled construction workers whose task was to assist in building naval bases in the theatres of war.

More than 325,000 men served with the Seabees in World War II, fighting and building on six continents and more than 300 islands. **In the Pacific, where 80% of Seabees were deployed was where most of the construction work was needed.** The Seabees could be found landing soon after the marines — building major airstrips, bridges, roads, warehouses, hospitals, gasoline storage tanks and housing, all while drawing enemy fire.

The Pacific war often found the Seabees in close support of invasion forces, taking part in unloading supplies, and quickly constructing or restoring harbors, airstrips and other facilities on newly captured islands. Their role in such operations as the invasion of Okinawa was central in bringing the war to its close.

As numbers grew the battalions were formed into regiments, the regiments into brigades, and brigades into a naval construction force for each theater of war. Special Construction Battalions and construction battalion detachments were also formed, containing men with specific construction skills. Eventually 190 battalions were created, in addition to detachments and maintenance units.

U.S. Navy Bureau of Yards and Docks recruited carpenters, machinists, electricians, etc. If interested, they were to apply to your nearest recruiting station.

The subsequent development of Espiritu Santo as an air base was rapid and extensive. A few days after the Guadalcanal landings, the 7th Battalion arrived on Santo and began building more extensive air facilities.

Army Air Forces and Marine Corps personnel on the island increased rapidly until Santo became a major South Pacific base for the support of air activities throughout the year-long campaign for possession of the Solomons.

Army Corps of Engineers

The history of United States Army Corps of Engineers can be traced back to 16 June 1775, when the Continental Congress organized an army with a chief engineer and two assistants.

The Corps of Engineers, as it is known today, came into existence on 16 March 1802, when President Thomas Jefferson signed the Military Peace Establishment Act whose aim was to *"organize and establish a Corps of Engineers ... that the said Corps ... shall be stationed at West Point in the State of New York and shall constitute a military academy."*

Many politicians wanted the Corps of Engineers to contribute to both military construction and works of a civil nature. Assigned the military construction mission on **1 December 1941** after the Quartermaster Department struggled with the expanding mission, the Corps built facilities at home and abroad to support the U.S. Army and Air Force.

During the 1930's, in view of Japan's growing power and the low state of American armaments, and with the independence of the Philippines scheduled for 1946, the War Department General Staff concluded that the United States should not attempt to hold initially in the western Pacific. Alaska, Hawaii, and Panama, often referred to as the "strategic triangle," should form the main line of defense.

The United States Army had been concerned with the possibility of war with Japan for many years before Pearl Harbor. Soon after World War I, American military leaders began to frame a strategy to be followed if war broke out. The first strategic plan, War Plan ORANGE, adopted in 1924, envisaged mainly a naval struggle, with the Army to seize the Japanese mandated islands in the central Pacific, reinforce the Philippines, and then prepare for an attack on Japan itself.

The last version of War Plan ORANGE, issued in 1938, embodied these views. It was assumed that after a period of strained relations, Japan would attack without notice. The Japanese would in all likelihood seize Guam and the Philippines. Enemy forces could be expected to make raids on Hawaii, Alaska, and the west coast of the United States. The Panama Canal might be wrecked by sabotage or by naval and air raids.

The Japanese attack on Pearl Harbor on 7 December 1941 found the Corps of Engineers, like the rest of the Military Establishment, in the midst of feverish defense preparations. The Corps had been assigned the task of building up defenses in Panama, Alaska, Hawaii, and other Pacific outposts; in areas ranging from the Arctic to the tropics, engineer units were engaged in a wide variety of urgent projects. Plagued by shortages of men and materials and difficult working conditions, these defense preparations were still far from finished when the nation was plunged into war. Along with these desperate efforts to build a bulwark on many fronts, the engineers were engaged in the vital mission of creating an organization and developing equipment that would enable them to carry out their many duties on the battle-fronts and behind the lines in case war broke out. By the time of Pearl Harbor much progress had been made in the relatively short time since the defense build-up began.

At home, the Corps conducted the planning, land acquisition, design, contracting and construction associated with a $15.3 billion mobilization program that included training camps, depots, hospitals and ammunition plants as well as the Manhattan Project, and the Pentagon.

Outside the United States, the engineers built - roads, bridges, airfields and pipe-lines; cleared mines; dredged harbors and repaired ports. In 1942 the Corps completed the 1,700-mile Alaska highway. During WWII the Corps built the 1,072-mile Ledo Road that follows the India-Burma border navigating along the mountain tops, passes and valleys. This road could supply the Chinese as an alternative to the Burma Road that had been cut off by the Japanese in 1942.

Engineer Combat Battalion

Also known as **"sappers"** were best known for pontoon bridge construction and clearing hazards in amphibious landings. Their duties also included serving as sappers deploying and deactivating explosive charges and unexploded munitions, mapmaking, camouflage, and a wide variety of construction services supporting frontline troops. They also fielded defensive .30 cal. and .50 cal. machine gun squads, anti-tank rocket and grenade launchers, and were required to fight as infantry when needed.

A **sapper** is a combatant or soldier who performs a variety of military engineering duties such as breaching fortifications, demolitions, bridge-building, laying or clearing minefields, preparing field defenses as well as building and working on road and airfield construction and repair. They are also trained to serve as infantry personnel in defensive and offensive operations.

A sapper's duties are devoted to tasks involving facilitating movement, defense and survival of allied forces and impeding those of enemies.

Pioneer Troops

In the Pacific theater, the Pioneer troops were formed, a hand-selected unit of volunteer Army combat engineers trained in jungle warfare, knife fighting, and unarmed jujitsu (hand-to-hand combat) techniques. Working in camouflage, the *Pioneers* cleared jungle and prepared routes of advance and established bridgeheads for the infantry as well as demolishing enemy installations.

Today the USACE is a U.S. federal agency under the Department of Defense and a major Army command is one of the world's largest public engineering, design, and construction management agencies. Although generally associated with dams, canals and flood protection in the United States, USACE is involved in a wide range of public works throughout the world. The Corps of Engineers provides outdoor recreation opportunities to the public and provides 24% of U.S. hydropower capacity.

The corps' mission is to ***"Deliver vital public and military engineering services; partnering in peace and war to strengthen our Nation's security, energize the economy and reduce risks from disasters."***

✦ ✦ ✦ ✦

In **1939**, the Army Air Corps had only 17 air bases across the country. Pearl Harbor changed that. During the first quarter of 1942, the Army ordered construction of over 200 air fields, pilot and technical schools and bombing ranges. By the end of 1943, there were 345 main bases, 116 subbases and 322 auxiliary fields. Most were located in rural areas. The Army Air Corp was active 2 July 1926 – 9 March 1942. During World War II, although not an administrative echelon, the Air Corps (AC) remained as one of the combat arms of the Army until **1947**, when it was legally abolished by legislation establishing the **Department of the Air Force**.

Building bombs and artillery shells – known as "ordnance" – was a good job. The plants paid 70- to 80-cents an hour, about the same as factory workers around the nation but well above what laborers on the farm and in small towns made. Merchants had been paying their workers around 30-cents an hour. Many commuted from farms and rural towns up to 60 miles away. There were three shifts each weekday and shifts on the weekends. A normal workweek was 48 hours long, and many worked overtime.

"Loose lips sink ships" was advise to servicemen and other citizens to avoid careless talk concerning secure information that might be of use to the enemy. The gist of this particular slogan was that one should avoid speaking of ship movements, as this talk (if directed at or overheard by covert enemy agents) might allow the enemy to intercept and destroy the ships.

✦ ✦ ✦ ✦

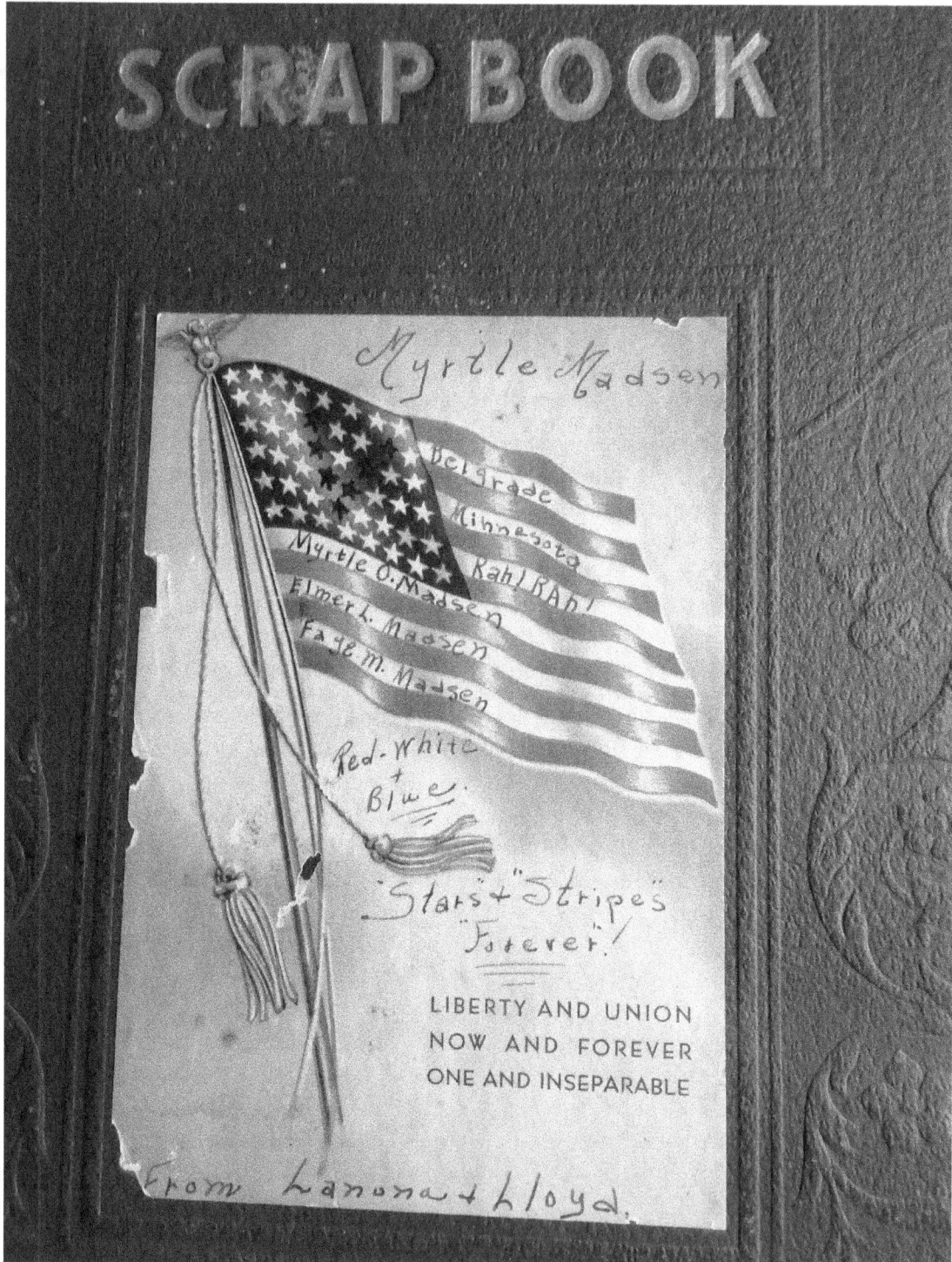

Above: Aunt Lanona Brandsrud, Mom's oldest sister, gave Mom a photo album with the American flag on the front and a saying: *"Liberty and Union now and forever - One and Inseparable"*. Mom kept all correspondence and newspaper clippings from and about Dad during the war in this scrapbook. Many families did the same hoping and praying they would again see one another.

The **BLUE STAR FLAG** was placed in a front window during the war and became a symbol of love, pride, hope and grave concern. The blue star was on a white background with a thick red border and yellow threaded fringe at the bottom. It also became a symbol of what Americans at home could do to increase a mother's chance of seeing her son's safe return: rationing, working in factories building needed materials, and even reminding all at home that *"loose lips sink ships"*.

The Blue Star Flag, often quickly visible from the windows of many houses up and down any given street in America, symbolized a pride in the commitment of America's youth and a reminder of the gravity of the entire war effort.

Grandma & Grandpa had three of these blue stars on one flag in their window during the war. Mom wore a Blue Star pin and a U.S. Army locket necllace containing Dad's picture.

It was not at all unusual for a window to display more than one flag (or a single flag with multiple stars), for a star was displayed for each son or daughter in service.

"Gold star mothers" replaced the blue banner star with the gold in memory of a fallen son who would not be coming home.

Following are the service records of the three Madsen brothers taken from the Belgrade, MN. Saboe-Larsen VFW Post #1825 service book:

Elmer (Mickey) Madsen entered service at age 27.

ELMER L. MADSEN
Entered Service: February 13, 1942.
Branch of Service: Army.
Trained at Camp Forrest, Tennessee.
Date of Embarkation: September 1, 1942
Theatre of Operations: Southwest Pacific.
Engagements: Guadalcanal, Northern Solomons, Luzon.
Decorations: Purple Heart, 1 Oak Leaf Cluster, Bronze
Star, Combat Infantry Badge.
Date Returned to United States: August 28, 1945.
Discharged: September 6, 1945 at Camp McCoy, Wisconsin.
Rank: Staff Sergeant.
Total Months Served: 43 months.

Entered Service: February 13, 1942
Branch of Service: Army
Trained at Camp Forrest, Tennessee
Date of Embarkation: September 1, 1942
Theatre of Operations: Southwest Pacific
Engagements: Guadalcanal, Northern Solomons, Luzon
Decorations: Purple Heart, 1 Oak Leaf Cluster, Bronze Star, Combat Infantry Badge
Date returned to United States: August 28, 1945
Discharged: September 6, 1945 at Camp McCoy, Wisconsin
Rank: Staff Sergeant
Total Months Served: 43 months

Robert (Bobby) Madsen entered the service at age 25.

ROBERT H. MADSEN
Entered Service: June 12, 1944.
Branch of Service: Army.
Trained at Buckley Field, Colorado; Kingman, Arizona;
Gulfport Field, Mississippi.
Date of Embarkation: March 1945.
Theatre of Operations: European.
Date Returned to United States: July 1945.
Discharged: June 7, 1946 at Fort Sheridan, Illinois.
Rank: Sergeant.
Total Months Served: 24 months.
Present Occupation: Service Station Operator.

Entered Service: June 12, 1944
Branch of Service: Army
Trained at Buckley Field, Colorado; Kingman, Arizona; Gulfport Field, Mississippi
Date of Embarkation: March 1945
Theatre of Operations: European
Date Returned to United States: July 1945
Discharged: June 7, 1946 at Fort Sheridan, Illinois
Rank: Sergeant
Total Months Served: 24 months
Present Occupation: Service Station Operator

Donald (Donny) Madsen entered the service at age 18.

DONALD W. MADSEN
Entered Service: December 1, 1942.
Branch of Service: Air Corps and Infantry.
Trained at St. Petersburg, Florida; Madison, Wisconsin;
Norfolk, Virginia.
Date of Embarkation: March 19, 1944.
Theatre of Operations: European.
Engagements: England, Central Europe, Northern France,
Normandy.
Decorations: 4 Battle Stars, Unit Citation, Good Conduct
Medal, European Ribbon, American Theatre Ribbon.
Date Returned to United States: December 6, 1945.
Discharged: December 19, 1945 at Camp McCoy, Wisconsin.
Rank: Corporal.
Total Months Served: 36 months.
Present Occupation: Truck Driver.

Entered Service: December 1, 1942
Branch of Service: Air Corps and Infantry
Trained at St. Petersburg, Florida; Madison, Wisconsin; Norfolk, Virginia
Date of Embarkation: March 19, 1944
Theatre of Operations: European
Engagements: England, Central Europe, Northern France, Normandy
Decorations: 4 Battle Stars, Unit Citation, Good Conduct Medal, European Ribbon,
        American Theatre Ribbon
Date Returned to United States: December 6, 1945
Discharged: December 19,1945 at Camp McCoy, Wisconsin
Rank: Corporal
Total Months Served: 36 months

III   Germany's rise to power

Conditions in Europe rapidly deteriorated **between 1936 and 1939**.

In **March 1936**, Germany violated the Treaty of Versailles and reoccupied the Rhineland. In **November 1937**, Italy joined Germany and Japan in the **Anti-Comintern Pact,** which united the three countries against the Soviet Union. Germany then annexed Austria in **March 1938** and, at the **Munich Conference** in **September 1938**, Great Britain and France agreed to give Germany the German-speaking part of Czechoslovakia (the Sudentenland) in return for "peace in our time." By **March 1939**, Hitler annexed the rest of the country, and an independent Czechoslovakia ceased to exist.

The **August 1939** signing of the **Nazi-Soviet Nonaggression Pact,** in which Germany and the Soviet Union agreed not to attack each other, gave Germany a green light to invade Poland on **September 1, 1939, the beginning of WWII**. This aggression in turn caused Great Britain and France, who had formed a military alliance with Poland that guaranteed Poland's independence, to declare war on Germany on **September 3, 1939**.

American response to the war

Although Franklin D. Roosevelt quickly announced that the United States would remain neutral, he did not ask the American people to be neutral in thought, as Wilson had done in 1914. Although most Americans still wanted to stay out of the war, they had little sympathy for Nazi Germany or Fascist Italy. Americans' attitudes were reflected in the change of policy that occurred with the Neutrality Act of 1939, which repealed the 1935 arms embargo on belligerents and provided for the export of military equipment on a cash-and-carry basis.

Denmark and Norway were invaded in **April 1940**, the Netherlands, Belgium, and Luxembourg fell in May, and France sued for peace in June. Any pretense of American neutrality ended as Great Britain stood alone. Defense spending and military production accelerated, with the focus on airplanes and motorized equipment.

The first peacetime draft in United States history was provided for in the **Selective Training and Service Act enacted September 16, 1940,** which registered men between the ages of 21 and 35 and planned to train more than 1.2 million troops and 800,000 reserves within a year. Later, when the U.S. entered World War II, all men from their 18th birthday until the day before their 45th birthday were made subject to military service, and all men from their 18th birthday until the day before their 65th birthday were required to register.

The Election of 1940

Germany's aggression and British requests for aid convinced Roosevelt to be "drafted" by the Democrats to run for an unprecedented third term.

In a fireside chat after the election, Roosevelt called on Americans to become the **"arsenal of democracy"** — remaining out of the war but giving the British what they needed to fight. To implement this idea, he submitted the **lend-lease bill** to Congress in **January 1941**. It gave the president the authority to lend, lease, sell, transfer, or exchange military equipment and other supplies to any country whose defense was deemed vital to American security.

Not long after the unexpected German invasion of Russia in **June 1941**, lend-lease aid was also extended to the Soviet Union. During the spring and summer of 1941, the United States steadily prepared itself for the possibility of war. Providing direct aid to the British and the Russians meant transporting supplies on merchant ships across the Atlantic Ocean.

Because German U-boats (submarines) sank millions of tons of shipping during the Battle of the Atlantic in 1941, the U.S. Navy began escorting ships further from American shores. American troops were sent to both Greenland and Iceland to forestall Germans from occupying and using these locations as bases of operations against the Western Hemisphere.

In August 1941, in a more public show of solidarity, Roosevelt and British Prime Minister Winston Churchill issued the **Atlantic Charter,** a joint statement of their war aims that called for self-determination, free trade and freedom of the seas, equal access to raw materials, and a new system of collective security.

By the **fall of 1941**, the United States and Germany were already fighting an undeclared naval war in the Atlantic. When a German submarine fired upon an American destroyer in September, Roosevelt ordered the Navy to "shoot on sight" any enemy warships in the western Atlantic.

After the destroyer Reuben James was torpedoed on **October 31** with the loss of 115 lives, Congress approved the president's request to arm merchant ships and to allow them to sail through combat zones to the ports of belligerents.

December 11, 1941, the United States Congress declared war upon Germany hours after Germany declared war on the United States after the Japanese attack on Pearl Harbor.

U-Boat attacks of WWII: 6 months of secret terror in the Atlantic

On **Jan. 13, 1942** German U-boat attacks officially started against merchant ships along the Eastern Seaboard of North America. From then until early August, Nazi U-boats dominated the waters off the East Coast, sinking fuel tankers and cargo ships with impunity and often within sight of shore.

In less than seven months, U-boat attacks would destroy 22% of the tanker fleet and sink 233 ships in the Atlantic Ocean and the Gulf of Mexico. The U-boats killed 5,000 seamen and passengers, more than twice the number of people who perished at Pearl Harbor.

While thousands of New Englanders looked to the sky for enemy airplanes, few had any idea about the carnage wreaked in the waters nearby.

The U.S. Navy lied to the public about the terrifying U-boat attacks. The news media agreed to government censorship, which helped to hide the military's incompetence in protecting shipping and the lives of merchant seamen.

New London, Conn., native Ralph Sturgis was one of the few who knew about the U-boat attacks. He ran an observation post on Fishers Island in the Long Island Sound. "I would watch boats go out, and probably an hour later get a radio message that the boat had been sunk," Sturgis remembered. "The Germans use to operate right off of the coast here and they use to sink the ships, it was really something."

German U-boats in the Gulf of Mexico

In the early days of U.S. involvement in World War II, German U-boats clouded Gulf waters with an ominous presence. With over 70 naval and merchant ships falling victim to Germany's "Gulf fleet," there was cause for real concern -- and for the safety of sailors and even residents of the Texas coast

Not long after Japanese *Admiral Isoroku Yamamoto* launched his fateful surprise attack at Pearl Harbor in late 1941, the High German command ordered the *10th U-boat flotilla* to begin war time operations in the Gulf of Mexico. The primary objective was to disrupt the vital flow of oil carried by tankers from ports in Texas and

Louisiana and to impede the flow of military hardware and supplies to the European front.

The Germans were exceedingly successful in their Gulf campaign sending 56 vessels to the bottom. The German submarine *U-166* was sunk by depth charges, 30 miles from the entrance to the Mississippi River. In fact, naval historians tell us that Germany's concentrated war effort in the Gulf of Mexico in **1942 and early 1943** represent one of the most celebrated sea campaigns of all time. At least two U-boat Captains earned Germany's Distinguished Iron Cross for their efforts, and the campaign is credited with effectively disrupting U.S. oil and gas supplies for the first half of the war.

While U-boat activity was largely limited to 1942-43, there was at one point no less than a fleet of 20 U-boats that patrolled Gulf waters regularly in search of allied supply ships. To prevent widespread panic, the U.S. War Department decided to keep the lid on the threat, but it wasn't long before merchant sailors and fishing vessel crews spread the word that not all ships in the Gulf were friendly.

German U-Boats sank dozens of ships off Florida's coast. In the cover of the night on **June 16, 1942**, a group of four Germans armed with explosives and disguised as Americans left their submarine and came ashore to Ponte Vedra Beach FL, just a few miles north of St. Augustine, according to the National Park Service. The spies were captured before any harm could be done but the incident was still cause for alarm and triggered Coast Guard personnel in St. Augustine to start patrolling the beach.

Shortly after dawn on **July 19, 1942** the German submerged U-84 torpedoed the ship, Baja California, steaming alone on a southerly heading, and brought World War II to within 55 miles of Marco Island.

Fifty-six ships sank in the Gulf of Mexico in 1942, compared with only one U-boat. In no other body of water did the German U-boats have more short-term success than in the Gulf of Mexico. With the success of the U-boats obvious, the **Gulf Sea Frontier Task Forces** ordered coastal defenses strengthened and documented vessels conscripted and placed into submarine patrol service.

World War II left a lasting legacy on the central Florida community. Before the war, the area's climate and terrain attracted nationally-known aviation enthusiasts, including Amelia Earhart and Charles Lindbergh, who came to Florida to fly. As war approached, the number of serviceable airfields as well as an average of over 350 days of good-flying weather per year made this area a significant home to aviation training both before and during the war.

Following Pearl Harbor, German submarines came to Florida's coast to hunt and sink cargo ships. People along the beach at Daytona saw numerous ships explode, sinking within eyesight of the Florida coast. Ship captains had to plead with local governments to get businesses along the coast to turn off their lights at night to prevent the ships from giving off a perfect silhouette for the waiting German submarines.

Final Solution to the Jewish Question

It is not known when the leaders of Nazi Germany definitely decided to implement the "Final Solution". The genocide, or mass destruction, of the Jews was the culmination of a decade of increasingly severe discriminatory measures.

The Final Solution was a Nazi plan for the extermination of the Jews during World War II. The *"Final Solution of the Jewish Question"* was the official code name for the murder of all Jews within reach, which was not limited to the European continent.

Nuremberg Laws in 1935

At the annual party rally held in **Nuremberg** in **1935**, the Nazis announced new **laws** which institutionalized many of the racial theories prevalent in Nazi ideology. The **laws** excluded German Jews from Reich citizenship and prohibited them from marrying or having sexual relations with persons of *"German or related blood"*.

Germany implemented the persecution in stages. Following Hitler's rise to power in **1933**, the government passed laws to exclude Jews from civil society, most prominently the Nuremberg Laws in 1935. Starting in 1933, the Nazis built a network of concentration camps in Germany for political opponents and people deemed "undesirable". After the invasion of Poland in 1939, the regime set up ghettos to segregate Jews. Over 42,000 camps, ghettos, and other detention sites were established.

Adolf Hitler's Nazi Germany, aided by its collaborators, systematically murdered some six million European Jews, around two-thirds of the Jewish population of Europe, between 1941 and 1945.

The Holocaust saw the killing of 90 percent of Jewish Poles, and two-thirds of the Jewish population of Europe. A large majority of these killings occurred in 1942.

The Office of Strategic Services (OSS)

The Office of Strategic Services (OSS) was established by a Presidential military order issued by President Roosevelt on **June 13, 1942**. The OSS was a wartime intelligence agency used to collect and analyze strategic information required by the Joint Chiefs of Staff and to conduct special operations not assigned to other agencies. During the war, the OSS supplied policymakers with facts and estimates, to coordinate espionage activities behind enemy lines for all branches of the United States Armed Forces. Other functions included the use of propaganda, subversion, and post-war planning. The OSS never had jurisdiction over all foreign intelligence activities. The FBI was left responsible for intelligence work in Latin America, and the Army and Navy continued to develop and rely on their own sources of intelligence. At the height of its influence during World War II, the OSS employed almost 24,000 people.

The National Security Act of 1947 established the first permanent peacetime intelligence agency in the United States, the Central Intelligence Agency (CIA), which then took up OSS functions.

IV   JAPAN'S RISE TO POWER

The Japanese islands are the only ones in the Pacific that have retained their independence and integrity since earliest times. According to legend, Japan was founded by the goddess of the sun and its rulers are her direct descendants. Before the middle of the sixteenth century the islands had a loosely organized feudal government headed by a **shogun, or military leader**, and virtually independent lords. After a period of internal conflict in the sixteenth century, the country came under new rulers who reformed the government and followed a policy of complete isolation from the rest of the world.

It was not until **Admiral Perry's visit in 1853** that Japan entered the community of nations, began to adopt western customs and techniques, and embarked on a policy of expansion. On **November 24, 1852**, Perry embarked from Norfolk, Virginia for Japan, in command of the East India Squadron in pursuit of a Japanese trade treaty. In 1852, Perry was assigned a mission by American President Millard Fillmore to force the opening of Japanese ports to American trade, through the use of **gunboat diplomacy** if necessary. The growing commerce between America and China, the presence of American whalers in waters offshore Japan, and the increasing monopolization of potential coaling stations by the British and French in Asia were all contributing factors.

The Americans were also driven by concepts of manifest destiny and the desire to impose western civilization on what they perceived as backward Asian nations. The Japanese were forewarned by the Dutch of Perry's voyage, but were unwilling to change their 220-year-old policy of national seclusion by opening the ports of Shimoda and Hakodate to American vessels.

There was considerable internal debate in Japan on how best to meet this potential threat to Japan's economic and political sovereignty. Perry attempted to intimidate the Japanese by presenting them a white flag and a letter which told them that in case they chose to fight, the Americans would destroy them. After negotiations, lasting several months, **the Convention of Kanagawa was signed on March 31, 1854**. It also ensured the safety of American castaways and established the position of an American consul in Japan. The treaty also precipitated the signing of similar treaties establishing diplomatic relations with other Western powers.

The Meiji Restoration was an event that restored practical imperial rule to Japan in **1868** under *Emperor Meiji* and led to enormous changes in Japan's political and social structure.   Although there were Emperors before the Meiji Restoration, the events restored practical abilities and consolidated the political system under the Emperor of Japan. a central government in Japan which exercised direct power through the entire "realm".

The military of Japan, being strengthened by nationwide conscription and the infusion of a samurai military spirit, became emboldened to see themselves as a growing world power after winning both the Sino-Japanese War and the Russo-Japanese War.

The Meiji Restoration accelerated industrialization in Japan, which led to its rise as a military power by the year **1905**, under the slogan of "Enrich the country, strengthen the military". The rapid industrialization and modernization of Japan both allowed and required a massive increase in production and infrastructure. Japan built industries such as shipyards, iron smelters, and spinning mills, which were then sold to well-connected entrepreneurs. Consequently, domestic companies became consumers of Western technology and applied it to produce items that would be sold cheaply in the international market.

Japan participated in World War I from **1914 to 1918** in an alliance with Entente Powers and played an important role in securing the sea lanes in the West Pacific and Indian Oceans against the Imperial German Navy. Politically, Japan seized the opportunity to expand its sphere of influence in China, and to gain recognition as a great power in postwar geopolitics. The Triple Entente was the understanding linking the Russian Empire, the French Third Republic, and the United Kingdom of Great Britain and Ireland after the signing of the Anglo-Russian Entente on 31 August 1907 against Germany and Austria-Hungary.

In the first week of World War·I Japan proposed to the United Kingdom, its ally since 1902, that Japan would enter the war if it could take Germany's Pacific territories. On **7 August 1914**, the British government officially asked Japan for assistance in destroying the raiders from the Imperial German Navy in and around Chinese waters. Japanese forces quickly occupied German-leased territories in the Far East. On **2 September 1914**, Japanese forces landed on China's Shandong province and surrounded the German settlement at Tsingtao (Qingdao). During October, acting virtually independently of the civil government, the Imperial Japanese Navy seized several of Germany's island colonies in the Pacific - the Mariana, Caroline, and Marshall Islands - with virtually no resistance. Japan was not doubted to have emerged as a great power in international politics by the close of the war.

The Shōwa era, refers to the period of Japanese history corresponding to the reign of the **Shōwa Emperor, Hirohito, from December 25, 1926 until his death on January 7, 1989.**

The Shōwa period was longer than the reign of any previous Japanese emperor. During the pre-1945 period, Japan moved into political totalitarianism, ultra-nationalism and fascism culminating in **Japan's invasion of China in 1937**.

A chronology of key events:

1853 - US fleet forces Japan to open up to foreign influence after over 200 years of self-imposed isolation.

1894-95 - Japan goes to war with China, and its better-equipped forces win victory in just nine months. China cedes Taiwan and permits Japan to trade on mainland.

1904 - Japan becomes first Asian country in modern times to defeat an European power when it routs Russia in Manchuria.

1910 - Japan annexes Korea after three years of fighting, becoming one of the world's leading powers.

1923 - British Empire ends 21-year alliance with Japan, signaling Western and US apprehension of Japan's growing power in East Asia.

Late 1920s - Extreme nationalism begins to take hold in Japan as world economic depression hits. The emphasis is on a preservation of traditional Japanese values, and a rejection of "Western" influence.

1931 - Japanese army invades Chinese province of Manchuria, installs puppet regime.

1936 - Japan signs alliance with Nazi Germany.

1937 - Japan goes to war with China, capturing Shanghai, Beijing and Nanjing amid atrocities like the **"Rape of Nanking"**, in which up to 300,000 Chinese civilians were killed.

1939 - Outbreak of Second World War in Europe. With fall of France in 1940, Japan moves to occupy French Indo-China.

1941 - Japan launches a surprise attack on US Pacific fleet at Pearl Harbor, Hawaii. US and main allies declare war on Japan.

1942 - Japan occupies succession of countries, including Philippines, Dutch East Indies, Burma and Malaya. In June, US aircraft carriers defeat the Japanese at the

Battle of Midway. The US begins a strategy of "'island-hopping", cutting the Japanese support lines as its forces advance.

1944 - US forces are near enough to Japan to start bombing raids on Japanese cities.

1945 - US planes drop atomic bombs on Hiroshima and Nagasaki in August. Emperor Hirohito surrenders and relinquishes divine status. Japan placed under US military government. All Japanese military and naval forces disbanded.

Rape of Nanking in 1937

During the Sino-Japanese War, Nanking, the capital of China, falls to Japanese forces, and the Chinese government flees to Hankow, further inland along the Yangtze River.

To break the spirit of Chinese resistance, Japanese General Matsui Iwane ordered that the city of Nanking be destroyed. Much of the city was burned, and Japanese troops launched a campaign of atrocities against civilians. In what became known as the "Rape of Nanking," the Japanese butchered an estimated 150,000 male "war prisoners," massacred an additional 50,000 male civilians, and raped at least 20,000 women and girls of all ages, many of whom were mutilated or killed in the process.

December 7, 1941 Attack on Pearl Harbor

In less than two hours the Japanese surprise attack had sunk and damaged most of the U.S. fleet moored in the harbor's Battleship Row. The assault killed 2,300 Americans and wounded another 1,347. Twelve vessels sank, including the two battleships Arizona and Oklahoma, another six battleships were severely damaged.

Japan's invasion force:

First Wave 7:40 AM

45	Fighters
54	Dive Bombers
40	Torpedo Bombers
50	High-level Bombers
——	
189	Aircraft

Second Wave 8:50 AM

36   Fighters
81   Dive Bombers
54   High-level Bombers
_____
171   Aircraft

Attacks end at 9:45 AM

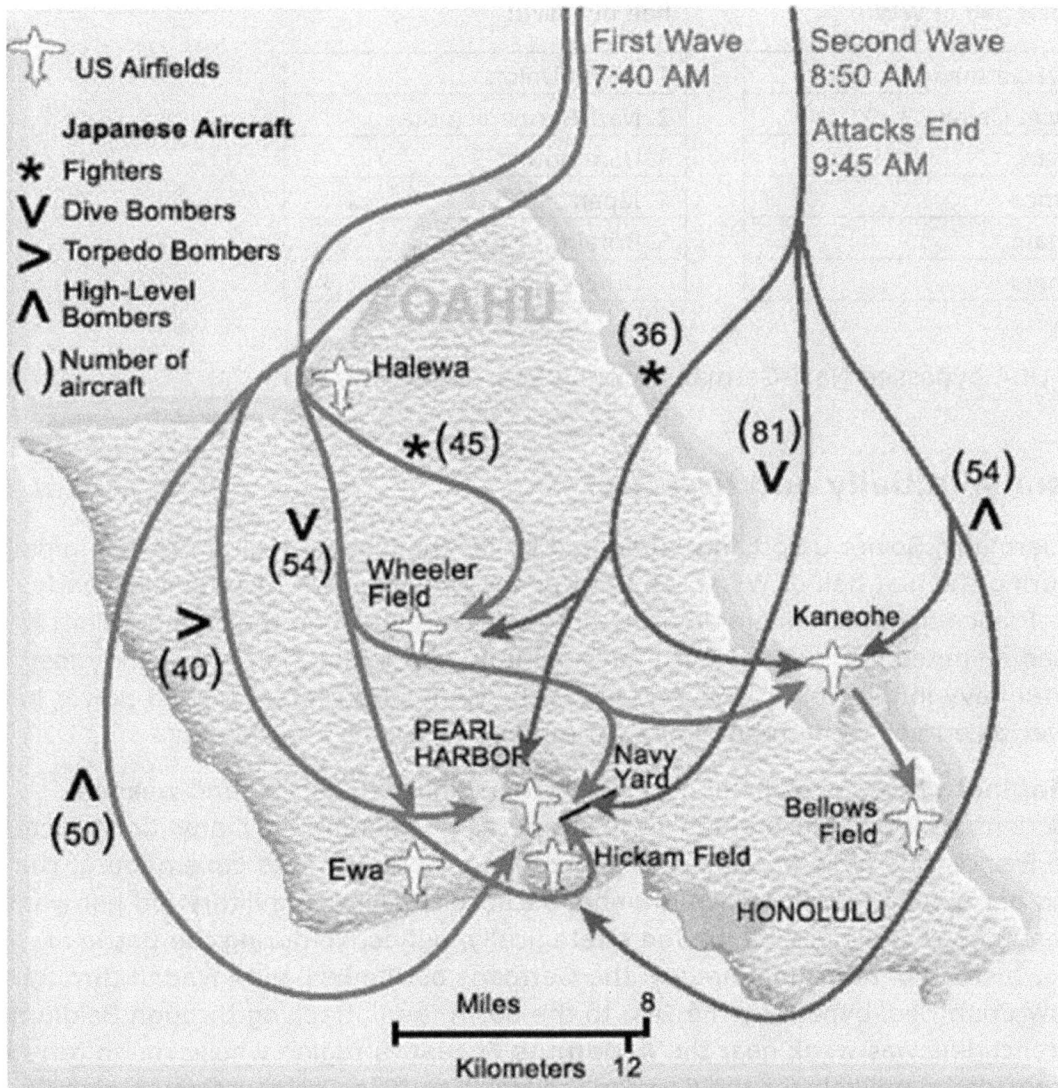

World War II, which began in 1939 and ended in 1945, was the deadliest and most destructive war in history.

Before the war, Germany, America, and the rest of the world were going through the Great Depression. The economy was very bad, unemployment was at an all-time high, and massive inflation caused money to lose its value. More than fifty nations in the world were fighting, with more than 100 million soldiers deployed. Countries like America and Britain were part of the Allied powers. Japan and Germany were part of the Axis powers.

Top military powers initially and first half of WWII:
1. Nazi-Germany
2. Soviet Union
3. Japan
4. France
5. Britain
Others

Top military powers second half of WWII:
1. Soviet Union
2. Nazi-Germany (note)
3. USA (note)
4. Japan
5. Britain
Others

Note: USA bypassed Nazi-Germany around year-end 1944/1945.

Reasons, initially and first half

Nazi-Germany, Soviet Union and Japan had by far the biggest military forces initially and during the first half of WWII. As the war theatres and war results also clearly show. France had a considerable army but relied too much on the Maginot line. It also had a limited but quite modern navy. Britain had a minor army but the most powerful navy in the world. USA had hardly no army or air force. Its sea power had however a certain strength but limited compared to Britain and Japan.

The **Maginot Line** was a line of concrete fortifications, obstacles, and weapon installations built by France in the 1930s to deter invasion by Germany. Constructed on the French side of its borders with Switzerland, Germany, and Luxembourg, the line did not extend to the English Channel because the French military did not want to offend neutral Belgium. It proved strategically ineffective during the Battle of France. Instead of attacking directly, the Germans outflanked and invaded through the Low Countries, bypassing the Line to the north, and attacking through Belgium. The French line was weak near the **Ardennes Forest**, a region whose rough terrain they considered unlikely for the Germans to traverse. The German Army took advantage of this weak point to split the French–British defensive front. The Allied forces to the north were forced to evacuate at Dunkirk, leaving the forces to the south unable to mount an effective resistance to the German invasion of France.

Reasons, second half

The Soviet Union managed to recover from its enormous early war losses and now became the biggest army. It also recovered from the enormous air force losses and developed a huge powerful air force that gained air superiority on the Eastern front. Nazi-Germany remained a very strong military power throughout the war. But was bypassed by Soviet some half way through the war and by the USA at the end of it.

The USA also mobilized enormously but had its ultimately built-up huge multi-million army available only in the last months of WWII. The USA also built-up the most powerful navy and bypassed both Britain's and Japan's navies. Japan remained strong throughout the war and was USA's opponent in the Pacific war. Britain's relative power fell. Even though it mobilized major forces, still had a mighty navy, and also a mighty air force. And remained as such one of the strongest military powers. France was defeated in 1940 by Germany.

As the question made focus only on "military power" the different countries' production capacity, access to crucial resources, etc., were not considered.

Technology also played a greater role in the conduct of World War II than in any other war in history and had a critical role in its final outcome. Many types of technology were customized for military use, and major developments occurred across several fields including:

- Weaponry: ships, vehicles, aircraft, artillery, small arms; and biological, chemical, and atomic weapons
- Logistical support: vehicles necessary for transporting soldiers and supplies, such as trains, trucks, ships, and aircraft
- Communications and intelligence: devices used for navigation, communication, remote sensing, and espionage
- Medicine: surgical innovations, chemical medicines, and techniques
- Rocketry: atomic bombs and automatic aircraft

1941 Japanese invasions

December 7, 1941 - Japanese bomb Pearl Harbor, Hawaii; also attack the Philippines, Wake Island, Guam, Malaya, Thailand, Shanghai and Midway.
December 8, 1941 - U.S. and Britain declare war on Japan. Japanese land near Singapore and enter Thailand.
December 9, 1941 - China declares war on Japan.
December 10, 1941 - Japanese invade the Philippines and also seize Guam.

December 11, 1941 - Japanese invade Burma.

December 15, 1941 - First Japanese merchant ship sunk by a U.S. submarine.

December 16, 1941 - Japanese invade British Borneo.

December 18, 1941 - Japanese invade Hong Kong.

December 22, 1941 - Japanese invade Luzon in the Philippines.

December 23, 1941 - General Douglas MacArthur begins a withdrawal from Manila to Bataan; Japanese take Wake Island.

December 25, 1941 - British surrender at Hong Kong.

December 26, 1941 - Manila declared an open city.

December 27, 1941 - Japanese bomb Manila.

Battle of Wake Island in Micronesia

The Battle of Wake Island began *simultaneously* with the attack on Pearl Harbor naval/air bases in Hawaii and ended on **23rd December 1941**, with the surrender of the American forces to the Empire of Japan. It was fought on and around the atoll formed by Wake Island and its minor islets of Peale and Wilkes Islands by the air, land, and naval forces of the Japanese Empire against those of the United States, with Marines playing a prominent role on both sides. Midway is northeast of Wake Island.

This island in Micronesia was held by the Japanese for the duration of the Pacific War theater of World War II; the remaining Japanese garrison on the island surrendered to a detachment of United States Marines on **4 September 1945**, after the earlier surrender on the battleship U.S.S. Missouri in Tokyo Bay to General Douglas MacArthur.

In **January 1941,** the United States Navy constructed a military base on the atoll. On 19th August, the first permanent military garrison, understrength elements of the 1st Marine Defense Battalion, totaling 450 officers and men were stationed on the island, supplemented by Marine Corps fighter plane squadron VMF-211, consisting of 12 F4F-3 Wildcat fighters. Forty-five Chamorro men (native Micronesians from the Mariana Islands and Guam) were employed by Pan American Airways at the company's facilities on Wake Island, one of the stops on the Pan Am Clipper trans-Pacific amphibious air service initiated in 1935.

On **8 December**, just hours after the attack on Pearl Harbor (Wake being on the opposite side of the International Date Line), 36 Japanese Mitsubishi G3M3 medium bombers flown from bases on the Marshall Islands attacked Wake Island. Following this attack, the Pan Am employees were evacuated, along with the passengers of the "Philippine Clipper", a passing Martin 130 amphibious flying boat that had survived the attack unscathed. The Chamorro working men were not allowed to board the plane and were left behind. Two more air raids followed the next day.

The main camp was targeted on **9 December**, destroying the civilian hospital and the Pan Am air facility.

Early on the morning of **11 December**, the garrison, with the support of the four remaining Wildcats, repelled the first Japanese landing attempt by the South Seas Force, which included three light cruisers, seven destroyers, two destroyers converted to patrol boats and two troop transport ships containing 450 landing force troops. "Battery L", on Peale islet, succeeded in sinking *Hayate* (destroyer) at a distance of 4,000 yd (3,700 m) with at least two direct hits to her magazines, causing her to explode and sink within two minutes, in full view of the defenders on shore. The four Wildcats also succeeded in sinking the destroyer *Kisaragi* by dropping a bomb on her stern where the depth charges were stored. Both Japanese destroyers were lost with nearly all hands (there was only one survivor, from *Hayate*), with ***Hayate* becoming the first Japanese surface warship to be sunk in the war.** *Kisaragi* and *Hayate* sank with 325 Japanese sailors. The Japanese force withdrew without landing. This was the first Japanese setback of the war against the Americans.

The second Japanese invasion force came on **23 December**, composed mostly of the ships from the first attempt with the major reinforcements of the carriers *Hiryū* and *Sōryū*, plus 1,500 Japanese marines. The landings began at 0235; after a preliminary bombardment, the ex-destroyers *Patrol Boat No. 32* and *Patrol Boat No. 33* were beached and burned in their attempts to land the invasion force. After a full night and morning of fighting, the Wake garrison surrendered to the Japanese by mid-afternoon. The Japanese captured all men remaining on the island, the majority of whom were civilian contractors employed by the Morrison-Knudsen (MK) Company. During World War II, MK built airfields, storage depots, and bases throughout the Pacific and built ships along the West Coast. Japanese forces captured 1,200 workers, including many MK employees, stationed on Midway and Wake Islands in late 1941. After the war MK expanded into a variety of foreign construction fields. Morrison-Knudsen (MK) was an American civil engineering and construction company.

Fearing an imminent invasion, the Japanese reinforced Wake Island with more formidable defenses. The U.S. Navy established a submarine blockade instead of an amphibious invasion of Wake Island. As a result, the Japanese garrison starved, which led to their hunting the Wake Island Rail, an endemic bird, 9 inches in length, to extinction.

The extinct **Wake Island Rail** (Gallirallus wakensis) was a flightless rail and the only native land bird on the Pacific atoll of Wake. It was found on the islands of Wake and Wilkes, but not on Peale, which is separated from the others by a channel of about 100 meters.

U.S. forces bombed the island periodically from 1942 until Japan's surrender in 1945. **Future President George H. W. Bush also flew his first combat mission as a naval aviator over Wake Island.** After this, Wake was occasionally raided but never attacked *in masse*.

V   AMERICAN HOME FRONT

Of the 16 million people in uniform

- 1 million were African Americans
- 44,500 were Native Americans
- 11,000 were Japanese-Americans
- 250,000 were women.
- Most of the rest – over 14 million – were Caucasian males

During the course of the war, 15 million men and women were called up into the military. At the time, the entire workforce consisted of only 73 million people. Over 20% of the pre-war workforce were now in the military, not working at their civilian jobs.

The 16th decennial census (years ending in 0 since 1790) of population began on April 1, 1940. The average income was $1,368 yearly, and the average unemployment rate in the 1930s was 18.26 percent, up from the average of 5.2 percent in the 1920s.

Unemployment Rates 1920-1948

Year	Rate
1920	5.2%
1928	4.2
1930	8.7
1932	23.6
1934	21.7
1936	16.9
1938	19.0
1940	14.6
1942	4.7
1944	1.2
1946	3.9
1948	3.8

After the **December 7, 1941**, Japanese attack on the American naval fleet at Pearl Harbor, Hawaii, the U.S. was thrust into World War II **(1939-45)**, and everyday life across the country was dramatically altered. Food, gas and clothing were rationed. Communities conducted scrap metal drives. To help build the armaments necessary to win the war, women found employment as electricians, welders and riveters in defense plants. Japanese Americans had their rights as citizens stripped from them. People in the U.S. grew increasingly dependent on radio reports for news of the fighting overseas. And, while popular entertainment served to demonize the nation's enemies, it also was viewed as an escapist outlet that allowed Americans brief respites from war worries.

African Americans in WWII

Over 2.5 million African-American men registered for the draft, and black women also volunteered in large numbers. While serving in the Army, Army Air Forces, Navy, Marine Corps and Coast Guard, they experienced discrimination and segregation but met the challenge and persevered. They served their country with distinction, made valuable contributions to the war effort and earned high praises and commendations for their struggles and sacrifices.

167,000 served in the Navy, initially as mess attendants and cooks. As such they were many times also assigned duties as gun crews. In 1942 general service was opened for African-Americans to serve in other capacities. In March 1944, the first thirteen African-American naval officers were commissioned. One of the first heroes of the war was Ship's Cook Third Class Doris Miller, from Waco, Texas, aboard the USS West Virginia at Pearl Harbor on December 7, 1941. His Navy Cross citation reads in part:

"... distinguished devotion to duty, extraordinary courage and disregard of his personal safety during the attack on the Fleet in Pearl Harbor on 7 December 1941. While at the side of his Captain on the bridge, Miller despite enemy strafing and bombing and in the face of serious ire, assisted in moving his Captain, who had been mortally wounded, to a place of greater safety and later manned and operated a machine gun until ordered to leave the bridge."

He was awarded the Navy Cross by Admiral Chester W. Nimitz, from Fredericksburg, Texas. Unfortunately, Doris Miller was killed in action when the USS Liscome Bay was sunk in November 1943 during operations in the Gilbert Islands.

The first ship named for an African-American was the USS Harmon (DE-678). It was named for Mess Attendant Leonard Roy Harmon, from Refugio, Texas, who was posthumously awarded the Navy Cross for his actions aboard the USS San Francisco during the Battle of Guadalcanal.

909,000 served in the Army, 78% of them served in service branches (engineer, quartermaster and transportation). The African-American combat units in the Pacific included the 93rd Infantry Division, the 24th Infantry Regiment (one of the original Buffalo Soldier regiments), ten anti-aircraft battalions and one coast artillery battalion. In the China-Burma-India Theater, 60% of the engineer units that built the Ledo Road from India to the connection with the Burma Road were African-Americans. Buffalo soldiers were a "colored" segregated unit of the U.S. Army that served in both World War I and World War II. The **Buffalo Soldiers** nickname was given to African American cavalrymen by Native Americans in the 19th century.

17,000 African-Americans served in the Marine Corps during the war, the majority as support troops in ammunition and depot companies. On Peleliu some of these support troops took up rifles and assisted the 1st Marine Division in the fighting on the island. Approximately 800 served on Iwo Jima bringing up ammunition and supplies as well as evacuating wounded. The only two African-American combat units formed by the Marine Corps were the 51st and 52nd Defense Battalions which garrisoned captured islands.

Defense Battalions

Unlike the mobile Marine forces involved in offensive actions, defense battalions were detached to key outposts, in the Pacific and remained at the station they defended. Most varied greatly in size and equipment. The battalions often had several coastal gun batteries, several anti-aircraft batteries, a detection battery (searchlights and radar), and machine gun units.

Almost 5,000 African-Americans served in the Coast Guard, 2,300 as steward's mates and gun crews and 2,400 served in shore establishments (USCG stations, beach patrols and headquarters). In 1943 the Coast Guard began a slow integration on ships and also that year the first African-American Coast Guard officer was commissioned, Joseph Charles Jenkins.

George Watson, U.S. Army, was the only African-American to be awarded the Medal of Honor in the Pacific during World War II. His unit was aboard a ship which was torpedoed on March 8th, 1943. Following the sinking of the ship, Watson repeatedly swam away from the life raft to save other men and bring them back to the raft until one time he swam away and never came back.

African-American women volunteered in large numbers. Many served as nurses in both the Army and Navy Nurse Corps. Others served in all branches of the armed forces. On the home front, women worked in factories building ships, tanks and airplanes; others supported war bond drives, raised victory gardens and assisted with scrap drives.

Although there were no famous units like the Tuskegee Airmen in the Pacific Theater, the African-Americans serving in the Pacific performed their duty just as proudly as their fellow countrymen in the European Theater. For more about the Pacific Theater and the part played by all Americans in that conflict, visit the National Museum of the Pacific War in Fredericksburg, Texas, a property of the Texas Historical Commission managed by the Admiral Nimitz Foundation.

Women in the Service

Women Airforce Service Pilots

The Women Airforce Service Pilots (WASP), called "Women's Army Service Pilots" by some sources, was a paramilitary aviation organization. The WASP's predecessors, the Women's Flying Training Detachment (WFTD) and the Women's Auxiliary Ferrying Squadron (WAFS) organized separately in **September 1942**. They were the pioneering organizations of civilian female pilots, employed to fly military aircraft under the direction of the United States Army Air Forces during World War II. **The WFTD and WAFS were merged on August 5, 1943, to create the paramilitary WASP organization.** The female pilots of the WASP ended up numbering 1,074, each freeing a male pilot for combat service and duties. They flew over 60 million miles in every type of military aircraft.

Women's Army Corp

The Women's Army Corps (**WAC**) was the women's branch of the United States Army. It was created as an auxiliary unit, the Women's Army Auxiliary Corps (**WAAC**) on **15 May 1942** by Public Law 554 and converted to full status as the WAC on **1 July 1943**.

The **WAAC** were first trained in three major specialties. The brightest and nimblest were trained as switchboard operators. Next came the mechanics, who had to have a high degree of mechanical aptitude and problem-solving ability. The bakers were usually the lowest scoring recruits and were stereotyped as being the least intelligent and able by their fellow WAACs. This was later expanded to dozens of specialties like Postal Clerk, Driver, Stenographer, and Clerk-Typist. WAC armorers maintained and repaired small arms and heavy weapons that they were not allowed to use. The WAC provided enlisted seamstresses to tailor WAC uniforms to their wearer

About 150,000 American women eventually served in the WAAC and WAC during World War II. They were the first women other than nurses to serve with the Army.

Woman's Land Army of America

The Woman's Land Army of America (**WLAA)**, later the Woman's Land Army (**WLA**), was a civilian organization created during the First and Second World Wars to work in agriculture replacing men called up to the military. Women who worked for the WLAA were sometimes known as farmerettes. The Women's Land Army (WLA) was formed as part of the United States Crop Corps, alongside the Victory Farm Volunteers (for teenage boys and girls), and lasted from **1943 to 1947**.

In the five years the WLA operated, the program employed nearly 3.5 million workers, which included both farm laborers. Though federally funded, the WLA operated on state and local levels, rather than through the national organization. The majority of WLA workers were seasonal labor consisting of White urban students, soldier's spouses, clerks, teachers, secretaries and other office workers. Women were paid an unskilled worker's wage, ranging from 25 to 50 cents per hour. To save on costs, which included paying for their own meals, many lived at home and commuted to their farm jobs.   However, women from distant urban areas lived in communal camps or buildings near their farm. Working in shifts allowed women to maintain their primary occupations.

In war, soldiers fight on the "front lines." During World War II, everyone in the U.S. was urged to fight on the "Home Front." The nation was called to war, and Americans responded. In that process, the government enlisted catch phrases that were used in the 1930s.

"Use it up, wear it out, make it do, or do without."

"If you don't need it, don't buy it."

VI   INCARCERATION

Shocked by the **December 7, 1941**, Empire of Japan attack on Pearl Harbor, Hawaii that propelled the United States into World War II, one U.S. government response to the war (1941-1945) began in early 1942 with the incarceration of thousands of Japanese Americans on the West Coast and the territory of Hawaii. Military and political leaders were suspect that Imperial Japan was preparing a full-scale attack on the West Coast of the United States. Due to Japan's rapid military conquest of a large portion of Asia and the Pacific between 1936 and 1942, some Americans feared that its military forces were unstoppable.

The government used data from the 1940 census, along with the cooperation of census officials, to obtain the necessary information to target and incarcerate the Japanese-Americans.

Approximately **120,000** *Issei* (first generation, Japanese immigrants) and *Nisei* (second generation, U.S. citizens) from the U.S. West Coast were incarcerated in War Relocation Authority (WRA) camps across the country--based on Executive Order 9066 (**Feb. 19, 1942**). Through separate confinement programs to the WRA, thousands of Japanese, German, and Italian citizens in the U.S. (and in many cases, their U.S. citizen relatives), classified as Enemy Aliens, were detained by the Department of Justice (DOJ) through its Alien Enemy Control Unit and, in Latin America, by the Department of State's Special War Problems Division.

The Department of Justice oversaw the processing of the cases and the internment program. Although many were released or paroled after hearings before a local alien enemy hearing board, for many the adversarial hearings resulted in internment that, in a few cases, lasted beyond the end of World War II. Of those interned, there was evidence that some had pro-Axis sympathies. Many others were interned based on weak evidence or unsubstantiated accusations of which they were never told or had little power to refute. Often families, including naturalized or American-born spouses and children, of those interned voluntarily joined them in internment.

Furthermore, on the basis of hemispheric security, the United States offered to intern allegedly dangerous enemy aliens living in Latin American countries and even recommended which enemy aliens should be interned. Over fifteen Latin American countries accepted the offer and eventually deported a total of over 6,600 individuals of Japanese, German, and Italian ancestry, along with some of their families, to the U.S. for internment. Few, if any, of those deported received any sort of a hearing so many did not know the specific reasons for their deportation.

65

Often these individuals were deported based on hearsay or for other political reasons.

Additionally, the U.S. Army held enemy aliens across the U.S. wherever the number of apprehensions was too few for the Immigration and Naturalization Service to operate a detention facility. The majority of nearly 130,000 Japanese Americans living in the U.S. mainland were forcibly relocated from their West Coast homes during the spring of 1942 including the states of California, Oregon, Washington and Arizona. Most did not have a job to go back home to or even a place to live in some cases after the war. It also operated the Fort Ontario Emergency Refugee Shelter in Oswego, New York, which was the only refugee camp set up in the United States for refugees from Europe. From 1944 to 1945, the shelter housed almost 1,000 European refugees, predominantly of Jewish descent.

These "West Coast" internees shared a common loss of freedom with the thousands of Japanese, German, and Italian Enemy Aliens and their U.S. relatives detained in DOJ camps through the Alien Enemy Control Unit Program. The DOJ, through the Federal Bureau of Investigations, began to target suspect Enemy Aliens in the U.S. as early as the night of December 7, 1941. Both legal resident aliens and naturalized citizens who were suspect were targeted [alongside enemy aliens], as were their families.

Within days of the Japanese attack on Pearl Harbor, the DOJ took into custody several thousand Axis nationals (during World War II, the Axis Nations consisted chiefly of Germany, Japan, and Italy). Although not legally administered in each case, and often spurred by prejudices, the action was intended to assure the American public that its government was taking firm steps to look after the internal safety of the nation.

The exclusion and incarceration of Japanese Americans began in March 1942. The War Relocation Authority, or WRA, was established to administer the camps. During the first phase, internees were transported on trains and busses under military guard to the hastily prepared temporary detention centers.

Twelve temporary detention centers were in California and one was in Oregon. They were set up on race tracks, fairgrounds, or livestock pavilions. Detainees were housed in livestock stalls or windowless shacks that were crowded and lacked sufficient ventilation, electricity, and sanitation facilities. Food was often spoiled. There was a shortage of food and medicine.

The second phase began midsummer and involved moving approximately 500 deportees daily from the temporary detention centers to permanent concentration camps. These camps were located in remote, uninhabitable areas. In the desert camps, daytime temperatures often reached 100 degrees or more. Sub-zero winters were common in the northern camps.

The internment camps were surrounded by barbed wire and guard towers. Armed guards patrolled the perimeter and were instructed to shoot anyone attempting to leave. The barracks consisted of tar paper over two-by-sixes and no insulation. Many families were assigned to one barracks and lived together with no privacy. Meals were taken communally in mess halls and required a long wait in line.

Through the relocation program the Japanese Americans suffered greatly. They first endured the shock of realizing they were not being sent to resettlement communities, as many had been led to believe, but to prison. They lost their homes and businesses. Their educations and careers were interrupted and their possessions lost. Many lost sons who fought for the country that imprisoned their parents. They suffered the loss of faith in the government and the humiliation of being confined as traitors in their own country.

Many young Japanese American men fought for the United States while their families were imprisoned. The highly decorated, all-Japanese American 100th Battalion /442nd Regimental Combat Team that fought in Italy is one example of this irony. Other Japanese Americans served as translators as well as ordinary soldiers in the Pacific theater.

Japanese Americans living in Hawaii were spared relocation because of the logistical difficulty of transporting a third of the state's population to the mainland. With their numbers exceeding the entire Japanese population on the mainland, Japanese Americans in Hawaii proved an essential part of the state's labor force and defense.

Alien Enemy Hearing Board

Early in 1942, the DOJ established a bi-level organization, which handled the individual cases of the alien enemies: The Alien Enemy Control Unit in Washington, D.C. and through Alien Enemy Hearing Boards with branches located in each of the federal judicial districts of the United States. Each Alien Enemy Hearing Board consisted of three civilian members from the local community, one of whom was an attorney. Representatives of the U.S. Attorney for that district, the INS, and the FBI attended each hearing as well. Alien Enemies taken into custody were brought before an Alien Enemy Hearing Board and were either released, paroled, or interned for the duration of the war. Within a few months, the United States looked toward the possibility of exchanging these Alien Enemies with Japan, Germany, and Italy.

Manzanar is most widely known as the site of one of ten American concentration camps where over 110,000 Japanese Americans were unjustly incarcerated during World War II from **December 1942 to 1945**. Located at the foot of the Sierra Nevada in California's Owens Valley, it is approximately 230 miles (370 km) north of Los Angeles.

Over 90 percent of the incarcerated were from the Los Angeles area, with the rest coming from Stockton, California; and Bainbridge Island, Washington. Many were farmers and fishermen. Manzanar incarcerated 10,046 at its peak, and a total of 11,070 people were incarcerated there.

The Heart Mountain War Relocation Center, named after nearby Heart Mountain and located midway between the towns of Cody and Powell in northwest Wyoming, was one of ten concentration camps used for the internment of Japanese Americans evicted from the West Coast Exclusion Zone during World War II.

Construction of the 650 military-style barracks and surrounding guard towers began in June 1942, and the camp opened on **August 11**, when the first Japanese Americans arrived by train from the Pomona, Santa Anita, and Portland assembly centers. The camp would hold a total of 13,997 Japanese Americans over the next three years, with a peak population of 10,767, making it the third-largest "town" in Wyoming before it **closed on November 10, 1945**.

Heart Mountain is best known for many of its younger residents' challenging the controversial draft of Nisei males from camp in order to highlight the loss of their rights through the incarceration. The Heart Mountain Fair Play Committee, led by Frank Emi and several others, was particularly active in this resistance, encouraging internees to refuse military induction until they and their families were released from camp and had their civil rights restored. Heart Mountain had the highest rate of draft resistance of all ten camps, with 85 young men and seven Fair Play Committee leaders ultimately sentenced and imprisoned for Selective Service Act violations. (At the same time, 800 Japanese American men — volunteers and draftees — joined the American military from Heart Mountain.

By the end of the war, over 31,000 suspected enemy aliens and their families, including a few Jewish refugees from Nazi Germany, had been interned at Immigration and Naturalization Services (INS) internment camps and military facilities throughout the United States. Some of these internment locations included Sharp Park Detention Station, California; Kooskia Internment Camp, Idaho; Fort Missoula Internment Camp, Montana; Fort Stanton Internment Camp and Santa Fe Internment Camp in New Mexico; Ellis Island Detention Station, New York; Fort Lincoln Internment Camp, North Dakota; Fort Forrest, Tennessee; and Crystal City Internment Camp, Kenedy Detention Station, and Seagoville Detention Station in Texas.

Closing the Camps

On **December 17, 1944**, President Roosevelt announced the end of the exclusion of Japanese Americans from the West Coast was no longer necessary and would end in **January 1945**, thus allowing the return home of the internees. Relocation after incarceration was difficult, especially since prejudice still ran high in the West Coast. Many Issei (first generation Japanese Americans) never regained their losses, living out their lives in poverty and poor health.

Heart Mountain didn't close all at once. The next day, the WRA proclaimed: "All relocation centers will be closed within a period of six months to one year after the revocation of the exclusion orders." They promised the incarcerated $25 and a train ticket anywhere in the U.S.

It took months for Heart Mountain to close. The incarcerated discovered, when released, that while the war was over, their struggle against prejudice was not. Racism was still very much alive in the United States, adding insult to injury as they tried desperately to rebuild their lives. Starting over was an incredibly difficult prospect.

Only 2,000 people had left Heart Mountain by **June 1945**. Wyoming officials tried to discourage Japanese Americans from remaining in Wyoming and had earlier passed laws that prevented them from owning land and voting. Nevertheless, the last trainload of the incarcerated left Heart Mountain on **November 10, 1945**.

Tule Lake, CA – Opened May 27, 1942. <u>Closed March 20, 1946</u>. Peak population 18,789.

Personal Justice Denied

In **1980**, under mounting pressure from the Japanese American Citizens League and redress organizations, President Jimmy Carter opened an investigation to determine whether the decision to put Japanese Americans into internment camps had been justified by the government.

President Carter signed Senate bill 1647 **July 31, 1980** establishing a seven-person commission that would work during the next 18 months to look into one of the disappointing and sometimes embarrassing occurrences in the history of our Nation. The only ones who were interned in these camps were the Japanese Americans. President Carter today announced the appointment of three persons as members of the **Commission on Wartime Relocation and Internment of Civilians**.

The Commission's report, titled *Personal Justice Denied*, found little evidence of Japanese disloyalty at the time and concluded that the incarceration had been the product of racism. It recommended that the government pay reparations to the internees.

August 10, 1988 President Ronald Reagan signed into law the **Civil Liberties Act of 1988**, which apologized for the internment on behalf of the United States government and authorized a payment of $20,000 to each camp survivor. The legislation admitted that government actions were based on "race prejudice, war hysteria, and a failure of political leadership.

VII   RATIONING

"Use it up, wear it out, make it do, or do without. If you don't need it, don't buy it."

On **January 30, 1942**, the Emergency Price Control Act granted the Office of Price Administration (OPA) the authority to set price limits and ration food and other commodities in order to discourage hoarding and ensure the equitable distribution of scarce resources. By the spring, Americans were unable to purchase sugar without government-issued food coupons. Vouchers for coffee were introduced in November, and by March of 1943, meat, cheese, fats, canned fish, canned milk and other processed foods were added to the list of rationed provisions.

Rationing regulated the quantity of commodities that consumers could obtain. Sugar rationing took effect in May 1943 with the distribution of **"Sugar Buying Cards"**. Registration usually took place in local schools. Each family was asked to send only one member for registration and be prepared to describe all other family members. Coupons were distributed based on family size, and the coupon book allowed the holder to buy a specified amount. Possession of a coupon book did not guarantee that sugar would be available. Americans learned to utilize what they had during rationing time.

While some food items were scarce, others did not require rationing, and Americans adjusted accordingly. "Red Stamp" rationing covered all meats, butter, fat, and oils, and with some exceptions, cheese. Each person was allowed a certain amount of points weekly with expiration dates to consider. "Blue Stamp" rationing covered canned, bottled, frozen fruits and vegetables, plus juices and dry beans, and such processed foods as soups, baby food and ketchup. Ration stamps became a kind of currency with each family being issued a "War Ration Book." Each stamp authorized a purchase of rationed goods in the quantity and time designated, and the book guaranteed each family its fair share of goods made scarce, thanks to the war.

Rationing also was determined by a point system. Some grew weary of trying to figure out what coupon went with which item, or how many points they needed to purchase them, while some coupons did not require points at all.

In addition to food, rationing encompassed clothing, shoes, coffee, gasoline, tires, and fuel oil. With each coupon book came specifications and deadlines. Rationing locations were posted in public view. Rationing of gas and tires strongly depended on the distance to one's job. If one was fortunate enough to own an automobile and drive at the then specified speed of 35 mph, one might have a small amount of gas remaining at the end of the month to visit nearby relatives.

Buying yards of cloth 3 feet wide requires 3 coupons per yard for wool and 2 coupons per yard for cotton becomes necessary. Sewing your families' clothes stretches your coupon budget. See the coupons required in the sample below.

Coupons required

Men and Boys	Adult	Child
Coat, jacket, blazer	13	8
Trousers	8	6
Shirt combinations - woolen	8	6
Shirt combinations - other material	5	4
Pair of socks or stockings	3	1
Pair of boots or shoes	7	3

Women and Girls	Adult	Child
Jacket, short coat	11	8
Dress, gown, frock - woolen	11	8
Dress, gown, frock - other material	7	5
Blouse, sports shirt, cardigan	5	3
Skirt or divided skirt	7	5
Pair of slippers, boots or shoes	5	3

Imagine how you would plan on spending your allocated coupons for the year for you, your spouse (if not overseas), and all of your children.

Children were allocated an extra 10 clothing coupons above the standard ration to allow for growing out of clothes during a year.

People were also urged to "Make do and mend" so that clothing factories and workers could be used to make items, such as parachutes and uniforms.

Everyone was given a Clothing Book with colored coupons in it. Every item of clothing was given a value in coupons. To buy clothes people handed over their Clothing Book to the shopkeeper who cut out one of the coupons. They then handed over money to the shopkeeper to pay for the clothes. The coupon system allowed people to buy one completely new set of clothes once a year.

Each page of coupons was a different color to stop people using up all their coupons at once. People were only allowed to use one color at a time. The government would tell people when they could start using a new color.

America has always been — and thought of itself as — a land of abundance. Even in the depths of the Depression, there was enough to eat, if only you could afford to buy it. But as soon as the U.S. entered the war in the winter of 1941–42, shortages began. By 1943, it had become every citizen's duty to cut back on meat, sugar, coffee, canned foods, fuel, shoes, and consumer goods — so "they'll have enough."

Every American was entitled to a series of war ration books filled with stamps that could be used to buy restricted items (along with payment), and within weeks of the first issuance, more than 91 percent of the U.S. population had registered to receive them. The Office of Price Administration (OPA) allotted a certain amount of points to each food item based on its availability, and customers were allowed to use 48 'blue points' to buy canned, bottled or dried foods, and 64 'red points' to buy meat, fish and dairy each month—that is, if the items were in stock at the market.

Due to changes in the supply and demand of various goods, the OPA periodically adjusted point values, which often further complicated an already complex system that required home cooks to plan well in advance to prepare meals.

Training sessions were held to teach women to shop wisely, conserve food and plan nutritious meals, as well as teach them how to can food items. The homemaker planned family meals within the set limits. The government's persuasion of people to give up large amounts of red meats and fats resulted in more healthy eating.

The government also printed a monthly meal-planning guide with recipes and a daily menu. *Good Housekeeping* magazine printed a special section for rationed foods in its **1943** cookbook. Numerous national publications also featured articles explaining what rationing meant to America.

Sugar rationing

Sugar was the first food to be rationed, in the spring of 1942. The war with Japan cut off U.S. imports from the Philippines, and cargo ships from Hawaii were diverted to military purposes. The nation's supply of sugar was quickly reduced by more than a third. To prevent hoarding and skyrocketing prices, the Office of Price Administration issued 123 million copies of War Ration Book One, which contained stamps that could be used to purchase sugar. No sugar could legally be bought without stamps, and sugar rationing would continue until supplies returned to normal in 1947.

Want to try out a ration 'sweets' recipe without sugar on your own?

Fruit Turnover

Ingredients: cups sifted flour, 3 tsps. Baking powder, ¾ tsp. salt, 1 tbsp. fat, ¾ cup of milk, or enough to make the dough soft.

Instructions:

Sift together the dry ingredients and then mix the fat in thoroughly. Add milk until a dough forms, then roll out onto a floured surgace. Cut the dough into circles, place fresh fruit on one side of the circle and fold over the other. Crimp the edges and bake until golden brown.

Sugar for canning

But canning required sugar, and sugar, too, was rationed. Women who canned could receive additional sugar, but they had to complete a special application. Canners certified that they expected to can a given quantity of fruit in the coming year and would can four quarts of fruit per pound of sugar allotted.

Home canning

Home-canned goods were exempted from the limits imposed by rationing, and victory gardeners were urged to grow enough fruits and vegetables to put aside for winter. Government pamphlets and agents of state agricultural extension services taught them how to can produce at home

Canned goods and ration points

Asking civilians to conserve food didn't do enough, though, and a year into the war, the government began rationing. In early 1943, the Office of Price Administration introduced a system for rationing canned goods — which were needed for troops overseas and also used scarce metals. Each person had 48 points' worth of ration stamps per month for canned, dried, and frozen foods.

Vegetables & Fruits		# of points
Peas	1 lb. 4 oz.	16
Corn	1 lb. 4 oz.	14
Pears	1 lb. 14 oz.	21
Peaches	1 lb. 14 oz.	21

Juices & Soups		# of points
Grapefruit juice	2 lb. 14 oz.	23
Tomato juice	1 lb. 7 oz.	17
Soup	10.5 oz.	6

Share the meat

The military needed huge amounts of food, too, to feed soldiers, and by late 1942 food at home was running short. Grocery stores started rationing canned goods to customers to prevent hoarding. Meat was in especially short supply. The government limited the amounts shipped to grocers and restaurants and set a "voluntary ration" of two and a half pounds of red meat per adult per week. But stores often could not get even that much, and residents of some cities faced a meatless Christmas.

Salvaging waste fats

Women were urged to save waste fat and greases and return them to butchers. The butcher would pay for the fat and sell it to rendering plants so that it could be processed into explosives. Since meats, oils, and butter were all rationed, women had to re-use fat for frying as often as possible before collecting it in a can and turning it in.

Salvaged kitchen fats and greases, according to one newspaper article, paid 4 cents a pound when taken to the meat market.

Fats and Oils

Unlike Americans in the twenty-first century, the U.S. population in the 1940s had no concerns about eating too much fat. On the contrary, they ate large quantities of high-calorie fats and oils. High-fat foods such as bacon and pork were staples of the U.S. diet and favored by U.S. troops. In 1942 U.S. farmers produced twelve billion pounds of fats. Lend-Lease exports quickly consumed these record amounts. There was real concern over shortages of fat. To prevent such shortages the U.S. Department of Agriculture (USDA) demanded that farmers plant more acres of peanuts, soybeans, and flax, all to be used for oil production. The USDA also required farmers to raise more hogs for lard and pork. In 1942, four million acres of peanuts were harvested, twice as much as in 1941. Soybean production nearly doubled, from about six million acres to eleven million acres. Processed soybeans provided cooking fats, oils, and margarine.

Victory gardens

People could avoid the limits imposed by rationing — and save food for soldiers — by planting "victory gardens." Some 20 million Americans planted gardens in their backyards, in empty lots, and on the rooftops of city buildings.

By 1944 Victory Gardens were responsible for producing 40% of all vegetables in the United States.

Excess food grown in these gardens were then canned and used during the winter. Victory gardens became a key symbol of the will of the American people on the home front to pitch in to win the war.

Scrap paper

Paper was needed for packing weapons and equipment before they were shipped overseas.

Scrap metal drives

To build tanks, ships, planes, and weapons required massive amounts of metal. A single tank needed 18 tons of metal, and one of the navy's biggest ships took 900 tons. Anything using metal — from chicken wire to farm equipment — was rationed. Americans were urged to turn in scrap metal for recycling, and schools and community groups across the country held scrap metal drives.

Gasoline rationing

Gasoline was rationed in 17 eastern states beginning in May 1942 and nationwide in December 1942 — not so much to save fuel as to save tires and the rubber they were made of. A nationwide speed limit of 35 miles per hour was also enforced to save wear on tires. To ration gasoline, the government issued coupon stamps. These "A" stamps were worth three to five gallons of gasoline per week for essential activities such as shopping, attending church, and going to the doctor. The letter on the stamp would have matched a sticker on the car's windshield. People using their cars for work could buy more gasoline, and truckers could buy all they needed.

All fuel is scarce — plan for winter now!

Although gasoline rationing had begun to conserve tires, by late 1942 other kinds of fuel were also in short supply. The military needed huge quantities of fuel for ships, tanks, and planes, and Americans at home had to make do with less. Fuel oil and kerosene were rationed beginning in 1942, and solid fuels followed in 1943. Citizens were warned of the coming shortage and advised them to "winterize" their homes — a term that most Americans were hearing for the first time.

Shoes

Soldiers needed shoes, too, and with rubber for soles in short supply, shoes were rationed beginning in early 1943. The 1943 Sears Roebuck catalog explained how people could buy rationed shoes via mail order.

America needs your scrap rubber

Most of the world's supply of natural rubber came from rubber tree plantations in Southeast Asia, which were quickly occupied by the Japanese in the first months of 1942. Factories converting to military production needed every scrap of rubber they could find, and citizens were asked to turn in old tires, raincoats, gloves, garden hoses, and rubber shoes for recycling. New tires became almost impossible to buy, and people tell stories of lining the insides of their tires with newspaper to make them last longer.

Examples of rubber usage.

A Gas Mask requires 1.11 pounds of rubber

A Life Raft requires 17 to 100 pounds of rubber

A Scout Car requires 306 pounds of rubber

A Heavy Bomber requires 1,825 pounds of rubber

Even Typewriters!

Major purchases such as automobiles, bicycles, and kitchen appliances required special certificates and proof of need. Because the military needed so many typewriters for communication, even they were rationed.

With many parents engaged in war work, children were taught the facts of point rationing for helping out in family shopping.

While life during the war meant daily sacrifice, few complained because they knew it was the men and women in uniform who were making the greater sacrifice.

War Bonds

These bonds were kind of like loans to the government. People would buy bonds and the government promised to return them with interest after **ten** years or more. During the war, the government needed all the extra money it could get to help pay for war equipment.

Durable work clothes replaced fashion for women's outfits. Specially designed garments in durable fabrics were made for the home front workers specially designed according whether they were used for factory, farm or home.

for factory, for farm and home

Specially designed garments in durable fabrics for home front workers

VIII FARMS

Sharp rise in demand

By 1941, as Europe's agricultural production became increasingly disrupted by the war, the demand for U.S. agricultural products began to rise sharply. On **March 11, 1941**, the Lend-Lease Act became law. The act authorized President Franklin D. Roosevelt (1882–1945; served 1933–45) to lend money and send weapons, equipment, and food to the Allies, the nations' combating the so-called Axis powers of Germany, Italy, and Japan. Under the Lend-Lease program, U.S. goods worth billions of dollars flowed to Great Britain, the Soviet Union, and China. Suddenly the American agricultural industry had to scramble to keep up with the food demands of the Allied countries.

With the commencement of the Lend-Lease program and the formal entrance of the United States into the war in late 1941, American farmers were expected to produce enough food for U.S. civilians, the U.S. Army and Navy, and Allied civilians and military forces overseas. Just as U.S. industry had mobilized to produce war products, farmers had to mobilize for massive increases in food production.

However, agricultural mobilization presented farmers with a set of challenges very different from those faced by industry leaders. Farmers dealt with living, growing commodities. Grain took a certain number of months to grow and mature; cattle and hogs took time to fatten up. Agricultural production had to proceed on nature's schedule, not the war's schedule. Containment pens allowed faster farm to market time.

Like the mobilization of industry for production of guns, warplanes, and ships, agricultural mobilization required immense effort and a complex set of strategies. Millions of acres of new fields had to be plowed and irrigated. Huge increases in the demand for fertilizers had to be met. Farm machinery had to be kept in excellent working condition, and new machinery for new crops often had to be procured.

Nearly 690,000 new tractors put two million horses and mules out of work. Greater numbers of cattle, hogs, and sheep meant grazing land had to be expanded; production of feed grains and corn had to increase, too. Transportation presented more challenges. To transport their goods to railroad shipping yards farmers needed trucks, gas, and tires—all items that were hard to obtain during wartime.

Keep them eating

Despite the challenges, most farmers were caught up in the patriotic fervor of wartime and vowed to "keep them eating," a common catchphrase during the war. To meet production goals farmers worked from sunup to sundown every day, often calling on the entire family to help in the effort. For average, hardworking "dirt" farmers, as they liked to call themselves, 1942 was a very good year. Most were inclined to go on with this effort, as the Department of Agriculture requested, "for the duration," meaning at least until the war ended.

Farmers also had to grow many nonfood crops. Before the war approximately 600 million pounds of wool were used for clothing each year. In 1942 about one billion pounds were used for military uniforms, jackets, heavy fleece-lined coats, and pants. Hemp for cordage had previously been imported from such countries as the Philippines, but those imports were halted during the war. Therefore, U.S. farmers needed to produce 150,000 tons of hemp, which required the planting of 300,000 additional acres.

It took only one-half acre of land and 6.5 man-hours of work to obtain the same amount of oil from soybeans as one and a third acre and 132 man-hours of work for cottonseed oil.

Although World War II ultimately raised the income and social status of America's farmers, the early 1940s were still difficult. During that period about five million small farmers who were barely making a living left their farms and sought work in the newly expanding war industries.

Farm workers pay

Pay was supposed to be at least 30 cents per hour or equivalent piecework rates (pay based on the amount harvested). Instead, rates were usually determined by locality and worker scarcity. Rates were higher in the West than in the East. Rates in the Pacific Northwest were 60 to 95 cents an hour, but in the Southeast, they were only 20 cents an hour. At harvest time. Workers were generally paid by the piece; for example, strawberry pickers were paid 42 cents per carrier full of strawberries. Generally, workers could pick between fourteen ($5.88) and eighteen carriers ($7.56) in a six-hour day.

Foreign workers and prisoners of war

In addition to workers from Mexico, farm workers were also brought to the United States from the Bahamas, Barbados, Jamaica, and Canada. In all, approximately

230,000 foreign workers came to the United States to relieve the farm labor shortage during World War II.

Approximately 265,000 prisoners of war (POWs) also helped relieve the farm labor shortage. In California, south of the San Francisco Bay area, Italian prisoners of war aided at harvest times. From 1944 to 1946 thirty-five hundred German and other prisoners of war from six POW camps in Oregon worked to harvest potatoes, onions, lettuce, and pears in that state.

Prosperity comes to American farms

Farmers experienced a peak of prosperity during the World War II years. Through the course of the war, the U.S. farm population fell by 17 percent. The remaining farmers prospered greatly. The number of farms decreased, but the size of farms increased.

Major scientific and technological advances, such as commercial fertilizers, substantially improved crop yields. Increased mechanization helped make up for the loss of workers who were enlisting in the military or taking factory jobs in the war industry. Farmers invested in new and improved tractors, trucks, and combines (a machine for cutting and threshing grains; threshing means separating out the seeds) that improved farm productivity. The federal government made a significant contribution to farmers' prosperity.

Food preservation

Dehydration processing plants were a significant war industry. At the plants, heat was used to remove all water content from food items. Foods were dehydrated for two reasons: to prevent spoilage and to reduce the size of food items so that more could be packed into each shipment. Eggs, meat, vegetables, and fruits all underwent dehydration. Three dozen eggs, susceptible to spoiling and breakage in transit, would reduce to one pound of easily transportable egg powder. Scrambled eggs from dehydrated egg powder tasted almost exactly like scrambled eggs from whole fresh eggs. Through dehydration a 700-pound steer could be reduced to a relatively small portion of dried beef, about enough to fill a medium-size suitcase. Dehydrated vegetables—including beans, tomatoes, potatoes, and cabbage—could be stored in boxes. They were favored over nondehydrated, canned vegetables, which took up more space and wasted tin, a scarce material during wartime.

What Is a Shipload of Food?

According to author Frederick Simpich in "Farmers Keep Them Eating," a *National Geographic* magazine article, the average U.S. freighter could carry the following amounts of goods:

- 6,000 barrels of dried eggs, equal to a year's work for 229,137 hens.

- 6,000 barrels of dried milk, a year's work for 2,783 cows.

- 16,522 cases of evaporated milk, a year's work for 304 cows

- 20,000 boxes of cheese, a year's work for

- 14,500 big cans of pork, the meat from 5,021 hogs.

- 16,800 boxes of **lard**, the fat of 27,632 hogs.

- 6,061 sacks of flour, the wheat from 838 acres.

- 26,111 cases of canned vegetables, equal to 40 acres of tomatoes, 100 acres of snap beans, and 102 acres of peas.

To fill this ship took the products from 3,824 average farms.

IX   INDUSTRY & LOGISTICS

List of selected US Corporations in the values of World War II production contracts.

1. General Motors

2. Curtiss-Wright (aircraft, aircraft engines)

3. Ford Motor Company

4. Convair (Aircraft)

5. Douglas Aircraft Company

7. Bethlehem Steel

8. Chrysler Corporation

10. Lockheed Corporation

11. North American Aviation, e.g. P-51 Mustang

12. Boeing

13. AT&T

16. U.S. Steel

17. Bendix Aviation

18. Packard, e.g. marine and aircraft engines

19. Sperry Corporation, e.g. bomb sights, radar

20. Kaiser Shipyards, e.g. Liberty ships

The high wages and new jobs were both a boom and a strain on the local economy. More money in people's pockets meant there was more to spend in town and at the markets, but it also meant that there were fewer people to work on the farms and behind the counters. Merchants had more money but were forced to pay more for their help and extend the hours they were open.

With thousands of new workers, communities experienced strains on their schools, housing, recreation facilities, police and other social services. Schools expanded their teachings and began offering more mathematics and a course in aeronautical engineering. When the war ended in August 1945, work forces at the plants were released in large numbers within weeks.

The women that were left behind picked up the slack, trading their aprons and knitting needles for overalls and hand tools. For the production of B-29 bombers alone, women accounted for one-third of all workers. The aircraft industry, which in

1939, employed less than 47,000 people and produced fewer than 6,000 planes, hit its peak in 1944. That year, the industry employed 2,102,000 workers and rolled out more than 96,000 planes.

In general terms, no 1940's automobiles were produced in 1943 or 1944. Automakers, for example, produced their last passenger cars on February 10, 1942. They then made aircraft — Chrysler built Martin designs, Ford made planes for Consolidated Aircraft, and General Motors produced aircraft for North American. In addition to airplanes and aircraft parts, the automakers also manufactured trucks, tanks, marine diesels, guns, and shells.

During the production freeze, automakers became around the clock defense contractors.

Ford built airplane engines for the British government. B-24 Liberator and gliders bombers for the U.S. Military. Ford also turned out tanks, armored cars, jeeps and engines for robot bombs. Ford's plants in Great Britain and Canada had joined the production efforts of the United States and produced everything from mobile canteens to four-wheel-drive trucks and autos, grenades, bombs and engine-powered landing craft.

At its vast Willow Run plant in Ypsilanti, Michigan, the Ford Motor Company performed something of a miracle 24-hours a day. The average Ford car had some 15,000 parts. The B-24 Liberator long-range bomber had 1,550,000. **One of the B-24s came off the line every 63 minutes**.

General Motors converted all of its production to the war effort and delivered more than $12 billion worth of goods, ranging from airplanes to tanks, marine diesel engines, trucks, machine guns, and shells. No other manufacturer delivered as much material to the Allied forces.

Chrysler made everything from fuse bomb noses, forging and machining shells, cartridge cases, tanks, anti-aircraft guns, aircraft engines, and they played a major role in the B-29 bomber. They also made assorted military vehicles such as command cars, ambulances, trucks, and weapons carriers.

Tanks and ships were also produced at record numbers. Medium tank production, in fact, advanced at such a rate that it actually had to be cut back before the war even ended. And shipbuilding also increased to handle merchant shipping, which rose from about one million tons in 1941 to 19 million tons only two years later.

America's manufacturing strength was crucial to the Allied victory in World War II. By the beginning of 1944, the output of American factories was twice that of all the Axis nations as manufacturers everywhere shut down normal operations and retooled for wartime.

America launched more vessels in 1941 than Japan did in the entire war. By the end of the war, more than half of all industrial production in the world would take place in the United States.

Kaiser Shipyards

Kaiser had seven major shipbuilding yards located on the United States west coast during World War II. Kaiser ranked 20th among U.S. corporations in the value of wartime production contracts. The shipyards were owned by the Kaiser Shipbuilding Company, a creation of American industrialist Henry J. Kaiser, (1882-1967), who established the shipbuilding company around 1939 in order to help meet the construction goals set by the United States Maritime Commission for merchant shipping. Henry Kaiser had previously completed construction of Hoover, Bonneville and Grand Coulee Dams ahead of schedule, but had never before built a ship.

Four of the Kaiser Shipyards were located in Richmond, California and were called the Richmond Shipyards. Together, these four Kaiser Shipyards produced 747 ships, including many of the famous Liberty ships and Victory ships— for carrying general cargo and military munitions, armaments and supplies, more than any other complex in the United States.

By the end of World War II, the number of shipyards building for the Maritime Commission comprised the following: 16 on the West coast, 16 on the East coast and 11 on the Gulf coast.

Henry Kaiser was known for developing new methods of ship building, which al-lowed his yards to outproduce other similar facilities and build 1,490 ships, 27 per-cent of the total Maritime Commission construction. Kaiser's ships were completed in two-thirds the time and a quarter the cost of the average of all other shipyards. Liberty ships were typically assembled in a little over two weeks, and one in less than five days. Kaiser's theories on mass-production created some mirth among conventional shipbuilders, but he continually reduced delivery times.

The U.S. government's greatest need was for Liberty ships to transport general cargo, military munitions, armaments and supplies, troops and cargo. The ships were built to a standardized design, with some 250,000 parts prefabricated throughout the country in 250-ton sections and welded together at the shipyards. At 441 feet long and 56 feet wide, the Liberty ships operated at a speed of 11 knots.

Built for just under $2 million, each could carry 2,840 Jeeps, 440 tankers, or 230 million rounds of rifle ammunition. Eighteen American shipyards built 2,710 Liberty ships between 1941 and 1945, easily the largest number of ships produced to a single design.

However, the quality of production of these simple vessels was very poorly suited and only useful for critical times of war. Although many were still used many years after WW2, more than 100 ships sank in the first ten years by hull and deck cracks due to brittle fracture. The reason for this was, that before the 1950s, the welding techniques that were used the first time for the mass-production of these ships, were not yet mature. Usually ships at this time were still riveted.

The Victory ships, officially adopted on 28 **April 1943**, were a more modern design compared to the earlier Liberty ship. They were slightly larger and had more powerful steam turbine engines giving higher speed to allow participation in high speed convoys.

Kaiser Shipyards shut down at the end of the war. **The Rosie the Riveter/World War II Home Front National Historical Park was dedicated October 25, 2000 on the site of one of the shipyards in Richmond, California.**

Kaiser Permanente

This program evolved from industrial health care programs for construction, ship-yard, and steel mill workers for the Kaiser industrial companies during the late 1930s and 1940s. **It was opened to public enrollment in July 1945.**

Harig Manufacturing Corp.,

First founded as a tool and die manufacturer in 1937. The company spent the war years filling military orders exclusively and even received a citation by the Armed Services for developing advanced tooling to manufacture the M1 rifle clip.

Kingsbury Toys

This toy company specialized in copying famous models of aircraft and assembly-line, autos, trucks, and buses. WWII saw Kingsbury shifting to war contracts and never returning again to toy production. The materials the toys were fashioned from — heavy gauge steel, flat steel springs, soft rubber, enamel paints, and automotive lacquer — were all needed for the war effort. And since toys were not high on the government's list of requirements, Kingsbury concentrated on making machinery to produce rifle bolts and shell casings.

Barnes International

Barnes' solution to a manufacturing problem became an entirely new metalworking process. What Barnes did was develop horizontal honing machines that precisely finished the bores of gun barrels for the best rifling operation. The effect of this new finishing method was demonstrated in the tremendous amount of money and time saved in maintaining fighting equipment for the U.S. The Navy, in particular, used these machines to service large-caliber naval guns after they had been fired a certain number of times.

These machines were designed so that it was possible to recondition guns in service without removing the gun barrel from the gun emplacement.

Barnes also built the world's largest machine for honing gun barrels and catapult tubes for aircraft carriers. The machine was 190-ft long, weighed 45 tons, and finished barrels up to 30-in, in diameter and 75-ft long. Small World War II aircraft carriers depended on their catapults to launch planes off of the flight deck.

Wartime production of lathes, mills, grinders, and other machine tools skyrocketed — peaking in 1942 — once industry realized it needed these machines to make planes, trucks, and tanks. **Collectively, more machine tools were manufactured between 1940 and 1943 than had been made between 1900 and 1940.**

Omaha's Glenn L. Martin Bomber Plant

The plant was actually closer to the small rural community of Bellevue than Omaha. When the plant began construction in the **spring of 1941** – well before Pearl Harbor – Bellevue had 1,184 residents occupying 306 buildings.

The plant was going to bring in 3,000 new workers. Some would come from the adjoining towns of Omaha, Ralston and Council Bluffs, but the plant would forever change Bellevue from rural to urban. Federal grants helped Bellevue with housing, schools, police and fire protection, but the town boomed and strained at the seams.

At its peak in **1945**, the plant employed over 13,000 workers. Over 40 percent of the workforce were women - 5,300 workers. **The plant recruited female workers with ads that said if they could sew they could learn to rivet. They became known as "Rosie the Riveter", a generic term for all working women of WWII.**

The Glenn L. Martin Company began producing bombers in January 1942, with the plant reaching full-scale production **8 June 1942**. Initially producing B-26 Marauder medium bombers, 1,585 Marauders were built at the Martin-Nebraska bomber plant. The plant's construction included a two-mile (3.2 km) concrete runway, six large hangars, and a 1,700,000-square-foot aircraft-assembly building.

Operation Silverplate

Silverplate was the code reference for the United States Army Air Forces' participation in the Manhattan Project during World War II. Originally the name for the aircraft modification project which enabled a B-29 Superfortress Bomber to drop an atomic weapon. The **Manhattan Project** was a research and development undertaking during World War II that produced the first nuclear weapons.

"Silverplate" eventually came to identify the training and operational aspects of the program as well. The original directive for the project had as its subject line "Silver Plated Project" but continued usage of the term shortened it to "Silverplate".

Production switched to B-29 Superfortress very heavy bombers in **1944**, and 531 Superfortresses' were produced before the end of World War II. Among these were the *Enola Gay* and *Bockscar*, the B-29's that dropped the first atomic weapons to be used in a military action (against the cities of Hiroshima and Nagasaki, Japan). Both aircraft were built and modified at the base.

Paul Tibbets personally selected the Enola Gay (Tibbets mothers name) from the assembly line. His crew dropped the first of two atomic bombs convincing the Japanese to surrender.

Glenn Martin Bomber plant employee Donita Mitchell remembers drinking tequila to celebrate the dropping of the bomb. It solved a mystery that had puzzled several of her co-workers. Why had some B-29s been shipped out without their normal bomb racks? Mitchell still has her dismissal letter, dated **Aug. 15, 1945**. *"You have served your Nation — and your Company — well,"* it said. *"They fired everybody with one letter,"* Mitchell said. Production ended on **18 September 1945**, when the last B-29 rolled out of the assembly building.

✦ ✦ ✦ ✦

Women Workers in World War II

- The female labor force grew by 6.5 million.

- In 1944, 37 percent of all adult women were employed.

- In 1944, women comprised 35.4 percent of the civilian labor force.

- In 1945, women comprised 36.1 percent of the civilian labor force.

- At the height of the war, there were 19,170,000 women in the labor force.

- Between 1940 and 1945, the female labor force grew by 50 percent.

- One in ten married women entered the labor force.

- The percentage of married women working outside the home increased from 13.9 to 22.5.

- The percentage of working women with children under 10 years of age increased from 7.8 to 12.1 from 1940 to 1944.

- At the height of the war, women comprised 4 percent of skilled workers.

- In 1944, skilled female workers made an average weekly wage of $31.21 while skilled male workers earned $54.65 weekly.

- From 1940 to 1944, the percentage of women workers employed in factories increased from 20 to 30 percent.

- From 1940 to 1944, the percentage of women workers employed as domestic servants declined from 17.7 to 9.5 percent.

- Female employment in defense industries grew by 462 percent from 1940 to 1944.

- Between 1943 and 1945, polls indicated that 61 to 85 percent of women workers wanted to keep their jobs after the war.

- Between 1943 and 1945, polls indicated that 47 to 68 percent of married women workers wanted to keep their jobs after the war.

Source: Susan M. Hartmann, **The Home Front and Beyond: American Women in the 1940s** (Boston: Twayne Publishers, 1982).

Propaganda

Tokyo Rose was a fabricated name given by Allied troops in the South Pacific during World War II to all female English-speaking radio broadcasters of Japanese propaganda. The programs were broadcast in the South Pacific and North America to demoralize Allied troops abroad and their families at home by emphasizing troops' wartime difficulties and military losses. Several female broadcasters operated under different aliases and in different cities throughout the Empire, including Tokyo, Manila, and Shanghai. The name "Tokyo Rose" was never used in any Japanese radio program, but it first appeared in U.S. newspapers in the context of these broadcasts in 1943.

Post War

The U.S. economy prospered after WWII, and veterans had little trouble finding work, partially because the pent-up demand for consumer goods was so high. In the five years after the war, national production increased as did worker income, and industries such as automotive had audiences hungry for new products.

X   Prelude and Brief Combat Narrative

This is Dad's journey with the 37th Infantry Division, 129th Infantry Regiment, based on dates on the backs of pictures he sent and brought back from the South Pacific during World War II. I have added history chronicles of the battles in the Pacific during the same time frame and at locations in very close proximity to where he was located. In my view, every one of those who served are heroes.

This journey has sure enhanced my appreciation of the sacrifices made and atrocities witnessed by all who served and those that assisted in the war effort. It has been a humbling experience for me in my research of Dad's travels in the Pacific and what he and everyone else affiliated with the war effort went through.

There wasn't a Veteran's Health Administration offering posttraumatic stress disorders (PTSD) treatment as this department was established in 1946. WWI shell shock diagnosis was replaced by Combat Stress Reaction (CSR), also known as "battle fatigue". It was called Battle Fatigue or Combat Stress Reaction (CSR) In World War II. Long battle surges were common in World War II and soldiers became battle weary and exhausted.

Combat Stress Reaction is an acute reaction that includes a range of behaviors resulting from the stress of battle that look like symptoms of mental illness such as panic, extreme anxiety, depression, and hallucinations. A lot of soldiers brought these behaviors home with them. The most common symptoms are fatigue, slower reaction times, indecision, disconnection from one's surroundings, and the inability to prioritize. Combat stress reaction is generally short-term.

Not until **1980** that **PTSD** was recognized as a disorder with specific symptoms that could be reliably diagnosed and was added to the American Psychiatric Association's Diagnostic and Statistical Manual of Mental Disorders.

Dad and soldiers like him returning home had to deal with the recurring nightmares and my mom had to constantly be aware of his nightmares and mood swings. Mom & Dad were inseparable and the "Best of Friends".

Brief Combat Narrative

The 37th Infantry Division arrived in the Fiji Islands in June 1942 to fortify the islands against possible invasion. The Division continued its training on the islands. With the end of ground fighting on Guadalcanal, the Division moved to that island in April 1943, continued training, and staged for the Munda campaign.

Two battalions joined the Marines on New Georgia, 5 July 1943, while the remainder of the Division landed, 22 July, and assisted the 43d Infantry Division in taking Munda airfield in heavy fighting. After mopping up on New Georgia, the Division returned to Guadalcanal, 9 September 1943, for rest and rehabilitation.

The Division's next assignment was Bougainville. Relieving Marine units, 8-19 November 1943, the 37th took over the perimeter defense of the area, constructed roads and bridges and engaged in extensive patrol activity. Defended Piva Airfield, Bougainville from heavy attacks. In March 1944, two Japanese divisions made eight major attacks, but Division lines held, which were the main Japanese attacks and penetrated the 129th's lines before the attack was defeated. This was the last Japanese offensive action in the Solomons. In April patrols cleared the Laruma Valley area of major enemy units. Spent remainder of time on Bougainville conducting construction and combat activities until 11 Oct 44, when it began training for operation in the Philippines.

Landing with the Sixth Army on the beaches of Lingayen Gulf, 9 January 1945, Encountered slight resistance landing at Lingayen Gulf. The 129th Infantry was attached to XIV Corps 21-24 Jan 45, then attached 40th Infantry Division 1-2 Feb 45 and 33rd ID 27 Mar -10 Apr 45. 129th IR was divisional reserve in drive to San Carlos and further on to Clark Field and Fort Stotsenburg where fierce resistance delayed capture of those objectives until 31 January. The division moved on toward Manila with 148th IR of the 37th ID, against small delaying forces, reaching the city's outskirts 4 Feb 45. While 145th IR stormed Quezon and Parian Gates, 129th IR crossed Pasig River in assault boats and stormed the Mint Building. Upon crossing the Pasig River, it ran into bitter Japanese opposition, and it took heavy street fighting to clear the city by 3 March 1945. After garrison duty and conducting mopping up activity in Manila, 5-26 March, the Division shifted to the hills of Northwest Luzon.   129th IR attached to 33rd ID from 37th ID and pushed up Highway 9 toward Baguio, encountering very heavy fighting in the Salat Area 23 Mar-10 Apr 44. 129th IR detached 33rd ID and joined 148th IR attacking up Highway 9, taking Three Peaks 11 Apr 45. Mount Mirador fell to the 129th after heavy fighting 17 Apr 45 culminated in the capture of Baguio, under combined assault of 33rd and 37th IDs 26 April 1945. relieved by 33rd ID and moved to San Jose 4 May 45 and rested until 29 May 45. Moved to Balete Pass-Santa Fe area 31 May 45 and pushed across Cagayen Valley against deteriorating Japanese resistance and took Cauayan 16 Jun 45. Continued to conduct mopping up duties and secure area until end of war. With the end of hostilities, 15 August, the Division was concerned with the collection and processing of prisoners of war, leaving November 1945 for the States and demobilization.

This was the address listed on a birthday envelope sent to Dad **February 17, 1943** from Mom and Faye. Faye was four months old at the time.

ELMER L. MADSEN

ASN 37162364

CO. H 129TH INFANTRY REGIMENT

37TH INFANTRY DIVISION

Commanders:

Maj. Gen. Robert S. Beightler commanded the 37th Infantry Division during its entire period of Federal service in World War II.

Col. John D. Frederick Commanding Officer of the 129th Infantry Regiment, assigned to the 37th Division in 1941, moving to a combat area at Espiritu Santo in the Pacific Theater. Commanded the 129th during its entire period of Federal service in WWII.

The type of patch Dad had on the left shoulder of his uniform was a red inner circle with a white outside background denoting the 37th Infantry Division.

Nickname: **Buckeye Division**. Shoulder Patch: Brilliant red circle on a circular background of white; the patch was adopted from the Ohio State flag which was a red circle on white near the center of the red, white and blue banner. (Troops refer to their division insignia as the "fried egg" patch). Song: None officially, although "Rodger Young" the Infantry song, was written about a Medal of Honor winner in the unit. Source: Ohio National Guard. History: Organized: Aug., 1917; overseas June, 1918. Actions: Baccarat Sector; Meuse-Argonne; Montfaucon; St. Mihiel; Ypres-Lys; crossing the Scheldt. Training: Inducted Oct., 1940, and assigned to Camp Shelby, Mississippi Maneuvers: June and Aug., 1941, under V Corps. Camp Claiborne, La. Transferred to Indiantown Gap, Pa., Feb 1942, and overseas May, 1942. Overseas training Fiji Islands. Commanding General: Maj. Gen. Robert S. Beightler, Oct., 1940, to present. Component Units: (As of May, 1942): 129th, 145th and 148th Infantry Regiments; 6th, 135th, 140th (L) and 136th (M) FA Battalions. Higher Commands: (combat) Sixth and Eighth Armies Awards Distinguished Unit Citation to Cos. E and P, 148th Inf., for action on Hill 700, Mar. 11-12, 1944 (Bougainville); DUC to Co. P, 129th Inf. Regt., for action at Empress Augusta Bay, Mar. 15 26, 1944; DUC to Hq. Co., 129th Infantry, for action battalion perimeter. Mar. 12-26, 1944; (Bougainville); DUC Hq. Co., 148th Inf. Regt., for action Hill 700. Mar. 11-12, 1944; DUC to CO. P. 145th Infantry Regiment, on Hill 700. Mar. 9-12, 1944.

Combat Highlights gives an abbreviated account of the brilliant action by the 37th Buckeyes, called the Heroes of Hill 700, crucial hill of the second battle of Bougainville, when the infamous Jap 6th Div. attempted to push the Ohio men into the sea. They were masters of Clark Field and Ft Stotsenberg, and liberators of Bilibid prison internees during their later Philippines campaign.

The 37th fought at Bairoka Harbor landing (New Georgia Island); Munda Airfield (New Georgia); Bougainville; Lingayen Gulf landing (Philippines); capture of Clark Field and Ft. Stotsenberg; seizure of San Fernando; penetration of Manila: crossing of the Pasig river; mopping up operations around Baguio, the Cagayen Valley and Baleta Pass, and liberation of 2000 internees at Bilibid Prison. The 37th slew 8000 Japs in two weeks at Bougainville; with the 1st Cavalry Division accounted for 10,000 more in Luzon; suffered 3800 casualties in the Manila operation.

The 129th Infantry Regiment (IR), Illinois National Guard, inducted into federal service at Sycamore, Ill. 5 March 1941 and assigned to the 33rd Division's Infantry Brigade. Trained various posts US and departed San Francisco P/E **24 August 1942**, detached to furnish cadre for the 37th Infantry regiment. A cadre is the complement of commissioned officers and non-commissioned officers of a military unit responsible for training the rest of the unit including themselves.

Dad is with the 37th Infantry Division, 129th Infantry Regiment and I can only assume he followed the path through the islands below.

Solomon Islands

The 37th Infantry Division arrived in the Fiji Islands in June 1942 to fortify the islands against possible invasion. The Division continued its training on the island. With the end of ground fighting on Guadalcanal, the Division moved to Guadalcanal in April 1943, continued training, and staged for the Munda campaign on New Georgia. Two battalions joined the Marines on New Georgia, 5 July 1943, while the remainder of the Division landed 22 July and assisted the 43rd Infantry Division in taking Munda airfield in heavy fighting. After mopping up on New Georgia, the Division returned to Guadalcanal 9 September 1943 for rest and rehabilitation.

Bougainville

The Division's next assignment was Bougainville. Relieving Marine units, 8-19 November 1943, the 37th took over the perimeter defense of the area, constructed roads and bridges and engaged in extensive patrol activity. In March 1944, two Japanese divisions made eight major attacks, but Division lines held.

Dad was wounded for the first time during this time frame. In April patrols cleared the Laruma Valley area of major enemy units. The Division remained on Bougainville and trained for the Luzon campaign.

Philippines

Landing with the Sixth Army on the beaches of Lingayen Gulf, 9 January 1945, the 37th raced inland against slight resistance to Clark Field and Fort Stotsenburg where fierce resistance delayed capture of those objectives until 31 January. The Division continued to drive to Manila against small delaying forces, and entered the city's outskirts, 4 February. Upon crossing the Pasig River, it ran into bitter Japanese opposition, and it took heavy street fighting to clear the city by 3 March 1945. After garrison duty in Manila, 5-26 March, the Division shifted to the hills of Northwest Luzon, where heavy fighting culminated in Baguio's capture, 26 April.

Rest and rehabilitation during May were followed by action in June in the Cagayan Valley against deteriorating Japanese resistance.

With the end of hostilities, 15 August, the Division was concerned with the collection and processing of prisoners of war, leaving November 1945 for the States and demobilization.

Dad would have been sent home the first part of August 1945 per an article in our hometown paper, The Belgrade Tribune stating, among other things, it took him thirty-three days to get home from Luzon. Arriving Saturday evening in the article would have been September 8, 1945.

The above synopsis shows the path taken by the 37th ID, 129th IR but these are just words. I liken it to a scenery picture you take on a vacation. Such beauty to the beholder, but only a picture to those you share it with. Unless you see it up close, smell it, touch it, hear it; just words on paper or a picture unappreciated for its connotation or simply, not understood. Compare this to a battlefield picture that you cannot smell, touch or hear what was happening. Just a picture...

So are the fights for freedom that our country has endured. Individuals who bore their grief with their families, took no part to seek assistance and slowly put their lives together in the best American tradition of stoic perseverance. Over the succeeding years having been comforted by family and friends through numerous inclusive activities, but in the silence of the wee hours of the morning, the only comfort being the indelible memories.

The words of 19th century writer Washington Irving: *"The sorrow for the dead is the only sorrow from which we refuse to be divorced. Every other wound we seek to heal, every other affliction to forget; but this wound we consider it a duty to keep open; this affliction we cherish and brood over in solitude."*

Just words and pictures in watered down history books that are taught in schools *(Founding Myths: Stories That Hide Our Patriotic Past by Ray Raphael)*. An eleventh grade Texas history teacher said it's *"definitely an attempt in many instances to whitewash our history, as opposed to exposing students to the reality of things and letting them make decisions for themselves"*. All that the future generations learn are dates and a little bit of the circumstances, condensed even more as time goes on.

The following narrative in no way tries to elevate my Dad's importance in his service during WWII in the Pacific. He was just a guy who was drafted, like so many others, into the service of his country. Every person involved, whether in a uniform or not, to do their part towards the war effort were heroes in their own way.

They all stepped out of their comfort zone to assist during WWII.

I have included a chronology of events of the path that the United States made in achieving the defeat of the Japanese Empire in the Pacific Theater. There were other air and naval battles and island skirmishes where thousands of Americans fought and lives were lost that are not included in this narrative.

World War II was the largest and most violent armed conflict in the history of mankind. However, the many years that now separates us from that conflict has exacted its toll on our collective knowledge and, unfortunately, receded in memory.

After Pearl Harbor the American public clamored for retaliation against Japan. Further, the stunning series of Japanese victories throughout the Pacific in the six months following 7 December 1941 demanded some military response as Japanese power in the Pacific went unchallenged. Meanwhile American and Australian Army units drove the enemy from easternmost New Guinea. Together the Guadalcanal and Papua Campaigns by early 1943 had committed more American troops to action against the Japanese than against the Germans, and American military strategists in the Pacific understandably wanted to follow their successes with additional operations to deny the Japanese any respite. Now, they argued, was the time to seize the initiative. Not only had Japanese momentum been halted, but the Japanese had not yet built elaborate defenses on their recently conquered islands. While the moment seemed advantageous for an offensive, decisions of grand strategy constrained American operations against Japan.

"THOSE WHO CANNOT REMEMBER THE PAST –
ARE CONDEMNED TO REPEAT IT"

While World War II continues to absorb the interest of military scholars and historians, as well as veterans, a generation of Americans have grown to maturity largely unaware of the political, social, economic and military implications of a war that, more than any other, united us as a people with a common purpose.

XI   Drafted into the Army

Drafted 13 February, 1942

Induction point - Fort Snelling, Minnesota

When the United States entered World War II in December 1941, Fort Snelling became the induction point for more than 300,000 men and women who joined the armed forces. At its height in **1942**, the Reception Center was capable of processing approximately 800 recruits each day. Recruits were sworn into the U.S. military, received medical examinations and vaccinations, were classified and assigned to a unit and were issued basic equipment. Most recruits stayed at Fort Snelling for only a short time before they were transferred to other military posts to begin their basic training. Announcement in the Belgrade Tribune, February 12, 1942.

Basic Training 4 April, 1942

Camp Forrest, located in Tullahoma, Tennessee, was one of the U.S. Army's largest training bases during World War II covering 78,000 acres. The Hardaway Construction Company of Columbus, Georgia, and the Creighton Construction Company of Nashville formed a temporary partnership to build the thirteen hundred buildings, the fifty-five miles of roads, and the five miles of railroad track that made up Camp Forrest and its 78,000 acres.

The camp served as a training facility for eleven infantry divisions, two battalions of Rangers, numerous medical and supply units, and a number of Army Air Corps personnel. It was an active army post between 1941 and 1946. Tullahoma was greatly affected by the installation of Camp Forrest. Because of maneuvers and operations, civilians had to adjust to blocked roads, traffic jams, crowded stores, the absence of mail delivery and driving at night without lights. Soldiers camped out on lawns and fields; many crops and fences were destroyed.

In **1940** the population in Tullahoma was 4,500. By the end of the war, the population had grown to 75,000. Many military people who moved in for construction and operation of the camp remained after the war. Housing at the induction and training center proved to be a recurring problem, and many soldiers bivouacked in tents during their assignment at the post. Dad quartered in one of these tents throughout his basic training.

Camp Forrest employed 12,000 civilians who ran the post exchanges, operated the nine-thousand square foot laundry, performed maintenance on military vehicles, repaired tanks and artillery pieces, and staffed the induction center where some

250,000 young men received their initial physical exams for the Army. Army trainees received instruction in house-to-house combat in the first village mock-up.

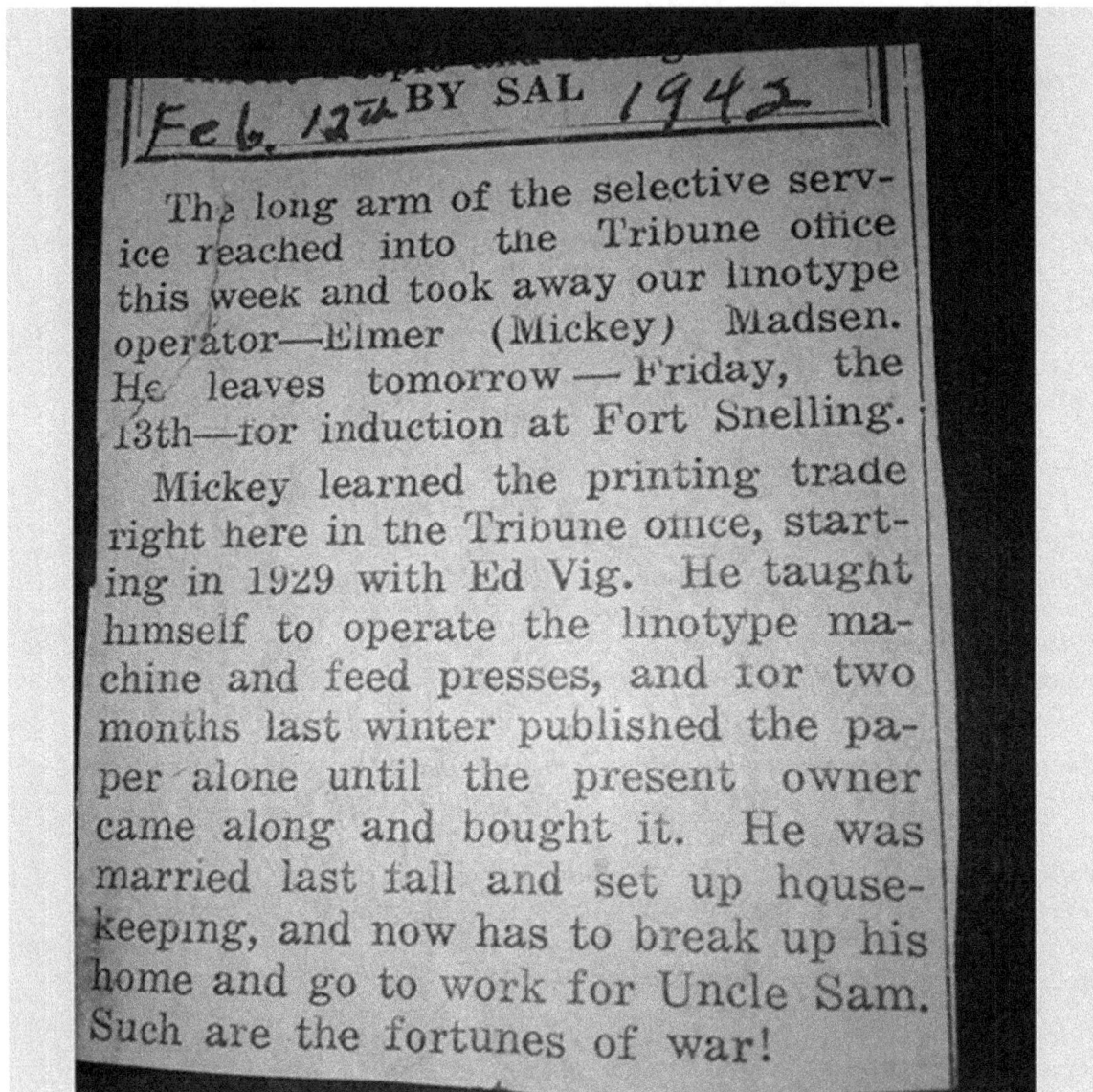

Feb. 12th BY SAL 1942

The long arm of the selective service reached into the Tribune office this week and took away our linotype operator—Elmer (Mickey) Madsen. He leaves tomorrow — Friday, the 13th—for induction at Fort Snelling.

Mickey learned the printing trade right here in the Tribune office, starting in 1929 with Ed Vig. He taught himself to operate the linotype machine and feed presses, and for two months last winter published the paper alone until the present owner came along and bought it. He was married last fall and set up housekeeping, and now has to break up his home and go to work for Uncle Sam. Such are the fortunes of war!

Lt. Col. Milton Thompson, the Battalion Commander of the 301st Troop Command and Environmental Branch Chief for the military department of Tennessee, is an African-American with more than 20 years in the Tennessee National Guard. *"The African-American barracks portion of Camp Forrest had conditions of separate living quarters, lack of uniforms, less pay and lack of other simple amenities that soldiers had to forfeit back then, yet they still wanted to serve and were willing to sacrifice their lives for freedom,"* he continued. *"Today the military has achieved integration in all branches of the armed services."*

Camp Forrest not only served to train thousands of our military but was also the first internment camp in our nation housing 800 plus Alien Civilians from January to November 1942. At this point in time over (late 1942 to early 1943) 24,000 prisoners of war were under the watchful eyes of the Guard at Camp Forrest. Many of these internees were incarcerated without legal process.

The camp was declared "surplus" in September 1945 and given "inactive" status in **February 1946**.

XII   Troop Train to California

The 1940s, Railroads in World War II

Railroads in World War II would greatly need the new diesel locomotives being produced by Electro-Motive Corporation (later EMD) beginning in the 1930s, as the U.S. needed to move hundreds of tons of goods, material and troops to fight against Germany and the Axis after it was bombed by the Japanese.

The 1940s also saw the peak of piston-driven steam locomotive technology. Because of wartime restrictions the government did not allow the building of new diesel locomotives because the steel and other metal components required was needed for the war effort. Instead, railroads were forced to buy steam locomotives to fill their motive power needs. It should be noted that railroads did have improved technology to move freight in the 1940s such as heavier freight cars and locomotives and the new diesel-electric locomotive.

Another new technology that helped railroads during the decade was the development of **Centralized Traffic Control, or CTC**. CTC gave a dispatcher complete control over a section of track, known as a block, to set switches and watch over signals. The new system allowed for a single track main line to achieve 75% capacity of a fully double-tracked line.

Year	1921	1940
Average freight car capacity (Tons)	42.5	50
Daily mileage per freight car	25.8	38.7
Daily ton-mileage per freight car	448	661
Average size of freight train by car	37.4	49.7
Average net tonnage per train	651	849
Average train speed	11.5	16.7
Net ton mileage per train hour	7,506	14,027

The Transportation Corps

Established **31 July 1942** by Executive Order 9082 (FDR) and began the largest mobilization in the country's history primarily to manage traffic and movement control.

The most common limiting factor in U.S. Army logistics has always been transportation. The Transportation Corps influenced the changing character of war more than any other service branch.

During the world war, the Transportation Corps transported 7,290,000 passengers, of which 94% were Army personnel, to overseas destinations. And it shipped 126,787,875 tons of cargo to some 330 destinations worldwide in 5,280 ocean-going vessels.

Typically, most Pullman troop sleepers (the box car type) ran in groups of three to one troop mess/diner car.

* In 1942, Pullman cars transported 8 million troops.
* It typically took 50 trains to transport one US Army division.
* Each train took a different route, and units were balanced on each train so should something happen to one train, the division could still function.

Troop trains

The railroads and the Pullman Company met the high demand.

Troop Trains were usually packed. They weren't designed for comfort like the crack trains such as the Broadway Limited and the Empire State Express. The Pullman Company converted 40-foot boxcars.

The whole idea of a troop train was to pack as many soldiers onto one train as possible. A Troop Sleeper, 40 feet long, is maybe 6-7 feet wide. They could pack 3 squads (8-14 men) in a single car. Not a small feat, considering the men had their rifles, helmets, and other equipment. An entire train could fit 2 companies (80-250 men in a company).

Army Units & Sizes

Detail of the chart below

[1] This column indicates what usually makes up the core of the unit - with larger formations there will be more supporting units as well such as units for headquarters, admin, signals, air-defense etc. which will increase the overall number of men involved.

[2] Regiment is not usually a deployed unit as a whole. It is more of an "administrative family" or permanent label of a group's identity. Units from a particular regiment may be spread around within an army.

Unit Name	Consists of [1]:	Approx Number of men:	Commanded by:
Army	2 or more Corps	100,000 to 150,000	Field Marshal or General
Corps	2 or more Divisions	25,000 to 50,000	General or Lt. Gen.
Division	3 or more Brigades or Regiments	10,000 to 15,000	Lt. Gen or Maj. Gen.
Brigade	3 or more Battalions	1500 to 3500	Maj. Gen, Brigadier or Col.
Regiment [2]	2 or more Battalions	1000 to 2000	Col.
Battalion	4 or more Companies	400 to 1000	Lt. Col.
Company	2 or more Platoons	100 to 250	Captain or Maj
Platoon (Troop)	2 or more Squads	16 to 50	1st Lt.
Squad	2 or more Sections	8 to 24	Sgt.
Section		4 to 12	Sgt.

The table is an attempt to summarize the relationships between and the sizes of various military units. These sizes (and sometimes names) will vary not only from country to country, but also by the nature of the unit and its particular circumstances. The numbers given for men in each unit is more representative of infantry units than armored units.

✦ ✦ ✦ ✦

18 August 1942 Left Camp Forrest, TN

Dad's trip diary by troop train from Camp Forrest, TN.

Dad kept a diary of his train ride on a 3x5 spiral note pad. 8 sheets written on both sides. **I am listing his notes from this note pad verbatim.**

"Tuesday - August 18   *Waited all day at Tent City for train. Left there at 1 AM.*

Wednesday - August 19   *A train of 35 cars waited for us. 16 coaches (Pullman). The next of the cars were box cars and flat cars loaded with truck and supplies. Left Camp Forrest at 2 AM. Got to Nashville at*

8:30 AM. At 2 PM we stopped at Bunceton, Tenn. Until 3 PM for an hour of physical exercise and close order drill.

Traveling very slow and side tracking for all trains. Six such trains will have left Tent City (129th Inf) by tonite.

Saw several lumber mills to-day, country is very dense with trees. Confederate Cemetery is near Nashville passed it to-day.

As we near Memphis Tenn. the country reminds one of Minnesota somewhat (except for lakes). The corn and cotton crop is not so good, see a herd of cattle now and then. Lots of Negroes. Arrived Memphis 9 PM.

Thursday - August 20   *Left Memphis at 12:30 AM. Followed the Mississippi River for a ways. Little Rock, Arkansas went thru there at 5 AM. Went to bed at 8 PM last nite. At 8:15 AM went thru Arkadelphia, Ark. There they had a large cotton seed oil refinery. 10:30 stopped at Prescot, Ark. for 10 minutes. All the way through Arkansas saw lots of lumber mills, lots of woods all the way through. It looks as if there has been lots of rain all along on this trip as there is water holes all along the way. The state of Arkansas ---*

Of the 8 double sided pages in the spiral note pad, page 3 is missing.

Friday - August 21   *5 AM - Abilene, TX. 8:15 AM - Stopped at Big Spring for exercises. As we get into the southwestern part of Texas we notice lots of sand, cactus and sage brush. Pecos, TX 2PM. First glimpse of the foothills. Van Horn, TX - 5 PM. Had supper and entered the foothills, also had haircut by amateur barber while train was moving, just a few nicks. Large movement of troops all over the south, every train that we meet on that passes us has soldiers. El Paso, Texas - 9:15 PM. Right on the Rio Grande river boarder town between U.S. and Mexico. Have been in the mountains for the past 3 hours, for the past hour traveled along the Rio Grande river, a stretch of land four miles wide has a very good crop, rich land altho irrigated. Here we ran into our first rain since the trip began. Left El Paso at 10 PM following the Rio Grande.*

Saturday - August 22   *During the nite went thru the southwestern corner of New Mexico. 5 AM - Douglas, Arizona, we should have changed our time last nite at supper time but no one thought of it, however they changed this morn. As we ride along the border of U.S. and Mexico we notice a range of high mountains in Mexico.*

9:15 Tucson, Arizona, very nice town, railway center. Large air base (Army). Stopped for one hour and had exercises. Along the way this morning we traveled on a plateau, saw large cattle ranches, lots of cactus and big yards. This is a mining town, lots of Mexicans all along the last 400 miles or so. About noon we hit the desert between Tucson and Yuma, Arizona and is it hot.

At 1:30 PM we went thru Casa Grande. Here we met a train load of Japs on their way to some concentration camp men, women and kids.

Yuma, Arizona 1015 PM. During the day temperature was 120 degrees. Mining town. Did not cool off until we hit a large lake at 2:30 Sun. morning.

Sunday - August 23   *Banning, Cal., 7:15 AM. Mining town also. Saw the first grain fields on this trip (course they were harvested). Also saw a few fruit trees, all land is under irrigation.*

Colton, Cal. 10:30 AM. Sunsweet Cal 11:20 AM. Had my first orange off an orange tree. Fruit trees and berry bushes of all kinds. We are now nearing the Pacific Ocean, 45 miles from Los Angeles, nice cool day.

1 PM Los Angeles One hour of exercises. Glendale, Cal. 3 PM saw lots of U.S. bombers. 3:10 passed thru Burbank, Cal. and saw Lockheed aircraft plant. Anti-aircraft guns on top of plant, soldiers patrolling all around plant with weapon trucks on which are mounted .50 caliber machine guns. The first 80 miles out of Los Angeles going north went thru 11 tunnels. Got to Mojave at 9 PM. From there followed the Mojave Desert for aways.

Went thru Bakersfield during the nite.

Monday - August 24   *Seeing lots of peach and orange orchards this morning, also quite a few cotton fields.*

Fresno, Cal. - 8:15 - half hour of exercises. Madera, 10:30 lots of dairy farms, all the farmers putting up alfalfa hay.

At 4:15 we arrived at Camp Stoneman, 40 miles northeast of San Francisco. Have not seen the Pacific Ocean yet."

24 August,1942

Arrived at Camp Stoneman, 40 miles north of San Francisco

2700 miles and 6 days on the troop train

XIII   Troop Ship and The South Pacific

September, 1942 Left Camp Stoneman California

Equator Line Crossing Ceremonies

Soldiers crossing the equator received Rights of Passage from a Pollywog to Shellback.

Dad brought his passage certificate home. See below.

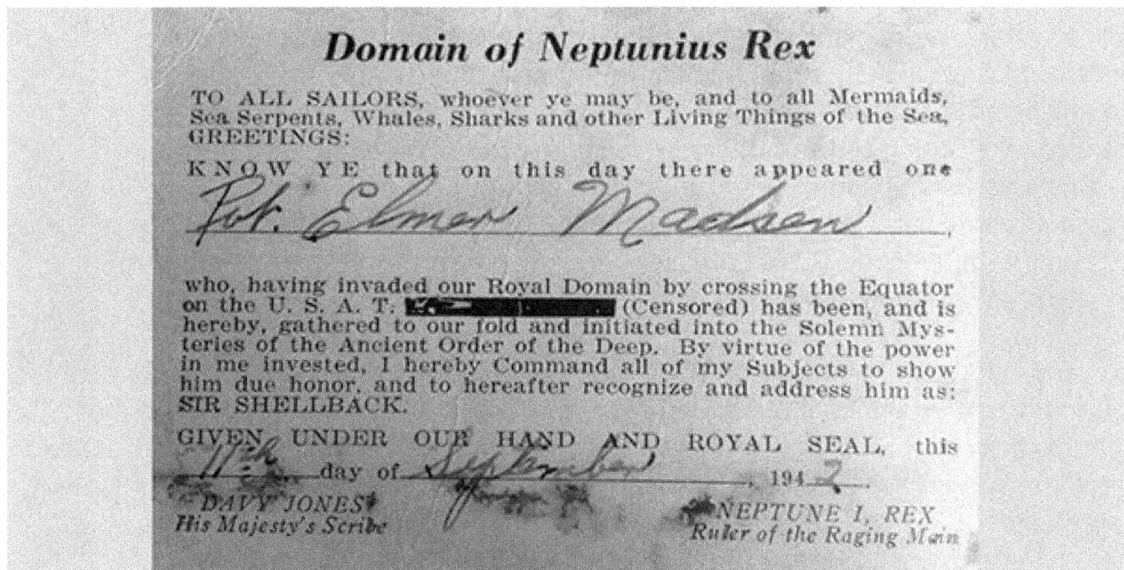

Domain of Neptunius Rex

TO ALL SAILORS, whoever ye may be, and to all Mermaids, Sea Serpents, Whales, Sharks and other Living Things of the Sea, GREETINGS:

KNOW YE that on this day there appeared one *Pvt. Elmer Madsen*,

who, having invaded our Royal Domain by crossing the Equator on the U. S. A. T. ▓▓▓▓ (Censored) has been, and is hereby, gathered to our fold and initiated into the Solemn Mysteries of the Ancient Order of the Deep. By virtue of the power in me invested, I hereby Command all of my Subjects to show him due honor, and to hereafter recognize and address him as: SIR SHELLBACK.

GIVEN UNDER OUR HAND AND ROYAL SEAL, this 11th day of September, 1942.

DAVY JONES
His Majesty's Scribe

NEPTUNE I, REX
Ruler of the Raging Main

✦ ✦ ✦ ✦

THE OCEAN AND ITS ISLANDS

The Pacific is the biggest and the deepest body of water on the earth. With a total area of 68,634,000 square miles, it is twice as large as the Atlantic and covers more than one-third of the surface of the entire globe. Measured along the equator it is about 10,000 miles wide, but its greatest width, 12,500 miles, is between Panama and Malaya where it extends half the distance around the earth. From Bering Strait on the north, where the ocean is only 56 miles wide and 300 feet deep, to the

Antarctic Circle, the Pacific measures 9,300 miles. So vast is its extent that if a giant bulldozer scraped off all the land on the surface of the earth to sea level and dumped it into the ocean, the Pacific would still have an average depth of two miles.

Though practically all the islands of the Pacific were formed by violent upheavals of the earth's crust and volcanic activity and consist essentially of hardened lava, their origin is often masked by a coating of coral rock, the remains of once-living plants and animals.

The most familiar of these is the coral polyp, a tiny marine animal that builds its own shell by extracting lime from sea water, thus providing the aviation engineers of World War II with the base for many of their airfields.

The coral polyp creates not only islands but atolls and reefs as well. The atoll, so characteristic of the eastern Pacific, consists of a chain of coral-encrusted islets, usually roughly circular or horseshoe-shaped in formation and enclosing a shallow lagoon; the reefs -- in this case, fringing reefs -- are platforms built upon the shoulders of volcanic peaks and extending between the shore and deep water. Reefs which are separated from the shore by a stretch of open water are called barrier reefs, and the largest of these, the 1,200-mile-long off the **Great Barrier Reef northeast coast of Australia**, is probably the greatest monument left by the tiny polyp.

The coral atoll with its many islets and reefs is actually the visible portion of a single land mass resting on a subterranean mountain. It is a haven in a wilderness of ocean that forever rolls high to boil whitely against the fringing reefs. In the lagoon, where the waters are blue and calm and where fish abound, lie safety and sustenance.

Troops stationed on a coral atoll during the war admired its beaches of dazzling sand where thousands of bird's nests, and its rows of graceful palm trees whose fruit is the lifeblood of the atoll. And everywhere they saw coral, shaped and colored in infinite variety, and incomparably beautiful.

It is the coral atoll that has become for many the typical South Sea island. Actually, there is no typical Pacific island. Some are made of the same stuff as continents, some of volcanic rock, and some of coral. In climate, size, height, and shape; in distribution of plant and animal life; in population, culture, and political affiliation, they vary so widely as to defy any simple classification.

Any grouping of the islands, whatever the basis chosen, must of necessity be a compromise. But since it is necessary, for convenience of description, to adopt some system, perhaps the most suitable would be that which was most familiar to the soldier of World War II.

The division of the Pacific world is broken down into five culture groups -- Australia, Indonesia, Micronesia, Melanesia, and Polynesia. See below.

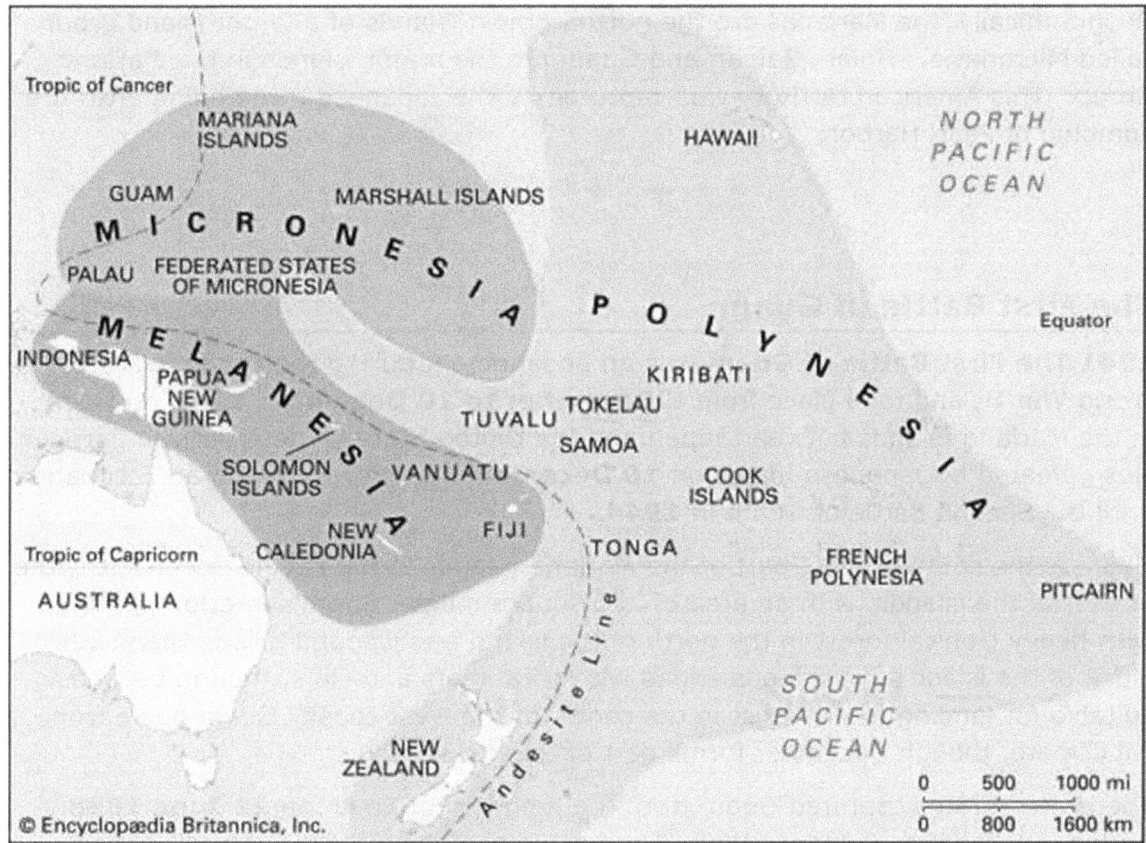

The surprise attack on Pearl Harbor opened a war which was fought all the way from Hawaii and Australia to Japan and the coast of Asia. It was a war waged in all the elements. Large fleets ranged the vast ocean searching for the enemy, aircraft flew hundreds and thousands of miles over water to drop their bombs, submarines hunted secretly in the lanes of empire for their prey, and troops fought desperately for islands with strange and unpronounceable names.

The **Mariana Islands** (also **the Marianas**) are a crescent-shaped archipelago comprising the summits of fifteen mostly dormant volcanic mountains in the western North Pacific Ocean. They lie south-southeast of Japan, west-southwest of Hawaii, north of New Guinea and east of the Philippines, demarcating the Philippine Sea's eastern limit. The Mariana Islands are the southern part of a submerged mountain range that extends 1,565 miles (2,519 km) from Guam to near Japan. Geographically, the Marianas are the northernmost islands of a larger island group called Micronesia. Tinian, Saipan and Guam are the major islands in the Mariana Group. This American territory was captured by the Japanese three hours after the bombing of Pearl Harbor.

✦ ✦ ✦ ✦

The First Battle of Guam

1941 The First Battle of Guam was an engagement during the Pacific War in World War II, and took place from **8 December to 10 December 1941** on Guam in the Mariana Islands between Japan and the United States. The American garrison was defeated by Japanese forces on **10 December**, which resulted in an occupation until the Second Battle of Guam in **1944**.

Guam is the southernmost part of the Mariana Islands in the Pacific Ocean. It is the largest of the islands, with an area of 225 square miles. Guam's interior is rugged, with heavy tropical forest in the north of the island and wooded hills in the south. Much of the island's coastline is edged with coral reefs and cliffs, though beaches suitable for landing troops exist in the center of the west coast. Guam has a tropical climate, though December forms part of the dry season.

The United States captured Guam from the Kingdom of Spain on **21 June 1898** during the Spanish–American War. The next year Spain sold the other islands in the Marianas chain to Germany. During World War I, Japanese forces captured the German islands in the Marianas during **October 1914** and established a garrison which was designated the South Seas Defense Force. Japan gained a mandate over the islands from the League of Nations in **December 1920**. Japanese colonists were permitted to settle in the Marianas, and by the late 1930s there were more colonists than natives in the Japanese islands.   In 1935 the Japanese Government banned westerners from entering its mandated islands in the Pacific, and in 1939 established the 4th Fleet to defend the region. In 1941 Guam had a population of 23,394, most of whom lived in or within 10 miles (16 km) of the island's capital of Agana. The island had about 85 miles (137 km) of improved roads and Apra Harbor was considered the best in the Marianas, but did not have an airfield.

Japanese plans for the Pacific War included capturing Guam within the war's first days. The United States Government did not believe that it would be possible or practical to defend Guam if it was attacked. The island was not seen as being useful in efforts to reinforce the Philippines. In 1941 the island was given a "Category F" defense rating; this ruled out the construction of new defenses and meant that when war broke out Guam's defenders would destroy all facilities of military value and withdraw.

U.S. Marine Corps Brigadier general William K. MacNulty fortified their positions and put up a valiant defense against the subsequent Japanese aerial assault of the island, while suffering losses and other casualties of near one third of their complement.

10 December 1941 Guam was taken over by the Japanese forces. Those on the island surrendered except for Six U.S. Navy seamen who decided to evade capture from the Japanese rather than surrender; five were eventually captured by the Japanese and beheaded. George Ray Tweed, a U.S. Navy radioman and one of the original six men, managed to survive with the help of local Chamorros. They moved him from village to village, sometimes endangering their own families for his protection. The Japanese knew that an unknown American could not hide without some form of help. Consequently, Chamorro suspects were questioned, tortured, and beheaded. Despite the horrific abuses, Chamorros loyal to the United States protected Tweed. The radioman managed to covertly endure throughout the two and one-half years of occupation.   The **Chamorro** people are the indigenous people of the Mariana Islands.

✦   ✦   ✦   ✦

Solomon Islanders helped carve airstrips out of jungle, Fijian and Tongan scouts performed heroic feats behind the Japanese lines on Bougainville. Papuans carried supplies over the Owen Stanley Range to the troops in New Guinea, and Filipino guerrillas met MacArthur's troops on the beaches at Leyte Philippines.

Volcanic wastes and coral atolls rising in a lonely ocean were scrutinized from the sea and charted with all the meticulous care of modern science. Islands, where few white men had ever been, were the subject of serious and lengthy debate at the council tables in Washington and London before they became major battlegrounds of the war and then, overnight, great bases on the road to Japan.

The New Guinea campaign of the Pacific War

Lasted **from January 1942 until the end of the war in August 1945.** During the initial phase in early 1942, the Empire of Japan invaded the Australian-administered territories of the New Guinea Mandate (23 January) and Papua (8 March) and overran western New Guinea (beginning 29/30 March), which was a part of the Netherlands East Indies.

During the second phase, lasting from late 1942 until the Japanese surrender, the Allies—consisting primarily of Australian and US forces—cleared the Japanese first from Papua, then the Mandate and finally from the Dutch colony. The campaign resulted in a crushing defeat and very heavy losses for the Empire of Japan.

As in most Pacific War campaigns, disease and starvation claimed more Japanese lives than enemy action. Most Japanese troops never even came into contact with Allied forces and were instead simply cut off and subjected to an extremely effective blockade by the US Navy. Garrisons were effectively besieged and denied shipments of food and medical supplies, and as a result, some claim that 97% of Japanese deaths in this campaign were from non-combat causes.

"Also formidable was the tenacity of the enemy, who would fight to the death in these stinking holes, starving, diseased and with their dead rotting and unburied beside them."   *John Vader, New Guinea: The Time Is Stemmed, p. 93*

XIV   History of World War II Medicine

Out of every Hundred soldiers receiving medical care, eight died in World War I and four died in World War II.

The Use of Atabrine to Fight Malaria During World War II

For hundreds of years quinine was used in the prevention and treatment of malaria. Quinine is found in the root, bark, and branches of cinchonas and other trees native to the Andes mountains in South America. Quinine remained in wider use than its synthetic counterparts until World War II, when the supply of quinine from countries in the South Pacific was cut off by Japanese military conquest.

 In the 1930s the first synthetic antimalarial drugs were developed. A synthetic drug invented by a German researcher before the war was distributed to American troops stationed on the South Pacific islands. This drug was sold under the name of Atabrine. Complaints against the yellow pills became common. Atabrine was bitter, appeared to impart its own sickly hue to the skin. Some of its side effects were headaches, nausea, and vomiting, and in a few cases, it produced a temporary psychosis.

Yet Atabrine was effective, if only the men could be made to take it. A great part of the problem was that the proper dosage had not yet been worked out. In an effort to ensure that the Atabrine was actually swallowed by the soldiers, medics or NCOs from the combat units stood at the head of mess lines to carefully watch marines and soldiers take their little yellow tablets.

The Use of Sulfanilamide in World War II

The discovery of Sulfanilamide greatly affected the mortality rate during World War II. First used in 1936, American soldiers were taught to immediately sprinkle sulfa powder on any open wound to prevent infection. Every soldier was issued a first aid pouch that was designed to be attached to the soldier's waist belt. The first aid pouch contained a package of sulfa powder and a bandage to dress the wound. One of the main components carried by a combat medic during World War II was sulfa powder and sulfa tablets.

The Use of Penicillin in World War II

From Ordinary Mold – The Greatest Healing Agent of this War

In 1941 John Davenport and Gordon Cragwall, representing the pharmaceutical company Pfizer, attended a symposium. At the symposium researchers from Columbia University presented clear evidence that penicillin could effectively treat infections. Inspired by the possibilities, the two men offered Pfizer's assistance.

Recognizing the potential of the Pfizer process for producing penicillin and desperate for massive quantities to aid in the war effort, the U.S. government authorized 19 companies to produce the antibiotic using Pfizer's deep-tank fermentation techniques, which Pfizer had agreed to share with its competitors. Many of these companies could not come close to Pfizer's production levels and quality. Ultimately Pfizer produced 90 percent of the penicillin that went ashore with Allied forces at Normandy on D-Day in 1944 and more than half of all the penicillin used by the Allies for the rest of the war, helping to save countless lives.

The Use of Plasma During World War II

Plasma is the liquid portion of the blood--a protein-salt solution in which red and white blood cells and platelets are suspended. Plasma, which is 90 percent water, constitutes 55 percent of blood volume. Plasma contains albumin (the chief protein constituent), fibrinogen (responsible, in part, for the clotting of blood), and globulins (including antibodies). Plasma serves a variety of functions, from maintaining a satisfactory blood pressure and volume to supplying critical proteins for blood clotting and immunity.

It also serves as the medium of exchange for vital minerals such as sodium and potassium, thus helping maintain a proper balance in the body, which is critical to cell function. Plasma is obtained by separating the liquid portion of blood from the cells.

In 1938, Dr. Charles Drew, a leading authority on mass transfusion and blood processing methods, set up a blood plasma system. By 1939, Dr. Drew had set up a blood bank at the Columbia Medical Center. He made a breakthrough discovery that blood plasma could replace whole blood, which deteriorated in a few days in storage. This discovery played a major role during World War II where many countries experienced extreme casualties. Dr. Drew's scientific research helped revolutionize blood plasma transfusion so that pooled plasma could readily be given on the battlefield, which dramatically improved opportunities to save lives.

Fearing the U.S. would be drawn into World War II, the American armed forces requested development of a similar blood collection system. In **February of 1941, Dr. Drew was appointed Director of the first American Red Cross Blood Bank. He established an effective plasma collection and preservation organization - a model for today's volunteer blood donation programs.**

Because of its ability to reduce death from shock caused by bleeding, dried plasma became a vital element in the treatment of the wounded on World War II battlefields. By the time the program ended in September 1945, the American Red Cross had collected over 13 million units of blood and converted nearly all of it into plasma. "If I could reach all America," said General Dwight D. Eisenhower, supreme commander of Allied Expeditionary Forces, "there is one thing I would like to do-- thank them for blood plasma and whole blood. It has been a tremendous thing." At war's end, some 1.3 million plasma units were returned to the American Red Cross, which made them available to civilian hospitals.

The Use of Morphine as a Pain Killer During World War II

Morphine, as a pain killer, was widely used during World War II. Morphine is processed from the opium poppy plant which in grown mainly in Turkey and India. Injecting morphine into the blood proved more addictive than smoking or eating opium.

During World War II, Squibb, a pharmaceutical company, developed a way for medics to administer on the front lines a controlled amount of morphine to wounded soldiers. What Squibb introduced was called a morphine syrette, which was like a miniature toothpaste tube that contained the morphine. Instead of unscrewing a top like you do on a toothpaste tube, it had a blind end that was sealed. A needle attached to the syrette was used by the medic to puncture the seal. The medic would come along, break the seal and inject the wounded soldier with the morphine syrette.

During World War II, Medics were allowed to administer morphine to alleviate pain, although the injection could also be given at the Battalion, or Collecting Stations. **If the drug was applied, the syrette was pinned to the casualties' collar to prevent overdosing of unconscious patients.**

Usually the 1/2 grain injection from the toothpaste tube shaped syrette, combined with physical exhaustion, was sufficient to knock the patient out, with the casualty often waking up in the hospital.

Doctrine of Medical Treatment in World War II

Governing all WW II medical planning were a series of general doctrinal rules, most of which remained valid long after 1945:

1. Commanders of all echelons are responsible for the provision of adequate and proper medical care for all noneffective [persons whose medical condition prevents them from performing their military duties] of their command;

2. Medical service is continuous;

3. Sick or injured individuals go no farther to the rear than their condition or the medical situation warrants;

4. Sorting of the fit from the unfit takes place at each medical installation in the chain of evacuation;

5. Casualties in the combat zone are collected at medical installations along the general axis of advance of the units to which they pertain;

6. Medical units must possess and retain tactical mobility to permit them to move to positions on the battlefield and enable them to move in support of combat elements;

7. Mobility of medical installations in the combat zone is dependent upon prompt and continuous evacuation by higher medical echelons;

8. The size of medical installations increases and the necessity and ability to move decreases the farther from the front lines these units are located;

9. Medical units must be disposed so as to render the greatest service to the greatest number.

Coordination of Medical Units in WW II

One problem with the medical organization used in World War II was the lack of an overall medical command and control headquarters at the third and fourth echelons of health-services support -- a problem not completely and adequately addressed by the Medical Department until well into the 1960s. This meant that health-services support for the corps was provided, for the most part, by units not under the control of the corps. In turn, the medical groups evacuated casualties to hospitals not under their control – hospitals that would sometimes receive patients from more than one corps. Close coordination by responsible officers, through communication and conferences on a continuing basis, was required to avoid disastrous results for the wounded.

XV Melanesia, Doolittle Raid, Battle of Midway

20 September 1942 Dad Arrived on Fiji Islands

The eastern portion of Melanesia consists of six major groups of islands: the Solomons, Santa Cruz, New Hebrides, New Caledonia, Loyalty, and Fiji.

The Solomon Islands, which stretch in a double northwest-southeast chain for 700 miles to the east of New Guinea, include seven major and many small islands, whose names sound the roll of notable American battles: Guadalcanal, Tulagi, New Georgia, Vella Lavella, and Bougainville. With their damp, hot climate, malarial mosquito, and well-nigh impenetrable jungle they constitute one of the most forbidding areas on earth.

Southeast of the Solomons lie the New Hebrides, and below them, New Caledonia. To the east and forming the eastern limit of Melanesia are the Fiji Islands, whose remarkably well-built natives were once the most famous cannibals of the South Seas.

The troop ship Dad was on landed at Fiji Island. There the soldiers continued their combat island warfare training.

After the initial Japanese offensive following Pearl Harbor. Fiji to the southeast of the Solomons found itself along with New Caledonia and the New Hebrides on the front line of the Pacific War. Suva (on Fiji) boasted one of the finest natural harbors in the South Pacific - 3 miles wide and cutting 2 miles inland. The Army, Marine, and Navy rushed air, ground, and naval assets to the island. Fiji boasted one of the few concrete air strips in the South Pacific and more were soon under construction. **In June 1942 the Seabees arrived.** The Japanese plan was to seize the South Pacific islands east of Australia cutting them and New Zealand off from the USA.

The United States and other Allied countries maintained military installations on Fiji during the war, but after the Solomons campaign, Fiji gradually became a remote rear area used for staging and logistics.

The Doolittle Raid

This was an air raid by the United States of America on the Japanese capital Tokyo and other places on the island of Honshu during World War II, the first air strike to strike the Japanese Home Islands. It was on **18 April, 1942** and demonstrated that Japan itself was vulnerable to American air attack, served as retaliation for the

Japanese attack on Pearl Harbor, and provided an important boost to American morale. The raid was planned and led by Lieutenant Colonel James "Jimmy" Doolittle of the United States Army Air Forces.

Sixteen B-25B Mitchell medium bombers were launched without fighter escort from the U.S. Navy's aircraft carrier USS *Hornet* (CV-8) deep in the Western Pacific Ocean, each with a crew of five men. The plan called for them to bomb military targets in Japan, and to continue westward to land in China because landing a medium bomber on the USS *Hornet* was impossible.

At the Battle of Coral Sea in the southwest Pacific and the Battle of Midway in the central Pacific, U.S. aircraft carriers stopped the Japanese advances in history's first carrier-versus-carrier battles. The Battle of Midway, along with the Guadalcanal Campaign, is widely considered a turning point in the Pacific War.

Battle of the Coral Sea

Fought from **4 to 8 May 1942**, was a major naval battle between the Imperial Japanese Navy and naval and air forces from the United States and Australia, taking place in the Pacific Theater of WWII.

The battle is historically significant as the first action in which aircraft carriers engaged each other, as well as the first in which neither side's ships sighted or fired directly upon the other. Also, the first air-sea battle in history.

In an attempt to strengthen its defensive position in the South Pacific, Japan decided to invade and occupy Port Moresby (in New Guinea) and Tulagi (in the southeastern Solomon Islands). The plan to accomplish this was called Operation MO and involved several major units of Japan's Combined Fleet. These included two fleet carriers and a light carrier to provide air cover for the invasion forces. It was under the overall command of Japanese Admiral Shigeyoshi Inoue.

The U.S. learned of the Japanese plan through signals intelligence and sent two United States Navy carrier task forces and a joint Australian-American cruiser force to oppose the offensive. These were under the overall command of American Admiral Frank J. Fletcher.

The Battle of the Coral Sea would prove to be a strategic victory for the Allies. **The battle marked the first time since the start of the war that a major Japanese advance had been checked by the Allies.**

The Japanese attempt to overtake Port Moresby resulted in the Battle of the Coral Sea. The Allies suffered higher losses in ships but achieved a crucial strategic victory by turning the Japanese landing force back, thereby removing the threat to Port Moresby, at least for the time being.

With both sides having suffered heavy losses in aircraft and carriers damaged or sunk, the two forces disengaged and retired from the battle area. Although a tactical victory for the Japanese in terms of ships sunk, the battle would prove to be a strategic victory for the Allies. The Japanese fleet carriers *Shōkaku* and *Zuikaku* – the former damaged and the latter with a depleted aircraft complement – were unable to participate in the Battle of Midway the following month, while *Yorktown* did participate, ensuring a rough parity in aircraft between the two adversaries and contributing significantly to the U.S. victory in that battle. The severe losses in carriers at Midway prevented the Japanese from reattempting to invade Port Moresby from the ocean and helped prompt their ill-fated land offensive over the Kokoda trail in Papua New Guinea.

Two months later, the Allies took advantage of Japan's resulting strategic vulnerability in the South Pacific and launched the Guadalcanal Campaign; this, along with the New Guinea Campaign, eventually broke Japanese defenses in the South Pacific and was a significant contributing factor to Japan's ultimate defeat in World War II.

The Battle of Midway

Was a decisive naval battle in the Pacific Theater of WWII fought between **4 and 7 June 1942**. Midway is 1,300 miles northwest of Honolulu, a lonely coral atoll, six miles in diameter, where the United States won its first important victory after Pearl Harbor. Together with Wake and Johnston Islands, Midway is important chiefly as a civil air station and military base.

Only six months after Japan's attack on Pearl Harbor and one month after the Battle of the Coral Sea, the United States Navy under Admirals Chester Nimitz, Frank Jack Fletcher, and Raymond A. Spruance decisively defeated an attacking fleet of the Imperial Japanese Navy under *Admirals Isoroku Yamamoto, Chuichi Nagumo, and Nobutake Kondo* near Midway Atoll, inflicting devastating damage on the Japanese fleet that proved irreparable. Military historian John Keegan called it *"the most stunning and decisive blow in the history of naval warfare."*

Japan's strategy was to lure the American aircraft carriers into a trap and occupying Midway was part of an overall "barrier" strategy to extend their defensive perimeter, in response to the Doolittle air raid on Tokyo on18 April 1942. This operation was also considered preparatory for further attacks against Fiji, Samoa, and Hawaii.

American cryptographers were able to determine the date and location of the planned attack, enabling the forewarned U.S. Navy to prepare its own ambush. There were seven aircraft carriers involved in the battle and all four of Japan's large aircraft carriers—*Akagi*, *Kaga*, *Soryu* and *Hiryu*, part of the six-carrier force that had attacked Pearl Harbor six months earlier—and a heavy cruiser were sunk, while the U.S. lost only the carrier Yorktown and a destroyer. After Midway and the exhausting attrition of the Solomon Islands campaign, Japan's capacity to replace its losses in materiel (particularly aircraft carriers) and men (especially well-trained pilots and maintenance crewmen) rapidly became insufficient to cope with mounting casualties, while the United States' massive industrial and training capabilities made losses far easier to replace. The Battle of Midway, along with the Guadalcanal Campaign, is widely considered a turning point in the Pacific War.

✦   ✦   ✦   ✦

Natives of the Solomon Islands

After World War II, anthropologists discovered that an unusual religion had developed among the islanders of the South Pacific. It was oriented around the concept of cargo, which the islanders perceived as the source of the wealth and power of the Europeans and Americans. This religion, known as the Cargo Cult, held that if the proper ceremonies were performed, shipments of riches would be sent from some heavenly place. The islanders saw that they worked hard but were poor, whereas the Europeans and Americans did not work but instead wrote things down on paper. In due time, a shipment of wonderful things would arrive.

These islands were used as staging areas to fight active and bloody battles, such as in Guadalcanal, which is within the Solomon Islands. Hence, Melanesia suddenly became an area of key tactical significance in WWII, providing a very dynamic example of "enculturation" in 20th century history.

CARGO CULTS

One day in the early 1940s, the relatively isolated group of islands was descended upon by hundreds of thousands of American soldiers who arrived by sea and by air. The world was at war, and America had plans to build bases on the Pacific islands. The newcomers recruited the locals' assistance in constructing hospitals, airstrips, jetties, roads, bridges, and corrugated-steel Quonset huts, all of which were strange and wondrous to the natives. But it was the prodigious amounts of war materiel that were airdropped for the US bases that drastically changed the lifestyle of the islanders. They observed as aircraft descended from the sky and delivered crates full of clothing, tents, weapons, tools, canned foods, and other goods to the island's new residents, a diversity of riches the likes of which the islanders had never seen. The natives learned that this bounty from the sky was known to the American servicemen as "cargo."

A Cargo Cult is a religious movement. A Cargo Cult is usually emerging in tribal or isolated societies after they have had an encounter with an external and technologically advanced society. Usually Cargo Cults focus on magical thinking and a variety of intricate rituals designed to obtain the material wealth of the advanced culture they encountered.

The natives interpreted the US military drill as religious rituals, leading them to conclude that these behaviors brought cargo to the islands. Hoping that the cargo would return by duplicating these behaviors, they continued to maintain airstrips and replaced their facilities using native materials. These included remarkably detailed full-size replicas of airplanes made of wood, bark, and vines, a hut-like radio shack complete with headphones made of coconut halves and attempts at recreating military uniforms and flags.

THE CARGO CULTS OF MELANESIA

In the Solomons, the Fijis, and New Guinea, were the dark-skinned Melanesians, fierce fighters who carved intricate and grotesque patterns in wood, ate human flesh, and were as addicted to exclusive men's clubs and secret societies as the American of today; and in the lush, beautiful islands of the eastern Pacific, where the Europeans came first, dwelt the tall, gold-skinned Polynesian who, with more time for leisure in a land where food abounded, created complex mythological and religious rites, and developed intricate social patterns.

Among the movements best known to students of Melanesia are the "Taro Cult" of New Guinea, the "Vailala Madness" of Papua, the "Naked Cult" of Espiritu Santo, the "John Frum Movement" of the New Hebrides and the "Tuka Cult" of the Fiji Islands. The Cargo Cult had a name for the deity in heaven. He was called John Fromm.   It is not certain how this name arose but quite possibly it was from American soldiers identifying themselves by their place of origin: i.e., I am "John from Indiana" or I am "John from Minneapolis". Some clever business began marketing products under the name John Fromm. For example, soap bars were labeled John Fromm Soap.

"Tuka Cult of Fiji Islands"

In the 1880s an oracle priest, Navosavakadua, mobilized Fijians of the hinterlands against the encroachment of both Fijian chiefs and British colonizers. British officials called the movement the Tuka cult, imagining it as a contagious superstition that had to be stopped. Navosavakadua and many of his followers, deemed "dangerous and disaffected natives," were exiled. Scholars have since made Tuka the standard

example of the Pacific cargo cult, describing it as a millenarian movement in which dispossessed islanders sought Western goods by magical means.

"John Frum movement of New Hebrides"

The movement gained popularity in the early 1940s, when 300,000 American Troops were stationed in New Hebrides during World War II, bringing with them an enormous amount of supplies (or "cargo"). After the war and the departure of the Americans, followers of John Frum built symbolic landing strips to encourage American airplanes to land and bring them "cargo". Several different Melanesian islands that had lived in almost complete isolation were suddenly contacted by mysterious-looking people with white skin during the war.

"John Frum Day" parade. Inhabitants of the remote Pacific Island of Tanna built an entire religion on trash left behind by American occupiers during World War II. To this day, every February 15, the local faithful perform elaborate military-inspired rituals in which worshipper's wave flags and march like GIs in hopes their god will deliver them more trade goods and supplies.

The natives were exposed to a level of sophistication, civilization and technology unlike anything they could possibly have expected before then. The people of Melanesia were unaware of the greater world around them. The idea that their population was very small, and there were far greater places to live than where they were, never even occurred to them.

The WWII soldiers who visited and assisted these islands also shared their own Christian teachings, including the idea of end times and Ascension. The war ended. The enemy of the U.S.A. never tried to invade the islands or use them as a staging area. The tactical significance of the islands disappeared. The promises of the "gods" were not kept. No one went back to give them more Cargo.

XVI　　New Hebrides of Melanesia

13 March 1943 Dad Landed on New Hebrides

Dad has a Sergeant patch on his right shoulder prior to Guadalcanal noticed from a picture he brought back from overseas. Again, he never discussed the war when I was growing up at home. He received this rank from the **37th Infantry Division** while providing cadre either on the Fiji Islands or on the New Hebrides Islands.

What do we mean when we say "cadre"? Webster defines cadre as a nucleus, especially of trained personnel, capable of assuming control and of training others. A properly supported cadre division generally implies that a small nucleus of the personnel required to fill a division would be assigned to the division for the purpose of managing parts of that division on a day-to-day basis and capable of deployment within 12 months of mobilization.

In early 1942, the Japanese reached the nearby Solomon Islands and the New Hebridean's lived in real fear that they would be next. The Americans, however, arrived first, totally unannounced, in **May 1942**.

It is a sight that can only be imagined; to wake up and glance out in the dawn light to the vast expanse of Mele Bay - filled with warships. A good number of the Vila population fled into the hills in the belief that the Japanese had arrived. It took some time to convince everyone otherwise, but the stealthy nature of the American arrival was imperative in its defensive strategy against the seemingly unbeatable Japanese.

The early 1940's were idyllic years for the native New Hebrideans. Vanuatu was attacked only once by a Japanese plane (that was shot down), resulting in but one casualty on Santo - Besse the cow. Thus, they never experienced the horrors of Japanese occupied New Guinea or Solomon Islands.

The G.I.s who landed in the New Hebrides, moving up for the bloody fighting on Guadalcanal, found the natives furiously at work.

The natives were preparing airfields, roads and docks for the magic ships and planes that they believed were coming from **"Rusefel"** (F.D. Roosevelt), the friendly king of America.

Development of Espiritu Santo

While the detachment of the 1st Battalion was building the air strip on Efate, New Hebrides, the Japs were engaged in constructing a field of their own on Guadalcanal. It was a construction race, and the Seabees won. Bombers took off from Efate within a month of the start of construction to harass the Japanese builders. But it was clear that the possession of Guadalcanal would have to be disputed with the enemy and Efate was not quite close enough to provide effective fighter support for our assault forces in the impending action. Another field, farther north, would have to be established.

After a reconnaissance had been made of the islands lying to the north of Efate, extending as far as the Santa Cruz islands, choice for the new airfield site fell upon Espiritu Santo, the northernmost island of the New Hebrides, 400 miles closer to the enemy's position.

✦ ✦ ✦ ✦

March 18, 1943 V-Mail to Dad's sister Alice.   The letter states he moved to a different island, which was from Fiji to the New Hebrides for additional training.

Obviously, from the way the letter is written they have not had any battle experience yet and don't know what the future holds for them. I have copied the first two paragraphs of the letter below:

Dear Alice and Axel,

Will write a few lines to let you know that we have moved to a different island but are still in the Tropics and the South Seas so that is the reason no one has heard from me for a while. Am feeling fine outside of a bad cold. Notice my new address.

I think I am going to like it better here than the other place, although I believe it is a little warmer. Here we have to do our own laundry but hope they can get some kind of a service set up. As yet have not had a chance to eat any of the tropical fruits, maybe they are not so plentiful. I don't know as I have not had time to look around yet.

Dad was here at Espiritu Santo, New Hebrides during this time. His division would have helped on the new air field and building of the supply depots. Before seeing any action, Dad took pictures of things he had never experienced before. Of the natives, their villages, the landscape and on the back of one picture of a banyan tree he wrote: *"This Banyan Tree is 100 feet tall with vines that you can swing on and climb"*.

V-Mail

Victory Mail, more commonly known as V-Mail, was launched **June 15, 1942** to expedite mail service for American armed forces overseas and assisted with logistical issues while acknowledging the value of communication.

Moving the rapidly expanding volume of wartime mail posed hefty problems for the Post Office, War, and Navy Departments. Officials found a model in the British Airgraph Service started in 1941 that microfilmed messages for dispatch.

V-Mail used standardized stationery and microfilm processing to produce lighter, smaller cargo. Because V-Mail stationery served as a letter and envelope in one, enclosed objects and photographs were prohibited.

To reduce the cost of transferring an original letter through the military postal system, a V-Mail letter would be censored, copied to film and printed back to paper upon arrival at its destination.

V-Mail correspondence was on small letter sheets, 7x9½ inches, that would go through mail censors before being photographed and transported as a thumbnail-sized image in negative microfilm. Upon arrival to their destination, the negatives would be printed to 60% of the original document's size, creating a sheet 4 1/4 x 5 1/4 inches.

Seabees

On **8 July** a small group of Seabees from the 1st Battalion detachment on Efate landed on Espiritu Santo and began work on the new field. They were accompanied by an infantry company of the U.S. Army who performed the unskilled work involved in the construction operations. Within twenty days the new field was in operation and offensive action against the japs in the Solomons was stepped up in intensity. On **7 August 1942**, the Marines made their landings on Guadalcanal and Tulagi.

The primary reason the Army was used to replace the Marines was the doctrine each service subscribed to. The Marines were a light assault force with a limited logistics pipeline. The Army had a massive support infrastructure behind it, thus had the staying power for long campaigns.

✦ ✦ ✦ ✦

The period July 1943 - October 1943 the 129th Regiment was assigned to garrison duty on Espiritu Santo. A garrison of troops are ones who stay on a base to run and secure supplies and equipment rather than being deployed. Like being held in reserve.

The island of Espiritu Santo belongs to the archipelago of the New Hebrides and is littered with WWII relics. A Quonset hut here, rusting bits of crashed plane there. Massive amounts of heavy equipment were bulldozed into the sea by departing Americans and the SS President Coolidge, a luxury liner turned troop carrier, sunk meters from shore. Exploring the interior area of land overgrown with dense forest and tangled vegetation and wreck strewn waters of Santo allows a glimpse into the past.

✦ ✦ ✦ ✦

By the time the U.S. entered WWII, the Japanese were already in the Solomon Islands and moving south towards Australia and New Zealand. To keep them from taking over all the western South Pacific, the allies established bases in the New Hebrides.

It was the last safe staging area to fight the Japanese and regain Guadalcanal in the Solomon Islands. Supplies came from the US via Hawaii, Fiji, sometimes New Zealand and Australia, to New Caledonia before arriving at Santo. **At one point the large, protected Segond Channel held nearly 100 ships over 1,000 tons.** The Segond Channel is located between southern Espiritu Santo bordering Luganville (Santo) and Aore Island. To the east is Million Dollar Point. During the war, this area was used as a seaplane takeoff area for Luganville Seaplane Base. The channel has very clear water visibility.

On **August 1, 1942** US Navy destroyers USS Gamble, USS Breese and USS Tracy laid a defensive mine field off the entrance to Segond Channel. Later that same day, USS Tucker (DD-374) accidentally struck a mine, unaware it had been laid and sunk three days later. Later, on **October 26, 1942** SS President Coolidge accidentally struck two mines and sank. As the war raged on further north, Santo was safe and relatively comfortable except for the heat, humidity, flies and disease-carrying mosquitos.

Espiritu Santo quickly became the second largest US base in the Pacific, behind Honolulu, with more than 40,000 troops stationed on the island at one time and nearly 500,000 personnel spending time here. The island went from no paved streets to having five airfields, a seaplane base, three hospitals, ten small camps and thirty-two miles or roads in a very short time.

Postwar, the U. S. military offered to sell all the surplus equipment to the local government at a very low price. However, in a gamble that failed, the local government refused to pay in the knowledge that the Americans could only fit a small amount of the equipment onto their ships. The thought in the back of their minds was that the Americans would just up and leave and the equipment would be theirs to have free of charge. This was a bad tactic as the Americans had other ideas.

When the war ended in 1945, the Americans made a hasty exit of the islands. But since supply and equipment stockpiles during the war had not been managed properly, ballooning to staggering levels - 9 million tons, many estimates say - a large amount was dumped under an initiative known as Operation Roll-Up. There were Quonset huts and fields filled with massive amounts of stuff. Planes, small boats, bulldozers, cranes, trucks of all sizes, forklifts, engines, bucket dredges, tires, iron girders and tons of earth-moving equipment had to be disposed of.

Between 1945 and 1947 entire planes, trucks, and bulldozers found graves underground or beneath the sea. Some things they buried. But others they pushed off barges into the harbor of Port Vila.

Some material was sold, but the majority was simply bulldozed into the sea at the entrance to Segond Channel. Thousands of tons of coral fill were pushed in on top of the submerged equipment which formed a ramp allowing more stuff to be dumped.

Thus, **Million Dollar Point** was created. Now days very popular for Scuba Diving.

The Japanese Empire at its peak in 1942.

Manchuria	Okinawa	Solomon Islands	Dutch East Indies
Korea	Ryukyu Islands	Bismarck Archipelago	Palau Islands
Eastern half of China	Guam	Burma	Caroline Islands
French Indo-China	Formosa	Siam	Gilbert Islands
Philippines	Marshall Islands	Wake Island	Iwo Jima
Malaya	Mariana Islands	New Guinea	Guadalcanal

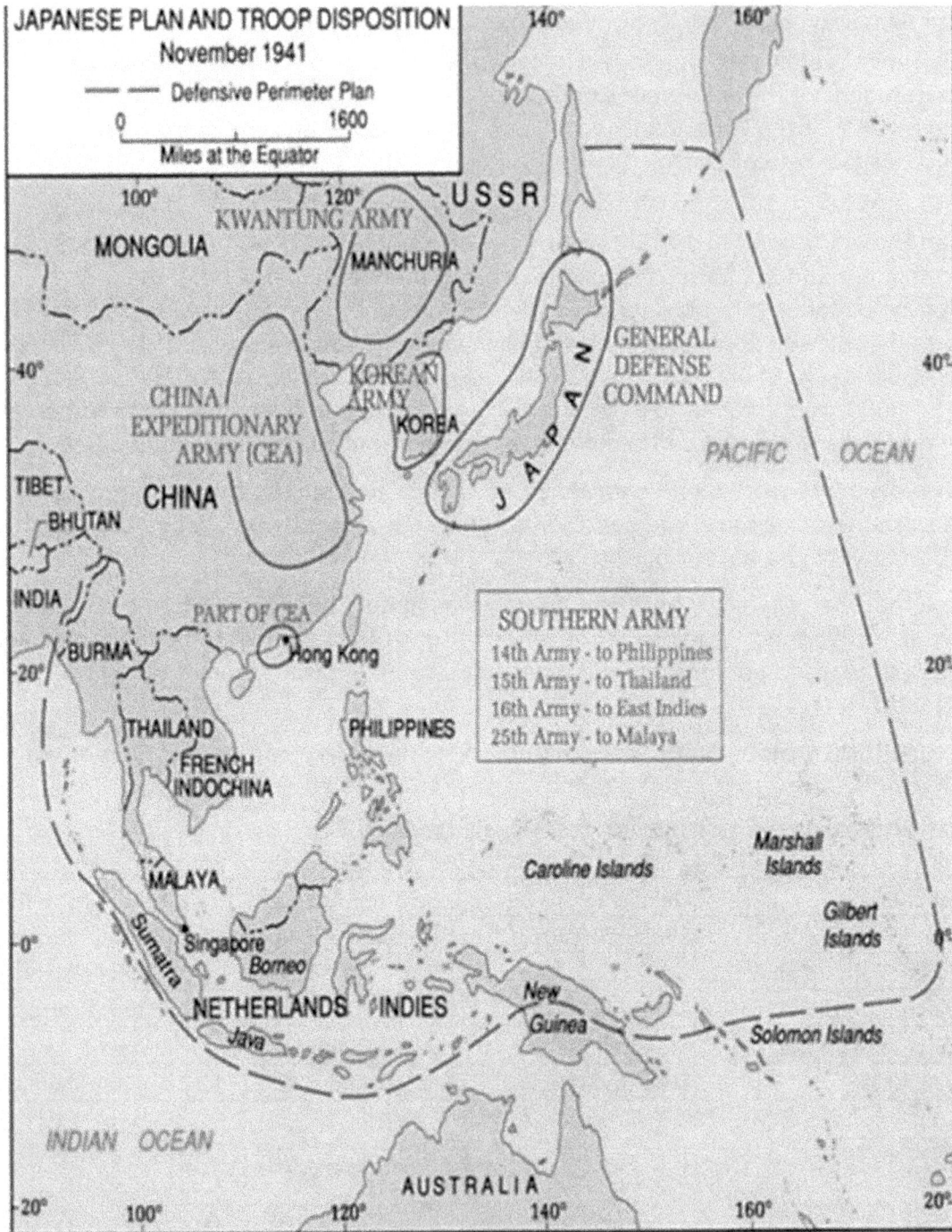

JAPANESE PLAN AND TROOP DISPOSITION
November 1941

— - — Defensive Perimeter Plan

0   1600
Miles at the Equator

USSR

KWANTUNG ARMY

MONGOLIA

MANCHURIA

KOREAN ARMY

CHINA EXPEDITIONARY ARMY (CEA)

KOREA

GENERAL DEFENSE COMMAND

JAPAN

PACIFIC OCEAN

TIBET

BHUTAN

CHINA

INDIA

BURMA

PART OF CEA

Hong Kong

THAILAND

FRENCH INDOCHINA

PHILIPPINES

SOUTHERN ARMY
14th Army - to Philippines
15th Army - to Thailand
16th Army - to East Indies
25th Army - to Malaya

Marshall Islands

Caroline Islands

Gilbert Islands

MALAYA

Sumatra

Singapore

Borneo

NETHERLANDS INDIES

New Guinea

Solomon Islands

Java

INDIAN OCEAN

AUSTRALIA

XVII   OPERATION CARTWHEEL

The Solomons, with their green mountains, forested shores, low-hanging clouds, and coral reefs, are beautiful when viewed from the air or from the calm inter island channels, but they present difficult terrain for military operations. They are covered by heavy, tropical rain forests. Mountains, deep rivers, swamps, heat, humidity, heavy rains, and mud, combined with the jungle, make all movements extremely difficult. Except along the sandy beaches vehicles cannot move until roads have been built.

Strategic Setting

In **March 1942** the Joint Chiefs of Staff achieved a workable solution by dividing the Pacific into two theaters. Each service received overall command in a theater. General Douglas MacArthur became commander of the Southwest Pacific Area (SWPA). Admiral Chester W. Nimitz commanded the second, the much larger Pacific Ocean Areas (which, in turn, was subdivided into the North, Central, and South Pacific Areas). Although the Solomon Islands west of Guadalcanal and the Russell Islands were in MacArthur's theater, Admiral King refused to divide his fleet or to put Halsey under MacArthur's direct control. This created an awkward command arrangement in which Halsey had operational control of all units involved in the Solomons, while MacArthur provided strategic direction.

In the South and Southwest Pacific Areas, the port of Rabaul on the island of New Britain in the Bismarck Archipelago blocked any American offensive toward the Philippines or Japan. The bulwark of Japanese defenses in the area, Rabaul was fortified with a large garrison and a network of air bases that protected Japanese warships and merchant vessels in its great natural harbor.

The ultimate fate of Rabaul became an issue of debate. General MacArthur insisted that this Japanese bastion be conquered. Other American strategists disagreed, arguing that capturing Rabaul would cost too many lives and would require troops and ships slated for the U.S. Navy's Central Pacific offensive, which was scheduled to begin in mid-November 1943.

Japanese Strategy

The Japanese military also recognized the importance of air power and airfields in the vast Pacific region. In **November 1942** they had built an airfield at Munda Point on New Georgia as an advance base to support the Guadalcanal fighting. The airstrip, less than 180 nautical miles from Guadalcanal, had become operational in

December 1942. Another strip was started shortly thereafter at Vila, on the nearby island of Kolombangara. However, by late 1942, the Japanese realized that their forces probably could not hold Guadalcanal. They correctly surmised that the Allies would strike next against Rabaul but did not know what form the attempt would take. They thus decided to attack aggressively in New Guinea to improve their position there, while mounting an active defense in the Solomons. Hurriedly they prepared defenses against anticipated Allied offensives in the central and northern Solomons. Ground troops were brought in to reinforce New Georgia, Kolombangara, and Santa Isabel.

Imperial Japanese Army commanders, arguing that holding the islands south of Bougainville would be costly and ultimately futile, wanted to wait for the Allies to attack Bougainville and the northern Solomons. The Imperial Navy disagreed. Naval planners wanted to delay the Allied advance for as long as possible, maintaining that New Georgia and Santa Isabel constituted a vital forward line of defense. With no one to arbitrate, each service did as it wished: the navy assumed responsibility for land defense of the central Solomons (although the army had to provide troops to cover naval commitments), the army for the northern islands.

Early 1943, therefore, found the Japanese holding the line in the Solomons while undertaking an offensive in New Guinea. Although the grueling struggle for Guadalcanal had worn down Japanese strength in the Solomons, the Japanese were still a tough foe. On New Georgia were approximately 10,500 troops, entrenched, determined, and waiting.

Planning and Preparations

During 1942, Allied operations in the Southwest and South Pacific were directed at encircling and, ultimately, capturing the great Japanese base at Rabaul (Operation CARTWHEEL). By early 1943 it was clear that this would require establishing a ring of air bases around Rabaul, and on **28 February 1943** the Joint Chiefs of Staff approved a plan (Elkton Plan) that included the invasion of Bougainville by Halsey's South Pacific Force. This would neutralize the Japanese airbases on the island and allow the Allies to establish their own airbases to provide fighter cover for Allied bombing raids on Rabaul. The Elkton Plan went forward even after the decision was made not to invade Rabaul itself, since it was still necessary to encircle and neutralize the Japanese base.

In early **January 1943** the Joint Chiefs ordered MacArthur to prepare and submit detailed plans for the carrying out of their **2 July 1942** directive. In response, representatives of MacArthur, Admiral Nimitz, and Admiral William F. Halsey (commander, SPA, and subordinate to Nimitz) flew to Washington in **March 1943** to present their plans to the Joint Chiefs. MacArthur and Halsey were to begin the initial advance toward Rabaul and capture various points along the northern coast of New Guinea, New Georgia, the northern Solomons, and the Bismarck Archipelago. A direct assault on Rabaul was postponed. The matter of timing was left to MacArthur and Halsey.

✦ ✦ ✦ ✦

Admiral Halsey flew to MacArthur's headquarters in Brisbane, Australia, where they discussed campaign strategy. MacArthur's headquarters issued plans on **26 April 1942** that laid out a two-pronged offensive, code-named CARTWHEEL, which would envelop and isolate the Japanese at Rabaul. One prong (MacArthur) would advance the northern shores of New Guinea and into the Bismarck Archipelago. The second prong (Halsey) would drive northwest from Guadalcanal and seize the along The **Bismarck Archipelago** is a group of islands off the northeastern coast of New Guinea in the western Pacific Ocean and is part of the Islands Region of Papua New Guinea.

The lengthy operational sequence designed to achieve the "reduction of Rabaul" initially consisted of thirteen separate, short, and often simultaneous advances. MacArthur would take Woodlark and Kiriwina Islands; then Halsey would take the New Georgia group in the Solomons.

Next, MacArthur would move along the New Guinea coast, seizing Salamaua, Lae, and Finschhafen. Halsey would follow by attacking the Shortland Islands and southern Bougainville, and then, farther up the New Guinea coast, MacArthur would capture Madang. CARTWHEEL would conclude with MacArthur's moving on to Cape Gloucester and Halsey's establishing himself on Bougainville's eastern coast. These phased advances were due to the need to build airstrips at each stage, so that Allied air forces could counter Japanese air power operating from Rabaul.

CARTWHEEL'S success rested on the ability of air, ground, and naval forces to work together in joint operations of unprecedented scope.

After this, the Allied forces sought to isolate and contain the main Japanese forces around Rabaul. When Japan surrendered in August 1945, it was found that there were still around 69,000 Japanese troops stranded in Rabaul.

After this, the Allied forces sought to isolate and contain the main Japanese forces around Rabaul. When Japan surrendered in August 1945, it was found that there were still around 69,000 Japanese troops stranded in Rabaul.

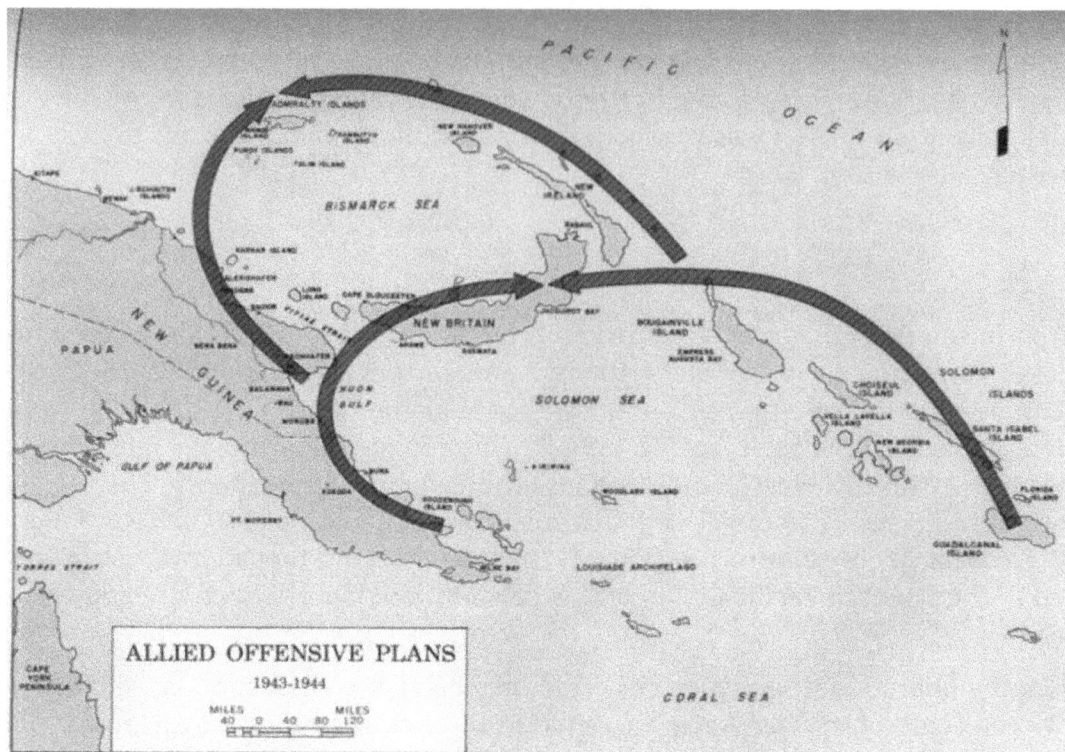

ALLIED OFFENSIVE PLANS
1943-1944

Operation Cartwheel (30 June 1943 - January 1944)

This operation was the name given to a series of interlocked invasions in New Guinea, New Britain and the Solomon Islands originally designed as preparation for the conquest of the Japanese base at Rabaul, but that eventually led to the isolation of that base.

The purpose of Cartwheel was to destroy the barrier formation Japan had created in the Bismarck Archipelago, a collection of islands east of New Guinea in the Solomon Sea. The Japanese considered this area vital to the protection of their conquests in the Dutch East Indies and the Philippines. For the Allies, Rabaul, in New Britain, was the key to winning control of this theater of operations, as it served as the Japanese naval headquarters and main base.

On **30 June 1943**, General MacArthur, strategic commander of the area, launched a simultaneous attack on New Guinea and on New Georgia, as a setup and staging maneuver for the ultimate assault, that on Rabaul. The landing on New Georgia, led by Admiral William Halsey, proved particularly difficult, given the large Japanese garrison stationed there and the harsh climate and topography. Substantial reinforcements were needed before the region could be controlled in **August 1943**.

Operation Cartwheel showed the effectiveness of a strategy which avoided major concentrations of enemy forces and instead aimed at severing the Japanese lines of supply and communication. Also, the ability to communicate and cooperate between commanders of the land and sea.

On **30 June 1943**, the same day that MacArthur's forces began attacking in New Guinea, Admiral Halsey's forces were landing four hundred miles away at several sites in the group of islands collectively known as New Georgia. Code-named TOENAILS, the invasion of the New Georgia islands presented several obstacles to the Army and Navy planners who had spent six months preparing for the operation. The strategic defeats suffered in the Battles of the Coral Sea and Midway checked Japan's advance in the Pacific. The engagements, which cost the Japanese over 400 carriers and land-based aircraft and five aircraft carriers, forced Tokyo to assume a defensive posture.

XVIII   Guadalcanal & The Eastern Solomons

The Solomon Islands 1943 Allied advances:

Guadalcanal **7 August 1942**
Russell Islands, Vella Lavella Island, Choiseul Island **21 February 1943**
New Georgia, Rendova, Kolombangara Islands **June – July 1943**
Bougainville **1 November 1943**

The Allies Take the Initiative

7 August, 1942 marked the first day of Operation Watchtower, the Allied campaign to wrest control of the island of Guadalcanal from Imperial Japan. It was also the beginning of the long and bloody Allied counteroffensive in the Pacific.

The Watchtower force, numbering 75 warships and transports (of vessels from the U.S. and Australia), assembled near Fiji on **26 July 1942** and engaged in one rehearsal landing prior to leaving for Guadalcanal on **31 July**. The commander of the Allied expeditionary force was U.S. Vice Admiral Frank Fletcher (whose flag was on the aircraft carrier USS *Saratoga*). Commanding the amphibious forces was U.S. Rear Admiral Richmond K. Turner. Vandegrift led the 16,000 Allied (primarily U.S. Marine) infantry earmarked for the landings.

The troops sent to Guadalcanal were fresh from military training and armed with bolt-action M1903 Springfield rifles and a meager 10-day supply of ammunition. Because of the need to get them into battle quickly, the operation planners had reduced their supplies from a 90-days to only 60 days. US Marines built defensive structures using pointed wood stakes, set in the ground at 45-degree angles. This was done due to the barbed wire shortage.

The men of the 1st Marine Division began referring to the coming battle as "Operation Shoestring".

The First U.S. Ground Offensive of World War II

The amphibious assault on Guadalcanal and Tulagi was the first US ground offensive of WWII. Designated Operation Watchtower, the hastily thrown together plan called for the 1st Marine Division, about 19,000 men, supported by American and

Australian warships and transport vessels, 82 ships of all types, to make the sea-borne assault. The Allied armada assembled near Fiji on July 26. A poorly planned and executed rehearsal, Operation Dovetail, was held on Koro Island in the Fijis, after which the fleet sailed for its objectives on the 31st.

As the Allied fleet neared Guadalcanal, it split: the Guadalcanal Group, made up of Combat Group A composed of the 1st and 5th Marine Regiments, the divisional artillery, and support units (11,300 men), under 1st Marine Division Commander Major General Alexander A. Vandegrift, headed for Junga Point on Guadalcanal. The Northern Group, built around four Marine infantry rifle battalions (2,400 troops) led by assistant division commander Brigadier General William H. Rupertus, steered for Tulagi, Florida, Gabutu, and Tanambogo.

The main Marine force that came ashore on Guadalcanal encountered more difficulty with the islands' foreboding jungle terrain, oppressively hot weather, and the confusion the inexperienced Americans had with offloading men and supplies than it did with the Japanese. It was a different and deadly story for General Rupertus's command, which hit the beaches at Tulagi, Florida, Gabutu, and Tanambogo that same day. Control of these small islands was deemed critical to the success of US landings on Guadalcanal and subsequent ability to resupply the Marines ashore.

Battle of Tulagi

On **May 3, 1942**, the Japanese invaded Tulagi. After taking Tulagi, the Japanese constructed a seaplane, ship refueling, and communications base on the island with supporting facilities on Gavutu, Tanambogo, and Florida Island.

Unlike their comrades who invaded Guadalcanal on **August 7, 1942**, United States Marines landing on Tulagi met fierce resistance. It was a harbinger of the bloody island fighting that marked combat in the Pacific during World War II.

The island of Tulagi is two miles long and a half mile wide; it lies just south of Florida Island and 22 miles directly north across Sealark Channel from Guadalcanal. A ridge rising over 300 feet above the sea marks the northwest-southeast axis of the island. About two-thirds of the way down from its northwest tip, the ridge is broken by a ravine and then rises again in a triangle of hills.

At 0652 on the morning of **August 7, 1942**, Japanese troops on Tulagi began to send a flood of radio transmissions in the clear reporting 20 enemy ships shelling the island accompanied by air attacks and seaborne forces. At 0805, Tulagi signaled that the island's defenders were destroying their papers and equipment and signed off with the message, "Enemy troop strength is overwhelming. We pray for enduring fortunes of war," and pledged to fight "to the last man". Making good on their promise, the Japanese on Tulagi did fight almost to the last man while exacting a heavy price on their American opponents.

About 1000, the Japanese mounted a fierce counterattack, driving a wedge between Company C and Company A, almost isolating the former from the rest of the battalion. Savage assaults against Company A's exposed flank were fended off. A second banzai attack, which might have successfully exploited the initial thrust, fell on the front of Company A and was bloodily repulsed. By 1500 the tenacious and often suicidal Japanese resistance on Tulagi was broken.

Cunningly constructed dugouts and tunnels carved into the hill's limestone cliffs and covered by machine-gun pits protected by sandbags made up this strong and well-concealed Japanese defensive position. The Japanese subsequently employed tactics that became hallmarks of their savage defense of Pacific island strongholds, including ambushes, the plentiful use of snipers, savage nocturnal counterattacks, and stealthy infiltration of American lines by small groups of Japanese soldiers.

While clearing the small island of Tulagi of its Japanese defenders, US Marines discovered dugouts and tunnels carved into the island's hillsides. These types of defenses were encountered many times during the American march across the Pacific toward the Japanese home islands.

Battle of Guadalcanal

Guadalcanal / Solomon Islands Date: **August 7, 1942- February, 9, 1943**

Background: Following their attack on Pearl Harbor (December 7, 1941), the Japanese Imperial Navy occupied scores of islands throughout the western Pacific Ocean. Japan's goal was to create a defensive buffer against attack from the United States and its Allies— one that would ensure Japan mastery over East Asia and the Pacific. **After the United States' strategic victories at the Battles of the Coral Sea (May 4-8, 1942) and Midway (June 4-7, 1942), expansion of the Japanese Empire halted.** The Japanese Imperial Navy was no longer capable of major offensive campaigns and the Allies could now start their own offensive in the Pacific.

The U.S. chose Guadalcanal, in the Solomon Island chain, as their first offensive campaign in the Pacific. The Solomons represented the farthest reach of Japanese territorial control in the Pacific and would be the first of many islands the U.S. would retake in a brutal three-year island-hopping campaign to reach and defeat Japan.

On **August 7, 1942**, U.S. forces landed on Guadalcanal, Tulagi, and Florida Islands in the Solomon Islands. The landings on the islands were meant to deny their use by the Japanese as bases for threatening the supply routes between the U.S. and Australia, and to secure the islands as starting points for a campaign with the eventual goal of isolating the major Japanese base at Rabaul while also supporting the Allied New Guinea campaign. The landings initiated the six-month-long Guadalcanal campaign.

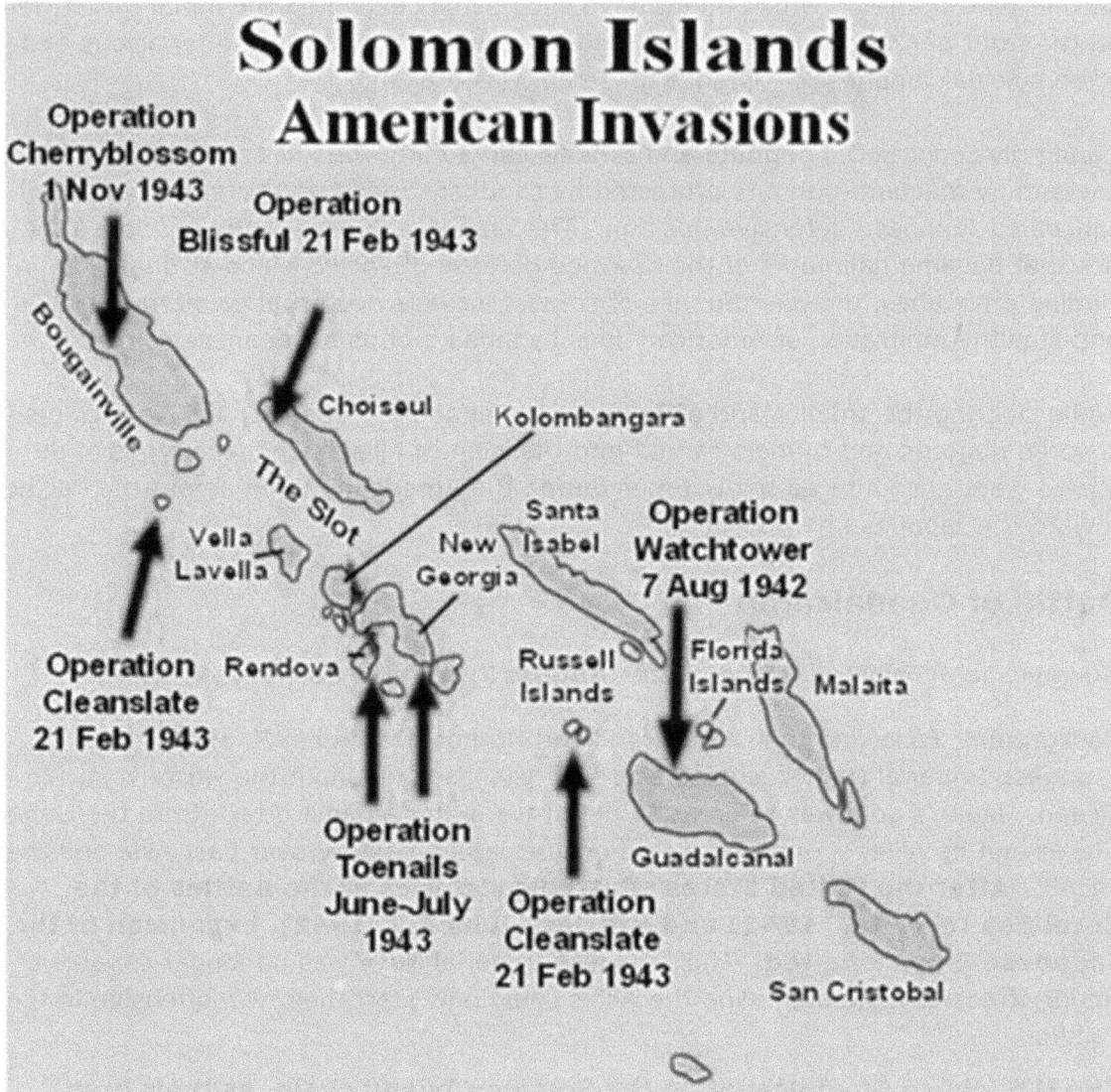

Solomon Islands American Invasions

Operation Cherryblossom 1 Nov 1943

Operation Blissful 21 Feb 1943

Bougainville

Choiseul

Kolombangara

The Slot

Vella Lavella

Santa Isabel

New Georgia

Operation Watchtower 7 Aug 1942

Operation Cleanslate 21 Feb 1943

Rendova

Russell Islands

Florida Islands

Malaita

Operation Toenails June–July 1943

Operation Cleanslate 21 Feb 1943

Guadalcanal

San Cristobal

Guadalcanal was a battle for a tiny island in the South Pacific no bigger than Delaware, but it became a turning point in the Allied fight against Japan during World War II. Nearly 7,000 Americans died fighting for control of Guadalcanal for six months between August 1942 and February 1943.

At the opening of the campaign there were few vehicular roads. Tulagi had some trails, and a trail had been built through the coconut groves on the north coast of Guadalcanal, but the only inland passages were native footpaths. There were no bridges suitable for artillery and heavy equipment.

The islands are unhealthful; malaria as well as dengue fever is common. The malarial (Anopheles) mosquito breeds in swamps, lagoons, sluggish streams, and puddles, and has seeded the natives heavily. In addition, fungus infections and sores were to plague all the troops. Only the utmost efforts at the prevention of disease would keep troops healthy. Living and combat conditions on Guadalcanal were to make systematic malaria control difficult.

Allied troops encountered a severe strain of dysentery soon after the landings, with one in five Marines afflicted by mid-August. Tropical diseases would affect the fighting strengths of both sides throughout the campaign.

Guadalcanal was used by the Japanese to assault shipping and communications lines between the U.S. and Australia and New Zealand. The Allied victory there gave the Americans a crucial foothold in the region.

The Guadalcanal campaign was fought on the ground, at sea, and in the air, pitted Allied forces against Imperial Japanese forces, and was a decisive, strategically significant campaign of World War II. The fighting took place on and around the island of Guadalcanal in the southern Solomon Islands and was the first major offensive launched by Allied forces against the Empire of Japan.

The Japanese sought to prevent Australia from becoming a threat by threatening Australian supply lines. Their first step was to secure Port Moresby, largest city of Papua New Guinea, and the island of Tulagi. They succeeded in capturing Tulagi, but the invasion of Port Moresby was called off due to a lack of air cover from aircraft carriers following the Battle of the Coral Sea.

In spite of this failure to capture Port Moresby, the Japanese continued to fortify other areas in the Solomons. They fully intended to accomplish their strategic objective of securing the Pacific by cutting off Australia from the United States.

They began construction of an airfield on Guadalcanal Island and garrisoned the Florida Islands, where they established a seaplane and communications base in support of the defense of their main base at Rabaul, on the island of New Britain. They also attacked New Guinea, facing off against Allied forces that mainly consisted of Australian units.

Having seen the importance of air superiority and the destructive capability of air power in the war up to this point, the Allies aimed straight for the Japanese airfield at Guadalcanal. It was nearly completed and capturing it would have prevented the Japanese from using it to provide air cover over the region.

Taking the Japanese by surprise on **7 August**, the Allied landing forces accomplished their initial objectives of securing Tulagi and nearby small islands, as well as an airfield under construction at Lunga Point on Guadalcanal, by nightfall on August 8.

The Japanese had been taken by surprise by this sudden invasion and had little recourse but to launch airstrikes from Rabaul against the Allied landings. They also attempted to reinforce their troops but recalled the ships when they realized that the Allies were landing troops in the thousands.

Guadalcanal, which is shaped like a Paramecium, is ninety miles long and averages over twenty-five miles in width. A backbone of forested mountains and quiescent volcanoes, rising in some places as high as 7,000 feet, runs the length of the island. Coral reefs and sharply rising mountains make the south coast inhospitable for ships. The north coast has no harbors, but Sealark Channel is calm. Many sandy beaches on the north coast are free of reefs and provide suitable landing areas for amphibious operations. From Aola Bay to the Matanikau River, between the mountains and Sealark Channel, there is a flat, narrow, grassy plain. Coconut plantations line most of the beach, and there are some stretches of high, tough kunai grass. There are few areas covered with the tall chest high kunai grass as encountered on Guadalcanal and Bougainville.

The plain is cut by many rivers and streams. They are generally deep, swift, and are frequently flooded by rains. Stagnant pools have formed at most of the river mouths through the accumulation of silt which, massing cones and sand bars, blocks the flow of water. There were several swampy areas (at times chest high) the Marines had to navigate on Guadalcanal.

There weren't any good maps of Guadalcanal, a deficiency that was, in fact, never remedied throughout the campaign. The Solomon Islands Campaign lasted six months and consisted of a number of major battles on land, at sea and in the air.

After some fierce fighting, the Marines cleared Tulagi and Florida by **9 August**. The main forces on Guadalcanal met little resistance on their way inland to secure the airfield at Lunga Point (soon to be renamed Henderson Field).   By **18 August** the airfield was ready for operation. Almost immediately, Japanese naval aircraft attacked transport and escort ships and Japanese reinforcements were sent to the area.

The airfield, renamed Henderson Field and located in the northwest corner of Guadalcanal, proved a key to the campaign. From its runway, a conglomerate of

Marine, navy, and army squadrons defended the local air space, eventually permitting resupply and reinforcement. **Air attacks denied the Japanese daylight access to the island and compelled them to resort to night runs by destroyers—dubbed the "Tokyo Express"—to reinforce and maintain their forces.** Over the next three months, the Japanese sought to recapture Henderson Field with successive counterattacks. Each time, they were repulsed. Four U.S. divisions, two Marine and two army, successfully defeated the Japanese in bloody fighting.

Over the following days, the first of many deadly naval battles occurred— the Battle of Savo Island **9 August 1942**. The fight for control of Guadalcanal (and with it, Henderson Field) and the seas around them continued for months with both sides continuing to lose men, ships and aircraft, but with no clear winner.

Battle of the Tenaru

Tenaru was the first of three separate major land offensives by the Japanese in the Guadalcanal Campaign. The Marines were defending the Lunga perimeter, which guarded Henderson Field, which was captured by the Allies in landings on Guadalcanal on **August 7, 1942**.

In response to the Allied landings on Guadalcanal, the *Japanese Imperial General Headquarters* assigned the Imperial *Japanese Army's 17th Army*, a corps-sized command based at Rabaul and under the command of *Lieutenant-General Harukichi Hyakutake*, with the task of retaking Guadalcanal from Allied forces.

Hyakutake sent the *35th Infantry Brigade under Major General Kiyotake Kawaguchi* was at Palau. The *4th (Aoba) Infantry Regiment* was in the Philippines. The *28th (Ichiki) Infantry Regiment*, under the command of *Colonel Kiyonao Ichiki*, was at sea en route to Japan from Guam. The different units began to move towards Guadalcanal immediately, but Ichiki's regiment, being the closest, arrived first.

Known as the *Ichiki Butai (Ichiki Detachment)*, they were an elite and battle-seasoned force but as was about to be discovered, they were heavily stricken with "victory disease" – overconfidence due to previous success. *Ichiki* was so confident in the superiority of his men that he decided to destroy the American defenders before the remaining majority of his force arrived, even writing in his journal "*18 August, landing; 20 August, march by night and battle; 21 August, enjoyment of the fruit of victory*".

Underestimating the strength of Allied forces (some 11,000 strong) on Guadalcanal, under the command of *Colonel Kiyonao Ichiki*, conducted a nighttime frontal assault on Marine positions at Alligator Creek (often called the "Ilu River" on U.S. Marine maps) on the east side of the Lunga perimeter in the early morning hours of **21 August**.

Ichiki's assault was defeated with heavy Japanese losses in what became known as the Battle of the Tenaru. The dead included *Ichiki,* though it has been claimed that he committed **seppuku** (harakiri or ritual suicide) after realizing the magnitude of his defeat, rather than dying in combat. All but 128 of the original 917 of the *Ichiki Regiment's First Element* were killed in the battle.

The Japanese realized after Tenaru that Allied forces on Guadalcanal were much greater in number than originally estimated and sent larger forces to the island for their subsequent attempts to retake Henderson Field.

The Battle of Tenaru introduced the U.S. Army and Marines to Japanese land battle tactics.

Victory at Tenaru despite savage, suicidal attacks by the outnumbered Japanese forces was both a great morale booster for the Allies and a *sobering realization of the enemy's determination to fight to the death.*

Battle for Henderson Field

This battle took place from **23–26 October 1942,** a land, sea and air battle, on and around Guadalcanal in the Solomon Islands.

Hyakutake's soldiers conducted numerous assaults over three days at various locations around the Lunga perimeter, all repulsed with heavy Japanese losses. At the same time, Allied aircraft operating from Henderson Field successfully defended U.S. positions on Guadalcanal from attacks by Japanese naval air and sea forces.

Japan conceded defeat in the struggle for the island and evacuated many of its remaining forces from Guadalcanal by the first week of **February 1943**.

Battle of Savo Island 8-9 August 1942

The Battle of Savo Island, also known as the First Battle of Savo Island and, in Japanese sources, as the **First Battle of the Solomon Sea**, and among Allied Guadalcanal veterans as **The Battle of the Five Sitting Ducks**, was a naval battle of the Pacific Campaign of World War II between the Imperial Japanese Navy and Allied naval forces.

The battle took place on **August 8–9, 1942** and was the first major naval engagement of the Guadalcanal campaign, and the first of several naval battles in the straits later named Ironbottom Sound, near the island of Guadalcanal. Ironbottom Sound was the name given due to the sheer number of ships sunk in the area. During the war, many naval engagements were fought in Savo Sound, the waters between Guadalcanal and the Florida Islands.

With airstrikes, the Japanese managed to destroy a US transport ship and heavily damage the destroyer USS Jarvis. During these engagements, the US Navy suffered heavy losses to their carrier-based fighters at the hands of Japanese fighter aces from Rabaul, among which were the famous aces *Hiroyoshi Nishizawa and Saburo Sakai*. It is possible that Nishizawa was the most successful Japanese fighter ace of the war; he personally claimed to have had 102 aerial victories at the time of his death, October 26, 1944. *Saburo Sakai* had 28 aerial victories (including shared) by official Japanese records.

In response to the Allies' amphibious landings, the Imperial Japanese Navy (IJN) also attacked the Allied forces landing at Guadalcanal. *Vice Admiral Gunichi Mikawa*, commander of the IJN's Eighth Fleet, sortied from Rabaul in the evening on **8 August, 1942**. The Sixth Cruiser Division, under *Rear Admiral Aritomo Goto*, rendezvoused with his fleet later. Altogether, this fleet was made up of 5 heavy cruisers, 2 light cruisers, and 1 destroyer.

Mikawa's fleet proceeded east past Buka Island and then south past Bougainville before turning east again to go through **New Georgia Sound (better known as The Slot)**. Although spotted by reconnaissance planes and an American submarine, the fleet did not come under attack. They proceeded towards Ironbottom Sound as the sun made its way toward the horizon on **8 August, 1942**.

Plan of Attack

Savo Island's position between Guadalcanal and the Florida Islands meant that there were only two routes into and out of Ironbottom Sound from The Slot. Regardless of which channel they decided to use, they would have to circle the eastern side of Savo Island and exit through the other passage in order to swiftly attack and escape.

Mikawa intended for his fleet to proceed through the southern entrance, attack any ships they could find, and exit through the north.

The Allied landing force, under the command of US Admiral Richmond Turner and British Admiral Richard Crutchley, was given several conflicting reports about a Japanese fleet sailing down The Slot.

A series of communication errors and inadequate reconnaissance caused Turner to perceive that the enemy fleet moving down The Slot was escorting seaplane tenders, which were not likely to come into close contact with his fleet. Based on information available at the time, Admiral Turner assessed that air attacks the following morning was more likely than a seaborne one that night.

Because they did not anticipate a Japanese counterattack that night, they reduced the alert level and allowed half their men to sleep in their bunks while the other half remained on duty. USS Blue and USS Ralph Talbot ran uncoordinated and unchanging patrol routes around each entrance into Ironbottom Sound. Both ships are Bagley-class destroyers.

The confusion and general tiredness of the Allied crews rendered them unprepared for an attack. These were exactly the circumstances in which *Mikawa's* sudden night attack worked best.

Shadowed by Darkness

Vice Admiral Mikawa sought to engage the Allies at night, because the Imperial Japanese Navy were well-versed in night fighting at sea. They had developed rangefinders and spotting equipment, trained their men in effective use of illumination targets at night. These factors enabled the IJN to dominate the seas at night which they would continue to do for a long time to come.

Fighting at night also brought with it an additional advantage: the darkness concealed them from enemy aircraft, which could not operate effectively at night. The Allied destroyers' lookouts did not spot the Japanese fleet in the dark, and their radars had been foiled by interference from the volcanic Savo Island. The Japanese fleet sped up once they had passed through the southern entrance. They had achieved surprise.

A Sound Beating

Mikawa's scout planes overhead began dropping the first of their parachute flares to illuminate the Allied ships as Japanese cruiser's million candle search lights snapped on, catching the Allied ships in their brilliantly blinding shafts of light. Within moments, the Eighth Fleet began raining deadly fire on three cruisers.

The Allied screen consisted of eight cruisers and fifteen destroyers under British Rear Admiral Victor Crutchley VC, but only five cruisers and seven destroyers were involved in the battle. In a night action, *Mikawa* thoroughly surprised and routed the Allied force. **In approximately 37 minutes, the Japanese Navy destroyed four heavy cruisers and killed more than 1,000 American and Australian sailors, handing the U.S. Navy the worst defeat in its history.** There were many reasons for the debacle, however the one common thread through the entire disaster was the poorly framed command and control relationships.

Mikawa's decision to withdraw under cover of night rather than attempt to destroy the Allied invasion transports was primarily founded on the high risk of Allied carrier strikes against his fleet upon daybreak. In reality, the Allied carrier fleet, similarly fearing Japanese attack, had already withdrawn beyond operational range. This missed opportunity to cripple (rather than interrupt) the supply of Allied forces on Guadalcanal contributed to Japan's inability to later recapture the island. At this early critical stage of the campaign, it allowed the Allied forces to entrench and fortify themselves in sufficient strength to successfully defend the area around Henderson Field until additional Allied reinforcements arrived later in the year.

The battle was the first of five costly, large scale sea and air-sea actions fought in support of the ground battles on Guadalcanal itself, as the Japanese sought to counter the American offensive in the Pacific. These sea battles took place every few days, with increasing delays on each side to regroup and refit, until the **November 30, 1942** *Battle of Tassafaronga*—after which the Japanese, eschewing the costly losses, attempted resupplying by submarine and barges. The final naval battle, the *Battle of Rennell Island*, took place months later on **January 29–30,**

1943 by which time the Japanese were preparing to withdraw and evacuate their remaining land forces from Guadalcanal.

Battle of the Eastern Solomons

The naval Battle of the Eastern Solomons took place on 24–25 August 1942, and was the third carrier battle of the Pacific campaign of World War II and the second major engagement fought between the United States Navy and the Imperial Japanese Navy during the Guadalcanal Campaign. As at the Battle of the Coral Sea and the Battle of Midway, the ships of the two adversaries were never within sight of each other. Instead, all attacks were carried out by carrier-based or land-based aircraft.

After several damaging air attacks, the naval surface combatants from both America and Japan withdrew from the battle area without either side securing a clear victory. However, the U.S. and its allies gained tactical and strategic advantage. Japan's losses were greater and included dozens of aircraft and their experienced aircrews. Also, Japanese reinforcements intended for Guadalcanal were delayed and eventually delivered by warships rather than transport ships, giving the Allies more time to prepare for the Japanese counteroffensive and preventing the Japanese from landing heavy artillery, ammunition, and other supplies.

The battle of the Eastern Solomons (**24-25 August 1942**) was the second battle in the series of six naval actions linked to the fighting on Guadalcanal and was a carrier battle that ended as a minor American victory.

After their first small-scale counterattacks on Guadalcanal had failed the Japanese began to move reinforcements to the island. A force of fast transports, cruisers and light cruisers under *Rear-Admiral Raizo Tanaka* was allocated to this task. *Tanaka's* force soon became known to the Americans as the 'Tokyo Express' and it would continue to operate for most of the Solomon Islands campaign. *Tanaka's* first run was a success, and 815 men were landed on Guadalcanal on the night of **18-19 August**. Although these troops were quickly lost in battle the Japanese decided to repeat the exercise and send another small force.

Japanese carriers and other large warships moved into a position near the southern Solomon Islands. From this location, the Japanese naval forces hoped to engage and decisively defeat any Allied (primarily U.S.) naval forces, especially carrier forces, that responded to the ground offensive. Allied naval forces also hoped to meet the Japanese naval forces in battle, with the same objectives of breaking the stalemate and decisively defeating their adversary. They met **24-25 August 1942**.

After several damaging air attacks, the naval surface combatants from both America and Japan withdrew from the battle area without either side securing a clear victory. However, the U.S. and its allies gained tactical and strategic advantage. Japan's losses were greater and included dozens of aircraft and their experienced aircrews. Also, Japanese reinforcements intended for Guadalcanal were delayed and eventually delivered by warships rather than transport ships, giving the Allies more time to prepare for the Japanese counteroffensive and preventing the Japanese from landing heavy artillery, ammunition, and other supplies.

Admiral Tanaka's force consisted of the transport *Kinryu Maru* (converted from a light cruiser), four destroyer transports, the seaplane carrier *Chitose* and Destroyer Squadron 2, led by the light cruiser *Jintsu*.

The main force was built around the fleet carriers *Shokaku* and *Zuikaku*. It also included eight battleships, four heavy cruisers and the light carrier *Ryujo*, which was to serve as bait. The Japanese hoped that the Americans would find the *Ryujo*, but not the larger carriers, and would attempt to attack her.

The main American fleet, under Admiral Fletcher, included the carriers Saratoga, Enterprise and Wasp, the new battleship North Carolina, four cruisers and ten destroyers. After a successful landing, they remained in the South Pacific area charged with four main objectives: guarding the line of communication between the major Allied bases at New Caledonia and Espiritu Santo; giving support to Allied ground forces at Guadalcanal and Tulagi against possible Japanese counteroffensives; covering the movement of supply ships aiding Guadalcanal; and engaging and destroying any Japanese warships that came within range.

✦ ✦ ✦ ✦

USS Saratoga

USS *Saratoga* (CV-3) was a *Lexington*-class aircraft carrier built for the United States Navy during the 1920s. Originally designed as a battlecruiser, she was converted into one of the Navy's first aircraft carriers during construction to comply with the Washington Naval Treaty of 1922. The ship entered service in 1928 and was assigned to the Pacific Fleet for her entire career.

In 1942, the USS Saratoga had a crew of 100 officers and 1,840 enlisted men and an aviation group totaling 141 officers and 710 enlisted men. By 1945, her crew totaled 3,373, including her aviation group.

The ship's flight deck was 866 feet 2 inches (264.01 m) long and had a maximum width of 105 feet 11 inches (32.28m). Her flight deck was widened forward and extended 16 feet (4.9m) aft during her refit in mid-1941.

When built, her hangar "was the largest single enclosed space afloat on any ship" and had an area of 33,528 square feet (3,114.9 sq. mi). It was 424 feet (129.2m) long and no less than 68 feet (20.7m) wide. Its minimum height was 21 feet (6.4m), and it was divided by a single fire curtain just forward of the aft aircraft elevator.

USS Saratoga was one of just three prewar US fleet aircraft carriers, along with Enterprise and Ranger, to serve throughout WWII. Saratoga was designed to carry 78 aircraft of various types, including 36 bombers, but these numbers increased once the Navy adopted the practice of tying up spare aircraft in the unused spaces at the top of the hangar. The ship was built with a 155 foot (47.2m), flywheel-powered, F MK II aircraft catapult, also designed by Norden, on the starboard side of the bow. This catapult was strong enough to launch a 10,000 lb. (4,500 kg) aircraft at a speed of 48 knots (89 km/h; 55 mph). It was intended to launch seaplanes.

Aircraft Carrier Catapults

November 5, 1915, Lieutenant Commander Henry C. Mustin launched himself from the armored cruiser USS North Carolina (CA-12) via catapult in a Curtiss Model AB-2, recording both the world's first catapulting of an aircraft from a ship and the first takeoff from a ship underway. The Model AB-2 was a biplane flying boat powered by a single engine mounted amongst the interplane struts and driving a pusher propeller.

Despite the prevailing ideas at the time that naval aviation was an outlandish endeavor, the flight was a success. At the time, launching a plane from a ship while underway had not been attempted. The questions of whether the plane would fly, or whether it would be possible to safely abort takeoff, were still big unknowns.

According to *U.S. Armored Cruisers: A Design and Operational History* by Ivan Musicant, the catapult bolted to the North Carolina's quarterdeck was made of narrow-gauge track, 50-feet long. It rose about four feet above the deck. The plane was launched on this track using 300 psi compressed air from the ship's torpedo air service. Although its catapult was rudimentary and crude, the AB-2 "flying boat" biplane zipped down the track and over the side of the ship at 50 mph.

The work performed on the *North Carolina* proved that "aeronautic ships" could carry and catapult planes at sea.

Mustin was also interested in the technical aspects of naval artillery and helped develop a telescopic sight that would aid in increasing the accuracy and range of naval gunnery. He made his first flight while on duty at the Philadelphia Navy Yard.

Mustin was named commandant of the Naval Aeronautic Station in April 1915. With USD $1 million in funding for the year, the station conducted antisubmarine patrols, worked on the development of a new bombsight and a gyroscopic sextant.

Mustin was outspoken about the potential of naval aviation, despite conclusions by officials that "aeronautics does not offer a prospect of becoming the principal means of exercising compelling force against the enemy." He lobbied to halt funding of dirigible projects and focus development on high-speed fighter aircraft.

Mustin began development of a "sea sled" carrier vessel. He conducted tests from November **1918 to March 1919**. The armistice with Germany and end of World War I on **11 November 1918** ended Mustin's sea sled development, although it would be revived during World War II and praised for its ingenuity.

Flywheel-powered

A flywheel used as a catapult is a mechanical device specifically designed to efficiently store rotational energy. This is the type flywheel on the USS Saratoga and other carriers of the day. Flywheels resist changes in rotational speed by their moment of inertia. The amount of energy stored in a flywheel is proportional to the square of its rotational speed. The way to change a flywheel's stored energy is by increasing or decreasing its rotational speed applying a torque aligned with its axis of symmetry.

Norden bombsight

The **Norden Mk. XV**, known as the **Norden M** series in Army service, was a bombsight in late 1942 used by the United States Army Air Forces (USAAF) and the United States Navy during World War II, and the United States Air Force in the Korean and the Vietnam Wars. It was the canonical tachometric design, a system that allowed it to directly measure the aircraft's ground speed and direction, which older bombsights could only measure inaccurately with lengthy in-flight procedures. The Norden further improved on older designs by using an analog computer that constantly calculated the bomb's impact point based on current flight conditions, and an autopilot that let it react quickly and accurately to changes in the wind or other effects.

Together, these features seemed to promise unprecedented accuracy in day bombing from high altitudes; in peacetime testing the Norden demonstrated a circular error probable (CEP)[a] of 23 meters (75 feet), an astonishing performance for the era. This accuracy allowed direct attacks on ships, factories, and other point targets. Both the Navy and the AAF saw this as a means to achieve war aims through high-altitude bombing; for instance, destroying an invasion fleet by air long before it could reach US shores. To achieve these aims, **the Norden was granted the utmost secrecy well into the war, and was part of a then-unprecedented production effort on the same scale as the Manhattan Project.**

USS Enterprise

A Yorktown-class carrier, she was launched in 1936 and was one of only three American carriers commissioned before World War II to survive the war (the others being *Saratoga* and *Ranger*). **She participated in more major actions of the war against Japan than any other United States ship.** These actions included the Attack on Pearl Harbor (18 dive bombers of VS-6 were over the harbor, 6 were shot down with a loss of eleven men, making her the only American Aircraft carrier with men at Pearl Harbor during the Attack and the first to receive casualties during the Pacific War), the Battle of Midway, the Battle of the Eastern Solomons, the Battle of the Santa Cruz Islands, various other air-sea engagements during the Guadalcanal Campaign, the Battle of the Philippine Sea, and the Battle of Leyte Gulf. *Enterprise* **earned 20 battle stars, the most for any U.S. warship in World War II, and was the most decorated U.S. ship of World War II. On three occasions during the Pacific War, the Japanese announced that she had been sunk in battle, resulting in her being named "The Grey Ghost".**

Enterprise was at sea on the morning of 7 December 1941 and received a radio message from Pearl Harbor, reporting that the base was under attack. The next evening, Enterprise, screened by six of her Grumman F4F Wildcat fighters, put into Pearl Harbor for fuel and supplies. Vice Admiral "Bull" Halsey ordered every able-bodied man on board to help rearm and refuel the Enterprise; the entire 24-hour process took only 7 hours.

RCA CXAM-1 Radar

Enterprise was one of fourteen ships to receive the early RCA CXAM-1 Radar. Radar detection range of aircraft depends on altitude, size, and number of aircraft. Surface ships are more difficult to detect due to ground clutter, and require shorter ranges. The CXAM is listed (in U.S. Radar, Operational Characteristics of Radar Classified by Tactical Application) as being able to detect single aircraft at 50 miles and to detect large ships at 14 miles. Other sources list CXAM detection range on aircraft out to 100 miles. *Lexington*'s CXAM-1 detected the incoming Japanese carrier aircraft strike at a range of 68 miles during the battle of the Coral Sea.

USS Wasp (CV-7) was a United States Navy aircraft carrier commissioned in 1940 and lost in action off Guadalcanal **15 September 1942** from three torpedo hits from a Japanese submarine.

Additionally, Wasp was launched with almost no armor, modest speed and, more significantly, no protection from torpedoes. Absence of side protection of the boilers and internal aviation fuel stores "doomed her to a blazing demise". Wasp was the first carrier fitted with a deck edge elevator.

Deck-edge elevators are used on airplane-carrier ships for transferring airplanes from one deck to another, they are mounted on the outer side of the ship in alignment with an opening therein to the main deck and are movable up and down on the side of the ships to serve the main decks and the flight decks.

Landing Vehicle Tracked (LVT)

The LVT had its origins in a civilian rescue vehicle called the *Alligator*. Developed by Donald Roebling in **1935**, the Alligator was intended to operate in swampy areas, inaccessible to both traditional cars and boats. Two years later, Roebling built a re-designed vehicle with improved water speed. The United States Marine Corps, which had been developing amphibious warfare doctrine based on the ideas of Lt. Col Earl Hancock "Pete" Ellis and others, became interested in the machine after learning about it through an article in *Life* magazine and convinced Roebling to design a more seaworthy model for military use.

The Bureau of Ships placed a contract for production of 100 units of a model using all-steel construction, for a more rugged and easily produced design, and the first LVT-1 was delivered in **July 1941**. Another 200 units were ordered even before the first production units were delivered. After more improvements to meet requirements of the Navy, made difficult by Roebling's lack of blueprints for the initial designs, the vehicle was adopted as "Landing Vehicle Tracked" or LVT.

The contract to build the first 200 LVTs was awarded to the Food Machinery Corporation (FMC), a manufacturer of insecticide spray pumps and other farm equipment, which built some parts for the Alligators. The initial 200 LVTs were built at FMC's Dunedin, Florida factory, where most of the improvement work had been done as well. The LVT-1 could carry 18 fully equipped men or 4,500 pounds (2,041 kg) of cargo.

June 1941, USMC recommended development of an LVT armed with a 37mm gun and three machine guns and armored against 0.50 (12.7mm) machine gun fire. Development was slow and ultimately involved a complete redesign of the LVT, the

LVT-2 Buffalo. Armored versions were introduced as well as fire support versions, dubbed *Amtanks*, which were fitted with turrets from Stuart series light tanks (LVT(A)-1) and Howitzer Motor Carriage M8s (LVT(A)-4).

However, the Marines soon recognized the potential of the LVT as an assault vehicle. A battalion of LVTs was ready for 1st Marine Division by **16 February 1942**. The LVTs saw their first operational use in Guadalcanal, where they were used exclusively for landing supplies. About 128 LVTs were available for the landings.

Production continued throughout the war, resulting in 18,616 LVT's delivered. 23 U.S. Army and 11 USMC battalions were equipped by 1945 with LVT's. British and Australian armies also used LVT's in combat during World War II.

✦ ✦ ✦ ✦

Battle of Santa Cruz Islands

The Battle of the Santa Cruz Islands, fought during **25–27 October 1942**, was the fourth carrier battle of the Pacific campaign of World War II and the fourth major naval engagement fought between the United States Navy and the Imperial Japanese Navy during the lengthy and strategically important Guadalcanal campaign.

 In similar fashion to the battles of Coral Sea, Midway, and the Eastern Solomons, the ships of the two adversaries were rarely in direct visual range of each other. Instead, almost all attacks by both sides were mounted by carrier or land-based aircraft.

The Japanese ground offensive on Guadalcanal was under way in the Battle for Henderson Field while the naval warships and aircraft from the two adversaries confronted each other on the morning of **26 October 1942**, just north of the Santa Cruz Islands. After an exchange of carrier air attacks, Allied surface ships were forced to retreat from the battle area with one carrier sunk and another heavily damaged. The participating Japanese carrier forces also retired because of high aircraft and aircrew losses plus significant damage to two carriers.

Although a tactical victory for the Japanese in terms of ships sunk and damaged, the loss of many irreplaceable, veteran aircrews would prove to be a long term strategic advantage for the Allies, whose aircrew losses in the battle were relatively low and could be quickly replaced.

The Battles of the **Eastern Solomons** and of the **Santa Cruz Islands** are the two great carrier battles of the period. These are not as famous as the Coral Sea or Midway but are two out of the five great carrier battles (with the very one-sided Battle of the Philippine Sea in 1944) of World War II. **Santa Cruz was the very last carrier battle of the War between roughly equal sides**, and it is where the carrier Hornet, which helped launch the Doolittle Raid against Tokyo (**18 April 1942**), was sunk.

The Japanese ground offensive on Guadalcanal was under way in the Battle for Henderson Field while the naval warships and aircraft from the two adversaries confronted each other on the morning of **26 October 1942**, just north of the Santa Cruz Islands. The high casualties for the Japanese prevented their carrier forces from further significant involvement in the battle for Guadalcanal, contributing to the eventual Allied victory in that campaign.

Battle of Tassafaronga

The Battle of Tassafaronga, sometimes referred to as the **Fourth Battle of Savo Island** was a nighttime naval battle that took place on **November 30, 1942** between United States (US) Navy and Imperial Japanese Navy warships during the Guadalcanal campaign. The battle took place in Ironbottom Sound near the Tassafaronga area on Guadalcanal.

In the battle, a US warship force of five cruisers and four destroyers under the command of Rear Admiral Carleton H. Wright attempted to surprise and destroy a Japanese warship force of eight destroyers under the command of *Rear Admiral Raizo Tanaka*. *Tanaka's* warships were attempting to deliver food supplies to Japanese forces on Guadalcanal.

Using radar, the US warships gained surprise, opened fire, and sank one of the Japanese destroyers. *Tanaka* and the rest of his ships, however, reacted quickly and launched numerous Type 93 "Long Lance" torpedoes at the US warships. The Japanese torpedoes hit and sank one US cruiser and heavily damaged three others, enabling the rest of *Tanaka's* force to escape without significant additional damage but also without completing the intended supply delivery mission.

Although a severe tactical defeat for the US, the battle had little strategic impact as the Japanese were unable to take advantage of the victory to further resupply or otherwise assist in their ultimately unsuccessful efforts to recapture Guadalcanal from Allied forces.

Battle of Rennell Island 29–30 January 1943

The Battle of Rennell Island took place on **29–30 January 1943**. It was the last major naval engagement between the United States Navy and the Imperial Japanese Navy during the Guadalcanal campaign of World War II. It occurred in the South Pacific between Rennell Island and Guadalcanal in the southern Solomon Islands.

In the battle, Japanese naval land-based torpedo bombers, seeking to provide protection for the impending evacuation of Japanese forces from Guadalcanal, made several attacks over two days on US warships operating as a task force south of this island. In addition to approaching Guadalcanal with the objective of engaging any Japanese ships that might come into range, the U.S. task force was protecting an Allied transport ship convoy carrying replacement troops there.

As a result of the Japanese air attacks on the task force, one U.S. heavy cruiser was sunk, a destroyer was heavily damaged, and the rest of the U.S. task force was forced to retreat from the southern Solomons area. Partly because they turned back the U.S. task force in this battle, the Japanese successfully evacuated their remaining troops from Guadalcanal by **7 February 1943**, leaving it in the hands of the Allies and ending the battle for the island.

By the end of the battle on **February 9, 1943**, the Japanese had lost two-thirds of the 31,400 army troops committed to the island, whereas the U.S. Marines and the U.S. Army had lost less than 2,000 soldiers of about 60,000 deployed. The ship losses on both sides were heavy. But by far the most significant loss for the Japanese was the decimation of their elite group of naval aviators. Japan, after Guadalcanal, no longer had a realistic hope of withstanding the counteroffensive of an increasingly powerful United States.

Japanese Tactics

In defense, the Japanese soldier was more skillful, and hence more formidable, than in offense. His strong points were well located and well organized, his weapons well sited, and his camouflage superior. His tenacity, his willingness to starve or be shot rather than surrender, may be denounced as fanaticism, but such qualities gave vital strength to his defense.

The pillboxes on Guadalcanal and the other islands were tough obstacles. Constructed with three or four layers of coconut logs and several feet of coral, they were largely subterranean. The few feet exposed above ground contained machine-gun and rifle firing slits, so well camouflaged that American soldiers often could not determine their location. These pillboxes were also on other islands in great numbers.

Photo Op showing empty pillbox

The Japanese, in an offensive, was wont to follow a fixed plan rigidly; they apparently lacked either the flexibility of mind or enough military technique to alter the plans when they went askew.

United States Tactics

Because the rough terrain and thick jungles prevented commanders from exercising close control over widely dispersed units, the columns deployed as late and as close to the enemy as possible. Where an entire battalion often moved over a single trail, a column of single files, deploying as late as possible, was best.

All divisions and regiments agreed that the wisdom of enveloping one or more of the enemy's flanks, rather than attacking frontally, had been repeatedly demonstrated.

Except in rare instances, advancing units usually halted early enough in the afternoon to establish all-round defenses and permit defensive artillery and mortar concentrations to be registered before the fall of darkness. Halting in the afternoon gave the troops time to dig foxholes and emplacements, string barbed wire, emplace and site heavy weapons, and camouflage the position as much as possible. By halting in daylight, troops in the jungle could also determine the location of the units on their flanks. If this was not done, inexperienced troops were apt to fire on each other during the night. All movement within a defensive area ceased after nightfall.

Infantry fighting was close work, as most targets lay less than fifty yards from the infantrymen. The nature of the terrain broke most engagements into "small unit scraps" in which "success is dependent upon the individual soldiers, NCO's, and platoon leaders' ability to act promptly and intelligently when confronted with a situation." This was true on most of the tropical islands.

American troops, in accordance with standard tactical doctrines, were relying heavily upon artillery for both offense and defense despite inaccurate maps, limited observation, and the difficulties of hauling ammunition.

Since infantrymen in their first battle were often apprehensive when their own artillery put fire over their heads to hit targets directly in front of them, forward observers usually laid the first registration shots deep in enemy territory, and then brought the fire back toward the American front lines.

Intelligence

Direct aerial observation and aerial photographs yielded valuable data. The Corps depended on ground patrols, usually of reinforced platoon strength, for close-in combat intelligence; finding routes of approach, enemy front lines, soft spots, and strong points. The quality of patrolling had been improving since D Day. Misled by the difficulty of walking through dark, rough jungle, patrols frequently overestimated the distances they had traveled.

Captured documents were still a fruitful source of data on enemy units, for the Japanese carelessly carried diaries and orders into the front lines. Prisoners of war, if well treated, usually gave voluminous testimony on all subjects.

Apparently, the Japanese belief that it is dishonorable to surrender had led the *Imperial Army* to neglect to instruct soldiers on what to do if captured, for the enemy soldiers, once taken prisoner, talked freely. **But very few Japanese soldiers ever gave themselves up voluntarily.**

Transportation

On the best motor roads of Guadalcanal, trucks could travel at twenty miles per hour if the roads were not muddy. Off the roads, they could scarcely move. On the jungle trails, the average march speed for troops was one mile per hour. Off the trails in the jungle, where troops had to hack their way through the undergrowth with machetes and bayonets, <u>a half mile per hour was a rapid march speed</u>.

Transportation problems were a major factor in the progress of the Guadalcanal battle. Where roads could be constructed, the jeep and 2-ton truck served well. Off the trails, troops had to hack their way through dense jungle with machetes, covering only a mile or two a day. The heavy rains that would fall during the battle created a logistic nightmare for both sides.

Rations and Clothing

The rations usually served to troops in combat were the C and K rations. These were nutritious but somewhat greasy for use in the tropics. The C ration consisted of prepared meals--meat and beans, stew, or meat and vegetable hash in the dinner ration, and biscuits, candy, and a concentrated beverage powder for breakfast--packed in tin cans. One day's ration weighed over five pounds and was bulky and heavy in a man's pack. The concentrated nonperishable K ration included a small can of cheese or meat paste, biscuits, candy, beverage powder, chewing gum, and two cigarettes. It was packed in waterproof paper packages, was lighter than the C and easier to pack. But most men found the cold K rations tiresome, and agreed that the C ration, whether hot or cold, was wearisome.

Men did not carry complete mess kits into action with them. A canteen cup and spoon sufficed each man. Both C and K rations could be eaten out of the containers with either hands or spoon. Means of washing mess kits thoroughly were not to be found at the front, and to eat from an improperly washed kit led to violent diarrhea.

The uniform most suitable for combat was, for the soldier, the two-piece green twill fatigue uniform rather than the one-piece coverall, and for the marine, the two-piece green utility suit. Shoes made of undressed leather, well covered with waterproofing grease and soled with rubber or a composition material, rendered the best service. Canvas leggings did not give good service. They held the damp and chafed the ankles, and the buckles, straps, and hooks caught in the underbrush. **The steel helmet was invaluable; besides protecting the head it served as an entrenching tool, cooking pot, and wash basin.**

It was essential that soldiers be thoroughly indoctrinated in the need for disposal of all waste materials, and that malaria discipline, including the use of mosquito nets, complete clothing after dusk, killing of mosquito larvae, and the regular use of atabrine tablets, be strictly enforced. Atabrine was an anti-malarial medicine.

Flamethrower

The American portable flame thrower made its first successful combat appearance against Japan on **15 January 1943** at Guadalcanal, five months after United States forces began the assault of this South Pacific island. Although the weapon was not available at first, its potentiality against enemy bunkers encountered on the islands defenses which defied ordinary weapons soon became apparent.

When the nozzles were lit, they threw out a roaring, hissing flame 20-30 feet long, swelling at the end to an oily rose, six feet in diameter.

During the island-hopping campaigns of the Pacific Theater, many servicemen believed flamethrowers made the difference between their lives and death. The operator was a target of the enemy. There had to be a joint effort of fire cover for the operator to raise up in order to operate the flame thrower. Without fire cover the operator was a sure target for snipers.

When soft-hearted Americans protested the use of flame weapons against the Japanese, Gen. George C. Marshall, then chief of staff of the Army, defended them.

"The vehement protests I am receiving against our use of flamethrowers do not indicate an understanding of the meaning of our dead."

✦　✦　✦　✦

When the Guadalcanal campaign began, it was the first amphibious land offensive invasion by the United States against any Axis power. It continued to be the *only* land offensive by the United States until the major Allied invasion of North Africa in November 1942. Under the "Europe first" doctrine of the Allied leadership, the material for Guadalcanal was assigned grudgingly. This made it "Operation Shoestring" to those involved. The future of the operation was also immediately put in doubt by the disaster of the Battle of Savo Island. Nevertheless, the American public was far more incensed about Japan than about Germany and was eager for news of American attacks, after many months of American forces being defeated and captured in the Philippines, and on Wake and Guam.

The U.S. made many initial mistakes, including not having the proper resources on the beaches to move men and material inland. The logistical challenges of transport and supply across the Pacific were immense. **Difficult jungle terrain, inhospitable weather, lack of infrastructure and a foe that fought to the death, gave the U.S. its first taste of what was to come throughout the Pacific Theater of War.** It seemed that every time the U.S. fought to victory, the Japanese would resupply Guadalcanal by night and be ready for more fighting the next day. But eventually, U.S. forces gained the upper hand and by **February 1943**, the Japanese withdrew their final men and surrendered the island to the Allies.

Over the next two and a half years, U.S. forces captured the Gilbert Islands (Tarawa and Makin), the Marshall Islands (Kwajalein and Eniwetok), the Mariana Islands (Saipan, Guam, and Tinian), Iwo Jima and Okinawa. With each island reclaimed from the Japanese, the U.S. moved closer to Japan. Growing superiority at sea and in the air, as well as in the number of fighting men, gave the U.S. increasing advantages. Nonetheless, wherever U.S. forces met Japanese defenders, the enemy fought long and hard before being defeated.

Strategically, the Japanese had an opportunity for a decisive victory but failed to achieve it, instead allowing the Americans to step away with a perception of victory, even only with a small margin. Additionally, the reinforcement of Henderson Field of Guadalcanal by Enterprise's aircraft became a precedent, making daylight supply runs to Guadalcanal impossible for Japanese shipping.

Now the Japanese were forced to making supply runs only under the cover of darkness. Victory required seven months of torturous fighting, but by **7 February 1943** the allies secured the Allied line of communications to Australia. The Allied High Command now could take advantage of its improved strategic position.

✦ ✦ ✦ ✦

Comfort Women

The phrase "comfort women" is a controversial term that refers to approximately 200,000 women who were recruited as prostitutes by the Imperial Japanese Army during World War II. Many of the young women were forced into servitude and exploited as sex slaves throughout Asia, becoming victims of the largest case of human trafficking in the 20th century.

During World War II, the Japanese established military brothels in the countries they occupied. The women in these "comfort stations" were forced into sexual slavery and moved around the region as Japanese aggression increased. Known as "comfort women," their story is an often-understated tragedy that continues to strike debate.

There were advertisements found in wartime newspapers; a failed attempt at attracting volunteers into prostitution. Instead, young women as young as 11 years old were kidnapped and forced into service where they faced rape, torture and extreme violence at military camps known as "comfort stations."

Most were teenagers and were raped by between 10 to 100 soldiers a day at military rape camps. Any woman refusing to provide comfort was immediately executed. At the later cycle of a woman's pregnancy they were no longer useful.

✦ ✦ ✦ ✦

Battle of the Aleutian Islands

In his classic *History of United States Naval Operations in World War II*, Navy Lieutenant Commander Samuel Eliot Morison wrote that the Aleutian Islands campaign could well have been labeled the *'Theater of Military Frustration'*. This phrase aptly describes the American effort to retake the Aleutian island of Attu from the Japanese in **1943**. It was a campaign handicapped not only by the island's fanatical defenders and the bitter Alaskan cold but also by the many miscalculations made by the Army itself.

It was clear to the Allied Forces that the Japanese occupation in the Aleutians provided a continuing threat to America's (and possibly Canada's) security. Any plans for Allied Forces to seize the offensive in the Central Pacific would be difficult to execute while Japan maintained flanking positions in the Aleutians. One should also consider that every day Japan's troops remained on American soil was beneficial to Japanese morale (especially after the losses incurred at the Battle of Midway), while it was detrimental to that of the American's. Perhaps this was the primary reason for what became the total blackout of news relating to events in the Aleutians...to keep the American public from becoming too overly concerned about events in Alaska that were perceived by some higher military and government authorities to be of not much importance considering the scope of WWII. Would the American public panic if they knew that Japan had actually occupied American soil at this time? Because of America's commitments elsewhere, the means of quickly resolving these issues were far from adequate.

The Islands

There are approximately 120 islands comprising the Aleutian chain that stretches from the tip of the Alaskan peninsula to within 90 miles of Kamchatka, Russia. The easternmost island, Unimak, is also the largest, measuring 65 by 22 miles. To the southwest is Unalaska, on the north coast of which is located Dutch Harbor. Unalaska is about 2,000 miles from both San Francisco and Honolulu. Continuing westward, in order, lie Umnak, Atka, and Adak. Kiska is 610 miles west of Dutch Harbor. Further west you will find Shemya, a small island located about 35 miles east of Attu. The Shemya landmass is only two by four miles, with the highest point being about 240 feet.

Attu, the westernmost Alaskan island, is nearly 1,100 miles from the mainland and 750 miles northeast of the northernmost of the Japanese Kurile Islands. Attu is about 20 by 35 miles and has some fairly high mountainous terrain beginning just a short distance from its shore line, rising abruptly to altitudes of 3000 feet, and stretching through to the interior of the island. One writer of the time wrote, *"Attu is the most lonesome spot this side of hell."*

All the Aleutians are volcanic in origin. They are uniformly rocky and barren, with precipitous mountains (usually covered with snow) and scant vegetation. There are no trees on the islands, with the exception of a few stunted spruces at Dutch Harbor, and no brush. The lowlands are covered with a spongy tundra or muskeg as much as three feet thick, making walking very difficult. Below the tundra is volcanic ash, finely ground and water soaked to the consistency of slime. In many places water is trapped in ponds under the tundra. A man on foot may readily break through the tundra, sinking in watery mud up to his knees. Men have fallen into these bogs and have been lost. Motor vehicles, even those with caterpillar treads, quickly churn the tundra into a muddy mass in which sunken wheels and treads spin uselessly.

The Aleutians, being unsuitable for agriculture, lacking in mineral resources, and with little possibility of commercial exploitation, received only slight attention after their acquisition from Russia in 1867. A chart of the coast lines was prepared by the United States Coast and Geodetic Survey office. The Aleutian island's shorelines are jagged with submerged rock formations rendering navigation hazardous. The better anchorages, such as Dutch Harbor, are located in the easternmost islands, while the worst are located in the westernmost islands. Attu has four relatively unguarded bays...Holtz, Chichagof (the best), and Sarana on the northeast side, with Massacre Bay on the southeast side.

Background

While the exact objectives of Japan's attack on the Aleutian Islands in **1942** isn't known, there are two main possibilities to ponder. One possibility is that Japan wanted to conquer the Aleutians to obtain access to Canada and America's northwestern states by way of Alaska. Many of Japan's military leaders considered these poorly defended outposts to be the logical route for an invasion of North America. Why Japan clung to its positions in the Aleutians after the battle of Midway is not known, but it is probable that Attu and Kiska were either going to provide the jumping-off places for future invasions of the North American continent, or merely provide advanced eastern observation posts and defenses for the Empire. General Simon Buckner had proposed to attack Japan via a northern route, through the Aleutians, thus giving some credence to Japan's concerns about protecting their northern flank, which formulates the second reason for Japan's wanting to hold on to Kiska and Attu. A line drawn from Kiska through Attu and down to Midway Island would define Japan's eastern line of homeland defense.

The Weather

Aleutian weather becomes progressively worse as you travel from the easternmost islands to the west. Attu weather is typified by cold, damp fog, often accompanied by snow or icy rain. The winds often reach velocities of more than 100 miles an hour. There are many days during the year where working outside is impossible. On Attu, five or six days a week are likely to be rainy, with hardly more than eight or ten clear days a year. The rest of the time, even if rain is not falling, fog of varying density is the rule rather than the exception. Shemya, located a short distance from Attu, suffers the same fate, but to not as great an extent due to the lack of mountainous terrain. This weather is highly localized, however, and areas of high visibility can be found within 20 miles of fog concentration.

The average rainfall is around 40 to 50 inches throughout the islands, with the heaviest rains in fall and early winter. Squalls, known as "williwaws," sweep down from the island's mountainous areas with great force, sometimes reaching gale proportions within 30 minutes. The mountains are concentrated on the north sides of the islands, which results in strong off-shore winds that in turn make it difficult to find a lee along the north coasts. The columns of spray and mist resulting from the williwaws frequently resemble huge waterfalls. In the winter, the williwaws can cause snow to be blown right up your pant legs, with many having observed the phenomenon of snow blowing from the ground up.

The Aleutian weather turned out to be a constant impediment to the military operations of the United States and Japan alike. Japan, however, enjoyed one advantage: the weather in this theater moves from west to east, resulting in Japan always knowing in advance the conditions which were likely to prevail in the islands.

The War in The Aleutians

Lieutenant General Hideichiro Higuda, commander of the *Japanese Northern Army*, said they wanted to break up any offensive action the Americans might contemplate against Japan by way of the Aleutians, to set up a barrier between the United States and Russia in the event Russia joined with the United States in its war against Japan (Russia at this time was neutral in terms of the Japanese conflict with America), and to make preparations through the construction of advanced airbases for future offensive actions.

Japan's intent was brought to light on **June 3, 1942**, when Japanese carrier-borne aircraft flew out of the Aleutian fog and bombed the American installations at Dutch

Harbor on the island of Unalaska. There were few casualties incurred with only minor damage to the Dutch Harbor facilities. Nevertheless, WWII now became more personal to those who lived in Alaska. News of this event took an inordinate amount of time to reach Americans living on the mainland's "lower 48."

The Japanese then made landfall at Kiska Island on **June 6** and Attu Island, approximately 200 miles away, on **June 7**. Japanese troops quickly established garrisons, or military bases, on both islands, which had belonged to the U.S. since it purchased Alaska from Russia in 1867.

By the **11th of June 1942** it was evident that Japan had landed substantial forces on both Kiska and Attu. The U.S. Navy's PatWing 4 (Patrol Wing 4) consisting of PBY Catalina's flying out of Atka, bombed the Japanese held positions on Kiska that same day.

On the **12th of June, 1942**, the U.S. Army's 11th Air Force heavy bombers made their first run over Kiska at 1200 feet, with hits on two cruisers and one destroyer.

On the **30th of August, 1942**, the allied forces captured Adak during a raging storm that prevented air cover during the assault. The first plane to land on the new Adak runway on **10 September 1942** was piloted by Col. William O. Eareckson. He pioneered low-level bombing raids against the enemy to counteract the effects of the consistently poor and unpredictable Aleutian weather.

On **March 26, 1943** Rear Admiral McMorris's Task Group Mike engaged the Japanese Northern Pacific Fleet which was attempting to re-supply the Japanese garrisons located on Attu and Kiska. This engagement, 150 miles west of Attu's Cape Wrangle, was to become known as the **Battle of the Komandorskies**. The defeat of the Japanese Northern Fleet by Task Group Mike ended Japan's attempts to gain a greater foothold in the Aleutians, and seemingly left the Japanese garrisons on Attu and Kiska to fend for themselves. U.S. airpower wasn't able to engage the Japanese during this skirmish as U.S. aircraft had been loaded with bombs with which to bomb Kiska. By the time the aircraft had changed-out their arsenal with weapons more suitable for naval engagements, the battle of the Komandorskies was over.

U.S. Bombers and fighters continued to bomb and strafe the islands of Kiska and Attu as the weather permitted. During **March of 1943**, 39 raids were made against Kiska.

In **early April** a spell of stormy weather with winds up to 108 m.p.h. grounded all planes for five days. Sixteen B-24, five B-25, and twelve P-38 sorties were ultimately flown against Kiska Island from Adak and Amchitka Islands. By the **21st of April** Kiska had been attacked 83 times. By the end of **April, 1943**, Adak, now the center of Army, Air Force, and Navy operations in the Aleutians, was maintaining a garrison of 19,067 Army personnel and 7,811 Navy. At Amchitka, where there were 10,260 Army and 903 Navy personnel, a 5,000-foot bomber strip had been completed during the month. By the end of the April 640 tons of bombs had been dropped.

The Battle of Attu, Alaska

Attu is about 20 by 35 miles and has some fairly high mountainous terrain beginning just a short distance from its shore line, rising abruptly to altitudes of 3000 feet. All the Aleutians are volcanic in origin. They are uniformly rocky and barren, with precipitous mountains (usually covered with snow) and scant vegetation. There are no trees on the islands, with the exception of a few stunted spruces at Dutch Harbor, and no brush. The lowlands are covered with a spongy tundra or muskeg as much as three feet thick, making walking very difficult. Below the tundra is volcanic ash, finely ground and water soaked to the consistency of slime. In many places water is trapped in ponds under the tundra. A man on foot may readily break through the tundra, sinking in watery mud up to his knees. Men have fallen into these bogs and have been lost. Motor vehicles, even those with caterpillar treads, quickly churn the tundra into a muddy mass in which sunken wheels and treads spin uselessly. The Aleutian island's shorelines are jagged with submerged rock formations rendering navigation hazardous.

Pre-invasion reconnaissance had shown that the Japanese were concentrated around Holtz Bay and Chichagof Harbor in the north and Massacre Bay in the south. Therefore, two landings were planned. The Northern Force, commanded by Lt. Col. Albert Hartl, consisted of the 1st Battalion, 17th Infantry Regiment, and its attached artillery and auxiliary units. The Northern Force's objective was to secure Holtz Bay and a valley lying to the southwest.

Admiral Rockwell planned an operation against Attu. The plan as it evolved was to land the 7th Division on Attu in two forces. One would land north and the other south of the enemy positions. They would then converge at the top of a peninsula which would isolate the enemy.

'The invasion took place from **11–30 May 1943**. It was a battle by the U.S. aided by Canadian reconnaissance and fighter-bomber support against Japan. Despite heavy naval bombardments of Japanese positions, the American troops encountered strong entrenched defenses that made combat conditions tough. Arctic weather conditions and exposure-related injuries also caused numerous casualties among U.S. forces.

The beaches quickly jammed up with supplies and bogged-down vehicles. The 7th soon realized they wouldn't be able to get their artillery or tracked vehicles across the muskeg. It was apparent the battle would have to be fought by the foot soldiers themselves. Troops in the front lines began to suffer greatly from the effects of the bitter cold. Hundreds of GIs would eventually have their feet amputated as a result of frostbite and trench foot (roughly a quarter of all casualties would be traced to frostbite). American troops, lost in the fog, walked into enemy cross-fires and would be pinned down for hours with no reasonable shelter from the cold.

The first wave of Americans on 11 May 1943 found snow running all the way down the beach. The first artillery pieces promptly sank into the tundra after being fired. The artillerymen found that moving their guns across the mucky muskeg was extremely difficult. Finally, the gunners were forced to emplace their 105mm howitzers only 75 yards from the beach.

Air support from the nearby CVE Nassau was eliminated by 90% cloud cover over the island. Those fighters that were able to find their way to the island more often than not strafed friendly units. A flight of F4F Wildcats attempted an attack against the Japanese defenders. As they flew through what was to become known as Jarmin Pass, a williwaw blew two of the planes against the mountain. A thick ground fog persisted to a considerable altitude that, while preventing the American invaders from seeing the Japanese defenders, provided protection for the Japanese (invisible in their white clothing) who could clearly see American troop movements below them.

The battle of Attu was essentially an infantry battle. The climate greatly limited the use of air power as the island was shrouded in fog more often than not, and experienced high winds almost every day. The terrain...steep jagged crags, knifelike ridges covered with snow, boggy tundra...made the use of mechanized equipment and of all motorized vehicles impractical. The American GI, thus reduced to moving only on foot, had to blast his way to victory with only the weapons he could carry with him. The American troops, some trained and equipped for fighting in desert climates, some totally inexperienced in combat, had found a most formidable enemy in the Japanese who were fully equipped, thoroughly acclimated, and fanatically determined to hold their strong, well chosen, defensive positions.

18 May The north and south forces linked up at Jarmin Pass. The west flank of clevesy Pass, leading to mountain peaks overlooking Chichagof Bay, was dominated by Cold Mountain. The east flank, which led to the Sarana Valley, was overlooked by Engineer Hill and an escarpment named Point Able. All of these positions were occupied by the dug-in Japanese, and the Americans spent the next four days trying to take them.

The last obstacle, Point Able, was slowly climbed by companies of the 32nd Infantry just after Engineer Hill was taken. The snow was thick, the cold bitter and the night so bright that soldiers silhouetted against the whiteness could be seen for 200 yards.

U.S. fighter pilots sent to strike the new Japanese positions mistook the advancing Americans for enemy soldiers and proceeded to bomb and strafe them. This tragic misidentification resulted in numerous casualties and delayed the advance for two hours.

Finally, an American rifle platoon managed to fight its way to the ridge's highest point. No sooner had GIs secured the position than they were attacked by about 45 Japanese, led by a saber-wielding officer. The Americans quickly cut down the attackers and completed their occupation of the ridge.

Japanese soldiers hidden on the ridges opened fire with machine guns and mortars and rapidly mowed down GIs who tried to run for cover; other Americans twisted ankles in potholes in the muskeg and fell.

Artillery fire did little but leave craters in the snow, while three Navy fighters attempting to bomb Japanese positions crashed as a result of heavy winds. Movement was only a few yards per hour, with men holding on to the jackets or cartridge belts of the men to their front in order not to be separated.

By the afternoon of **May 19**, companies from the 17th and 32nd regiments had begun a slow ascent up the snowy slope of Cold Mountain. Despite heavy fire from above, the Americans gradually moved up the slope that faced Massacre Valley. In the long daylight and short nights of spring in the Aleutians, evening on Attu began after 2200 hours and ended just after 0100. Although brief, the night was bitter. The Americans froze in their lightweight uniforms, while the Japanese, bundled in fur-lined coats and boots, huddled around their kerosene stoves. Some of the GIs who had spent the night on the floor of Massacre Valley were later found frozen stiff, having burned the stocks of their rifles in a futile attempt to keep warm.

The Japanese attempted to stay in their holes, but the GIs ousted them using grenades and bayonets. American attempts to reach the north side of the mountain, however, were held up until high explosives and smoke rounds were fired into the enemy positions. Again, mistaking the smoke for gas, the Japanese were either killed while putting on their masks or simply fled toward Chichagof Harbor.

Badly outnumbered and sensing possible defeat, the Japanese now killed their own wounded by injecting them with morphine. To make sure the job was completed, they then threw hand grenades into their own medical tent.

But after two weeks of relentless fighting, American units managed to push the Japanese defenders back to a pocket around Chichagof Harbor, an inlet on the northeast coast of the island of Attu.

By nightfall on **May 28** the bulk of the American forces were poised for the final assault on Chichagof Harbor. That evening of **May 28**, a small American patrol from the 17th Infantry penetrated Japanese lines, seeking any information that might help the impending U.S. attack. When the patrol got about 500 yards into enemy territory, the GIs could hardly believe what they saw groups of frenzied Japanese jumping up and down, yelling at the top of their lungs and guzzling bottles of sake. They were dispatching their own wounded, either through morphine injections or self-inflicted pistol shots.

On **29 May 1943** at about 0330, *Yamasaki's* remaining troops took advantage of the lingering fog and managed to break through the American lines. Ten minutes later, with the artillery battery located on Engineer Hill in sight, the Japanese commander ordered a Banzai attack. A thousand screaming Japanese soldiers came running through the bivouac area of the 32nd Infantry. They carried rifles, grenades, even bayonets attached to sticks.

After the main Japanese assault began, diversionary forces attacked the 17th Infantry in Chichagof Valley. Screaming *'We'll drink your blood,'* the Japanese butchered any GIs they could get their hands on. The main body of Japanese then stormed into the lower valley, where an American aid station was set up. They swept through the station, slashing the tent ropes and killing the wounded, who were trapped in their sleeping bags by the fallen canvas.

When they had finished destroying the aid station, the main Japanese force headed down toward Clevesy Pass, occupied mostly by engineer, medical and artillery troops. The only warning these troops had was from retreating GIs shouting, *'The Japs are coming!'*

The sleeping Americans quickly rallied their forces and threw the Japanese back into the fog after intense close combat. The failure to carry out their plan effectively destroyed the Japanese morale. Five hundred of the remaining Japanese committed mass suicide (gyokusai) with grenades held close to their stomachs, chests, and foreheads. *Yamasaki* attempted a final but fruitless charge later in the day with what remained of his force. During this charge he lost his own life to a .30-caliber bullet. The battle for Attu was over.

By the evening of **31 May**, the island was fully in American hands, but at a terrible price for both sides. Out of the Japanese defenders, 2,351 were killed and only 29 were taken prisoner. The American figures were 549 killed, 1,148 wounded and about 2,100 listed as casualties from exposure, trench foot and shock.

The casualties incurred during the invasion of Attu were appalling. The Americans suffered 3,829 casualties, roughly 25% of the invading force, second only in proportion to Iwo Jima. Of these, 549 were killed; 1,148 injured; 1,200 with severe cold injuries; 614 with disease; and a remaining 318 to miscellaneous causes. On the Japanese side 2,351 men were counted by American burial parties, and hundreds more were presumed already buried. Total prisoners taken: 28 (none of whom were officers). The Japanese fought to virtually the last man.

Battle of Kiska Alaska

This battle was a tactical maneuver which completed the Aleutian Islands campaign. On **August 15, 1943**, the 7th Division (U.S.) and the 13th Infantry Brigade (Canada), landed on opposite shores of Kiska which had been occupied by Japanese forces since June 1942. The Japanese, however, had secretly abandoned the island garrison two weeks prior (**28 July**) ending the Japanese presence in the Aleutian Islands. The Allied landings were unopposed. Despite this, after over two days in thick fog and in a confused state of affairs, U.S. and Canadian forces mistook each other as the Japanese.

Allied casualties during the invasion nevertheless numbered close to 200, all from friendly fire, booby traps set out by the Japanese to inflict damage on the invading allied forces, or disease. There were seventeen Americans and four Canadians killed from either friendly fire or booby traps, fifty more were wounded as a result of friendly fire or booby traps, and an additional 130 men came down with trench foot.

✦ ✦ ✦ ✦

PT 109

A notable incident in the later campaign was the ramming and sinking of torpedo boat PT-109 by the destroyer *Amagiri*, on **2 August 1943** off New Georgia. Since PT-109 was commanded by **John F. Kennedy**, who was credited with heroism, this became part of the story of his Presidency.

PT-109 was a PT boat (Patrol Torpedo boat) last commanded by Lieutenant, junior grade (LTJG) John F. Kennedy (later President of the United States) in the Pacific Theater during World War II. Kennedy's actions to save his surviving crew after the sinking of *PT-109* made him a war hero, which proved helpful in his political career. The incident may have also contributed to his long-term back problems.

Abandoning their sinking ship, Kennedy and his men swam first to the very tiny Plum Pudding island. They later abandoned Plum Pudding Island and swam to tiny Olasana Island in search of food and water. On Olsana, Kennedy found coconuts and fresh water which were of some small help to his men. On Olsana Island, Kennedy was discovered by the two islander men, Biuku Gasa and Eroni Kumana. The canoe couldn't accommodate all of the PT-109 crewmen safely, and the islanders and English-speaking crew had difficulty communicating with each other. In absence of writing utensils, Biuku Gasa suggested that Kennedy should inscribe a message on the husk of a coconut he had plucked from a nearby palm tree. This carved message, after rowing their dugout canoe at great risk through 35 nautical miles (65 km) of hostile waters patrolled by the Japanese, was then delivered to the nearest Allied base at <u>Rendova</u>. They enabled the ensuing return to Olasana and the successful American rescue operation. This coconut remained on President Kennedy's desk at the White House during his term in office.

Message carved on the coconut shell reads **"NAURO ISL...COMMANDER...NATIVE KNOWS POS'IT...HE CAN PILOT...11 ALIVE...NEED SMALL BOAT...KENNEDY"**.

✦ ✦ ✦ ✦

Together the Guadalcanal and Papua New Guinea Campaigns by early 1943 had committed more American troops to action against the Japanese than against the Germans

Although the Solomon Islands west of Guadalcanal and the Russell Islands were in MacArthur's theater, Admiral King refused to divide his fleet or to put Halsey under MacArthur's direct control. This created an awkward command arrangement in which Halsey had operational control of all units involved in the Solomons, while MacArthur provided strategic direction.

Code Talkers

The name code talkers are strongly associated with bilingual Navajo speakers specially recruited during WWII by the Marines to serve in their standard communications units in the Pacific Theater. Code talking, however, was pioneered by Cherokee and Choctaw Indians during WWI.

As 1942 dawned, WWII was not going well for America and her Allies. Japanese carrier-borne bombers and fighters had crippled the United States Navy's proud Pacific Fleet at Pearl Harbor; attacked American bases in the Philippines and on Guam; and were intent on seizing other island bases in the south and central Pacific.

Japanese cryptographers were proving themselves amazingly adept at breaking top-secret military codes almost as rapidly as newer, more complicated procedures could be devised. Many of the Japanese code breakers had been educated in the United States where they had learned to speak English and had become familiar with American colloquialisms, including slang terms and profanity. As a result, American battle plans became known to the enemy almost immediately, often before they had become operational, and there appeared to be no immediate workable solution.

After viewing a demonstration of messages sent in the Navajo language, the Marine Corps was so impressed that they recruited 29 Navajos in two weeks to develop a code within their language. United States Marine Corps Platoon 382, made up of the first 29 Navajo Code Talkers, **April 1942**.

Navajo Code Talkers – American History

At Camp Pendleton, the Navajos, in addition to their other duties, were required to devise a new Marine Corps military code which, when transmitted in their own language, would completely baffle their Japanese enemies. The code's words had to be short, easy to learn, and quick to recall. After working long and hard on the project, the men devised a two-part code. The first part, a 26-letter phonetic alphabet, used Navajo names for 18 animals or birds, plus the words ice for I, nut for N, quiver for Q, Ute for U, victor for V, cross for X, yucca for Y, and zinc for Z. The second part consisted of a 211-word English vocabulary and the Navajo equivalents. This code, when compared with conventional Marine Corps codes, offered considerable savings in time, since the latter involved lengthy encoding and deciphering procedures by Signal Corps cryptographic personnel using sophisticated electronic equipment.

Exactly how the Navajos did their job remained a mystery to many Marine Corps staff officers. However, their proficiency, both under training conditions and later in actual combat, proved that the Navajos were completely reliable and erased the initial distrust felt by some Marine officers.

August 1942 Guadalcanal

Several of the Navajos remained in California as instructors; two became recruiters; and one did not complete the course. The remainder of the original contingent reported for combat duty in **August 1942** to Major General Alexander Vandegrift's First Marine Division on Guadalcanal. The general became so impressed by the code talkers' performance that he requisitioned Washington for 83 additional Navajos to be assigned to his division alone. By the time the Guadalcanal campaign ended that December, General Vandegrift had no doubt about the Navajos' dependability.

Meanwhile, a second, much larger contingent of Navajos had been recruited and sent to boot camp in San Diego. Following completion of their basic training, the men were assigned to the top-secret code-talker program at Camp Pendleton. By **August 1943**, nearly two hundred young Navajos had been trained at the camp. In all, 421 Navajos had completed wartime training at Camp Pendleton's code talker school, and most had been assigned to combat units overseas.

When the war was over the Code Talkers continued to protect the code – and their part in the victory – until it was declassified twenty-three years after the conclusion of WWII.

✦ ✦ ✦ ✦

War Dogs

As early as 1935, the Marines were interested in war dogs. They had experienced the enemy's sentry dogs used in Haiti and in the other "Banana Wars" in Central America where dogs staked around guerrilla camps in the jungle sounded the alarm at the approach of the Marines. Jungle scouting and perimeter watch would be prime skills honed in the War Dog Training Center that Gen Holcomb approved and announced on **Nov. 24, 1942**.

Although prior to Pearl Harbor, the citizens of the U.S. were opposed to getting involved with the war that was going on in Europe and Asia, the Marines thought they would have to fight the Japanese in the Pacific. The Marines knew they were going to be fighting in tropical climates where the vegetation provided jungle-like coverage. In such conditions, dogs would be ideal sentries and couriers. It was no surprise later that the Marine Corps had the first large dog unit in the nation's history to see action against the enemy.

The Doberman Pinscher Club of America began a national dog recruiting effort. It was Capt. Boyd who would go with 19 enlisted men for five weeks of Army dog basics at Fort Robinson, Nebraska. Just after Christmas 1942, Boyd was back at

Camp Lejeune as the first CO of the equally new dog detachment. He'd stay until the end of the war. As training progressed Its strength was some 50 men and a few less dogs, mostly Doberman pinschers and German shepherds, but there was never an official Marine Corps breed nor birth. Doberman pinschers had the temperament, were short-haired, aggressive but controlled and were offered quite readily by their owners.

Arriving in Camp LeJeune NC, the new canine recruits were first entered in a forty-page dog service record book. The Marine Corps was the only branch of the service to have such a record for their dogs. Each Dog Record Book is about 4" x 6" in size and 40 pages in length. A new book was opened for each dog "when he (she) first reported to the Dog Detachment Training Center for duty." In making entries, "neatness, clearness, and strict economy of space" was expected to be observed, and each book had to be returned to the Dog Detachment Training Center at Camp Lejeune, North Carolina, when the dog was "separated from the service," which explains how these little documents came to be preserved. The dog community, like Lucky Strike's green cigarette package, had gone to war. These dogs were trained to find Japanese snipers, carry messages, and protect against ambushes.

The dogs could detect a human scent up to one-half mile away. *During the war, the Japanese ambushed none of the War Dog platoons.*

USMC war dog "Caesar von Steuben" would prove the value of a dog's role in war several times over the course of his service in World War II. Caesar was one of the first War Dogs entering the war in the Pacific on Bougainville.

The following was written by Rebecca Frankel for National Geographic. (May 18, 2014)

On one morning in November 1943, in the jungles of the Pacific island of Bougainville, Marine PFC Rufus Mayo was in a panic, scanning the scene around him. Desperate for help, he yelled to another marine – where was Caesar?

At dawn the Japanese had mounted an attack on the Marines. The dog handlers had brought their dogs into their foxholes, resting easier knowing their dogs were there to keep watch. Caesar, a large German shepherd, had heard the attackers coming before the men had heard them, and in his instinctive reaction to protect his handler, Mayo, sleeping beside him, the dog had launched out of the foxhole.

When Mayo realized what was happening he shouted at Caesar to stop and come back. But when the dog turned to obey, a Japanese soldier opened fire, sending three bullets into his body. A battle ignited, and, in the chaos, Caesar went missing. Afterward, Mayo and another Marine searched for the dog. They found a trail of blood, leading them back to the battalion's command. The dog had managed to return to his other handler, PFC John Kleeman, and collapsed behind a bush.

Mayo rushed to him, cradling him gently. The Marines around them moved quickly, breaking down two poles and attaching a blanket to build a makeshift litter to carry the dog to the hospital tent.

While the doctors worked to remove the bullets, his handlers paced outside. Two bullets could be removed, but the surgeon felt it was too risky to take out the third, which had lodged near the dog's heart. In the end, the dog would prove stronger than the bullet, and after only three weeks of rest and recovery, he was back on active duty.

During one deployment, heavy rains rendered the marines' walkie-talkies unusable, and Caesar ran messages back and forth repeatedly between his handlers while evading sniper fire. On another occasion, Caesar saved Mayo, his handler, from a grenade attack. In a letter home, the handler wrote to his family, "I would not give Caesar up for a general's commission."

Like the other 10,000 dogs that would serve in the United States military during World War II, Caesar was a very valuable asset.

XIX   Papua New Guinea & Surrounding Islands

New Guinea is the second largest island in the world after Greenland. Its north coastline extends nearly 1,600 miles from twelve degrees south latitude to just south of the equator. A major mountain range cuts across the island's center from the eastern end of New Guinea to Geelvink Bay on the west and makes passage overland through the jungled mountains by large units nearly impossible. The protective shelter of the mountainous spine, around the Port Moresby area, is wet from January to April but otherwise dry. On the windward side, scene of most of the ground fighting during 1942-1945, rainfall runs as high as 300 inches per year. As one veteran recalled, *It rains daily for nine months and then the monsoon starts."*

Disease thrived on New Guinea. Malaria was the greatest debilitating sickness, but dengue fever, dysentery, scrub typhus, and a host of other tropical sicknesses awaited unwary soldiers in the jungle. The Allied armies were caught flat-footed during WWII when 18,000 of their troops became ill with scrub typhus in the Pacific Theater. Scattered, tiny coastal settlements dotted the flat malarial north coastline, but inland the lush tropical jungle swallowed men and equipment.

The terrain was a commander's nightmare because it fragmented the deployment of large formations. On the north shore a tangled morass of large mangrove swamps slowed overland movement. Monsoon rains of eight or ten inches a day turned torpid streams into impassable rivers. There were no roads or railways, and supply lines were often native tracks, usually a dirt trail a yard or so wide tramped out over the centuries through the jungle growth. Downpours quickly dissolved such footpaths into calf-deep mud that reduced soldiers to exhausted automatons stumbling over the glue-like ground. Fed by the frequent downpours, the lush rainforest jungle afforded excellent concealment to stubborn defenders and made coordinated overland envelopments nearly impossible.

Infantrymen carrying sixty pounds of weapons, equipment, and pack staggered along in temperatures reaching the mid-90s with humidity levels to match. Thus the U.S. Army faced a determined Japanese foe on a battleground riddled with disease and whose terrain made a mockery of orthodox military deployments.

The battle casualties tell only part of the struggle fought out against nature in the jungle wilds. Men on both sides collapsed, exhausted from the debilitating tropical heat and humidity; soldiers shook violently from malarial chills or from a drenching in tropical downpours. Others simply went mad. The neuropsychiatric rate for

American soldiers was the highest in the Southwest Pacific theater (43.94 per 1,000 men). The same monotonous field ration-bully beef and biscuits for the Australians, C-rations for the Americans-left soldiers undernourished and susceptible to the un-countable tropical diseases that flourished in the warm, moist jungle.

The struggle for New Guinea began with the capture by the Japanese of the city of Rabaul at the northeastern tip of New Britain Island in **January 1942** (the Allies responded with multiple bombing raids, of which the Action off Bougainville was one). Rabaul overlooks Simpson Harbor, a considerable natural anchorage, and was ideal for the construction of airfields. Over the next year, the Japanese built up the area into a major air and naval base.

The Battle of Rabaul

Also known by the Japanese as **Operation R**, was fought on the island of New Britain in the Australian Territory of New Guinea, in **January and February 1942**. It was a strategically significant defeat of Allied forces by Japan in the Pacific campaign of World War II.

Rabaul was the headquarters and main supply base for both the Japanese Southeastern Army and the Southeastern Fleet and lay directly northwest of Bougainville. Air units based at Rabaul were the responsibility of the Eleventh Air Fleet. Despite extensive losses, the Imperial Japanese Navy continued to reinforce its air units with approximately 50 planes a month flown in from Truk in the Caroline Islands.

In all of New Britain, the Imperial Japanese Army could muster more than 97,000 men. To defend the region around Rabaul in **November 1943**, the Imperial Japanese Army had more than 76,000 men. There were four natural harbors there, with Simpson Harbor and its excellent docking facilities capable of handling 300,000 tons of shipping.

Over the next year, the Japanese built up the area into a major air and naval base and proceeded to land on mainland New Guinea advancing toward Port Moresby located on southern part of Papua.

By late **November 1943** the Japanese force in Rabaul had been reduced by airpower, a hefty part of it on **5 November 1943** from Halsey's aircraft carriers Saratoga and Princeton, and thereafter no Japanese heavy ships ever came to Rabaul.

The Japanese *8th Area Army* (equivalent to a Euromerican army), under *General Hitoshi Imamura* at Rabaul, was responsible for both the New Guinea and Solomon Islands campaigns. The Japanese *18th Army* (equivalent to a Euromerican corps), under *Lieutenant General Hatazō Adachi*, was responsible for Japanese operations on mainland New Guinea.

Battle of Milne Bay

Offering a sheltered harbor, Milne Bay, on the south-eastern tip of Papua was selected for development as an Allied base, the key component of which was three airstrips in 1942. These facilities also made it a key stepping stone for the Japanese in their drive towards Port Moresby. The Battle of Milne Bay **25 August – 7 September 1942**. The Elite Japanese naval troops, known as *Kaigun Tokubetsu Rikusentai* (Special Naval Landing Forces), with two small tanks attacked the Allied airfields at Milne Bay that had been established on the eastern tip of New Guinea.

The battle is often described as the first major land battle of the war in the Pacific in which Allied troops decisively defeated Japanese land forces.

These troops were steadily pushed back as the Australians brought forward veteran Second Australian Imperial Force units that the Japanese had not expected. Allied air superiority helped tip the balance, providing close support to troops in combat and targeting Japanese logistics. Finding themselves heavily outnumbered, lacking supplies and suffering heavy casualties, the Japanese withdrew their forces, with fighting coming to an end on **7 September 1942**.

"Thenceforth, the Battle of Milne Bay became an infantry struggle in the sopping jungle carried on mostly at night under pouring rain. The Aussies were fighting mad, for they had found some of their captured fellows tied to trees and bayoneted to death, surmounted by the placard, 'It took them a long time to die'." -Samuel Eliot Morison, Breaking the Bismarcks Barrier, p.38

Battle of Papua New Guinea

30 June 1943 MacArthur attacks Papua New Guinea.

The colonial capital of Port Moresby on the south coast of Papua was the strategic key for the Japanese in this area of operations. General Douglas MacArthur, Supreme Commander Allied Forces South West Pacific Area, was determined to hold it. MacArthur was further determined to conquer all of New Guinea in his progress toward the eventual recapture of the Philippines.

Due north of Port Moresby, on the northeast coast of Papua, are Huon Gulf and the Huon Peninsula. The Japanese entered Lae and Salamaua, two locations on Huon Gulf, unopposed in early **March 1942**.

Aircraft based at Port Moresby and Milne Bay fought to prevent the Japanese from basing aircraft at Buna and attempted to prevent the Japanese reinforcement of the Buna area.

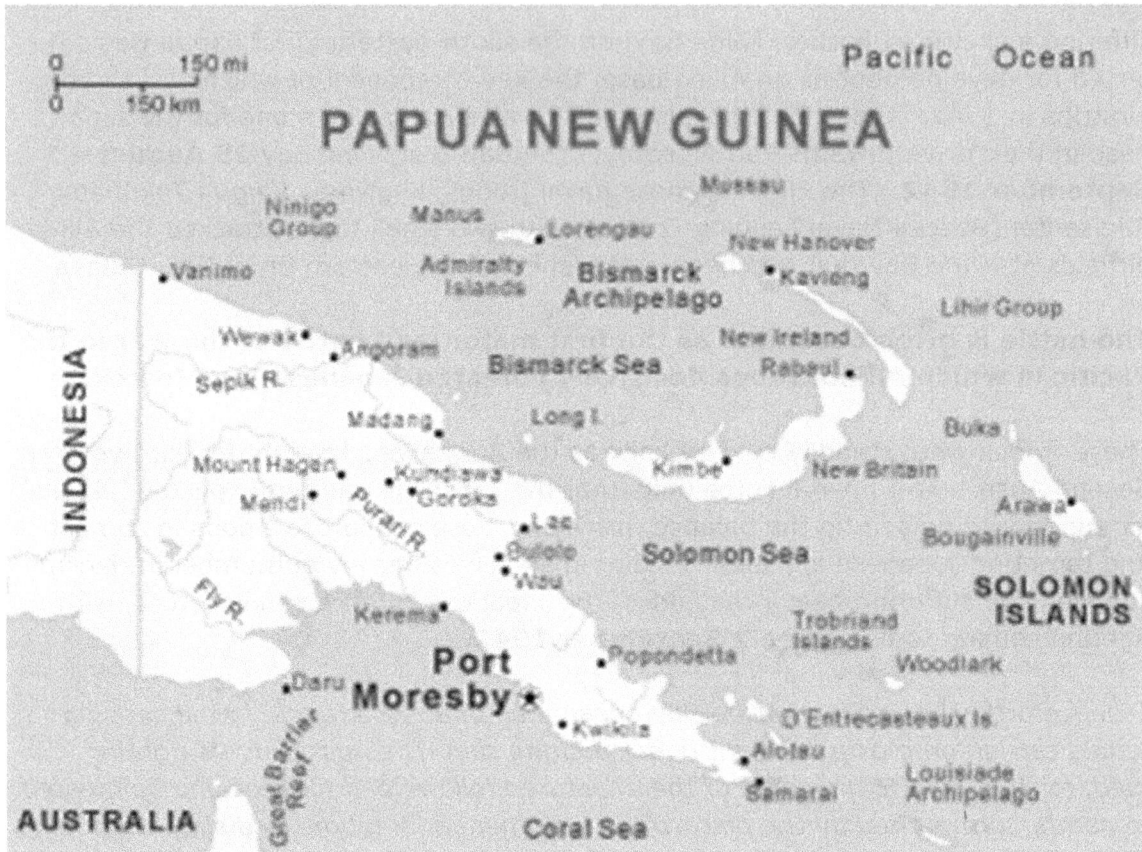

Battle of Buna-Gona

This was an Allied attack on the Japanese beach-head on the northern coast of Papua (along with the battles of Gona and Sanananda). This beach-head, next to Popondetta, had been established to allow the Japanese to launch an overland assault over the Kokoda Trail to Port Moresby. This attack came within thirty miles of Port Moresby, before an Australian counterattack forced the Japanese back along the trail.

MacArthur's rollback began with the **16 November 1942 – 22 January 1943 Battle of Buna-Gona.** The experience of the green US 32nd Infantry Division, just out of training camp and utterly unschooled in jungle warfare, was nearly disastrous. Instances were noted of officers completely out of their depth, of men eating meals when they should have been on the firing line, even of cowardice.

MacArthur relieved the division commander and on **30 November 1942** instructed Lieutenant General Robert L. Eichelberger, commander of the US I Corps, to go to the front personally with the charge *"to remove all officers who won't fight ... if necessary, put sergeants in charge of battalions ... I want you to take Buna, or not come back alive."*

The Allied objective was to eject the Japanese forces from these positions and deny them their further use. The Japanese forces were skillful, well prepared and resolute in their defense. They had developed a strong network of well-concealed defenses.

Operations in Papua and New Guinea were severely impacted by terrain, vegetation, climate, disease and the lack of infrastructure. In turn, these imposed significant logistical limitations. Mortar crews were attacking Japanese positions less than 50 yards away.

Allied air power interrupted the Japanese capacity to reinforce and resupply the beachheads from Rabaul. This ultimately made the Japanese position untenable. There was widespread evidence of the Japanese defenders cannibalizing the dead.

Scanty, ill-informed intelligence led MacArthur to believe that Buna could be taken with relative ease. MacArthur never visited the front during the campaign. He had no understanding of the conditions faced by his commanders and troops yet he continued to interfere and pressure them to achieve unreasonable outcomes. Terrain and persistent pressure for haste meant that there was little, if any, time given for reconnaissance.

Pressure applied by MacArthur has been attributed to both prolonging the duration of the battle and increasing the number of Allied casualties.

The battle is noteworthy for a number of reasons.

- The resolve and tenacity of the Japanese in defense was unprecedented and had not previously been encountered.

- It was to mark the desperate nature of fighting that characterized battles for the remainder of the Pacific war.

- For the Allies, there were a number of valuable but costly lessons in the conduct of jungle warfare. Allied losses in the battle were at a rate higher than that experienced at Guadalcanal. For the first time, the American public was confronted with the images of dead American troops.

- Natives were used as stretcher bearers to carry the wounded American soldiers from the front lines at Buna, New Guinea. The wounded are on their way to makeshift hospitals in the rear.

✦ ✦ ✦ ✦

The Photo That Won World War II: 'Dead Americans at Buna Beach,' 1943

Here, LIFE.com recalls one of those pivotal battles, the Battle of Buna-Gona, through pictures made by the **master photojournalist George Strock**—including one of the most famous and influential photographs ever taken in any war, anywhere: the disquieting image of three dead Americans half-buried in the sand at a place called Buna Beach. Caption from LIFE: "Three dead Americans on the beach at Buna."

What is ultimately so notable about Strock's picture, however—beyond its sheer technical excellence, and its quiet power—is that when it was published in LIFE magazine in **September 1943**, it was the first time that any photograph depicting dead American troops had appeared in any American publication during WWII.

This photo was taken in **January 1943** and approved to be published by President Roosevelt for the **September 1943 issue**. The story behind how the photograph came to be published, meanwhile, speaks volumes about LIFE magazine's national stature during the war, and the strained relationship that always exists (and, in an elemental way, *should* always exist) between journalists and government officials.

For months after Strock made his now-iconic picture, LIFE's editors pushed the American government's military censors to allow the magazine to publish that one photograph. The concern, among some at LIFE and certainly many in the government, was that Americans were growing complacent about a war that was far from over and in which an Allied victory was far from certain.

In the **Sept. 20, 1943**, issue of LIFE, in which Strock's photo first appeared (and in which it was given a full page to itself), the magazine's editors made the case to LIFE's readers for publishing the picture—even if it took the better part of a year to bring the censors and President Franklin Roosevelt himself around to their way of thinking:

Here lie three Americans [the editorial began].

What shall we say of them? Shall we say that this is a noble sight? Shall we say that this is a fine thing, that they should give their lives for their country?

Or shall we say that this is too horrible to look at?

Why print this picture, anyway, of three American boys' dead upon an alien shore? Is it to hurt people? To be morbid?

Those are not the reasons. The reason is that words are never enough. The eye sees. The mind knows. The heart feels. But the words do not exist to make us see, or know, or feel what it is like, what actually happens. The words are never right.

The reason we print it now is that, last week, President Roosevelt and [Director of the Office of War Information] Elmer Davis and the War Department decided that the American people ought to be able to see their own boys as they fall in battle; to come directly and without words into the presence of their own dead.

And so here it is. This is the reality that lies behind the names that come to rest at last on monuments in the leafy squares of busy American towns.

Behind the Picture: Ben Cosgrove Oct 31, 2014 and Liz Ronk, who edited this gallery, is the Photo Editor for LIFE.com.

✦　✦　✦　✦

Battle of Wau 29–31 January 1943

Wau is a village in the interior of the Papuan New Guinea peninsula, approximately 30 miles southwest of Salamaua. An airfield had been built there during an area gold rush in the 1920s and 1930s. This airfield was of great value to the Australians during the fighting for northeast Papua. The Australians decisively turned back the Japanese assault.

Within a few days, the enemy was retreating from the Wau Valley, where he had suffered a serious defeat, harassed all the way back to Mubo. About one week later, the Japanese completed their evacuation of Guadalcanal.

It is indicative of the extent to which Japanese ambitions had fallen at this point in the war that a 50% loss of ground troops aboard ship was considered acceptable.

Battle of Bismarck Sea

General Imamura and his naval counterpart at Rabaul, *Admiral Jinichi Kusaka*, commander Southeast Area Fleet, resolved to reinforce their ground forces at Lae for one final all-out attempt against Wau. If the transports succeeded in staying behind a weather front and were protected the whole way by fighters from the various airfields surrounding the Bismarck Sea, they might make it to Lae with an acceptable level of loss, i.e., at worst half the task force would be sunk in route.

On **23 Dec 1942**, *Japanese IGHQ (Imperial General Headquarters)* gave the order to transfer 100,000 troops from Japan and China to New Guinea island as reinforcements. It was a large exercise in Japanese logistics, but a successful landing of these troops at Lae could possibly turn back the Australian and American offensive, and perhaps even take Port Moresby. On **28 Feb 1943**, a convoy of eight destroyers and eight troop transports set sail with 6,900 troops from Rabaul under the cover of about 100 aircraft.

After a few unsuccessful Allied attempts at attacking the convoy by Catalina and Beaufort aircraft, an attack by 13 Flying Fortress bombers at 1000 hours on 3 March scattered the convoy, making the ships vulnerable to follow-up attacks by Beaufighters and Mitchell bombers. The weather changed direction and *Kimura's* slow-moving task force was spotted by an Allied scout plane. By the time the Allied bombers and PT boats finished their work on **3 March 1943**, Kimura had lost all eight transports and four of his eight destroyers.

The action was a near total loss for the Japanese. Only 800 out of the 6.900 soldiers made their way to Lae, at the cost of all eight transports, four of the eight destroyers, twenty aircraft, and over 2,000 lives.

An officer in one of the assault ships, later remembered:

...planes and PTs went about the sickening business of killing survivors in boats, rafts or wreckage. Fighters mercilessly strafed anything on the surface ... The PTs turned their guns on, and hurled depth charges at the three boats which, with over a hundred men on board, sank. It was a grisly task, but a military necessity since Japanese soldiers do not surrender and within swimming distance of shore, they could not be allowed to land and join the Lae garrison.

✦ ✦ ✦ ✦

Bristol Beaufighter

The **Bristol Type 156 Beaufighter** (often referred to simply as the "Beau") is a multi-role aircraft developed during the Second World War by the Bristol Aeroplane Company in the United Kingdom. Upon its entry to service, the Beaufighter proved to be well suited to the night fighter role, in part due to its large size allowing it to accommodate both heavy armaments and early airborne interception radar without major performance penalties. As its wartime service continued, the Beaufighter was used in many different roles; rocket-armed ground attack aircraft and torpedo bomber. The Royal Australian Air Force (RAAF) made extensive use of the type in the maritime anti-shipping role, such as during the Battle of the Bismarck Sea.

B-25 Mitchell bomber

The **North American B-25 Mitchell** is an American twin-engine, medium bomber manufactured by North American Aviation (NAA). North American Aviation (NAA) continued design and development in 1940 and 1941. Both the B-25A and B-25B series entered USAAF service. The B-25B was operational in 1942. Combat requirements lead to further developments. Before the year was over, NAA was producing the B-25C and B-25D series at different plants.

Also, in 1942, the manufacturer began design work on the cannon-armed B-25G series. The NA-100 of 1943 and 1944 was an interim armament development at the Kansas City complex known as the B-25D2. Similar armament upgrades by U.S-based commercial modification centers involved about half of the B-25G series. Further development led to the B-25H, B-25J, and B-25J2. The gunship design concept dates to late 1942.

Three factors conspired to create disaster for the Japanese. **First**, they had woefully underestimated the strength of the Allied air forces. **Second**, the Allies had become convinced that the Japanese were preparing a major seaborne reinforcement and so had stepped up their air searches. **Third**, and most important of all, the bombers of MacArthur's air forces, under the command of Lieutenant General George C. Kenney, had been modified to enable new offensive tactics. Their noses had been refitted with eight 50-caliber machine guns for strafing slow-moving ships on the high seas. In addition, their bomb bays were filled with 500-pound bombs to be used in the newly devised practice of **skip bombing**.

Skip bombing

Skip bombing was a low-level bombing technique independently developed by several of the combatant nations in World War II, notably Britain, Australia and the United States. General George Kenney has been credited with being the first to use skip bombing with the U.S. Army Air Forces.   The bombing aircraft flew at very low altitudes (200–250 ft (61–76 m)) at speeds from 200–250 mph (320–400 km/h). They would release a "stick" of two to four bombs, usually 500 lb. (230 kg) or 1,000 lb. (450 kg) bombs preferably equipped with four- to five-second time delay fuses. The bombs would "skip" over the surface of the water in a manner similar to stone skipping and either bounce into the side of the ship and detonate, submerge and explode next to the ship, or bounce over the target and miss.

The Air Force used modified B-25 bombers to develop skip-bombing. 'The Boeing [B-25] is most terrifying,' wrote one survivor in his diary.

The first time skip bombing was used in action by U.S. pilots was against Japanese warships at Rabaul on New Britain on October 2, 1942, where B-25 bombers attacked and destroyed the enemy vessels. With the continuing success against shipping in Rabaul Harbor throughout October and November 1942, both the tactic and the term 'skip bombing' had become popular in the Fifth Army Air Force.

Unguided, unpowered bombs are vastly cheaper than torpedoes of equivalent explosive power. Torpedoes take up to several minutes to reach their targets after launch, enough time for an agile ship with an attentive crew to turn and avoid the attack or minimize its damage; skipped bombs, however, reach their targets in seconds. The main drawback of skip bombing was that it took a great deal of skill to perfect; sometimes the bombs would detonate too soon, or in some cases, sink too deep before its delay-fused explosion.

✦ ✦ ✦ ✦

Bombing of Wewak, New Guinea

The Bombing of Wewak was a series of air raids by the USAAF Fifth Air Force, on **17–21 August 1943**, against the major air base of the Imperial Japanese Army Air Force on the mainland of New Guinea, at Wewak. The four raids, over a five-day period, represented a decisive victory for the Allies: the Japanese Fourth Air Army lost about 100 planes on the ground and in the air, reducing its operational strength to about 30 planes. Ten aircraft from the U.S. Fifth Air Force were lost.

By **August 1943**, the *Fourth Air Army*—which had been formed in June for the New Guinea campaign—had 130 operational aircraft. This was one third of its full complement of planes and represented an operational strength of 50%. According to Japanese historian *Hiroyuki Shindo*: "*...the major causes of this low operational rate were widespread illness among the aircrews, along with ... the lack of aircraft replacements.*"

The raids caught the Japanese unprepared. Their New Guinea airbases were inadequate in terms of the concealment of planes, in hangars and other shelters, and they relied almost completely on a visual warning system, which did not allow enough time for aircraft on the ground to take off or be taken under cover. These problems were compounded by the poor quality of runways, a shortage of maintenance staff and a lack of heavy equipment at forward bases.

✦ ✦ ✦ ✦

Japanese Commanders

Combined Fleet   *Fleet Admiral Isoroku Yamamoto*
Third Fleet   *Vice Admiral Jissaburo Ozawa*
Southeast Area   *Rear Admiral Jinichi Kusaka*

Operation I-Go

Fleet Admiral Isoroku Yamamoto promised the emperor that he would pay back the Allies for the disaster at the Bismarck Sea with a series of massive air strikes. For this, he ordered the air arm of *Vice Admiral Jisaburo Ozawa's* Third Fleet carriers to reinforce the Eleventh Air Fleet at Rabaul. To demonstrate the seriousness of the effort to the Supreme War Council, multiple shifts of high-ranking personnel were also affected: Both *Yamamoto* and *Ozawa* moved their headquarters to Rabaul.

I-Go was to be carried out in two phases, one against the lower Solomons and one against Papua. **The first strike, on 7 April 1943, was against Allied shipping in the waters between Guadalcanal and Tulagi. At 177 planes, this was the largest Japanese air attack since Pearl Harbor**. *Yamamoto* then turned his attention to New Guinea: 94 planes struck Oro Bay on **11 April**; 174 planes hit Port Moresby on **12 April**; and in the largest raid of all, 188 aircraft struck Milne Bay on **14 April**.

I-Go demonstrated that the Japanese command was not learning the lessons of air power that the Allies were. The Allied reduction of Rabaul was only made possible by relentless air strikes that took place day after day, but *Yamamoto* thought the damage inflicted by a few attacks of large formations would derail Allied plans long enough for Japan to prepare a defense in depth.

Also, *Yamamoto* accepted at face value his fliers' over-optimistic reports of damage: they reported a score of one cruiser, two destroyers and 25 transports, as well as 175 Allied planes, a figure that should certainly have aroused some skepticism. Actual Allied losses amounted to one destroyer, one oiler, one corvette, two cargo ships and approximately 25 aircraft. These meager results were not commensurate with either the resources expended or the expectations that had been promoted.

The Guadalcanal campaign was a significant strategic combined arms Allied victory in the Pacific theater. Along with the Battle of Midway, it has been called a turning point in the war against Japan.

The Japanese had reached the peak of their conquests in the Pacific. The victories at Milne Bay, Buna-Gona, and Guadalcanal marked the Allied transition from defensive operations to the strategic initiative in the theater, leading to offensive operations such as the Solomon Islands, New Guinea, and Central Pacific campaigns, that eventually resulted in Japan's surrender and the end of World War II.

XX   New Georgia and the Solomon Islands

A Frightful Battlefield

The New Georgia Group in the Central Solomons, on the west side of "The Slot," is 125 miles long and 40 miles wide. It includes 12 large habitable islands, several dozen small ones, barrier islands, fringing coral reefs and innumerable uncharted coral heads.

Like most of the other large Solomon Islands, the New Georgia group is thickly covered by some of the most difficult jungle terrain in the world. So thick is the top canopy that twilight prevails even in broad daylight. The ground beneath is covered with many steep ridges and small rivers—most of which are unseen in aerial photography. Where the terrain flattens near the coastline and the rivers deposit silt carried down from the interior highlands, mangrove swamps usually result.

Just south of the equator, the islands are always hot and rainy, with high daytime temperatures often in excess of 100 degrees. Humidity runs near 100%, and as a result the usual tropical diseases, malaria and dengue fever, proliferate. Constant moisture promotes many debilitating fungal skin conditions, commonly referred to as "jungle rot." Metal rusts seemingly overnight, and in WW II cloth and leather literally rotted off the soldiers' equipment. Large insects, land crabs, poisonous snakes, monitor lizards and alligators abound."

New Georgia was nothing but rain, mud, swamps, English speaking Japanese – and furious fighting.

July 16, 1943: the **37th Infantry Division**, lest the 3rd Battalions of the 145th and 148th Infantry Regiments, begin landing on New Georgia. **This would be the first combat campaign for the Buckeye Division, and victory would not come easily. Over the course of the next three years, the Buckeye Division would earn itself a reputation of being one of the best Army units to fight in the Pacific. Taking part in 3 combat campaigns, taking over 10,000 casualties, and seeing 59 days of combat, the 37th played an important role in securing victories in the Northern Solomon Islands and the Philippines.**

Located in the central Solomons, New Georgia comprises about a dozen large islands and numerous smaller ones, all surrounded by coral reefs, barrier islands, and shallow lagoons. With only a few narrow passages through the offshore obstacles, the seas surrounding New Georgia proper are hazardous. Because reefs made

Munda Point inaccessible to large ships, Halsey and his commanders chose to seize the offshore island of Rendova Island as a preliminary to the main invasion. Close enough to Munda for supporting artillery, Rendova Island would serve as a forward base from which the main invasion could be launched and supported.

Code-named OPERATION TOENAILS, under the command of South Pacific Commander Admiral William F. "Bull" Halsey, and initially led by Rear Admiral Richmond Kelly Turner, the attack on New Georgia had to overcome significant obstacles including terrain, limited resources in men and materiel, and coordination of multiple landing forces. The main objective was the Japanese airfield at Munda Point on the main island of New Georgia.

Given the lack of sufficient landing areas near the airfield and needing to protect supply lines from Japanese naval and air attacks, the operation would be conducted in two phases:

The First Phase, 30 June – 3 July 1943, consisted of initial landings on Rendova Island, Segi Point on New Georgia and Wickham Anchorage on Vanguru Island to protect the flow of supplies and men coming from Guadalcanal for the attack. Heavy rains, however, reduced visibility almost to zero, and high winds and rough seas wreaked havoc with the landing operation. Amphibious vehicles had to follow the sound of breaking waves to find the shore.

The operation, as the official Army history candidly recounts, *"was exactly what might be expected from a night landing in bad weather,"* with the marines landing in *"impressive disorganization."* In the ensuing chaos, six landing craft became lodged on the coral reef, while others discharged troops at the wrong site and then had to reload. Over the next four days, marines and soldiers, supported by 105-mm. howitzers from the 152d Field Artillery Battalion, rooted out the Japanese from Wickham Anchorage (southeast end of island).

The Western Force's first landing on **30 June** was the predawn insertion of two companies of the 169th Infantry on two small islands bracketing the passage through the coral reef to the future landing site on New Georgia Island. About 0700 the 172d Infantry began landing on Rendova. There was confusion and disorganization, but the regiment quickly overwhelmed a 120-man Japanese detachment and established a 1,000-yard-deep beachhead.

All troops, including General Harmon, were ashore in half an hour. Moving supplies ashore and inland quickly became the main problem. As rain turned the ground into red clay mud, heavy traffic ruined the island's single mile-long road, making it so muddy that a bulldozer sank. Inadequately marked supplies, dumped on the beach by troops wading ashore, piled up and became intermixed. So many trucks became mired in the mud that Hester had to stop their shipment to the beachhead, and movement of supplies off the beach became slow and laborious.

Reinforcements, the majority splashing ashore on Rendova, continued to disembark at all four beachheads until **5 July 1943**, when virtually the entire New Georgia Occupation Force was assembled. The first phase of TOENAILS had succeeded.

The Second Phase, 2 July – 5 August 1943, consisted of moving the 43rd Infantry Division from Rendova Island to New Georgia for the attack on Munda Airfield. Major General John Hester, commanding that division, was given the difficult task of also commanding all ground forces with only a division headquarters staff.

The Northern Landing Force, **5 July 1943**, consisting of the 1st Battalion of the 1st Marine Raider Regiment and the 3rd Battalions of the 37th Infantry Division's 145th and 148th Infantry Regiments were soon slowed by the dense jungle.

Admiral Turner restructured the Western Force for the main invasion of New Georgia. Commanded by Hester, the force was subdivided into five parts, including two landing groups. The second was the Northern Landing Group, commanded by Col. Harry B. Liversedge, USMC, and consisting of one battalion each from the 145th and 148th Infantry, 37th Division, and the 1st Raider Battalion, 1st Marine Raider Regiment. Liversedge's mission was to invade New Georgia's northwest shore at Rice Anchorage and defeat the Japanese in the area directly north of Munda between Enogai Inlet and Bairoko Harbor, called Dragons Peninsula. This would interdict the Japanese supply line to Munda and prevent Japanese troops on nearby Kolombangara from reinforcing Munda.

The Commander of XIV Corps, Lieutenant General Oscar W. Griswold, took over command on **July 16**. He committed the area reserves, consisting of the remainder of the 37th Infantry Division reinforced with the 161st Infantry Regiment of the 25th Infantry Division, to move into position north of the 43rd Infantry Division.

By **22 July 1943**, total U.S. land forces on New Georgia, Rendova, and smaller islands amounted to 32,000 Army troops and 1,700 Marine personnel.

With the final attack on Munda Airfield scheduled to begin on **July 25**, U.S. Army forces consolidated their positions and sent out aggressive patrols to provide exact locations of enemy defenses. The larger XIV Corps headquarters was able to vastly improve logistical support. Supply dumps were located closer to the front lines, as were rest centers to treat the hundreds of new psychological casualties caused by combat fatigue; the corps surgeon also better coordinated the evacuation of the wounded.

To the north, Colonel Liversedge's forces landed after midnight on **5 July** at Rice Anchorage, several miles northeast up the coast from the Bairoko-Enogai area. Shallow water and a narrow landing beach hindered the landing more than the inaccurate Japanese shelling.

Liversedge planned for two companies from the 3d Battalion, 145th Infantry, to defend the landing site, while the rest of the battalion, the 1st Marine Raider Battalion, and the 3d Battalion, 148th Infantry, moved to Dragons Peninsula. There the 3d Battalion, 148th, would veer southwest and take up a blocking position along the Munda-Bairoko trail. Remaining forces would clear the peninsula and take Bairoko.

Because speed was so important, Liversedge's force was lightly armed and provisioned, carrying only three days' worth of rations.

Moving out early on **5 July 1943**, the men soon learned that, contrary to earlier intelligence reports, following the rough trails, hacked out of the jungle by coast watchers and native New Georgians, to Dragons Peninsula would be exceedingly tough. Constant rain plagued the first weeks of the campaign, making more dismal the task of struggling up and down jungle hills seemingly composed in equal parts of sharp coral and thick clinging vines. The rain also added unforeseen tasks; one stream soon became a nine-foot-deep river to cross. The men in the 148th's weapons company, laboring under the weight of their heavy machine guns and 81-mm. mortars, were soon far to the rear.

Despite the capture of Enogai, Liversedge's tactical situation remained difficult. Already five days behind schedule and with many wounded, he was so short of supplies that he was receiving resupply by air. The marine battalion was at one-half of its effective strength. Liversedge needed to capture Bairoko to cut the Japanese line of communications to Munda.

Battle of Bairoko

This was a battle between American and Imperial Japanese Army and Navy forces on **20 July 1943** during the New Georgia Campaign in the Solomon Islands during the Pacific War. In the battle, U.S. Marine Raiders—supported by two U.S. Army infantry battalions—attacked a Japanese garrison guarding the port of Bairoko on the Dragons Peninsula on New Georgia. The day-long assault on well-prepared Japanese defensive positions by the Americans was unsuccessful. With the forces available to him, Liversedge was unable to take Bairoko and retired to Enogai. Japanese supply lines would remain operating during the campaign against Munda.

After calling-off the assault, the Americans withdrew to nearby Enogai. The American forces remained in the Enogai area until the end of the New Georgia Campaign. The Japanese used Bairoko to resupply and reinforce their troops who were guarding an airfield at Munda Point on New Georgia. After the U.S. and its allies successfully captured the airfield, the Japanese evacuated New Georgia and abandoned Bairoko on **24 August, 1943**.

Battle of Munda Airfield

The plan for taking Munda was not complicated. General Hester envisioned the 169th and 172d marching from Zanana to the Barike River, a distance of no more than three miles. The only passage through the jungle was a narrow footpath just north of Zanana that led west. Called Munda Trail, it wound through the middle of the high ground-a series of convoluted ridges that ran inland and northwest for 3,000 yards and concealed the main Japanese defenses. On paper, the plan seemed simple. For the green troops, however, who would be using inadequate maps to find their way through a labyrinth of coral jottings, draws, and swamps, all so densely overgrown with exotic jungle flora that visibility was measured in yards and enemy positions were invisible, the reality proved quite different.

The 169th received a brutal introduction to jungle warfare. On **6 July** the men spent an exhausting day following native guides along the narrow, vine-choked Munda Trail. That night the worn-out 3d Battalion failed to establish proper defenses and fell prey to Japanese harassment. The tired and nervous troops spent a sleepless night firing at imagined Japanese raiding parties. The next morning the battalion continued along Munda Trail, running into a well-camouflaged trail block established by a Japanese infantry platoon. Dug-in machine guns on high ground with supporting riflemen stopped the advance. Frontal assaults against hidden enemy positions resulted only in the loss of platoon leaders and a company commander. Finally, after the mortar platoon of the 3d Battalion, 169th, cut down trees to create fields of fire, observers crept to within thirty yards of the Japanese to direct 81-mm. mortar fire on enemy positions on what was now called Bloody Hill. The battalion spent another sleepless night as the target of Japanese harassment.

The 3d Battalion stormed the Japanese position the next day and eradicated it before advancing west with the remainder of the regiment and joining the 172d on the line of departure along the Barike River. That night the 3d Battalion, along with the rest of the regiment, endured yet another evening of Japanese torment. It was too much. Overwhelming fatigue and stress combined with imagination and anxiety to produce something resembling widespread panic. The official Army history recounts that ominously, there now appeared the first large number of shaken, hollow-eyed men suffering from a strange malady, later diagnosed as "combat neuroses". Before the end of July, the 169th would suffer seven hundred such cases of battle fatigue.

When the Japanese made their presence known to the three battalions, or when the Americans thought there were Japanese within their bivouacs, there was a great deal of confusion, shooting, and stabbing. Some men knifed each other. Men threw grenades blindly in the dark. Some of the grenades hit trees, bounced back, and exploded among the Americans. Some soldiers fired round after round to little avail. In the morning no trace remained of the Japanese dead or wounded. But there were American casualties; some had been stabbed to death, some wounded by knives. Many suffered grenade wounds, and 50 percent of these were caused by fragments from American grenades.

After an hour-long bombardment of suspected Japanese positions on 9 July, the offensive jumped off. Progress was slow. The difficult terrain, the absence of tactical intelligence regarding Japanese defenses, and the physical depletion of the troops all hindered the advance. Weighted down with equipment and ammunition, the men forded the rain-swollen river and its twisted tributaries. Between streams, they slogged through mangrove swamps, struggling to stay upright while trying to find their way without accurate maps. Soldiers in the lead platoons had to cut their way through the tangles of rattan vines that knotted the jungle. Narrow trails forced units to advance in single-file columns, churning the trails into mud and allowing a few hidden Japanese to slow the advance. By the late afternoon, the 172d had gained approximately 1,100 yards. Farther inland, the 169th made little progress, still shaken from the previous night. Advancing along Munda Trail the next day, the 169th struck the first line of the Japanese main defenses.

Despite the slow advance, both regiments soon had overextended supply lines. The primeval jungles of New Georgia, and the Solomons in general, were thankless places to build roads. The 118th Engineer Battalion spared no effort to construct a road-more accurately, a jeep trail-from Zanana to the front, but even its indefatigable exertions could not speed road building in a jungle crisscrossed with streams. As the road's terminus gradually fell farther and farther behind the advancing troops, ammunition, food, water, and other supplies had to be hand-carried to the front and casualties carried to the rear. Half of the combat troops soon were performing such duties, and Allied cargo planes were pressed into service to parachute supplies to the troops.

General Hester recognized that logistical shortcomings were restraining his advance and decided to shorten his supply line. He ordered the 172d to push through the mangrove swamp behind Laiana, two miles east of Munda and establish a new beachhead. Concurrently, the 169th was involved in a savage fight to occupy the high ground north of Munda. The combat location was eerily reminiscent of World War I. More than once, infantrymen, following their artillery barrage, clambered over shattered trees and shell craters to attack Japanese machine gunners in pillboxes with only rifles and bayonets. Also evoking echoes of the Western Front were high casualties and progress that was measured in yards. After five days of attacks, the 169th's 3d Battalion had penetrated 500 yards into the Japanese defenses. The battalion paid for its achievement with 101 casualties in the first twenty-four hours after the penetration. There on Reincke Ridge, in the high ground south of Munda Trail, the regiment regrouped and prepared to assault the main defensive line on imposing Horseshoe Hill.

General Griswold arrived on Rendova Island with an advance section of his head-quarters on **11 July** and quickly assessed the situation. "Things are going badly," he radioed Harmon on the morning of **13 July**. The 43d Division looked "about to fold up." He recommended that the remainder of the 37th Division, then in re-serve, and the 25th Division on Guadalcanal be committed immediately to combat. Harmon, whom Halsey recently had placed in charge of New Georgia ground opera-tions, instructed Griswold to be prepared to assume command and promised rein-forcements. Griswold took command at midnight on **15-16 July**.

Ground operations were well behind schedule and the troops worn. Griswold decid-ed not to renew the offensive until the supply situation improved and his troops were reorganized and reinforced. To improve logistics, he designated a specific off-shore island to serve as a supply dump for each division. Griswold also accelerated expansion of the Laiana beachhead, as well as the engineers' furious road-building effort, which allowed supplies to be stockpiled nearer the front line.

Reinforcements were badly needed. By **17 July** the 43d Division's casualties were 90 dead and 636 wounded. More than a thousand men had contracted diseases. Diarrhea was a common affliction, while dysentery cases and malaria relapses were prevalent. One-quarter of the men were suffering from varying degrees of skin fun-gus. Additionally, between fifty and one hundred men left the line each day as neu-roses cases. In the opinion of the XIV Corps surgeon, who flew in on **14 July**, there was no doubt that the major reason for these "nonbattle casualties" was combat fatigue-extreme exhaustion exacerbated by atrocious living conditions. Little could be done until rest camps could be built on the offshore islands; the high incidence of casualties due to disease and combat fatigue would continue throughout the campaign.

Griswold's corps offensive began on **25 July** with five regiments attacking abreast. The 43d Division with two regiments in line (103d on the coast, 172d-later the 169th-on its right) moved along the coast.

Farther inland, the 37th Division (north to south: 148th, 161st, and 145th Regi-ments) made the main attack, combining a frontal assault with a flanking move-ment designed to envelop the Japanese northern flank, take Bibilo Hill, and swoop down on Munda.

On **July 25**, the attack by XIV Corps commenced with the 43rd Infantry Division grinding its way through the main Japanese defenses near the coast and Major **General Robert S. Beightler's 37th Infantry Division advancing on the right flank to envelop Munda Airfield from the north.** For several days, the divisions fought a brutal close quarter battle against the Japanese, as small units sought to find and destroy well concealed and fortified positions. By **July 29**, hard-learned battle experience began to pay off as the regiments broke through the last remaining Japanese strong points on the high ground around Munda Airfield. The battle-weary units captured the airfield on the morning of **August 5, 1943**.

Achieving Munda would not be easy. In defense were approximately three Japanese infantry battalions in fortified positions. Also, off the American right flank were survivors of a unit that had attacked the 169th Infantry during the night of **17-18 July**. Driven off with heavy losses, they now lurked in the jungle awaiting an opportunity.

Most foreboding was information from the 172d Infantry, which, with the support of Marine tanks, had cleared the Laiana beachhead of Japanese during the logistic buildup. These operations revealed the nature of the main Japanese defenses: machine gunners and riflemen ensconced in sturdy pillboxes with interlocking fields of fire. The pillboxes were tough obstacles. Constructed with three or four layers of coconut logs and several feet of coral, they were largely subterranean. The few feet exposed above ground contained machine-gun and rifle firing slits, so well camouflaged that American soldiers often could not determine their location.   Pillboxes like this were found throughout the islands all the way to Okinawa.

When the offensive resumed, therefore, so did the demanding, draining, and deadly task of assaulting hidden Japanese positions one by one-a style of warfare that chewed up rifle companies and became all too familiar to American ground troops in the Pacific. Because the enemy was virtually invisible in his pillboxes and rarely fired indiscriminately, reconnaissance squads and platoons frequently could not determine the extent of Japanese defenses; details of Japanese positions often remained unknown until the attack.

Once infantrymen located an enemy position, they called in artillery fire which made the position visible amidst the jungle growth, if not destroying it outright. When full reconnaissance was not possible, troops had to attack the terrain-seize and occupy pieces of ground while calling in mortar fire on likely pillbox sites. A tactic of necessity, attacking the terrain could be risky against more than light opposition. The operations officer of the 145th Infantry noted, *"Enemy strong points encountered in this fashion often times resulted in hasty withdrawals which were costly both in men and weapons."*

Further, although they lacked antitank guns, the Japanese soon adopted measures to knock out tanks lacking infantry support. American troops quickly learned the importance of close infantry-armor coordination for successfully assaulting Japanese positions. Likewise, although flamethrowers proved useful in attacking pillboxes, the operator had to expose his head and torso and was likely to be shot unless supporting infantry provided suppressive fire. Just as in tank infantry operations, troops learned that mutual cooperation and support between riflemen and flamethrower operators were vital to success. Once integrated with the infantry, both tanks and flamethrowers were important infantry-support weapons on New Georgia, especially because the irregular shape of the front line and the poor quality of available maps often made artillery support impractical.

Over the next several days, the regiments clawed their way forward through the Japanese defenses. Concurrent with the change in American command, the Japanese withdrew to a final defensive line in front of the airfield. They had suffered heavy casualties and, unbeknownst to the Americans, their main defenses had been shattered.

On **4 August 1943** Bibilo Hill fell. The next day the Americans overran Munda, with 43d Division infantrymen killing or driving the remaining Japanese from their bunkers, tunnels, and pillboxes. From Bibilo Hill, General Wing informed General Hodge, "Munda is yours at 1410 today." Operational within two weeks, Munda's 6,000-foot runway soon made it the most-used airfield in the Solomons.

The capture of Munda airfield on **5 August 1943** was only one phase of the New Georgia campaign. There were still Japanese on New Georgia, as well as on the surrounding islands of Arundel, Baanga, Gizo, Kolombangara, and Vella Lavella. These islands had to be taken or neutralized before the Americans could continue up the Solomons chain. Most Japanese moved to Arundel, Kolombangara, and Baanga, leaving behind only a small detachment to contest the American advance. U.S. troops spent two weeks eliminating these forces and finally occupied Bairoko on **25 August 1943**.

American casualties were 1,094 dead and 3,873 wounded, excluding the even greater number of disease, combat fatigue, and neuropsychiatric casualties. 1671 Japanese killed.

Sea Battle at Vila on Kolombangara

A Japanese "Tokyo Express" reinforcement force—commanded by *Sho-sho (Rear Admiral) Shunji Izaki* and comprising one light cruiser, five destroyers and four destroyer made a run down "The Slot" from the upper Solomons to land troops at Vila on Kolombangara (off the northwest coast of New Georgia) by way of Kula Gulf on the night of **12 July 1943**.

An Allied force—commanded by Rear Admiral Walden L. Ainsworth and comprising the United States Navy three light cruisers and ten destroyers—were deployed in a single column with five destroyers in the van followed by the light cruisers and then by five destroyers in the rear.

Admiral Ainsworth's mission was to protect the north shore beachhead of New Georgia from attack by the "Tokyo Express" and if possible to prevent Imperial reinforcements from landing. The damage after the sea battle was the Americans lost three light cruisers and one destroyer. Except for one light cruiser, the Japanese force escaped damage, and the transport destroyers successfully landed 1,200 men at Vila. The Emperor's men had won a tactical victory, but of the action the naval historian Samuel Eliot Morison wrote: *"A string of such victories added up to defeat."*

Battle of Mbanga (Baanga) Island

The battle of Baanga Island (**12-22 August 1943**) saw the Americans occupy a small island near Munda after unexpectedly fierce Japanese resistance. Baanga Island is a long narrow island that runs in a north-south direction, just off the western coast of New Georgia, close to Munda. During the battle for Munda the island had been garrisoned by about 100 men, but it was an obvious refuge for retreating troops, and by the time the Americans attacked the island it was probably defended by around 400 men. The Japanese also had two 120mm guns on the island and could use them to bombard Munda airfield.

The Japanese presence on Baanga Island was detected on **11 August** as the Americans extended their control of the area around Munda. The size of the defending force was underestimated and on **12 August** a single company of American troops attempted to land on the island. They came under heavy fire as they left their landing craft and after suffering 50% casualties were forced to re-embark.

The Americans now prepared for a larger scale assault on the island. A number of 155mm guns were moved to Munda and two battalions from the 169th Infantry Regiment were allocated to the attack. On **14 August**, covered by an artillery bombardment, the 169th landed on the east coast of the island. This time the Americans were able to establish a beachhead on the island, but as they advanced west they ran into a line of Japanese defenses and the advance came to a halt.

More troops were clearly needed, and so on **16 August** two battalions from the 172nd Infantry moved to the island.   More artillery was also moved into place, and by **19 August** most of the Japanese guns had been knocked out. That night the

Japanese began to evacuate the remaining troops to Arundel Island. By **22 August** the Americans occupied the island.

Battle of Arundel Island and Kolombangara

27 August – 20 September 1943

Arundel Island is at the southern end of the Kula Gulf, between New Georgia and Kolombangara. Before the fall of Munda, the Japanese had only used it as a barge staging post, but it now gained greatly in importance. Both sides realized that it was a valuable defensive outpost for the Japanese base at Kolombangara - if it fell into American hands the airfield at Vila on Kolombangara would come within range of their artillery. The Japanese also saw it as a useful evacuation point for troops still trying to escape from New Georgia.

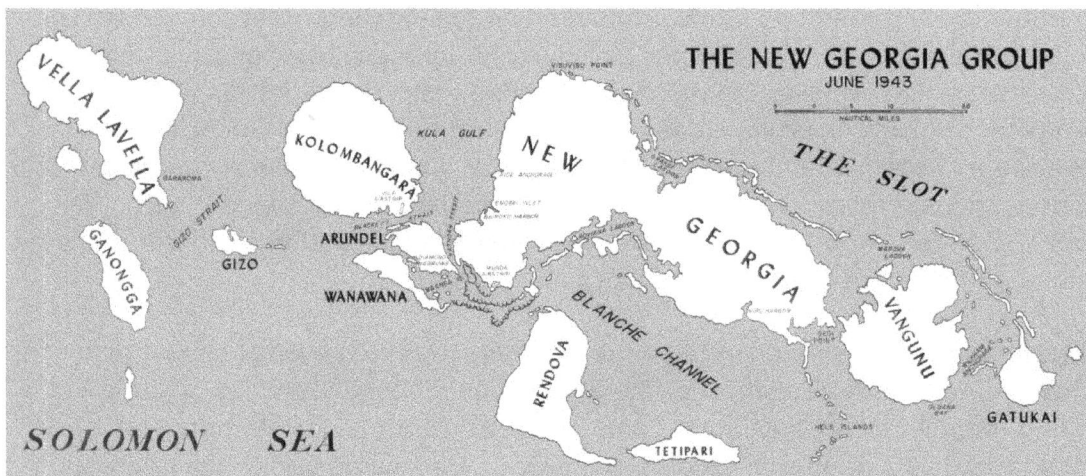

Admiral Halsey also wanted Arundel Island taken because of its important position. But there, too, because of recent undetected reinforcements and because of the difficulty of its terrain-perhaps the worst in New Georgia-Japanese resistance proved stronger than expected. While combat on Arundel was viewed primarily as *"mopping up small groups of Japanese,"* one 43d Division battalion commander later described the fighting on Arundel as *"the most bitter combat of the New Georgia campaign."* The fighting continued through the first three weeks of September when remaining Japanese troops withdrew at night, this time to Kolombangara.

There were about 12,000 Japanese troops on Kolombangara, the next stronghold in the Solomons chain and site of another Japanese airfield. In mid-July as the advance toward Munda floundered and the Japanese reinforced Kolombangara, Halsey's staff suggested a deviation from the original TOENAILS plan: instead of seizing Kolombangara, seize Vella Lavella, only fifteen miles northwest of Kolombangara and weakly held by the Japanese. Halsey endorsed the idea, recognizing that it exploited both American mobility and local air and sea superiority. He would gain his objective, a better airfield nearer to Bougainville, while avoiding a costly battle. Japanese forces on Kolombangara would be left to "die on the vine."

The bypassed Japanese troops on Kolombangara did not wither on the vine. During three nights between **28 September and 3 October**, more than 9,000 troops escaped to southern Bougainville in a well-organized evacuation effort. The evacuation of Kolombangara largely ended the campaign for New Georgia and the surrounding islands, a joint campaign that had proved much more involved and costly in its ground operations than had been anticipated.

A quote by Edward Mondroski of A Company, 145th Infantry Regiment, probably sums up the campaign and its hardships best: *"I never washed my face and I never took off my shoes. I never changed clothes for 43 days along with thousands of other veterans who were there. We fought for one airfield [Munda] for 43 days and never once were we able to clean up. We looked like tramps…"*

The strategy and tactics of the New Georgia campaign were among the least successful of any Allied campaign in the Pacific.

In 1950 Samuel Eliot Morison concluded his final evaluation of the New Georgia Campaign:

Before 1942 hardly anybody had ever heard of New Georgia, and after 1943 few people would ever hear of it again. Nothing important had ever happened there before, and nothing important afterwards. But for an intense five-month period from June through November 1943, the New Georgia Group of islands would see fierce fighting on land, sea and in the air—and some of the worst American strategic and tactical planning of the war.

The needless complexity of the operation was bewilderingly wasteful and was often poorly led by Army officers at all levels who had little or no foreknowledge of the terrain and whose troops were woefully inexperienced and physically unprepared. These Americans also had the misfortune of facing one of the most wily and resolute Japanese generals of the Pacific War, Minorou Sasaki."

Battle of Vella Lavella

The Battle of Vella Lavella was a naval battle of the Pacific campaign of World War II fought on the night of **6 October 1943**, near the island of Vella Lavella in the

Solomon Islands. It marked the end of a three-month fight to capture the central Solomon Islands, as part of the Solomon Islands Campaign.

The battle took place at the end of the ground campaign on Vella Lavella, as the Japanese sought to evacuate the 600-strong garrison from the island. The garrison had become hemmed into a small pocket on the northern end of the island around Marquana Bay. While a force of around 20 auxiliary ships and barges evacuated the stranded soldiers, a force of nine Japanese destroyers fought a short, but sharp engagement with six US Navy destroyers to the north of the island diverting attention from the evacuation. As a result of the engagement, the Japanese evacuation effort was successfully concluded. Each side lost one destroyer sunk.

✦ ✦ ✦ ✦

September 9, 1943 V-Mail to Aunt Effie Madsen, Grandpa's sister-in-law. The letter includes a redacted phrase as soldiers were not allowed to be specific in their letters home. Dad was on New Georgia at this time. Read the middle paragraph where he talks of Labor Day, which was September 6, 1943 as the "toughest & most miserable days" he has put in. He has two more years of the same. **Next stop Bougainville**.

Dear Effie,

Not much to write about so will just send a V-Mail this time in answer to your last two letters I got last week.

So, you are working hard these days, too bad you have trouble with your legs as that makes it that much harder. Say Effie, you better plan on taking a vacation when I get home and spend some time with Myrt and I.

Tuesday, I came in from a [redacted] …. It was one of the toughest and most miserable days I have ever put in. Boy that's one Labor Day I will never forget. I am not allowed to write anymore of it. Had a good meal when we came in and after a day's rest feel pretty good again.

Had a letter from Myrt and the folks today. Guess Dady hasn't been feeling so well lately. Faye now has four teeth. Imagine I will have quite a time getting acquainted with her when I get back. Will close now, I am feeling fine and in good health. Greetings to all, Love, Elmer

After the New Georgia campaign, the 37th Division returned to Guadalcanal to regroup prior to leaving for Bougainville. As per Major General Robert S. Beightler: *"The 37th Infantry Division left New Georgia and arrived on Guadalcanal 4 November 1943 and departed 11 November 1943 arriving on Bougainville 13 November 1943 and leaving there 13 December 1944."*

XXI   Island Battles of Operation Cartwheel

Battle of Treasury Islands

The Battle of the Treasury Islands was a Second World War battle that took place between **27 October and 12 November 1943** on the Treasury Islands group, part of the Solomon Islands. The battle formed part of the wider Pacific War and involved New Zealand and US forces fighting against Japanese troops. The majority of the ground forces were provided by the New Zealand 3rd Division.

The Allied invasion of the Japanese held island group intended to secure Mono and Stirling Islands so that a radar station could be constructed on the former and the latter be used as a staging area for an assault on Bougainville.

Consisting of two islands, Mono and Stirling, the Treasuries are located 300 miles (480 km) north of Guadalcanal, and 60 miles (97 km) from Vella Lavella, and just 18 miles (29 km) from the Shortland Islands. The Shortland Islands are a group of five islands belonging to the Western Province of the Solomon Islands, close to the island of Bougainville.

The islands were endowed with a deep natural harbor – Blanche Harbor – which the Allies determined would be useful for supporting landing operations at Cape Torokina on Bougainville. Mono Island, due to its high features, also offered the prospect of serving as a radar station to provide early warning for aerial and naval surface attacks during the Cape Torokina operation. The Allies also hoped that the landing would convince the Japanese that their next move would be on the Shortlands or on Buin, on the southern tip of Bougainville, instead of the Cape Torokina – Empress Augusta Bay area.

A total of 3,795 men landed in the assault wave with the remainder of the Allied force landing in four waves during the following 20 days, to reach a total of 6,574 men. It was the second combat operation undertaken by the New Zealanders in the Pacific, following the Land Battle of Vella Lavella, which had taken place the previous month. The New Zealand infantry were supported by US combat support and service support units including a naval construction battalion (the 87th), a signals unit, a naval base unit, and a coastal artillery battalion (the 198th) to provide anti-aircraft fire support.

Battle of Choiseul Island

The **Raid on Choiseul,** located southeast of Bougainville, was a small unit engagement that occurred from **October 28 to November 3, 1943**, during the Solomon Islands campaign. United States Marines from the 2nd Parachute Battalion, led by Lt Col. Victor "Brute" Krulak, landed on Japanese occupied Choiseul in the northern Solomon Islands and carried out raids on Japanese army and navy forces over a 40 kilometer (25 mi) area over the course of seven days. The Allies hoped that the raid would cause the Japanese to believe the landings would be on the east side of Bougainville.

On **November 2**, the raid was momentarily stalled when a Japanese ambush trapped between 40 and 50 marines. Three marines were severely wounded, one of them fatally. The Marines were rescued by the motor torpedo boat *PT-59*, under the command of Lieutenant John F. Kennedy.

Battle of Cape St George

The **Battle of Cape St. George** was a naval battle of the Pacific campaign of World War II fought on **25 November 1943**, between Cape St. George, New Ireland, and Buka Island (now part of the North Solomons Province in Papua New Guinea). It was the last engagement of surface ships in the Solomon Islands campaign. During the engagement, a force of five US Navy destroyers led by Captain Arleigh Burke interdicted a similar sized Japanese force that was withdrawing from Buka towards Rabaul, having landed reinforcements on the island. In the ensuing fight, three Japanese destroyers were sunk and one was damaged, with no losses amongst the US force.

The naval battles extend beyond the Guadalcanal Campaign through the rest of the campaign in the Solomons. **That ended Japanese efforts to resupply or evacuate the Japanese forces that had become trapped on Bougainville. Meanwhile, the main Japanese base for the whole area, at Rabaul, had itself become trapped and isolated.**

Battle of the Tarawa Atoll

The **Battle of Tarawa** was a battle in the Pacific Theater of World War II that was fought on **20–23 November 1943**. It took place at the Tarawa Atoll in the Gilbert Islands, and was part of Operation Galvanic, the U.S. invasion of the Gilberts.

The Battle of Tarawa was the first American offensive in the critical central Pacific region. It was also the first time in the Pacific War that the United States faced serious Japanese opposition to an amphibious landing.

Tarawa is a **coral atoll**, a triangular shaped coral reef including a coral rim that partially encircles a large lagoon spanning 193 square miles (500 sq. km) with a wide southern reef. The coral of the atoll sits atop the rim of an volcano which has eroded or subsided partially beneath the water. The lagoon forms over the volcanic crater or caldera while the higher rim remains above water or at shallow depths that permit the coral to grow and form the reef. North Tarawa consists of a string of islets, with the most northern islet being Buariki. The islets are separated in places by wide channels that are best crossed at low tide.

United States Marines landed on Tarawa and suffered heavy losses from Japanese soldiers occupying entrenched positions on the atoll. Previous landings had met little or no initial resistance, but on Tarawa the 4,700 Japanese defenders were well-supplied and well-prepared, and they fought almost to the last man, exacting a heavy toll on the United States Marine Corps. Tarawa is southeast of the Marshall Islands.

The Japanese had built an airfield on the southern reef and were dug into a labyrinth of pillboxes and bunkers interconnected by tunnels and defended by wire and mines.

The U.S. had suffered similar casualties throughout the duration of other previous campaigns, for example over the six months of the Guadalcanal Campaign, but the losses on Tarawa were incurred within the space of 76 hours. Nearly 6,400 Japanese, Koreans, and Americans died in the fighting, mostly on and around the small island of Betio, in the extreme southwest of Tarawa Atoll. **November 20 1943**, destroyers and battleships from the U.S. staged a heavy assault on the three-mile-long island.

As the battle progressed a US landing craft moved in on the island and got stuck on a reef because of the low-tide. This left the craft only 500 feet from shore and sitting in open Japanese fire. Wading through waist-deep water walking over piercing, razor-sharp coral, many were cut down by merciless enemy gunfire yards from the beach. Those who made it ashore huddled in the sand, hemmed in by the sea to one side and the Japanese to the other. Out of the 800 Marines attempting to breach the island only 450 made it to shore.

The enemy had sat quiet waiting for opportune moments and many of the Marines left wading to shore were struck down by gunfire. More reinforcements were brought in by the Americans and the battle started to tilt in their direction with this and the loss of communication the Japanese felt. The Japanese were taught to fight or commit suicide so they turned all their attention to attacking the Marines over the next day. The Marines asked for reinforcements they didn't get but managed to stand the attack and win. Of the nearly 5,000 Japanese soldiers and workers on the island, only 146 were captured, the rest were killed.

Below is a first-person account of the Battle of Tarawa from *"The Bloody Battle of Tarawa, 1943"* Eyewitness to History.

Robert Sherrod was a seasoned war correspondent having covered the Army campaign in the Aleutian Islands and the Navy raid on Wake Island. However, nothing from these experiences prepared him for the brutal terror of Tarawa. His observations of one of the costliest battles in US Marine Corps history were published as a book in early 1944.

In the early hours of November 20, Sherrod was among a contingent of Marines aboard a Navy transport - the Blue Fox, - waiting for the order to board a landing craft for the beach. We join his story as the bombardment of the island begins:

"Now, at 0505, we heard a great thud in the southwest. We knew what that meant. The first battleship had fired the first shot. We all rushed out on deck. The show had begun...

Within three minutes the sky was filled again with the orange-red flash of the big gun, and Olympus boomed again. The red ball of fire that was the high-explosive shell was again dropping toward the horizon. But this time there was a tremendous burst on the land that was Betio. A wall of flame shot five hundred feet into the air, and there was another terrifying explosion as the shell found its mark. Hundreds of awestruck Marines on the deck of the Blue Fox cheered in uncontrollable joy...

The next flash was four times as great, and the sky turned a brighter, redder orange, greater than any flash of lightning the Marines had ever seen. Now four shells, weighing more than a ton each, peppered the island. Now Betio began to glow brightly from the fires the bombardment pattern had started.

That was only the beginning. Another battleship took up the firing - four mighty shells poured from its big guns onto another part of the island. Then another battleship breathed its brilliant breath of death. Now a heavy cruiser let go with its eight-inch guns, and several light cruisers opened with their fast-firing six- inch guns. They were followed by the destroyers, many destroyers with many five-inch guns on each, firing almost as fast as machine guns. The sky at times was brighter than noontime on the equator. The arching, glowing cinders that were high-explosive shells sailed through the air as though buckshot were being fired out of many shotguns from all sides of the island. The Marines aboard the Blue Fox exulted with each blast on the island...

The first streaks of dawn crept through the sky. The warships continued to fire. All of a sudden, they stopped. But here came the planes-not just a few planes: a dozen, a score, a hundred. The first torpedo bombers raced across the smoking conflagration and loosed their big bombs on an island that must have been dead a half hour ago! They were followed by the dive bombers, the old workhorse SBD's and the new Helldivers, the fast SB2C's that had been more than two years a-borning. The dive bombers lined up, many of thousands of feet over Betio, then they pointed their noses down and dived singly, or in pairs or in threes. Near the end of their dives they hatched the bombs from beneath their bellies; they pulled out gracefully and sailed back to their carriers to get more bombs. Now came the fighter planes, the fast, new Grumman Hellcats, the best planes ever to squat on a carrier. They made their runs just above the awful, gushing pall of smoke, their machine guns spitting hundreds of fifty-caliber bullets a minute.

Surely, we all thought, no mortal men could live through such destroying power.

Surely, I thought, if there were actually any Japs left on the island (which I doubted strongly), they would all be dead by now."

At 0635, Sherrod and a 30-man, Marine assault force board a Higgins landing craft and head for the enemy beach. It takes an hour and a half for the landing craft to reach its rendezvous point off the beach where it joins other assault boats for the landing.

It is here that Sherrod gets his first warning that something is going terribly wrong with the attack. He can see no landing craft on the beach - four assault waves should have previously gone ashore. At this point, the commander of the landing craft announces that he can go no further as the water is too shallow. The assault team will have to transfer to a tank-like amphtrack for the rest of the journey. We rejoin Sherrod's account as the Marines scramble aboard the amphtrack under intense enemy machinegun fire:

"We jumped into the little tractor boat and quickly settled on the deck. 'Oh, God, I'm scared,' said the little Marine, a telephone operator, who sat next to me forward in the boat. I gritted my teeth and tried to force a smile that would not come and tried to stop quivering all over (now I was shaking from fear). I said, in an effort to be reassuring, 'I'm scared, too.' I never made a more truthful statement in all my life.

Now I knew, positively, that there were Japs, and evidently plenty of them, on the island. They were not dead. The bursts of shellfire all around us evidenced the fact that there was plenty of life in them!... After the first wave there apparently had not been any organized waves, those organized waves which hit the beach so beautifully in the last rehearsal. There had been only an occasional amphtrack which hit the beach, then turned around (if it wasn't knocked out) and went back for more men. There we were: a single boat, a little wavelet of our own, and we were already getting the hell shot out of us, with a thousand yards to go. I peered over the side of the amphtrack and saw another amphtrack three hundred yards to the left get a direct hit from what looked like a mortar shell.

'It's hell in there,' said the amphtrack boss, who was pretty wild-eyed himself. 'They've already knocked out a lot of amphtracks and there are a lot of wounded men lying on the beach. See that old hulk of a Jap freighter over there? I'll let you out about there, then go back to get some more men. You can wade in from there.' I looked. The rusty old ship was about two hundred yards beyond the pier. That meant some seven hundred yards of wading through the fire of machine guns whose bullets already were whistling over our heads.

The fifteen of us - I think it was fifteen - scurried over the side of the amphtrack into the water that was neck-deep. We started wading.

No sooner had we hit the water than the Jap machine guns really opened up on us. There must have been five or six of these machine guns concentrating their fire on us... It was painfully slow, wading in such deep water. And we had seven hundred yards to walk slowly into that machinegun fire, looming into larger targets as we rose onto higher ground. I was scared, as I had never been scared before. But my head was clear. I was extremely alert, as though my brain were dictating that I live these last minutes for all they were worth. I recalled that psychologists say fear in battle is a good thing; it stimulates the adrenalin glands and heavily loads the blood supply with oxygen.

I do not know when it was that I realized I wasn't frightened any longer. I suppose it was when I looked around and saw the amphtrack scooting back for more Marines. Perhaps it was when I noticed that bullets were hitting six inches to the left or six inches to the right. I could have sworn that I could have reached out and touched a hundred bullets. I remember chuckling inside and saying aloud, 'You bastards, you certainly are lousy shots.'

After wading through several centuries and some two hundred yards of shallowing water and deepening machinegun fire, I looked to the left and saw that we had passed the end of the pier. I didn't know whether any Jap snipers were still under the pier or not, but I knew we couldn't do any worse. I waved to the Marines on my immediate right and shouted, 'Let's head for the pier!' Seven of them came. The other seven Marines were far to the right. They followed a naval ensign straight into the beach - there was no Marine officer in our amphtrack. The ensign said later that he thought three of the seven had been killed in the water."

✦ ✦ ✦ ✦

A bloody Thanksgiving as wounded Marines are returned to the ship in rubber boats. There were 2296 wounded in the Battle of Tarawa. During the 3-day Battle, some 1,000 U.S. Marines died and another 687 U.S. Navy sailors lost their lives when the USS Liscome Bay was sunk by a Japanese torpedo.

F6F Hellcats from the USS LEXINGTON shot down 17 out of 20 Japanese planes heading for Tarawa Atoll, Gilbert Islands, Comdr. Edward Steichen, **November 1943**.

The lessons learned at Tarawa would be applied to all subsequent amphibious assaults as the United States worked its way across the Central Pacific.

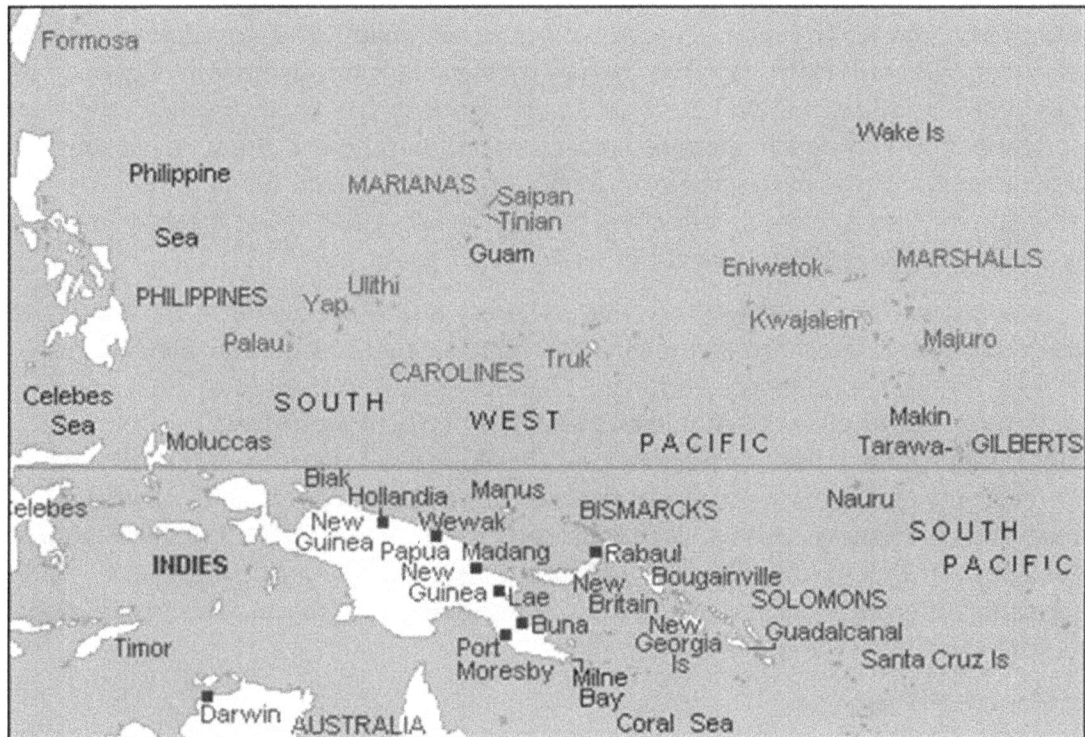

Marshall Islands in Micronesia

After the Gilberts fell to the Americans in late **November 1943**, *Admiral Mineichi Koga* of the Japanese Combined Fleet was unsure of which islands the Americans would strike. Without any carrier aircraft to inform him, he ordered *Admiral Masashi Kobayashi* to disperse his 28,000 troops primarily to the outer Marshall Islands of Maloelap, Wotje, Jaliuit, and Mili. However, Allied intelligence intercepted Imperial code, informing the Americans of which islands were more heavily defended. The Americans decided to invade the least protected but strategically important islands of **Majuro, Kwajalein, and Eniwetok** of the Marshall Islands. The Marshall Islands are northeast of New Guinea and south southeast of Midway.

Battle of Majuro

31 January 1944. The island was seen as an important base for conducting air operations against the rest of the Marshall Islands and eventually the Marianas, west of the Marshall Islands. The force took the lightly defended island in one day without any casualties.

Battle of Kwajalein

31 January 1944. The same day as the Majuro invasion, the 4th Marine Division under Major General Harry Schmidt began their assault on Kwajalein. Schmidt's troops first landed on Roi-Namur, a group of islands in the northern part of the atoll. Major confusion and delays were caused by poor weather and American troops inexperienced in amphibious operations, but the pre-invasion naval and air bombardment was extremely effective. Out of roughly 3,000 Japanese soldiers, only about 300 were left to guard the island.

On the southern island of Kwajalein, Major General Charles Corlett's 7th Infantry Division landed on southern Kwajalein with relative ease. Although the Japanese pillboxes, bunkers, and intense infantry offensives slowed the Americans, more troops, more experience in amphibious landings, effective pre-landing bombardment, and Japanese defenses on the opposite side of the atoll from where the Americans landed contributed to the capture of Kwajalein and its surrounding islands on **7 February 1944**. Of the entire force of about 8,000 Japanese guarding Majuro and Kwajalein, only 51 survived, and 253 were taken prisoner. The Americans suffered 348 men killed, 1,462 wounded, and 183 missing in the eight days it took to take the atoll.

Battle of Eniwetok

Eniwetok's islands and islets housed enough room for airfields critical for the upcoming invasion of the Marianas. On **17 February 1944**, a naval bombardment of Eniwetok Atoll began. This marked the beginning of Operation Catchpole. The same day, the 22nd Infantry Regiment under Colonel John Walker landed on the northern island of Engebi. The landings were a logistical nightmare, with American troops, gear, and supplies scattered along the beach. Walker and his Marines took the island on **18 February** with 85 dead and 166 wounded. On **19 February**, the 106th Infantry Regiment, under Lieutenant General Thomas E. Watson, landed on the main island of Eniwetok after a heavy bombardment. However, the Japanese spider holes and bunkers repelled much of the bombardment by battleships. The landing group also faced the same logistical problems as the 22nd Infantry Regiment. Japanese forces concentrated in the southwest corner of the island counterattacked the American flank, forcing the Americans to attack mainly at night.

Eniwetok Island was captured on **21 February** with the loss of 37 Americans and nearly 800 Japanese. On another one of Eniwetok's islands, Parry Island, the Americans used heavy gunfire support from battleships before the 22nd Marine Regiment, under Watson, waded ashore at Parry Island on **22 February**. They captured the island and the entire atoll on **23 February**. 313 Americans died, 879 were wounded, and 77 were reported missing on Eniwetok, while the Japanese suffered 3,380 dead and 105 captured. This marked an end to the Marshall Islands campaign.

In the Gilberts, Makin and Tarawa, the Americans emerged victorious, but were caught unprepared, suffering 2,459 dead and 2,286 wounded. Japan suffered a total of 5,085 dead and 247 captured.

The Marshalls, by contrast, were a much easier landing. The Americans used the lessons learned at Tarawa by outnumbering the enemy defenders nearly 6 to 1 with heavier firepower (including use of armor-piercing shells) after the islands took nearly a month of heavy air and naval bombardment. In the Marshalls, the Americans lost 611 men, suffered 2,341 wounded, and 260 missing, while the Japanese lost over 11,000 men and had 358 captured.

After the Gilberts and Marshalls were taken, the Allies built naval bases, fortifications, and airfields on the islands to prepare for an assault on the Marianas. The Japanese defeat forced military leaders to draw back to a new defensive perimeter, the Absolute National Defense Zone, which included the Marianas and Palau. These islands were heavily fortified for an upcoming assault because if captured, they would put American heavy bombers within range of Tokyo.

Battle of Cape Gloucester, New Britain

This battle took place on the island of New Britain, Territory of New Guinea, between late **December 1943 and April 1944**. Columns of troop-packed LCIs (Landing Craft, Infantry) trail in the wake of a Coast Guard-manned LST (Landing Ship, Tank).

This operation was conceived with several phases, with the broad Allied scheme of maneuver being to secure all of New Britain west of the line between Gasmata and Talasea on the north coast. Within this plan, one of the phases, codenamed Backhander, was a landing around Cape Gloucester aimed at the capture, and expansion of two Japanese military airfields. This was to contribute to the increased isolation and harassment of the major Japanese base at Rabaul, while a secondary goal was to ensure free Allied sea passage through the straits separating New Britain from New Guinea.

Perceiving that the Allies could not bypass Rabaul as they attempted to advance towards the Japanese inner perimeter and would instead seek to capture it as quickly as possible, Japanese strategy on New Britain sought to maintain a sizeable force for the defense of Rabaul, thus reducing the forces available for the defense of western New Britain.

The main landing came on **26 December 1943** when U.S. Marines landed either side of the peninsula. The western landing force cut the coastal road, while the main force, landing on the eastern side, advanced north towards the airfields. Further fighting followed into early **January 1944** as the U.S. troops extended their perimeter south from the airfields, with mopping up operations in the vicinity continuing into **April 1944**.

Cape Gloucester is on the west side of New Britain with Rabaul on the east end. The 1st Marine Division was relieved around Cape Gloucester on **23 April 1944**, and were replaced by the 40th Infantry Division. After this, a period of relative quiet followed on New Britain as the US confined their operations largely to the western end of the island, having decided at a strategic level to bypass Rabaul, while the Japanese stayed close to their base around Rabaul at the opposite end of the island.

In assessing the operation historian Samuel Eliot Morison has argued that it was of limited strategic importance in achieving the Allied objectives of Operation Cartwheel. Indeed, Morison characterizes it as a *"waste of time and effort"*.

✦ ✦ ✦ ✦

The Coast Watchers

It was on Bougainville, as well as on other islands of the Solomons chain, that the Australian coast watchers played their most decisive role in transmitting vital advance warnings to Allied forces in the lower Solomon Islands. Japanese war planes and ships summoned in urgency to smash the beachhead at Guadalcanal had to pass over Bougainville, the big island in the middle of the route from Rabaul.

In 1941, as the war with Japan commenced, there were 100 coast watchers in the Solomons. There were 10 times that number as the war ended, later including Americans. Assembled first as a tight group of island veterans in 1939 (although there had been coast watchers after World War I) under Lieutenant Commander A. Eric Feldt, Royal Australian Navy, their job was to cover about 500,000 miles of land, sea, and air.

Bazooka: aka Bunker Busters

The bazooka was a marvel of science and engineering—the world's first shoulder fired antitank rocket. Using a shaped charge rocket, it was a powerful weapon that enabled Marines and Soldiers to defeat enemy armor and field fortifications. Of vital importance was the bazooka's simplicity of operation and maintenance in the most rugged combat conditions.

In **June 1942**, the US Army officially adopted the Launcher, Rocket, Antitank, M1. **General Electric** built the first 5,000 weapons in a crash program to equip Army troops for the North African campaign. When Soldiers first got their first look at the rocket launcher, they dubbed it **"the bazooka"** after a musical instrument developed by entertainer Bob Burns.

A detachment for the experimental rocket platoon went in with the Marine forces during the Bougainville operation in **October 1943**. In the South Pacific, Marines encountered many problems with the new bazookas. The battery-operated firing circuit was delicate and the rocket motors often failed because of high temperatures and humidity. But the weapon showed promise as a bunker buster for the infantry Marine.

With the introduction of the M1A1 and its more reliable rocket ammunition, the bazooka was effective against some fixed Japanese infantry emplacements such as small concrete bunkers and pillboxes. Against coconut and sand emplacements, the weapon was not always effective, as these softer structures often reduced the force of the warhead's impact enough to prevent detonation of the explosive charge.

In the few instances in the Pacific where the bazooka was used against tanks and armored vehicles, the rocket's warhead easily penetrated the thin armor plate used by the Japanese and destroyed the vehicle. Overall, the M1A1, M9, and M9A1 rocket launchers were viewed as useful and effective weapons during World War II, though they had been primarily employed against enemy emplacements and fixed fortifications, not as anti-tank weapons.

The first widespread use of the bazooka in Pacific combat was during the Marianas campaigns in the summer of 1944. They proved extremely effective against Japanese field fortifications and tanks. For example, early in the morning of **17 June 1944**, the enemy launched a tank attack with infantry support against the 2nd Marine Division on Saipan. About thirty tanks crashed into the Sixth Marine Regiment's defensive positions. Bazooka teams hunted Japanese tanks in this intense, close quarter fight. The bazooka teams usually won, for Japanese tanks are weak.

215

General Dwight Eisenhower later described it as one of the four "Tools of Victory" which won World War II for the Allies together with the atom bomb, Jeep and the C-47 Skytrain transport aircraft.

The C-47 Skytrain Transport

The C-47 Skytrain was a product of the Douglas Aircraft Company and achieved its first flight prototype form on **December 23rd, 1941**.

The original DC-3 was modified from commercial airliner to military transport which required some changes to her base design – the passenger cabin was revised to carry 27 combat-ready personnel in more spartan conditions. The passenger seats were removed to make room for bench-style seating where the passenger now faced centerline, seated in bucket seats. Pratt & Whitney radial engines were then added in place of the Wright "Cyclones" found in the DC-3. This transport was manned by a crew of three and could carry a variety of loads up to 6,000 pounds, including, troops, wounded, medical personnel, guns, ammunition, and even a jeep.

XXII   Bougainville

The Solomon Island chain is more than 500 miles long. Bougainville is one of the most northern islands in the chain, as well as the largest, 130 miles long and on average 30 miles wide, with an area of about 3800 square miles.

Bougainville's strategic importance lay with its location just over 200 air miles from Rabaul. Topographically, Bougainville possessed two central mountain ranges, the Emperor Range in the north and the lower, less rugged one to the south, the Crown Prince Range, with the former having two active volcanoes—Mount Balbi at over 10,000 feet and Mount Bagana.   The lower slopes and coastal plains are covered in dense jungle. Streams and small rivers are often fringed with crocodile-frequented mangrove swamps, but larger rivers have steep, bare banks swept clean by flooding.

The two sides of the island are markedly different. The northeast side has a narrow coastal plain crossed by fewer streams. The numerous beaches are good, but there are many coral reefs. The southwest side is more rugged and densely vegetated. Broad, shallow Empress Augusta Bay, twenty-two miles across, indents the central-southwest coast, its northwest side defined by Cape Torokina and the southwest by Mutupina Point. This would be the American landing site.

Except for some roads in the south that could accommodate wheeled transport, overland movement was limited to primitive trails through the dense jungle interior. Most important of the island routes were the Numa Numa Trail which extended southwest from Numa on the northeast coast to Empress Augusta Bay, and the East-West Trail running from Buin on the southern tip to Gazelle Harbor below Empress Augusta Bay.

The climate is hot and humid with a wet or northwest season in the summer months and a dry or southeast season in the winter months, but the 100-inch average annual rainfall may fall equally in any month. Malaria is endemic and blackwater fever, dengue fever, and dysentery are prevalent. The natives suffer from tuberculosis, yaws, and hookworm.

Japanese troops landed in the area around Buka Passage, the northern most end of the island, on **30 March 1942**, seizing the airfield as a useful satellite to the bases at Rabaul. Occupation of the rest of the island was leisurely; for example, Kieta (southeast side) was not occupied until **July 1942**.

By 1943, Bougainville and the other islands of the Northern Solomons had gained strategic importance. Bougainville had adequate facilities for basing fleet units and aircraft. Its capture would contain Japanese forces at Rabaul and help neutralize the major enemy base at Truk.

Japanese strategy

Yamamoto sorely wanted to regain the strategic initiative and, perhaps, win one additional major victory since the lightning campaign of 1941-1942. Such a decisive Japanese victory might yet compel the Allies to seek a negotiated peace and allow the Japanese to keep their new Pacific empire.

Also, the continued possession of Bougainville was to provide the leaders in Tokyo the necessary time for the Imperial Japanese Army to supply and execute land offensives in China and through Burma's western boundary into India. Victories in these operations might derail Allied war-plans in the Pacific Theater.

Ironically, on **April 18, 1943**, during a morale-boosting trip to the Northern Solomons, *Yamamoto's* personal, twin-engine Mitsubishi G4M "Betty" bomber was shot down by Guadalcanal-based American Lockheed P-38 Lightning fighters over the southern tip of Bougainville. *Admiral Mineichi Koga* took over the Combined Fleet after *Yamamoto's* death.

Bougainville was to become the staging area for renewed attacks to the south and east. As the troops from Kolombangara and the other Central Solomon Islands were brought back to safer Japanese areas, they were concentrated on Bougainville. After the loss of Guadalcanal and New Georgia and the evacuation of Kolombangara, Bougainville was deemed the best option to accomplish the two goals of protecting Rabaul and serving as an eventual springboard to strike southeastward again.

✦ ✦ ✦ ✦

Depth Charges

A depth charge is an anti-submarine warfare weapon. It is intended to destroy a submarine by being dropped into the water nearby and detonating, subjecting the target to a powerful and destructive hydraulic shock. The canister would sink through the water, and its explosive charge would be detonated at a preselected depth by means of a hydrostatic valve. Most depth charges use high explosive charges and a fuse set to detonate the charge, typically at a specific depth. Depth charges can be dropped by ships, patrol aircraft, and helicopters.

The depth charge rarely exploded close enough to sink the submarine, but its shock waves loosened the submarine's joints and damaged its instruments, thus forcing it to the surface, where it could be finished off by naval gunfire. An attacking ship would try to drop a pattern of depth charges around a submarine to increase the chances of one exploding near enough to damage the sub.

Dropping depth charges off the stern via a rack or track was standard practice for anti-submarine warfare (ASW) vessels in both World Wars. For the heavier depth charges, such as the Mark 4 and the Mark 7, this was the only method used, while the smaller depth charges could be used with "Y" and "K" guns. Destroyer and Destroyer Escorts generally had two racks while smaller ships had one. The "Y" gun allowed you to propel two depth charges from one depth charge projector, going to both sides of the ship. The "K" gun was a single projectile allowing use on both sides of the ship.

Surface ships usually used ASDIC (sonar) to detect submerged submarines. However, to deliver its depth charges a ship had to pass over the contact to drop them over the stern; sonar contact would be lost just before attack, rendering the hunter blind at the crucial moment. This gave a skillful submarine commander an opportunity to take evasive action.

Hedgehog

In **1942** the forward-throwing "hedgehog" mortar, which fired a spread salvo of bombs with contact fuses at a "stand-off" distance while still in sonar contact, was introduced and proved to be effective.

The **Hedgehog** (also known as an *Anti-Submarine Projector*) was a forward-throwing anti-submarine weapon that was used in the World War II. The spigot design allowed a single device to fire warheads of varying size. The device, which was developed by the Royal Navy, fired up to 24 spigot mortars ahead of a ship when attacking a U-boat. It was deployed on convoy escort warships such as destroyers and corvettes to supplement the depth charges.

By the end of the war, statistics showed that on average, one in every five attacks made by Hedgehog resulted in a kill (compared to less than one in 80 with depth charges). In the Pacific Theater, USS *England* sank six Japanese submarines in a matter of days with Hedgehog in **May 1944**.

In **June 1943**, the deficiencies of Japanese depth-charge tactics were stupidly revealed in a press conference held by U.S. Congressman Andrew J. May, a member of the House Military Affairs Committee, who had visited the Pacific theater and received many intelligence and operational briefings. May mentioned the highly sensitive fact that American submarines had a high survivability rate because Japanese depth charges were fused to explode at too shallow a depth. An example of "loose lips sink ships".

Torpedo's

The first automotive torpedo was developed in 1866, and the torpedo boat was developed soon after. In 1898, while the Spanish–American War was being fought in the Caribbean and the Pacific, Assistant Secretary of the Navy Theodore Roosevelt wrote that the Spanish torpedo boat destroyers were the only threat to the American navy, and pushed for the acquisition of similar vessels. On **4 May 1898**, the US Congress authorized the first sixteen **torpedo boat destroyers** and twelve *seagoing torpedo boats* for the United States Navy. The first torpedo boat destroyers, the *Bainbridge* class, featured two torpedo tubes and two 3-inch (76 mm) guns, displacing 400 short tons.

Designed in **1930**, the Mark 14 torpedo had the misfortune of being developed in the Great Depression when there was little or no money available for painting barracks, let alone funding new and expensive weapon systems. The Mark 14 was put into production even though it had been inadequately tested – in fact no live-fire tests were ever conducted.

When submarine commanders went to war in the Pacific, they discovered that more often than not their torpedoes exploded prematurely, ran too deep, were duds, or, frighteningly, circled back and tried to sink their own submarines.

In **1942**, submarines in the three regional Pacific Ocean commands had fired 1,442 torpedoes and sunk only 211 ships totaling almost 1.3 million tons (post-war analysis of Japanese records reduced these figures to 109 ships and 41,871 tons). The new Commander, Submarines, Pacific Fleet, Rear Adm. Charles Lockwood looked at the tally sheet for March 1943. The results continued to be disappointingly low. The problem: duds and premature explosions of torpedoes. In 1942, Lockwood had forced the powerful Bureau of Ordnance (BuOrd) to admit to and fix faults in the Mark 14 torpedo's depth gauge, the cause of torpedoes running too deep. Now he braced himself for another bruising battle with BuOrd, this time over the magnetic "exploder," also called a pistol, which was meant to detonate the torpedo beneath the keel of enemy ships.

In **July 1943**, Admiral Lockwood officially ordered what many of his commanders were already doing: deactivate the magnetic exploder and only use the contact pistol, which would detonate the torpedo when it actually contacted the side of an enemy ship.

Yet even *that* didn't completely solve the dud and premature explosion problem. In July 1943, Lt. Cmdr. Lawrence Daspit of the *Tinosa* fired eleven torpedoes under near perfect conditions that were duds. In August, Lockwood ordered field tests in which torpedoes with warshots were fired at an undersea cliff and the duds retrieved for study, and torpedoes containing dummy warheads were dropped from a cherry picker onto a steel plate set at different angles. The tests revealed defects in the contact pistol as well. This information was passed onto BuOrd which eventually redesigned the contact pistol.

In his book, *Silent Victory*, historian Clay Blair Jr. wrote, "After twenty-one months of war, the three major defects of the Mark 14 torpedo had at last been isolated. . . . Each defect had been discovered and fixed in the field – always over the stubborn opposition of the Bureau of Ordnance."

By the end of World War II, the Mark 14 torpedo was a reliable weapon which remained in service for almost 40 years. The effective Firing Range: 4500 yards at 46 knots, 9000 yards at 31 knots. It was supplemented by the Mark 18 electric torpedo in the last two years of the war.

Imperial Japanese Type 93 "Long Lance Torpedo"

When U.S. Navy warships began exploding in the middle of the night, America realized it had a problem. In the autumn of 1942, Guadalcanal, in the Solomon Islands near Australia, became the focal point of the Pacific War. For six months,

U.S. and Japanese forces savagely battled on land, air, and sea to determine who would control the island and its strategic airfield.

For the U.S. Navy, which had belittled the Japanese as incompetent, Guadalcanal came as a shock. The disaster at Pearl Harbor could be explained by surprise and treachery, but the Navy left two dozen warships in "Ironbottom Sound" off Guadalcanal.

One reason was the "Long Lance", the Japanese torpedo that was the most powerful weapon of its kind in the early years of World War II. Developed in the late 1920s, the Long Lance, as Americans nicknamed it (the Japanese designation was the "Type 93"), was a remarkable device. In modern parlance, it would be an asymmetric weapon, designed to compensate for Japanese inferiority to more economically powerful Western nations. In some ways, it was the equivalent of hypersonic ship-killing missiles that China and Russia would use to counter the superior U.S. Navy.

When the Second World War began, the Japanese plan was to exercise patience to defeat a stronger foe. Under the "decisive battle" strategy, Japan would seize the Philippines, and as the U.S. Navy sailed across the Pacific to recapture Manila, it would be harried and worn down by persistent aircraft, submarines and destroyer attacks. Once the American battle fleet had been sufficiently weakened, the Japanese battle fleet would sortie out and sink it in a huge Jutland-style naval battle near the Philippines.

To accomplish this, the Imperial Japanese Navy relentlessly trained its surface ships in night torpedo attacks that would allow its ships to sneak up on and destroy the enemy. The Imperial Navy lacked radar, but lookouts were rigorously trained and equipped with powerful night binoculars. Yet all would be for naught without a good torpedo, and the Long Lance more than met the need.

The Long Lance was a big torpedo for its time, some two feet in diameter almost thirty feet long and weighing almost three tons. It was armed with a 1,080-pound warhead that was 50 percent larger than most other torpedo warheads. Most important was the Long Lance's propulsion system. Most other nations fielded torpedoes propelled by steam, diesel or electric propulsion. But the Japanese opted for a pure oxygen-based system (inspired by an earlier British design) that could send the Long Lance out to twelve miles at a speed of 48 knots, or an incredible 24 miles—about the same range as a battleship's gun—at a speed of 36 knots. The Long Lance also didn't leave telltale bubbles on the surface to warn enemy ships a torpedo was approaching.

The Americans quickly felt the sting of the Long Lance. At the Battle of Savo Island, a task force of Japanese heavy cruisers (the Americans wouldn't have dreamed of using heavy warships in a night torpedo attack) and destroyers surprised an Allied force, sinking three American and one Australian heavy cruiser. The subsequent withdrawal of the U.S. Navy nearly doomed the U.S. Marine garrison on Guadalcanal. At the Battle of Tassafaronga on the night of November 30, 1942, the Imperial Navy's "Tokyo Express" force of destroyers sank one and badly damaged three U.S. Navy heavy cruisers, at a cost of just one destroyer.

The problem wasn't just the Long Lance. It was also superiority of Japanese sensors, namely the **Mark I human eyeball**. The U.S. Navy placed its faith in newly developed radar for surface ships, but the primitive radar of late 1942 was unreliable and its operators inexperienced. Japanese lookouts consistently spotted U.S. ships first at incredible ranges. Once spotted, Imperial cruisers and destroyers could launch torpedoes that unlike naval guns, betrayed neither flash nor sound, thus preserving the element of surprise while denying the enemy a target.

The Japanese edge eroded as American radar, crew experience and tactics improved.

Gato-class Submarines

The Gato-class were a class of submarines built for the United States Navy and launched in **1941–1943**; they were the first mass-production US submarine class of World War II. Gato's name comes from a species of small catshark. The Gatos and their successors formed the core of the submarine service that was largely responsible for the destruction of the Japanese merchant marine and a large portion of the Imperial Japanese Navy in World War II.

They were to scout out ahead of the fleet and report on the enemy fleet's composition, speed, and course, then to attack and whittle down the enemy in preparation for the main fleet action, a titanic gun battle between battleships and cruisers. This was an operational concept born from experience in World War I. In order to operate effectively in this role, a submarine had to have high surface speed, long range and endurance, and a heavy armament. *Gato*-class boats would be fully capable of routinely operating at 300 feet having **24 torpedoes**. 10 torpedo tubes - 6 forward 4 aft tubes, 1 × 3-inch (76 mm) / 50 caliber deck gun, Bofors 40 mm and Oerlikon 20 mm cannon.

P-38 Lightning Fighter

The P-38 was used for interception, dive bombing, level bombing, ground attack, night fighting, photo reconnaissance, radar and visual path finding for bombers and evacuation missions, and extensively as a long-range escort fighter when equipped with drop tanks under its wings. The P-38 was used most successfully in the Pacific Theater of Operations and the China-Burma-India Theater of Operations as the aircraft of America's top aces, Richard Bong (40 victories), Thomas McGuire (38 victories) and Charles H. MacDonald (27 victories).

The following are interesting facts of the P-38:

-- The P-38 was the first fighter to fly faster than 400 mph.
--- It was the only American fighter aircraft in production throughout the entire American involvement in WWII.
-- The P-38 was nicknamed the 'fork-tailed devil' by the German Luftwaffe and 'two planes, one pilot' by Japanese fighter pilots.

-- The aircraft used nose-mounted guns, unlike most other US fighters. This meant the P-38 had better useful gun range than other aircraft, whose wing-mounted guns had crisscross trajectories.

 -- The P-38s guns were so effective they could reliably hit targets at up to 1,000 yards.
-- Most other fighters were only effective at 100-250 yards.
-- The engines rotated outward from the cockpit. This made the platform more stable for shooting guns, however, if the pilot lost an engine, the operating engine was so powerful that it could uncontrollably roll the aircraft inverted.
-- The P-38 was the first American fighter to extensively use stainless steel and flush-mounted rivets.
--- The cockpit windows couldn't be opened in flight because they caused buffeting on the plane's tail. This made the cockpit very hot in the Pacific theater, and pilots often times flew in just shorts, tennis shoes, and a parachute.
-- Charles Lindbergh was a key figure in improving the performance of the P-38. Working as a civilian contractor in the South Pacific, he developed throttle settings and engine leaning techniques that significantly increased the range of the aircraft.

-- The P-38 downed over 1,800 aircraft in the Pacific theater.
-- In total, over 10,000 P-38s were produced during the war, making it one of the most successful fighters and interceptors of its time.

Destroyers

On 7 December 1941, the day the United States entered World War II, the United States Navy had 100 destroyers seven years old or newer. This number included 27 *Benson* and *Gleaves*-class destroyers.

The **Benson class** was a class of destroyers of the U.S. Navy built 1939–1943. The thirty 1,620-ton *Benson*-class destroyers were built in two groups. The first six were authorized in fiscal year 1938 (FY38) and laid down at Bethlehem Steel, Quincy, Massachusetts and three naval shipyards. The remaining 24 "repeat *Bensons*" were authorized in 1940–42 and built at four Bethlehem Steel yards. They were laid down after the first group was commissioned.

The **Gleaves-class destroyers** were a class of 66 destroyers of the United States Navy built 1938–42, designed by Gibbs & Cox. The first ship of the class was USS *Gleaves*. They were the production destroyer of the US Navy when it entered World War II.

The *Benson*- and *Gleaves*-class destroyers were the backbone of the pre-war Neutrality Patrols and brought the action to the enemy by participating in every major naval campaign of the war.

However, none were equipped with torpedoes comparable to the (then unknown) Type 93 torpedoes ("Long Lance torpedo") of the Imperial Japanese Navy, and only destroyer leaders had more than four main guns—inferior to the six guns on a Japanese *Fubuki*-class destroyer (the first 24 ships of the *Benson/Gleaves* class were built with five guns, but excessive top-weight led to one being removed).

After World War II broke out across Europe in 1939, the United States Navy began sketches for a five-gun ship— on an enlarged hull. Introduced in 1942, the 175 *Fletcher* class "2100 tonners", became the U.S. Navy's signature destroyer in the Pacific War. By the end of World War II, the U.S. Navy had also commissioned 112 six-gun destroyers derived from the *Fletcher* design; 67 *Allen M. Sumner* class 2200 tonners and 45 *Gearing* class 2250 tonners. The *Allen M. Sumner* class' hull was slightly wider than the *Fletcher* class', while the *Gearing*-class design was a lengthened version of the *Allen M. Sumner*s.

By 1945, as the threat from *kamikazes* increased and the threat from the Japanese surface fleet decreased, torpedoes and guns were partially (or completely in the case of torpedoes on some ships) removed from most US destroyers in favor of light anti-aircraft guns against the kamikazes. Destroyers had acquired the hazardous radar picket mission by this time. Collectively, these destroyer designs are sometimes regarded as the most successful of World War II.

A radar picket is a radar-equipped station, ship, submarine, aircraft, or vehicle used to increase the radar detection range around a force to protect it from surprise attack, typically air attack. Radar picket vessels may also be equipped to direct friendly fighters to intercept the enemy. Often several detached radar units encircle a force to provide increased cover in all directions. Airborne radar pickets are generally referred to as airborne early warning.

Radar picket ships first came into being in the US Navy during World War II to aid in the Allied advance to Japan. The number of radar pickets was increased significantly after the first major employment of kamikaze aircraft by the Japanese in the Battle of Leyte Gulf in October 1944. Fletcher- and Sumner-class destroyers were pressed into service with few modifications at first. Later, additional radars and fighter direction equipment were fitted, along with more light anti-aircraft (AA) guns for self-defense, usually sacrificing torpedo tubes to make room for the new equipment, particularly the large height-finding radars of the era. Deploying some distance from the force to be protected along likely directions of attack, radar pickets were the nearest ships to the Japanese airfields. Thus, they were usually the first vessels seen by incoming waves of kamikazes and were often heavily attacked.

The radar picket system saw its ultimate development in World War II in the Battle of Okinawa. A ring of 15 radar picket stations was established around Okinawa to cover all possible approaches to the island and the attacking fleet. Initially, a typical picket station had one or two destroyers supported by two landing ships, usually **landing craft support (large) (LCS(L))** or **landing ship medium (rocket) (LSM(R))**, for additional AA firepower. Eventually, the number of destroyers and supporting ships were doubled at the most threatened stations, and combat air patrols were provided as well.

In early 1945, 26 new construction *Gearing*-class destroyers were ordered as radar pickets without torpedo tubes, to allow for extra radar and AA equipment, but only some of these were ready in time to serve off Okinawa. The radar picket mission was vital, but it was also costly to the ships performing it. Out of 101 destroyers assigned to radar picket stations, 10 were sunk and 32 were damaged by kamikaze attacks. The 88 LCS(L)s assigned to picket stations had two sunk and 11 damaged by kamikazes, while the 11 LSM(R)s had three sunk and two damaged.

The destroyer USS Charles Ausburne (DD-570) left Okinawa 10 September 1945, and arrived at Washington, D.C., 17 October to receive her Presidential Unit Citation for 11 Battle Stars and thereby decommissioned.

Builder: Consolidated Steel Corporation, Orange, Texas. Commissioned 24 November 1942. Length – 376 feet 6 inches, Beam – 39 feet 8 inches, Speed 35 knots (40mph), Complement – 329, officers and enlisted
Armament: 5x5" 38 caliber guns, 10x40mm Anti-aircraft guns, 7x20mm Anti-aircraft guns, 10x21" torpedo tubes, 6x depth charge projectors, 2x depth charge tracks.

✦ ✦ ✦ ✦

Battle of Empress Augusta Bay

In early October, the Japanese had approximately 37,500 troops on Bougainville and nearby islands. There were 25,000 soldiers in southern Bougainville and the Shortland Islands, 5,000 on the east coast, 5,000 on Bougainville's northern end and on Buka Island, and a small number around Empress Augusta Bay on the west coast. After deliberation, Halsey targeted Torokina in the Empress Augusta Bay area. Despite the heavy surf at Empress Augusta Bay and its proximity to Japanese airfields on southern Bougainville (65 miles) and Rabaul (215 miles), Halsey surmised that the imposing mountain range surrounding the bay's coastal plain would delay the Japanese counterattack three to four months.

Admiral William F. Halsey, Commander South Pacific, ordered Task Force 39 (which included four cruisers and eight destroyers of Captain Arleigh Burke's Destroyer Squadron 23), under Rear Admiral A.S. Merrill, to bombard airfields on Buka and Bonis northwest of Bougainville. The cruisers were officially categorized as 'light cruisers', however they were nearly the size of the Japanese heavy cruisers and were armed with twelve radar-aimed 6-inch (152 mm) rapid fire guns.

The **Cleveland Class** was a group of light cruisers built for the U.S. Navy during World War II and were the most numerous class of light cruisers ever built. The preferred cruiser of the US Navy, the twelve 6" radar-aimed guns could hurl 10 rounds per minute as opposed to 3 rounds per minute on US heavy cruisers using 8" guns.

Halsey intended the bombardments to keep the enemy off-balance and prevent air harassment of the landing force. The task force then steamed more than 200 miles to strike at the Shortland Islands, while Rear Admiral F.C. Sherman's Task Force 38 took over the bombardment of Buka, eliminating the threat from those airfields.

As invasion preparations proceeded, Lt. Gen. George C. Kenney's Fifth Air Force flying from New Guinea conducted major air attacks against Rabaul during **October and November 1943**, while the Air Command, Solomons, kept the five Japanese fields on Bougainville under such pressure that they were useless by invasion day. Meanwhile, on **27 October 1943**, New Zealand and American troops captured the Treasury Islands, south of Bougainville. That same day the 2d Marine Parachute Battalion landed on Choiseul, a large island in the Solomons near Bougainville. As part of a deception plan to mislead the Japanese as to where the main invasion would occur, the marines harassed the Japanese on the northern half of the island for twelve days before withdrawing. Perceiving threats everywhere except in the west, the Japanese concentrated their defenses accordingly, largely ignoring the western shore.

The Japanese commander on Bougainville, *Lieutenant General Harukichi Hyakutake*, initially believed that the landing at Empress Augusta Bay was a diversion, and would be followed by a direct assault on the south of the island. However, he conducted several small and unsuccessful attacks against the beachhead in early November after being ordered to do so by the *Eighth Area Army* using units from his *17th Army* and forces dispatched directly from Rabaul. The United States forces subsequently expanded their beachhead and defeated the Japanese forces in the area in a series of battles in November and December.

The battle was significant as part of a broader Allied strategy—known as Operation Cartwheel—aimed at isolating and surrounding the major Imperial base at Rabaul. The intention was to establish a beachhead on Bougainville, within which an airfield would be built.

The Japanese responded with air attacks and a powerful naval force from Rabaul commanded by *Admiral Sentaro Omori*: 2 heavy cruisers, 2 light cruisers, 6 destroyers. The Japanese formation was hastily assembled from whatever ships were on hand, many of which had never trained or fought together before.

The Americans made radar contact at 0230 on **2 November**. From the leading position in the American formation Commodore Arleigh Burke sent the four destroyers of DesDiv 45 forward for a torpedo attack and at 0245 fired a salvo toward the enemy. Almost simultaneously, the *Sendai*-led division fired 18 torpedoes. Each attack was detected and both groups maneuvered away from the torpedoes. The Japanese fleet became separated in the confusion into three groups, north, center and south.

At around 0250, when it became apparent that DesDiv 45's torpedo attack had failed to achieve complete surprise, the American cruisers opened fire, quickly disabling *Sendai*. DesDiv 45 maneuvered north and concentrated on the northern group, DesDiv. 46 engaged the center group while the cruisers divided their fire between all three groups.

Although the Japanese ships were equipped with anti-air and surface detection Type 21 Radar, they could only rely on optical tracking of their targets. With difficulty, they pinpointed the American cruisers and opened fire at 0313. At 0320 the Japanese Cruiser Squadron fired a total of 10 torpedoes and all missed their targets. Without fire control radar, the Japanese depended heavily on flares to illuminate their targets. CruDiv 12 repeatedly maneuvered to avoid starshells fired by the opposing ships but was finally successfully illuminated by brilliant flares dropped by Japanese snooper aircraft.

All during the battle the American destroyers experienced difficulty maintaining contact with each other and several times came close to firing on friendly ships, underscoring the difficulty in fighting night actions even when equipped with radar and IFF systems (Identification Friend or Foe).

By 0337, *Commander Omori*, believing that he had sunk a heavy cruiser and worried about being caught in daylight by U.S. carrier aircraft, ordered a retreat. Admiral Merrill's cruisers closed to bombard the retreating Cruiser Division to the south but difficulties in positive identification hampered this effort and CruDiv 12 turned away to the north allowing the Japanese cruisers to slip away in the darkness.

At daylight the pursuit was broken off and all ships, many low on fuel and ammunition, were ordered to rendezvous. The rest of the day was spent defending the landing beaches from air attack. This ended the Japanese warship threat to the Allied landing forces at Bougainville.

Division Signals

For an infantry division to fight effectively, its commander must be in contact with his subordinate units at all times. To do this during the war, the divisional signals had to provide the commander with communications, whether by dispatch runner, over the telephone and wireless, War Dogs if available or any other necessary means. Communications had to be maintained around the clock, under all conditions, and no matter how difficult.

Underground surgery rooms behind the front lines on Bougainville doctors operate on soldiers before being transported safely out of harm's way or patching the soldier to allow him back to the battle.

Due to the island terrain, muddy conditions and lack of usable roads supplies had to be hand carried to the front lines.

First Battle of Bougainville

The task of seizing the Cape Torokina region on the island was assigned to the I Marine Amphibious Corps, commanded by Lieutenant General Alexander A. Vandegrift and later by Major General Roy S. Geiger. For this operation IMAC included the -following assault units: 3d Marine Division, Major General Alan H. Turnage; **37th Infantry (Army) Division, Major General Robert S. Beightler;** 2d Marine Raider Regiment (Provisional), Lieutenant Colonel Alan Shapley; 1st Marine Parachute Regiment, Lieutenant Colonel Robert H. Williams and 8th New Zealand Brigade Group, Brigadier R. A. Row.

Given the primitive jungle trails and harsh mountainous terrain of the Emperor and Crown Prince mountain ranges the Cape Torokina area was almost isolated from the strong Japanese garrisons in northern and southern Bougainville.

November 1, 1943, the allied invasion of Bougainville would begin with an offensive-defensive mission. There was no thought of pushing across this 250-square-mile island and eliminating the 25,000 Japanese in a brutal, costly, slow action. Instead, the plan was to take only a small piece of Bougainville, perhaps six square miles, including the deepest, best port at Empress Augusta Bay. Within those six square miles, a major airfield would be built, from which American planes could range over the South Pacific as far forward as the Philippines, assuring security from the air for the convoys and task forces that would invade the Philippines in October 1944.

The Bougainville campaign basically resembled that of Guadalcanal: it had a limited objective --- the capture and defense of a strategic airfield site. The acquisition of a base on Bougainville was part of the overall plan of isolating the highly strategic Japanese naval and air base of Rabaul on the island of New Britain. The initial landing on Bougainville was intended primarily as a Marine Corps operation. Once a beachhead was secured the Marines were to be withdrawn and replaced by Army troops.

The plan was to establish a beachhead, then bring in supplies and equipment to build a landing strip for fighters. Invasion forces consisted of 14,321 troops (including the 1st Marine Dog Platoon with their 24 Dobermans and German Shepherds) in 12 transports, preceded by a minesweeper group. Destroyer Squadron 45, four minelayers and two salvage tugs provided further support.

On Bougainville, the US troops were opposed by *Lieutenant General Harukichi Hyakutake's Japanese 17th Army*, which formed part of *General Hitoshi Imamura's 8th Area Army*, based at Rabaul. The main infantry forces opposing the Marines were the *6th Division*, under *Lieutenant General Masatane Kanda*.

At 0645 on **1 November 1943**, U.S. troops go over the side of Coast Guard manned combat transports to enter the landing barges at Empress Augusta Bay and head to shore as the first wave of the assault force moved ashore. Despite heavy surf that caused one transport to run aground and eighty-six landing craft to swamp and that rendered some beaches too dangerous to use, most supply ships were emptied within eight hours and 14,000 marines landed before nightfall. By the end of D-day, the marines had established a shallow, 4,000-yard beachhead.

The initial landing was made by the U.S. 3rd Marine Division, the 37th Infantry Division, and Americal landed at Cape Torokina, the northwest corner in Empress Augusta Bay. The bay had been chosen because it was at the outer limit of Allied fighter plane range. Despite prior bombardment by both ships and planes, the invasion force met heavy fire from the defenders. Japanese positions were camouflaged in the low-lying areas by the Kunai grass where they dug into the coral rock both flatland and hillsides and laid over the fox holes with a stick framework.

Although this shore fire did not prevent the landing, it did cause much confusion. The situation was further complicated by heavy surf. As a result, squads, platoons, even companies landed far out of position and in sectors assigned to other units. The dense jungle, moreover, did nothing to facilitate reorganization.

Because of the difficult terrain the beachhead was not expanded very rapidly. Three days after the landing the perimeter was only an average of 1,500 yards from the beach. Following the initial resistance the advance had been unopposed. The Marines now faced another enemy; the jungle and the swamps. Any advance inland was a matter of clawing, hacking, and wading one's way foot by foot.

The 37th Infantry Division landing at Cape Torokina would advance using the Mission Trail to Piva Trail, Coconut Grove and Piva Forks on their way to intersect with the Numa Numa Trail.

The landing met with several obstacles. The Japanese defense of the beaches was stronger than anticipated. The 40,000 troops on the island had been reported stationed mainly around the airfields, and aerial reconnaissance photos did not reveal the extensive system of bunkers in the jungles above the beaches. The Marines who landed west of the mouth of the Koromokina River encountered steep slopes and shoals on which more than 80 of their amphibious craft foundered. Those landing east of the Koromokina were caught in crossfire from machine guns on the offshore islet of Puruata and on Cape Torokina east of the beach. A small contingent of Marines knocked out the gun emplacement on the cape after it had destroyed or damaged 14 landing craft; the 3d Marine Raiders captured Puruata.

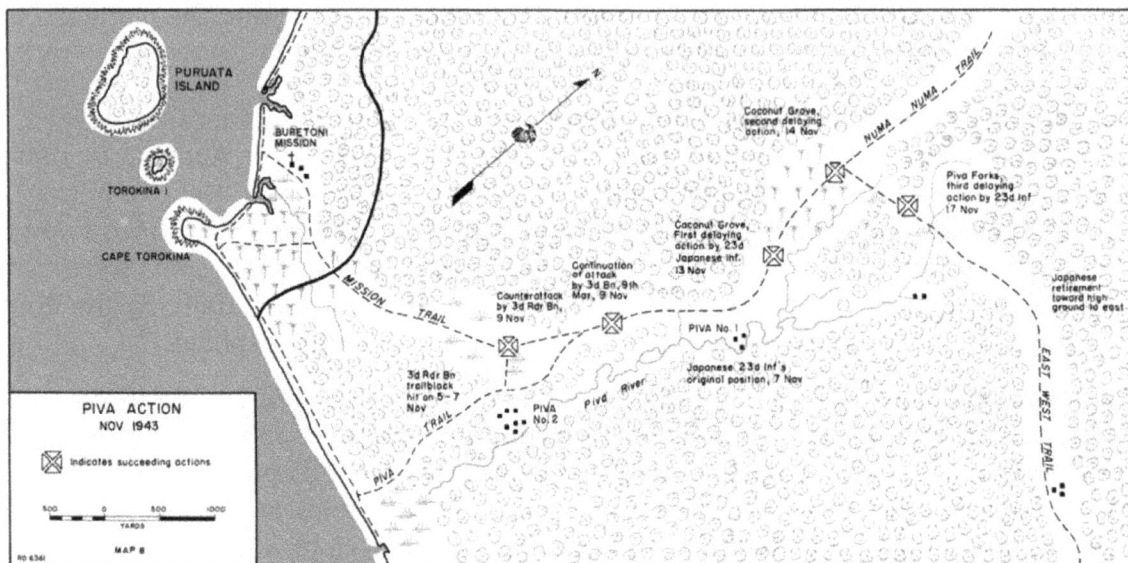

The evening of the landing, Army reconnaissance aircraft reported that a large Japanese surface force was heading for Bougainville. Task Force 39 intercepted it about 0230 the following morning 45 miles west of Empress Augusta Bay. The American ships, executing maneuvers at breakneck speeds in the darkness to avoid Japanese long-range torpedoes, sank two enemy ships after three hours of heavy fire. With two other ships damaged in collisions while trying to avoid American torpedoes, the scattered Japanese chose to retreat. The American force had only two ships hit, both of which sustained moderate damage.

The Japanese Response

The initial Japanese reaction to the Bougainville landing was to send a force of 19 ships to strengthen Rabaul. However, a **November 5** air attack from Task Force 38 heavily damaged seven cruisers and two destroyers, prompting the withdrawal of the cruisers and eliminating worries about surface attacks on the Bougainville amphibious forces.

Even so, the night of **Nov. 6-7**, four Japanese destroyers eluded the Americans and landed 475 troops west of the Marine beachhead. The Japanese hoped to catch the Marines between them and the other troops on the island, but the enemy forces never coordinated their actions. The Marines routed out the counter-landing detachment after two days of artillery barrages.

Fewer than 100 Japanese escaped into the jungle; the rest were killed. The Marines sustained under 50 casualties. Another punishing attack from Task Force 38 on Rabaul **Nov. 11** cost the Japanese 68 fighters and three ships. Nevertheless, Japanese carrier air groups from Rabaul made repeated attacks on the American landing force and the Navy ships, which continued to ferry in reinforcements, supplies and munitions. The strikes did little damage to the American forces, but the Japanese lost so many planes--121 out of 173--that the remaining carrier-based squadrons were withdrawn **November 13**.

The landing force drove away the rest of the Japanese defenders, while the dog platoon, moving ahead of the main body, sniffed out snipers along the trails of the bog-ridden jungle. In spite of the resistance, and two Japanese air assaults launched from Rabaul bases during the day (which were driven off by AirSols fighters), the Marines succeeded. By nightfall, all 14,000 troops, together with 6,200 tons of fuel, rations, and ammunition, were landed along a 200-yard perimeter.

From the initial landing until the end of the Marine participation in the campaign, the story of Bougainville is one of a beachhead expanding slowly, inexorably against nature and the Japanese. Behind the perimeter engineers and Seabees struggled to construct air facilities on one of the most unpromising pieces of real estate in the entire Pacific.

The Japanese for the most part dug into the jungle and the ridges and waited for the Americans to carry the fight to them. Not until months after the Marines had left did they make a determined effort to oust the invader and by then it was too late. Only once did the Japanese attempt to throw out the Marines. During the night of **6/7 November**, the enemy made an abortive counter landing at Atsinima Bay, some distance beyond the Marines, left flank, then anchored on the Koromokina River. In the meantime, the Japanese attempted an attack on the perimeter by infiltrating forces down the Piva Trail.

Battle of Piva Trail

This two-pronged attack was ineffectual. The amphibious landing force was too small to really disrupt the American hold on the perimeter. More important, American naval and air forces thwarted any enemy attempt to send reinforcements to their beleaguered troops. Despite a determined resistance by the Japanese landing force (approximately 500 men, it was practically annihilated after three days of heavy fighting. The attack via the Piva Trail was also stymied after three days of heavy fighting. By **10 November**, two battalions of the 9th Marines reached Piva Village and found that the Japanese had withdrawn. From then on the Japanese operated strictly on the defensive against the Marines and Army units which were gradually building up their strength on the island. The enemy from his well-placed positions now began utilizing the tactics of counterattack, sniping, and infiltration, with an occasional Banzai charge. This inspired the Japanese proceeding in country which gave the defenders every advantage, this made for some bitter and bloody fighting. The Japanese inability to commit sufficient troops for the task at hand, however, insured their ultimate failure.

Battle of Coconut Grove

The battle took place on **13–14 November 1943**. a small party of Construction Battalion personnel, with a covering infantry patrol, led by Commander William Painter, Civil Engineer Corps of United States Naval Reserve did a reconnaissance for an airfield site. Finding a suitable area located to the north of the perimeter, they set about preparations for the construction of landing strips.

Further patrols were undertaken up the Piva Trail, beyond the coconut grove near the East-West Trail junction, which failed to establish contact with the Japanese. Due to tremendous difficulties encountered in movement and supply through the swamps, it was impossible to advance the perimeter of the beachhead far enough to cover the proposed airfield site selected by Commander Painter. It was therefore decided to establish a strong outpost, capable of sustaining itself until the lines could be advanced to include it, at the junction of the Numa Numa and East-West Trails, in order to avoid a fight for the airfield site should the Japanese occupy it first.

On the afternoon of **12 November**, General Allen Hal Turnage—commander of the 3rd Marine Division—directed the 21st Marine Regiment to send a company patrol up the Numa Numa Trail at 0630 on **13 November**. The patrol was to move up the Numa Numa Trail to its junction with the East-West Trail and reconnoiter each trail for a distance of about 1,000 yd (910 m), with a view of establishing a strong outpost in the vicinity in the near future with Company E, 21st Marines led by Captain Sidney Altman assigned to the mission.

On **13 November** at 0730, Company E was ordered proceed out the Numa Numa Trail and begin to set up the outpost, without the rest of the battalion. At 0800 they proceeded up the Numa Numa Trail without incident. When the company had reached a point about 200 yd (180 m) south of its objective, it was struck by heavy fire coming from a Japanese ambush at 1105. A runner was sent to Smoak, informing him of the situation. Company E sustained a number of casualties from mortar fire as well as rifles and machine-gun.

Smoak—upon receiving the message from the Company E runner at 1200—was leading the rest of the battalion about 1,200 yd (1,100 m) south of the trail junction, having been delayed by the late arrival of the forward observer team and difficulty in supplying his troops in their swampy assembly area. One platoon of Company F was left behind to provide security for the forward observer's wire team.

By 1245, the battalion was 200 yd (180 m) to the rear of Company E, whereupon Smoak learned that Company E was pinned down by heavy fire and was taking casualties and reinforcement was needed immediately. The Japanese ambush position was located south of the trail junction. Smoak promptly ordered forward Company G—under the command of Capt. William McDonough—to reinforce Company E, **while Company H—led by Maj. Edward Clark—was ordered to provide <u>81 mm (3.19 in) mortar</u> support for the attack.** Company F—led by Capt. Robert Rapp—less the platoon protecting the wire team, was ordered into reserve and await orders.

By 1630, Smoak decided to dig in for the night, with his companies suffering fairly heavy casualties, Company F was missing and communications with regimental headquarters and the artillery had been broken. Throughout the night, sporadic enemy rifle fire occurred, with no attempt to attack the Marine positions. On the morning of **14 November**, all companies established outposts about 75 yd (69 m) in front of the perimeter and sent out patrols. At 0905, airstikes were called in, with 18 TBF Avengers from VMTB-143 bombing and strafing the area after artillery marked the target with smoke. Immediately after the airstrike, Company E moved back into its original position in the line. Smoak then ordered an attack, with Company E on the left and Company G on the right while Companies F and H would hold in reserve. The attack was to be a frontal assault, supported by five M3 Stuart tanks of the 2nd Platoon, Company B, 3rd Tank Battalion.

Artillery preparation was later recognized as of prime importance against the Japanese system of defenses, with their well dug-in, concealed, and covered foxholes, equipped with a high percentage of automatic weapons, in turn covered by equally invisible riflemen in trees and <u>spider-holes</u>, it had become evident that severe losses would be sustained by attacking infantry, regardless of the size of the force, unless attacks were preceded by artillery or mortar preparation or bombing or by all three.

A spider hole is U.S. military parlance for a camouflaged one-man foxhole, used for observation. They are typically a shoulder-deep, protective, round hole, often covered by a camouflaged lid.

After the preparatory barrage, the attack commenced at 1155. The Japanese immediately reoccupied their positions and opened fire with rifles and machine guns. Several tanks of 3rd Tank Battalion became confused and fired into our own troops, and accidentally ran over several men. Two tanks were damaged by enemy anti-tank fire. Complete loss of control and wild shooting occurred for about five minutes, with Smoak moving forward in person and gave orders to cease fire and to halt the advance. The tanks—except the two damaged by enemy anti-tank weapons—were ordered to return to an assembly position in reserve. At this time, it was discovered that the Marines had overrun the enemy positions, and that some Japanese were still present in dugouts. These were quickly reduced by riflemen with grenades. By 1400, all enemy resistance had been overcome.

After the Battle of the Coconut Grove on **13–14 November**, American patrols reported sporadic contacts with Japanese forces. Documents obtained from a Japanese officer who was killed in an ambush provided US forces with details of Japanese dispositions in the area, showing that a roadblock had been set up by elements of the Japanese 23rd Infantry Regiment on both the Numa Numa and the East–West Trails. General Roy Geiger, commander of I Marine Amphibious Corps, set in place plans for the expansion of the beachhead perimeter that had been established around Torokina to a new defensive line further inland designated as "Easy". Geiger specified that the line was to be obtained by 20 November 1943.

The battle paved the way on **15 November** for an advance on all fronts, extending the perimeter of the Torokina beachhead to about 1,000 yd (910 m) on the left (west) flank and about 1,500 yd (1,400 m) north in the center, to the inland defense line known as "Dog".

On **18 November**, US patrols discovered a Japanese roadblock on the Numa–Numa Trail about 1,000 yd (910 m) in front of the beachhead perimeter lines, while another patrol found a roadblock halfway between the two branches of the Piva River along the East–West Trail.

Battle of Piva Forks

Also known as the **Battle of Numa–Numa Trail** Occurred between **18 and 25 November 1943**. The Battle of Piva Forks began on **18 November**, ending seven days later, took place amidst the context of the expansion of a beachhead that US forces had established around Torokina on the western side of the island. This was a rather bitter and difficult battle in which units of the 3d Marines bore the brunt of the fighting. After engaging the Americans in very close combat, the Japanese broke off the fight, leaving behind more than 1,200 dead, and withdrew into the hinterland. There they set about the preparation of strong defensive positions beyond the range of American artillery. Clashes between Marine patrols and Japanese forces continued for some time.

In response to the US forward movement, the Japanese placed road blocks along the main axes of advance to delay the Americans; finding their way towards the Piva River checked near the junction of the Numa Numa and East–West Trails, the US forces sought to remove the obstacles by force. On the morning of **20 November**, after the initial US attack was repulsed, the Japanese counterattacked attempting to outflank the Marine positions along the Numa Numa Trail.

The 2nd Battalion, 3rd Marine Regiment advanced across the west fork of the Piva River, to capture the Japanese positions between the two forks of the Piva River. A river crossing was made made by the engineers using a hastily constructed bridge of mahogany. Moving forward under light opposition from scattered snipers and several machine gun nests, the enemy outposts were discovered to have been abandoned and had been booby-trapped. The 2nd Battalion, 3rd Marine Regiment set up positions astride the East–West Trail between the two forks of the Piva River.

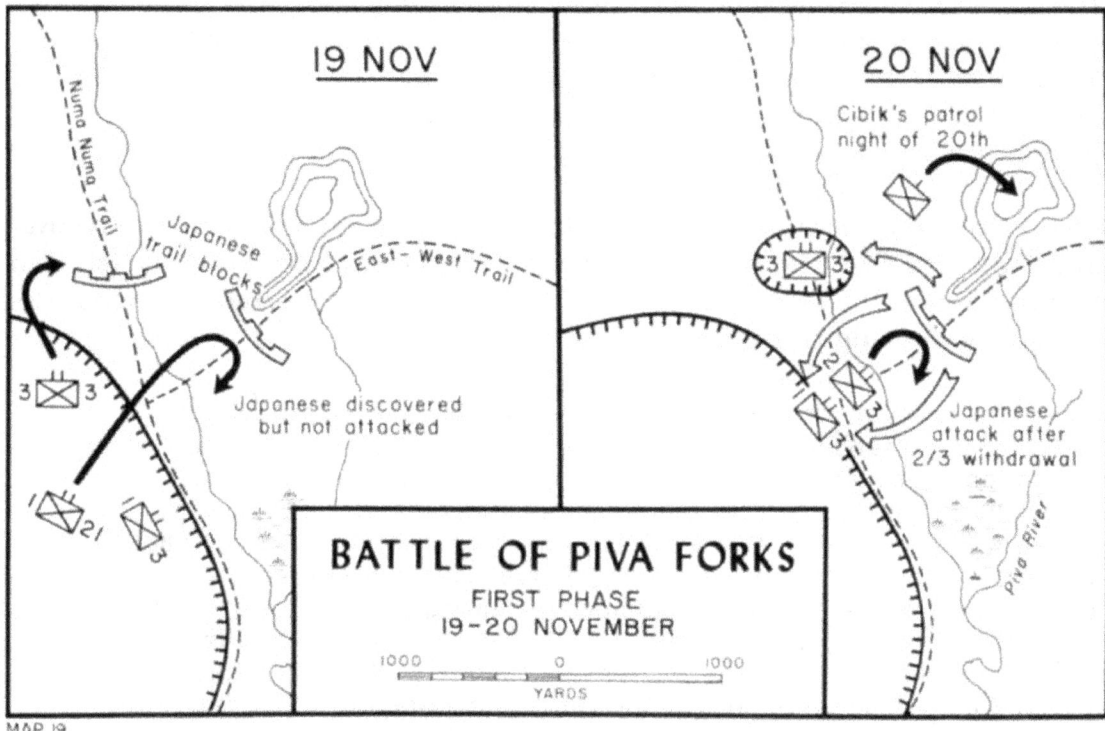

BATTLE OF PIVA FORKS
FIRST PHASE
19-20 NOVEMBER

On **19 November**, the 21st Marine Regiment took up blocking positions behind the 3rd Marine Regiment. **The 3d Marines were supported by the 9th, and 21st Marines, and the raiders, while the 37th Infantry Division provided road blocks, patrols, and flank security.** Support was also provided by the Army's heavy artillery, the 12th Marines, and the defense battalions. All the troops were now entering a new phase of the campaign, during which the fight would be more for the hills than for the trails.

One account makes clear the overwhelming difficulties facing the Marine battalions:

"water slimy and often waist deep, sometimes to the arm pits . . . tangles of thorny vines that inflicted painful wounds men slept setting up in the water . . . sultry heat and stinking muck."

After seizing that position, the next objective was a 400-foot ridge that commanded the whole area — and, in fact, provided a view all the way to Empress Augusta Bay. As the first high ground the Marines had found, it would clearly produce a valuable observation post for directing the artillery fire of the 12th Marines.

19 November 1943. Where the Army-Marine artillery barrages fell, however, there was desolation. Major Schmuck, a company commander in one of the assault battalions, later remembered: *"For 500 yards, the Marines moved in a macabre world of splintered trees and burned-out brush. The very earth was a churned mass of mud and human bodies. The filthy, stinking streams were cesspools of blasted corpses. Over all hung the stench of decaying flesh and powder and smoke which revolted [even] the toughest. The first line of strong points with their grisly occupants was overrun and the 500-yard phase line was reached."*

19 & 20 Nov 1943 at the intersection of the East-West Trail and the Numa Numa Trail Dad's mortar squad, with the 37th Infantry Division, assisted in achieving and defending both of these Japanese blocks. Dad was wounded the first time during this fight.

This began a four-day epic battle, **20-23 November**. The Marines got to the top, realized the importance of the vantage point to the Japanese, dug in defensive positions, and got ready for the enemy counterattacks that were sure to come. The Japanese were not through. As the Marines moved forward a Nambu machine gun stuttered and the enemy artillery roared, raking the Marine line. A Japanese counterattack hit the Marines' left flank. **It was hand-to-hand and tree-to-tree.** One company alone suffered 50 casualties, including all its officers. Still the Marines drove forward, finally halting 1,150 yards from their jump-off point, where resistance suddenly ended. The *Japanese 23d Infantry* had been totally destroyed, with 1,107 men dead on the field. The Marines had incurred 115 dead and wounded. The battle for Piva Forks had ended with a dramatic, hard fought victory which had "broken the back of organized enemy resistance".

Late in the afternoon of **20 November**, a small, 400 ft (120 m) high ridge was discovered that would provide observation of the entire Empress Augusta Bay area and dominated the East–West Trail and the Piva Forks area. A platoon—under the command of First Lieutenant Steve J. Cibik—was ordered to occupy the ridge with detachments of signals and a section of heavy machine guns. The trek began with a struggle up the steep ridge late in the afternoon, with signal wire being reeled out as the platoon climbed the ridge. Reaching the summit just before sunset, they set about establishing defensive positions, with machine guns sited along likely avenues of attack.

With daybreak on **21 November**, it was discovered that the crest of the ridge was a Japanese outpost position, used during the day as an observation post and abandoned at night. Approaching Japanese soldiers who were preparing to take up positions were fired upon and they withdrew and fled down the hill. The enemy having regrouped and having been reinforced launched numerous attacks against Cibik's platoon, which itself had been reinforced by more machine guns and mortars and was able to hold onto the crest despite fanatical attempts by the Japanese to reoccupy the position.

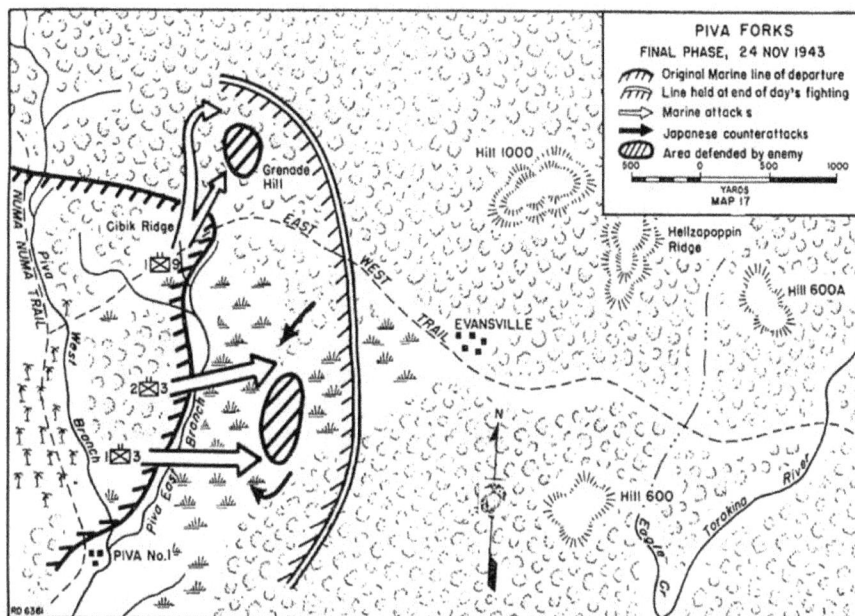

PIVA FORKS
FINAL PHASE, 24 NOV 1943

There were "fanatical attempts by the Japanese to reoccupy the position" in the form of "wild charges that sometimes carried the Japanese to within a few feet of their foxholes on the crest of the ridge." The Marines were ready, machine guns in place. *One of them killed 74 out of 75 of the enemy attackers within 20-30 yards of the gun.* By **26 November** the battle had subsided following the capture of a knoll overlooking the East–West Trail by US forces. The **18–25 November** Battle of Piva Forks effectively wiped out an entire Japanese infantry regiment.

The US Marines overcame this and continued their advance towards two forks in the Piva River. By **26 November** the battle had subsided following the capture of a knoll overlooking the East–West Trail by US forces. This represented the last of the significant features west of the Torokina and the conclusion of the battle marked a temporary end to significant Japanese opposition to the US beachhead around Torokina.

After the initial US attack was repulsed, the Japanese counterattacked before the US Marines overcame this and continued their advance towards two forks in the Piva River. By **26 November** the battle had subsided following the capture of a knoll overlooking the East–West Trail by US forces. This represented the last of the significant features west of the Torokina and the conclusion of the battle marked a temporary end to significant Japanese opposition to the US beachhead around Torokina.

The last major battle for the Marines on Bougainville was the engagement at "Hellzapoppin Ridge," where some of the toughest fighting of the first battle of

Bougainville occurred. The Japanese were dug in on the steep slopes and crest of the ridge. After the discovery of the Japanese positions, it was found that the only way to dislodge the enemy was by a frontal assault. Between **12 and 18 December** the Marines, primarily the 21st Marines, struggled to gain the ridge. Time and again they would get a foothold, only to be forced to abandon it a little later. After a series of air strikes on the last day of the battle, the Marines were able to reach the crest. Over 200 of the defenders had died by the time struggle ended.

Within the Allied horseshoe perimeter is Piva Uncle Airfield to be used for bombers and Piva Yoke Airfield was to be used for fighter aircraft. The Torokina Airfield along the coast was for fighter aircraft. **15 December 1943 the** Allied perimeter line of defense was complete. **The 129ᵗʰ Infantry Regiment is on the left side of this perimeter and Dad's 37ᵗʰ Infantry Division is on the center line passed the Piva Yoke and either side of Lake Kathleen on the end of the center line.** See map below for the airfields location.

Toward the end of December Allied forces advance to the east moving from the Numa Numa Trail following the East-West Trail. Army units began replacing Marine Corps personnel and shortly after the first of the New Year most Marines were redeployed elsewhere. Their mission was completed; a precious beachhead had been secured on which American naval and air bases were rapidly being constructed. The price paid by the Marine Corps for the seizure of the Bougainville base sites was 732 killed and 1,259 wounded. The valor and courage displayed by the Marines demonstrated by the fact that three Marines received the Medal of Honor: Private First-Class Henry Gurke, Sergeant Robert A. Owens, and Sergeant Herbert J. Thomas; all posthumously.

On the Defensive at Bougainville

Throughout the campaign for the Northern Solomons, the Marine Corps took part in every action, either through the presence of Marine units or by exercise of landing force command. However, many of the troops involved at one time or another came from the U.S. Army or from the Imperial Forces of New Zealand. Because of this thread of continuity, it seems appropriate that the entire campaign, diverse and long as it was, be treated as an entity. However, it is more correct that the Army should recount the story of the repulse of the major Japanese counteroffensive on Bougainville in the spring of 1944. The U.S. Army exercised command and furnished the XIV Corps which fought so gallantly and bore the brunt of the action in the decisive defeat of the Japanese forces seeking to eliminate the beachhead established by the I Marine Amphibious Corps.

It was obvious that the Japanese had assumed–and hoped–that the American troops would go after them in the jungle terrain, where the Japanese could inflict heavy casualties on the Americans as they hacked their way, yard by yard, through those jungles. By **March 1944**, the Japanese realized that the Americans were going to sit this one out, manning defensive lines. If they wanted to kill their enemy and, most important, take out the vital airfield, the Japanese would have to attack head-on.

XIV Corps Defenses

At the beginning of March, the XIV Corps' perimeter was somewhat larger than it had been when Griswold took over. It included, in a horseshoe-shaped line on the inland side, some 23,000 yards (13 miles) of low hills and jungle. The beach frontage totaled 11,000 yards (6 miles). Depth of the position was about 8,000 yards (4 1/2 miles). **The main ground combat elements of the corps were the American and 37th Divisions, which numbered about 27,000 men.** All together, 62,000 men, including naval units, were attached or assigned to the XIV Corps.

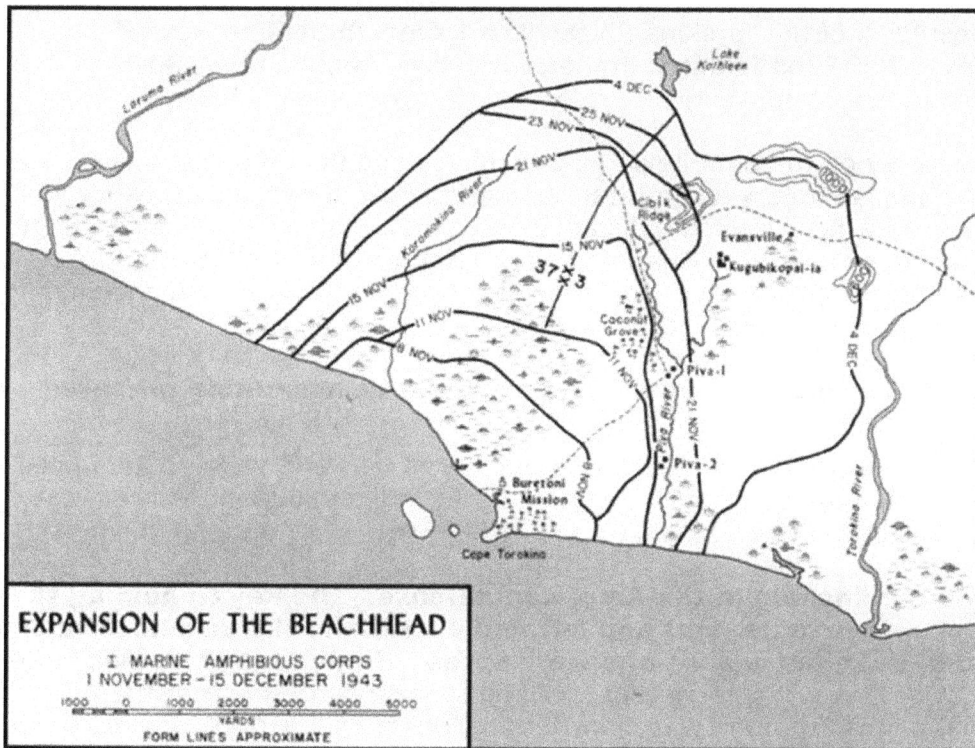

EXPANSION OF THE BEACHHEAD

I MARINE AMPHIBIOUS CORPS
I NOVEMBER – 15 DECEMBER 1943

FORM LINES APPROXIMATE

Map showing lines of expansion dates of Nov 8 11 15 21 23 25 and Dec 4.

All the infantry regiments were placed on the front lines. A total of twelve rifle battalions held frontages varying from 2,000 to 2,400 yards. Usually each regiment held one battalion in reserve.

The 37th Division defended the left (northwest) sector from a point on the beach 5,500 yards (3 miles) northwest of Cape Torokina to the area of Hill 700, about 2,000 yards east of Lake Kathleen. The 148th Infantry, on the division left, and the 129th Infantry, in the center, held low ground. Lake Kathleen is a caldera in the volcanic mountaintop just west of hill 700.

The sector of the 145th, now commanded by Col. Cecil B. Whitcomb, extended from low ground in the vicinity of the Numa Numa Trail eastward past the south shore of Lake Kathleen and up along the military crest of Hill 700, a frontage of about 3,500 yards. The 3d Battalion, on the left (west), held the low ground just south of Lake Kathleen and Cannon Hill, an eminence slightly lower and to the west of Hill 700. **On the right the 2d Battalion held Hill 700 with two rifle companies (E and G) and machine gun sections of H Company in line, F Company in reserve, and H Company's 81-mm. mortars grouped on the reverse (south) slope.**

The Americal Division's line ran from just east of Hill 700, where the 164th Infantry's left flank tied in with the 145th's right, over Hills 608, 309, and 270, then along the west bank of the Torokina River. Near its mouth the line crossed over to the east bank. The 182nd Infantry, in the division's center, held Hills 309 and 270 on the main perimeter line.

The 132nd Infantry on the right held low ground. In addition, a detachment of the 182nd Infantry, plus artillery and mortar observers, maintained an outpost on Hill 260, an eminence which was some distance east of the main line of resistance and overlooked the Torokina River. Griswold had ordered this hill held so that it could be used as an American artillery and mortar observation post, and so that the enemy could not use it to observe American positions.

Unlike at New Georgia, now the Japanese would be assaulting prepared defenses.

The American perimeter was dotted with a number of hills and valleys. The famed Hill 700 was right in the center of the perimeter, towering above the entire area with a clear view of the airfield.

Hill 700 was the linchpin of the American defenses, the key to holding the perimeter positions to its right and left and eventually the airfield. The 3rd Marine and 37th Infantry divisions were spread thinly along this two-mile perimeter, with forces in reserve that could be sent forward wherever the Japanese might break through. Patrols were sent out to find and fix Japanese troop concentrations. A few prisoners were taken, and several quickly confessed that the Japanese command had finally understood the U.S. defensive concept and tactical plan with Hill 700 as its heart.

All units had been developing and strengthening positions on the main line of resistance, which now consisted of rifle pits and earth, log, and sandbag pillboxes, with minefields. Various devices were employed to give illumination at night: searchlights, either shining directly or reflecting a spread beam off clouds; flares tied in trees and set off by pull wires; flashlights; thermite grenades; and cans full

242

of sand and gasoline. Grenades, with wires attached, were set up as booby traps along obvious approach routes. Oil drums, each with scrap metal packed around a **Bangalore torpedo** (*an explosive charge placed within one or several connected tubes*), were wired for electrical detonation. Fields of fire fifty yards or more, deep enough to prevent the enemy from throwing hand grenades at the American positions from cover and concealment, had been cleared. Almost all the infantry regiments possessed extra machine guns and had issued two BARs to each rifle squad.

All regiments had constructed reserve positions. The naval construction battalions, the 3rd Marine Defense Battalion, Army engineer units, and others maintained provisional infantry units as part of the corps reserve, which also included the 82nd Chemical Battalion, the 754th Tank Battalion, and the 1st Battalion, 24th Infantry.

Beyond the coastal plain the ground rises abruptly from ridge to ridge, each higher than the preceding one, up to the summits of the Crown Prince Range. The Americans on Hills 608 and 700 held positions that were dominated by the higher ground in Japanese hands—Blue Ridge, three thousand yards north of Hill 700, and Hills 1000 and 1111, just southeast of Blue Ridge. These hills gave the enemy an excellent view over all the perimeter except the reverse slopes of the American-held hills.

In **March 1944**, some 16,000 Japanese who had been waiting for the Americans to strike at Buin, on the other side of the island, trekked through the jungle and struck in full fury, making 8 major attacks. The enemy assault consisted mainly of the infamous *6th Division*, perpetrators of the rape of Nanking.

At 0600 on March 8, the inevitable massive Japanese attack began and it did not wane until March 13 when Hill 700, which had been partially overrun by the Japanese, was retaken by 37th Division forces, who annihilated thousands of Japanese in the recapture phase.

The American beachhead was on a coastal plain lying at the foot of the towering Crown Prince Range, volcanic mountains held by the Japanese. The enemy also occupied the rest of Bougainville–giving them a white elephant compared to the Americans' potent mouse. The two American divisions could not spread their perimeter beyond the nearest foothills overlooking the beachhead. The best they could do was to hang on to the lesser heights that dominated the airfield and to deny those hills to enemy artillery.

Hostile fire was coming from Japanese positions on Blue Ridge, Hills 1001, 1111, 500 and 501 and the Saua River valley. Fire from only a few pieces could hit the airfield from those positions, but those meager rounds hinted at the Japanese destructive potential if they could place their cannon on the hills that the 37th Division defended, mainly Hill 700.

Shells continued to fall–not only on the airstrip but also on the 145th, the 6th Field Artillery Battalion, the 54th Coast Artillery Battalion, and the 77th and 36th Seabees. Casualties were light, but the Americans were tense. The inaccuracy of the Japanese fire made even the least strategic American installation subject to those wild haymakers. Helmeted repairmen kept the airstrip in operation, filling up holes and smoothing out shell craters. Planes landed and took off with casual disdain. A few planes were destroyed, however, and the possibility of declaring the bomber strip off-limits was seriously considered.

The defense of the hill was committed to the 145th Infantry. The point of the attack was within the sector of the 2nd Battalion, but the whole regiment was eventually engaged in the fight, with the entire division behind it in support. The artillery of the 37th Division and of the entire corps area had been placed so that it could be used in support of an action on any part of the perimeter. The Reconnaissance Troop took a place in the line. The 117th Engineers laid aside their picks and shovels and, taking up rifles, took the place of infantry. The 2nd Battalion of the 148th Infantry made the counterattack that cleaned off the ridge. Quartermaster troops, ordnance men and medics brought up supplies and ammunition and carried away the wounded. The MPs patrolled the roads and fought off the souvenir hunters. The straggler line was used not to keep the front troops from coming back but to keep the sightseers from going forward. The game was over.

Of the eight Japanese major attacks, 4 were assaults on the 37th Division. These included the **8 March 1944** attack on Hill 700, the "Hill of Heroes", where the battle raged in an area no more than 100 yards long and 50 yards wide and where an attack was driven into the lines of the 145th Infantry Regiment. This attack wasn't reduced until **13 March 1944**. A main attack occurred on **11 March 1944** toward Piva Airfield which hit the 129th Infantry Regiment**. A 23 March 1944 general attack penetrated the 37th's lines before it was defeated.**

The American troops were also supported by air and naval units. The US Navy force assigned to the island comprised the six destroyers of Destroyer Squadron 22, a squadron of PT boats, a small number of Landing Craft Infantry fitted as gunboats and several armed landing craft. The air units on Bougainville (designated AirSols) had 64 SBD Dauntless dive bombers and 32 TBF Avenger torpedo bombers available for ground support tasks.

From the advance bases on Bougainville, American forces disrupted the vital Japanese lines of sea and air communications in the Southwest Pacific. As a result, thousands of Japanese troops were cut off from their sources of supplies. By early 1944, the enemy's offensive capability in this area of the Pacific had been effectively neutralized, thus enabling American forces to advance along the northern coast of New Guinea and into the Philippines. The seizure of potential base sites on Bougainville by the Marines had assured other American troops of easier going in the Pacific war.

✦ ✦ ✦ ✦

SBD Dauntless dive bombers

The SBD ("Scout Bomber Douglas") was the United States Navy's main carrier-borne scout plane and dive bomber from mid-1940 through mid-1944. The SBD was also flown by the United States Marine Corps, both from land air bases and aircraft carriers. The SBD is best remembered as the bomber that delivered the fatal blows to the Japanese carriers at the Battle of Midway in **June 1942**. The type earned its nickname "Slow, But Deadly" (with the SBD initials) during this period. It possessed long range, good handling characteristics, maneuverability, potent bomb load, great diving characteristics, good defensive armament and ruggedness.

TBF Avenger torpedo bombers

The Avenger entered U.S. service in 1942, and first saw action during the Battle of Midway. Despite the loss of five of the six Avengers on its combat debut, it survived in service to become one of the outstanding torpedo bombers of World War II.

There were three crew members: pilot, turret gunner and combined radioman/bombardier/ventral gunner. One .30 caliber machine gun was mounted in the nose, a .50 caliber (12.7 mm) gun was mounted right next to the turret gunner's head in a rear-facing electrically powered turret, and a single .30 caliber hand-fired machine gun mounted ventrally (under the tail), which was used to defend against enemy fighters attacking from below and to the rear. This gun was fired by the radioman/bombardier while standing up and bending over in the belly of the tail section, though he usually sat on a folding bench facing forward to operate the radio and to sight in bombing runs. Grumman designed the Avenger to also use the new Sto-Wing patented "compound angle" wing-folding mechanism, intended to maximize storage space on an aircraft carrier. The Avenger had a large bomb bay, allowing for one Bliss-Leavitt Mark 13 torpedo, a single 2,000 pound (907 kg) bomb, or up to four 500 pound (227 kg) bombs.

The innovative wing folding mechanism (STO-Wing), developed by Leroy Grumman in early 1941 and first applied to the XF4F-4 Wildcat, manufactured by the Grumman Aircraft Engineering Corporation, is designated an ASME Historic Mechanical Engineering Landmark. The STO-Wing was applied to the Wildcat, the Hellcat and the TBF Avenger. The Grumman folding wing is still in use today, notably on the larger carrier-based aircraft built by Grumman.

✦ ✦ ✦ ✦

The Japanese Plan of Attack

Preparations for the counterattack were made during the first months of **1944**. As the bulk of the 17th Army was stationed in northern and southern Bougainville, engineers needed to develop roads and bridges to allow the troops to move to the hills inland from the American perimeter. All of the units selected for the offensive had departed their bases by mid-February, and advanced along the eastern and western coasts of the island.

General Hyakutake organized most of his infantry into three forces, each named for its commander. The **Iwasa Unit** assembled behind Hill 1111, the **Magata Unit** behind Mount Nampei, a shoulder-shaped ridge extending outward from the Crown Prince Range just northwest of Blue Ridge. The **Muda Unit** assembled at Peko, a village on the East-West Trail about 5,400 yards east-northeast of Hill 260. The artillery group was placed in the vicinity of Hill 600.

The plan of maneuver involved two thrusts from the north coupled with an attack from the northeast, all on a complicated schedule. Briefly, the *Iwasa Unit* was to attack and secure Hill 700 on Y Day (set, after some delays in moving into position, for **8 March**), reorganize on **9 and 10 March**, and advance to the Piva airfields.

During this period the *Muda Unit* was to capture Hills 260 and 309, whereupon it and one battalion of the *Iwasa Unit* were supposed to attack Hill 608 from the southeast and northwest on **12 March**.

All these attacks were preliminary to an effort which was to be delivered, starting 11 March, by the *Magata Unit* against the 129th Infantry in its low ground west of Hill 700. Magata's men, after cracking the 129th's line, were to advance against the Piva airstrips in conjunction with Iwasa's advance. Then all units were to drive southward on a broad front to capture the Torokina fighter strip by 17 March. Haste was essential, since the *17th Army* had brought with it but two weeks' rations. Hindsight indicates that the Japanese plan was unsound.

✦ ✦ ✦ ✦

By **8 March** almost everything was ready. The rhetorical manifestoes by which Japanese officers exhorted their troops were issued. *General Hyakutake* expressed himself along these lines:

"The time has come to manifest our knighthood with the pure brilliance of the sword. It is our duty to erase the mortification of our brothers at Guadalcanal.

Attack! Assault! Destroy everything! Cut, slash, and mow them down. May the color of the red emblem of our arms be deepened with the blood of the American rascals. Our cry of victory at Torokina Bay will be shouted resoundingly to our native land.

We are invincible! Always attack. Security is the greatest enemy. Always be alert. Execute silently."

Not to be outdone, *General Kanda* had this to say:

"We must fight to the end to avenge the shame of our country's humiliation on GUADALCANAL. There can be no rest until our bastard foes are battered and bowed in shame. Till their blood adds luster to the badge of the Sixth Division. Our battle cry will be heard afar."

Again, the most apt comment is in **Proverbs XVI: 18**. *Pride goes before destruction, a haughty spirit before a fall.*

Allied strategy

In early **June 1943**, the Joint Chiefs of Staff completed a survey, which concluded a direct invasion of New Britain would be too costly. Rabaul should be neutralized instead. The next month, General George C. Marshall, the US Army Chief of Staff, communicated to MacArthur that with the Southwest Pacific Area Commander capturing Wewak on the northeast New Guinea coast and Manus in the Admiralty Islands Group along with Admiral William F. "Bull" Halsey's South Pacific Force's eventual seizure of Kavieng on New Ireland to the north of Rabaul he believed that Rabaul could be encircled and effectively neutralized using US airpower.

Allied planners at the Quebec Conference of the Combined Chiefs of Staff in **August 1943** formalized the strategy codenamed **Operation Cartwheel** to neutralize Rabaul. A large part in the success of the War in the Pacific was the flexibility of the Allied planners in their strategy to eventually end up on the island of Japan. Planning a lot of times would be done 'on the fly' due to local intelligence gathering, another important part of the flexibility of battle.

Admiral Halsey and his South Pacific Force staff's strategic outlook and tactical planning had to evolve to establish a beachhead on Bougainville without a bloodbath. Largely due to the combat exhaustion of the US Army's 25th Infantry Division on New Georgia and the commitment of the 2nd Marine Division to Nimitz's Central Pacific offensive. **Halsey's South Pacific Force was left with only the**

3rd Marine Division and the 37th Infantry Division, the latter largely an Ohio National Guard unit that had also seen action on New Georgia.

The 37th Infantry Division had been made a part of the XIV Corps, US Army, in July 1943, and as such had participated in the seizure and final conquest of the New Georgia Group, in conjunction with the Marine Raider Regiment, 9th Marine Defense Battalion, 2nd Marine Air Wing, and other Army troops. By late summer island after island had been occupied, Kolombangara had been by-passed and Japanese troops on Vella Lavella had been rendered impotent. In September 1943 the 37th Division was attached to Task Force 31, and by command of Rear Admiral Theodore S. Wilkinson (CTF-31) was later attached in November to IMAC (I Marine Amphibious Corps).

The American perimeter was dotted with a number of hills and valleys. The famed Hill 700 was right in the center of the perimeter, towering above the entire area with a clear view of the airfield. Hill 700 was the linchpin of the American defenses, the key to holding the perimeter positions to its right and left and eventually the airfield. The 3rd Marine and 37th Infantry divisions were spread thinly along this two-mile perimeter, with forces in reserve that could be sent forward wherever the Japanese might break through.

*The battle at Hill 700 was the first defensive action of the **37th Division** and the 3rd Marine Division as part of General Griswold's XIV Corps. Heretofore the division had been on the offensive. Its mission on Bougainville had been to set up a perimeter and defend the airfield.* Japanese capture of the hill would have imperiled the whole installation at Empress Augusta Bay.

Imagine having hundreds of Japanese charging uphill and stepping on their dead comrade's bodies trying to overtake these defenses. Mortars, Grenades, Bangalore torpedo's, M1's, and Browning Automatic rifles (BAR's) were used to slow down and eventually stop the enemy. Pillboxes were just 5-10 feet apart along the line of defense and around the various hills. This arrangement allowed for firing cover for each pillbox and a means of communication.

✦   ✦   ✦   ✦

Browning Automatic Rifle (BAR)

30-caliber, gas operated, automatic, 20 round detachable box-magazine
Effective firing range 100-1500 yards with sight adjustments.

M1 Garand Rifle (M1)

30-caliber, gas operated, semi-automatic, 15 or 30 round detachable box magazine Effective firing range 300 yards. Dad said he carried an M1.

The M1 and BAR are designed for two very different purposes. The M1 is simply an individual weapon that for its time was fairly advanced, particularly given its wide distribution. The BAR was designed as a squad support weapon having more fire-power being capable of automatic fire and having a much larger magazine.

✦ ✦ ✦ ✦

The following is an excerpt from the article Dad brought back from his units' Chicago Reunion. The name of the article is **"The Second Battle of Bougainville"**.

The Japanese forces were the Seventeenth Army, of which the major element was the 6th Division-a regular outfit known for its infamous role in the Rape of Nanking in 1937. It was augmented by the usual complement of service and special troops. The soldiers of the 6th division wore patches on their left sleeves, awarded in "recognition" for their record in the Chinese war.

They were well equipped, sturdy, determined, and healthy. They went into battle carrying an exhortation from their Army commander who proclaimed:

"The time has come to manifest our knighthood with the pure brilliance of the sharp sword. It is our duty to erase the mortification of our brothers at Guadalcanal. Attack, assault, and destroy everything. Cut, slash, and mow them down. May the color of the red emblem of memory on our arms be deepened with blood of the American rascals. Our cry of victory at Torakina Bay will be shouted resoundingly to our native land. We are invincible. Always attack. Security is the greatest enemy. Always be alert. Execute silently. Always be clear."

✦ ✦ ✦ ✦

Second Battle of Bougainville

8 March to 25 March, 1944

For the next two months Nov – Dec 1943, as the marines expanded their beachhead, the Japanese continued to believe that the main assault on Bougainville would come elsewhere. By **March 1944** the Japanese had realized their error and assembled a counterattack force. This force, some 15,000 to 19,000 strong, moved across the mountains to attack what Japanese intelligence had reported to be 30,000 Americans and their airfields within the beachhead.

The movement of Japanese troops and supplies from all over Bougainville toward Empress Augusta Bay had been detected, however, and attack plans learned from decrypted Japanese Army messages and captured documents. Papers taken from the bodies of Japanese soldiers killed in previous fighting also allowed the Allies to build up an accurate appreciation of the Japanese plan of attack as well as the order of battle of the forces involved. Intelligence information detailing the Japanese plans was then distributed to American soldiers holding the perimeter through various means, including notices posted on unit bulletin boards. There would be no surprise.

The Japanese plan called for two simultaneous preliminary attacks followed three days later by a major thrust. The attacks along the horseshoe-shaped perimeter were aimed at the middle (Hill 700), and at both points where the horseshoe's legs began to curve (low-lying creeks in the west, Hill 260 on the east side). The Japanese enjoyed possession of high ground beyond the perimeter, which permitted them to see American positions, but their wildly optimistic plans (one document specified the location on which General Griswold would surrender to the Japanese) negated any advantage. Overall, the Japanese plan called for dispersed and unsupported attacks and was governed by an unrealistic timetable and operational plan.

By this time, however, General Griswold's XIV Corps manned the perimeter. **With a strength of approximately 62,000 men, including the Americal (General Hodge) and 37th Divisions (Maj. Gen. Robert S. Beightler), XIV Corps was a powerful force.** While Griswold did not have as many troops as he might have wished to defend his 23,000-yard perimeter (13 mile- half circle), he refused to abandon tactically important pieces of high ground to shorten the line. Remembering the lessons learned at Munda on New Georgia, General Griswold was content to let the Japanese come to him.

American manpower, combined with extensive defensive preparations and strong fire support, made the Japanese task almost hopeless. Unlike at New Georgia, now the Japanese would be assaulting prepared defenses. Attacking units would confront booby traps, illumination devices, and minefields, then concertina wire shielding rifle pits and pillboxes. In the latter were rifle squads with more than the usual number of automatic rifles and probably extra machine guns. Fields of fire fifty or more yards deep had been cleared to prevent the enemy from sneaking within hand-grenade range. Searchlights as well as oil drums-each containing a Bangalore torpedo surrounded with scrap metal-provided additional obstacles for an attacker.

Perhaps most important, the line was manned by six veteran U.S. Army infantry regiments.

Stanley Frankel, the US Army's 37th Infantry Division historian, wrote about the Japanese counteroffensive against the US Army's XIV Corps perimeter at Cape Torokina on Bougainville in March 1944.

"The curtain was about to rise on one of the bloodiest, most fanatical Banzai attacks made by the Japanese in the South Pacific War… against a civilian army of battling clerks, farmers, mechanics, school-boys, business men."

✦ ✦ ✦ ✦

The goal of the offensive was to completely destroy the Allied beachhead, with the Japanese wrongly believing that their forces were approximately as large as the combat units deployed to defend the Allied positions. The Allies detected the Japanese preparations for the attack shortly after they began in early 1944 and strengthened the perimeter's defenses. None of the three Japanese forces **(Iwasa, Muda & Magata)** which conducted the attack were able to penetrate far into the Allied perimeter, though there was intense fighting for several positions.

The Bougainville terrain is covered by trees, thick undergrowth, deep and steep ravines with lots of water. In setting up a defensive position there had to be sufficient shooting lanes. Supply routes had to be made to have easier access to the front lines. These areas were cleared using bulldozers clearing underbrush in dense jungle growth and preparing the airfields.

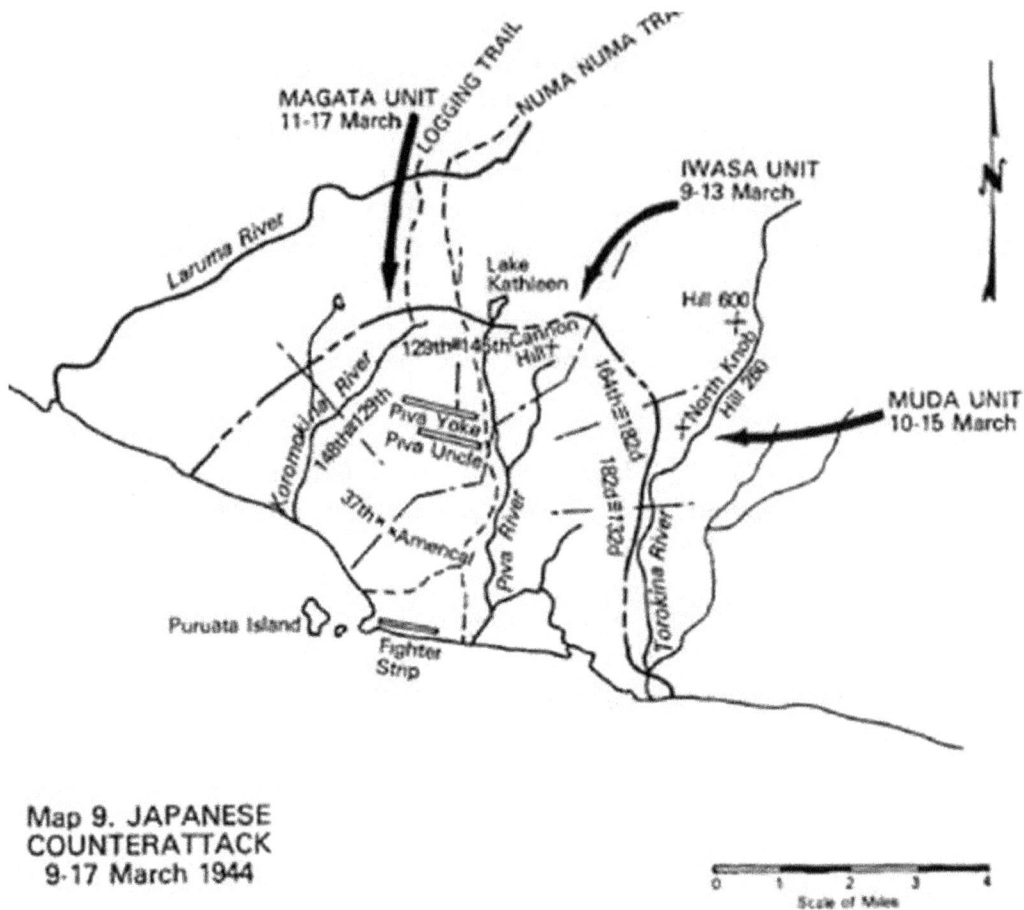

Map 9. JAPANESE
COUNTERATTACK
9-17 March 1944

Hill 700

The American perimeter was dotted with a number of hills and valleys. The famed Hill 700 was right in the center of the perimeter, towering above the entire area with a clear view of the airfield. Hill 700, the first Japanese target, was a commanding position with **65 to 75-degree slopes** in all directions situated at the eastern end of the 145th Infantry's sector. American intelligence estimates, though not ruling out an enemy attack here, had tended to discount its probability. The steepness that increased the difficulty of attack also complicated the defense, for the forward (north) slope fell away too sharply to permit it to be completely covered with grazing fire. The sector stretched 3,500 yards west past the southern shore of

Lake Kathleen and ended in low ground near the intersection of a major inland trail with the American perimeter.

Magata Force

Near midnight during the night of **8-9 March**, two Japanese companies attacked a platoon position on the northern slope of Hill 700. They were repulsed before they could reach the saddle between the hill's eastern and western high points. A few hours later an entire Japanese infantry regiment attacked the same position in columns of battalions. Artillery fire caught the third battalion in the open and decimated it, but the attackers seized the saddle, establishing mortar and machine-gun positions. From here on **9 March** they were able to interdict the sector's major supply road, forcing the Americans to hand-carry supplies and hand-evacuate casualties.

Hostile fire was coming from Japanese positions on Blue Ridge, Hills 1001, 1111, 500 and 501 and the Saua River valley. Fire from only a few pieces could hit the airfield from those positions, but those meager rounds hinted at the Japanese destructive potential if they could place their cannon on the hills that the 37th Division defended, mainly Hill 700. Short-range patrols discovered that the enemy was assembling in front of the 2nd Battalion, and it was thought that the major attack would be against Hill 700.

The attacks along the horseshoe-shaped perimeter were aimed at the middle (Hill 700), and at both points where the horseshoe's legs began to curve (low-lying creeks in the west, Hill 260 on the east side). The Japanese enjoyed possession of high ground beyond the perimeter, which permitted them to see American positions, but their wildly optimistic plans (one document specified the location on which General Griswold would surrender to the Japanese) negated any advantage. Overall, the Japanese plan called for dispersed and unsupported attacks and was governed by an unrealistic timetable and operational plan. The 129th and 148th infantry sectors had been relatively quiet, although patrols invariably ran into enemy squads and platoons.

The sector of the 37th Division's 129th Infantry, where *Colonel Magata* de-livered his attack, was generally flat and low. In contrast with the *Iwasa Unit,* which assaulted up very steep slopes, Magata's soldiers possessed easy routes of approach along Numa Numa Trail and various streams. The 129th, in the center of the 37th Division's line, held about 3,900 yards of curving front from a point slightly east of the Numa Numa Trail west and

southwest to the right flank of the 148th Infantry. **Several small streams, all tributaries of the Koromokina River, flowed through the area in a generally southerly direction. Taylor Creek cut through the 129th's lines less than 1,000 yards west of the Numa Numa Trail. Cox Creek entered the line about 750 yards southwest of Taylor Creek's penetration.** The Logging Trail, cut and used extensively by XIV Corps engineers in the relatively peaceful days before March, entered the main perimeter just west of Taylor Creek.

The 129th Infantry, commanded by Col. John D. Frederick, held its front with two battalions in line. The 2nd Battalion, on the right, faced north, its left (west) flank joined to the right of the 3rd Battalion between Cox Creek and another branch of the Koromokina River.

In general, the 129th's positions were stronger than the 145th's since the terrain permitted grazing fire except in the numerous ravines and gullies that were scattered throughout the area.

The Japanese plan called for two simultaneous preliminary attacks, *Iwasa and Muda forces*, followed three days later by a major thrust, The *Magata force.*

Earth-and-log-pillboxes, mutually supporting and arranged in depth, formed the backbone of the main line of resistance, which was wired in behind single barbed wire and double-apron barbed wire fences. Antipersonnel mines had been laid in front of the wire. The entire front was covered by interlocking bands of machine gun fire. Additional rows of double-apron barbed wire extended diagonally from the main line of resistance to channel Japanese attacks into the machine gun fire lanes. In addition to division artillery, mortars, and the 75-mm. pack howitzers of the 129th's Cannon Company, the front was supported by 37-mm. antitank guns (firing canister) and 40-mm. antiaircraft guns.

The 2nd Battalion, under Lt. Col. Preston J. Hundley, had in line three rifle companies, F, G, and E from left to right. Cox Creek lay in F Company's sector, the Logging Trail and Taylor Creek in G's, and the Numa Numa Trail in E's.

At noon March 8 the last patrol was reported in by the 145th, and the combined guns of the 135th Field Artillery, the 6th Field Artillery, the 140th Field Artillery, the 136th Field Artillery, and two battalions of the Americal Division artillery were readied for area fire on the Japanese as they moved from assembly areas behind Hills 1111 and 1000 toward the American lines. The Japanese *3rd Battalion, 23rd Infantry*, and the *13th Infantry* (less one battalion) crowded toward Hill 700 to join the *2nd Battalion, 23rd Infantry*, which had filtered in earlier. For two hours, thousands of rounds of American medium and heavy artillery blanketed the target zone. Later, a prisoner admitted that the Japanese *3rd Battalion, 23rd Infantry,* was practically annihilated during this bombardment; he said the rest of the troops escaped a similar fate by moving close enough to American lines to get within that umbrella of safety. Anticipating this ruse, U.S. artillery observers had called for fire closer and closer to the 37th's front lines. **Dad is in this area with the 37th Infantry Division.**

Still, the enemy was in an excellent position. Once the Japanese closed in on the Americans, it was difficult for the U.S. artillery to reach an enemy hiding literally under the front lines. Mortars pounded away in the dark with unobserved results. The 136th Field Artillery alone expended 1,239 rounds that day. Those manning the observation posts yelled back that the enemy was scrambling up the hill after the artillery had subsided. Several booby traps and warning devices were exploded near the positions of Companies E and G, 145th Infantry, and the men in the perimeter holes replied with small arms and mortars. The enemy retaliated with rifles and knee mortars. Fog and rain made the darkness impenetrable.

During that night attack, a device cooked up by Staff Sgt. Otis Hawkins proved invaluable. As soon as the first Japanese started jimmying the barbed wire on the perimeter, Hawkins ordered mortar flares fired and wires pulled, setting off gallon buckets of oil ignited by phosphorus grenades. With help from this artificial lighting, Hawkins directed 600 rounds of 60mm mortar fire, and the riflemen picked off many Japanese who had counted on darkness and confusion to help them achieve their goal.

The Japanese assaulted an isolated mortar observation post from Company E, situated on a knoll on the outer perimeter and affectionately dubbed 'Company E Nose.' Holding fast, the hopelessly overwhelmed soldiers from the 2nd Battalion, 145th Infantry, lived or died where they stood. The enemy managed to cut three of the four double aprons of protecting wire before a sergeant, investigating the noise, crawled out of his pillbox and discovered them. Just as the Japanese placed a Bangalore torpedo under the fourth double apron, the sergeant opened up with his Browning Automatic Rifle (BAR) and caught eight Japanese in the wire. Holding off additional Japanese with his BAR, he called in a 60mm mortar concentration, adjusted it in and around the wire, ducked back to his pillbox and then had a steady concentration dropped around—and often behind—his pillbox during the night. The sergeant and his men survived. In a close by area, under cover of heavy rain and darkness, using Bangalore torpedoes and dynamite to blast holes in the wire, and pushing one full battalion directly at the forward U.S. emplacements, the Japanese had shoved their foot in the door.

At 5 p.m., March 9, the 1st and 2nd battalions, 145th Infantry attacked again, assuming that the Japanese resistance had been sufficiently softened. Using Bangalore torpedoes, bazookas and pole charges, the infantrymen strove for the enemy pillboxes on the crest of Hill 700. The main line of resistance was tenuously re-established with the exception of a 30- or 40-yard gap in the lines. Four pillboxes remained in Japanese possession.

By afternoon of **10 March**, this day on the Numa Numa Trail and ineffective action (which also featured enemy fire on McClelland Road and a 36-plane strike against Japanese positions), the American units in contact with the enemy had become intermingled. Sorting and reorganizing them consumed much of the afternoon, so that it was 1700 before elements of the 1st and 2d Battalions, 145th, after a ten-minute mortar preparation, delivered a coordinated attack. The Americans used Bangalore torpedoes, rocket launchers, and pole charges in the face of artillery, mortar, machine gun, and rifle fire. The fighting was close work; several pillboxes were recaptured and then lost. As darkness fell, however, the Americans had achieved some success. The Japanese penetration was now reduced by more than half. By 1930, G, F, A, C, B, and E Companies held the line; the 37th Reconnaissance Troop, which General Beightler attached to the 145th at 1815, was in reserve.

There was no shortage of firepower. The Japanese would also be on the receiving end of available American artillery, which consisted of 8 howitzer battalions (6 105-mm. and 2 155-mm.), 2 155-mm. gun batteries, and 8 90-mm. gun batteries, along with 6 cannon companies with 75-mm. pack howitzers that arrived in early March. Also available was the "Bougainville Navy," which included all destroyers assigned for fire support under Griswold's command, as well as plentiful air support.

✦ ✦ ✦ ✦

The following is an excerpt from an officer who was at this battle.

"The Jap 23rd Infantry would be on the front of the 145th. Then, the two punches were to meet on the Piva River. It is also interesting to note that we found that they had already issued the orders as to how to execute the officers of the corps, how they were to line them up even as to the names.

*They were to take the air strip at Piva and then to line the officers up and execute us. March the tenth was a particular day of emphasis for the Japs and this is the day they hit us on Hill 700. We had with us a battalion of chemical mortars 4.2 [inch]21 but we also had shrapnel of that caliber designed for that mortar. In that battalion there were **forty-eight mortars and on the night of the big attack— March the tenth—we fired those forty-eight mortars twenty rounds per minute for four hours.** The barrels were red hot but we knew we had to stop the Japs. I may say that the jungle is hard on ammunition. It was necessary for us to clean the ammunition. [For] this I used the natives do to so. But, on the tenth the*

Japs took Hill 400 and pushed in our main line of resistance. In, the zone of the 145th they were right on our main line. But, on the twelfth they had withdrawn back from the main line."

The night of March 10, as *Colonel Magata* prepared to deliver his attack against the 129th Infantry, *General Iwasa* sent the rest of his command against the 145th's front from Cannon Hill to the crest of 700. The Japanese came in closely packed waves, shouting, the 37th Division reported, imprecations (cursing) in Japanese. The fields of fire at Cannon Hill and Pat's Nose were better than at 700, and the 145th, heavily supported by artillery and mortars, handily repulsed *Iwasa* everywhere except on the saddle, where the Japanese captured one more pillbox. Brig. General Charles F. Craig, the assistant division commander, visited the regimental intelligence section, with two men who had joined him, had a brush with the enemy on top of Hill 700; his companions were bayoneted and evacuated to the battalion aid station. Returning alone to the site of the struggle, Orick slipped a noose of telephone wire over the foot of a Japanese officer killed in the struggle and then pulled him from the crest of the hill. On his body were found plans for the attack on the beachhead, with maps and directions. That information was rushed to the Division G-2 section. Japanese officers regularly had instructions, maps and directions on their body.

As dawn broke on **11 March**, a day on which *Muda* was active at Hill 260 and the *Magata Unit* began its attack against the 129th Infantry, General Beightler was obviously concerned over the 145th's failure to reduce the enemy salient.

In the meantime, the Japanese made valorous efforts to put more troops onto the saddle. The Americans resisted with vigor and with all the fire power at their disposal. Charging, literally, over the piled heaps of their dead comrades, the enemy soldiers fought hard but vainly, and failed either to budge the Americans or to strengthen the saddle.

Three 105-mm. howitzer battalions, the 145th Infantry Cannon Company, 4.2-inch chemical mortars, the 81-mm. mortars of D, H, and M Companies of the 145th, and the 60-mm. mortars of all the rifle companies of the 2d Battalion, 148th, fired a preparation from 1320 to 1330. Then elements of the 148th attacked. Two platoons from E Company moved east from Pat's Nose in an effort to envelop the saddle from north and south while a third platoon delivered a holding attack westward from the crest of Hill 700. The whole target was blanketed by artillery smoke shells. The 145th supported the attack with overhead fire. The platoon making the envelopment from the north gained the crest, losing eight dead, whereupon the platoon leader and four enlisted men seized a communication trench, then a pillbox. But the Japanese killed the five men and the attack halted about

1900. The troops dug in on the ground they had gained. During the night the Japanese harried the Americans but failed to penetrate the line.

During the early days of the *17th Army's* attack the 129th Infantry received mortar and artillery fire, engaged in fire fights and patrol clashes, and strengthened its positions, but was not heavily engaged in battle. But on **11 March** *Colonel Magata* moved forward from his assembly area behind Mount Nampei to begin the attack that was designed to pierce the 129th Infantry and capture the Piva airfields not far away. Outposts and patrols reported increasing numbers of Japanese troops in front of the 129th, and the artillery fired on them off and on all day.

When an antipersonnel mine in front of E Company was exploded about 1600, Colonel Frederick ordered in the outposts. Shortly afterward Japanese troops were reported advancing down the Logging Trail toward the perimeter. Starting at 1800, when all outposts and patrols had come in, division artillery and mortars laid a ten-minute concentration to the front of Colonel Hundley's battalion. A patrol from G Company went out to examine the impact area, now cleared of underbrush and foliage, but came under Japanese fire and returned to the perimeter to report that it had located no less than fourteen enemy machine guns.

Pictures Dad brought back of dead Japanese piled on top of each other as they assaulted hill 700 **March 11-15** using their dead comrades as stepping stones. Estimated 5,469 Japanese dead around the extended perimeter of hill 700 and as many as 8,000 Japanese dead in entire Jungle after shelling.

In the gathering dusk *Magata's* troops—the *1st Battalion, 45th Infantry,* on the left (east) and the *3rd Battalion* on the right—opened up on the 2nd Battalion, 129th, with machine guns and rifles. The Americans replied with rifles, mortars, machine guns, and a 40-mm. antiaircraft gun, which along with a .50-caliber machine gun put searching fire up the Logging Trail. Machine guns in the frontline pillboxes abstained from firing so as not to reveal their locations to the enemy. This fire fight continued until 1920, then died down to flare up sporadically throughout the night.

General Beightler, at 2100, ordered his regimental commanders to keep their troops alert, for documents captured that day (apparently on Hill 700) indicated that the Japanese planned to attack in strength the next day. At the same time, as Japanese soldiers began working their way through the American wire. C Company, 82nd Chemical Battalion, was attached to the 129th Infantry, and at 0420 the next morning **12 March,** its 2nd Platoon moved its 4.2-inch mortars into position behind the Antitank Company, 129th, which was supporting the rifle companies.

By dawn of **12 March**, though the Japanese had made earnest efforts to get through the lines, they found they had been held for very small gains. As the coming of daylight clarified the situation, the 2nd Battalion, 129th, found that the Japanese had succeeded in cutting through G Company's wire and effecting two minor penetrations. In the 2nd Platoon sector, where Taylor Creek and the Logging Trail entered the perimeter, the Japanese had captured two pillboxes (one an alternate, unoccupied position), and to the right (east) they had seized five pillboxes.

The Japanese tried to exploit their penetrations and break out to the south but were held back by American artillery, rocket launchers, mortar, machine gun, rifle fire, grenades, and flame throwers. Then the 129th prepared to counterattack and re-store the line. Colonel Frederick ordered C Company out of regimental reserve and forward to support G Company at 0723. By 0810, when C Company moved into position behind the 2nd Platoon of G Company, one platoon of the Antitank Compa-ny had attacked the western penetration and retaken one pillbox. During the rest of the morning another Antitank Company platoon moved in behind E Company; 81-mm. mortars of D Company, 129th, took up positions to support the 2nd Battal-ion; and B Company moved forward behind C.

At 1255, after a mortar concentration, three rifle platoons (two from C and one from G), plus two flame throwers, attacked the western penetration and by 1405 had retaken the second pillbox. The Japanese retaliated with a counterattack that was promptly repulsed. When nearly all the officers in both companies were wounded, sergeants took over command. By the end of the day the Japanese still held the five pillboxes, which the Americans had not attacked, in the 3rd Platoon's sector. Two Americans had been killed, twenty-two wounded in the day's action as compared with one killed and six wounded the day before.

American artillery and mortars shelled the enemy during the night. Searchlights tried to illuminate him with direct beams but failed as he took refuge in the ravines and draws. The searchlights then achieved more success by raising their beams so that they were reflected from the clouds.

The *1st* and *3rd Battalions* of the *45th Infantry* struck again at G Company about 0400 of **13 March** and gained one more pillbox before they were stopped. To elim-inate this penetration, Colonel Frederick requested tanks. Corps headquarters, at 0815, released the 1st Platoon of C Company, 754th Tank Battalion, to the 129th. General Griswold released the tanks with the express proviso that they could not be used as stationary defenses. They must be employed in an attack to recapture the lost pillboxes. At 0812 General Beightler ordered the 129th not to deliver any piecemeal infantry attacks but to wait for the tanks and organize a coordinated tank infantry assault. He issued this order just fifteen minutes after C Company, 129th, made a local counterattack which regained one pillbox.

Four tanks and elements of B, C, and G Companies attacked at 1000 after a ten-minute artillery preparation. Although the ground was generally level, the tanks had difficulty in bringing their guns to bear because the Japanese were down in ra-vines with steep slopes. After two pillboxes had fallen, the tanks withdrew. The attack was renewed at 1315. After another hour the tanks had almost exhausted their fuel and ammunition, and the attack was suspended while the 2nd Platoon, C Company, 754th Tank Battalion, came up to replace them. The new tanks and the same infantry units attacked at 1730. This time the tanks and infantry managed to demolish all the Japanese-held pillboxes. By 1930, at a cost of eighteen wounded, the original line was almost restored. Colonel Magata withdrew his battalions to rest, reorganize, reconnoiter, and make ready for another attack.

 On the **14ᵗʰ March**, a day that was quiet except for small arms fire and occasional shelling, the 2nd Battalion repaired its positions, strung new wire, planted mines in the ravines that provided covered routes of approach, and fired its mortars. Patrols went out and reported the presence of strong bodies of the enemy not far from the perimeter. The Americans were sure that the Japanese withdrawal was only tempo-rary.

Temporary it was, for at 0400 of **15 March** the *1st* and *3rd Battalions* of the *45th Infantry* and the *2nd Battalion, 81st Infantry,* renewed the assault. They again achieved a small local success in the Cox Creek sector held by the 2nd Platoon of F Company. By dawn they had seized one pillbox and penetrated to a depth of about one hundred yards. F Company, supported by one platoon of C Company and aided by a 36-plane air strike in front of the battalion line, counterattacked with flame throwers and bazookas to recapture the pillbox by 1153. But the enemy, still hold-ing a salient in the line, was digging positions in the roots of banyan trees and ap-peared to be pushing in reinforcements and more weapons.

General Craig, arriving in the sector to observe and inform General Beightler, as he had on Hill 700, asked for tanks. General Griswold sent a platoon. A tank-infantry attack, delivered at 1500 with artillery and mortar support, made small gains. A second, at 1635, killed or drove off all the enemy at a cost of seven killed, fifty-six wounded, and one tank damaged. One hundred and ninety Japanese corpses lay within the American lines, and four enemy soldiers were captured. The Japanese suspended their assaults on **16 March** but renewed them on the **17th March** and effected a small penetration in F Company's sector which tanks and infantry promptly eliminated.

✦ ✦ ✦ ✦

Iwasa Force

Attack on the central perimeter at Hill 700

While the *Iwasa Unit* arrived at its attack position on 8 March, its assault on the American perimeter was delayed until the next day, **9 March**. Hill 700, in the 37th Division's sector, was held by the 2nd and 3rd Battalions of the US Army's 145th Infantry Regiment. Several small skirmishes were fought between these units and elements of the Japanese *23rd Infantry Regiment* on 8 March, and the 37th Division's artillery bombarded areas from where the Japanese could potentially launch an attack on the 2nd Battalion, 145th Infantry.

The *23rd Infantry Regiment* belatedly began to attack just after midnight on **9 March** but was unable to penetrate far into the American defenses. After daybreak on **9 March**, elements of the 1st and 2nd Battalions of the 145th Infantry Regiment counterattacked the Japanese and regained most of the terrain which had been lost.

The *Iwasa Unit* attacked again at 6:45 am on **10 March** but did not make any progress. At 5:00 pm that day parts of the 1st and 2nd Battalions of the 145th Regiment launched a well-coordinated attack and managed to recapture more of the area lost on 9 March. The remaining men of the *Iwasa Unit* conducted an offensive against Hill 700 on the night of **10/11 March**, but only managed to capture a single pillbox. Further Japanese attacks on the morning of **11 March** were unsuccessful.

General Beightler, the commander of the 37th Division, was frustrated by the 145th Infantry's failure to re-establish its original perimeter and reinforced the regiment on **11 March** with the 2nd Battalion, 148th Infantry Regiment. During that day the commander of the 145th Infantry was also relieved of command after Beightler learnt that he was suffering from extreme combat fatigue.

Following an artillery bombardment, elements of the 2nd Battalion, 148th Infantry Regiment attacked the Japanese positions during the afternoon and captured some ground. This battalion made further progress against Japanese-held pillboxes the next day, **12 March**, and the original perimeter lines were recaptured. The *Iwasa Unit* began to withdraw from the area on **13 March** after suffering heavily in its unsuccessful attack behind a screen of combat patrols and fire.

The Japanese had suffered heavy losses during the fighting around Hill 700, and the Americans counted 309 bodies near the area recaptured on **11 and 12 March**; two prisoners were also taken.

The 37th Division's fatalities amounted to five officers and 73 enlisted men. The artillery expended a considerable amount of ammunition in

defense of Hill 700: 20,802 105-mm. rounds; about 10,000 75mm. rounds; 13,000 81-mm. and 811 4.2-inch mortar shells.

Dad wrote on the Back of a picture he brought home: **"1944 Bougainville Decorated with Purple Heart - me second from right." Between March 9-17 was when Dad was wounded and received this, his first Purple Heart.**

✦ ✦ ✦ ✦

Muda Force

Hill 260

While *General Iwasa* was meeting defeat at Hill 700, *Colonel Muda* was attacking the American outpost on Hill 260 in preparation for operations against Hills 309 and 608 in the Americal Division's sector. The *Muda Unit*--principally one battalion and two companies of the *13th Infantry*--completed its assembly at Peko and moved forward. Peko is a village on the East-West Trail about 5,400 yards east-northeast of Hill 260.

Situated in the Americal Division's sector, Hill 260 was located about 800 yards (730 m) outside the main perimeter line, on the southern approaches to the Torokina perimeter. Hill 260 was a geographically isolated outpost. The East-West Trail crossed the Torokina just east of 260 and, bending south of South Knob, entered the main perimeter line between Hills 309 and 608. A small north-south stream, called the Eagle River by the Americans, flowed between 260 and the main perimeter before running into the Torokina River. In the early part of March only one trail led from the main line to South Knob. The last hundred yards to the top consisted of a steep stairway rivetted into the southwest slope. A small vehicular bridge had been built over the Eagle. The entire area, including the east and west slopes of 260, was heavily jungled.

On the night of **9-10 March** small enemy forces infiltrated between Hill 260 and the main line of resistance, while an assault force assembled east of 260 and made ready to attack

The US forces had established an outpost on the feature which was occupied by a reinforced platoon from G Company of the 182nd Regiment and a party of artillery observers; the total strength of this isolated force on **10 March** was about 80 men.

An hourglass-shaped feature consisting of two rounded hills to the north and south – dubbed "North Knob" and "South Knob" – the position was essentially a saddle, albeit one separated by a very narrow handle running northwest to southeast. Each knob is about half the size of a football field. The handle between them is slightly lower and so narrow that there was room for only a trail. North and South Knobs lie so close together--less than 150 yards apart--**that to hit one knob with artillery or mortar fire inevitably showered the other with fragments**. The slopes to the east and west are very steep. Just north of the hill a major jungle trail ran east-west, while to its rear a small river ran north-south. Hill 260 truly was, as the 182d Infantry commander said, "a sore thumb stuck out into the poison ivy."

A key objective in the battle for Hill 260 was the Observation Post (called "OP tree") built 150 feet high in a tall banyan tree, able to survey the island for miles around. The heavily forested hill was protected by a network of pillboxes and bunkers, which had been constructed out of sandbags and logs. American mortar and artillery forward observers could view the banks of the Torokina below, the East-West Trail, and Hills 250 and 600 to the northeast. Conversely, in Japanese hands Hill 260 would have provided good observation of Hills 608 and 309 and of the corps' rear area between them. At the conclusion of the fighting, nothing was left of the banyan tree but a ruined stump.

During the night of **9-10 March**, small numbers of enemy infiltrated between Hill 260 and the main line, while a larger force massed nearby. Active operations for the day were concluded by an enemy bayonet assault which F Company repulsed by fire.

The following is an excerpt from an officer who was at this battle.

"On Hill 260 there was an instant which is well worth recording. We had five men in an outpost and the Japs came up the hill so fast that the men—the five men in this outpost—could not defend themselves adequately. Three of the men we finally got out alive [but] the other two were killed. One of our soldiers became so excited that he failed to pull the pin [of his grenade] and he hit a Nip in the forehead and knocked him out. Later he killed him with his rifle. When we got these men out of this outpost, they were really in such a mental state that we were afraid that we would have to evacuate them."

A few minutes after 0600 on **10 March**, during the 182d's normal stand to for the two hours before daylight, fire from Japanese mortars, machine guns, and rifles began striking the American positions on 260. At 0638 an officer of the 246th Field Artillery Battalion, American Division, reported from his post in OP Tree that the Japanese had attacked and were all around the base of his tree. He was not heard from again. The attack, which the Americans estimated was made by one company, was actually delivered by all or part of the *3d Battalion, 13th Infantry.* It overran most of the American positions, captured OP Tree, and drove the six survivors of the American garrison to North Knob.

General Griswold ordered the hill held, and two companies promptly were dispatched from the perimeter. One company reinforced North Knob, and then pushed a platoon southward along the ridge while the second worked its way up from the southwest. Several flamethrower-supported assaults achieved partial success, but the Japanese strength on South Knob thwarted recapture.

Repeated American attacks over the next four days could not retake South Knob. Preceded by lavish artillery fire, and using flamethrowers, each attempt achieved some measure of success (one attack liberated the besieged artillery observers), but casualties from concealed Japanese machine guns, supply shortages, and the lack of additional troops all prevented the troops from consolidating a strong position. <u>One company in the 182nd was reduced from 150 to 25 men within a single day.</u>

With supplies on the North Knob running low, on **12 March**, efforts were made by US troops to bring ammunition, food and water forward; requiring soldiers to carry the heavy loads forward under fire; this was an arduous task, and in order to offer some protection to the carrying parties, they moved forward with protection parties offering covering fire. By midday, a sufficient quantity of supplies had been brought forward for the Americans to launch an attack with one company providing support by fire while another carried out a flanking move to attack the South Knob from the west with flamethrowers and indirect fire support. After initial gains, this attack was held up and eventually the company had to be withdrawn for the night after reinforcements from the 132nd Infantry Regiment failed to reach them before dark.

The US forces made further attempts to secure Hill 260 on **13 March**, but several attacks were defeated after the American troops crested the South Knob. As local US commanders calculated the cost of continuing to hold Hill 260, the Americal Division sought permission to withdraw, but this was refused by the XIV Corps headquarters.

After another attempt failed on **14 March**, the Americans changed tactics. Casualties already numbered 98 killed, 24 missing, and 581 wounded (including fatigue cases). Patrols had not detected any other Japanese troops in the area, and those on South Knob were too few to attack elsewhere, so recapturing South Knob did not merit additional casualties.

From **14** until **18 March 1944**, when General McCulloch launched a series of coordinated attacks, the Americans shelled South Knob heavily and made several ingenious attempts to burn out the Japanese with gasoline. They threw gallon cans of gas by hand and tried to ignite them with white phosphorous grenades. They jury-rigged a 60-mm. mortar for throwing cans. Finally, they took two hundred feet of flexible pipe and snaked it to within nine feet of an enemy emplacement; with oxygen pressure they pumped gasoline from a drum through the pipe and over the enemy and ignited it with a white phosphorous grenade. All the while mortars and artillery hammered away, the artillery firing at the reverse slopes while the mortars covered the hilltop. The 182d Infantry's Cannon Company emplaced its 75-mm. pack howitzers on Hill 309 for direct fire and did its best to knock down OP Tree. By **14 March** South Knob, jungled no longer, was a bare, blasted slope. At 1900, **17 March**, OP Tree fell to the ground. During the action more than ten thousand 105-mm. rounds struck South Knob. When all was over, the Americans reported counting 560 enemy dead. American casualties totaled 98 killed, 24 missing, and 581 wounded.

In the aftermath of the battle for Hill 260 on Bougainville, the blasted ground was covered with Japanese dead. Here, American soldiers dump lime on Japanese corpses to fight the effects of jungle heat and humidity.

The carnage on Hill 260 after three weeks of battle left the hill buried in corpses, ruined vegetation, trash, and discarded military equipment. Some of this was burned off using flamethrowers. Trenches were dug and several dead Japanese soldiers would be dumped in the hole and covered up. The smell of dead and decaying bodies was putrid. Markings were left to indicate a mass burial both along Hill 260 and Hill 700.

This was the last attack for several days, for the Japanese overhauled their plans. They had decided to abandon the attacks on Hills 260 and 700 in favor of a massed attack by the depleted regiments of the *17th Army* against the 129th Infantry.

Artillery and mortar fire, patrol skirmishes, and fire fights continued, especially in the sector of the 2nd Battalion, 129th Infantry. After a four-day lull in Japanese assaults from **18-22 March,** *Magata* put together a force of almost 5,000 infantrymen by amalgamating elements of the *Iwasa* and *Muda* Units to replace his own 45th Regiment's casualties.

The Japanese commanders decided to concentrate their efforts in the northern sector along the perimeter sector held by the 129th Infantry Regiment where Cox Creek abuts it. They began moving the *Iwasa* and *Muda* Units to link up with the *Magata* Unit, in order to launch an all-out assault. This movement was not completed until **23 March**, and a general attack began after sundown with shelling and skirmishes prior to a series of assaults through the ravines. Forewarned by captured plans, the US troops were again fore-warned after intercepting a wireless communication from *17th Army* Headquarters to Tokyo pinpointing the time and place of the attack.

A heavy American artillery barrage fell on the main Japanese assault forces as they formed up and disrupted their advance with heavy casualties. **The 37th Division artillery and the various mortars promptly opened fire and largely broke up the Japanese assault before it got started.** But the enemy succeeded in again piercing the 1st Platoon of F Company in the Cox Creek area, this time a little to the west of the earlier penetration. About one hundred Japanese soldiers captured four pillboxes and pushed to a low ridge about twenty-five yards from the battalion command post. Nearly all *Hyakutake's* remaining units attacked. This proved the final element of the Japanese counterattack. The Japanese succeeded in capturing a number of forward positions.

The Antitank and K Company platoons, plus the 3rd Platoon, A Company, 754th Tank Battalion, attacked northwest from the command post **24 March** at 0725 and within twenty minutes had gained possession of the ridge. At 0930 the attackers reorganized and drove in again, supported this time by 37th Division artillery, three battalions of the Americal Division artillery, the 129th Infantry Cannon Company, and twenty-four 4.2-inch mortars, which fired into the ravines. The Americans burned, dug, and blasted the Japanese out of their ravines, trenches, foxholes, and pillboxes while the seven artillery battalions, their fire directed by General Kreber and augmented by the heavy mortars, shelled the concentrated enemy troops in front of the American lines. By 1400 General Griswold had dispatched more reserves to the area but they were not needed. The Japanese were dead or dispersed, the line restored. *Hyakutake's* counteroffensive was over.

Hyakutake received permission from *General Hitoshi Imamura*, Commanding General, Imperial Japanese Army, 8th Area Army, to withdraw, and so the remnants of his army began their retreat on **28 March, 1944**. *Yamashita's* troops withdrew from the 129th's front pursued by the Fijians and two American battalions from the corps reserve, and on the same day he told *Imamura* that further attacks would be fruitless. *Imamura* left the next move to *Hyakutake* but ordered him to resort to guerrilla warfare and raise as much of his own food as possible. *Hyakutake*, though not abandoning his desire to counterattack, elected to withdraw to the posts whence he had come. The *Iwasa* and *Muda* Units withdrew south to Buin, while *Magata's* 1,500 survivors went north via the Numa Numa Trail.

As the Japanese retreated, XIV Corps artillery rained down almost 15,000 rounds on enemy troop concentrations.

The *17th Army*, in spite of its serious losses, was still an effective fighting force; late March and early April saw several sharp fights when the XIV Corps fanned out to pursue the enemy and enlarge the perimeter.

Throughout the campaign, and often under barely tolerable conditions, American soldiers, sailors, airmen, and marines of all ranks exhibited the skill, determination, and endurance that ensured victory. The staunch and deadly repulse of the Japanese counterattack on Bougainville showed an experienced army corps functioning efficiently at all levels.

 "Winning at all costs" was ingrained in the Japanese soldier's psyche. What they weren't taught was what to do if they were captured (most were killed). When Japanese prisoners were treated with respect and provided comfort food and shelter they opened up and told their captors everything they knew of upcoming Japanese initiatives.

This ended the last Japanese offensive effort in the Solomons. Had it succeeded, it would have seriously affected the course of the war in the Solomons by requiring the commitment of more men, ships, and planes to recapture Empress Augusta Bay.

This battle was the final major Japanese offensive in the Solomon Islands campaign.

✦ ✦ ✦ ✦

Following this engagement, the Japanese force withdrew from the Empress Augusta Bay area, and only limited fighting took place until late 1944 when Australian troops took over from the Americans and began a series of advances across the island which continued until the end of the war in August 1945.

Following is an excerpt of "The 2ⁿᵈ Battalion as part of a pursuing force **April 2-4, 1944**". After the battle of Hill 700 in March, the pursuing force started to search for the retreating Japanese.

"The island of Bougainville, like most of the other South Pacific islands is geologically speaking, new, which accounts for the fact that the hills and mountains rise very abruptly. Slopes on the hillsides frequently vary from 45 degrees to vertical. Ridges often are barely wide enough for a foot path, with very steep slopes falling off on either side. Rivers and streams are short and usually not deep but are very rapid until the coastal plain is reached. River bottoms are rocky and strewn with boulders. The entire area, including the steepest hillsides, is covered with a

rain forest type jungle. The floor of the jungle is continually damp and in shadow from the overhead canopy. Brush and small trees growing to a height of ten or twelve feet and vines hanging from the branches of the taller trees prohibit observation for more than a few feet in any direction except where vegetation does not exist, such as across a river. The jungle floor, while apparently flat, is cut by numerous deep, narrow, eroded washes.

Weather during the operation was normal for this climate; clear except for thunder showers during the early morning and late afternoon; usually two hours of rain began at about 1600 hours every day. The temperature, except during the rains, was hot and humid but dropped rapidly to cool (50-60 degrees) at night.

The battalion was at, due to the anticipated hand carry, certain deliberate reductions of equipment. Only one 60 mm mortar per rifle company was carried. Only two 81 mm mortars and four machine guns of the heavy weapons company were carried and these were light machine guns rather than heavy ones. The weapons unit personnel not carrying weapons were used to carry extra ammunition and rations and to assist in carrying the crew served weapons listed above.

The river banks were found to have near vertical embankments of from 20 to 40 feet, however, sufficient vines and tree roots were available to permit the men to scramble down. The greatest difficulty was encountered in lowering the weapons. This was finally accomplished by a chain of men holding themselves to the roots and vines with one hand or tying themselves to the roots with their belts and lowering the weapons and ammunition from one man to another."

At no time in its campaigns in the Pacific did the 37th Division meet enemy soldiers equal to these in valor or ability. This was the real test of the fighting power of the division. The 37th Infantry Division spent the remainder of time on Bougainville conducting combat and construction activities until 11 Oct 44, when it began training for operation in the Philippines. By early December, the division was packing and preparing for departure. It landed at Huon Gulf, New Guinea 18 Dec 44 and Manus Island 22 Dec 44 in route to Lingayen Gulf in the Philippines.

Japanese staff work during the battle had been good. They had correctly evaluated the importance of the hill and had cleverly approached it through the defiles in the mountains. They had performed magnificently in transporting supplies and ammunition over the mountains and through the jungles. They had hand-carried large guns and placed them on almost inaccessible mountains. They fought up a steep slope that would have been difficult to climb empty-handed. They attacked in force on a narrow front and took advantage of a dark, rainy night to penetrate a key section of the American lines. The Japanese took tremendous losses without wavering. They held their positions until exterminated.

The next few weeks of October brought sporadic fighting as XIV Corps pursued the beaten Japanese. During these operations the 1st Battalion, 24th Infantry Regiment, became the first black American infantry unit to engage in combat during the war in the Pacific. The 25th Regimental Combat Team of the 93d Division also joined in the final operations. For several months after major combat operations had ended, American troops patrolled and hunted the remnants of Japanese units through Bougainville's vast jungles.

In November 1944 command of all island operations passed from General Griswold to Lt. Gen. Sir Stanley Savige of the Australian Army, and by mid-December Australian forces had relieved all American units. The Aussies attempted to wipe out the remaining Japanese forces trapped on the island. They suffered over 500 dead and more than 1500 wounded and failed to defeat the Japanese holdouts. At the end of the war, more than 15,000 Japanese troops surrendered to the Australians.

Although for the U.S. Army the Northern Solomons Campaign was declared officially concluded in November 1944 (the Australians would conduct major campaigns in 1945), for practical purposes the end had come with the destruction of the Japanese counterattack in March 1944. Long before November, the Allies were looking ahead to the Philippines.

✦ ✦ ✦ ✦

Final Analysis of the Solomon Islands

The Northern Solomons is one of the more unheralded of the U.S. Army campaigns of World War II, largely overshadowed by its predecessor, Guadalcanal, and by its more publicized successor, Leyte in the Philippines. Furthermore, with hindsight the campaign for the northern Solomon Islands might be described simply as bringing to bear preponderant American strength on isolated Japanese positions. Such a summary does describe accurately what American strategy skillfully achieved through sustained joint operations: the isolation and subsequent defeat in detail of Japanese forces. Nevertheless, such brevity fails to convey either the complexity or the totality of the American effort in the Solomons. American forces had advantages in the Northern Solomons Campaign, which they exploited for the greatest benefit.

There were several reasons for the American difficulties during the campaign's early stages. First, the drive through the Solomons was not a top Allied priority, so Halsey's forces competed with other Allied theaters for resources. Competition prodded commanders to undertake operations as soon as was possible to show that they deserved more resources. More significantly, American planners underestimated the task they faced in conquering New Georgia, miscalculating both the strength of Japanese defenses and the severe hardships that jungle fighting would impose on American troops. This grave failure to identify, and prepare for, the two most important external influences on the American ground campaign can hardly be overemphasized in explaining the ground offensive's subsequent breakdown. Considering the earlier savage and lengthy fighting on Guadalcanal and at Buna on New Guinea, this seems an incomprehensible lapse. The eventual commitment of XIV Corps, with its additional combat power and administrative and logistical capabilities, underscored recognition that the original task assigned to the 43d Division simply had been too great for its resources to accomplish.

Also contributing to the offense's woes were the overburdening of General Hester's staff, the virtual absence of useful intelligence, and, not least, the inexperience of some units like the 43d Division. Even after these problems were surmounted, the Navy's inability to stop nighttime Japanese troop movements meant that some of the fruits of the New Georgia campaign were lost. In the Solomons, Japanese soldiers who escaped generally fought again another day.

But with hard-won experience came increased efficiency and effectiveness for American units, staffs, and commanders. Helping matters was the skill of important commanders. General Griswold inherited command at a critical moment and helped rescue a disintegrating tactical situation on New Georgia. Simultaneously, the replacement of Admiral Turner by Admiral Wilkinson brought to the fore an extremely talented amphibious commander, as evidenced by the Vella Lavella and Bougainville landings, who also could excel in a joint environment. Likewise, the decision to bypass Kolombangara was evidence of a mature theater headquarters staff at work, while the ever-increasing efficiency with which amphibious and ground operations were carried out illustrated the same high quality of subordinate staffs. Finally, the staunch and deadly repulse of the Japanese counterattack on Bougainville showed an experienced army corps functioning efficiently at all levels.

At the "sharp end," troops learned to counter enemy defenses as well as reduce the jungle environment's physical and emotional toll by swiftly applying lessons learned in combat. Among those strength-sapping hardships that all soldiers endured were utter physical and mental exhaustion, malnourishment, and poor sanitation, along with a host of debilitating diseases-dysentery, malaria, and jungle rot, to name three that flourished in the pernicious climate of the Solomons.

Not for the last time, American soldiers learned that tough terrain and a determined foe make a potent combination. Words fail to convey the demands placed on the men who served at the front or to praise their efforts men like Medal of Honor recipient, S. Sgt. Jessie R. Drowley, 132d Infantry, who, in January 1944 during an action to expand the corps perimeter on Bougainville, rescued two wounded men under fire and then, despite being wounded horribly, led an assault on an enemy pillbox.

Special mention, too, is deserved to the Army engineers and Navy Seabees. In extremely short periods of time, they constructed the numerous airfields that played a vital role in providing air cover for operations throughout the Southwest Pacific.

There are two requirements for defeating an enemy who occupies a strong defensive position: superior firepower and men willing to go forward and attack the enemy. On New Georgia in particular, the latter was often in greater supply than the former. Unlike the ground war in Europe, in which vast quantities of artillery often were employed at long range with devastating effect on visible targets, jungle fighting in the Solomons usually pitted small groups against a camouflaged enemy, occupying well-prepared defensive positions, at extremely close range.

Irregular frontline positions often made artillery support equally dangerous to friend and foe. Only in a few cases, most notably the Bougainville counterattack, did the Americans have the advantage of fighting defensively in prepared positions, supported by artillery and without the need to navigate through the dense jungle foliage. Through experience, infantrymen learned to work closely with tanks and flamethrowers when attacking enemy positions. Allied superiority in men and materiel throughout the campaign never relieved the individual soldiers of the arduous and most dangerous job of moving forward and killing the enemy at close quarters.

Inexperienced troops, unfamiliar with the realities of Pacific island combat and the demands it placed on individual initiative and fortitude, did have difficulties. Such was the experience of the 43d Division on New Georgia, where the untested unit suffered one of the highest rates of neuroses casualties of any American division during the war. But the division's loss of 1,500 men in a three-month period reflected most of all the extreme hardship the troops endured. Poorly prepared, ill supplied, and surrounded by a fetid jungle that was almost as dangerous as the enemy, these men fought a grim war of attrition in the Pacific War's equivalent of World War I trenches. Acquiring their knowledge in combat, even men physically unscathed by combat paid dearly. Still, the 43d Division reconstituted after New Georgia and, as a veteran unit, later fought well in the Philippines.

The risk that the United States incurred in the Pacific by dispersing its forces and conducting two strategic offensives brought substantial rewards. Especially at CARTWHEEL'S operational level, the Japanese could not counter the Allied agility. Japanese efforts to use their "interior lines" in the Pacific, by shifting forces to block alternately MacArthur's and Halsey's offensives, were insufficient. Never more than a hindrance to Allied campaign progress, tactically such Japanese efforts only provided the Allies with many opportunities to inflict considerable damage on their off-balance foe. Allied forces generally made the most of these opportunities.

As attrition depleted Japanese air and naval forces and interdiction of supply lines isolated ground units, the Japanese lost the initiative. Confronted with increasingly strong and aggressive Allied forces in the South and Southwest Pacific, they would never regain it. Allied destruction of Japanese men, materiel, and mobility throughout the northern Solomons and New Guinea left the Japanese mired in a multi-front war they could not win.

During the nineteen months of the Northern Solomons Campaign, the measure of the war with Japan changed dramatically. The invasion of New Georgia in **June 1943** had signaled a new phase of the war, the beginning of a sustained American strategic offensive. Less than a year later, the failed Japanese counterattack on Bougainville and CARTWHEEL'S successful isolation of Rabaul heralded the beginning of the end-the eagerly awaited American return to the Philippines. The Northern Solomons Campaign constituted a major step toward that goal.

It promised to be a campaign in a miserable location. And it was. There were centipedes three fingers wide, butterflies as big as little birds, thick and nearly impenetrable jungles, bottomless man grove swamps, crocodile infested rivers, millions of insects, and heavy daily torrents of rain with enervating humidity. "Never had men in the Marine Corps and Army had to fight and maintain themselves over such difficult terrain as was encountered on Bougainville."

✦ ✦ ✦ ✦

A Marine veteran of Guam and Iwo Jima recounted, *"Of all the 28 months I spent overseas, nothing compared to Bougainville for miserable living conditions.... Bougainville had to be the closest thing to a living hell that I ever saw in my life."*

The Pacific campaigns before and after Bougainville – Guadalcanal, Tarawa, the Marshall Islands, Saipan, Guam, Peleliu, Iwo Jima, and Okinawa – seemed to be much more "headline grabbing" amphibious operations than the largely forgotten six month long Marine and Army efforts at Cape Torokian on Empress Augusta Bay of Bougainville. Possible explanations for Bougainville being overshadowed stem from a paradigm shift in Allied strategy in the South Pacific. A new strategic initiative to invade Japanese-held areas where they were the least defended.

After the war a Japanese intelligence officer admitted "the Americans, with minimum losses, attacked and seized a relatively weak area, constructed airfields, and then proceeded to cut the supply lines to troops in that area. Without engaging in a large-scale operation, our strongpoints were gradually starved out. The Americans flowed into our weaker points and submerged us, just as water seeks the weakest entry to sink a ship."

The following is an excerpt from "The Second Battle of Bougainville" by Captain John Guenther.

*"The tactics of the Japanese officers who led the Seventeenth Army will always be a mystery. On occasion after occasion they attacked over the same ground, often literally stepping over the bodies of their dead which had been cut to pieces in preceding assaults. On occasion after occasion they queued up, one battalion behind the other, waiting for the breakthrough, only to have their long column almost blasted from the earth by the thousands of shells our artillery poured into them. **By the most conservative corps estimate almost 8,000 Japanese soldiers died in this attack, the majority of them before the 37th Division's front.** Later on, our patrols located a number of rude cemeteries, one with more than 300 graves. Prisoners of war attested to the frightfulness of our artillery and its devastation to the Japanese rear areas. The 4.2-inch mortars, too, proved to be superb weapons.*

Scores of thousands of Japan's finest troops have been sacrificed in these remote islands, overridden by the superior might of the United States. The coup de grace was delivered at Bougainville when the professionals of the Japanese Regular Army ran into an American garrison largely composed of one-time farmers, factory workers, miners and clerks, who out-scouted, out-maneuvered, out-fought, and above all out-lived the best the enemy could throw against them."

The Solomon Islands Campaign cost the Allies approximately 7,100 men, 29 ships and 615 aircraft. The Japanese lost 31,000 men, 38 ships and 683 aircraft. Over the next two and a half years, U.S. forces captured the Gilbert Islands (Tarawa and Makin), the Marshall Islands (Kwajalein and Eniwetok), the Mariana Islands (Saipan, Guam, and Tinian), Iwo Jima, Philippines and Okinawa. With each island reclaimed from the Japanese, the U.S. moved closer to Japan. Growing superiority at sea and in the air, as well as in the number of fighting men, gave the U.S. increasing advantages. Nonetheless, wherever U.S. forces met Japanese defenders, the enemy fought long and hard before being defeated.

XXIII   Graves Registration Units

From: Warfare History Network, Graves Resignation Units by Mason B. Webb

The grim but necessary task of caring for the war dead was the responsibility of the Army's graves registration units.

The very nature of war means that some participants will be killed and others will be wounded. While battlefield medics and the surgical teams who care for the wounded have been hailed as unsung heroes, and books and articles have been written about them, very little has been said about the men of the U.S. Army Quartermaster Branch's Graves Registration units.

Also, before the introduction of M1940 identification tags, the so-called "dog tags" of World War II, and the more recent science of DNA, being able to identify a particular dead soldier was a haphazard affair. Before going into battle, Civil War soldiers sometimes wrote their names and the names of their next of kin on a scrap of paper that they put in a pocket or pinned to their uniforms.

During World War II, Graves Registration Service (GRS) teams were deployed to land shortly after the first wave of amphibious troops hit the beaches to remove the dead from view, as it was felt that subsequent reinforcements, for morale purposes, should be spared the sight of dead comrades. Except for perhaps a few soldiers who had previously been employed in a morgue or funeral home, the handling of corpses, especially of those who had died a bloody and violent death, was a new and unpleasant assignment for GRS troops.

As procedures for collecting the combat dead evolved, it became the responsibility, whenever possible, of the frontline infantry and /or medics to retrieve their fallen comrades and evacuate them through battalion and regimental areas to the division collection point, where GRS men were standing by for the next step in the processing operation; in some cases, it was GRS personnel who were also tasked with the retrieval.

Retrieving battlefield remains proved to be extremely problematic in some theaters of operation. A Quartermaster Branch report noted that problems of Graves Registration services in the Pacific area were more complex than in Europe due to the extended area over which fighting took place. "In New Guinea, for example," the report said, "consolidation of cemeteries has become necessary, due to the fact that group burials took place at widely scattered points and temporary battlefield cemeteries were established close to the actual combat area. Some New Guinea natives refuse to disinter bodies, and this means that at times the actual digging must be done by limited Graves Registration personnel. The task of locating isolated graves is sometimes complicated by the rapid growth of vegetation, the tall kunai grass in some areas, and the dense jungle undergrowth in others.

Confronting Graves Registration Service units in New Guinea is also the arduous task of recovering bodies from air crashes. Expeditions have been sent out from all bases to locate crashed aircraft and transport the bodies back for burial in military cemeteries. These expeditions into the densely forested, mountainous interior of the country sometimes cover great distances and must be accomplished on foot with the aid of native carriers.

Retracing the Bataan Death March

Even after the fighting was long concluded, challenges remained. According to the Quartermaster Corp' official history of the Graves Registration Service, in **May 1945** the Army's 601st Graves Registration Company undertook its most difficult assignment when it began retracing the route of the infamous Bataan Death March to recover and identify the remains of Americans who died during that journey.

From Mariveles, a town at the southern tip of Bataan, Highway No. 3 stretches northward through the towns of Balanga, Orani, and Bacolor, and runs 120 miles north to the town of San Fernando, Where the six-day march ended. All along this route lay the bodies of Americans, English, Dutch, and Filipinos, unclaimed and unidentified after nearly four years of war. With the capitulation of the Japanese on Bataan early in the spring of 1945, the Army set to work to track down all information that might lead to the identification and proper burial of the remains of Bataan's heroic defenders.

The problems faced by the Army were many. There were no official Army records of either the men on the march or the men who had died at the hands of the Japanese. Men of the 601st had no idea what three years of tropic rains and rapid growth of vegetation would do to hastily-dug graves. Also, there remained the greatest problem of all – proper identification of bodies. Swollen streams and tropical rains washed away many of the shallow, makeshift graves and, in some instances, scavenger animals had taken their toll. Six months after the job was started, very few bodies had been positively identified.

✦ ✦ ✦ ✦

According to Army Field Manual 10-63 ("Graves Registration," 1945, which superseded FM-630, 1941), one Graves Registration company was assigned to each corps having at least three divisions. Given the size of command they were expected to service, the GRS companies were, during large engagements, chronically understaffed and overworked.

Once the dead had been brought to the collection point, a medical examination was made to establish the cause and certainty of death and attempts at identification were conducted if the deceased had not otherwise been identified. In most cases the dog tags provided sufficient information but, when the tags were missing, the deceased soldier's pockets were searched for other evidence, such as a letter from home or a photo of a wife or girlfriend. In some cases, a note written by the dead soldier's superior or comrades before the body was evacuated provided the needed information.

Sometimes a distinguishing feature, such as a birthmark or tattoo, or even laundry marks on clothing and serial numbers on watches, helped in the identification process.

In too many instances, however, a soldier's identity could not be discerned (perhaps because of being too badly mangled, fragmented, burned, or intermixed with other remains) and his grave would be simply marked "Unknown". Identifying a group of victims, say, of an airplane crash or a crew incinerated inside a tank was always problematic, and every effort such as examining fingerprints and dental records was exhausted before declaring the dead "Unknown". After the deceased's commanding officer had a chance to examine the fallen soldier's personal effects to ensure that no items that would cause embarrassment or additional heartache for the next of kin (such as pornography or letters from, or photographs of, a mistress), the effects were sealed in a personal effects bag and shipped first to the Army Effects Bureau at the Kansas City Quartermaster Depot in Kansas City, Missouri. Great care was taken to ensure that the personal effects bags were not stolen or pilfered.

In addition to taking charge of bodies retrieved from the battlefield, GRS units were also involved in taking care of the remains of service personnel who died in field hospitals of combat- or non-combat related causes.

The GRS units had, as part of their personnel roster, draftsmen whose duty it was to draw accurate maps of all the graves. Field Manual 10-63 specifies that GRS companies were "not authorized nor equipped to perform embalming".

On occasion, GRS personnel found themselves in danger from the battle still going on around them. Enemy snipers were as fond of picking off noncombatant medics and GRS men as they were shooting at fighting men.

Personnel who died at sea, if it were not practical to return them to land, were "buried" at sea in weighted mattress covers; the latitude and longitude of the burial locations were then reported to high authority.

Obviously, when dealing with dead and horribly mangled human remains, many of which may be in an advanced stage of decomposition, the mental effect on Graves Registration soldiers is certain to be great. Ways to reduce mental stress include chain of command involvement and assistance from chaplains, psychologists, and social workers.

The mission remains the same:

To spare no effort in the recovery, identification, return, and burial of deceased personnel, and to assist families during an emotionally difficult time or bereavement.

XXIV   Island Reclamation and Biological Weapons

Battle of Truk

Operation Hailstone was a massive naval air and surface attack launched on **February 16–17, 1944**, during World War II by the United States Navy against the Japanese naval and air base at Truk in the Caroline Islands, a pre-war Japanese territory.

Truk was a major Japanese logistical base as well as the operating "home" base for the Imperial Japanese Navy's Combined Fleet. Some have described it as **the Japanese equivalent of the U.S. Navy's Pearl Harbor**. The atoll was the only major Japanese airbase within range of the Marshall Islands and was a significant source of support for Japanese garrisons located on islands and atolls throughout the central and south Pacific. The base was the key logistical and operational hub supporting Japan's perimeter defenses in the central and south Pacific.

To ensure air and naval superiority for the upcoming invasion of Eniwetok, Admiral Raymond Spruance ordered an attack on Truk. Vice Admiral Marc A. Mitscher's Task Force 58 had five fleet carriers (Enterprise, Yorktown, Essex, Intrepid, and Bunker Hill) and four light carriers (Belleau Wood, Cabot, Monterey, and Cowpens), embarking more than 500 planes. Supporting the carriers was a large fleet of seven battleships, and numerous cruisers, destroyers, submarines, and other support ships.

Fearing that the base was becoming too vulnerable, the Japanese had relocated the aircraft carriers, battleships, and heavy cruisers of the Combined Fleet to Palau a week earlier. However, numerous smaller warships and merchant ships remained in and around the anchorage and several hundred aircraft were stationed at the atoll's airfields.

The U.S. attack involved a combination of airstrikes, surface ship actions, and submarine attacks over two days and appeared to take the Japanese completely by surprise. Several daylight, along with nighttime, airstrikes employed fighters, dive bombers, and torpedo aircraft in attacks on Japanese airfields, aircraft, shore installations, and ships in and around the Truk anchorage. A force of U.S. surface ships and submarines guarded possible exit routes from the island's anchorage to attack any Japanese ships that tried to escape from the airstrikes.

In total the attack sank three Japanese light cruisers, four destroyers, three auxiliary cruisers, two submarine tenders, three other smaller warships (including submarine chasers), one aircraft transport, and 32 merchant ships. Some of the ships were destroyed in the anchorage and some in the area surrounding Truk lagoon. Many of the merchant ships were loaded with reinforcements and supplies for Japanese garrisons in the central Pacific area. Very few of the troops aboard the sunken ships survived and little of their cargoes were recovered.

In the campaigns of 1943 and the first half of 1944, the Allies had captured the Solomon Islands, the Gilbert Islands, the Marshall Islands and the Papuan Peninsula of New Guinea. This left the Japanese holding the Philippines, the Caroline Islands, Palau Islands and Mariana Islands.

Battle of The Philippine Sea

The Battle of the Philippine Sea took place between **19 and 20 June 1944**. This battle was said to be the last great carrier battle of World War Two. The Battle of Midway in 1942 had done a great deal to damage Japan's carrier force, but even into 1944, Japan statistically had a larger carrier force than America. Despite America's huge military capability, the Japanese Navy still represented a threat to her – especially in America's desire to advance to the Marianas.

As the Americans moved relentlessly east through the Central Pacific, the Japanese came to the conclusion that only a major sea battle with America would redress the balance at sea. Without control of the sea, the Japanese believed, the Americans could no longer maintain their advance as all their successes had been amphibious based. Without control of the sea, the Americans could no longer move her troops to shore.

The Japanese had planned for an attack on the Marianas with *'Operation A-Go'*. Her *Commander-in-Chief, Admiral Toyoda*, had developed a complex plan to lure the American fleet to either the Palau's or the Western Carolinas. Once in either region, America's ships would be in range of Japan's land-based air force. *Toyoda* envisaged that they would finish off America's naval power in the Central Pacific. *Toyoda* decided that part of his fleet would be used to lure the Americans to either the Palau's or the Western Carolinas. Little attempt would be made to conceal the movement of the Japanese force that was to be the bait – a force commanded by *Vice-Admiral Ozawa*.

The next stage in the American campaign was an attack on the Marianas, which was scheduled for June 1944. The main Mariana Islands consist of Tinian, Saipan and Guam. The Northern Attack Force, led by Vice-Admiral Richmond Turner, was assembled at Hawaii in readiness to attack Saipan. The Southern Attack Force, commanded by Rear-Admiral R L Conolly assembled at Guadalcanal and Tulagi in preparation for an attack on Guam. There were 71,000 assault troops in the Northern Force and 56,000 in the Southern; a combined total of 127,000.

The attack on Saipan was scheduled for **June 15th** and the two forces, Northern and Southern, moved to their forward bases at Eniwetok and Kwajalein respectively. The invasion fleet was protected by a vast force – 7 battleships, 12 escort carriers, 11 cruisers and 91 destroyers or destroyer escorts. Task Force 58 had already started to soften up targets on Saipan on June 11th. Task Force 58 was commanded by Vice-Admiral Marc Mitscher who flew his flag on the 'USS Lexington'. The Americans had planned for air superiority over Saipan before the assault took place. Over 200 Hellcat fighters from Mitscher's carriers attacked Japanese positions on the island on a regular basis.

The ships in Task Force 58 were divided into four battle groups.

1. **TG58-1** with the carriers Hornet and Yorktown had 265 aircraft in it.
2. **TG58-2** was led by the carrier Bunker Hill and had 242 planes at its disposal.
3. **TG58-3** had the carriers Enterprise and Lexington in it and could call on 227 aircraft.
4. **TG58-4** was led by the carrier Essex and had 162 aircraft in it.

Each battle group was protected by battleships and cruisers. In all, Task Force 58 could call on 896 planes – nearly all were the Grumman F6F Hellcat – a plane with a deserved reputation in combat and a major contributor to secure air superiority over the Pacific Theater.

Some facts of the Grumman F6F Hellcat:

* Grumman F6F Hellcat was faster at all altitudes than Japanese Zero Type 52 Fighter
* Standard armament on the F6F-3 consisted of six .50 in (12.7 mm) M2/AN Browning air-cooled machine guns with 400 rounds per gun.
* **The Grumman F6F Hellcat accounted for 75% of all aerial victories recorded by the U.S. Navy in the Pacific.**
* The Grumman F6F Hellcat claimed 13:1 kill ratio against the A6M Zero, 9.5:1 against the Nakajima Ki-84, and 3.7:1 against the Mitsubishi J2M during the last year of the war.

Performance

- Maximum Speed: 380 mph
- Combat Radius: 945 miles
- Rate of Climb: 3,500 ft./min.
- Service Ceiling: 37,300 ft.
- Power Plant: 1× Pratt & Whitney R-2800-10W "Double Wasp" engine with a two-speed two-stage supercharger, 2,000 hp

Such was the improvement in communications since the Battle of Coral Sea in 1942, that each battle group could operate on its own very effectively but could support any other one (or fight as a complete unit) when required to do so. By the evening of June 13th, the planes from Task Force 58 had gained air superiority over the Japanese in Saipan and Tinian. On the same day, 16-inch and 14 –inch guns from American battleships pounded targets on the shoreline.

Toyoda had placed a great deal of faith in the 500 Japanese planes based on the Marianas. They had now been destroyed or had moved out of the battle zone. This was a serious blow to the Japanese – and one that they failed to inform *Ozawa* of as he attempted to 'lure' out the Americans. On June 13th, *Toyoda* gave the go-ahead for *'Operation A-Go'* to start.

On June 15th, American forces landed at Saipan – the Northern Force. Therefore, the coming naval battle was to be in the vicinity of Saipan. The Japanese ordered more ships to the region to support *Ozawa* – including the battleships *Yamato and Musashi*. They were accompanied by two heavy cruisers, one light cruiser and three destroyers. It seems that at this point any intention to lure the Americans to a specific spot was dropped and that a simple full-scale sea battle was envisaged. All the Japanese ships met together on June 16th.

On June 18th, the American submarine 'Cavalla' spotted the Japanese fleet 780 miles to the west of Saipan. As it approached the Americans, the Japanese split the fleet in three:

A Force had three large carriers attached to it and could muster 430 planes
B Force had two carriers and one light carrier in it and had 135 planes in it.
C Force had three light carriers in it and had 88 aircraft in it.

The Japanese launched sea planes from their large warships and the whereabouts of Task Force 58 was soon known. In just one hour, the Japanese sent out 244 planes.

Admiral Raymond Spruance, commander of the 5th Fleet, had sent up Grumman F6F Hellcat fighters at dawn to give his fleet aerial cover. At 1000 hours on 19 June, American radar picked up a very large swarm of Japanese planes approaching. More planes were launched from the American carrier force – 300 in all.

The American planes intercepted the Japanese between 45 and 60 miles from the American fleet. Many Japanese planes were shot down. Japan had lost many experienced naval pilots at Coral Sea and Midway and this experience had never been fully replaced. Many who fought in this battle had not finished their training and paid the price.

In the first Japanese strike, 42 planes were shot down out of a total of 69, an attrition rate of 61%. In Europe, Bomber Command and the USAAF deemed a bomber loss of 5% as being unacceptable. From the second strike, out of 128 planes, about 20 got through the US fighter cover but hit the massed guns of American battleships, cruisers and destroyers. A few got passed the battleship line and attacked the carriers. Only minor damage was done to the 'Bunker Hill' and 'Wasp'. Out of the 128 planes that attacked this time, only 30 returned.

Along with these losses, *Ozama* suffered another when the carrier *'Shokaku'* was sunk by the submarine USS Cavalla. This carrier had been in on the attack on Pearl Harbor in December 1941, so her loss did a lot to lower morale. The *'Taiho'*, hit by an earlier torpedo attack, also went down when fumes from ruptured petrol tanks were ignited and tore open the hull of the carrier.

In all, the Japanese had launched 373 planes from its carriers and only 130 returned – nearly a two-thirds rate of loss. Only 102 were serviceable to any degree. Only 29 Americans planes were destroyed. The aerial part of the battle was nicknamed the **Great Marianas Turkey Shoot** by American aviators for the severely disproportional loss ratio inflicted upon Japanese aircraft by American pilots and anti-aircraft gunners.

A carrier fleet without planes was useless. The Battle of the Philippine Sea effectively spelt the end of whatever carrier strength the Japanese Navy had. However, *Ozawa* was never fully aware of what had happened to his plane force carried by his carriers. Those pilots that had returned had brought back stories of four American carriers being sunk and many US planes destroyed! He prepared to continue the battle.

However, he was never given the chance. At 1630, 77 dive-bombers, 54 torpedo-planes and 85 fighters took off from American carriers to attack the Japanese fleet. *Ozawa* had very few planes with which to fight back and his losses were severe. The carriers *'Hiyo'*, *'Zuikaku'* and *'Chiyoda'* were hit. The battleship *'Haruna'* was also hit. The Japanese lost a further 65 planes and by the end of the attack, *Ozama's* fleet only had 35 planes left. The total American loss in this attack was 14 planes. *Ozama* realized that he had no hope of continuing the fight and signaled *Toyoda* that he was retreating to Okinawa. He had lost 375 planes in total.

The battle was the last of five major "carrier-versus-carrier" engagements between American and Japanese naval forces, and pitted elements of the United States Navy's Fifth Fleet against ships and aircraft of the Imperial Japanese Navy's Mobile Fleet and nearby island garrisons. **This was the largest carrier-to-carrier battle in history**.

The outcome is generally attributed to American improvements in training, tactics, technology (including the top-secret anti-aircraft proximity fuse), and ship and aircraft design.

✦   ✦   ✦   ✦

Anti-aircraft Proximity Fuse

A **proximity fuse** is a fuse that detonates an explosive device automatically when the distance to the target becomes smaller than a predetermined value. Proximity fuses are designed for targets such as planes, missiles, ships at sea and ground forces. They provide a more sophisticated trigger mechanism than the common contact fuse or timed fuse. It is estimated that it increases the lethality by 5 to 10 times, compared to these other fuses.

During the course of the battle, American submarines torpedoed and sank two of the largest Japanese fleet carriers taking part in the battle and a third by aircraft bombings. The American carriers launched a protracted strike, sinking one light carrier, damaging other ships and shot down approximately 600 Japanese aircraft. Most of the Japanese aircraft returning to their carriers ran low on fuel as night fell and 80 planes were lost. Although at the time the battle appeared to be a missed opportunity to destroy the Japanese fleet, the Imperial Japanese Navy had lost the bulk of its carrier-borne air strength along with experienced pilots and would never recover.

USS Albacore (SS 218)

USS Albacore (SS-218) was a Gato-class diesel–electric submarine which served in the Pacific Theater of Operations during World War II, **winning the Presidential Unit Citation and nine battle stars for her service**. During the war, she was credited with sinking 13 Japanese ships (including two destroyers, a light cruiser, and the aircraft carrier *Taihō*) and damaging another five; not all of these credits were confirmed by postwar JANAC accounting. **She also holds the distinction of sinking the highest warship tonnage of any U.S. submarine.** She was lost in 1944, probably sunk by a mine off northern Hokkaidō on **7 November 1944**.

Length 311 ft 9 in., Beam 27 ft. 3 in., Range 11,000 nautical miles (20,000 km) speed 21 knots (39 km/h) surfaced, 9 knots (17 km/h) submerged, Test depth 300 feet with a complement of 6 officers, 54 enlisted, Armament 10 x 21-inch torpedo tubes 6 forward, 4 aft, 24 torpedoes.

✦ ✦ ✦ ✦

Battle of Biak Island

The Battle of Biak was part of the New Guinea campaign of World War II, fought between the United States Army and the Japanese Army from **27 May to 17 August 1944**. It was part of General Douglas MacArthur's Southwest Pacific command's offensive drive to clear New Guinea in preparation for an invasion of the Philippines. **It was the first major effort by the Japanese to allow uncontested landings for the purpose of creating a kill zone inland.** The airfields are at the southern end of the island. The island of Biak dominates the entrance to Geelvink Bay, near the western end of New Guinea.

The island was held by 11,000 Japanese troops under the command of *Colonel Kuzume Naoyuki*. He decided instead to allow the Americans to come ashore unopposed so that they would stroll unwarily into the trap he had prepared for them. This would turn the area around the vital airfield there into a martial honeycomb of caves and pillboxes filled with riflemen, automatic weapons, artillery, batteries of mortars, and a single company of nine Type 95 Ha-Go light tanks. *Kuzume* also stockpiled these positions with enough ammunition, food and water to sustain his defense for months. Water was less than abundant on Biak, where heat and humidity would take a toll equal to enemy gunfire.

After a brief attack on **27 May** at the beachhead by a group of Japanese light tanks, defeated by a group of M4 Shermans, the regiment moved inland quietly confident and expecting little opposition. This perception all changed when they reached the airfield, where from out of low-lying terrain and the ridges above came a terrible storm of heavy weapons fire that pinned them to the ground. It was not until dark that amphibious tractors could be brought up to extricate them from the trap. The next day they reached the end of Mokmer airstrip. Sorido airstrip was the objective.

The Americans broke through the Japanese defenses on **22 June**, with a coastal strip from Bosnek to Sorido captured, including the three airfields at Sorido (4500 ft), Borokoe (4500 ft) and Mokmer (8,000 ft). There were about 3,000 Japanese remnants trying to organize a final counterattack up to **17 August**.

The capture of Biak Island cost the Americans nearly 3,000 casualties, with 474 killed and 2,428 wounded. The Japanese fought to annihilation, with 6,100 killed and 450 submitting to being captured. In addition, some 4,000 Japanese were unaccounted for, missing in action and presumed dead. The Japanese tactics of allowing the landing and delaying their firing until there were a great many targets were repeated at the Battle of Peleliu, the Battle of Iwo Jima, and the Battle of Okinawa.

Battle of the Marianas

In **June 1944** the US Fifth Fleet approached the Marianas with 535 combat ships and transports carrying 127,571 men. *Admiral Toyoda* moved his warships from Biak to the Marianas. Allied planes bombed the Marianas for three days. From the Marianas, Japan would be well within the range of an air offensive relying on the new Boeing B-29 Superfortress long-range bomber with its operational radius of 1,500 miles.

After naval bombardments of Saipan, the marines began landing on **June 15**. Japan had 31,629 men defending Saipan, but they were not well armed. On **June 19** Admiral *Ozawa Jisaburo* commanded four air attacks by the *First Mobile Fleet*.

On that day US planes bombed the Japanese airfield on Guam. American submarines sank *Ozawa's* flagship and an aircraft carrier. The Japanese fleet fled north, but the Allied task force led by Admiral Raymond Spruance in two days sank three aircraft carriers and damaged four others. Japan lost 476 airplanes and 445 pilots while the United States lost 130 planes and 76 aviators.

Battle of Saipan

The Battle of Saipan was a battle of the Pacific campaign of World War II, fought on the island of Saipan in the Mariana Islands from **15 June to 9 July 1944**. The naval force consisted of the battleships Tennessee and California, the cruisers Birmingham and Indianapolis, the destroyers Norman Scott, Monssen, Coghlan, Halsey Powell, Bailey, Robinson and Albert W. Grant.

The invasion surprised the Japanese high command, which had been expecting an attack further south. *Admiral Soemu Toyoda*, *Commander-in-Chief of the Japanese Navy*, saw an opportunity to use the *A-Go* force to attack the U.S. Navy forces around Saipan. On **15 June**, he gave the order to attack. But the resulting battle of the Philippine Sea was a disaster for the Imperial Japanese Navy, which lost three aircraft carriers and hundreds of planes.

The garrisons of the Marianas would have no hope of resupply or reinforcement. Without resupply, the battle on Saipan was hopeless for the defenders, but the Japanese were determined to fight to the last man. The nicknames given by the Americans to the features of the battle — "Hell's Pocket", "Purple Heart Ridge" and "Death Valley" — indicate the severity of the fighting.

The Japanese used the many caves in the volcanic landscape to delay the attackers, by hiding during the day and making sorties at night. The Americans gradually developed tactics for clearing the caves by using flamethrower teams supported by artillery and machine guns.

By 1615 on **9 July**, Admiral Turner announced that Saipan was officially secured. *Saito* — along with commanders *Hirakushi* and *Igeta* — committed suicide in a cave. *Vice-Admiral Chuichi Nagumo*, the naval commander who led the Japanese carriers at Pearl Harbor, also committed **seppuku** (suicide) in the closing stages of the battle. He had been in command of the Japanese naval air forces stationed on the island.

Seppuku is the ceremonial disembowelment, which is usually part of a more elaborate ritual and performed in front of spectators, consists of plunging a short blade into the abdomen and drawing the blade from left to right, slicing the abdomen open. If the cut, done with a movement, is done deep enough, it can cut the descending aorta, inducing a massive blood loss inside the abdomen, with a very fast death. The knifes blade below is 6 inches.

In the end, almost the entire garrison of troops on the island — at least 30,000 — died. For the Americans, the victory was the costliest to date in the Pacific War: out of 71,000 who landed, 2,949 were killed and 10,464 wounded. **Future Hollywood actor Lee Marvin was among the many Americans wounded.**

The Second Battle of Guam

The Second Battle of Guam (**21 July – 10 August 1944**) was the American recapture of the Japanese-held island of Guam, a U.S. territory in the Mariana Islands captured by the Japanese from the U.S. in the **1941** First Battle of Guam during the Pacific campaign of World War II.

Guam, ringed by reefs, cliffs, and heavy surf, presents a formidable challenge for an attacker. Underwater demolition teams reconnoitered the beaches and removed obstacles from **14–17 July**. Despite the obstacles, on **21 July**, the American forces landed on both sides of the Orote Peninsula on the western side of Guam, planning to secure Apra Harbor. The 3rd Marine Division landed near Agana to the north of Orote at 08:29, and the 1st Provisional Marine Brigade landed near Agat to the south. Japanese artillery sank 20 U.S. LVTs and inflicted heavy casualties on the landing troops, especially of the 1st Provisional Marine Brigade, but by 09:00 men and tanks were ashore at both beaches.

Saipan, Tinian, and Guam were chosen as targets due to their size, their suitability as a base for supporting the next stage of operations toward the Philippines, Taiwan and the Ryukyu Islands; the deep-water harbor at Apra on Guam was suitable for the largest ships; and airfields for Boeing the B-29 Superfortresses could be built from which to bomb Japan.

The U.S. Army's 77th Infantry Division had a more difficult landing on **23–24 July**. Lacking amphibious vehicles, they had to wade ashore from the edge of the reef where the landing craft dropped them off. The men stationed in the two beachheads were pinned down by heavy Japanese fire, making initial progress inland quite slow. By **29 July**, the Americans secured the peninsula.

Japanese artillery sank 20 U.S. LVTs and inflicted heavy casualties on the landing troops, especially of the 1st Provisional Marine Brigade, but by 0900 men and tanks were ashore at both beaches.

By nightfall, the U.S. Marines and soldiers had established beachheads about 6,600 feet (2,000 m) deep.   Japanese counterattacks were made throughout the first few days of the battle, mostly at night, using infiltration tactics. Several times the Japanese penetrated the American defenses and were driven back with heavy losses of men and equipment. On **28 July**, the two beachheads were linked, and by **29 July**, the Americans secured the peninsula.

Lieutenant General Hideyoshi Obata took over the command of the Japanese defenders after *Lieutenant General Takeshi Takashina* was killed on **28 July**. The Japanese counterattacks against the American beachheads, as well as the fierce fighting, had exhausted the Japanese.   At the start of August, they were running out of food and ammunition and had only a handful of tanks left. *Obata* withdrew his troops from the south of Guam, planning to make a stand in the mountainous central and northern part of the island, "to engage in delaying action in the jungle in northern Guam to hold the island as long as possible".

Rain and thick jungle made conditions difficult for the Americans, but after an engagement with the main Japanese line of defense around Mount Barrigada from **2–4 August**, the Japanese line collapsed. The Japanese had another stronghold at Mt. Santa Rosa, which was secured on **8 August**.

On **10 August**, organized Japanese resistance ended, and Guam was declared secure, but 7,500 Japanese soldiers were estimated to be at large. The next day, *Obata* committed ritual suicide at his headquarters on Mount Mataguac after he had sent a farewell message to Japan.

Guam was turned into a base for Allied operations after the battle. Five large airfields were built by the Navy Seabees, and Army Air Forces B-29 bombers flew from Northwest Field and North Field on Guam to attack targets in the Western Pacific and on mainland Japan.

A few Japanese soldiers held out in the jungle after the fighting on Guam. On **8 December 1945**, three U.S. Marines were ambushed and killed. On **24 January 1972**, Japanese *Army Sergeant Shoichi Yokoi* was discovered by hunters on the island. He had lived alone in a cave for 28 years, near Talofofo Falls. Despite hiding for twenty-eight years in an underground jungle cave, he had known since **1952** that World War II had ended. He feared coming out of hiding, explaining, *"We Japanese soldiers were told to prefer death to the disgrace of getting captured alive."*

Battle of Peleliu

Palau, Micronesia is a chain of some 200 islands 535 miles east of the Philippines and forms the western edge of Micronesia. Peleliu and Angaur Islands of the Palau Islands are on the southern end of Palau.

Marines, soldiers and sailors fought the Japanese in one of the most savage and costly battles in World War II. The assault on the island of Peleliu compares to the most famous battles in American history in terms of ferocity and valor. Yet this battle has been all but forgotten except by a few military historians and the valiant men who fought there.

The Battle of Peleliu, was fought from **September to November 1944** during the Mariana & Palau Campaign. US Marines of the 1st Marine Division, and later soldiers of the US Army's 81st Infantry Division, fought to capture an airstrip on the small coral island.

Major General William Rupertus, (USMC commander of the 1st Marine Division) predicted the island would be secured within four days. However, after repeated Imperial Army defeats in previous island campaigns, Japan had developed new island-defense tactics and well-crafted fortifications that allowed stiff resistance, extending the battle through more than two months.

In the United States, **this was a controversial battle because of the island's questionable strategic value and the high casualty rate, which exceeded that of all other amphibious operations during the Pacific War.** The National Museum of the Marine Corps called it *"the bitterest battle of the war for the Marines"*.

There was disagreement among the U.S. Joint Chiefs over two proposed strategies to defeat the Japanese Empire. The strategy proposed by General Douglas MacArthur called for the recapture of the Philippines, followed by the capture of Okinawa, then an attack on the Japanese mainland. Admiral Chester Nimitz favored a more direct strategy of bypassing the Philippines, but seizing Okinawa and Taiwan as staging areas to an attack on the Japanese mainland, followed by the future invasion of Japan's southernmost islands. Both strategies included the invasion of Peleliu, but for different reasons.

The 1st Marine Division had already been chosen to make the assault. President Franklin D. Roosevelt traveled to Pearl Harbor to personally meet both commanders and hear their arguments. MacArthur's strategy was chosen. However, before Mac-Arthur could retake the Philippines, the Palau Islands, specifically Peleliu and Angaur, were to be neutralized and an airfield built to protect MacArthur's right flank. The assault on Peleliu was planned as a supporting attack for Gen. MacArthur's return to the Philippines.

III Amphibious Corps, commanded by Major General Roy S. Geiger, would conduct the amphibious assault using the veteran 1st Marine Division, commanded by Major General William H. Rupertus, as the main attack forces. The Army's 81st Infantry Division would serve as the floating reserve until released to assault the nearby island of Angaur.

By **1944**, Peleliu Island was occupied by about 11,000 Japanese of the 14th Infantry Division with Korean and Okinawan laborers. *Colonel Kunio Nakagawa*, commander of the division's 2nd Regiment, led the preparations for the island's defense. *Colonel Nakagawa* used the rough terrain to his advantage, by constructing a system of heavily fortified bunkers, caves and underground positions all interlocked into a "honeycomb" system. The old "banzai charge" attack was also discontinued as being both wasteful of men and ineffective. These changes would force the Americans into a war of attrition requiring increasingly more resources.

Nakagawa's defenses were based at Peleliu's highest point, Umurbrogol Mountain, a collection of hills and steep ridges located at the center of Peleliu overlooking a large portion of the island, including the crucial airfield. The Umurbrogol contained some 500 limestone caves, interconnected by tunnels. Many of these were former mine shafts that were turned into defense positions. Engineers added sliding armored steel doors with multiple openings to serve both artillery and machine guns. Cave entrances were built slanted as a defense against grenade and flamethrower attacks. The caves and bunkers were connected to a vast system throughout central Peleliu, which allowed the Japanese to evacuate or reoccupy positions as needed, and to take advantage of shrinking interior lines. All the caves had either natural or carved-out rifle slits along their side passages, almost impossible to see from the outside.

The battleships Pennsylvania, Maryland, Mississippi, Tennessee and Idaho, heavy cruisers Indianapolis, Louisville, Minneapolis and Portland, and light cruisers Cleveland, Denver and Honolulu led by the command ship Mount McKinley, subjected the tiny island, only 6 square miles (16 km^2) in size, to a massive three-day bombardment, pausing only to permit air strikes from the three aircraft carriers, five light aircraft carriers, and eleven escort carriers with the attack force. A total of 519 rounds of 16 in (410 mm) shells, 1,845 rounds of 14 in (360 mm) shells and 1,793 500 lb. (230 kg) bombs were dropped on the islands during this period.

The Americans believed the bombardment to be successful, as Rear Admiral Jesse Oldendorf claimed that the Navy had run out of targets. In reality, the majority of the Japanese positions were completely unharmed. Even the battalion left to defend the beaches was virtually unscathed. During the assault, the island's defenders exercised unusual firing discipline to avoid giving away their positions. The bombardment managed only to destroy Japan's aircraft on the island, as well as the buildings surrounding the airfield. The Japanese remained in their fortified positions, ready to attack the American landing troops.

Along the beaches were log cradles, concrete tetrahedrons, and barbed wire intermingled with mines. There were extensive antitank defenses consisting of ditches and mined obstacles placed two-or-three-deep and flanked by pillboxes which could only be hit by a tank already in the trap.

Unlike the Japanese, who drastically altered their tactics for the upcoming battle, the American invasion plan was unchanged from that of previous amphibious landings, even after suffering 3,000 casualties and two months of delaying tactics against the entrenched Japanese defenders at the Battle of Biak. On Peleliu, American planners chose to land on the southwest beaches because of their proximity to the airfield on South Peleliu.

On the morning of **September 15**, the 1st Marine Division landed on the southwest corner of Peleliu. U.S. forces had refined their amphibious strategy over a year of hard fighting, and by this time had it down to a science: Massive naval bombardment of land-based targets preceded troop landings, which were supported by strafing and bombing runs by carrier-based aircraft. The troops arrived on shore in waves, gathering on an island's beaches until they had sufficient numbers to push inland. These methods had worked in earlier landings and were expected to work again on Peleliu.

The following excerpt is taken from "Peleliu: The Forgotten Battle by Major Henry J. Donigan.

Few anticipated what was awaiting the Marines on that clear, bright morning. They would find a rugged coral island with the airfield shaped like an Arabic numeral "4" occupying the wide, flat southern portion immediately east of the landing beach. The limestone ridges and most of the island outside the airfield were thickly wooded with occasional wild palms and open grass areas. Northeast of the flat ground the terrain forked to a series of coral islets and tidal mangrove swamps with the coral and limestone ridges of the Umurbrofols running in a parallel prong to the northeast. This was the terrain in which the Marines would fight, the true nature of which had not been revealed by photo intelligence. No one anticipated the impenetrable coral, which made digging almost impossible and absorbed the sun like molten lava. It would also slice the body as one hugged the ground in a struggle to survive. Nor did anyone anticipate the unimaginable heat and humidity that prevailed during the battle.

The heat on Peleliu was incredibly intense. A blazing sun, reflected off the white sand and coral, turned the entire arena into a furnace. The temperature on D-day was a- scorching 105 degrees and would soar to 115 degrees on subsequent days. Heat casualties mounted, and water ran critically short as Marines quickly depleted their canteens in the first hours of battle. There was little if any shade. Faces blistered and lips cracked. The wounded suffered. Helmets without cloth covers were too hot to touch. Everyone was weakened and near exhaustion. Most units were not resupplied until D+1. Water came from the ships in 55-gallon drums and Marines drank vehemently, only to find the water contaminated-tainted with oil, causing many to get violently sick.

The ferocious barrage that preceded the Marines lifted as the first wave of amphibious tractors (amtracs) approached the beach and landed at 0832. Records show that few Japanese were injured by the preparatory fires. As if on signal, the first wave was subjected to a furious volume of preregistered indirect and flanking direct fires. Amtracs and DUKWs of the follow-on waves were hit crossing the reef shelf and sank or burned. The Japanese guns on the southern point of the island were particularly deadly, badly carving up the flank of the 7th Marines and casting platoons and companies into confusion. The Army's 81st Infantry Division reserve battalion was committed to close the gap much earlier than anticipated.

Bill Tapscott described his experience landing with the 7th Marines on Peleliu: "As soon as I got on the beach, I fell face down … There was firing going on all around us-line mines [sic?], knee mortars, dropping shells on us, everything in the world … I don't know how in the world the Japanese survived, they were really dug in … this island is nothing but coral rock. You could drop a bomb on it and all it would o was ricochet. It had to be a direct hit … our planes were still bombing…coming pretty close to us."

From the heavy cruiser Portland, the gunnery officer watched as a steel door in the limestone ridge opened to let a gun fire on the beach, and the ship returned five salvos of 8-inch fire each time the Japanese gun fired again. He commented in frustration, "You can put all the steel in Pittsburgh on that thing and not get it."

Sherman tanks of the 1st Tank Battalion began to land with the fourth assault wave to reinforce the fragile beachhead. This was much earlier than in any previous Marine amphibious operation. However, the enemy fire was so furious that of the 30 tanks that landed on D-day, over half received from one to four hits from high explosive shells before reaching shore. Fortunately, only a few were knocked completely out of action.

About 1650 the Japanese launched a bold, well-planned, tank-infantry attack across the northern portion of the airfield at a time when the farthest advance of Marine units were a mere 200 yards inland, far short of the airfield. There were many gaps in the Marine line. Mustering most of their tanks, about 13, the Japanese smashed fortuitously into the seam between the 1st and 5th Marines, breaking through all the way to the beach. They opened fire on the wounded in the evacuation station. At this point, five Marine tanks surged forward out of protective cover positions and engaged in a violent tank battle over the heads of Marines cowering low in their holes. It was the only tank battle of its kind that the Marines would fight in the Pacific War. When the fight was over, all 13 Japanese tanks were destroyed, and all enemy troops participating in the attack were dead.

Morale now soared across the division as many of the Japanese withdrew into the Umurbrogols, which the 1st Marines were now calling "Bloody Nose Ridge". The lines pushed deeper into the moonlike terrain as the regiments prepared their night defensives, reorganized their positions, and assessed the general situation. Unable to dig foxholes into the coral island, the men used depressions, coral rubble, and any other suitable cover to fortify their night positions.

✦ ✦ ✦ ✦

Tom Lea, one of the few combat correspondents ashore, reported no less than four banzai charges, though these were local attacks and not massed suicide assaults. He told of Japanese entering the lines wearing the helmets of dead Marines, sneaking into fighting positions, cutting Marines' throats.

On D+1, with the landing phase complete, the assault phase of the operation commenced. There were no further counterattacks and the Japanese on the southern portion of the island were isolated and without communications.

Marine veteran Eugene B. Sledge, author of With the Old Breed at Peleliu and Okinawa, remembers the attack across the airfield vividly: "[the noise was deafening] … [The Japanese fired heavy weapons from the 300-foot-high ridges dominating the airfield from the north] … shells screeched and whistled, exploding all around us … it was more terrifying than the landing … we were exposed, running … through a veritable shower of deadly metal … tracers went by me on both sides at waist height … steel fragments spattered down on the hard rock like hail on a city street. I saw Marines stumble … as they got hit … The farther we went, the worse it got. The noise … pressed on my ears like a vise. [I waited] the shock of being struck down at any moment. It seemed impossible that any of us could make it across. We passed several craters that offered shelter, but I remembered the order to keep moving. Because ot the superb discipline and excellent esprit of the Marines, it never occurred to us that the attack might fail. How far we had come in the open I'll never know … It must have been several hundred yards. The attack across Peleliu's airfield was the worst combat experience I had during the entire war. It surpassed all the subsequent horrifying ordeals on Peleliu and Okinawa."

By nightfall, it was clear that the Japanese-infested Umurbrogols were the enemy center of gravity and controlled the rest of the island by fire. It was obvious that the ridges had to be taken, and it would take the resources of the entire division to do it. The division commander ordered a general assault for the morning of D+2.

*Gen. Rupertus remained optimistic that the Marines were on the verge of victory. In fact, on **16 September** he released the 81st Division as the floating reserve to* *commence its assault on Angaur. There they encountered only a reinforced Japanese battalion, a force much smaller than estimated. The "Wildcats" had little difficulty declaring the island secure in 4 days. Angaur would have two 6,000-foot runways ready to support the war effort by **17 October**.*

The 1st Marines launched its attack on D+2, with one attached battalion from the 7th Marines, to reduce the Umurbrogol ridges. They advanced straight up the precipitous slope of Bloody Nose, gaining 500 yards, but at a terrible and bitter cost. The enemy-filled caves were given names such as the "Horseshoe", "Death Valley", and Walt's Ridge".

✦ ✦ ✦ ✦

Author George McMillan wrote a description of Bloody Nose Ridge. *"[There were] no roads, hardly any trails. There was no secure footing on the ridge. It was impossible to dig in. The jagged rock slashed shoes and clothes and tore their bodies every time they hit the deck. Casualties were higher simply because it was impossible to get under the ground away from Jap mortar barrages. Each blast hurled chunks of coral multiplying many times the fragmentation effect of every shell."*

Marine fighters from VMF-114 began operating from Peleliu's captured airfield on D+3, flying some of the shortest close air support missions on record. Corsairs took off from the strip to drop napalm on the ridges 15 seconds beyond the runway. So close were these missions that the planes' wheels were never retracted, allowing them to return immediately to the airfield to quickly rearm. The men on the ground were heartened by their bravery.

The cost of the fighting to the 1st Marines was staggering. It was being chewed up in a brutal, methodical reduction of Japanese positions in a grinding, slow-moving frontal assault. Marine artillery was now playing a big supporting role, firing directly into the openings of Japanese caves and emplacements.

The fight took on a special savagery. Many officers had been killed. Many others who were wounded pressed on. Col. Lewis B. "Chesty" Puller, one of the most highly decorated Marines in history and already the holder of three Navy Crosses, led his 1st Regiment while being carried at times from place to place on a stretcher. He continued to locate himself perilously close to the frontlines. Despite his regiment's incredible losses, he pushed his battered battalions forward in an unrelenting assault. Like all who fought on Peleliu, he possessed a fanatical hatred for the Japanese, aggravated by the loss of his brother during the recent fight for Guam. For most, the hatred of the Japanese had become highly personal.

They fought through a maze of rubble where every crag, gulch, and ridge sheltered enemy positions. There was no room for maneuver. Marines scaled vertical faces to reach cave mouths so that the highly effective flamethrower, satchel charge, or grenade could be used to subdue the fanatical enemy. Gains were measured in yards and the number of destroyed enemy positions. Attacks ranged from well-coordinated assaults using air-delivered napalm, bazookas, tanks, and mortars to desperate night fighting where Marines repulsed Japanese infiltrators with rocks, ammo boxes, bare fists, and bayonets. It was primordial violence. As the attack pressed on, one battalion commander called back to Puller stating that his situation was desperate. He reported, "I'm afraid we can't go on, *Colonel; There's nobody left here.* "Puller replied, "You're there ain't you …?" With that, the fight continued.

Typical of the stiff fighting for Bloody Nose was the attack on Walt's Ridge led by Capt. Everett P. Pope, commanding Company C. Rowland P. Gill wrote this account:

"Pope led his 90-man command across a fire-swept causeway, through a swamp, and with a rush pushed the company atop a hill which proved not to be a hill, but a long coral ridge exposed to severe flanking fire. The company couldn't penetrate the coral to dig foxholes and as a result was mercilessly pounded by enemy fire. By nightfall, the company strength was down to 15 men and the captain. All night they held, repulsing the final enemy charge with chunks of coral. Finally, the survivors were ordered off the ridge which took another two weeks to seize and hold."

On D+5, **20 September**, Gen. Rupertus ordered an all-out assault on Walt's Ridge. Armored vehicles, guns, and mortars were pushed forward close to the frontlines. Air support was used to the maximum extent possible. This was an all-out effort; there was nothing in reserve. The attack failed. Heavy losses were incurred, and the exhausted survivors fell back to where they could safely cover the enemy positions.

The 1st Marines had taken on one of the roughest assignments ever given to a Marine regiment, conducting one of the most fiercely aggressive fights ever waged against an equally determined and savage adversary. They had destroyed over 145 Japanese caves and pillboxes and killed 3,942 Japanese. The price was high. The regiment had suffered 1,749 casualties in 8 days of fighting.

The relief of the 1st Marines by the 321st Regimental Combat Team, was a major turning point in the battle. It marked the opening of a new phase of operations. Yet the struggle would go on for 2 more months.

Gen. Rupertus was finally convinced that it was time for a change in tactics. There would be no more fruitless attacks into the ridges from the south. Rather a sweep would be conducted up the western coast around the enemy's last-ditch defenses in search of a better way to get into the final pocket of enemy resistance. The main Japanese strongholds would be reduced by concentrating firepower on a small area of the ridges, seizing that position, and then advancing a few more yards, slowly repeating this process over and over again.

The initial gains of the fresh Army regiment were dramatic. The soldiers advanced north up the west road parallel to the Umurbrogols, covered on the flank by a battalion of the 7th Marines. After a week of stalled frontal assaults into Bloody Nose by the 1st Marines, the 321st Infantry had advanced a mile and a half up the western road with patrols probing an additional mile up the road by **24 September**.

Battle of Ngesebus Island

On D+13, **27 September**, the 5th Marines launched a bold shore-to-shore amphibious assault supported by Peleliu-based Marine aircraft and 16 tanks to seize Ngesebus, capture its airfield, and prevent the landing of further enemy reinforcements. This was one of the only amphibious assaults of the war that was supported exclusively by Marine aircraft. Ngesebus is connected to Peleliu by a causeway on the north end of Peleliu.

There were numerous pillboxes and fortified positions that required leadership, skill, and tenacity to destroy. Such pillboxes had concrete walls partitioning them into three-to-four-man compartments, with each compartment having its own firing ports. Each section had to be destroyed individually. It took a combination of rifle fire, grenades, 75mm armor piercing shells, and finally a flamethrower to kill all of the Japanese inside.

On **27 September**, the same day that Ngesebus was assaulted, a symbolic flag raising was held at the division command post. However, with the north now secured, there was still one job let-to isolate the only Japanese remaining on Peleliu in the middle section of the Umurbrogols. It was here that the Japanese commander continued to lead from his command post deep inside the limestone rock. The division proceeded to encircle this area in what became known as the "Umurbrogol Pocket". Clearing it out would be a matter of advancing by inches and sealing up the seemingly endless cave entrances.

The succeeding weeks of fighting after the relief of the 1st Marines began to whittle down the strength of the 5th and 7th Marines. By D+20, **5 October**, the 7th Marines had lost about as many men as the 1st Marines and were finished as a regimental-size assault force.

Col. "Bucky" Harris of the 5th Marines, like Puller earlier in the fight, led from a stretcher. Both the 5th and 7th Regiments had experienced a far bigger dose of Peleliu's heat, humidity, rain, and backbreaking terrain than the 1st Marines. *Eugene Sledge comments about this stage of the battle: "[It was] a nether world of horror from which escape seemed less and less likely as casualties mounted and the fighting dragged on and on. Time had no meaning; life had no meaning. The fierce struggle made savages of us all. We existed in an environment totally incomprehensible to those behind the line …"*

The original plan for the seizure of Peleliu provided for the turnover of command from the III Amphibious Corps and 1st Marine Division, to the commanding general, 81st Infantry Division at the end of the assault phase. In accordance with the plan, the relief of the 1st Marine Division commenced on D+30, **15 October 1944**, with units of the 81st Division relieving the Marines in place in the pocket. The "Wildcats" would fight on for another 6 weeks before declaring on **27 November** that all organized enemy resistance had ceased. However, numerous isolated incidents of fighting continued on the island for some time with the last known Japanese soldier coming out of the caves in 1955.

Admiral Halsey sent a message to mark the turnover: *"The sincere admiration of the entire Third Fleet is yours for the hill blasting, cave smashing extermination of 11,000 slant-eyed gophers. It has been a tough job, extremely well done."*

After the end of the invasion, which took over two months, 10,695 of the 11,000 Japanese soldiers stationed on the island had been killed, only some 200 captured. U.S. forces suffered some 9,800 casualties, including 1,794 killed.

Eugene Sledge wrote of the sacrifice made on Peleliu: *"[We] suffered so much for our country. None came out unscathed. Many gave their lives, their health, and some their sanity. All who survived will long remember the horror that they would rather forget. But they suffered and they did their duty so a sheltered homeland can enjoy the peace."*

Lessons of Peleliu

The Battle of Peleliu resulted in the highest casualty rate of any amphibious assault in American military history: Of the approximately 28,000 Marines and infantry troops involved, a full 40 percent of the Marines and soldiers that fought for the island died or were wounded, for a

total of some 9,800 men (1,800 killed in action and 8,000 wounded). The high cost of the battle was later attributed to several factors, including typical Allied overconfidence in the efficacy of the pre-landing naval bombardment, a poor understanding of Peleliu's unique terrain, and overconfidence on the part of Marine commanders, who refused to admit their need for support earlier on at Bloody Nose Ridge.

Battle of Angaur

In conjunction of the Battle of Peleliu was the Battle of Angaur **from 17 September—22 October 1944**. Angaur is a tiny limestone island, just 3 mi (4.8 km) long, separated from Peleliu by a 7 mi (11 km) strait, from which phosphate was mined. In mid-1944, the Japanese had 1,400 troops on the island.

Once the assault on Peleliu was "well in hand", the 322nd Regimental combat team (RCT) would land on the northern Beach Red, and the 321st RCT on the eastern Beach Blue, both of the 81st Infantry Division.

The island's defense commander, *Major Goto* was killed on 19 October fighting to keep possession of a cave. The last day of fighting was **October 22** with a total of 36 days of fighting and blasting the Japanese resistance from their caves with explosives, tanks, artillery and flamethrowers. The 81st Infantry Division had finally taken the whole of Angaur, albeit suffering more casualties than they had inflicted. US had 260 killed, 1354 wounded. Japan had 1350 killed and 50 captured.

Battle of Formosa (Taiwan)

The Formosa (east of China) Air Battle, **12–16 October 1944**, was a series of large-scale aerial engagements between carrier air groups of the United States Navy Fast Carrier Task Force (TF 38), and Japanese land-based air forces of the Imperial Japanese Navy (IJN) and Imperial Japanese Army (IJA). On **October 12** a US task force of 1,068 planes supported by B-29s from China attacked the Japanese air force in Formosa (Taiwan), destroying more than 500 planes.

It was estimated that an invasion of Formosa would require about 12 divisions from the Army and Marines. Meanwhile the entire Australian Army was engaged in the Solomon Islands, on New Guinea, in the Dutch East Indies, and on various other Pacific islands. The invasion of Formosa would require much larger ground forces than were available in the Pacific in late 1944 and would not have been feasible until the defeat of Germany freed the necessary manpower.

The battle consisted of American air raids against Japanese military installations on Formosa (Taiwan) during the day and Japanese air attacks at night against American ships. Japanese losses exceeded 300 planes destroyed in the air, while American losses amounted to fewer than 100 aircraft destroyed and two cruisers damaged. This outcome effectively deprived the Japanese Navy's Combined Fleet of air cover for future operations, which proved decisive during the Battle of Leyte Gulf Philippines later in October.

Surviving Japanese pilots returned with tales of a stunning victory. It was reported that practically the whole U.S. Third Fleet had been sunk and that the American carrier force was left in shambles. Though some members of the IJN command were initially skeptical of such reports, this narrative was carried forward by members of the cabinet until it reached *Emperor Hirohito*. He congratulated the Navy and Army for their success. Actually, the Formosa Air Battle represented a rout of Japanese air forces and a turning point for future naval operations. Upon realizing the scale of the Japanese defeat suffered on **12 October** alone, *Admiral Fukudome* lamented, *"Our fighters were nothing but so many eggs thrown at the stone wall of the indomitable enemy formation."*

Between the aforementioned carrier air group losses, which deprived *Admiral Jisaburō Ozawa's* ships of their pilots, and losses of experienced land-based attack units like the T Air Attack Force, there remained no real prospect of providing air cover over the Japanese fleet for the coming Battle of Leyte Gulf.   *Admiral Soemu Toyoda*, when posed the question *"What would you say was the primary cause for the lack of success in the Formosa operation?"* responded, *"Our weakness in air, and the fact that our pilots under Admiral Ozawa were not sufficiently trained."*

Battle of The Ryukyu Islands

In late **September 1944** the Joint Chiefs of Staff (JCS) in Washington decided to invade Okinawa, the largest island in the Ryukyu Islands, as part of a strategy to defeat Japan. The effort was code-named Operation ICEBERG. Okinawa had initially emerged as an objective in the spring of 1943, when the Allies believed that an invasion of the home islands might be necessary to force Tokyo's surrender. Possession of Okinawa would give the American forces additional, better-positioned air bases for intensifying the air campaign against the home islands and also provide important anchorages and staging areas for the huge, ambitious effort needed to invade Japan.

Beginning in late **September 1944** American aircraft and submarines began to tighten a noose around the Ryukyus, making surface shipping extremely hazardous for the Japanese. Heavy bombers of the Fourteenth and Twentieth Air Forces and carrier planes from Admiral William F. Halsey's Third Fleet struck repeatedly at Japanese positions in the Philippines, Taiwan, and the Ryukyu Islands. On **29 Sep-**

tember B-29 bombers conducted the initial reconnaissance mission over Okinawa and its outlying islands. On **10 October 1944** nearly two hundred of Admiral Halsey's planes struck Naha, Okinawa's capital and principal city, in five separate waves. The city was almost totally devastated. Amphibious landings would be postponed. The American war against Japan was coming inexorably closer to the Japanese homeland.

✦   ✦   ✦   ✦

Japan's biological weapons program

Japan's biological weapons program was born in the 1930's, in part because Japanese officials were impressed that germ warfare had been banned by the Geneva Convention of 1925. If it was so awful that it had to be banned under international law, the officers reasoned, it must make a great weapon.

Unit 731, a research program, was one of the great secrets of Japan during and after World War II: a vast project to develop weapons of biological warfare, including plague, anthrax, cholera and a dozen other pathogens. Led by *Lieutenant-General Ishii Shiro*, 3,000 Japanese researchers working at Unit 731's headquarters in Harbin infected live human beings with diseases such as the plague and anthrax and then eviscerated them without anesthesia to see how the diseases infected human organs.

The Japanese Army, which then occupied a large chunk of China, evicted the residents of eight villages near Harbin, in Manchuria, to make way for the headquarters of Unit 731. One advantage of China, from the Japanese point of view, was the availability of research subjects on whom germs could be tested. The Unit 731 headquarters contained many jars with specimens. They contained feet, heads, internal organs, all neatly labeled. "I saw samples with labels saying 'American,' 'English' and 'Frenchman,' but most were Chinese, Koreans and Mongolians," said a Unit 731 veteran who insisted on anonymity. Medical researchers also locked up diseased prisoners with healthy ones, to see how readily various ailments would spread.

A Russian mother and daughter left in a gas chamber, for example, as doctors peered through thick glass and timed their convulsions, watching as the woman sprawled over her child in a futile effort to save her from the gas.

To ease the conscience of those involved, the prisoners were referred to not as people or patients but as "Maruta", or wooden logs. Before Japan's surrender, the site of the experiments was completely destroyed, so that no evidence is left.

Japan Confronting Gruesome War Atrocity by Nicholas D. Kristof:
From the New York Times: Unmasking Horror – A special report;

He is a cheerful old farmer who jokes as he serves rice cakes made by his wife, and then he switches easily to explaining what it is like to cut open a 30-year-old man who is tied naked to a bed and dissect him alive, without anesthetic.
"The fellow knew that it was over for him, and so he didn't struggle when they led him into the room and tied him down," recalled the 72-year-old farmer, then a medical assistant in a Japanese Army unit in China in World War II. "But when I picked up the scalpel, that's when he began screaming."

"I cut him open from the chest to the stomach, and he screamed terribly, and his face was all twisted in agony. He made this unimaginable sound, he was screaming so horribly. But then finally he stopped. This was all in a day's work for the surgeons, but it really left an impression on me because it was my first time."

Unit 731 of the Japanese Imperial Army conducted research by experimenting on humans and by "field testing" plague bombs by dropping them on Chinese cities to see whether they could start plague outbreaks. They could. Victims were often taken to a proving ground called Anda, where they were tied to stakes and bombarded with test weapons to see how effective the new technologies were. Planes sprayed the zone with a plague culture or dropped bombs with plague-infested fleas to see how many people would die.

No one knows how many died in the "field testing." The Japanese Army regularly conducted field tests to see whether biological warfare would work outside the laboratory. Planes dropped plague-infected fleas over Ningbo in eastern China and over Changde in north-central China, and plague outbreaks were later reported. It is becoming evident that the Japanese officers in charge of the program hoped to use their weapons against the United States. They proposed using balloon bombs to carry disease to America, and they had a plan in the summer of 1945 to use kamikaze pilots to dump plague-infected fleas on San Diego.

The human experimentation did not take place just in Unit 731, nor was it a rogue unit acting on its own. While it is unclear whether Emperor Hirohito knew of the atrocities, his younger brother, Prince Mikasa, toured the Unit 731 headquarters in China and wrote in his memoirs that he was shown films showing how Chinese prisoners were *"made to march on the plains of Manchuria for poison gas experiments on humans."*

The Japanese Imperial Army *Noborito Institute* in Kawasaki Japan cultivated anthrax and pasteurella pestis, furthermore, it produced 20 tons

of cowpox viruses which is the quantity to be equivalent to the whole area of the United States. The plan of deployment of these biological weapons on fire balloons was planned in **1944**. The *Emperor Hirohito* did not admit deployment of biological weapon on the occasion of a report from *Staff Officer Umezu* on **October 25, 1944**. Consequently, the biological warfare was not realized.

Fire Balloons

Japan's so-called **Fu-Go** or fire-balloon campaign released the first of over 9300 of these bomb-bearing balloons **on November 3, 1944**. At least 342 reached the United States found in Alaska, Arizona, California, Colorado, Idaho, Iowa, Kansas, Michigan, Montana, Nebraska, Nevada, North Dakota, Oregon, South Dakota, Texas, Utah, Washington and Wyoming, as well as Mexico and Canada. Some were shot down. Some caused minor damage when they landed, but no injuries. One hit a power line and temporarily blacked out the nuclear weapons plant at Hanford, Washington. Made of rubberized silk or paper, each balloon was about 33 feet in diameter. Barometer operated valves released hydrogen if the balloon gained too much altitude or dropped sandbags if it flew too low.

By **early 1945**, Americans were becoming aware that something strange was going on. Balloons had been sighted and explosions heard, from California to Alaska.

Despite the high hopes of their designers, the balloons were ineffective as weapons: causing only six deaths (from one single incident) and a small amount of damage. The only combat deaths from any cause on the US mainland were the five kids and their Sunday school teacher going to a picnic in eastern Oregon.

What U.S. military investigators sent to the blast scene immediately knew, but didn't want anyone else to know, was that the strange contraption was a high-altitude balloon bomb launched by Japan to attack North America.

January 1, 1945 issue of Newsweek ran an article titled "Balloon Mystery", and a similar story appeared in a newspaper the next day. The **Office of Censorship** then sent a message to newspapers and radio stations to ask them to make no mention of balloons and balloon-bomb incidents. They did not want the enemy to get the idea that the balloons might be effective weapons or to have the American people start panicking. Cooperating with the desires of the government, the press did not publish any balloon bomb incidents. Perhaps as a result, the Japanese only learned of one bomb's reaching Wyoming, landing and failing to explode, so they stopped the launches after less than six months. The last one was launched in **April 1945**.

When the United States prepared to attack the Pacific island of Saipan in the late spring of **1944**, a submarine was sent from Japan to carry biological weapons. The submarine was sunk without knowing what it carried.

As the end of the war approached in 1945, Unit 731 embarked on its wildest scheme of all. Codenamed Cherry Blossoms at Night, the plan was to use kamikaze pilots to infest California with the plague.

Toshimi Mizobuchi, who was an instructor for new recruits in Unit 731, said the idea was to use 20 of the 500 new troops who arrived in Harbin in **July 1945**. A submarine was to take a few of them to the seas off southern California, and then they were to fly in a plane carried on board the submarine and contaminate San Diego with plague-infected fleas. **The target date was to be Sept. 22, 1945.**

It is unclear whether Cherry Blossoms at Night ever had a chance of being carried out. Japan did indeed have at least five submarines that carried two or three planes each, their wings folded against the fuselage like a bird.

But a Japanese Navy specialist said the navy would have never allowed its finest equipment to be used for an army plan like Cherry Blossoms at Night, partly because the highest priority in the summer of 1945 was to defend the main Japanese islands, not to launch attacks on the United States mainland.

If the Cherry Blossoms at Night plan was ever serious, it became irrelevant as Japan prepared to surrender in early August 1945. In the last days of the war, beginning on **August 9, 1945**, Unit 731 used dynamite to try to destroy all evidence of its germ warfare program, scholars say.

The Aftermath; No Punishment, Little Remorse.

✦ ✦ ✦ ✦

The US armada is moving toward the Philippines with 840 ships, 1,600 planes on 47 aircraft carriers,

and in addition as many bombers and long-range fighters came from:

China, Tinian, Morotai, and Peleliu.

XXV   Philippines

Japan Offensive 1941-42

Just hours after the dawn attack on Pearl Harbor (Dec. 7) but across the international dateline making it December 8, 1941, the Japanese attacked Malaya,
Hong Kong, and the Philippines. Japanese planes flying from Taiwan destroyed or damaged seventeen B-17s and thirty fighter planes at Clark Field in the Philippines. War historians considered the bombing of Fort Stotsenburg on **8 December 1941** at 1230 as one of the most destructive air raids in World War II, because almost all the American war planes were wrecked on the ground. In thirty minutes, the air might of America in the Far East was completely destroyed.

General *Honma Masahuru* led the invasion of Luzon that began on **22 December** from the north with about 48,000 troops, followed two days later by about 26,000 from the south. They captured Manila on **2 January 1942**. These invasions were so successful that troops were transferred to the attack on Java, Indonesia which was moved up one month.

The Americans and Filipinos defended Bataan while General MacArthur was ordered to Australia in March. With fewer forces, *Honma's* army did not take Bataan until April. The Corregidor island fortress held out until **7 May 1941**.

Filipino Guerillas

Across all the islands, efforts of local resistance groups against the Japanese should not go unmentioned, as they rivaled the effectiveness of the French resistance. By 1944, 180,000 Filipinos had served in the resistance in some way, with one in six of them serving in Luis Tarluc's Hukbalahaps. The Huks, as they were referred to by Americans, were a band of Marxists that were consisted mostly of the middle class whose devotion were attributed to their faith in MacArthur. **The Huks and other resistance groups, after Hollandia, sent Australia nearly 4,000 radio messages every month, detailing from military maneuvers to the guest list at the Manila Hotel.**

MacArthur, in return, sneaked equipment, transmitters, and even commando teams to the guerillas by submarines. The Japanese secret police put a price on resistance leaders and publicly beheaded those caught, but the Filipinos only fought on with greater determination. One such leader was Lieutenant Colonel Guillermo Nakar, a former member of the 14th Infantry of the Philippine Army. After being caught sending intelligence info to MacArthur's forces, he was tortured and beheaded. Instead of shutting down his cell's operations out of fear, however, "a new leader rose to carry on the fight", recalled MacArthur. As American troops advanced in Luzon, guerilla forces cut telephone wires to disrupt Japanese communications, while key bridges behind Japanese lines were dynamited.

A highly effective guerilla campaign by Philippine resistance forces-controlled sixty percent of the islands, mostly jungle and mountain areas. MacArthur supplied them by submarine and sent reinforcements and officers. Filipinos remained loyal to the United States, partly because of the American guarantee of independence, and also because the Japanese had pressed large numbers of Filipinos into work details and even put young Filipino women into brothels.

Col. Russell W. Volckmann, commander of the US Army Forces in the Philippines, Northern Luzon, the much-decorated Colonel led his Filipino troops in raiding the Japs and piping information to Gen. MacArthur.

When Col. Volckmann took command of approximately 8,000 Filipino guerillas in **June 1943**, his forces had been harassing the Japs by ambushing trucks, destroying bridges and dumps, and raiding for arms and ammunition. Then they laid low, under orders from Gen. MacArthur, and established an extensive intelligence network over Luzon.

Four days before the landing on Lingayen in **January 1945**, they were again destroying roads, bridges, and communications, attacking airfields, supply dumps, and convoys, and communications, attacking airfields, supply dumps, and convoys, and generally raising havoc in the Jap's rear. Taking the offensive, they drove the Japs out of San Fernando, La Union, and continuing south toward Manila.

Finally, grown to 20,000 strong, he led them in annihilating the *79th Independent Brigade* (*Gen. Ariki*), and the *19th Division* (*Gen. Osaki*) before joining our 32nd and 6th Divisions in pocketing *Yamashita*.

✦   ✦   ✦   ✦

BATAAN DEATH MARCH

The invasion of the Philippines by the Japanese started on **8 December 1941**, ten hours after the attack on Pearl Harbor. One day difference due to the International Date Line.

The U.S.-Filipino resistance in the Philippines lasted until **9 April 1942**, when U.S. Gen. Edward P. King surrendered to the Japanese. About 12,000 Americans and 63,000 Filipinos who had been pushed back onto the Bataan Peninsula and Corregidor Island became prisoners of war and were subjected to the infamous Bataan Death March.

The Japanese forced the prisoners to march 85 miles in six days to a prison camp near Cabanatuan, with only one meal of rice during the entire journey. Guards shot any man who fell or faltered during the five-day march. Along the way, the Japanese singled out prisoners, sometimes in groups, and shot them to death as examples to the others. By the end of the march, which was punctuated with atrocities committed by the Japanese guards, 10,000 men – 1,000 American and 9,000 Filipino – died. Those that survived the march would spend the next **40 months** in horrific conditions in confinement camps where thousands perished from disease, starvation and atrocities while held captive.

The Bataan Death March did not really have much of an impact, if any, on the actual outcome of World War II. And it did not have much of an impact on how the war was fought. The only real importance of this is in how it affects the way we remember the war and of course it affected the people involved.

Battle of Leyte Gulf

The Battle of Leyte Gulf, **23–26 October 1944**, was a decisive air and sea battle of World War II that crippled the Japanese Combined Fleet, permitted U.S. invasion of the Philippines, and reinforced the Allies' control of the Pacific. It was fought in waters near the Philippine islands and east of Leyte, Samar and Luzon between combined American and Australian forces and the Imperial Japanese Navy.

Leyte Gulf is generally considered to be the largest naval battle of World War II and, by some criteria, possibly the largest naval battle in history.

It was fought in waters near the Philippine islands of Leyte, Samar and Luzon between combined American and Australian forces and the Imperial Japanese Navy. On **20 October**, United States troops invaded the island of Leyte as part of a strategy aimed at isolating Japan from the countries it had occupied in Southeast

Asia, and in particular depriving Japanese forces and industry of vital oil supplies. The Imperial Japanese Navy (IJN) mobilized nearly all of its remaining major naval vessels in an attempt to defeat the Allied invasion but was repulsed by the U.S. Navy's Third and Seventh Fleets. The IJN failed to achieve its objective, suffered heavy losses, and never sailed to battle in comparable force thereafter. The majority of its surviving heavy ships, deprived of fuel, remained in their bases for the rest of the Pacific War and suffered under heavy sustained aerial attack.

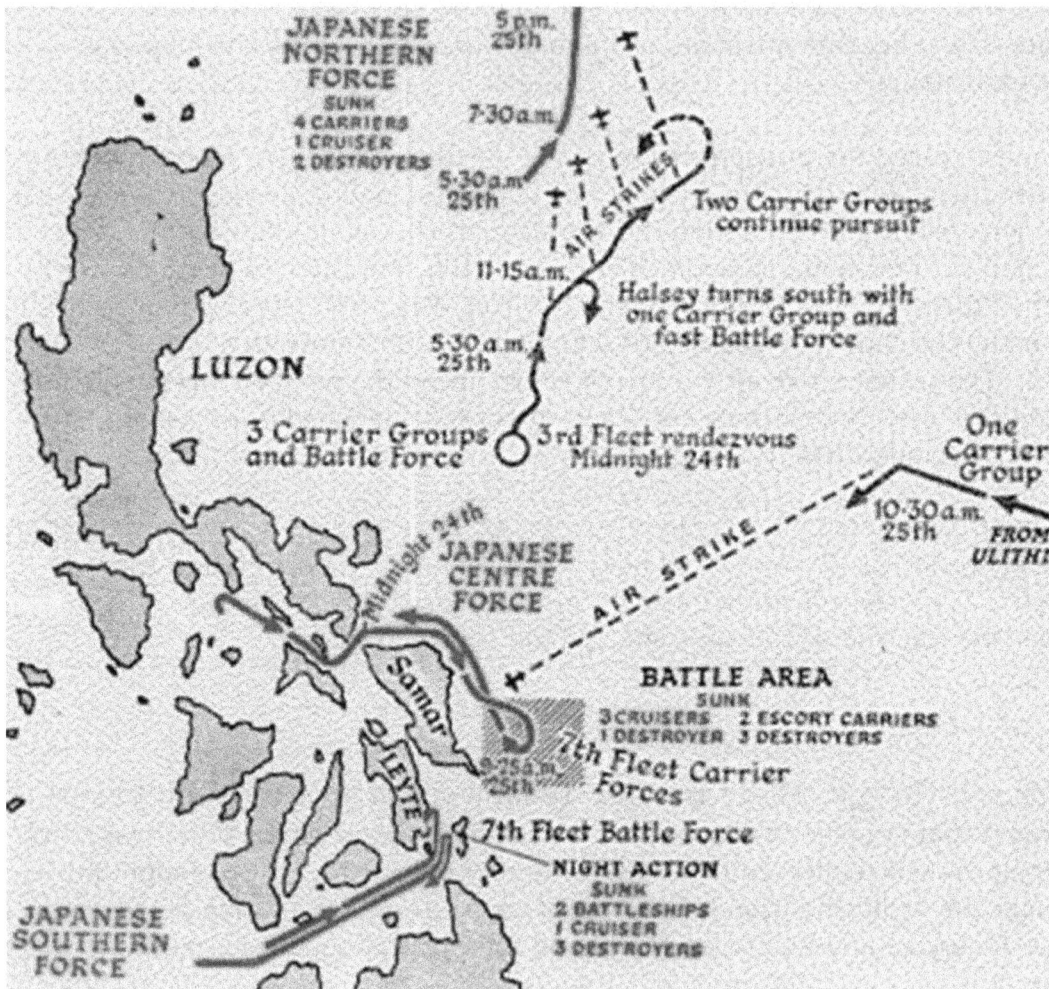

Shō-Gō 1 were divided into three combat groups.

- **"Northern Force"** commanded by *Vice Admiral Jisaburō Ozawa's* ships was designed to lure the main American covering forces away from Leyte. Northern Force would be built around several aircraft carriers, but these would have very few aircraft or trained aircrew. The carriers would serve as the main bait. As the U.S. covering forces were lured away, two other surface forces would advance on Leyte from the west.

- **"Southern Force"** under *Vice Admirals Shoji Nishimura and Kiyohide Shima* would strike at the landing area via the Surigao Strait.
- **"Center Force"** under *Vice Admiral Takeo Kurita*—by far the most powerful of the attacking forces—would pass through the San Bernardino Strait into the Philippine Sea, turn southwards, and then also attack the landing area.

The Battle of Leyte Gulf consisted of several separate engagements between the opposing forces: **the Battle of the Sibuyan Sea, the Battle of Surigao Strait, the Battle of Cape Engaño and the Battle off Samar.**

Battle of the Sibuyan Sea

The battle of the Sibuyan Sea (**23-24 October 1944**) was the opening phase of the battle of Leyte Gulf and saw American submarines and carrier aircraft attack Admiral Kurita's I Striking Force.

The "*Center Force*" under *Vice Admiral Takeo Kurita*—by far the most powerful of the attacking forces—would pass through the San Bernardino Strait **23 October 1944** into the Philippine Sea, turn southwards, and then also attack the landing area of Leyte.   As it sortied from its base in Brunei, Kurita's powerful "*Center Force*" consisted of five battleships, ten heavy cruisers, two light cruisers and 15 destroyers.

The U.S. 3rd Fleet flew 259 sorties—mostly by Hellcats—against *Center Force* on **24 October**. This weight of attack was not nearly sufficient to neutralize the threat from *Kurita*. It contrasts with the 527 sorties flown by 3rd Fleet against *Ozawa's* much weaker *Northern Force* on the following day, **October 25.**

The Americans could put the **MK-37 radar-directed fire control system** and its computer in ships as small as destroyers. This allowed them to land accurate hits while maneuvering. The freedom to maneuver was exploited by the American units, as they could predict the fall of Japanese shells. The Japanese visual-aiming system produced "bracketing" multiple shots. Ships' captains would see sets of shells fall and notice that subsequent shells would be predictably placed. The ship would be able to maneuver away from a bracket that was closing in.

Kurita's Center Force battleships were driven away from the engagement by torpedo attacks from American destroyers; they were unable to regroup in the chaos, while three cruisers were lost after attacks from U.S. destroyers and aircraft, with several other cruisers damaged. Due to the ferocity of the defense, *Kurita* was convinced that he was facing a far superior force and withdrew from the battle, ending the threat to the troop transports and supply ships.

The *Musashi* was the second in the *Yamato* class of World War II battleships of the Imperial Japanese Navy. Launched on November 1, 1940, she, along with her sister ship *Yamato*, were recognized as the heaviest and most powerfully armed battleships of their time. Armed with nine 46-centimeter (18.1 in) main guns. Their secondary armament consisted of four 15.5-centimeter (6.1 in) triple-gun turrets formerly used by the *Mogami*-class cruisers. They were equipped with six or seven floatplanes to conduct reconnaissance. She was commissioned on August 5, 1942, being named after the ancient Japanese province of the same name.

At about 0800 on **24 October**, the *Center Force* was spotted entering the narrow Sibuyan Sea by planes from USS Intrepid. Two hundred and sixty planes from carriers Intrepid and Cabot of Task Group 38.2 attacked at about 10:30 a.m., scoring hits on *Nagato, Yamato, Musashi,* and severely damaging *Myōkō*. The second wave of planes concentrated on *Musashi,* scoring many direct hits with bombs and torpedoes. As she retreated, listing to port, a third wave from USS Enterprise and USS Franklin hit her with eleven bombs and eight torpedoes. *Kurita* turned his fleet around to get out of range of the planes, passing the crippled *Musashi* as he retreated. He waited until 1715 before turning around again to head for the San Bernardino Strait. *Musashi* finally rolled over and sank at about 1930. *Kurita* made his way through the San Bernardino Strait in the night, to appear off Samar in the morning.

Launched in 1942 alongside its sister ship, the *Yamato*, the *Musashi* became the flagship of the main fleet of the Imperial Japanese Navy the following year. The two ships were among the largest and most powerful ever built, measuring 862 feet (263 meters) long and weighing in at 73,000 tons. Their maximum height reached some 183 feet (56 meters), about the height of a 16-story building. Armed with 56-centimeter main guns¬¬—the largest and most powerful of any warship—the *Yamato* and *Musashi* were designed to help Japan combat the much larger naval force of the United States during World War II.

Battle off Cape Engano

25 October 1944

Admiral Halsey was convinced the *Northern Force, Jisaburō Ozawa's* ships, constituted the main Japanese threat, and he was determined to seize what he saw as a golden opportunity to destroy Japan's last remaining carrier strength. Halsey and his staff officers ignored information from a night reconnaissance aircraft operating from the light carrier Independence that *Kurita's* powerful surface force had turned back towards the San Bernardino Strait. When Rear Admiral Gerald F. Bogan—commanding TG 38.2—radioed this information to Halsey's flagship, he was rebuffed by a staff officer, who tersely replied *"Yes, yes, we have that information."* The entire available strength of 3rd Fleet continued to steam northwards, leaving the San Bernardino Strait completely unguarded. It left the landings on Leyte covered only by a handful of escort carriers and destroyers.

Ozawa's "Northern Force" had four aircraft carriers (*Zuikaku, Zuihō, Chitose,* and *Chiyoda*), two battleships partially converted to carriers (*Hyūga* and *Ise*—the aft turrets had been replaced by hangar, deck and catapult, but neither carried any planes in this battle), three cruisers (*Ōyodo, Tama,* and *Isuzu*), and nine destroyers. He had only 108 planes.

The U.S. Third Fleet was formidable and completely outgunned the Japanese *Northern Force*. Halsey had six fleet carriers (Intrepid, Franklin, Lexington, Bunker Hill, Enterprise, and Essex), five light carriers (a sixth, Princeton was destroyed by a Japanese air attack just as its planes were taking off to attack *Center Force*) (Independence, Belleau Wood, Langley, Cabot, and San Jacinto), six battleships (Alabama, Iowa, Massachusetts, New Jersey, South Dakota, and Washington), seventeen cruisers and sixty-three destroyers. He could put more than 1,000 planes in the air.

On the morning of **October 25**, *Ozawa* launched 75 planes to attack the Americans, doing little damage. Most were shot down by the American covering patrols. A handful of survivors made it to Luzon.

The American carriers launched their first wave, 180 aircraft, at dawn, before the *Northern Force* had been located. The search aircraft made contact at 0710. At 0800 the American fighters destroyed the defensive screen of 30 aircraft. Air strikes began and continued until the evening, by which time the American aircraft had flown 527 sorties against the *Northern Force*, sinking *Zuikaku* and *Zuiho*, "seaplane tender" *Chiyoda*, and destroyer *Akitsuki*. "Seaplane tender" *Chitose* was disabled, as was the cruiser *Tama*. *Ozawa* transferred his flag to *Oyodo*.

With all the Japanese carriers sunk or disabled, the main targets remaining were the converted battleships *Ise* and *Hyuga*. Their massive construction proved resistant to the air strikes. *Ise* and *Hyuga* returned to Japan, where they were sunk at their moorings in 1945.

The first use of *kamikaze* aircraft took place following the Leyte landings. A *kamikaze* hit the Australian heavy cruiser HMAS Australia on **21 October 1944**.

Organized suicide attacks by the "Special Attack Force" began on **25 October** during the closing phase of the Battle off Samar.

Halsey's 3rd Fleet consisted of fifteen fleet carriers, seven modern fast battleships, twenty-one cruisers and fifty-eight destroyers. The air groups of the ten U.S. carriers present contained 600–1,000 aircraft. His orders were to protect the landing fleets at Leyte Gulf but also to seek out a chance to defeat and destroy the Japanese fleet.

Battle of Surigao Strait

The Battle of Surigao Strait, 25 October, is significant as the last battleship-to-battleship action in history. **The Battle of Surigao Strait was one of only two battleship-versus-battleship naval battles in the entire Pacific campaign of World War II (the other being the naval battle during the Guadalcanal Campaign).** Surigao Straight is south of Leyte Gulf between Leyte and Dinagat Island.

Nishimura's "Southern Force" consisted of the battleships *Yamashiro* and *Fusō,* the cruiser *Mogami,* and four destroyers. They were attacked by bombers on **24 October** but sustained only minor damage.

Because of the strict radio silence imposed on the Central and Southern Forces, *Nishimura* was unable to synchronize his movements with *Shima and Kurita*. When he entered the narrow Surigao Strait at about 2:00 a.m., *Shima* was 25 miles (40 km) behind him, and *Kurita* was still in the Sibuyan Sea, several hours from the beaches at Leyte.

As they passed the cape of Panaon Island, they ran into a deadly trap set for them by the 7th Fleet Support Force. Rear Admiral Jesse Oldendorf had six battleships (Mississippi, Maryland, West Virginia, Tennessee, California, and Pennsylvania, all but the Mississippi having been resurrected from Pearl Harbor), eight cruisers (heavy cruisers USS Louisville, the flagship, Portland, Minneapolis, and HMAS Shropshire, light cruisers USS Denver, Columbia, Phoenix, Boise), 28 destroyers and 39 Patrol/Torpedo (PT) boats. To pass the strait and reach the landings, *Nishimura* would have to run the gauntlet of torpedoes from the PT boats, evade two groups of destroyers, proceed up the strait under the concentrated fire of six battleships in line across the far mouth of the strait, and then break through the screen of cruisers and destroyers.

At about 0300, *Fusō* and the destroyers *Asagumo, Yamagumo,* and *Mishishio* were hit by torpedoes launched by the destroyer groups. *Fusō* broke in two but did not sink. Then at 0316, USS West Virginia's radar picked up *Nishimura's* force at a range of 42,000 yards (38 km) and had achieved a firing solution at 30,000 yards

(33 km). She tracked them as they approached in the pitch-black night. At 0352, West Virginia unleashed her eight 16-inch (406 mm) guns of the main battery at a range of 22,800 yards (**12.95 miles**), striking the leading Japanese battleship with her first salvo. At 0354, USS California and USS Tennessee opened fire.

Radar fire control allowed these American battleships to hit targets from a distance at which the Japanese could not reply because of their inferior fire control systems.

Yamashiro and *Mogami* were crippled by a combination of 14-inch (356mm) and 16-inch (406 mm) armor-piercing shells. *Shigure* turned and fled but lost steering and stopped dead. *Yamashiro* sank at 0419, with *Nishimura* on board. His surviving ships retreated west. The Japanese fleet had been shelled so relentlessly that it had little time to react and retaliate.

At 0425, *Shima's* two cruisers (*Nachi* and *Ashigara*) and eight destroyers reached the battle. Seeing what they thought were the wrecks of both *Nishimura's* battle-ships (actually the two halves of *Fusō*), he ordered a retreat. His flagship, *Nachi,* collided with *Mogami,* flooding the latter's steering-room. *Mogami* fell behind in the retreat and was sunk by aircraft the next morning. The bow half of *Fusō* was de-stroyed by *Louisville,* and the stern half sank off Kanihaan Island. Of *Nishimura's* seven ships, only *Shigure* survived.

Around dawn on **25 October**, *Ozawa's Northern Force* launched 75 aircraft to attack the 3rd Fleet. Most were shot down by American combat air patrols, and no damage was done to the U.S. ships. A few Japanese planes survived and made their way to land bases on Luzon. When Halsey turned TF 34 southwards at 1115, he detached a task group of four of its cruisers and nine of its destroyers under Rear Admiral DuBose and reassigned this group to TF 38. At 1415, Mitscher ordered DuBose to pursue the remnants of the Japanese Northern Force.

The Battle of Leyte Gulf was one of the last major naval engagements between U.S. and Japanese surface forces in World War II. After this, the Philippines were liber-ated by the U.S., which cut the Japanese off from their oil-producing colonies in Southeast Asia, while her major shipyards and repair facilities were in Japan. The Imperial Japanese Navy never again sailed into battle in such force; most ships re-turned to bases in Japan and remained largely inactive for the rest of the war.

The battle took place above the Philippine Trench, with most of the hull losses occurring in waters of over 7,000 m (23,000 ft) deep. Though the sinking locations are approximate, the battle produced some of the deepest shipwrecks on record.

The **Philippine Trench** reaches one of the greatest depths in the ocean, third only to the Mariana trench and the Tonga trench. Its deepest point is known as

Galathea Depth and reaches 34,580 feet (6.5 miles). It has a length of approximately 820 miles and a width of about 19 miles from the center of the Philippine island of Luzon trending southeast to the northern Maluku island of Halmahera in Indonesia.

Deepest reaches in the oceans. #1 Marianas trench (1,580 mi) long and 69 km (43 mi) wide on average. It reaches a maximum-known depth of 10,994 metres (36,070 ft). #2 Tonga trench depth 35,433 ± 33 ft. #3 Philippine trench depth 34,580 feet (6.5 miles).

In the combined Battle of Leyte Gulf, 10,000 Japanese sailors and 3,000 Americans died. Although the battleship *Yamato* and the remaining force returned to Japan, the battles marked the final defeat of the Japanese Navy, as the ships remained in port for most of the rest of the war and ceased to be an effective naval force.

Due to the long duration and size of the battle, accounts vary as to the losses that occurred as a part of the Battle of Leyte Gulf and losses that occurred shortly before and shortly after.

Listed Japanese losses include only those ships sunk in the battle. After the nominal end of the battle, several damaged ships were faced with the option of either making their way to Singapore, which was close to Japan's oil supplies but could not undertake comprehensive repairs or making their way back to Japan where there were better repair facilities but scant oil. The cruiser *Kumano* and battleship *Kongō* were sunk retreating to Japan. Cruisers *Takao* and *Myōkō* were stranded, unrepairable, in Singapore. Many of the other survivors of the battle were bombed and sunk at anchor in Japan, unable to move without fuel.

The Imperial Japanese Navy had suffered its greatest loss of ships and crew ever.

One account of the losses lists the following vessels:

Allied losses

The United States lost six warships during the Battle of Leyte Gulf:

- One light aircraft carrier: USS Princeton
- Two escort carriers: USS Gambier Bay and USS St. Lo **(the first major warship sunk by a kamikaze attack)**
- Two destroyers: USS Hoel and USS Johnston
- One destroyer escort: USS Samuel B. Roberts
- Four other American ships and HMAS Australia were damaged.
- All of these ships have their own stories of battle not discussed here.

Japanese losses

The Japanese lost 26 warships during the Battle of Leyte Gulf:

- One fleet aircraft carrier: *Zuikaku* (flagship of the decoy *Northern Forces*).
- Three light aircraft carriers: *Zuihō*, *Chiyoda*, and *Chitose*.
- Three battleships: *Musashi* (former flagship of the Japanese Combined Fleet), *Yamashiro* (flagship of the *Southern Force*) and *Fusō*.
- Six heavy cruisers: *Atago* (flagship of the *Center Force*), *Maya*, *Suzuya*, *Chokai*, *Chikuma*, and *Mogami*.
- Four light cruisers: *Noshiro*, *Abukuma*, *Tama*, and *Kinu*.
- Nine destroyers: *Nowaki*, *Hayashimo*, *Yamagumo*, *Asagumo*, *Michishio*, *Aki-zuki*, *Hatsuzuki*, *Wakaba*, and *Uranami*.

Its failure to dislodge the Allied invaders from Leyte meant the inevitable loss of the Philippines, which in turn meant Japan would be all but cut off from its occupied territories in Southeast Asia. These territories provided resources that were vital to Japan, in particular the oil needed for her ships and aircraft. This problem was compounded because the shipyards and sources of manufactured goods, such as ammunition, were in Japan itself. Finally, the loss of Leyte opened the way for the invasion of the Ryukyu Islands and Okinawa in 1945.

✦ ✦ ✦ ✦

Battle of Leyte Island

The **Battle of Leyte** was the amphibious invasion of the Gulf of Leyte located in the southern Philippine islands by American forces and Filipino guerrillas under the command of General Douglas MacArthur who fought against the Imperial Japanese Army in the Philippines led by General Tomoyuki Yamashita from **17 October - 26 December 1944**. The operation launched the Philippines campaign of **1944–45** for the recapture and liberation of the entire Philippine Archipelago and to end almost three years of Japanese occupation.

In **1899**, Major General MacArthur (father of Douglas MacArthur) established his headquarters at the Pamintuan residence, near what would become Clark Field on Luzon. This area became the cradle of pre-war American Army bases and airfields. Clark Field became the Army Air Corps headquarters overseas. The only American air base west of Hawaii, it became the largest American overseas airbase in the world, and largest American base in the Philippines.

General MacArthur kept his promise when he landed 60,000 troops on the Philippine island of Leyte on **October 20, 1944** and 140,000 more would follow. This landing force was accompanied by 700 vessels. That summer 80% of the Japanese ships going to the Philippines had been sunk.

Leaving the Philippines in Japanese hands would be a blow to American prestige and a personal affront to MacArthur, who in 1942 had famously pronounced "I shall return."

General Douglas MacArthur and staff, accompanied by Philippine President Sergio Osmena (L), land at Red Beach, Palo, Leyte, 20 October 1944.

US Army General Douglas MacArthur restages his landing from an LVCP on Leyte, Philippine Islands, for the press on White Beach in the 1st Calvary Division sector. With him are Lieutenant General Richard K. Sutherland, MacArthur's chief of staff, and Lloyd Lehrbas, the general' aide. LST-740 and LST-814 are behind him. He originally landed on **20 October 1944**, under marginal enemy fire on Red Beach in the 24th Infantry Division sector. Both the Japanese and the Americans were shocked to see him wade ashore on A-Day, the day of the invasion. The Japanese taunted him verbally and opened fire with a Nambu machine gun, but he was not hurt and reportedly did not duck. Philippine President in exile, Sergio Osmena, accompanied the first landing. The Higgins Boat (LCVP) ran aground, and the party had to walk to shore. MacArthur was upset that his carefully prepared uniform was wet, but the shot was iconic.

Coast Guard-manned landing ships had U.S. soldiers line up to build sandbag piers out to the ramps to speed up unloading operations. There was plenty of sand for the soldiers to use to fill the empty burlap bags. This was done following every amphibious landing during the war by the Seabees.

On 23 October began the biggest naval battle in history. American submarines sank two heavy cruisers including the flagship of *Admiral Kurita Takeo*, who escaped to the *Yamato* battleship. The gigantic Musashi battleship was sunk the next day. Admiral *Ozawa* managed to lure Admiral William Halsey's Third Fleet to the north, but *Ozawa* lost three aircraft carriers, a destroyer, and 280 planes in one day. Admiral Thomas Kinkaid's Seventh Fleet ambushed Nishimura Shoji's task force in the Surigao Strait. In addition to four battleships and four carriers, in the six-day battle the Japanese lost thirteen cruisers, eight destroyers, and six submarines. Of the 55,000 Japanese soldiers fighting for Leyte about 49,000 were killed.

Battle of Leyte's Ormoc Bay

The Battle of Ormoc Bay was a series of air-sea battles between Imperial Japan and the United States in the Camotes Sea on the west side of Leyte in the Philippines from **11 Nov.-21 Dec. 1944**.

The Battle of Leyte on land was fought in parallel with an air and sea campaign in which the Japanese reinforced and resupplied their troops on Leyte while the Allies attempted to interdict them and establish air-sea superiority for a series of amphibious landings in Ormoc Bay—engagements collectively referred to as the Battle of Ormoc Bay.

General *Tomoyuki Yamashita*, believed that the United States Navy had suffered severe casualties and that the Allied land forces might be vulnerable. Accordingly, he began to reinforce and resupply the garrisons on Leyte; over the course of the battle the Japanese ran nine convoys to the island, landing around 34,000 troops. Ormoc City at the head of Ormoc Bay on the west side of Leyte was the main port on the island and the main destination of the convoys.

Decryption of messages sent using the PURPLE cipher alerted the Allies to the concentration of Japanese shipping around Leyte, but they initially interpreted this as an evacuation. However, by the first week of November the picture was clear, and the Allies began to interdict the convoys.

Type B Cipher Machine

In 1937, the Japanese completed the next generation "Type 97 Typewriter". The Ministry of Foreign Affairs machine was the ***"Type B Cipher Machine"***, codenamed **Purple** by United States cryptanalysts. The year 1937 was year 2597 in the Japanese Imperial calendar. Thus, it was prefixed "97" from the year it was developed.

In operation, the enciphering machine accepted typewritten input (in the Roman alphabet) and produced ciphertext output, and vice versa when deciphering messages. The result was a potentially excellent cryptosystem. The cipher was broken by a team from the US Army Signals Intelligence Service, then directed by William Friedman in 1940. Lt Francis A. Raven, USN discovered that the Japanese had divided the month into three 10-days periods, and within each period they used the keys of the first day with small predictable changes. The Japanese believed it to be unbreakable throughout the war, and even for some time after the war.

✦ ✦ ✦ ✦

As *Yamashita* began to suffer continuing losses on Leyte he urgently worked with the Admiralty in Tokyo to establish a series of re-supply missions. Between **23 October and 11 December 1944** there would ultimately be nine missions in all and they were collectively code-named "Operation TA". In charge was *Vice Admiral Mikawa Gunichi*. It was the same *Admiral Mikawa* who had scored a one-sided victory when he led a surface fleet in the Battle of Savo Island in August 1942. This time *Mikawa* would not be as lucky.

TA-1 (Japanese)

TA-1 took place during the Battle for Leyte Gulf and had the advantage that American attentions were too pre-occupied with the epic battle on Leyte's east coast to notice the redeployment of Japanese resources on the west. The plan was to transport troops and equipment from Luzon, Mindanao and the Visayas to the western port city of Ormoc on Leyte.

TA-1 consisted of five transports, screened by the light cruiser *Kinu* and two destroyers. It took out of Manila on **24 October** but was doomed from the start. Though it ended up safely landing two regiments of soldiers, carrier planes from the U.S. Third and Seventh fleets doubled up on it and the *Kinu*, both destroyers and two of the transports were sunk in the Sibuyan Sea about 150 miles short of their destination. It was not an auspicious beginning for Operation TA.

TA-2 (Japanese)

Rear Admiral Kimura was in charge of TA-2 on 28 October and he upped the ante on protection for his fleet of four large, modern transports, providing six destroyers made up of three echelons. The first landed one anti-tank battalion at Ormoc and returned safely to Manila. The second also landed troops successfully because of poor visibility from the air but later in the day *Kimura* lost one of his four transports to a U.S. Army B-24 when it was caught in a clear patch without clouds. Nevertheless, the operation was considered a success resulting from increased destroyer protection.

Incidentally, it was the very same *Rear Admiral Kimura* who, just one month before the Japanese attack on Pearl Harbor, paid a **"goodwill" call at Pearl Harbor** aboard his flagship *Siritoko*. Several of his crewmembers went ashore and were seen snapping photos of sites of interest from all angles.

TA-3 and TA-4 (Japanese)

On **8–9 November 1944**, the Japanese dispatched two convoys from Manila to Ormoc Bay. The convoys were spotted on **November 9** and attacked by land-based aircraft of the Fifth Air Force. On 10 November the 38th Bomb Group, based on Morotai, sent 32 B-25 Mitchells escorted by 37 P-47 Thunderbolts to attack TA-4 near Ponson Island. The B-25s attacked at minimum altitude in pairs, sinking the two largest transports, *Takatsu Maru* and *Kashii Maru*, disabling a third, and sinking two of the patrol craft escorts at a cost of seven bombers, for which the group was awarded the Distinguished Unit Citation. But the Japanese transports had been able to put ashore the 10,000 soldiers they had been carrying, be it with only a fraction of the supplies.

On **11 November**, U.S. 3rd Fleet commander Admiral William F. Halsey ordered an attack by 350 planes of Task Force 38 on the combined convoys. Four destroyers and four transports were sunk, with many of the 4,000 soldiers on board killed. *Rear Admiral Mikio Hayakawa* went down with destroyer *Shimakaze*, and some 1,000 sailors from the 8 ships were killed.

TA-5 (Japanese)

Convoy TA-5 left Manila on **23 November** for Port Cataingan and Port Balancan. Of the six transports, five were sunk by air attack.

U.S. Destroyer sweeps

Bad weather in late November made air interdiction less effective, and the U.S. Navy began to send destroyers into Ormoc Bay. Canigao Channel was swept for mines by the minesweepers. Four destroyers of Destroyer Squadron 22 under the command of Captain Robert Smith entered the bay on **27 November**, where they shelled the docks at Ormoc City.

TA-6 (Japanese)

Two transports escorted by three patrol vessels, two Subchasers and Patrol Boat No. 105, left Manila on 27 November. They were attacked by American PT boats in Ormoc Bay on the night of **28 November** and by air attack as the survivors left the area. All five ships were sunk, but not before they were able to unload most of its badly-needed supplies to the troops on Leyte.

TA-7 (Japanese)

A convoy of three transports departed Manila on **1 December**, escorted by two destroyers under the command of *Lieutenant Commander Masamichi Yamashita*. Two groups of transport submarines also took part in the operation.

The convoy was docked at Ormoc City when it was engaged at 00:09 on **3 December** by three ships of U.S. Destroyer Division 120 (DesDiv 120) under the command of Commander John C. Zahm. The destroyers were the Allen M. Sumner (DD-692), U.S.S. Cooper (DD-695) and U.S.S. Moale (DD-693).

The U.S. ships sank the transports as they were unloading but came under heavy attack from *Yokosuka P1Y* "Frances" bombers, shore batteries, submarines that were known to be in the harbor, and the Japanese destroyers. *Kuwa* was sunk and *Commander Masamichi Yamashita* was killed (different than *Gen. Tomiyuchi Yamashita* on Luzon). At 00:33, the two surviving U.S. destroyers (U.S.S. Cooper was cut in two by a torpedo) were ordered to leave the bay, and the victorious Japanese successfully resupplied Ormoc Bay once more.

TA-8 (Japanese)

This convoy carried 4,000 troops destined for Ormoc Bay, but which were unloaded at San Isidro, 30 miles north of Ormoc, after receiving news of the U.S. troop landings near Ormoc. All five transports were sunk on **7 December** by air attack, and the escorting destroyers were damaged. Some 350 sailors were killed.

TA-9 (Japanese)

Convoy TA-9 landed some 4,000 troops at Palompon north of Omroc Bay, but escorting destroyers entered the bay on **11 December** where two, *Yūzuki* (by air attacks) and *Uzuki* (by PT boats), were sunk and the third, *Kiri*, was damaged. This phase of the Battle of Ormoc Bay has gone down in history as the only naval engagement during the war in which the enemy brought to bear every type of weapon: naval gunnery, naval torpedoes, air attack, submarine attack, shore gunnery, and mines.

Leyte's Ormoc Bay U.S. troop landings

On **7 December 1944**, the 77th Infantry Division, commanded by Major General Andrew D. Bruce, made an amphibious landing at Albuera, 3.5 mi (5.6 km) south of Ormoc City. The 77th Division's 305th, 306th, and 307th Infantry Regiments came ashore unopposed, but naval shipping was subjected to *kamikaze* attacks, resulting in the loss of destroyers *Ward* and *Mahan*.

By fighting this series of engagements in Ormoc Bay, the U.S. Navy was eventually able to prevent the Japanese from further resupplying and reinforcing their troops on Leyte, contributing significantly to the victory in the land battle. The final tally of ships lost in Ormoc Bay is: U.S. — three destroyers, one high speed transport, and two LSMs (amphibious assault ships); Japan — six destroyers, 20 small transports, one submarine, one patrol boat and three escort vessels.

A heavily forested north-south mountain range dominates the interior of Leyte and separates two sizable valleys, or coastal plains. The larger Leyte Valley extends from the northern coast to the long eastern shore and contains most of the towns and roadways on the island. The other, Ormoc Valley, situated on the west side, was connected to Leyte Valley by a roundabout and winding road, Highway 2. The mountainous southern third of Leyte was mostly undeveloped. High mountain peaks over 4,400 ft (1,300 m), as well as the jagged outcroppings, ravines, and caves typical of volcanic islands offered formidable defensive opportunities. The timing late in the year of the assault would force combat troops and supporting pilots, as well as logistical units, to contend with monsoon rains.

Ormoc Bay is on the west side of Leyte. By the end of A-day, **20 October**, the Sixth Army had moved 1 mi (1.6 km) inland from the east and five miles wide. In the X Corps sector, the 1st Cavalry Division held Tacloban airfield, and the 24th Infantry Division had taken the high ground on Hill 522 commanding its beachheads. In the XXIV Corps sector, the 96th Infantry Division held the approaches to Catmon Hill, and the 7th Infantry Division held Dulag and its airfield.

A typhoon began on **8 November**, and the heavy rain that followed for several days further impeded American progress. At least 10,000 people were thought to have died in the central Philippine province of Leyte after **Typhoon Haiyan**, one of the strongest storms ever to make landfall, lashed the area, swallowing coastal towns, a senior police official said. With winds up to 315km/h (195mph) tearing roofs off buildings, turning roads into rivers full of debris and knocking out electricity pylons. About 70-80% of the buildings in the area in the path of Haiyan in Leyte province was destroyed, said chief superintendent Elmer Soria. He said the storm surge caused sea waters to rise 20 feet when the typhoon hit.

Despite the storm and high winds, which added falling trees and mud slides to enemy defenses and delayed supply trains, the infantry continued its slow and halting attack supported by artillery fire, with companies often having to withdraw and recapture hills that had been taken earlier.

Leyte's population of over 900,000 people—mostly farmers and fishermen—could be expected to assist an American invasion, since many residents already supported the guerrilla struggle against the Japanese in the face of harsh repression.

American efforts had become increasingly hampered by logistical problems. Mountainous terrain and impassable roads forced Sixth Army transportation units to improvise resupply trains of Navy landing craft, tracked landing vehicles, airdrops, artillery tractors, trucks, even carabaos and hundreds of barefoot Filipino bearers.

The troops that were fighting in the mountains were frequently supplied by airdrops by the 11th Air Cargo Resupply Squadron from supplies that were available in the Leyte area. From about the middle of November until the latter part of December, 1,167,818 pounds of supplies were either dropped or delivered by air. 282 plane loads of supplies were dropped, a total of 2,776 parachutes being used. Because of the nature of the terrain and the proximity of the Japanese, the proportion of airdropped supplies that could be recovered varied from 65 to 90 percent.

The 727th Amphibian Tractor Battalion made daily, often multiple, trips with ammunition and rations between Capoocan and Calubian. From Calubian, the 727th tractors would navigate the Naga River to Consuegra and then traverse overland to Agahang. On their return trip, they would evacuate the casualties. Not surprisingly, the complex scheduling slowed resupply as well as the pace of assaults, particularly in the mountains north and east of Ormoc Valley and subsequently in the ridgelines along Ormoc Bay.

By **11 December**, the Japanese had succeeded in moving more than 34,000 troops to Leyte and over 10,000 short tons (9,100 t) of material, most through the port of Ormoc on the west coast, despite heavy losses to reinforcement convoys, including engagements at Ormoc Bay, because of relentless air interdiction missions by US aircraft.

The troop movements fought their way across Leyte and advanced through the following battles. The campaign in the Leyte Valley on the east coast from Dulag north to Pinamopoan. Advance Towards the Ormoc Valley on the west coast, Battle of Breakneck Ridge, Battle of Kilay Ridge, Battle of Shoestring Ridge, Battle of the Ridges, Battle of the Airfields, Fall of Ormoc. This was the westward march to the coast over the course of fifty-five days. These battles are not discussed in detail here but nonetheless are memorialized of soldier's lives lost.

The campaign for Leyte proved the first and most decisive operation in the American reconquest of the Philippines. Japanese losses in the campaign were heavy, with the army losing four divisions and several separate combat units, while the navy lost 26 major warships and 46 large transports and hundreds of merchantmen.

The struggle also reduced Japanese land-based air capability in the Philippines by more than 50%. Some 250,000 troops still remained on Luzon, but the loss of air and naval support at Leyte so narrowed *Gen. Yamashita's* options that he now had to fight a passive defensive of Luzon, the largest and most important island in the Philippines.

In effect, once the decisive battle of Leyte was lost, the Japanese gave up hope of retaining the Philippines, conceding to the Allies a critical bastion from which Japan could be easily cut off from outside resources, and from which the final assaults on the Japanese home islands could be launched.

✦ ✦ ✦ ✦

Kamikaze

Kamikaze were suicide attacks by military aviators from the Empire of Japan against Allied naval vessels in the closing stages of the Pacific campaign of World War II. Designed to destroy warships more effectively than was possible with conventional attacks. **According to a U.S Air Force webpage: Approximately 2,800 Kamikaze attackers sank 34 Navy ships, damaged 368 others, killed 4,900 sailors, and wounded over 4,800.**

Kamikaze aircraft were essentially pilot-guided explosive missiles, purpose-built or converted from conventional aircraft. Pilots would attempt to crash their aircraft into enemy ships in what was called a *"body attack"* in planes laden with some combination of explosives, bombs, torpedoes and full fuel tanks.

Ensign Kiyoshi Ogawa flew his aircraft into USS Bunker Hill during a kamikaze mission on **11 May 1945.**

The following is an English translation of the Ensigns last letter:

Father and Mother,
It has been decided that I also will make a sortie as a proud Special Attack Corps member. Looking back, when I think of your raising me in your arms for more than twenty years, I am filled with a sense of gratitude. I truly believe that no one else has lived a happier life than me, and I am resolved to repay the Emperor and my father for your kindness.

Beyond those boundless white clouds, I will make my attack with a calm feeling. Not even thoughts of life and death will come to mind. A person dies once. It will be an honorable day to live for the eternal cause.

Father and Mother, please be glad for me.

Above all, Mother, please take care of your health, and I wish for everyone's prosperity. As I will be at Yasukuni Shrine, Father and Mother, I always and forever will be living near you and will be praying for your happiness.

I will go smiling, both on the day of my sortie and forever.

The USS Bunker Hill was hit by this kamikaze pilot on **11 May 1945**. 389 personnel were killed or missing, 264 wounded from a crew of 2,600. These attacks, which began in **October 1944**, followed several critical military defeats for the Japanese. They had long since lost aerial dominance due to outdated aircraft and inexperienced pilots.

As Leyte Island was still too distant for efficient preparations against Luzon, MacArthur made the decision to seize Mindoro, an island half the size of New Jersey and lightly defended by the Japanese.

Through December 1944, the islands of Leyte and Mindoro were cleared of Japanese soldiers. During the campaign, the Imperial Japanese Army conducted a suicidal defense of the islands.

In 1944 Japan produced about 18,000 planes even though their plan was for 40,000. By the end of the war the United States would have 40,893 planes and 60 aircraft carriers.

✦ ✦ ✦ ✦

Battle of Mindoro Island

Mindoro was invaded by the U.S. forces on **15 December 1944**. Despite kamikaze attacks, the landings were otherwise unopposed as there were only 1000 Japanese troops on the island. Airfields were seized by the end of that first day and preparations began for the taking of Luzon.

There was no significant opposition from the Imperial Japanese Navy, nor from the Japanese Army and Navy Air Forces, except for *kamikaze* (suicide) attacks on American ships. The Japanese force in Mindoro was not large and was eliminated in three days. The Army was assisted in the campaign by guerrillas from the local Filipino population.

The U.S. captured Mindoro to establish airfields there, which would be in fighter range of Lingayen Gulf in northern Luzon Island, where the next major amphibious invasion of the Philippines was planned. Ground-based fighter cover was necessary for this operation. Mindoro could also serve as the advanced base for U.S. troops going to fight in Luzon.

"The gun crews of a Navy cruiser covering American landing on the island of Mindoro, Philippines Dec. 15, 1944, scan the skies in an effort to identify a plane overhead. Two 5" (127mm) guns are ready while inboard 20mm anti-aircraft crews are ready to act."

Invasion of Lingayen Gulf

During World War II, the **Lingayen Gulf off Luzon** proved a strategically important theater of war between American and Japanese forces. On **22 December 1941**, the Japanese 14th Army—under *Lieutenant General Masaharu Homma*—landed on the Eastern part of the gulf at Agoo, Caba, Santiago and Bauang, where they engaged in a number of relatively minor skirmishes with the defenders, which consisted of a poorly equipped contingent of predominantly American and Filipino troops, and managed to successfully invade and occupy the gulf. Following the defeat, the next day General Douglas MacArthur issued the order to retreat from Luzon and withdraw to Bataan. For the next three years, the gulf remained under Japanese occupation prior to the Lingayen Gulf Landings.

The Invasion of Lingayen Gulf, **6–9 January 1945**, was an Allied amphibious operation in the Philippines. a large Allied force commanded by Admiral Jesse B. Oldendorf began approaching the shores of Lingayen. U.S. Navy and Royal Australian Navy warships began bombarding suspected Japanese positions along the coast of Lingayen from their position in Lingayen Gulf for three days. On **9 January**, the U.S. 6th Army landed on a 20 mi (32 km) beachhead between the towns of Lingayen and San Fabian.

Beginning on **6 January 1945**, a heavy naval and air bombardment of suspected Japanese defenses on Lingayen began. Underwater demolitions began, but found no beach obstacles, and encountered sparse opposing forces. Aircraft and naval artillery bombardment of the landing areas also occurred, with *kamikazes* attacking on **7 January**.

Despite their success in driving out the Japanese forces stationed there, they suffered relatively heavy losses; particularly to their convoys, due to *kamikaze* attacks. From **4–12 January**, a total of 24 ships were sunk and another 67 were damaged by *kamikazes.* Following the landings, the Lingayen Gulf was turned into a vast supply depot for the rest of the war to support the Battle of Luzon.

On **January 6, 1945**, *Lieutenant Junior Grade Tadasu Fukino* piloted a *Suisei* dive bomber (Allied code name of Judy) that crashed into the heavy cruiser *Louisville* (CA-28) in Lingayen Gulf off the coast of Luzon Island in the Philippines. The suicide attack killed 36 men and wounded 56 others.

Tadasu Fukino wrote the following last letter to his mother after he had arrived in the Philippines and before his final mission:

December 31, 1944
Mother,
I truly have caused you only trouble for a long time. In addition to being undutiful to you in various ways, now again I will not even take care of you. Please forgive my prior undutifulness.

Last fall you surely were worried when I chose the Navy Air path. Using common sense, there were several other paths with little danger. Regarding the path of service to the country, perhaps those would have been adequate. However, as for this country of Japan, great numbers of us splendidly have obtained shining glory only after we have endured endless sorrows and griefs. Moreover, precisely because of this, hereafter Japan will be a country that flourishes. I have been able to advance and take this glorious path without any regrets precisely because I believed you to be a strong mother who has made this country of Japan prosper splendidly by valiantly enduring these sorrows. Even though I was able to go forward on the path of a warrior who will repay the country in some little way, it is primarily because of you, Mother.

You can say with pride that I went to a glorious death in the honorable Navy Air way and performed some little service.

I will be content with beautiful white clouds in the skies as a grave marker. Now I go to die for the Emperor and for the mountains and rivers of my beloved Japan. Well, so long.   Tadasu

The Kamikaze willingly joins the Special Attack Corps, an airman's highest honor.

✦ ✦ ✦ ✦

Battle of Luzon

9 January – 15 August 1945, was a land battle of the Pacific Theater of Operations of World War II by the Allied forces of the U.S., its colony the Philippines, and allies against forces of the Empire of Japan. The battle resulted in a U.S. and Filipino victory. The Japanese force was estimated at this time to be about 260,000 soldiers, with no hope of reinforcement.

The battle was fought on the island of Luzon in the northern Philippines and pitted the Allied forces under General Douglas MacArthur against a large Japanese force under Japanese *General Tomoyuki Yamashita*. Because of the vital nature of the Philippines as a key route to sources of rubber and oil as well as the proximity of the islands to Japan, the Japanese High Command had reinforced the islands with a total of 430,000 troops distributed across the islands, 260,000 of which were on Luzon.

The destruction of much of the Japanese carrier fleet earlier in **June 1944** at the battle of the Philippine Sea and the subsequent loss of the remaining surface fleet in **October 1944** at the Battle of Leyte Gulf, with the additional destruction of Japanese air power, left the defense of the Philippines in the hands of ground-based forces.

In 1944 Sarasota County Florida received the honor of having a US Navy ship named after it. The USS Sarasota was built by the Permanente Metals Corporation of Richmond, California, between April and June 1944. Built as a Naval attack transport ship, it was acquired by the US Navy on August 16, 1944 and commissioned the same day. The first commander of the USS Sarasota was James I. Macpherson.

USS Sarasota (APA/LPA-204) was a Haskell-class attack transport that saw service with the US Navy in World War II, Korean War Era and after. She was of the VC2-S-AP5 Victory ship design type. **This is the troop ship that landed the 37th Infantry Division on Luzon 9 January 1945.**

The **Victory ship** was a class of cargo ship produced in large numbers by North American shipyards during World War II to replace losses caused by German submarines. They were a more modern design compared to the earlier Liberty ship, were slightly larger and had more powerful steam turbine engines giving higher speed to allow participation in high speed convoys and make them more difficult targets for German U-boats. A total of 531 Victory ships were built.

Haskell-class attack transports (APA) were amphibious assault ships of the United States Navy created in 1944. They were designed to transport 1,500 troops and their combat equipment, and land them on hostile shores with the ships' integral landing craft.

✦ ✦ ✦ ✦

*The USS Sarasota arrived in Lingayen Gulf **7 January** and dropped anchor. He wrote on the front of the card:* **"Landed on Luzon January 9, 1945 with the initial landing at 0900".** *Dad brought back a Christmas Day dinner menu card (1944) while aboard the USS Sarasota troop ship.*

This is the Christmas Holiday menu from the USS Sarasota:

Sweet Pickles, Ripe Olives
Cream of Turkey Soup, Saltines
Roast Young Turkey, Baked Virginia Ham
Creamed Mashed Potatoes, Creamed Sweet Potato Souffle
Giblet Gravy, Apple Dressing
French Peas, Hot Parker House Rolls, Salad
Mincemeat Pie, Ice Cream
Fruit Punch, Mixed Nuts, Candy
Cigarettes, Cigars

✦ ✦ ✦ ✦

At 0930 on **9 January 1945** about 68,000 GIs under General Walter Krueger of the U.S. 6th Army—following a devastating naval bombardment—landed at the coast of Lingayen Gulf meeting no opposition. A total of 203,608 soldiers were eventually landed over the next few days, establishing a 20 mi (32 km) beachhead, stretching from Sual, Lingayen and Dagupan (XIV Corps) to the west and San Fabian (I Corps) to the east.

The total number of troops under the command of MacArthur was reported to have even exceeded the number that Dwight D. Eisenhower controlled in Europe. Within a few days, the assault forces had quickly captured the coastal towns and secured the 20-mile-long (32 km) beachhead, as well as penetrating up to five miles (8 km) inland.

9 January 1945. Operation Mike 1, the US landings on Luzon at Lingayen Gulf, is begun. General Swift's I Corps lands from the ships of TF 78 around San Fabian. The assault units are from 43rd and 6th Infantry Divisions.

Part of General Griswold's XIV Corps land between the villages of Lingayen and Dagupan. These assault units are from the 37th and 40th Divisions and head southeasterly through San Carlos to Bayambang and south to Clark Field. (Map below)

Ultimately ten U.S. divisions and five independent regiments would see action on Luzon, making it the largest campaign of the Pacific War, involving more troops than the U.S. had used in North Africa, Italy or southern France.

These attacks trapped the Japanese defenders in a giant pincer movement, but they put up bitter resistance at the battles for Manila, Balete Pass and the Cagayan Valley. *Yamashita's* forces, despite their large number, were under-supplied with artillery, armor and other equipment, forcing him to fight a delaying action against the Americans with no real hope of victory. As such, *Yamashita* withdrew to mountainous zones of northern Luzon, where the terrain afforded him some degree of protection and advantage.

After the 129th Regiment landed at Liugayen Gulf, Luzon **9 January, 1945**, it was attached to the 40th Infantry Division **1-2 February, 1945** and the 33rd Infantry Division **27 Mar – 10 April, 1945**.

The 37th Infantry Division raced inland against slight resistance to Clark Field and Fort Stotsenburg (about 50 miles inland). Upon arrival there was fierce resistance until 31 January. The division continued to drive to Manila against small delaying forces and entered the city's outskirts 4 February. Dad was on this drive to Manila. (see map below)

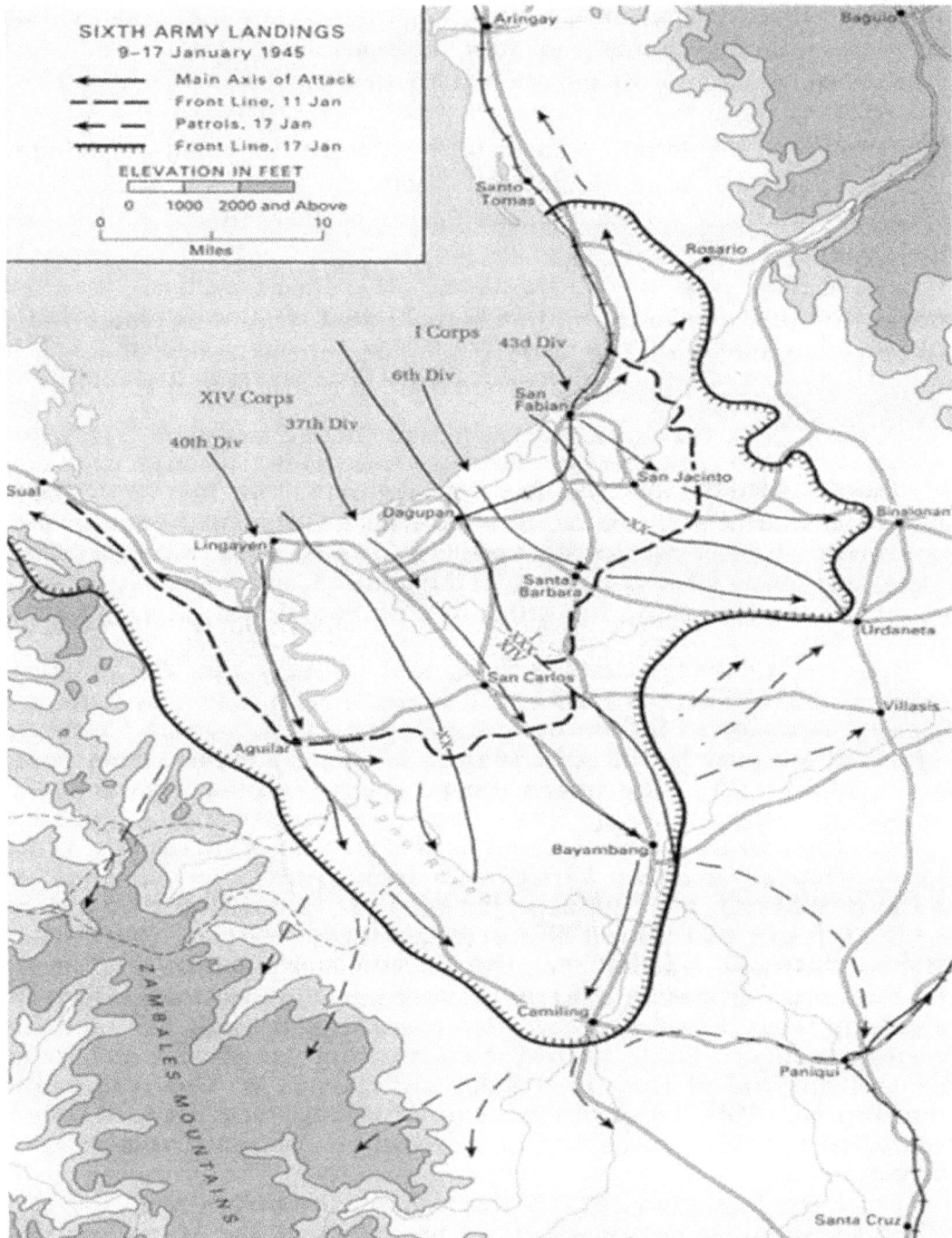

SIXTH ARMY LANDINGS
9–17 January 1945

Main Axis of Attack
Front Line, 11 Jan
Patrols, 17 Jan
Front Line, 17 Jan

ELEVATION IN FEET

0   1000   2000 and Above

0   10
Miles

I Corps
43d Div
6th Div
XIV Corps
37th Div
40th Div

Aringay
Baguio
Santo Tomas
Rosario
San Fabian
San Jacinto
Binalonan
Sual
Dagupan
Lingayen
Santa Barbara
Urdaneta
San Carlos
Villasis
Aguilar
Bayambang
Camiling
Paniqui
ZAMBALES MOUNTAINS
Santa Cruz

✦ ✦ ✦ ✦

The following is an excerpt pertaining to the 37th Division in the Philippines from "The Second Battle of Bougainville" written by Captain John C. Guenther. Dad brought this back from the last military reunion he attended in Chicago prior to his passing.

"The 37th were masters of Clark Field and Ft Stotsenberg, and liberators of Bilibid prison and Santa Tomas internees during their later Philippines campaign. The 37th fought at Bairoka Harbor landing (New Georgia Island); Munda Airfield (New Georgia); Bougainville; Lingayen Gulf landing (Philippines); capture of Clark Field and Ft. Stotsenberg; seizure of San Fernando; penetration of Manila: crossing of the Pasig river; mopping up operations around Baguio, the Cagayen Valley and Baleta Pass, and liberation of 2000 internees at Bilibid Prison."

The 148th Infantry took San Carlos **10 January 1945** and the division assembled and then advanced against strong Japanese opposition toward Clark Field and Fort Stotsenberg. The 145th and 148th Infantry reached the Culayo-Magalang line and the runways of Clark Field **26 January 1945** and captured their objectives with the 129th Infantry on **31 January 1945**.

By **January 1945**, the Japanese had all but abandoned Subic Bay on the west side of the Bataan Peninsula which is on the west side of Manila Bay. The U.S. Fifth Air Force had dropped 175 tons of bombs on Grande Island evoking only light fire from the skeleton Japanese force manning the anti-aircraft guns. The commander of Japanese forces in the Philippines, *General Tomoyuki Yamashita*, had withdrawn his forces into defensive mountain positions.

The 8th Army commanded by General Robert L. Eichelberger landed at Subic Bay on **29 January** and at Batangas on **31 January**. Subic Bay is on the northwest corner of the Bataan peninsula and Batangas is on southwest corner of Manila Bay.

✦ ✦ ✦ ✦

Battle of Clark Field and Fort Stotsenburg

January 24-31, 1945. On **January 24, 1945** two U. S. Army Infantry Divisions approached Clark Field. The 40th Division advanced along the hills to the north of Clark Field while **the 37th Division advanced heading west and southwest from Bambam to Mabalacat, Dau and Angeles across the Clark Field.**

Dad was wounded at Clark Field by a Jap mine in the road. This is where Dad would get his second purple heart.

The Battle of Luzon pitted the Americans against Japan's 2nd Tank Division and produced perhaps the most numerous armored confrontations of the Pacific War. Japanese tanks would conceal themselves in villages lying in ambush for their American adversaries. One of these types of engagements occurred at Sapangbato during the Americans' approach in the Clark Field – Fort Stotsenburg sector on **29 January 1945. Moving in were elements of the 3rd Battalion, 129th Infantry Regiment, 37th Infantry Division supported by four tank battalions.**

Opposing them in the Clark Field – Fort Stotsenburg sector were mixed forces of 30,000 Army and Navy troops known as the *Kembu Group* under commanding *General Rikichi Tsukada*.

Armored forces consisted of eight Type 97 Chi-Ha Kai medium tanks and two Ho-Ro self-propelled guns which were attached to the 2nd Mobile Infantry Regiment of the 2nd Tank Division. Six tanks of the Tank Company were hidden in the village while the SP Gun Company supported them from positions near Runway No. 4 of Clark Field. They dug trenches, caves and interconnecting gun pits throughout the area. The Japanese made the decision to defend the base at all costs.

Type 97 Chi-Ha tank chassis had a Type 4 Ho-Ro mounted the Type 38 150mm howitzer. Surrounding the front of the howitzer was 25mm of armor plating – the open rear leaving the crew susceptible to close combat and shrapnel.

The village of Sapangbato, Angeles lightly defended, was quickly overcome. It is believed that the presence of tanks in the infantry attack facilitated the Japanese's decision to withdraw.

The Executive Officer of the 754th Tank Battalion realized one platoon was running low on fuel, ammunition, and began to withdraw to its headquarters approximately five miles out. Six tanks of the *Iwashita Independent Tank Company* began to pursue them from within the village. Both platoons from Company D, 754th Tank Battalion met just outside the village, where the withdrawing platoon deployed off the road to return fire and the reserve platoon deployed in battle formation. The Japanese tanks succeeded in destroying three tanks before losing four of their tanks to the reserve platoon of Company D. The other two withdrew and, with the rest of their tanks, were encountered as static defenses in the hills of Mt. Pinatubo where they were subsequently destroyed. The surviving defenders retreated into the Zambales Mountains, had to be flushed out one by one, and continued to resist until **20 February 1945**. Damage to base facilities was extensive. Mt. Pinatubo is part of the Zambales Mountains. Clark Air Base is on the eastern edge. The Zambales Mountains stretch from the Lingayen Gulf south to Subic Bay.

Many wrecked Japanese airplanes existed at the Clark Airfield and were studied by ATIU (Air Technical Intelligence Unit) that based itself at Clark to repair and test *them. Forty-five Ki-45 Nicks were captured at Clark, also a Ki-67 Peggy, eight Ki-44 Tojo, Ki-43 Oscar and others.*

Afterwards, the 40th Infantry Division guarded the Clark Field area and conducted mopping up operations, while the 37th continued to advance southward towards Manila.

✦ ✦ ✦ ✦

The military would send news releases picked up by the local newspapers. I have an article from Dad's hometown paper, The Belgrade Tribune. The same heading, *"News about the Boys in the Service"*, was used whenever there was news about a local soldier. The following is one such article.

With the 129th Infantry Regiment on Luzon Island. – Award of the Oak Leaf Cluster in Lieu of a second Purple Heart medal has been made to Staff Sergeant Elmer L. Madsen for wounds sustained in action against the Japanese in the Philippine campaign. Madsen, a mortar squad leader in the 129th Infantry regiment, was wounded slightly in the thigh by a land mine fragment while taking part in an attack on Fort Stotsenburg. His regiment, after a six-day battle, wiped out enemy resistance in the fort area, securing the use of the air strip installations at nearby Clark Field.

Staff Sergeant Madsen has been overseas 31 months, serving also in the Fijis and the Solomons. He landed with his regiment – part of the 37th Infantry division – at Lingayen Gulf on "D" Day helping to make the initial beachhead. He received the Purple Heart for shoulder wounds on Bougainville last year.

✦ ✦ ✦ ✦

Palawan Massacre

On **14 December 1944** near the city of Puerto Princesa in the Philippine province of Palawan Allied soldiers, imprisoned near the city, were killed by Imperial Japanese soldiers.

In order to prevent the rescue of prisoners of war by the advancing Allies units of the *Japanese 14th Area Army* (under the command of *General Tomoyuki Yamashita*) brought the POWs back to their own camp. An air raid warning was sounded to get the prisoners into the shelter trenches, the 150 prisoners of war at Puerto Princesa entered those trenches, and the Japanese soldiers set them on fire using barrels of gasoline. Only 11 men escaped the slaughter. Evidence of the episode has been recorded by two of the eleven survivors: Glenn McDole and Rufus Willie Smith from the 4th US Marines.

The incident sparked a series of POW rescue campaigns by the US, such as the raid at Cabanatuan on January 30, 1945, the raid at Santo Tomas Internment Camp on February 3, 1945, the raid of Bilibid Prison on February 4, 1945, and raid at Los Baños on February 23, 1945.

Raid at Cabanatuan

The Raid at Cabanatuan was a rescue of Allied prisoners of war (POWs) and civilians from a Japanese camp near Cabanatuan City, in the Philippines. On **January 30, 1945** United States Army Rangers, Alamo Scouts and Filipino guerrillas liberated more than 500 from the POW camp.

After the surrender of tens of thousands of American troops during the Battle of Bataan, many were sent to the Cabanatuan prison camp following the Bataan Death March. At its peak, the camp held 8,000 American soldiers (along with a small number of soldiers and civilians from other nations including the United Kingdom, Norway, and the Netherlands), making Cabanatuan the largest POW camp in the Philippines. This number dropped significantly as able-bodied soldiers were shipped to other areas in the Philippines, Japan, Japanese occupied Formosa and Manchukuo to work in slave labor camps. As Japan had not yet ratified the Geneva Convention, the POW's were transported out of the camp and forced to work in factories to build Japanese weaponry, unload ships and repair airfields.

The Japanese transferred most of the prisoners to other areas, leaving just over 500 American and other Allied POWs and civilians in the prison. Facing brutal conditions including disease, torture, and malnourishment, the prisoners feared they would all be executed by their captors before the arrival of General Douglas MacArthur and his American forces returning to Luzon.

In late **January 1945**, a plan was developed by Sixth Army leaders and Filipino guerrillas to send a small force to rescue the prisoners. A group of over a hundred Rangers and Scouts and a couple of hundred guerrillas traveled 30 miles (48 km) behind Japanese lines to reach the camp.

In a nighttime raid, under the cover of darkness and a distraction by a P-61 Black Widow, the group surprised the Japanese forces in and around the camp. Hundreds of Japanese troops were killed in the 30-minute coordinated attack; the Americans suffered minimal casualties. The Rangers, Scouts, and guerrillas escorted the POWs back to American lines. The rescue allowed the prisoners to tell of the death march and prison camp atrocities, which sparked a new rush of resolve for the war against Japan.

Long before the American invasion began, *General Yamashita* divided his Luzon forces into three groups, each centered around a remote geographical region.

The largest of these groups and under the direct command of *Yamashita* was **Shobu Group**, located in northern Luzon with about 152,000 troops.

A much smaller force, **Kembu Group**, with approximately 30,000 troops, occupied the Clark Air Field complex as well as the Bataan Peninsula and Corridor.

The third major force, **Shimbu Group**, consisted of some 80,000 soldiers occupying the southern sections of Luzon, an area that included the island's long Bicol Peninsula as well as the mountains immediately east of Manila.

Most *Shimbu* units were in the latter area and controlled the vital reservoirs that provided most of the capital area's water supply.

General Yamashita long had plans to move the Shobu Group into the triangular redoubt in northern Luzon with apexes at Baguio, Bontac, and Bambang.

Yamashita's troops had been preparing defenses in the mountains since late December and *Yamashita* had initiated a general withdrawal into the mountains before the end of **January 1945**.

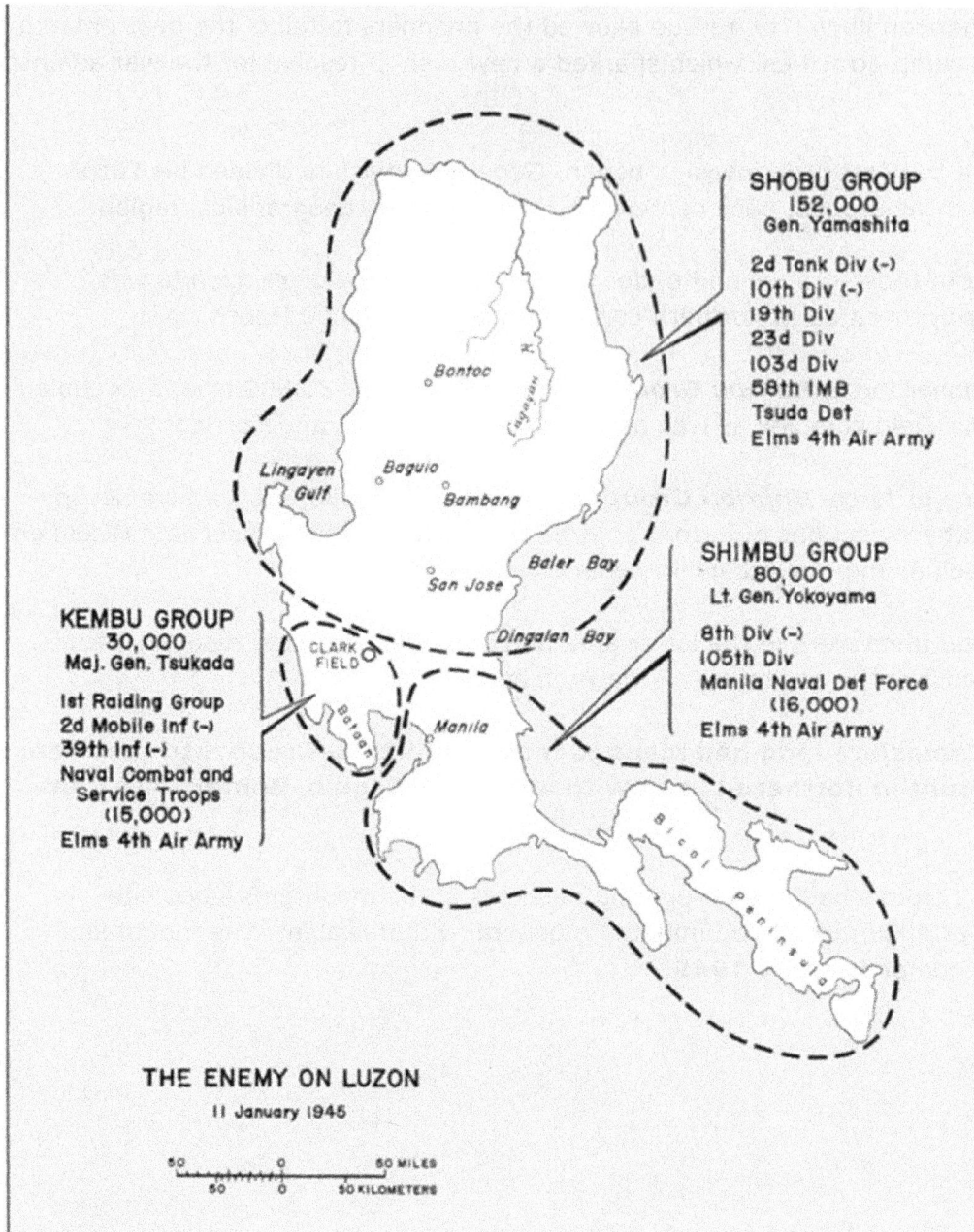

SHOBU GROUP
152,000
Gen. Yamashita

2d Tank Div (-)
10th Div (-)
19th Div
23d Div
103d Div
58th IMB
Tsuda Det
Elms 4th Air Army

SHIMBU GROUP
80,000
Lt. Gen. Yokoyama

8th Div (-)
105th Div
Manila Naval Def Force
(16,000)
Elms 4th Air Army

KEMBU GROUP
30,000
Maj. Gen. Tsukada

1st Raiding Group
2d Mobile Inf (-)
39th Inf (-)
Naval Combat and
Service Troops
(15,000)
Elms 4th Air Army

Bontoc

Lingayen Gulf

Baguio

Bambang

Baler Bay

San Jose

Dingalan Bay

CLARK FIELD

Bataan

Manila

Bicol Peninsula

Cagayan R.

THE ENEMY ON LUZON
11 January 1945

50   0   50 MILES
50   0   50 KILOMETERS

✦ ✦ ✦ ✦

Tank Combat

Tank combat in the Pacific War of 1941–45 is not widely discussed. There has long been a presumption that the terrain conditions in many areas, especially the mountainous tropical jungles of the Southwest Pacific and Burma, were not well suited to tank use. Yet the terrain of the Pacific battlefields varied enormously, from the fetid jungles of New Guinea to the rocky coral atolls of the Central Pacific. In many of the critical campaigns of 1944–45, the terrain was suitable for tank use and they became a critical ingredient in the outcome of the fighting. The largest tank-vs-tank battles of the Pacific War were fought in the Philippines in **January–February 1945** pitting the Japanese 2nd Armored Division against several US Army tank companies and infantry units.

The Imperial Japanese Army tank regiments formed an armored spearhead for the Japanese offensive operations in the tropical jungles of Singapore, Malaysia, Burma, and the Philippines, and proved remarkably successful in areas long thought to be impassable to tanks. In spite of these early successes, the IJA tank force stagnated after early 1942. Japanese strategic planning saw little need for tank forces to defend the Pacific islands in its new outer defense belt, and the Imperial Japanese Navy (IJN) was responsible for the Pacific island defenses. The IJA returned to its focus on the China theater, as well as unresolved campaigns in Burma and New Guinea where tank use was restricted by terrain. The armored divisions formed in 1941–42 were primarily oriented towards defending the Manchurian frontier against a potential Soviet incursion. But with the Soviet Union officially neutral, and with enormous demands on Japan's limited industrial resources, tank manufacture was downgraded in priority and neglected through the middle years of the war.

Both the US Army and US Marine Corps began to deploy the M4 medium tank into the Pacific theater towards the end of 1943, first at Tarawa in November, and subsequently in all of the major campaigns. While the use of medium tanks proved difficult at best in the tropical forests of New Georgia and the Southwest Pacific, the islands of the Central Pacific had coral and volcanic terrain that was much more favorable for tank operations.

The Marine Corps began deploying tanks on roughly the same scale as the US Army in Europe, with each division having a supporting tank battalion. The first use of complete Marine medium tank battalions occurred in the summer of 1944 in the Marianas campaign, with the Marines deploying two tank battalions on Saipan in June 1944. Tank–infantry tactics became a hallmark of Marine offensive capability in the final year of the war. Saipan was also the first clash between the M4 Sherman and the *Japanese Type 97-kai Shinhoto Chi-Ha.*

Although the IJA had very weak technical intelligence on the American tank force, by the summer of 1944 the technological imbalance between Japanese and American tanks was becoming painfully clear. It was too late to introduce technological improvements into the Japanese tank force, and in the event, nearly all of the new-generation tanks were hoarded for the final defense of the Japanese

Home Islands. Instead, Japanese commanders began to examine new tactics to make their tank units a useful tool in the upcoming island campaigns. This debate was still under way in the autumn of 1944 when the US Army began its campaign to liberate the Philippines.

Tanks on Luzon, Japanese View

Yoshiharu Iwanaka's 2nd Tank Division was ready to meet the Americans in the Philippines. It contained about **200 tanks**, mostly Type 97 Chi-Ha and Shinhoto Chi-Ha, but also a few light Type 95 Ha-Go and obsolete Type 89s. In **October of 1944**, the division lost two tank companies (about 30 vehicles) which were sent to Leyte to defend against the American invasion.

The commander of the Japanese defenses of the Philippines, *Tomoyuki Yamashita*, understood that defending against the American invasion is an unrealistic task. However, he planned on lasting as long as possible to allow the main forces to retreat into the mountains, where dealing with them would be much more difficult.

On **16 January 1945**, *Yamashita* ordered the 7th Tank Regiment to attack the American foothold. The order was supposed to be carried out by a tank company and a motorized infantry battalion. Moving out at night, they were caught in an anti-tank gun ambush and suffered serious losses. In the morning, the Americans attacked themselves, targeting the main forces of the Japanese regiment, quartered in a small city called Urdaneta. In this battle, only one Japanese tank platoon had any luck, taking up favorable positions and knocking out two Shermans before they were knocked out in return. The other Japanese tankers had no such luck; their 47 mm shells could only penetrate a Sherman in the sides and rear.

The remainder of the *7th Regiment* (34 tanks out of 60 authorized) retreated to San Manuel. The Americans were not in a hurry to attack them. Instead, they spent five days grinding Japanese defenses into dust with bombs and artillery. The Shermans only attacked on the dawn of **January 26th**. One by one, they shot up the Japanese tanks from a safe distance. By the evening, the regiment shrank to 7 tanks, the crews of which carried out the Japanese tradition in an unescapable situation and launched a suicide attack.

Unlike them, the commander of the Japanese *10th Tank Regiment* ordered his crews to abandon their tanks and fight their way back to their main force on foot.

The *6th Tank Regiment*, located in the southern part of Luzon on the day of the landing, moved out north and quartered themselves in the town of Munoz. The tankers defended against their first attack on **January 27th**. American infantry fell back once they encountered resistance, but aircraft started their hunt for Japanese tanks. The second attack, this time with the use of Shermans, started on **January 30th**. As a result, the city was completely surrounded and the Japanese regiment had only 20 tanks left. The order to retreat was only given a week later. At night, the surviving Japanese soldiers fought their way out through a storm of American fire, with only one in five making it out alive.

In this battle, the Japanese faced C Company from the 44th Tank Battalion. **The "Tank News" newspaper of the 6th Army called it "the hottest tank on tank battle in the Pacific".** American soldiers had to not only shoot but also fight hand to hand. In the morning, the Americans discovered 10 knocked out tanks in front of their positions, one light tank, a couple of trucks, an all-terrain vehicle, and 245 dead Japanese soldiers. C Company got off with one killed, 11 wounded, and 2 damaged tanks.

The last tank battle in Luzon happened in **April of 1945**. The attacking Americans were nearing the HQ of the *14th Japanese Army* in Baguio. At that point, *General Yamashita* only had three medium and two light tanks left from the *5th Company of the 10th Regiment*. Since they had no chance of dealing with the Americans in open battle, *Yamashita* ordered a suicide attack, attaching explosives to the front armor of one medium and one light tank. According to Japanese records, they managed to burn up two Shermans in that fight, and crews of knocked out Japanese tanks left their vehicles and rushed at the enemy, swinging their swords.

Battle for Manila, American View

The Americans knew that the Philippines held a large amount (for the Pacific theatre, anyway) of tanks. To be safe, American units were reinforced with not only Sherman battalions, but tank destroyed battalions armed with M10 Wolverines. It's worth noting that the Wolverines were excessive: the weak armor of Japanese tanks could be penetrated by regular Sherman guns without effort.

One of the priority tasks for MacArthur's troops was the taking of Manila. The general expected that this would minimize the casualties among the city's civilian population and American prisoners of war that were held in the capital. In addition, the liberation of Manila was supposed to encourage the Filipino's to more actively resist the Japanese, especially since the previous few years gave them more than enough reasons for hatred.

Battle for Manila, Japanese View

Interestingly enough, *Yamashita* wanted to give up Manila as much as MacArthur wanted to take it. He considered the city a trap and its defense a waste of already diminishing resources. He may have had his way, if not for a peculiarity of Japanese warfare. The Navy always looked down on the Army, and the commander of the Manila defenses was *Rear Admiral Sanji Iwabuchi*, former commander of the battleship *Kirishima* that was sunk by the Americans in 1942. He decided to restore his honor for his lost ship and die a samurai's death. In order to do this, the city must be defended, and not abandoned on the order of some Army man.

According to some sources, *Iwabuchi* had about 4000 soldiers that fell behind their land units and 15,000 poorly organized sailors with no land experience at his disposal. The Rear Admiral also had a single tank, an American M3 Stuart that was captured when Manila was taken in January of 1942. These were the forces that *Iwabuchi* was going to use to defend the city, to the last Japanese, American, or Filipino, whichever came first.

Three tank battalions participated in the battle for Manila at first (711th, 754th, and the aforementioned 44th), as well as a tank destroyer battalion. The "flying column" of tankers from the 44th Battalion managed to carry out MacArthur's orders and penetrate the Japanese defenses, reaching the University of Santo Tomas building by **February 3rd**, which housed nearly 4000 prisoners of war.

Then the clearing out of the city began. This was done with the forces of the 37th Infantry Division with support of tanks from the 44th and 754th battalions. The history of the latter contains the phrase *"This was a new type of fighting for tanks and infantry. Tanks were used as mobile artillery in a very limited space."* Japanese mines made a lot of trouble for the Americans. Despite all of engineers' efforts, tanks blew up on streets that were allegedly cleared of mines.

On **February 7th**, one of the American tankers wrote in his journal: "Manila is on fire". Houses were burning as well as tanks; the attempt of two platoons from the 44th Battalion to move forward ended tragically. The Japanese attacked the tanks with 20 mm and 125 mm naval guns, as well as grenadiers carrying mines and Molotov cocktails. Three Shermans burned up, two more were damaged. Other American units also reported suicide attacks with Molotov cocktails. Another tank received three hits from a 5-inch gun. The Sherman's armor could not withstand such a caliber and the tank was completely destroyed. 4 tankers died.

To protect the 800,000 civilians in Manila from excess deaths, MacArthur implemented harsh restrictions on American artillery and air support. This did not have the desired effect. By the end of the battle, the city lay in ruins.

On, **February 13th 1945**, the Americans reached the old city. Its thick stone walls (Intramuros) were immune to 75 mm shells. One of the most resilient buildings was the police station: it cost the 754th Battalion several days and three lost tanks. Another memorable structure was the building known in Manila as the "German house". After an extensive shelling, tanks and infantry tried to get close to it, only to have one Sherman be knocked out by a mine and pelted with Molotov cocktails.

✦   ✦   ✦   ✦

Battle of Manila

The **Battle for Manila** from **3 February to 3 March 1945**, fought by U.S. and Japanese forces, was part of the Philippines' 1945 campaign. The one-month battle which culminated in a terrible bloodbath and total devastation of the city was the scene of the **worst urban fighting in the Pacific War - Pacific theater**, ended almost three years, **1942-1945** of Japanese military occupation in the Philippines.

Cities such as Manila (the second most destroyed Allied city in WWII) were reduced to rubble. Between 500,000 and 1,000,000 Filipinos died during the occupation.

MacArthur added additional forces to the drive on the capital. On **15 January 1945** he launched Operation MIKE VI which was a second amphibious assault, forty-five miles southwest of Manila. On **31 January**, X-ray Day, two regiments of the 11th Airborne Division, under the command of Maj. Gen. Joseph M. Swing, landed unopposed. The paratroopers seized a nearby bridge before the surprised Japanese defenders had a chance to demolish it, and then the paratroopers turned toward Manila. The division's third regiment, the 511th Parachute, dropped in by air to join the advance, which by the following day was speeding north along the paved highway toward the capital to the cheers of throngs of grateful Filipino civilians along the way.

Originally the 11th Airborne Division, one of Lt. Gen. Robert L. Eichelberger's Eighth Army units, had been slated to contain Japanese troops throughout southwestern Luzon. But acting on MacArthur's orders, Eichelberger pushed the division north. On **3 February** one battalion of the 511th encountered determined Japanese resistance near the town of Imus, five miles south of Manila, where some fifty defenders clung to an old stone building despite a fierce bombardment by the battalion's 75-mm. howitzers. Observing that the artillery had had little effect, T. Sgt. Robert C. Steel climbed onto the building's roof, knocked a hole through it, poured in gasoline, and then threw in a phosphorous grenade. As the Japanese dashed out, Steel's men shot them down.

Another three miles up the road lay the Las Pinas River bridge. It was set for demolition and guarded by a small detachment of Japanese who were dug in along the north bank. Despite the fierce firefight less than an hour before at Imus, the Japanese were surprised by the appearance of the Americans. The paratroopers secured the span before it could be blown. With one battalion guarding the bridge, another passed over on trucks toward Manila, hoping to enter the city from the south.

By dawn on **4 February** the paratroopers ran into increasingly heavy and harassing fire from Japanese riflemen and machine gunners. At the Paranaque River, just south of the Manila city limits, the battalion halted at a badly damaged bridge only to be battered by Japanese artillery fire from Nichols Field. The 11th Airborne Division had reached the main Japanese defenses south of the capital and could go no further.

The "race" for Manila was now between the 37th Division and the 1st Cavalry Division, with the cavalry in the lead. Since the operation had begun in late January, its units had been fortunate enough to find bridges and fordable crossings almost everywhere they went. On **2 February** Chase's flying column was dashing toward Manila, sometimes at speeds of fifty miles per hour, with individual units competing for the honor of reaching the city first. **The 37th Division was slowed down by difficult crossings which forced it to either ferry its artillery and tanks across or wait for the engineers to build bridges.**

3 February 1945, the battle for the liberation of Manila started. The *Manila Naval Defense Force*, under *Rear Admiral Iwabuchi Sanji*, composed of around 15,000 troops, defended Manila to the last man. There was only one Japanese tank attached to naval forces in the defense. Tanks played a vital role for the American operations. The 44th Tank Battalion and 640th Tank Destroyer Battalion of the 1st Calvary Division and the 754th Tank Battalion and 711th Tank Battalion of the 37th Division played a significant role in liberating Manila, the capital city of the Philippines.

On **3 February** elements of the 1st Cavalry Division pushed into the northern outskirts of Manila, with only the steep-sided Tuliahan River separating them from the city proper. A squadron of the 8th Cavalry reached the bridge just moments after Japanese soldiers had finished preparing it for demolition. As the two sides opened fire on one another, the Japanese lit the fuse leading to the carefully placed explosives. Without hesitation, Lt. James P. Sutton, a Navy demolitions expert attached to the division, dashed through the enemy fire and cut the burning fuse. The way to Manila was clear.

That evening of **3 February**, the 8th Cavalry passed through the northern suburbs and into the city itself. The troopers had won the race to Manila. As the sun set over the ocean behind the advancing Americans, a single tank named "Battling Basic" crashed through the walls surrounding Santo Tomas University, the site of a camp holding almost 4,000 civilian prisoners. The Japanese guards put up little re- sistance, and soon the inmates, many of whom had been incarcerated for nearly two years, were liberated.

Santo Tomas Internment Camp

Also known as the **Manila Internment Camp**, was the largest of several camps in the Philippines in which the Japanese interned enemy civilians, mostly Americans, in World War II located four city blocks south of the Pasig River. The campus of the University of Santo Tomas in Manila was utilized for the camp which housed more than 3,000 internees from **January 1942 until February 1945**. Conditions for the internees deteriorated during the war and by the time of the liberation of the camp by the U.S. Army many of the internees were near death from lack of food. Since **4 January 1942**, a total of thirty-seven months, the university's main build- ing was used to hold civilian POWs and classrooms for sleeping quarters. Out of 4,255 prisoners, 466 died in captivity. 3,785 prisoners were released on   **3 Feb- ruary 1945**.

Male internees lost an average of 53 pounds during the 37 months of their internment at Santo Tomas. The evacuation of the internees began on **February 11**. Sixty-four U.S army and navy nurses interned in Santo Tomas were the first to leave that day and board airplanes for the United States. Flights and ships to the United States for most internees began on **22 February.**

Using intelligence provided by Filipino guerrillas, American units were able to find intact bridges and shallow rivers everywhere they went. **The 37th Division con- tinued to drive to Manila against small delaying forces, and entered the city's northern outskirts, 4 February 1945. Upon crossing the Pasig River, it ran into bitter Japanese opposition.**

Old Bilibid Prison Camp

The prisoner of war camp known as Old Bilibid Prison Camp was located in the heart of Manila, not far distant from Santo Tomas University, where the Allied civilians were interned during the Japanese occupation of the Philippines. **4 February 1945 Billibid Prison was liberated by the 37th Division. 1,000 prisoners of war, mostly former defenders of Bataan and Corregidor held at Bilibid Prison, was abandoned by the Japanese.** Billibid Prison buildings in a spoked wheel design as shown below.

As reported by the AP on a **February 6** news article: *"Musty, filthy old Bilibid, erstwhile Japanese prison of horrors, was a begrimed citadel of American freedom today. The Thirty-seventh division infantry opened its doors Sunday for the liberation of its half-starved, ill-clothed 800 prisoners of war and 500 civilian internees, including women and children."*

Army medics speak with and feed three emaciated, newly liberated American POWs at Billibid prison.

At Santo Tomas University, ten blocks to the north, there had been some fighting prior to the complete liberation of its some 3700 internees by the 1st cavalry division. This was not so at Bilibid. The Japanese fled their infamy there. Old Bilibid was in such a deplorable condition that the ancient Spanish prison had been abandoned by the Filipino government before the war. But the Japanese made full use of its torture chambers. Many an accused man was taken from Santo Tomas to Bilibid. If he came back at all, he came back a broken and shattered shell of himself. Prisoners confined to the prison itself and not taken to the torture chambers, however, received generally better treatment than in other war prisons.

The 37th Division ferried across the Pasig River in assault boats about a half mile to the right of the Jones Bridge due to enemy forces protecting the bridge. The General Post Office is on the other side of the river and is surrounded by water. Upon crossing the river, the 37th Division stormed The Mint Building (Bureau of Treasury) and ran into bitter Japanese opposition.

This difficult and hazardous maneuver demanded a daylight crossing of the Pasig River at a point, 375 feet in width, followed immediately by direct assault on a strongly fortified bastion under constant enemy observation and defended by heavy fire from many automatic weapons. Colonel Frederick led his regiment with such outstanding success that it not only seized its initial objective but continued to advance for seven hundred yards into the Walled City itself. It took heavy street fighting to clear the city by 3 March, 1945.

Although the approach to the city had been relatively easy, wresting the capital from the Japanese proved far more difficult. Manila, a city of 800,000, was one of the largest in Southeast Asia. While much of it consisted of ramshackle huts, the downtown section boasted massive reinforced concrete buildings built to withstand earthquakes and old Spanish stone fortresses of equal size and strength. Most were located south of the Pasig River which bisects the capital, requiring that the Americans cross over before closing with the enemy. Even a half-hearted defense was bound to make Manila's recapture difficult. The Americans soon realized that they couldn't hope to save a large part of the city from being wrecked, while at the same time root-out the Japanese. They prepared fanatical resistance.

✦ ✦ ✦ ✦

Dad brought pictures home of him and fellow soldier Leonard Martinson kneeling with their rifles in a pose on one of the islands.

Dad and Martinson became very good friends during the war. Leonard Martinson from Audubon, MN was killed in Manila while fighting next to Dad.

For several years after the war I was told Dad visited Martinson's widow to keep a promise they both shared while together in the war:

Whoever makes it back will visit the other's widow on their wedding anniversary date. 2 ½ hours NW of Belgrade, Minnesota and one hour east of Fargo, North Dakota. 192 miles one way. This trip was made by Dad and Mom for several years after the war.

They were together through basic training, across the Pacific to the Fiji Islands, New Hebrides, Guadalcanal, New Georgia, Bougainville, and finally, the Philippines. Now, back to the states in spirit only.

✦ ✦ ✦ ✦

The 148th Infantry reached Manila **4 Feb 45.** After crossing the Pasig River, the division began the house-to-house combat which slowly reduced the city.

On 5 February the 37th Division began to move into Manila, Griswold divided the northern section of the city into two sectors, with the 37th responsible for the western half, toward Manila Bay, and the 1st Cavalry responsible for the eastern part. By the afternoon of the 8th, 37th Division units had cleared most Japanese from their sector, although the damage done to the residential districts was extensive. The Japanese added to the destruction by demolishing buildings and military installations as they withdrew. But the division's costliest fighting occurred on Provisor Island, a small industrial center on the Pasig River. The Japanese garrison, probably less than a battalion, held off elements of the division until 11 February. Almost three days for this small island to fall. Building to building, floor to floor, and hand to hand combat.

Every building was a fortress, almost every street corner a machine gun nest. Thousands of mines had been planted by the Japanese, and there were numerous booby-traps.

On **23 Feb 45** the assault was begun on Intramuros after heavy artillery preparation. The 145th stormed the Quezon and Parian Gates and the 148th Infantry cleared the Legislative Building.

On **28 February 1945**. A M4 Sherman tank finally breached the defenses of Fort Santiago, Intramuros (the heart of Manila), entering through the Santa Lucia Gate.

The only Japanese tank that is part of the defenses was a M3 Light Tank, captured in 1942 and used by Japanese, was recaptured by units of the 1ˢᵗ Cavalry Brigade in front of the Manila Hotel. The Japanese abandoned it, removing all the weapons.

Regarding Manila as indefensible, *General Yamashita* had originally ordered the commander of *Shimbu Group, General Yokoyama Shizuo*, to destroy all bridges and other vital installations and evacuate the city as soon as strong American forces made their appearance. However, *Rear Adm. Iwabachi Sanji*, the naval commander for the Manila area, vowed to resist the Americans and countermanded the order. Determined to support the admiral as best he could, *Yokoyama* contributed three Army battalions to *Iwabachi's* 16,000-man *Manila Naval Defense Force* and pre-pared for battle. The sailors knew little about infantry tactics or street fighting, but they were well armed and entrenched throughout the capital. *Iwabachi* resolved to fight to the last man.

Following the initial American breakthrough on **4 February**, fighting raged throughout the city for almost a month. The battle quickly came down to a series of bitter street-to-street and house-to-house struggles. In the north, General Griswold continued to push elements of the XIV Corps south from Santo Tomas University toward the Pasig River.

Iwabuchi's sailors, marines and army reinforcements, having initially successfully resisted American infantrymen armed with flamethrowers, grenades and bazookas now faced direct fire from tanks, tank destroyers, and howitzers, who attacked one building after another and killed the Japanese, and often the trapped civilians, inside the structures.

Subjected to incessant pounding, and facing certain death, the beleaguered Japanese troops took out their anger and frustration on the civilians caught in the crossfire, committing multiple acts of severe brutality, which later would be known as the Manila Massacre.

The Manila Massacre

Although the Americans were under orders to advance without causing too much destruction in the city, influenced by MacArthur's liking for the city, the city still suffered dearly from American artillery and air attacks during the month-long urban fighting; an estimated 1,000 Filipinos were killed from American tank and artillery fire. However, a much greater part of damage, both material as well as in human lives, were caused by the Japanese. Before *Yamashita* had left Manila for his new headquarters in Banguio, he left *Vice Admiral Denshichi Okochi* instructions to destroy the port facilities and declare Manila an open city. However, *Okochi* defied his orders. With a division-equivalent of mostly naval personnel, *Okochi* and his men engaged in a horrendous pillaging act. During lulls in the battle for control of the city, Japanese troops took their anger and frustration out on the civilians in the city. Violent mutilations, rapes, and massacres occurred in schools, hospitals and convents, including San Juan de Dios Hospital, Santa Rosa College, Santo Domingo Church, Manila Cathedral, Paco Church, St. Paul's Convent, and St. Vincent de Paul Church.

Dr. Antonio Gisbert told of the murder of his father and brother at the Palacio del Gobernador, saying, *"I am one of those few survivors, not more than 50 in all out of more than 3000 men herded into Fort Santiago and, two days later, massacred. Hospitals were set afire with patients tied to their beds."*

The Bayview Hotel was used as a designated "rape center". According to testimony at the *Yamashita* war crimes trial, 400 women and girls were rounded up from Manila's wealthy Ermita district and submitted to a selection board that picked out the 25 women who were considered most beautiful. These women and girls, many of them 12 to 14 years old, were then taken to the hotel, where Japanese enlisted men and officers took turns raping them. Women of all ages raped and murdered. Babies' eyeballs were gouged out and smeared on walls. 100,000 Filipinos would be murdered mercilessly in Manila and all-around Luzon in the last days of Japanese control.

The fighting for Intramuros continued from **23-28 February**. Already having decimated the Japanese forces by bombing, American forces now used artillery to try and root out the Japanese defenders. However, the centuries-old stone ramparts, underground edifices, the Sta. Lucia Barracks, Fort Santiago, and villages within the city walls all provided excellent cover.

The last pocket of Japanese resistance at the Finance Building, which was already reduced to rubble, was flushed out by heavy artillery on **3 March**. For the rest of the month the Americans and the Filipino allies mopped up resistance throughout the city.

"That the artillery had almost razed the ancient Walled City could not be helped. To the XIV Corps and the 37th Division at this state of the battle for Manila, American lives were understandably far more valuable than historic landmarks. The destruction stemmed from the American decision to save lives in a battle against Japanese troops who had decided to sacrifice their lives as dearly as possible," a U.S. battle report stated.

The Intramuros is the place where the occupying Japanese Imperial Army made their last stand against American soldiers and the Filipino guerillas. The battle destroyed its magnificent churches, universities, houses and government buildings, most of which dated back to the Spanish Colonial Period. **3 March 1945** Japanese resistance in Manila comes to an end after a bitter month-long fight. The 20,000 defenders have been wiped out and the town devastated.

The battle left 1,010 U.S. soldiers dead and 5,565 wounded. An estimated 100,000 Filipinos were killed, both deliberately by the Japanese and accidentally by crossfire. About 16,000 Japanese soldiers died, mostly sailors from the Japanese *Manila Defense Force*.

In the month-long battle, the Americans and Japanese inflicted worse destruction on Manila than the German Luftwaffe had visited upon London, which resulted not only in the destruction of the city, but in a death toll comparable to that of the Tokyo Firebombing or the atomic bombing of Hiroshima. The city joined Stalingrad as being the host to some of the fiercest urban fighting during the war. Few battles in the closing months of World War II exceeded the destruction and the brutality of the massacres and savagery of the fighting in Manila.

After garrison duty in Manila, 5-26 March, the 37th Division shifted to the hills of Northwest Luzon. The 129th Infantry was detached to Bauang and attached to the 33rd Infantry Division 26 Mar-10 Apr 45. Bauang is on the west coast of Luzon south of San Fernando. The 145th Infantry remained in Manila when the 129th division moved to northwest Luzon for the offensive against Baguio and did not rejoin it until **2 Jun 45**.

19 March 1945i n the northward attacks along the west coast, I Corp takes Bauang south of San Fernando on east side of Lingayen Gulf Luzon with the help of Filipino guerillas. **The 37th Infantry Division relieves the 130th at Burgos, east of Bauang.**

✦ ✦ ✦ ✦

Battle of San Fernando

The **Battle of Bacsil Ridge** was fought on **19 March 1945** was one of the continued main battles of the Philippines Campaign was between the Filipino soldiers under the 121st Infantry Regiment, Philippine Commonwealth Army, USAFIP-NL, under the command of Russell W. Volckmann, and the Japanese Imperial forces under *General Tomoyuki Yamashita*, which resulted in the capture of San Fernando, La Union on **23 March 1945**, and Bacnotan, La Union after two months of fighting. Against 6,000 Japanese troops, the Filipino soldiers fought valiantly and forced the enemy into northern Luzon resulting in 3,322 Japanese killed, 407 captured and 877 Filipino casualties.

On Luzon, **10 April**, the advance of the XIV Corps reaches Lamon Bay and the coastal town of Mauban is captured. Mauban is within the Quezon province on the southeastern end of Luzon.

Fort Drum

In Manila Bay US forces land on Fort Drum **13 April 1945**, "the Concrete Battleship", and begin to pour 5,000 gallons of fuel oil into the fortifications. This is then set on fire and burns for five days eliminating the Japanese garrison. On **16 April** a landing on Fort Frank finds it abandoned. This completes the capture of the islands in Manila Bay.

While Beightler's division was garrisoning Manila, the I Corps had been pressing the *Shobu* Group south and west of Baguio, and the XIV Corps, later replaced by the XI Corps, had been squeezing remnants of the *Shimbu* Group east of Manila. Innis Swift's I Corps had the difficult task of assaulting the *Shobu* Group's stronghold in northern Luzon, a mountainous triangular redoubt with apexes at Baguio, Bontac, and Bambang.

Swift had three divisions operating against the Japanese. The 33rd Division south and west of Baguio. The 32nd Division to the southeast of Baguio. The 25th Division to the east and south of Baguio. Swift was supported by a force of 18,000 Filipino guerrillas, who had secured much of the west coast of Luzon north of Bauang and were driving on Baguio from the northwest.

Handheld metal detectors became a common use on the Philippines as a mine sweeper throughout the war to locate land mines.

The principal role for the US Army tank battalions in the Philippines was infantry support. One of the problems in tank operations on Luzon was the frequent switch of tank companies from one infantry regiment to another, with no previous joint training and a lack of standardized tactical practices.

✦ ✦ ✦ ✦

Battle of Baguio

The 129th Infantry, under the command of John Frederick, and the 6th Field Artillery Battalion began leaving Manila on March 26, traveling the 180 miles to Bauang by train, truck, and ship. On March 30, it replaced the 130th Infantry Regiment on Route 9, and by 1 April was at Salat, less than a mile short of the Japanese MLR (Main Line of Resistance) position at Sablan. In the following days the 129th pushed east as far as Salat, fifteen miles from Baguio. They ran into Japanese resistance and for ten days sparred with the Japanese in the surrounding mountains.

Beightler planned to drive directly along Route 9 with the 129th regiment in column and concentrate his fire support at each enemy position he encountered. The 148th Infantry, at Naguilian some miles to the rear, would be in reserve.

The Allied forces had made it virtually impossible for the Japanese to bring any food into the Baguio area. Almost inevitably the principal sufferers were the front-line troops. By mid-March the best-fed Japanese combat troops on the Baguio front were getting less than half a pound of rice per day as opposed to a minimum daily requirement of nearly two and a half pounds. Before the end of the month the troops on the main line of resistance were down to less than a quarter of a pound of rice a day. Starvation and diet-associated diseases filled hospitals and sapped the strength of the combat units. Generally, effective frontline strength was far lower than reported ration strength indicated. Medical supplies were consumed rapidly, and by the end of March, for example, there was virtually no malaria prophylaxis left in Baguio area hospitals.

Beightler's ammunition had been rationed, and therefore, in contrast to previous operations, he was unable to go splashing artillery and mortar shells on possible enemy concentrations, possible gun positions, and possible routes of approach. Instead, targets had to be defined and each round made to count. For Beightler, a disciple of area barrages, the parsimony in the availability of shells was hard to take.

Beightler compensated for the restrictions on artillery fire by expanding his use of air support. His previous experience with such support was limited, for in the New Georgia, Bougainville, and Manila operations little had been available, and even that often had been patently ineffective. Now more support was available, and Beightler, short of artillery shells, decided to use it. As he saw the capabilities of close air support, Beightler increasingly called for airstrikes to pound Japanese positions in front of him and on his flanks. Techniques were refined to coordinate airstrikes with ground action, and by the end of the Baguio operation Beightler did not hesitate to call in airstrikes on targets, sometimes as close as 400 yards from his front-line troops. Thereafter, close air support assumed a definite place in Beightler's tactics. *"Air support,"* Beightler later wrote, *"saved us many casualties and materially speeded our progress."*

By late March, Innis Swift's I Corps assault against the Japanese redoubt had stalled. It was ordered that all three divisions hold in place until reinforcements could be provided.

129th IR attached to 33rd ID from 37th ID and pushed up Highway 9 toward Baguio, encountering very heavy fighting in the Salat Area 23 Mar-10 Apr 44. 129th IR detached 33rd ID and joined 148th IR attacking up Highway 9, taking Three Peaks 11 April 1945.

Beightler ordered Frederick to move his 129th Regiment against the Japanese at Sablan. From April 11 to 14, the 129th Regiment battled the Japanese, with Beightler constantly urging Frederick to push aggressively to keep the Japs off balance and achieve a quick breakthrough. Supported by air strikes, artillery barrages, and tanks that led the way, Frederick's 3rd

and 1st Battalions secured several key peaks, advanced nearly a mile along the road, and repulsed several minor counterattacks, breaking the Japanese defenses in the Sablan area. The fighting was often quite fierce, and Frederick's men relied heavily on close artillery and tank fire to knock out Japanese machine gun, mortar, and antitank gun positions. Frederick used the tactics of pounding heavily with the power weapons to save infantry lives.

The main effort was to be made on Route 9 by the 37th Division. The 33d Division would advance along all three approaches to Baguio in its area, placing emphasis on the Galiano road since an attack there would support the 37th Division's action and the terrain on the Galiano approach, at least east from Asin, appeared the easiest in the 33d Division's zone. The 33d Division made its 136th Infantry, reinforced by the 33d Reconnaissance Troop and the 2d Battalion of the 66th Infantry, USAFIP(NL), responsible for continuing pressure along Route 11 and up the three river valleys to the east. The 123d Infantry would push northeast over the Tuba Trail. The 130th Infantry would concentrate on the Galiano road. **The 129th Infantry was to lead the 37th Division attack down Route 9, with the 148th Infantry initially held in reserve.**

On the Tuba Trail troops spent most of their time bogged down by rain, fog, incredibly bad terrain, and steady, determined Japanese resistance. Thus, neither of the 33d Division's two right flank regiments was able to make a direct contribution to the success of the drive on Baguio; subsequent events proved that the units on Route 11 did not even keep in place the Japanese forces that faced them as of **12 April**. Therefore, the description of the drive to Baguio of necessity centers on the operations along Route 9 and the Galiano road.

Although the two-division attack was not to start until 12 April, the 37th Division, in order to maintain momentum and contact, moved on 11 April against the Japanese known to be entrenched at and near Sablan. During the period 11-14 April the 129th Infantry broke through the Japanese defenses at Sablan in a battle marked by extremely close artillery and medium tank fire support. On **14 April** the 148th Infantry took over and by the end of the next day had secured Route 9 through Calot. During those two days the regiment also captured many ammunition and other supply dumps that the *19th Division* had left behind when it had redeployed through Baguio to the north. The Japanese had neither the time nor the means to move these supplies north, and their loss would ultimately prove serious. **Equally serious was the fact that from 11 through 15 April the 37th Division's artillery, supporting aircraft, and attached tank units had destroyed nearly all the artillery pieces available to the Japanese *58th IMB.***

The seizure of Yagyagan was to assume considerable importance, for from that barrio a trail led southwest down steep slopes to Asin on the Galiano road. The 130th Infantry, 33d Division, had been stalled by determined Japanese resistance west of Asin. If the 37th Division could secure the Yagyagan trail entrance, part of the 130th Infantry could move around to Route 9 and fall upon the Asin defenses in a neat envelopment.

To secure the trail entrance and to assure its own progress along Route 9, the 37th Division had to break through known Japanese defenses where, just a mile southeast of Yagyagan, the highway dipped across the gorge of the Irisan River. The six-day battle that ensued at the Irisan Gorge proved to be the critical action of the entire drive to Baguio. It was, indeed, one of the few cohesive actions on the Baguio front after the capture of the Routes 3-11 road junction by the 43d Division in late January, and it serves as an example of much of the fighting on the Baguio front starting from late February on.

At the Irisan River crossing, in general, all Japanese positions in the area were of a hasty nature, with the possible exception of some caves in which antitank guns were emplaced to control the east-west stretch of Route 9. But most emplacements, especially those for machine guns, the Japanese had chosen with an excellent eye for terrain, and installations on every ridge were mutually supporting when the terrain permitted.

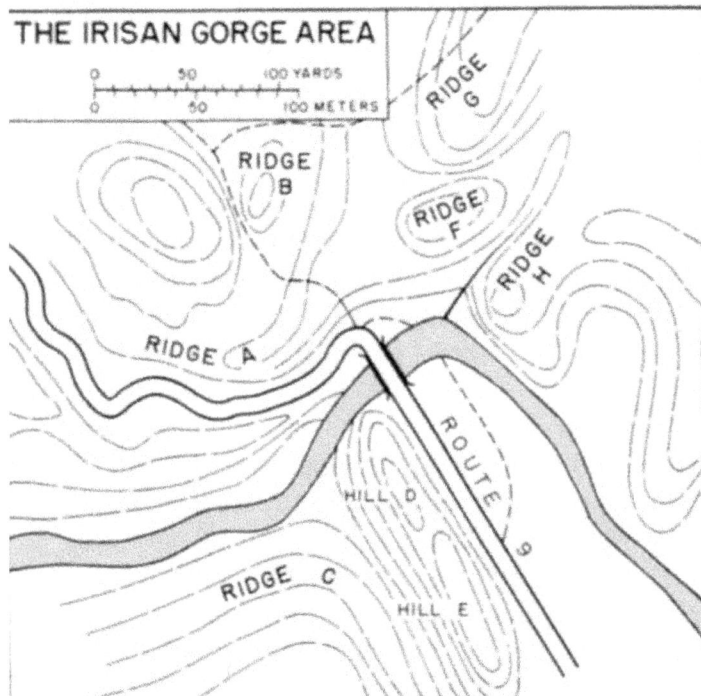

THE IRISAN GORGE AREA

April 14 Beightler replaced the tired 129th Infantry with the 148th Infantry. By the evening of **April 16**, the 148th had pushed beyond Yagyagan. About a mile southeast of Yagyagan, the 148th encountered the major Japanese defensive position on Route 9; the Irisan Gorge, which was about 5 miles west of Baguio. The bridge spanning the Irisan River had already been destroyed by the Japanese. Eight nearby ridges all occupied by the Japanese, dug into the side of these ridges, dominated the gorge. The terrain was heavily wooded, and all of the trails leading to the Japanese strongpoints were narrow, difficult to climb, and covered by machine guns, anti-tank guns and spider holes. Route 9 on both sides of the bridge could be easily swept by Japanese fire and cross fire from the surrounding ridges, making any attempt to rebuild it suicide without first seizing the ridges.

The morning of **April 17** Beightler learned he was in for a tough fight at the gorge. Two companies from the 2nd battalion of the 148th Infantry, reinforced by tanks, tank destroyers, and self-propelled guns, were moving along Route 9 just west of the bridge. Going around the last curve in the road to the river, the Japanese opened fire.

This battle involved one of the last tank-versus-tank engagements of the Philippines campaign, between M4 Shermans of the U.S. Army's Company B, 775th Tank Battalion and *Type 97s* of the *IJA's 5th Tank Company, 10th Tank Regiment.*

The battle at the Irisan Gorge, from **16 April,** was not cleared until **21 Apr 1945** when the advance resumed. The Japanese lost close to 500 killed in the fighting at the gorge. Beightler's losses were forty killed and 160 wounded.

The victory at Irisan Gorge freed Beightler to push rapidly on to Baguio. For this purpose, he replaced the 148th Regiment with the rested 129th on **April 22**, and by nightfall the latter had advanced to the junction of Route 9 and the Galiano road. Swift ordered Beightler to hold his position on Route 9, clear the area north of Route 9 between Sablan and the Irisan Gorge, and block the trail to Trinidad to forestall a possible counterattack.

Mount Mirador fell after heavy combat to the 129th after heavy fighting 24-26 April 45 and culminated in the capture of Baguio and Camp John Hay Airfield, under combined assault of 33rd and 37th Infantry Divisions 27 April 1945.

There was no need to worry about a Japanese counterattack. *Yamashita* had left Baguio for Bambang on **April 19**, and early on **April 23** *Utsunomiya*, short of supplies and lacking artillery support, concluded strengthening their defensive positions. The Japanese *10th Division and 2nd Tank Division* were finished as effective combat units.

Once under way, the Japanese retreat was rapid. A patrol of the 129th Infantry, 37th Division, entered Baguio on 24 April, and two days later the regiment secured most of the city against negligible opposition. The 123d Infantry reached Tuba on **24 April** after an unopposed march southwest from Mt. Mirador; a battalion left in the Mt. Calugong area straggled into Tuba from the west during the next two days. On **27 April** patrols of the 33d Division moved into Baguio proper from the south and southwest, making contact with the 129th Infantry and thus marking the end of the drive to Baguio.

As a campaign to destroy Japanese, the drive to Baguio was only partially successful because the halt I Corps ordered on **22 April** had permitted *General Utsunomiya* to extricate some 10,000 troops from his defenses in front of Baguio and from the city proper. Given the information available to it, I Corps was undoubtedly justified in its decision to halt, although the 33d Division, again disappointed at being forced to hold, could not but take a dim view of the order. The 33d Division did not know that General Swift was planning to redeploy the 37th Division to the Bambang front and that he therefore could not risk involving General Beightler's command in a major fight.

When the 37th Division captured Baguio on 26 April, the 25th and 32nd Divisions were still struggling to reach Santa Fe, 20 miles south of Bambang.

Between 27 April and 5 May, the 37th Division secured the Trinidad area, mopped up isolated pockets of Japanese in the high ground north of Route 9, cleared Route 11 from Baguio north to Trinidad, and patrolled northeast three miles on Route 11 from Trinidad to Acop's Place. The division encountered organized resistance only near Trinidad.

On **April 30,** the 148th Infantry was placed under the control of the 25th Division and sent to the Balete sector. It remained with the 25th Division until **May 25**, helping it complete the seizure of Balete Pass and then capture Santa Fe.

The 33d Division, until **5 May**, mopped up along Tuba Trail and Route 11 north to Baguio, then moved on to occupy the crest of high ground two to three miles east and southeast of the city. The 130th Infantry, advancing by company-sized combat patrols, began marching over secondary roads to Balinguay, 7 miles east-southeast of Baguio.

As The 148th left the Baguio front, what was left of the 37th Infantry Division was relieved by the 33rd ID and moved to San Jose 4 May 45 and

rested until 29 May 45. The 37ᵗʰ moved to Balete Pass-Santa Fe area north of Manila 31 May 45 where they rested and revitalized.

With the departure of the 37th Division, the 33d Division found itself with a holding mission designed to secure the Baguio-Bauang-San Fernando area. The division was also responsible for patrolling ten miles northeast along Route 11 from Baguio, and for reconnoitering eastward along the Baguio-Aritao supply road from Route 11 at Kilometer Post (KP) 21, the highway and supply road junction.

Contrasted with the 129ᵗʰ and 148ᵗʰ Regiments, the 145ᵗʰ had submitted a relatively small number of recommendations for decorations for bravery in the battle for Manila, and a disproportionate number of these had been for officers. Believing that ample decorations had a major effect on morale, Beightler on **April 19** asked Whitcomb (145ᵗʰ commander) to submit more commendations and to include more enlisted men.

While at San Jose, Beightler received 1,800 new recruits in three groups of 600 each. Many were young, eighteen and nineteen years old, and had received only basic training. Most had no firsthand knowledge of supporting weapons. Beightler assigned each group to a battalion of the 129ᵗʰ Infantry, the only regiment presently with the division, and prescribed an intensive training program. Demonstrations were held to illustrate the proper way to assault a strongpoint. Patrolling techniques were taught, and live ammunition was used in close proximity to the troops. Beightler knew they soon would be in combat and he wanted them to be ready.

After mopping up isolated pockets of Japanese troops, the 33ʳᵈ Division captured the San Nicholas-Tebbo-Itogon route on **12 May 1945**.

✦ ✦ ✦ ✦

Battle of Balete Pass

Because of its strategic importance as the only access between Pampanga and Cagayan Valley, Balete Pass became the scene of much bloody fighting during the final stages of World War II. Japanese *Shobu* soldiers headed *by General Tomoyuki Yamashita* tried to hold their positions while Filipino and American soldiers under the leadership of Colonel Robert Lapham, were determined to dislodge them from **February to March 1945**. By the closeness of hostilities, the blood of almost 17,000 Japanese fighting units and the US-Filipino allied forces mingled with the soil.

Balete Pass in Nueva Vizcaya (east southeast of Baguio and north of San Jose), the retreating Japanese under *General Tomoyuki Yamashita* dug in and held on for three months against the American and Filipino forces who eventually drove them out. Dalton Pass/Balete Pass is a rugged piece of terrain where a part of the Caraballo Sur reaches south and joins the Sierra Madre. The terrain above the rivers have deep sharp-sided towering ridges. Route 5 rises to 3,000 feet at Balete Pass, dipping down north of the pass to approximately 2,500 feet at Santa Fe. Twisting northward along the noses of innumerable great and small ridges. ROUTE 5, winding south from Santa Fe and across Balete Pass. Most paths were along the valley's used by cart drawn water buffalo and other narrower paths used as horse trails through extremely rugged, nearly vertical terrain. The Japanese are dug in along all of these ridges.

Fighting on Luzon and on the Pacific Islands; uphill, downhill, repeat.

✦ ✦ ✦ ✦

A letter dated **May 11, 1945**. Per the V-Mail letter to Dad's sister Alice, Dad was in the hospital in San Jose during the divisions rest and rehab after contracting Malaria (I found this out from relatives a few years after his death). Letters written by soldiers to loved ones at home were not allowed to be specific. Dad arrived at the hospital on **4 May** and was released to rejoin his group for the **31 May '45** push north at Santa Fe. The letter follows:

Dear Alice and Axel,

Just a V-Mail this time as I have no other writing paper. Has been sometime since I received your last letter of March 16 but for over a month we have really been on the go and I have had very little time for letter writing. Now I am in a hospital for a swelling I had in my left side but it is nearly gone now and I expect to go back to my outfit one of the first days. I came here on the fourth but have not been a bit sick as I guess it is nothing serious anyway this is a good time to catch up on some letter writing and believe me I'm sure way behind. I haven't received any mail since coming here so I should have lots of it when I get back.

I suppose by now all the farmers have all their spring work done and everything is nice and green. Here the days aren't quite as hot as when we first came but gosh are the nights ever cold. When sleeping on the ground a person just can't get enough to cover with to keep warm. For over the past week we have had more rain than all of the rest of the time. I have been on the island so nights are beginning to be quite miserable. Guess this will have to be all for now and I hope to hear from you soon. Greeting to all and I still have hopes of being home before fall. Love, Elmer

✦ ✦ ✦ ✦

Located 3,000 feet above sea level, Balete Pass is also the gateway to the Cagayan Valley Region (north end of Luzon) and the **Ifugao Rice Terraces**.

The **Banaue Rice Terraces** are 2,000-year-old terraces that were carved into the mountains of Ifugao in the Philippines by ancestors of the indigenous people. They are frequently called the **"Eighth Wonder of the World"**. It is commonly thought that the terraces were built with minimal equipment, largely by hand. The terraces are located approximately 5000 feet above sea level. They are fed by an ancient irrigation system from the rainforests above the terraces. It is said that if the steps were put end to end, it would encircle half the globe.

The **carabao** is a swamp-type domestic water buffalo native to the Philippines. Water buffalo were probably introduced to the Philippines by Malay immigrants around 300 to 200 BCE. It is considered the **national animal of the Philippines**.

Water Buffalo were used to plow the rice fields, help harvest the rice and pull wagons and carts.

Beightler's next mission was to drive up the Cagayan Valley, smashing any Japanese formations in his path and denying Yamashita valuable foodstuffs. About 200 miles in length and 30 miles across at its widest point, the valley extends north from the Oriung Pass to Aparri at the northern end of Luzon. It is edged in by the Sierra Madre Mountains in the east and the Cordillera Mountains in the west. The valley generally follows the course of the Cagayan River, which is fed by many tributaries along its entire length. There were many towns in the valley, and the road network was fairly extensive.

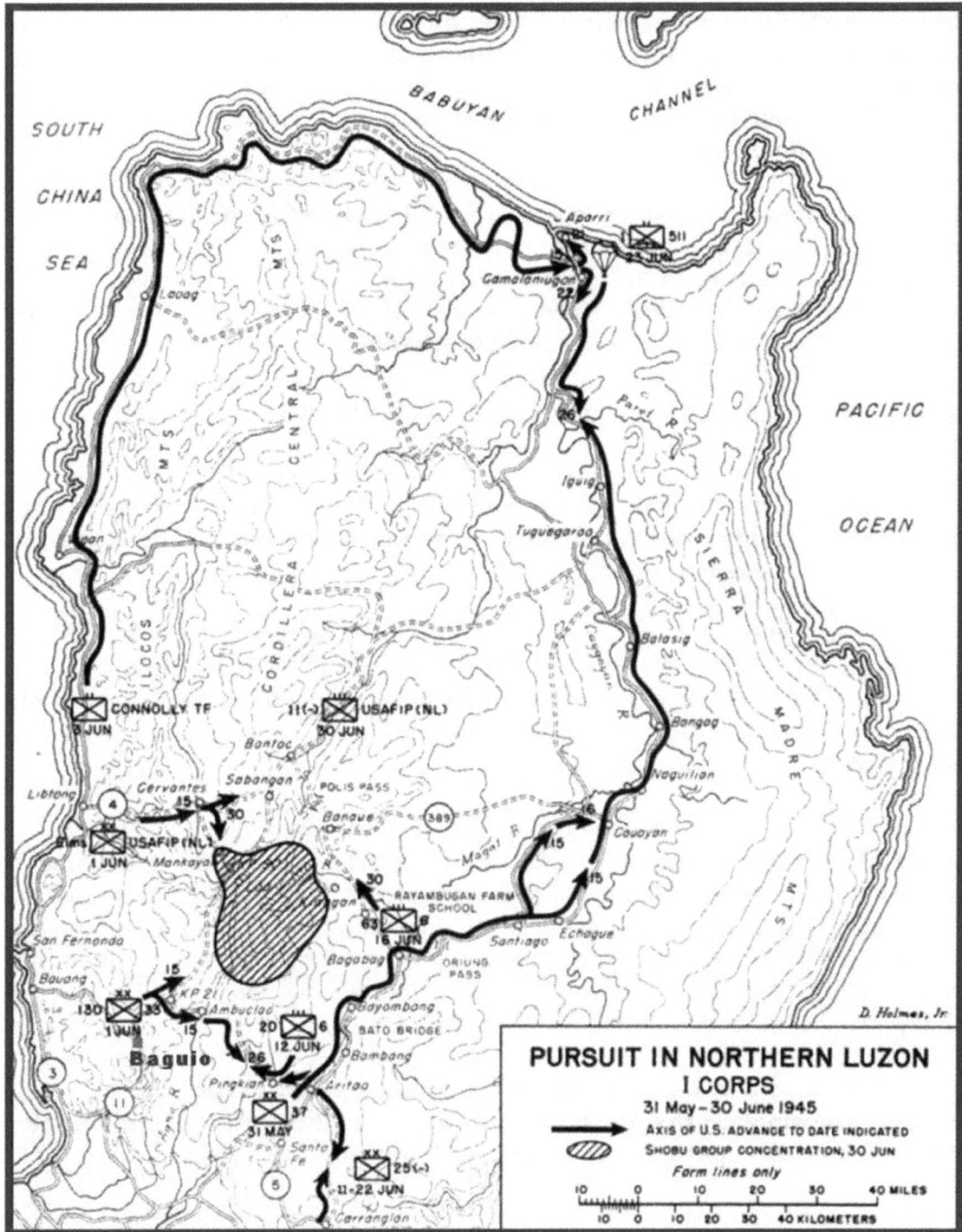

PURSUIT IN NORTHERN LUZON
I CORPS
31 May–30 June 1945

AXIS OF U.S. ADVANCE TO DATE INDICATED

SHOBU GROUP CONCENTRATION, 30 JUN

Form lines only

The 129th Infantry Division passed through the 25th Division on May 29 and 30, and, following a brief bombardment, Frederick's men moved forward from their jumping-off point, 1000 yards north of Santa Fe, on May 31.

They will continue along the line to the northeast fighting along the Cagayen River to the Paret River on the northeast end of Luzon. The Japanese *2nd Tank Division* and *10th Division* had not yet moved in strength into their defense positions south of Bagabag, and thus Frederick's men encountered only light opposition.

The few Japanese troops in the area scarcely slowed Frederick, capturing Aritao on 5 Jun 45.and on 6 June he seized Bambang. Brushing aside token resistance at Bato Bridge, Frederick sped north and reached Bayombong, 8 miles beyond Bambang, on June 7. Located along the north-south line alongside the Sierra Madre Mountains.

Beightler replaced the 129th Infantry with the 145th Infantry the morning of **June 8**. On **June 9** the 145th Infantry secured Bagabag and then immediately headed northeast along Route 5 toward Oriung Pass, the last obstacle before the Cagayan Valley. The pass was defended by a battalion from the *103rd Division*, the only unit the Japanese had been able to rush south to occupy it. Although outgunned and outmanned, the battalion put up a hard fight.

The 145th entered the pass at dawn on **June 10** and were immediately hit by machine gun and mortar fire from the wooded draws on both sides of the pass. They were stopped cold with heavy casualties, beginning a fierce battle that lasted through the evening of **June 12**. US firepower prevailed with the use of artillery, tanks, tank destroyers, and airstrikes.

Once the 145th was through Oriung Pass, they kept moving, and by nightfall on **June 13** had reached Santiago, 20 miles northeast of Bagabag. Continuing the advance in the morning of **June 14**, they were at Echague by nightfall, 8 miles east of Santiago. The advance continued over the next days, and by **June 16** both the 145th and the 148th Regiments took Cauayan (15 miles north of Echague) and took Ilagan **19 Jun 1945.** The Cagayan Valley is where the division drove 225 miles in 26 days against deteriorating Japanese resistance.

23 June there is a U.S. paratroop landing near Aparri, part of the 11th Airborne Division, on the north coast of Luzon at the mouth of the Cagayan River. They head south and meet the 37th Division at the Paret River by 26 June.

At the end of the war a feature story in Yank, the official Army publication, characterized the 37th as "The Heavyweight" on Luzon.

While the 33rd Division had breached the defenses north of Baguio, the 6th Division was moving up Route 4, a task force consisting of ranger units and Filipino guerrillas had made its way along the western and northern coasts of Luzon to Aparri, and Philippine Army units had cleared much of the Cagayan Valley west of the Cagayan River from Cauayan north to Aparri on the Philippine Sea northern coastline of Luzon.

Bessang Pass was fought from **9 January through 15 June 1945** in Cervantes located on the left of the *Shobu Group* concentration. The *Shobu* concentration was the triangular defense of *General Yamashita* in the north, namely the Balete Pass, Villaverde Trail and Bessang Pass.

Yamashita did not plan to make a major stand in the Cagayan Valley. With the collapse of the Baguio apex of the *Shobu Group's* original defensive triangle, he decided in early May to concentrate his remaining forces in northern Luzon in a stronghold deep in the Cordillera Mountains. There he would fight on to occupy as many US troops as possible and, it was hoped, help delay the US invasion of the Japanese home islands. Therefore, he planned to evacuate most of his troops in the valley as quickly as possible and leave the Japanese *103rd Division* until August so the food and military supplies located there could be moved to the redoubt he was preparing between Baguio and Bontac toward the coast of Lingayen Gulf.

Unable to maintain the perimeter of his original last-ditch area, *Yamashita* on **June 15** ordered his units to withdraw into a shrunken stronghold in the inhospitable valley of the Asin River between Routes 4 and 11 with his headquarters near. The only large organized Japanese unit left in the Cagayan Valley was the *Yuguchi Force*, an understrength regiment from the *103rd Division*.

This is the area of *Yamashita's* last stand. Route 11 intersects Route 4 on the north. Route 5 runs from Santa Fe through Bambang and angles right at Bagabag as it continues north (dark shaded area on the lower center of the above map).

The Battle of Bessang Pass was fought from **9 January through 15 June 1945** in Cervantes, a municipality in the province of Ilocos Sur, located 260 km north of Manila. The area serves as a gateway to the Cordillera mountains and the city of Baguio. It was part of the triangular defense of *General Yamashita* in the north, namely the Balete Pass, Villaverde Trail and Bessang Pass. Its fall on **14 June 1945** paved the way for the entrapment of *Yamashita's* forces in the Cordillera until the general's surrender in **September 1945**.

13 June, the 6th Division's 63d Infantry began probing northwest up Route 4 from Bagabag. The reconnaissance foreshadowed a push that *Yamashita* especially feared, since Route 4 provided direct access to the deep Cordillera Central. The *105th Division,* with defenses across Route 4 at the Rayambugan Farm School, did not have sufficient strength to hold the highway, *Yamashita* knew.

Events in the Cagayan Valley were also moving faster than Yamashita had expected. By **15 June** the 11th and 14th Infantry Regiments, USAFIP(NL), had cleared almost all the valley west of the Cagayan River from Cauayan north to Aparri and had gained complete control over Route 11 from Bontoc to the valley. Meanwhile the Connolly Task Force, after an uneventful march, had neared Aparri and on **11 June**, with the help of the 11th Infantry, USAFIP(NL), had begun an attack to clear the last Japanese from the Aparri area.

By **15 June**, then, the *Shobu Group's* phased withdrawal had progressed so poorly that nowhere in northern Luzon did *Yamashita* have the strength he had expected when he had formulated his plans in early May. He realized that he could not hope to hold along any of the three perimeters he had established in May, and he therefore issued new orders calling for ultimate withdrawal into a last-stand area that he would set up along the inhospitable valley of the Asin River, between Routes 4 and 11. This triangle shape is about 7 miles by 4 miles by 5 miles.

On **15 June** Krueger ordered Beightler to move rapidly and not concern himself much with his flanks or threats to his supply line. "Advance aggressively northward in the Cagayan Valley, capture and secure the Naguillian-Cabatuan-Cauayan area and prepare for further advance to the north when directed."

On **17 June** Beightler renewed his advance up Route 5, with the 148th Infantry in the lead. There was little opposition as it moved north from Cauayan on **17 June**. By nightfall it was at Naguilian, 10 miles north of Cauayan. **On 19 June** the regiment reached Bangag, 12 miles north of Naguilian.

Yamashita's mid-June plans called for his units to start withdrawing slowly toward a new perimeter. When this last-stand perimeter collapsed, *Yamashita* planned, all remaining forces would hole up in the barren Asin Valley between Toccucan and Kiangkiang, there to fight to the death.

Most of the Japanese combat troops left in the valley north of Cauayan were members of the *Yuguchi Force,* an understrength RCT of the *103d Division.* Upon the fall of the division's defenses at Oriung Pass, the *Yuguchi Force* had started south from the vicinity of Aparri, apparently intending to cross to the west side of the Cagayan River near Cauayan and make its way to Yamashita's last-stand area via Route 389 to Banaue, on Route 4. By **15 June** the *Yuguchi Force's 177th IIB* was at Tuguegarao, forty-five miles north of Cauayan, and the rest of the unit was strung out along

Route 5 for some twenty miles north of Tuguegarao. **25 June** Tuguegarag is captured by the US forces in the Cagayan Valley. The surviving Japanese units on the east side of the island are now mostly concentrated in the Sierra Madre area to the east of the Cagayan Valley.

Advancing northward in the valley the 37th took Ilagan against deteriorating resistance, and eventually made contact at the Paret River with the 511th Infantry and parachute Regiments marking the end of Japanese resistance in the Cagayan Valley. The 37th Division (which gained control over the 11th Infantry, USAFIP(NL); the airborne regiments; and the Connolly Task Force) now began mopping up and patrolling eastward into the Sierra Madre, where perhaps as many as 10,000 Japanese, the bulk of them service personnel, hid out.

As Beightler wrote Ludwig Conelly at the end of May: *"The so-called mopping-up operations often assume the nature and costliness of regular offensives."* **Fierce, dug-in to the bitter end enemy fighting.**

During July and the first two weeks of August, Beightler's job was to neutralize the approximately 13,000 Japanese troops scattered in the Sierra Madre east of the Cagayan Valley. At the same time, other US units were putting pressure on the 52,000 Japanese troops in Yamashita's redoubt located west of the Cagayan Valley in the Cordillera Mountains (see map above). In their retreat from the Cagayan Valley into the Sierra Madre, the Japanese had used five valleys formed by tributaries of the Cagayan River. Beightler put all nine of his infantry battalions along Route 5, assigning each a section averaging 12 miles in length to move east into the Sierra Madre Mountains. To minimize casualties, he decided to push slowly and use the maximum of artillery fire and air attacks to pressure the Japanese and push them out of the valleys.

There were several hundreds of wounded and starving Japanese troops taken to the prisoner-of-war assembly areas. *"Don't provide trucks,"* one Japanese commander said. *"Those who can't walk will be left there to die. Not to worry."* Beightler *"blew his top"* at the cold-blooded attitude of the Japanese officer and ordered that *"every last Japanese soldier would be brought out, the weakest first by truck"*.

Yamashita would continue to use delaying tactics to maintain his army in Kiangan (part of the Ifugao Province), until **2 September 1945**, several weeks after the surrender of Japan. At the time of his surrender, his forces had been reduced to under 50,000.

The area behind *Yamashita's* new last-stand perimeter boasted excellent defensive terrain, and *Yamashita* estimated that most of his units had sufficient ammunition for machine guns, mortars, and small arms to hold the region for a long time. But the situation in regard to other supplies his supply officers termed "distressing." When I Corps had started up Route 5 at the end of May, *Shobu Group* had just begun to move food and additional military supplies up Route 4 from the Cagayan Valley and Route 5. The group had virtually no medical supplies left; it had no stocks of clothing; its food would be completely exhausted by mid-September. The *Shobu Group* could look forward only to slow death by starvation and disease if it were not first annihilated by the force of Fil-American arms.

Sixth Army had greatly underestimated the Japanese strength left in northern Luzon, and Eighth Army's estimates, made upon its assumption of command, were but little closer to fact. Actually, at the end of June, close to 65,000 Japanese remained alive in northern Luzon, 13,000 of them in the Sierra Madre and 52,000 in the last-stand area between Routes 4 and 11. Although organization, control, and morale were deteriorating, and although most of the troops were ill armed and poorly supplied, the Japanese in the last-stand area were still capable of effective resistance when the occasion demanded. The task confronting the U.S. Army and guerrilla units in northern Luzon was of far greater magnitude than any headquarters estimated at the end of June.

XIV Corps plans for operations against the remainder of the *Shobu Group* differed only in detail from those I Corps had previously employed. Reduced to their simplest terms, both sets of plans called for the exertion of unremitting pressure against the *Shobu Group* wherever *Shobu Group* troops were to be found.

East of the Cagayan River the 37th Division, and for a time a regiment of the 6th Division, hampered by supply problems and torrential rains, patrolled vigorously, forcing Japanese troops ever farther into the Sierra Madre. From 1 July through 15 August the 37th Division and attached units killed about 1,000 Japanese, east of the Cagayan, itself losing approximately 50 men killed and 125 wounded.

With the end of hostilities, 15 August, the 37ᵗʰ Division was concerned with mopping up, securing its area, and the collection and processing of prisoners of war, leaving November 1945 for the States and demobilization. (Dad left Luzon on 28 August)

On the northwest and Cordillera mountain region of Luzon, opposition was stronger and better organized. The 15th Infantry, secured the Sabangan junction of Routes 4 and 11 on **9 July**, and on the next day the 11th Infantry occupied Bontoc. The

19th Division's defenses began to fall apart before attacks of the 66th Infantry on **10 July**; Mankayan fell on the **20 July**. The 66th Infantry secured the junction of Routes 11 on **25 July**, making contact the same day with troops of the 15th Infantry coming down Route 11 from Sabangan. The *19th Division* now began withdrawing into the upper Agno Valley to block the northern, western, and southern approaches to Toccucan, at the western end of *Yamashita's* last-stand area in the Asin Valley. The 15th and 121st Regiments immediately began attacks toward Toccucan, but found the *19th Division* remnants still capable of effective resistance. By **15 August** the USAFIP(NL)'s leading units were four miles short of Toccucan on the northwest and a mile and a half short on the west.

Throughout July and the first half of August the main effort continued to be the 6th Division's attack from Route 4 toward Kiangan. Here, all operations were virtually stopped about 1 July by incessant, torrential rains that turned the road toward Kiangan into an impassable quagmire. The problems of the 6th Division were aggravated because the *Fifth Air Force*, in "co-operation" with the Japanese, had made a- shambles, of sections of the old road, destroying all bridges and causing many landslides. Finally, rear-guard troops of the *105th Division* also slowed progress.

The 63d Infantry, 6th Division, reached Kiangan on **12 July**, there capturing all types of Japanese military supplies in large quantities. But then even heavier rains came down, and from **16 through 20 July** the regiment was marooned at Kiangan, barely supported by hand-carrying parties. On the 24th, the 20th Infantry took over and began an advance toward Kiangkiang and the Asin River.

Rain-swollen streams, flooded rice paddies, and nearly impassable trails restricted the 63d's activities to patrolling, and as of **15 August** the regiment had not established contact with the main body. Meanwhile, the Japanese had bitterly opposed the 6th Division's efforts to advance west from Kiangan toward the Asin Valley. Instead of mopping up, the division soon found itself involved in mountain fighting as rough as that experienced at any time or at any place throughout the Luzon Campaign. At the end of hostilities on **15 August** the 20th Infantry, 6th Division, was scarcely three miles beyond Kiangan along the trail to Kiangkiang.

In a month and a half of bitter fighting in incredibly steep terrain and in the most miserable type of weather Filipino and American forces had failed to project any strength into the Asin Valley. This last month and a half of the operation in northern Luzon had cost the Allied forces engaged approximately 1,650 casualties. Eighth Army estimated that *Shobu Group* casualties for the same period were 13,500 men killed or dead of starvation and disease.

Although there are still many Japanese on the island who will go on fighting until the end of the war, much of the mopping up will be left to Filipino units aided by US Eighth Army troops, who will take over responsibility for Luzon in addition to their present tasks in the other Philippine islands in order to free Sixth Army to prepare for the invasion of Japan.

How much longer the *Shobu Group* could have kept Filipin and American troops out of the Asin Valley is a moot question. *Yamashita* had estimated in June that he had sufficient supplies to hold out until mid-September, and from the scale of effort Eighth Army was able and willing to put into the campaign from **1 July to 15 August**, it appears that *Yamashita* would have met his deadline. When food was exhausted, he planned to have his most effective remaining troops attempt a breakout from the Asin Valley to the mountains of far northwestern Luzon where, he hoped, more food might be found. Men not participating in the breakout were to stage banzai attacks on all fronts to cover the effectives' escape. Expecting that, successful or not, the breakout would mark the complete disintegration of his forces, *Yamashita* planned to commit hara-kiri during the melee. Thus, the end of the war came about a month before *Yamashita* was ready to admit final defeat.

The effectiveness of the *Shobu Group* operations in northern Luzon must be assessed within the context of *Yamashita's* concept of the strategic goal of the Luzon Campaign. From the first, *Yamashita* had known that he had insufficient strength to hold all Luzon or to prevent MacArthur's forces from ultimately occupying all the island. *Yamashita* was convinced as early as **December 1944**, the most he could accomplish, was to delay Allied progress toward Japan by pinning down as many American divisions on Luzon as possible.

He also realized that his strength, the condition of the roads, bridges, and railroads on Luzon, and the preponderance of Allied air power, would make it impossible for him to mount a decisive counterattack against the invasion forces of the Sixth Army. Any attack employing less than his entire strength would, he knew, be foredoomed to disastrous failure, but he lacked the capability of concentrating all his forces. He was certain, therefore, that counterattacks could result only in the rapid, piecemeal destruction of the *14th Area Army*. Such destruction would, of course defeat his main purpose--conducting protracted delaying actions on Luzon.

It had been this reasoning that had led *Yamashita* to establish his three separate defensive positions in Luzon's mountains. He had concentrated his principal strength, the *Shobu Group,* in northern Luzon because the size of that area and the nature of its terrain afforded him the best opportunities for extended delaying operations. Moreover, food requisite to such operations was available in the Cagayan and Magat Valleys, the defense of northern Luzon would deny the Allies the use of the Cagayan Valley airfields, and his best and strongest units were already in northern Luzon.

As of **30 June,** the *Shobu Group* was no longer capable of effective or significant offensive effort. At the end of June, the *Shobu Group* still had 65,000 men of its peak strength of over 150,000. Of the 65,000, 52,000 comprised an organized force still firmly under Yamashita's control in the Asin Valley sector.

After the end of the war, roughly 50,500 Japanese troops came out of the mountains of northern Luzon, nearly 40,000 of them from the Asin Valley last-stand area. Thus, the war ended with about one-third of the *Shobu Group's* peak strength still alive and still capable of conducting organized, stubborn delaying operations. **The conclusion can hardly be avoided that the *Shobu Group,* in the seven and a half months from 9 January 1945, had indeed executed a most effective delaying action.**

Yamashita would continue to use delaying tactics to maintain his army in Kiangan (part of the Ifugao Province), until **2 September 1945**, several weeks after the surrender of Japan. ***General Yamashita* of the Imperial Forces, Philippines, came out of the mountains to surrender to the 32D 'Red Arrow' Infantry Division near Kiangan, Luzon, on 2 September 1945.**

XXVI   Iwo Jima, Japan Air Raid, Humane Support

Battle of Iwo Jima

19 February – 26 March 1945

Iwo Jima is a very small Pacific island – just over 4.5 miles long and 2.5 miles wide which lies at the foot of the Bonin chain of islands, an archipelago of over 30 subtropical islands, south of the main Japanese island of Honshu. 540 nautical miles directly south of Tokyo, Japan. Bonin comes from the Japanese word meaning "no people" or uninhabited.

Despite its size, Iwo Jima was considered to have great tactical importance. There were two airfields on the island – under Japan's control; they could be used by Japanese fighter planes to attack American bombers on their flights to Japan. Under American control, the airfields could be used as emergency landing bases for damaged airplanes in the bombing raids. They could also be used for American fighter planes to escort the bombers, as they needed smaller runways for take-off.

Knowing that the island was of such importance, the Japanese were determined to keep control of it. There were about 22,000 soldiers under the command of *Lieutenant-General Kuribayashi*. These men had the time to build strong defensive positions throughout the island but especially in the north. **Positions on the island were heavily fortified, with a dense network of bunkers, hidden artillery positions, and 18 km (11 miles) of underground tunnels.** *Kuribayashi* knew that his options for launching attacks were extremely limited because of the small size of the island. His options to do anything other than defend ferociously were extremely limited.

American intelligence sources were confident that Iwo Jima would fall in one week. In light of the optimistic intelligence reports, the decision was made to invade Iwo Jima and the operation was given the code name Operation Detachment. American forces were unaware that the Japanese were preparing a complex and deep defense, radically departing from their usual strategy of a beach defense. So successful was the Japanese preparation that it was discovered after the battle that the hundreds of tons of Allied bombs and thousands of rounds of heavy naval gunfire had left the Japanese defenders almost undamaged and ready to inflict losses on the U.S. Marines.

The American invasion, designated **Operation Detachment**, had the goal of capturing the entire island, including the three Japanese-controlled airfields (including the South Field and the Central Field), to provide a staging area for attacks on the Japanese main islands.

The American ground forces were supported by extensive naval artillery, and had complete air supremacy provided by U.S. Navy and Marine Corps aviators throughout the entire battle.

✦ ✦ ✦ ✦

Japanese preparations

By **June 1944**, *Lieutenant General Tadamichi Kuribayashi* was assigned to command the defense of Iwo Jima. *Kuribayashi* knew that Japan could not win the battle, but he hoped to inflict massive casualties on the American forces, so that the United States and its Australian and British allies would reconsider carrying out the invasion of Japan Home Islands.

While drawing inspiration from the defense in the Battle of Peleliu, *Kuribayashi* designed a defense that broke with Japanese military doctrine. Rather than establishing his defenses on the beach to face the landings directly, he created strong, mutually supporting defenses in depth using static and heavy weapons such as heavy machine guns and artillery. *Takeichi Nishi's* armored tanks were to be used as camouflaged artillery positions. Because the tunnel linking the mountain to the main forces was never completed, *Kuribayashi* organized the southern area of the island in and around **Mount Suribachi** as a semi-independent sector, with his main defensive zone built up in the north. The expected American naval and air bombardment further prompted the creation of an extensive system of tunnels that connected the prepared positions, so that a pillbox that had been cleared could be reoccupied. This network of bunkers and pillboxes favored the defense. For instance, The **Nanpo Bunker** (Southern Area Islands Naval Air HQ), which was located east of Airfield Number 2, had enough food, water and ammo for the Japanese to hold out for three months. The bunker was 90 feet deep and had tunnels running in various directions. Approximately 500 55-gallon drums filled with water, kerosene, and fuel oil for generators were located inside the complex. Gasoline powered generators allowed for radios and lighting to be operated underground.

Hundreds of hidden artillery and mortar positions along with land mines were placed all over the island. Among the Japanese weapons were 320 mm spigot mortars and a variety of explosive rockets.

Nonetheless, the Japanese supply was inadequate. Troops were supplied 60% of the standard issue of ammunition sufficient for one engagement by one division, and food and forage for four months.

Numerous Japanese snipers and camouflaged machine gun positions were also set up. *Kuribayashi* specially engineered the defenses so that every part of Iwo Jima was subject to Japanese defensive fire.

He also received a handful of *kamikaze* pilots to use against the enemy fleet. Three hundred and eighteen American sailors were killed by *kamikaze* attacks during the battle. However, against his wishes, *Kuribayashi's* superiors on Honshu ordered him to erect some beach defenses. These were the only parts of the defenses that were destroyed during the pre-landing bombardment.

American preparations

Each warship was given a three-day bombardment window and fired for approximately six hours before stopping for a certain amount of time. Poor weather on D minus 3 led to uncertain results for that day's bombardment. On D minus 2, the time and care that the Japanese had taken in preparing their artillery positions became clear. When heavy cruiser USS Pensacola got within range of shore batteries, the ship was quickly hit 6 times and suffered 17 crew deaths. Later, 12 small craft attempting to land an underwater demolition team were all struck by Japanese rounds and quickly retired. While aiding these vessels, the destroyer USS Leutze was also hit and suffered 7 crew deaths. On D minus 1, Adm. Blandy's gunners were once again hampered by rain and clouds. Gen. Schmidt summed up his feelings by saying, *"We only got about 13 hours' worth of fire support during the 34 hours of available daylight."*

The limited bombardment had questionable impact on the enemy due to the Japanese being heavily dug-in and fortified. However, many bunkers and caves were destroyed during the bombing giving it some limited success. The Japanese had been preparing for this battle since March 1944, which gave them a significant head start. By the time of the landing, about 450 American ships were located off Iwo Jima. The entire battle involved about 60,000 U.S. Marines and several thousand U.S. Navy Seabees.

Amphibious landing

Allied amphibious landing on Iwo Jima begins 19 February 1945.

During the night, Vice Adm. Marc A. Mitscher's Task Force 58, a huge carrier force, arrived off Iwo Jima. Also in this flotilla was Adm. Raymond A. Spruance, overall commander for the invasion, in his flagship, the heavy cruiser USS Indianapolis. "Howlin' Mad" Smith was once again deeply frustrated that Mitscher's powerful carrier group had been bombing the Japanese home islands instead of softening up the defenses of Iwo Jima. Mitscher's fliers did contribute to the additional surface-ship bombardment that accompanied the formation of the amphibious craft.

Unlike the days of the pre-landing bombardment, D-Day dawned clear and bright. At 0859, one minute ahead of schedule, the first wave of Marines landed on the beaches of the southeastern coast of Iwo Jima.

Situation on the beaches

Unfortunately for the landing force, the planners at Pearl Harbor had completely misjudged the situation that would face Gen. Schmidt's Marines. The beaches had been described as "excellent" and the thrust inland was expected to be "easy". In reality, after crossing the beach, the Marines were faced with 15-foot-high slopes of soft black volcanic ash. This ash allowed for neither a secure footing nor the construction of foxholes to protect the Marines from hostile fire. However, the ash did help to absorb some of the fragments from Japanese artillery

Marines were trained to move rapidly forward; here they could only plod. The weight and amount of equipment was a terrific hindrance and various items were rapidly discarded. First to go was the gas mask.

The lack of a vigorous response led the Navy to conclude that their bombardment had suppressed the Japanese defenses and in good order the Marines began deployment to the Iwo Jima beach. *Gen. Kuribayashi* was far from beaten, however. In the deathly silence, landed US Marines began to slowly inch their way forward inland, oblivious to the danger. After allowing the Americans to pile up men and machinery on the beach for just over an hour, *Kuribayashi* unleashed the undiminished force of his countermeasures. Shortly after 1000, everything from machine guns and mortars to heavy artillery began to rain down on the crowded beach, which was quickly transformed into a nightmarish bloodbath.

Moving off the beaches

Amtracs, unable to do more than uselessly churn the black ash, made no progress up the slopes; their Marine passengers had to dismount and slog forward on foot. Men of the Naval Construction Battalions (CBs or Seabees), braving enemy fire, eventually were able to bulldoze passages up the slopes. This allowed the Marines and equipment to finally make some progress inland and get off the jam-packed beaches. *"Even so, in virtually every shell hole there lay at least one dead Marine ..."*

By 1130 hours, some Marines had managed to reach the southern tip of Airfield #1, whose possession had been one of the (highly unrealistic) original American objectives for the first day. The Marines endured a fanatical 100-man charge by the Japanese but were able to keep their toehold on Airfield No. 1 as night fell.

Action on the right flank

The right-most landing area was dominated by Japanese positions at the Quarry. The 25th Marine Regiment undertook a two-pronged attack to silence these guns. Their experience can be summarized by the ordeal of 2nd Lt. Benjamin Roselle, part of a ground team directing naval gunfire:

Within a minute a mortar shell exploded among the group ... his left foot and ankle hung from his leg, held on by a ribbon of flesh ... Within minutes a second round landed near him and fragments tore into his other leg. For nearly an hour he wondered where the next shell would land. He was soon to find out as a shell burst almost on top of him, wounding him for the third time in the shoulder. Almost at once another explosion bounced him several feet into the air and hot shards ripped into both thighs ... as he lifted his arm to look at this watch a mortar shell exploded only feet away and blasted the watch from his wrist and tore a large jagged hole in his forearm: "I was beginning to know what it must be like to be crucified," he was later to say.

The 25th Marines' 3rd Battalion had landed approximately 900 men in the morning. Japanese resistance at the Quarry was so fierce that by nightfall only 150 were left in fighting condition, an astounding 83.3% casualty rate.

By the evening, 30,000 Marines had landed. About 40,000 more would follow. Aboard the command ship Eldorado, "Howlin' Mad" Smith saw the lengthy casualty reports and heard of the slow progress of the ground forces. To the war correspondents covering the operation he confessed, *"I don't know who he is, but the Japanese general running this show is one smart bastard."*

Subsequent combat

In the days after the landings, the Marines expected the usual Japanese *banzai* charge during the night. This had been the standard Japanese final defense strategy in previous battles against enemy ground forces in the Pacific. However, *Ku-*

ribayashi had strictly forbidden these *"human wave"* attacks by the Japanese infantrymen because he considered them to be futile. Towards the end of the battle, with their demise imminent, he changed his story.

The fighting on the beachhead at Iwo Jima was very fierce. The advance of the Marines was stalled by numerous defensive positions augmented by artillery pieces. There, the Marines were ambushed by Japanese troops who occasionally sprang out of tunnels. At night, the Japanese left their defenses under cover of darkness to attack American foxholes, but U.S. Navy ships fired star shells to deny them the cover of darkness. On Iwo Jima (and other Japanese held islands), Japanese soldiers who knew English were used to harass and or deceive Marines in order to kill them if they could; they would yell "corpsman" pretending to be a wounded Marine, in order to lure in U.S. Navy medical corpsmen attached to Marine infantry companies.

The Marines learned that firearms were relatively ineffective against the Japanese defenders and effectively used flamethrowers and grenades to flush out Japanese troops in the tunnels. The eight Sherman M4A3R3 medium tanks equipped with a flamethrower ("Ronson" or "Zippo" tanks), proved very effective at clearing Japanese positions. The Shermans were difficult to disable, such that defenders were often compelled to assault them in the open, where they would fall victim to the superior numbers of Marines.

Marines began to face increasing numbers of nighttime attacks; these were only repelled by a combination of machine-gun defensive positions and artillery support. At times, the Marines engaged in hand-to-hand fighting to repel the Japanese attacks. With the landing area secure, more troops and heavy equipment came ashore, and the invasion proceeded north to capture the airfields and the remainder of the island. Most Japanese soldiers fought to the death.

Raising the flag on Mt. Suribachi

By the morning of **23 February 1945**, Mount Suribachi was effectively cut off above ground from the rest of the island. The Marines knew that the Japanese defenders had an extensive network of below-ground defenses, and that in spite of its isolation above ground, the volcano was still connected to Japanese defenders via the tunnel network. They expected a fierce fight for the summit. Two small patrols from two rifle companies from 2/28 Marines were sent up the volcano to reconnoiter routes on the mountain's north face.

Popular accounts (embroidered by the press in the aftermath of the release of the photo) had the Marines fighting all the way up to the summit. Although the Marine riflemen expected an ambush, one patrol encountered only small groups of

Japanese defenders on top of Suribachi. The majority of the Japanese troops stayed in the tunnel network, only occasionally attacking in small groups, and were generally all killed. The recon patrols made it to the summit and scrambled down again, reporting any contact to the 2/28 Marines commander, Colonel Chandler Johnson. Johnson then called for a reinforced platoon size patrol from E Company to climb Suribachi and seize and occupy the crest. The patrol commander, 1st Lt. Harold Schrier, was handed the battalion's American flag to be raised on top to signal Suribachi's capture, if they reached the summit. Johnson and the Marines anticipated heavy fighting, but the patrol encountered only a small amount of small arms fire on the way up the mountain. Once the top was secured by Schrier and his men, a length of Japanese water pipe was found there among the wreckage, and the American flag was attached on the pipe and then raised and planted on top of Mount Suribachi which became the first foreign flag to fly on Japanese soil. **Photographs of this "first flag raising" scene, taken by Marine photographer Louis R. Lowery, were not released until late 1947.**

Participants to the first flag raising were: 1st Lt. Harold Schrier (kneeling behind radioman), Pfc. Raymond Jacobs (radioman), Sgt. Henry "Hank" Hansen (cloth cap, looking downward while he is helping to steady the flagstaff with his left hand), Pvt. Phil Ward, securing the lower part of the flagstaff, Platoon Sgt. Ernest "Boots" Thomas (seated), PhM2c. John Bradley, USN (securing the flagstaff above Ward), Pfc. James Michels (holding M1 carbine), and Cpl. Charles W. Lindberg (standing above Michels).

As the flag went up, Secretary of the Navy James Forrestal had just landed on the beach at the foot of Mount Suribachi and decided that he wanted the flag as a souvenir. Colonel Johnson, the battalion's commander, believed that the flag belonged to the 2nd Battalion 28th Marines, who had captured that section of the island. Johnson sent Pfc. Rene Gagnon, a messenger for E Company, to take a second larger flag up the volcano to replace the first flag. **It was the replacement flag attached to another heavy pipe went up that Rosenthal took *Raising the Flag on Iwo Jima*.**

Northern Iwo Jima

Despite Japan's loss of Mount Suribachi on the south end of the island, the Japanese still held strong positions on the north end. The rocky terrain vastly favored defense, even more so than Mount Suribachi, which was much easier to hit with naval artillery fire. Coupled with this, the fortifications constructed *by Kuribayashi* were more impressive than at the southern end of the island. Remaining under the command of *Kuribayashi* was the equivalent of eight infantry battalions, a tank regiment, two artillery and three heavy mortar battalions. There were also about 5,000 gunners and naval infantry.

The overall objective at this point was to take control of Airfield No. 2 in the center of the island. However, every *"penetration seemed to become a disaster"* as *"units were raked from the flanks, chewed up, and sometimes wiped out. Tanks were destroyed by interlocking fire or were hoisted into the air on the spouting fireballs of buried mines"*. As a result, the fighting bogged down, with American casualties piling up. Even capturing these points was not a solution to the problem since a previously secured position could be attacked from the rear by the use of the tunnels and hidden pillboxes. As such, it was said that *"they could take these heights at will, and then regret it"*.

On the evening of **8 March**, *Captain Samaji Inouye* and his 1,000 men charged the American lines, inflicting 347 casualties (90 deaths). The Marines counted 784 dead Japanese soldiers the next day. The same day, elements of the 3rd Marine Division reached the northern coast of the island, splitting *Kuribayashi's* defenses in two.

The island was officially declared secure at 0900 on **26 March 1945**. Once the island was officially declared secure, the Army's 147th Infantry Regiment was ostensibly there to act as a garrison force, but they soon found themselves locked in a bitter struggle against thousands of stalwart defenders engaging in a last-ditch guerilla campaign to harass the Americans. Using well-supplied caves and tunnel systems, the Japanese resisted American advances. For three months, the 147th slogged across the island, using flamethrowers, grenades, and satchel charges to dig out the enemy, killing some 1,602 Japanese soldiers in small unit actions.

Aftermath

Of between 20,530 and 21,060 Japanese defenders entrenched on the island, from 17,845 to 18,375 died either from fighting or by ritual suicide. Only 216 were captured during the course of battle. After Iwo Jima, it was estimated there were no more than 300 Japanese left alive in the island's warren of caves and tunnels. In fact, there were close to 3,000. **The Japanese *bushido* (samurai) code of honor, coupled with effective propaganda which portrayed American G.I.s as ruthless animals, prevented surrender for many Japanese soldiers.** Those who could not bring themselves to commit suicide hid in the caves during the day and came out at night to prowl for provisions. Some did eventually surrender and were surprised that the Americans often received them with compassion, offering water, cigarettes, alcohol, or coffee. The last of these holdouts on the island, two of *Lieutenant Toshihiko Ohno's* men, *Yamakage Kufuku and Matsudo Linsoki*, lasted four years without being caught and finally surrendered on 6 January 1949.

Though ultimately victorious, the American victory at Iwo Jima had come at a terrible price. According to the official Navy Department Library website, "The 36-day (Iwo Jima) assault resulted in more than 26,000 American casualties, including 6,800 dead." Iwo Jima was also the only U.S. Marine battle where the American casualties exceeded the Japanese. **USS Bismarck Sea was also lost, the last U.S. aircraft carrier sunk in World War II.**

After the heavy losses incurred in the battle, the strategic value of the island became controversial. It was useless to the U.S. Army as a staging base and useless to the U.S. Navy as a fleet base. However, Navy Seabees rebuilt the landing strips, which were used as emergency landing strips for USAAF B-29s.

In a postwar study, Japanese staff officers described the strategy that was used in the defense of Iwo Jima in the following terms:

In the light of the above situation, seeing that it was impossible to conduct our air, sea, and ground/ operations on Iwo Island [Jima] toward ultimate victory, it was decided that to gain time necessary for the preparation of the Homeland defense, our forces should rely solely upon the established defensive equipment in that area, checking the enemy by delaying tactics. Even the suicidal attacks by small groups of our Army and Navy airplanes, the surprise attacks by our submarines, and the actions of parachute units, although effective, could be regarded only as a strategical ruse on our part. It was a most depressing thought that we had no available means left for the exploitation of the strategical opportunities which might from time to time occur in the course of these operations. — Japanese Monograph No. 48

The Battle of Iwo Jima was the costliest in Marine Corps history, with almost 7,000 Americans killed in 36 days of fighting.

✦ ✦ ✦ ✦

Mainland Japan Incendiary Air Raid

General Curtis LeMay, who had planned the strategic bombing of Hamburg, took over the bombing operations in the Marianas in **January 1945** and became concerned that the high explosives that had devastated German industries were not as effective in Japan. It was determined that two-thirds of industrial facilities were vulnerable to such attacks as they were concentrated in several large cities and a high proportion of production took place in homes and small factories in urban areas. Precision bombing was not nearly as devastating as fire bombing in these areas due to the make-up of construction of their buildings.

Napalm, used by the Americans for flamethrowers and incendiary bombs, was increased in production from 500,000 lbs. in 1943 to 8 million lbs. in 1944. Much of the napalm went from nine U.S. factories to bomb-assembly plants making the M-69 incendiary and packing 38 of them into the E-46 cluster bomb. These were shipped across the Pacific and stored for future use.

On the night of **24 February 1945,** the US Air Force launched <u>174 B-29s</u> in the first incendiary air raid on Tokyo that devastated about one square mile. Then LeMay ordered the pilots to fly at low altitudes of less than 8,000 feet with fewer guns in order to carry more bombs.

On the night of **March 9,** the <u>279 B-29s</u> doing this dropped 1,700 tons of bombs that contained a mixture of oil, phosphorus, and napalm, killing about 90,000 people and burning sixteen square miles, a quarter of Tokyo. **The Japanese later called this event Night of the Black Snow.**

The next night LeMay sent <u>313 bombers</u> with napalm to attack Nagoya, Japan's third largest city. That week 45 square miles of industrial areas were burned.

In **April** <u>B-29 raids</u> bombed the Nakajima aircraft factory twice, the Koizuma aircraft factory, arsenals, and urban areas.

After Germany surrendered on 8 May 1945, the United States shifted more forces to the Pacific War.

On **23 May** a raid by <u>520 B-29s</u> bombed the industrial area south of the Imperial Palace, and two days later Tokyo was hit again by <u>564 B-29s</u>.

Yokohama was attacked by <u>450 bombers</u> on **29 May**.

✦ ✦ ✦ ✦

Humanitarian Crisis

While war still raged in Europe and the Pacific, America got ready to help the displaced persons (or DPs, as they came to be known). In **November 9, 1943,** at President Franklin D. Roosevelt's invitation, representatives of 44 nations met at the

White House and established the **United Nations Relief and Rehabilitation Administration (UNRRA)**, an international agency to plan and coordinate *"measures for the relief of victims of war."*

The following are some of the humanitarian crisis' our soldiers saw and responded to.

" A member of a Marine patrol on Saipan found a family of Japanese hiding in a hillside cave. The mother, four children and a dog, took shelter from the fierce fighting in that area." Cpl. Angus Robertson, **June 21, 1944**

Tenderness in a July 1944 photograph, American Marine lifts a nearly dead infant downhill to another Marine.

Filipino women rescued by American soldiers, Intramuros, Manila, Philippines, **March 1945.**

A little Japanese girl drinks from the canteen of a US Marine who found her in a cave on Okinawa. She couldn't have been more than 4 years old.

U.S. Marine feeds two children on Okinawa. These children about 4-6 years old.

Showing the humanitarian side of the war. Two US Marines share a foxhole with an Okinawan war orphan in a **April 1945** *photo.*

Bat Bombs

Bat bombs were an experimental World War II weapon developed by the United States. The bomb consisted of a bomb-shaped casing with over a thousand compartments, each containing a hibernating Mexican free-tailed bat with a small, timed incendiary bomb attached. Dropped from a bomber at dawn, the casings would deploy a parachute in mid-flight and open to release the bats, which would then roost in eaves and attics in a 20–40-mile radius. The incendiaries would start fires in inaccessible places in the largely wood and paper constructions of the Japanese cities that were the weapon's intended target.

The bat bomb was conceived by a Pennsylvania dentist named Lytle S. Adams, a friend of First Lady Eleanor Roosevelt. Adams submitted it to the White House in **January 1942**, where it was subsequently approved by President Roosevelt on the advice of Donald Griffin (American professor of Zoology).

The plan was to release bat bombs over Japanese cities having widely dispersed industrial targets. The bats would spread far from the point of release due to the relatively high altitude of their release and would then hide in buildings across the city at dawn. Shortly thereafter, built-in timers would ignite the bombs, causing widespread fires and chaos.

By **March 1943**, a suitable species had been selected. The project was considered serious enough that Louis Fieser, the inventor of military napalm, designed 0.6 ounce (17 g) and one ounce (28 g) incendiary devices to be carried by the bats. A bat carrier similar to a bomb casing was designed that included 26 stacked trays, each containing compartments for 40 bats. The carriers would be dropped from 5,000 feet (1,525 m). Then the trays would separate but remain connected to a parachute that would deploy at 1,000 feet

A series of tests to answer various operational questions were conducted. In one incident, the Carlsbad Army Airfield Auxiliary Air Base near Carlsbad, New Mexico was set on fire on **May 15, 1943**, when armed bats were accidentally released. The bats roosted under a fuel tank and incinerated the test range.

Following this setback, the project was relegated to the Navy in **August 1943**, who renamed it **Project X-Ray**, and then passed it to the Marine Corps that December.

The National Defense Research Committee (NDRC) observer stated: *"It was concluded that X-Ray is an effective weapon."* The Chief Chemist's report stated that, on a weight basis, X-Ray was more effective than the standard incendiary bombs in use at the time: *"Expressed in another way, the regular bombs would give probably 167 to 400 fires per bomb load where X-Ray would give 3,625 to 4,748 fires."*

More tests were scheduled for **mid-1944** but the program was cancelled by Fleet Admiral Ernest J. King when he heard that it would likely not be combat ready until **mid-1945**. By that time, it was estimated that $2 million had been spent on the project. It is thought that development of the bat bomb was moving too slowly and was overtaken in the race for a quick end to the war by the atomic bomb project. Adams maintained that the bat bombs would have been effective without the devastating effects of the atomic bomb. He is quoted as having said: *"Think of thousands of fires breaking out simultaneously over a circle of forty miles in diameter for every bomb dropped. Japan could have been devastated, yet with small loss of life."*

Saipan Suicides

Suicide Cliff is a cliff above Marpi Point Airfield near the northern tip of Saipan, Northern Mariana Islands. It is a location where thousands of Japanese civilians and soldiers committed suicide by jumping to their deaths in 1944 in order to avoid capture by the United States, as Japanese propaganda emphasized brutal treatment of Japanese such as American mutilation of Japanese war dead. Many Japanese feared the 'American devils raping and devouring Japanese women and children. The precise number of suicides there is not known but has been estimated at around 8,000 deaths.

Banzai Cliff overlooks the Pacific Ocean. Towards the end of the Battle of Saipan in 1944, hundreds of Japanese civilians and soldiers jumped off the cliff to their deaths in the ocean and rocks below to avoid being captured by the Americans. Some who jumped did not die and were rescued by American ships.

✦ ✦ ✦ ✦

The United Nations Relief and Rehabilitation Administration (**UNRRA**)

 was an international relief agency representing 44 nations and largely dominated by the United States. **Founded in 1943, it became part of the United Nations in 1945, and it largely shut down operations in 1947.** Its purpose was to *"plan, co-ordinate, administer or arrange for the administration of measures for the relief of victims of war in any area under the control of any of the United Nations through the provision of food, fuel, clothing, shelter and other basic necessities, medical and other essential services"*.

The recipient nations had been especially hard hit by starvation, dislocation, and political chaos. It played a major role in helping Displaced Persons return to their home countries in Europe in **1945-46**. Its UN functions were transferred to several UN agencies, including the International Refugee Organization and the World Health Organization. As an American relief agency, it was largely replaced by the Marshall Plan, which began operations in 1948 and was an American initiative to aid Western Europe.

The United Nations (**UN**) is an intergovernmental organization tasked to promote international cooperation and to create and maintain international order. **A replacement for the ineffective League of Nations**, the organization was established on **24 October 1945** after World War II with the aim of preventing another such conflict. At its founding, the UN had 51 member states.

The Economic Commission for Europe and the Economic Commission for Asia and the Far East was established in **1947** by the

United Nations Economic and Social Council to assist in dealing with regional problems.

The International Refugee Organization (IRO), beginning operations on **July 1, 1947**, was a temporary specialized agency of the United Nations that, between its formal establishment in 1946 and its termination in January 1952, assisted refugees and displaced persons in many countries of Europe and Asia who either could not return to their countries of origin or were unwilling to return for political reasons. Among the services supplied by the IRO were the care and maintenance of refugees in camps, vocational training, orientation for resettlement, and an extensive tracing service to find lost relatives.

XXVII   Battles in the Southern Philippines

The Philippines are made up of 7,107 islands

The Eighth Army's future area of operations was vast, stretching over 600 miles from west to east and some 400 miles from north to south. Within this expanse, all south of the largest island in the Philippines, Luzon, were thousands of smaller isles which together constituted the bulk of the archipelago. At the extreme south was Mindanao, the second largest island in the Philippines, while the major islands lying between Mindanao and Luzon included Bohol, Cebu, Negros, and Panay, (collectively known as the Visayas) which stretched in an east-west line from American bases on Leyte to just southeast of another American enclave on Mindoro, which had been seized in **December 1944**.

Outside of the central islands, the Sulu Archipelago extended southwest from Mindanao's Zamboanga Peninsula almost to Borneo in the Netherlands East Indies. Farther west, Palawan island lay between Borneo and Mindoro and fronted on the South China Sea. All of the larger islands possessed imposing terrain, ranging from sea-level mangrove swamps to rain forest-covered and ravine-scarred mountains that jutted thousands of feet high, and all offered formidable opportunities to a determined defender. Enemy garrisons dotted the islands, generally concentrated around ports and smaller seacoast towns. Additional dangers awaited in the forms of disease and a generally enervating environment. For Eighth Army planners, moreover, the very number of contemplated operations and the distances between the sites would demand skill, with staffs forced to juggle assets and to schedule events in sequence with an eye to the limited shipping capabilities available to support such scattered and simultaneous operations.

The success of the Palawan, Zamboanga, and Sulu operations would not only assure a more effective blockade of the South China Sea and provide adequate air support for the invasion of Borneo but would also result in the creation of a virtually complete aerial blockade of the East Indies and southeast Asia, assuming the success of concurrent offensives by forces of the Southeast Asia Command. Moreover, these opening offensives would draw a ring around the Japanese in the rest of the Southern Philippines, leaving them isolated and without chance of reinforcement or escape. They were designed for the purpose of liberating Filipinos, re-establishing lawful government.

Weather also played a part in the decision to launch early attacks into the Southern Philippines. Planners knew how important it was to have the campaigns in the southern islands well under way before the summer rains began, and they recognized the importance of having airfield construction in hand before wet weather created engineering problems like those that so delayed air base developments on Leyte in late 1944.

On **6 February 1945**, after Sixth Army troops had been in Manila but three days, MacArthur ordered the seizure of Palawan. A week later he issued additional instructions for the occupation of the Zamboanga Peninsula and the Sulu Archipelago.

Commander of the Eighth Army General Eichelberger stressed aggressiveness and innovative tactics so that small units could capitalize on surprise and exploit opportunities that arose in the confusion of combat. Such training would pay great dividends during the reconquest of the southern Philippines, where the majority of the amphibious assaults would be conducted by battalions and companies and success would hang on small groups of men pushing through the jungle and engaging the Japanese in fierce small unit actions.

Opposing the Eighth Army was the *Japanese Thirty-Fifth Army,* initially commanded by *Lt. Gen. Sosaku Suzuki*, who would later be killed in **mid-April 1945** during an effort to sail from Cebu to Mindanao. Although his troops numbered approximately 100,000, they were scattered throughout the Eighth Army area of operations and his number of trained combat troops was much lower, perhaps about 30,000. *Suzuki's* best unit, the *30th Infantry Division,* was stationed on Mindanao, but even that division had lost half of its troops as reinforcements to the battle for Leyte. The strongest Japanese defenses were at Cebu City on Cebu, on the Zamboanga Peninsula in western Mindanao, and around Davao City in southern Mindanao. Most of the understrength and ill-equipped Japanese garrisons did not anticipate large pitched battles with U.S. Army forces. Instead they somewhat complacently expected to be bypassed and left alone until the end of the war. Nevertheless, as events would show, they were prepared to resist if attacked and ultimately proved dangerous foes under any circumstance.

Battle of Mindanao Island

The Battle of Mindanao, located in the southern Philippine Islands, was fought by United States forces and allied Filipino guerrillas against the Japanese from **10 March - 15 August 1945** on the island of Mindanao in the Philippines. The battle was waged to complete the recapture of the southernmost portions of the archipelago.

Mindanao Island, the second largest (after Luzon) in the Philippines, in the southern part of the archipelago, surrounded by the Bohol, Philippine, Celebes, and Sulu seas. Irregularly shaped, it measures 293 miles (471 km) north to south and 324 miles (521 km) east to west. The island is marked by peninsulas and is heavily indented by the Davao and Moro gulfs in the south and by Iligan Bay in the north. The long, semicircular Zamboanga Peninsula (west) extends southwesterly toward the Sulu Archipelago and Borneo, and the Cotabato and Surigao peninsulas extend south and north, respectively.

Rugged, faulted mountains and volcanoes occur in many areas. Mount Apo, at 9,692 feet (2,954 metres), is an active volcano in the southern part of the central highlands; it is the highest peak in the Philippines. The island has narrow coastal plains, and broad, fertile basins and extensive swamps are formed by the Mindanao and Agusan river systems. Lake Lanao (Lake Sultan Alonto), created by a lava dam, has an area of 134 square miles (347 square km).

The campaign for Mindanao posed the greatest challenge for the liberating Allied forces, primarily for three reasons: the island's inhospitable geography; the extended Japanese defenses; and the strength and condition of the Japanese forces, which contained the significantly remaining concentration of combat troops in the Philippines.

Mindanao, the second largest island in the Philippines, offered very little inspiration for soldiers who would have to fight there. It boasted a long and irregular coastline, and the topography was generally characterized as rugged and mountainous. Rain forests and numerous crocodile-infested rivers covered the terrain, the rest by either lake, swamp or grassland. These grassland regions—along with dense groves of abacá trees, a source of hemp fiber—offer the worst obstacles, limiting vision and sapping the strength of soldiers.

Abaca trees on Mindanao were not grown in rows like the modern-day plants. They were growing wild on this island in 1945 making it hard to navigate. The plant, native to the Philippines, achieved importance as a source of cordage fiber, otherwise known as Manila hemp. They look like banana trees but without the banana. Abaca trees offered the worst obstacles, limiting vision and sapping the strength of soldiers.

The strongest of the Japanese defenses were concentrated around the Davao Gulf area, which was heavily mined to counter an amphibious landing. Artillery and anti-aircraft batteries extensively ringed the coastal shoreline defenses. Believing that the Americans would ultimately attack from Davao Gulf and also anticipating that they would be eventually driven from the city, the Japanese also prepared defensive bunkers inland behind its perimeter where they could retire and regroup, with the intention of prolonging the campaign as much as possible.

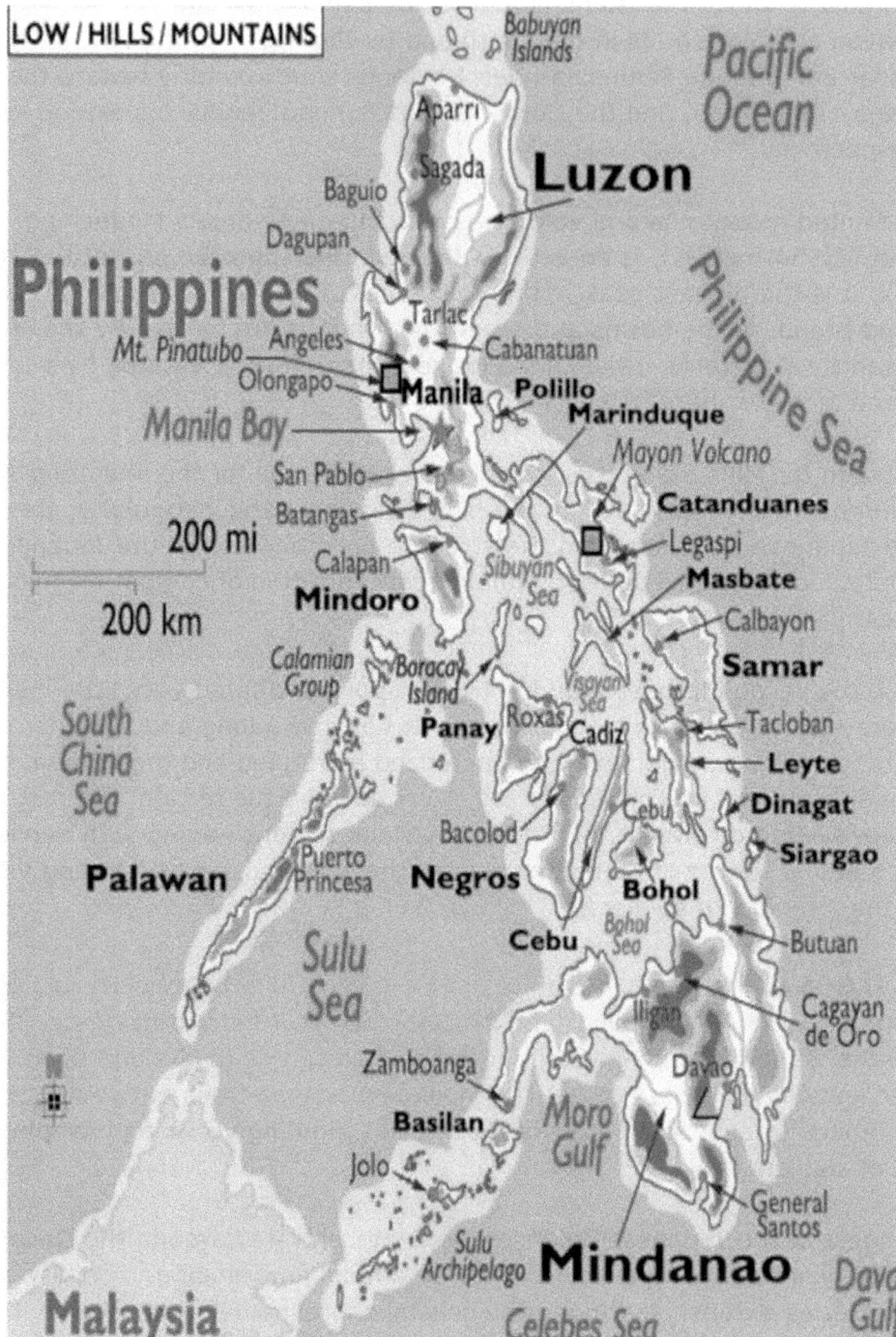

On **10 March 1945**, the U.S. Eighth Army—under Lieutenant General Robert L. Eichelberger, instead of the expected headlong frontal assault on the Japanese defenses at Davao Gulf, the plan called for securing a beachhead at Illana Bay in the undefended west, then driving eastward more than a 100 miles (160 km) through jungles and mountains to strike from the rear. The objective, which called for achieving surprise and pressing forward quickly and aggressively by the invading forces, Eichelberger deemed, could unhinge the Japanese both physically and psychologically.

As Rear Admiral Noble's TG 78.2 moved toward Illana Bay to prepare the landings at Parang, Colonel Wendell Fertig, commander of guerrilla forces in Mindanao, sent word that his guerrillas controlled Malabang and its airstrip in Illana Bay (Illana Bay is on the west side). Starting on **5 April**, Colonel Jerome's Marine aviators from Dipolog moved to the Malabang airstrip, and with targeting information from the guerrillas, proceeded to bomb the Japanese positions. By **11 April**, the remaining Japanese forces fled toward Parang, and friendly forces were in complete control of Malabang.

On the same day Eichelberger's forces were ordered to invade Mindanao, remnants of Major General Jens A. Doe's 41st Infantry Division carried out the seizure of Zamboanga, the large peninsula that extended to the southwest, concurrent with the recapture of Palawan Island located west of Mindanao. A sizable force—numbering about 8,900 men of *Lt. Gen. Tokichi Hojo's* 54th Japanese Independent Mixed Brigade (IMB)—had established strong defensive positions around Zamboanga City at the southern tip of the peninsula.

Marine Aircraft Groups Zamboanga (MAGSZAM) under Col. Clayton C. Jerome was flying sorties off the airstrip to cover naval bombardment and landing preparations off Zamboanga City. After the bombing of the landing areas by the 13th Air Force and a three-day bombardment by the U.S. Navy, the 162nd and 163rd Infantry Regiments landed 3 miles (4.8 km) west of Zamboanga City at San Mateo. Japanese opposition to the landings were minimal, and the 41st Division troops quickly captured the city, which was decimated by the pre-invasion bombardments.

The next day, **11 March**, the Americans encountered strong resistance when they attacked Japanese positions in the hills overlooking the coastal plain. For two weeks, American infantry—ably supported by Marine aviation and naval gunfire—fought the Japanese along a 5-mile (8.0 km) front, in terrain so rugged that tanks could not be used, and in positions heavily fortified with deep earthen emplacements, barbed wire, minefields, and booby traps.

On **23 March**, after heavy fighting, the center of the Japanese line finally broke, and in the next three days, the 162nd Infantry continued eliminating resistance in the central sector. The 186th Infantry replaced the 163rd and continued the attack. The 54th Japanese IMB (Imperial Mixed Brigade) was forced to pull out a week later, harried by guerrilla units, retreating through the peninsula and into the jungle.

While the Parang landings in Illana Bay proceeded on **17 April** and the 24th Division quickly heading inland, the Eighth Army planners assumed correctly that the Japanese might destroy the bridges along Highway 1, and they decided to use the 533rd Engineer Boat and Shore Regiment, 3rd Engineer Special Brigade to exploit the Mindanao River. This waterway ran roughly parallel to Highway 1 and was navigable for 35 miles (56 km). A small fleet of gunboats—under the command of Lieutenant Colonel Roberto Amputs—sailed upriver and seized Kabacan and the junction of Highway 1 and Sayre Highway on **22 April**. This startled the nearby Japanese garrisons, and they fled north and west. The Mindanao River became the main line of supply, as troops and rations were disgorged far upriver.

With General Woodruff's 24th Division moving so rapidly, the Americans were almost on top of the Japanese around Davao (right, east side of above map) before *General Morozumi* learned too late that the western landing was, in fact, not a diversion. Upon reaching Digos on **27 April**, the Americans quickly overwhelmed the defending Japanese, who were prepared only to repel an assault from the sea, not from their rear. The 24th Division immediately turned north and headed toward Davao City.

On **3 May 1945**, the first combat elements of the 24th Division entered Davao City against less opposition than had been expected. The Japanese had contented themselves with destroying the city as best they could before their withdrawing inland. While it took just 15 days, despite severe heat and humidity and constant rain, with an entire division travelling 115 miles (185 km) and seizing the last major Philippine city under Japanese control, the real battle for Mindanao had begun. Up to this point, X Corps had deliberately bypassed the main Japanese defenses, which they planned to turn to eliminate them.

By **17 May**, exhausted and bloodied, the 24th Division renewed its offensive, and this time, the 19th Infantry Regiment, supported by Fertig's guerrillas, blew open the Japanese eastern flanks before capturing the villages of Tacunan, Ula, Matina Biao, Magtuod and Mandug on **29 May**. The Japanese *100th Division* collapsed and retreated. But soon fighting erupted into pursuit and mopping-up operations against bypassed Japanese pockets, which later claimed the life of the 19th Infantry's commander, Colonel Thomas "Jock" Clifford Jr.

Meanwhile, the 31st Division had forged ahead to the town of Kibawe on Highway 1, some 40 miles (64 km) away, since **27 April**, with the 124th Infantry Regiment of Colonel Edward M. Cullen at point, where the first monsoon rains started creating havoc on the advance. Running into a Japanese battalion hurrying south, Lieutenant Colonel Robert M. Fowler's 2nd Battalion, with Battery B, 149th Field Artillery attached, engaged the Japanese with much needed artillery fire, killing at least 50 and sending the rest fleeing.

On **3 May**, the 31st Division reached Kibawe, against stiffening Japanese resistance. The town led to a supposed Japanese supply trail that twisted and turned south, until it reached the ocean shore village of Talomo in Davao City. The treacherous terrain proved equally dangerous to both sides as they struggled in the ensuing battle for the Talomo trail on **11 May**. About 1,000 Japanese held the trail, but jungle rain forests, torrential rains and abysmal trail conditions were the real factors. Airdropped supplies to the isolated infantrymen were common as the trail was impassable to motor vehicles. By **30 June**, the 167th Infantry managed to move only 5 miles (8.0 km) beyond the Pulangi river, even with the assistance of Filipino guerrillas. It lost 80 men and 180 wounded to the Japanese, who themselves suffered about 400 dead.

On **6 May**, the 124th Infantry Regiment continued to move up Sayre Highway without the Talomo trail reconnaissance operation in full swing, and in doing so, it moved into its toughest fight of the Mindanao campaign. A Japanese battalion, ordered by *Morozumi* to delay the 124th at Maramag some 30 miles (48 km) south to enable the regrouping of his *30th Division*, did so with such ferocity, that it took six days for the 124th to reach Maramag. The battle area from Talomo to Maramag was later renamed Colgan Woods by the troops in remembrance of Captain Thomas A. Colgan, an Army chaplain who was killed during one of his repeated efforts to aid wounded soldiers in the line of fire. The battle was one of the many brutal struggles in the Pacific theater that never made any headlines.

Firing from dugout positions, camouflaged spider holes with connecting tunnels, and virtually invisible pillboxes, the defending Japanese chose to die in place rather than retreat. Banzai charges struck the 124th, fighting without supporting artillery, first on **7 May** and then on the night of **14 May**. The latter ended in a rout, as American automatic weapons stopped the attackers, killing 73 Japanese, marking the end of the battle. In the fighting for Colgan Woods and Maramag, the 124th Infantry lost 60 men and 120 wounded from **6–12 May 1945**.

The final stages of the battle for Mindanao culminated with the 155th Infantry Regiment of Colonel Monaks J. Mungkamar occupying Malaybalay on **21 May** and taking control of the Sayre Highway, together with the 108th Infantry Regiment of

Colonel Maurice D. Stratta after a stiff fight with the Japanese. *Morozumi's 30th Division* continued their retreat up the Agusan Valley, after a vicious encounter with the pursuing 31st Division on **5 June**, where they eventually made it into the jungle. Farther south on Mindanao, smaller X Corps units seized Sarangani and Balut islands, situated off its southern tip, and on **12 July**, the 1st Battalion, 24th Division's 21st Infantry arrived at the northwest shore of Sarangani Bay to reinforce a reconnaissance patrol, which located a strong Japanese force in the interior and proceeded to pursue the Japanese through the jungle. Japanese forces retreated into Klaja Karst in the municipality of Buayan, where they made their last stand against mixed American forces and Filipino guerrillas that were operating in the area. Operations in these areas continued until mid-August, when American planes heavily bombed the land, resulting in large Japanese casualties. Some Japanese who have survived the bombings escaped to the forest but were hunted down by the soldiers. The Japanese resistance in Mindanao was finally over.

A chronicler for the 24th Division wrote:

*The soldiers of the 24th Infantry, considered the post-Davao operations to be the hardest, bitterest and, most exhausting battle of the ten island campaigns. In addition to the tenacious defense put up by the Japanese, another punishing aspect of the subsequent combat was the proliferous fields of abaca. To the foot soldiers fighting in the Davao province, the word abaca was synonymous with hell...Countless acres around Davao are covered with these thick-stemmed plants, fifteen to twenty feet high; the plants grow as closely together as sugar cane, and their long, lush, green leaves are in a welter of green so dense that a strong man must fight with the whole weight of his body for each foot of progress...In the abaca fields, visibility was rarely more than ten feet. No breeze ever reached through the gloomy expanse of green, and more men - American and Japanese - fell prostrate from the overpowering heat than bullets. **The common way for scouts to locate an enemy position in abaca fighting was to advance until they received machinegun fire at a range of three to five yards.** For the next two months, in such an environment, the 24th Division fought the Japanese. While the infantry sought out the Japanese defenses, platoons and squads worked through the abaca and surrounding jungle to seek out enemy bunkers and spider holes.*

While mopping up operations by small American units and Filipino guerrillas continued for some time, General Eichelberger announced the end of organized Japanese resistance. Throughout Mindanao, pockets of Japanese troops, protected by the impenetrable terrain of the island's unexplored jungle expanses, survived until the end of the war, when some 22,250 troops and 11,900 civilians emerged to surrender. That signaled the total liberation of the Philippines. Some 12,865 Japanese troops were killed, and another 8,235 appeared to have succumbed to starvation and disease. The Americans lost 820 men and 2,880 wounded for the entire campaign.

The seemingly low cost in battlefield casualties for the Americans in the Mindanao campaign stemmed, aside from the overall brilliance and skill of the Eighth Army planners and leaders, from increasing assistance by Filipino guerrillas, which in military terms, constituted a valuable "force multiplier" for the Eighth Army units. Before landings, guerrillas harassed Japanese units, provided valuable intelligence about enemy dispositions and the relative suitability of landing beaches. And after each landing, the Filipinos fought alongside the Americans and pursued the Japanese through the island's interior.

Battle of Basilan Island

16 March 1945. Part of the U.S. 41st Division lands on Basilan Island, above Sulu Archipalago. Here, as on the other small islands, the pattern will be for the US forces to subdue the Japanese in the first few days fighting and then mostly to withdraw, leaving the mopping up to Filipino guerrillas. Fighting continues along the *Shimbu* line southeast of Manila and in the I Corps sector to the north, especially on the Villa Verde track.

Battle of Visayas Islands

Visayas Provinces

Western Visaysa:

      Aklan, Antique, Capiz, Guimaras, Iloilo, Negros Oriental

Central Visayas:

      Bohol, Cebu, Negros, Occidental, Siquijor

Eastern Visayas:

      Biliran, Eastern Samar, Leyte, Northern Samar, Samar, South Leyte

The **Visayan Islands** are one of the three principal geographical divisions of the Philippines, along with Luzon and Mindanao. It consists of several islands, primarily surrounding the Visayan Sea, although the Visayas are considered the northeast extremity of the entire Sulu Sea.

The major islands of the Visayas are Panay, Negros, Cebu, Bohol, Leyte, Samar, Masbate, Romblon, and Palawan.

Battle for Cebu City

The Battle for Cebu City on Cebu island in the southern Philippines was a major engagement that occurred between **March 26 and April 8, 1945**, during the second Philippines Campaign. Cebu Island is southwest of the island of Leyte. The battle resulted in an Allied victory over the occupying Japanese Army and the liberation of Cebu City. The island was garrisoned by a force of between 14,500 and 15,000 Japanese troops. These were situated mainly in Cebu City and on the central east coast.

The Americal Division's 132nd and 182nd Infantry Regiments, totaling about 5,000 men, were landed on **Cebu island** at Talisay Beach, 4 miles (6.4 km) southwest of Cebu City. The 182nd came ashore southwest of the city, while the 132nd landed at a wide gravel beach to the northeast opposite a palm grove. **Meeting no Japanese opposition, the U.S. forces nevertheless suffered heavily from mines and booby traps as they crossed the beach. It was the first time in the Philippines campaign that U.S. troops had encountered such weapons.**

8 April 1945 the island and Cebu City was overtaken by the Allies. American troop strength: 14,900 US and 8,500 Cebuano guerrillas. American casualties: 410 killed, 1700 wounded, 8000 sick most of which succumbed to an outbreak of infectious hepatitis. Japanese troop strength: 14,500 - 15,000. Japanese casualties: 9,000 killed, estimated 2,000 committed suicide, 2,000 captured.

Negros Island

29 March there are US landings in the Negros Island near Bacolod. Negros Island is west of Cebu Island. The landing force is from the 185th Regiment. **8 April** the US forces are reinforced by the landing of a second regiment in the northwest of Negros near Bacolod.

The Japanese on this island will fight very fiercely aided by booby-trapped terrain, defended their fortified positions by day, and conducted harassing attacks at night. Soon, the 40th Division started using small infiltrating units to creep past tank traps and minefields, then scrambled uphill across open fields of fire to attack Japanese positions.

By **4 June**, the Japanese began a general withdrawal, retreating further into the unexplored mountains of Negros. Eight weeks later, the 40th Division overcame these final defenses and scattered the rest of the Japanese into the jungle.

Masbate Island

3 April part of the US 40th Division land on Masbate to help the Filipino guerrillas who have controlled part of it for several days. Masbate Island is north of Negros Island.

9 April the 163rd Regiment of the 41st Division lands on Iloilo, a province located in the region of Western Visayas. The 185th Infantry landed unopposed about twelve miles west of Iloilo, a principal city of Panay and the third largest commercial center in the Philippines. The first assault wave was greeted on shore by troops of Colonel Peralta's guerrilla forces, drawn up in parade formation. Numbering over 22,500 men, about half of them armed, the Panay guerrillas controlled much of their island. There is no Japanese resistance.

Invasion of Palawan Island

Like most of the Philippine Islands, Palawan was a hostile site for an invading force. Well over 200 miles in length and up to 30 miles wide, the numerous reefs, sand banks, and mangrove swamps of the island's coast offered few suitable landing sites. Farther inland, the coastal plain gave way to heavily forested mountains that offered great defensive potential to Japanese forces.

After two days of punitive air strikes by the US 13th Air Force and a fierce naval bombardment by 7th Fleet warships offshore, the first assault wave from the 186th Regimental Combat Team began moving ashore at Puerto Princesa on the morning of **28 February 1945 and ending 22 April**, under the eyes of Gen. Eichelberger, who watched from a B-17 heavy bomber flying overhead.

As expected, the absence of suitable landing areas slowed the largely unopposed unloading operation, but the process would have been even slower if not for the outstanding efficiency of the Army Shore Party and Boat Company from the 2nd Engineer Special Brigade, units who ably supervised and managed the movement of troops and supplies at the beach landings.

Holdovers from *Lt. Gen. Sōsaku Suzuki's 35th Army*—would not put up a fight at Puerto Princesa and had withdrawn into the hills to the northwest. More disturbing was the revelation of a massacre of approximately 150 American prisoners of war the previous December on Palawan.

The 186th RCT encountered little opposition until its third day ashore on **3 March** when fierce fighting erupted as soldiers entered the hills that lay about 10 mi (16 km) north of the harbor. Five days of savage combat eliminated the strongly defended Japanese pockets. In the weeks that followed, Gen. Eichelberger also directed smaller units of the 186th RCT to seize the small islands situated to the northern and southern parts of Palawan.

On **9 March**, a 186th RCT reconnaissance team landed on Dumaran Island to the northeast of Palawan and found it unoccupied. Then on **9 April** a month later, Company F, 186th Infantry, landed on Busuanga Island, killed 10 Japanese, and reported the island secured. Subsequently, the regiment also seized nearby Culion and Coron. To the south, parties from the 2nd Battalion landed on Balabac on **16 April** and at Pandanan on **22 April**. Both landings were unopposed.

Casualties on Palawan were unbalanced. U.S. Army forces lost 12 killed and 56 wounded, while Japanese dead numbered almost 900 and another 140 wounded, which were approximately ½ of the Palawan garrison.

Mopping up activities on Palawan lasted until late April, when the remaining Japanese simply withdrew farther into the trackless mountain jungles of Palawan—a pattern that repeated during all of the major operations in the southern Philippines—after which many were stalked and killed by U.S. troops and Filipino guerrillas.

11 April   Units of the Americal Division land on Bohol Island just east of Cebu Island. The convoy taking the Filipino and American liberation forces to Bohol consisted of a flotilla of six landing ships (medium), six landing crafts (infantry) and two landing crafts (support). Upon arrival, the reinforced battalion combat team advanced rapidly to the east and northeast with the mission of destroying all hostile forces in Bohol. The bulk of the Japanese force was destroyed and beaten in the ten days of action.

14 April The US XIV Corps continues its advance onto the Bicol Peninsula in the southwest of Luzon, Bicol Region which is north of Leyte. The general headquarters of the Philippine Army and Constabulary under the Commonwealth regime was built and stationed in Calauag during and after the war from 1945 to 1946 against the Japanese. **19 April 1945**, the United States and Filipino forces liberated the town from Japanese occupation.

Masacre at Palawan: American POWs

Among the American prisoners remaining in the Philippines were 346 men who were sent 350 miles on **August 1, 1942**, from the Cabanatuan POW camps north of Manila, and from Bilibid Prison in Manila itself, to Puerto Princesa on the island of Palawan located on the western perimeter of the Sulu Sea. The POWs were shipped there to build an airfield for their captors. Although the prisoners' numbers fluctuated throughout the war, the brutal treatment they received at the hands of their Japanese guards was always the same. The men were beaten with pick handles and kickings and slappings were regular daily occurrences. Prisoners who attempted to escape were summarily executed.

The Palawan compound was known as Camp 10-A and the prisoners were quartered in several dilapidated, unused Filipino buildings. Food was minimal; each day, prisoners received a mess kit of wormy Cambodian rice and a canteen cup of soup made from camote vines boiled in water (camotes are a Philippine variant of sweet potatoes). Prisoners who could not work had their rations cut by 30%.

When six Americans POWs were caught stealing food in **December 1942**, they were tied to coconut trees, beaten, whipped with a wire and beaten again with a wooden club 3 inches in diameter. After this brutal episode, they were forced to stand at attention while a guard beat them unconscious, after which the prisoners were revived to undergo further beatings. A Japanese private named *Nishitani* punished two Americans, who were caught taking green papayas from a tree in the compound, by breaking their left arms with an iron bar.

Medical care was nonexistent, and one Marine, **13 March 1943**, Pfc Glenn McDole of Des Moines, Iowa underwent an appendectomy with no anesthesia and no infection-fighting drugs. Infection set in and McDole's abdomen ruptured. The only American doctor in the camp sewed it but when the thread did not hold, he had to sew shirt buttons along the incision site.

The prisoners suffered from malaria, scurvy, pellagra, beriberi and tropical ulcers, as well as from injuries suffered at their work or from the physical mistreatment perpetrated by their Japanese guards. When Red Cross supplies finally were received in January 1944, the enemy had removed the medicines and drugs from the parcels for their own use.

In **September 1944**, 159 of the American POWs at Palawan were treturned to Manila. The Japanese estimated that the remaining 150 men could complete the arduous labor on the airfield, hauling and crushing coral gravel by hand and pouring concrete seven days a week. The total area to be cleared was approximately 2,400 yards by 225 yards, with the actual airstrip measuring 1,530 yards long and 75 yards wide. The men also repaired trucks and performed a variety of maintenance tasks in addition to logging and other heavy labor. Late in September, *General Shiyoku Kou*, in charge of all POWs in the Philippines, ordered the remaining 150 Americans returned to Manila, but that order was not carried out until mid-October, even though transportation was available.

The daily sightings of American aircraft led the prisoners to believe that their deliverance was not far off. After initially refusing the prisoners' request, the Japanese reluctantly allowed the Americans to paint American Prisoner of War Camp on the roof of their barracks. This gave the prisoners some measure of protection from American air attacks. The Japanese then stowed their own supplies under the POW barracks.

In **November 1944** with the constant presence of Allied aircraft overhead, the Japanese ordered the prisoners to construct three shelters on the beach side of the camp; each 150 feet long, 4 feet high, covered with bamboo logs and dirt for their own protection during air raids. The Japanese had ordered that the entrances at each end of the shelters be only large enough to admit one man at a time. While not totally bombproof, they did offer a significant level of protection. There were also several shelter holes that could hold two or three men.

On **14 December** Japanese aircraft reported the presence of an American convoy, which was actually headed for Mindoro, but which the Japanese thought was destined for Palawan. Two American Lockheed P-38 Lightning fighter aircraft were sighted and the POWs were ordered into the air raid shelters by Japanese *1st Lt. Yoshikazu Sato*, whom the prisoners called the Buzzard, where they remained closely guarded.

Suddenly, in an orchestrated and obviously planned move, 50 to 60 Japanese soldiers under *Sato's* leadership doused the wooden shelters with buckets of gasoline and set them afire with flaming torches, followed by hand grenades. The screams of the trapped and doomed prisoners mingled with the cheers of the Japanese soldiers and the laughter of their officer, *Sato*. As men engulfed in flames broke out of their fiery deathtraps, the Japanese guards machine gunned, bayoneted and clubbed them to death. Most of the Americans never made it out of the trenches and the compound before they were barbarously murdered but several closed with their tormentors in hand-to-hand combat and succeeded in killing a few of the Japanese attackers.

Glenn McDole stood in the opening of one of the trenches and informed the others of what was happening. He saw the Japanese approaching with torches and buckets full of gas, which they poured onto prisoners in the first trench and then ignited the bamboo logs, shooting anyone who tried to escape. McDole and the other men in his trench had managed to dig a tunnel leading to a cliff with a sixty-foot drop to the beach and it was through this tunnel that McDole fled and hid under a pile of garbage for two excruciating days. He then took cover in a sewer outlet. On **18 December**, he swam five miles to the beach, where he climbed aboard a fishing trap. McDole and another escapee, Sergeant Bogue, reached the free Philippines on Christmas Eve.

About 30 to 40 Americans escaped from the massacre area, either through the double-woven, barbed-wire fence or under it, where some secret escape routes had been concealed for use in an emergency. They fell and/or jumped down the cliff above the beach area, seeking hiding places among the rocks and foliage. Marine Sergeant Douglas Bogue recalled: *"Maybe up to forty were successful in getting through the fence down to the water's edge. Of these, several attempted to swim across Puerto Princesa's by immediately but were shot in the water. I took refuge in a small crack among the rocks, where I remained, all the time hearing the butchery going on above. They even resorted to using dynamite in sorcing some of the men from their shelters. I knew that as soon as it was over up above they would be down probing among the rocks, spotting us and shooting us. The stench of burning flesh was strong. Shortly after this they were moving in groups among the rocks dragging the Americans out and murdering them as they found them. By the grace of God, I was overlooked."*

Radioman 1st Class Joseph Barta, who had worked in his family's poultry business before joining the Navy in 1934, later testified: *"At first I did not get into my shelter. But a Jap officer drew his saber and forced me to get under cover. About five minutes later, I heard rifle and machine-gun fire. Not knowing what was happening, I looked out and saw several men on fire and being shot down by the Japs. One of them was my friend Ron Hubbard. I and several other fellows in the hole went under the fence. Just as I got outside the fence, I looked back and saw a Jap throw a torch in the other end of our hole, and another one threw in a bucket of gasoline."* Of the 146 enlisted men and four officers held in the Palawan prison camp, only 11 men survived the massacre on **14 December 1944**.

After Palawan was liberated by the 186th Infantry Regiment of the 41st Division, the men of the Army's 601st Quartermaster Company, under Major Charles Simms, excavated the burned and destroyed dugouts to properly inter the dead Americans. The unit reported 79 individual burials during **March 1945** and many more partial burials. Its report stated: 26 skeletons, some still with flesh on the bones, were found piled four and five high in one excavation. The skulls of these skeletons either had bullet holes or had been crushed by some blunt instrument. These were the dead from the compound thrown into the shelters by the Japanese after the massacre. The report also stated: Most of the bodies were found in the shelters huddled together at a spot furthest away from the entrance. This would indicate that they were trying to get as far away from the fire as possible.

Japanese atrocities against Allied military and civilian personnel after capture were well-documented by war's end. Although the famous Nuremberg Trials held in Europe received the lion's share of interest, especially from the world press, the Military Tribunal for the Far East managed to capture the Americans' attention. **However heinous the crimes of the Nazi government, they rarely involved Americans, while the Japanese were brutal and criminal in their treatment of captured Americans and other Allied military personnel.**

MacArthur essentially controlled the War Crimes Trials in the Pacific Theater. On **August 2, 1948** the Palawan Massacre trial began in Yokohama, Japan. On trial were several staff officers who had exhibited criminal liability through their failure to take command responsibility. Most of the accused Japanese had very little direct involvement with the atrocities perpetrated at Puerto Princesa. Their attitude was described as callous indifference to the fate of the prisoners in their hands.

Of certain importance in the trial was the introduction of a written order sent to each Japanese branch camp commander in May 1944. It stated that *"during an attack on a branch camp by the Allies, the main force shall keep strict guard over POWs and if there is any fear that the POWs would be retaken due to the tide of Battle turning against us, decisive measures must be taken without returning a single POW"*.

☆☆☆☆

Sulu Archipelago

Alongside the Zamboanga operation, smaller units of the 41st Division invaded the Sulu Archipelago, a long stretch of islands reaching from the Zamboanga Peninsula to north Borneo. The Sulu Archipelago runs southwest of Mindanao to the northeast tip of Borneo. Rapidly taken in succession were Basilan, Malamaui, Tawi-Tawi, Sanga and Bangao. On **15 April**, strong resistance at Jolo was encountered. Jolo Island is about midway between Zamboanga and Tawitawi. Anchoring their stubborn defense around Mount Daho, some 3,750 Japanese troops held off the 163rd Infantry, supported by Filipino guerrillas. By **22 April**, the Allies took the position after hard fighting and the rest of the Japanese troops fled and held out in the west for another two months. The 163rd suffered 35 dead and 125 wounded by **mid-June 1945**, while some 2,000 Japanese perished.

2 April 1945 Part of the US 163rd regiment is landed on Tawitawi, the extreme southwestern tip, in the Sulu Archipelago.

Battle of Borneo

The Borneo Campaign of 1945 was the last major Allied campaign in the South West Pacific Area during World War II. Borneo is the third largest island in the world and the largest in Asia. In a series of amphibious assaults between **1 May and 21 July 1945**, the Australian I Corps attacked Imperial Japanese forces occupying the island. Allied naval and air forces, centered on the U.S. 7th Fleet under Admiral Thomas Kinkaid, the Australian First Tactical Air Force and the U.S. Thirteenth Air Force also played important roles in the campaign. They were resisted by Imperial Japanese Navy and Army forces in southern and eastern Borneo, under *Vice-Admiral Michiaki Kamada*, and in the north west by the Thirty-Seventh Army, led by *Lieutenant-General Baba Masao*.

The battle involved a series of three amphibious landings by Australian forces on various points on the mainland. The landing had been preceded by heavy bombing and shelling by Australian and US air and naval forces. Japanese opposition to the landings was sporadic initially, although as the campaign progressed a number of considerable clashes occurred and both sides suffered relatively significant casualties.

The two 20th Brigade battalions were now joined by the 2/13th Battalion, which had conducted an unopposed landing at Lutong on **20 June**, before continuing their advance down the southwestern coast, passing through Miri and Seria on their way towards Kuching. At Seria they found the 37 oil wells ablaze, having been deliberately lit by the Japanese defenders, and engineers from the 2/3rd Field Company were called up to put out the fires, a task which took over three months to complete. Having secured its objectives, the 20th Brigade then began patrolling operations, using landing craft to move quickly along the various rivers and streams that punctuated the western coastline.

The Battle of Balikpapan in southeast Borneo was the concluding stage of the Operation Oboe. The landings took place on **1 July 1945**. The Australian 7th Division, composed of the 18th, 21st and 25th Infantry Brigades, with KNIL troops (Royal Netherlands East Indies Army), made an amphibious landing a few miles north of Balikpapan. The Japanese were outnumbered and outgunned, but like the other battles of the Pacific War, many of them fought to the death.

The Australians gains of North Borneo were negated by the sudden conclusion of the war in August 1945.

XXVIII Battle of Okinawa, the B-29 Superfortress

The path to the Battle of Okinawa arose from a long and bloody direction to get closer to the mainland of Japan and was the final stepping stone to an invasion.

Operation Iceberg would be the culmination of Admiral Chester W. Nimitz's island-hopping campaign that had taken the United States Navy and Marine Corps, in three years, all the way across the Central Pacific. Now, with Nimitz himself head-quartered at Guam and the elements of what would become the greatest naval armada ever assembled being outfitted at their various staging areas from California to Australia, the Americans were poised to enter their end game with Japan.

After the reduction of Iwo Jima on March 14, 1945, square in the sights of this American juggernaut was the tiny island of Okinawa, the anchor at the end of a long chain of outer islands that led 400 miles back to Kyushu, the southernmost of the Japanese home islands.

The Battle of Okinawa started on **23 March 1945** with all major combat operations ending on **23 June 1945**. The Okinawa campaign was the last and biggest of the Pacific island battles of World War II. Code named Operation Iceberg, was a series of battles fought in the Japanese Ryukyu Islands, centered on the island of Okinawa, and included **the largest amphibious assault in the Pacific War during World War II**, starting **1 April 1945**.

Okinawa Island is the largest of the Okinawa Islands and the Ryukyu Islands of Japan. The island is approximately 70 miles long and an average 7 miles wide. It is roughly 640 kilometers (400 mi) south of the rest of Japan.

Okinawa is a subtropical island that stays hot and muggy year-round with almost continual precipitation. The precipitation did not have an effect on either side's weapons or equipment due to experience in maintaining the weapons and gear in such conditions. The effect of the precipitation on morale was dramatic for the American troops. In addition, the physical effects increased disease while decreasing operational efficiency by increasing the prevalence of mud preventing any sort of mechanized support. The terrain on Okinawa was covered in foliage and trees and was littered with hills, one of which reaches 505 meters (1640 feet) at its highest point. The combination of these factors gave the advantage to the defender on this long island. The Japanese also used the coral and limestone as natural cover and concealment.

The island's airfields were indispensable to the launching of bombers and long-range escorts for the preparatory bombing for the land invasion of mainland Japan. This battle involved the Japanese Army, minimal Japanese naval efforts (due to a lacking naval power), and the last of its airpower concentrated in mass kamikaze formations.

The allied power consisted of a combined force that was largely American with some British naval support, along with the Joint Services of the U.S. Army, Marine Corps, and Navy. The bombardment of Okinawa commenced on **23 March** and lasted until the morning of the land invasion (codenamed Operation Iceberg) on **1 April 1945.**

The land battle took place over about 81 days beginning on **April 1, 1945**. The first Americans ashore were soldiers of the 77th Infantry Division, who landed in the Kerama Islands, 15 mi (24 km) west of Okinawa on **March 26**. The Kerama Islands are a group of 22 islands southwest of Okinawa Island, part of the Ryukyu Islands.

As L-day for Operation Iceberg approached, Vice Admiral Kelly Turner, commander of the Joint Expeditionary force designated TF51, suggested the seizure of a tiny group of islands 15 miles west of Okinawa called Kerama Retto, the largest and most easterly of which would host a two-mile-long runway for seaplanes and a sheltered, deep water anchorage that could hold as many as 75 ships.

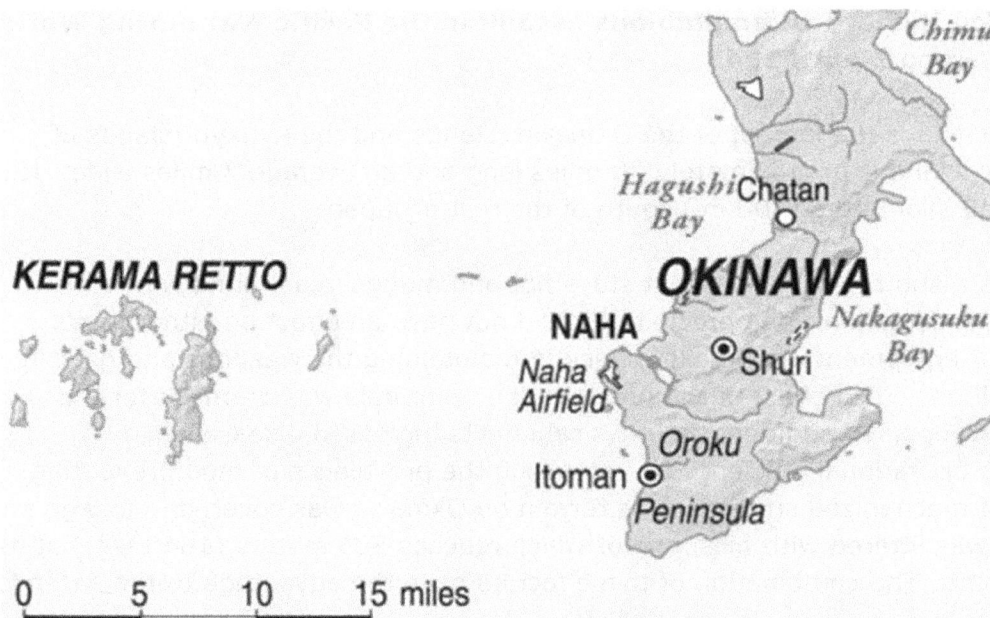

Chosen for that job was XXIV Corps' 77th Infantry Division. Veterans of the Philippines fighting, they were involved with the conquest of Leyte and were ramrodded by Major General Andrew D. Bruce. As the operation unfolded, the 77th would break up into four Battalion Landing Teams (BLT's) and assault each island in the Kerama group simultaneously. In addition, the 420th Artillery Group would land on tiny Keise Shima, about halfway between Kerama and Okinawa, where their guns would be within range to support the coming landings on the Hagushi beaches.

From **March 18-20**, the 77th completed loading duties and embarked into its various landing craft. All the elements of TG51.1 began coming together as Rear Admiral Ingolf N. Kiland took the Western Island Attack Group out to sea on **March 21**. From there, aboard his flagship Mount McKinley, Kiland could observe his entire command: a 19-ship transport squadron with their attendant destroyers and destroyer escorts, a tractor flotilla of 29 large landing craft, gunboats and patrol ships, a hospital ship, two repair ships, two Victory ships filled with ammunition, an antimine group with their nets and buoys, tankers, and a whole range of miscellaneous surface craft that included two tug boats. In short, Kiland had everything he needed to make a proper, self-contained island assault.

On **March 23**, the destroyer Haggard found a prowling Japanese submarine that Lt. Cmdr. V.J. Sobalie immediately ordered depth charged. Forced to the surface by the sub-sea explosions, *R-41* breached just in time to be rammed by Haggard and sent to the bottom again in pieces.

The next day, **March 24**, Admiral Mitscher sent 112 planes on a strike against a Japanese convoy, 150 miles northwest of Okinawa, sinking all eight ships.

Battle of Kerama Retto

Lt. Gen. Mitsuru Ushijima, the commanding officer of the Japanese on Okinawa, was convinced that the Americans would not waste their strength or allow themselves to be distracted in taking Kerama Retto. So, in dire need of every fighting man he could get, *Ushijima* ordered the islands stripped of the 2,335 soldiers stationed there. That left behind a gaggle of 975 men as well as Korean slave laborers.

Despite the weakness of the remaining force, *Ushijima* still had plans for the Kerama Islands, intending to use them as a base for 350 explosive-laden suicide boats that would be launched against the ships of the American landing force.

As it turned out, the operation took the enemy completely by surprise, **26 March 1945**, with most of the landings being unopposed and the few Japanese defenders retreating inland to caves and tunnels, bringing the islands' terrorized native inhabitants with them. The soldiers, who had been ordered by Ushijima to offer minimum resistance to any enemy attack, had regaled the civilian population with stories of the horrible fate that awaited them at the hands of the barbaric Americans.

In the afternoon, a total of 58 more Japanese were killed in a host of small-unit encounters, with every enemy soldier needing to be rousted from caves and prepared positions almost man to man. By early evening, however, most of the island had been secured. Yet nearly 300 Japanese combatants and 400 civilians were still holed up in what remained.

Landing on Tokashiki Island

Close to the northern end of the island of Tokashiki, the largest member of a tiny group of islands called Kerama Retto, Corporal Alexander Roberts and the rest of the 306th Regimental Combat Team rested for the night beneath the starry skies of the northern Pacific. It was a welcome respite from the previous three days of tension-filled landings and clashes with resisting Japanese troops.

Suddenly, *the eerie silence of the night was interrupted by a series of dull explosions and the subsequent screams and wails of the injured from farther inland. The next morning, Roberts and his fellows, in seeking out the source of the sounds, discovered a small valley filled with over 150 dead and dying Japanese civilians. As a result of official warnings of the barbarous practices of the invading Americans, fathers had throttled their families before disemboweling themselves. In some places, three generations lay mangled together beside the bodies of their patriarchs who themselves had been torn apart by the self-inflicted blasts of hand grenades. As the American soldiers did what they could dispensing food and medical care, survivors who had killed their loved ones only hours before wept with the realization of the enormity of their error.*

Such a scene was only the beginning of the tragedies to be visited upon the Japanese people already overburdened with the human cost of years of war. The toll in human lives would only escalate as the titanic struggle for the Pacific entered its final phase and the desperation of Japan's military leaders led them to envision a final stand involving every last member of their beleaguered nation.

On **March 27**, the last islands in the Kerama group were invaded, with the garrisons on Amuro and Kuba Shima offering no resistance. At midmorning, units of the 1st BLT that had taken Geruma the day before landed at Beach Purple, just north of Hitachi Point on the west coast of Tokashiki, the largest of the Kerama islands.

Tokashiki is six miles long with its western side, called the Roadstead, offering the anchorages Rear Admiral Kiland sought for the fleet; otherwise, its topography was much like its sister islands: rocky and scrubby with a few rough hills.

Two battalions linked up and began a sweep northward over the island's goat trails. At its southern tip, the 306th's reserve BLT, the 3rd, came ashore to secure the rear. That night, the 1st and 2nd rested just outside the town of Tokashiki in the extreme northeast, where they and Corporal Roberts later discovered the remnants of the island's civilian inhabitants, murdered by the Japanese.

By the end of **March 27**, the entire western portion of the Kerama group was secured. The importance of its seizure had already become apparent. In their sweep of the islands, soldiers of the 77th discovered the shallow-draft *"suicide boats"* the Japanese intended to use to *"attack … transports, loaded with essential supplies and material and personnel [to be] carried out by concentrating maximum strength immediately upon the enemy's landing."*

Made of plywood and powered by an 85 horsepower Chevrolet engine, the 18-foot-long boats were intended to emerge from their camouflaged hideouts carrying two depth charges each and guided by a Japanese officer right up to an unsuspecting American vessel to unload its deadly cargo. Presumably, the boat's pilot would have a chance of getting away as the depth charges had a five-second delayed fuse.

Unfortunately for *Ushijima*, the attack against Kerama Retto ruined his plans for the suicide boats, prompting General Bruce to declare that their interdiction alone made the whole operation worth it.

In the course of the three-day operation, the Americans lost 155 soldiers and sailors killed in 15 separate landings while the cost to the Japanese defenders was 530 killed. By **March 29**, the purpose for which Kerama Retto was seized in the first place was already being fulfilled. On that day, 30 planes flew in to establish anti-submarine patrols, and combat-ship refueling operations had begun in the Roadstead, a boat pool and ammunition dump set up and nets raised and tended. All was in readiness for the invasion of Okinawa two days later.

✦   ✦   ✦   ✦

This is the text of an interview with Kinjo Shigeaki (85) about his experience as a survivor of the compulsory mass suicides which occurred on Tokashiki Island, Okinawa in late March 1945. The interview took place on April 23rd 2014.

Interviewed by Michael Bradley Translation by Maehara Naoko

I am from the Kerama Islands, about 30 km off the coast of Naha, the capital of Okinawa. There are about 10 islands in the group.

On the 26th March 1945 the Americans began to land on some of the islands. We lived on Tokashiki and were told by Japanese soldiers to move to Nishiyama in the north of the island, where the Japanese soldiers had their camp. We were ordered to travel after dark so the Americans wouldn't see us. There was no shelling from the Americans that night, but it was raining heavily. I don't know how many hours we walked, maybe four or five. We were nearly in Nishiyama when the sun rose.

About 700 or 800 people had gathered in Nishiyama. We were packed together tightly and women and children were crying. Surrounded by Japanese soldiers, we feared that something bad was about to happen. The village head was an ex-soldier himself. We waited for a long time. I don't know how many hours passed but eventually the village head gave the order. We were to call out Banzai (Long Life!) to the emperor three times. We knew that this was what Japanese soldiers did when they were going to die on the battlefield. The village head didn't exactly tell us to commit suicide, but by telling us to shout Banzai, we knew what was meant.

Soldiers distributed grenades among us. We were told that after you pull out the pin, you had to wait three seconds before the grenade exploded. (It didn't seem to matter that it was prohibited at that time to distribute arms to civilians.) There weren't enough grenades to go around because there were so many of us. Actually, my family didn't get one. Anyway, once the grenades were given out, that was taken as a sign and the killing began immediately. The grenades were detonated, but there were few of them, so most people survived the blasts. Then people began to use clubs or scythes on each other – various things were used.

It was the father's role to kill his own family, but my father had already died. I was only 16 years and one-month old, high school age. (Although, I wasn't in high school.) My older brother and I didn't discuss how we would do it, but we both knew we had been ordered to kill ourselves and our family.

I don't remember exactly how we killed our mother, maybe we tried to use rope at first, but in the end, we hit her over the head with stones. I was crying as I did it and she was crying too. My younger sister would have been about to become a 4th grader in elementary school and my little brother would have been about to start 1st grade. I don't remember exactly how we killed our little brother and sister but it wasn't difficult because they were so small – I think we used a kind of spear. There was wailing and screaming on all sides as people were killing and being killed. If there were knives, knives were used.

After we finished, my brother and I discussed which of us would die next. Just then, a boy ran up to us. He was about 15 or 16 and he said, "Let's fight the Americans and be killed by them, rather than dying like this." The Americans of course had lots of weapons and we knew that we would be killed instantly if we tried to attack them. But we decided that rather than killing ourselves then and there, we would let the Americans finish us off. So, we left that place of screaming and death and set off to find the Americans.

However, the first person we met was not an American but a Japanese soldier. We were shocked and wondered why he was still alive when we had been told to kill each other. Why was it that only the locals had to commit suicide while Japanese soldiers were allowed to survive? We felt betrayed. After the war, I coined the phrase, 'Gunsei, Minshi,' which means 'the army survives, the people die.' Anyway, after seeing this soldier I was no longer willing to commit suicide.

I stayed in the mountains while the Americans bombed the island from the air. Houses, schools, post offices—all the buildings were destroyed. A fire bomb burnt down an entire village. I lived in the mountains for a couple of weeks. There was no food. I went to the beach. I couldn't fish but I dived into the sea and got some turban shells (snails), or whatever I could find that was edible. I also found some paths made by American soldiers. Here and there they'd dropped some food cans which I was able to use. Apart from these things, there was no food. Everybody became emaciated with malnutrition. After a couple of weeks, the American soldiers were getting close to us. I observed that they didn't shoot girls when they ran towards them. But I did see them shoot a man, a relative of my father's – he was hit in the stomach and died where he fell. I was hiding in the grass. Finally, I was discovered by an American soldier who pointed a gun at me. I raised my hands.

I was brought by the soldiers to a truck and the truck went into the sea. At first, I thought they were going to drown us but it turned out to be some kind of amphibious vehicle. Anyway, they brought us from Aharen to Tokashiki village. There were 20 prisoners, maybe more, in that truck. At Tokashiki village we were given food. I realized that many people had survived the slaughter of Nishiyama. I later learned that some 300 people had died there that day – overall, about 600 had died in two mass suicides in the Kerama islands. It's important to remember that such mass suicides occurred only in places where the Japanese army was present.

The POW camp where we stayed in Tokashiki was across a little track from where the Americans had their tents. Because I was young I often went to the soldiers' camp and they would ask me, "Are you Japanese?" When I said yes they would point their guns at me but if they asked, "Are you Okinawan" and I said yes, they wouldn't point them. I realized that they distinguished between Japanese and Okinawans.

After the war my inner struggle began. It was hard to continue living, thinking about the horrific things I'd done. I felt so terribly guilty. It was during this desperate time that a Mr Tanahara, a Christian introduced me to the Bible – Gideon's bible. I'd never even seen, let alone read, a Bible before but flicking through it, my attention was grabbed by words like, "life" "Salvation" and "death". I was intrigued so I got a bible myself and started reading it. It gave me comfort.

In 1948 I sailed from Tokashiki in a small traditional boat to Itoman on the Okinawan mainland to be baptized at Itoman Church. I later went to high school for a year and in 1951 entered Aoyama Gakuin University in Tokyo. I became a minister in Itoman Church in 1955 and was involved in setting up Okinawa Christian Junior College. In 1958 I went to graduate school in Manhattan to study theology.

Fortunately, not all of the natives panicked. A great many – in company with Korean forced laborers who'd escaped their masters – gave themselves up.

✦   ✦   ✦   ✦

Kerama was used as a staging area for the assault on Okinawa.   The operation provided a protected anchorage for the fleet and eliminated the threat from suicide boats. The main Okinawa landing was made by the XXIV Corps and the III Amphibious Corps on the Hagushi beaches on the western coast of Okinawa on **L-Day, 1 April 1945**. Kerama Island is on the lower west side of Okinawa.

Battle of Okinawa

The battle of Okinawa has been referred to as the **"typhoon of steel"**. The nicknames refer to the ferocity of the fighting, the intensity of Japanese *kamikaze* attacks, and the sheer numbers of Allied ships and armored vehicles that assaulted the island. The battle was one of the bloodiest in the Pacific, with approximately 160,000+ casualties on both sides including drafted Okinawans wearing Japanese uniforms. 149,425 Okinawans were killed, committed suicide or went missing, a significant proportion of the estimated pre-war 300,000 local population.

Japanese air opposition had been relatively light during the first few days after the landings. However, on **6 April**, the expected air reaction began.

13 April 1945: About 350 miles from the Japanese mainland, U.S. invasion forces establish a beachhead on Okinawa island.   Pouring out war supplies and military equipment, the landing crafts fill the sea to the horizon, where stand the battleships of the U.S. fleet.

Five thousand of the American dead in the Battle of Okinawa are sailors killed in *kamikaze* attacks. An additional thousand more Americans will be pulled off the line with shell shock from enduring the prolonged Japanese artillery bombings. Japan's Okinawa casualties will number more than a hundred thousand dead soldiers.

Chiran high school girls wave farewell with cherry blossom branches to a departing kamikaze pilot in a Nakajima Di-43-IIIa Hayabusa. This was a single-engine land-based tactical fighter used by the Imperial Japanese Army Air Force. The Allied reporting name was "Oscar" but it was often called the "Army Zero" by American pilots because it bore a certain resemblance to the Mitsubishi A6M Zero.

The HMS Formidable of the Royal Navy burns after a **May 4** Kamikaze attack. Eight crew members were lost and 55 injured, but the Formidable survived the war.

Between the American landing on **April 1 and May 25**, seven major *kamikaze* attacks were attempted, involving more than 1,500 planes.

Cherry Blossom Squadrons

The pilots of the Cherry Blossom Squadrons trained to guide Ohka rocket-powered glider bombs into American ships in the last year of World War II. Ohka means "cherry blossom" in Japanese, and each Ohka weapon had a cherry blossom painted on each side of its nose, which contained 2,800 pounds of explosives and a pilot. The mother planes, Mitsubishi Type 1 (Betty) bombers, carried one Ohka each to within a few miles of a target before being released, and Zero fighters served as escorts to protect the mother planes. American fighters destroyed most of the mother planes before the Ohka weapons could be released, so the rocket-propelled human bombs inflicted little damage on American ships near Okinawa. Over 50 Ohka pilots and about 320 pilots and crewmen of the mother planes lost their lives during the war. Below is the Ohka Cherry Blossom Kamikaze glider.

+ + + +

Sgt. Willard Chamberlin with 1st Marine Division at Okinawa during WW II

War Tales by **DON MOORE**

Willard Chamberlin was a Marine mess sergeant and rifleman who saw action at Okinawa, the biggest battle in the Pacific during the closing days of World War II. He quit high school in 1943, when he was just 17-year-old, and joined the Marines with his parents' permission. Before the war was over he had three brothers who also served in the Army, Navy and Air Corps. After graduating from cook and bakers school the teenage leatherneck was sent to San Diego where he shipped out aboard a transport for the war zone in the South Pacific.

"I was a cook in the 3rd Amphibious Corps attached to a battalion of 155 'Long Tom' field guns, part of the 1st Marine Division. There was a lot of speculation aboard ship we were going to Formosa. We ended up in an LST (landing ship) off the beach at Okinawa. Just before we arrived they told us where we were going, what we were going to do and what was expected of us. "Shortly after we got there a Japanese kamikaze (suicide pilot) came down and hit the water right next to our ship and blew up. The explosion rocked our LST so badly the chains holding some of the 155-millimeter cannons broke and the weight aboard our ship shifted," he said. "The captain of our LST ran the ship on the beach, opened the bow doors and we stepped onto the sand without getting our feet wet," Chamberlin recalled. "There was no enemy resistance." Within two weeks Marines had taken the north end of the 70-mile-long island without too much fighting.

"I was told to cook some food for the troops. So, I set up on the beach and made soup and coffee for the Marines. While cooking on the beach an object flew right by my head and buried itself in the sand at my feet. The object was dug up and we found it was a piece of shrapnel about 20-inches long, 5-inches wide and 2-inches thick. I was told the Japanese had no guns that would fire a shell that size. It was from one of our battleships off shore," he said. The Marines and Army hadn't been on the island long when the Japanese Air Force came calling.

"The Marines captured one of the two runways built by the Japanese located on the north end of the island early on. One night we heard Japanese planes fly over. We could tell they were Japanese planes because their engines sounded different than our planes," Chamberlin said. "They flew right in and landed on the runway the Marines had just taken. They ran down to where our planes were parked and blew six of them up before we got 'em."

The U.S. Army's job was to capture the south end of the 70-mile long island. It was a big assignment since the better part of 100,000 enemy troops inhabited the caves, hills and foxholes on the lower part of Okinawa. The fighting was so fierce the Marines were sent south to help the Army finish the job. "The Japanese had their cannons in caves. They were on tracks and they could pull them out of a cave to fire at American forces and then push them back into the hill to protect their guns from the enemy," Chamberlin said. "The Army was having a terrible time taking Kakazu Ridge. The Marines were told to take the hill. When we got done with the hill there wasn't a blade of grass on it."

"One of these caves had massive steel doors to protect the Japanese artillery. We couldn't blow the doors off with our guns. So, <u>we drilled into the 20-inch thick steel doors</u> and placed charges in the holes that blew the doors off the front of the cave," he said.

"The Japanese military headquarters was in a building near the south end that had walls that were 10-feet thick. They also had underground tunnels running off in all directions from this headquarters."

The further south the Marines and Army moved on Okinawa the tougher the fighting got.

"I saw the final stages of the fight for Okinawa that ended up on the beach at the south end of the island. I was on a hill overlooking the beach. The Marines had trapped most of the Japanese that remained on the island in the water. They had no place to go," Chamberlin said.

"All the Japanese soldiers were swimming around in the ocean. The Marines set up speakers and told them to come ashore and surrender. They wouldn't, so the Marines opened up on them with machine-guns and killed 'em all."

"In the midst of the fighting Lt. Gen. Simon Bolivar Buckner, the commanding general of the Marines on Okinawa was killed by Japanese artillery. He was the highest-ranking general killed in the Pacific. It happened shortly after he walked right by me on his way to the front lines."

"He was told by a Marine to go no further because they had been in hand-to-fights with the enemy. Buckner told the Marine, 'I'm the general and I'll do whatever I want.' He was standing between two coral formations when a Japanese artillery round hit and killed him instantly," Chamberlin said.

"Our general, Roy Geiger, took over for Buckner. Although most people think the battle of Okinawa lasted 82 days, it actually lasted an additional 10 days because Gen. Geiger ordered us to clean out any Japanese still left on the island," he said.

✦ ✦ ✦ ✦

The four principal Japanese airfields are located on the southern end of Okinawa.

Operation *Ten-Go* was the attempted attack by a strike force of 10 Japanese surface vessels, led by the super battleship *Yamato* and commanded by *Admiral Seiichi Itō*. This small task force had been ordered to fight through enemy naval forces, then beach *Yamato* and fight from shore using her guns as coastal artillery and crew as naval infantry. The Ten-Go force was spotted by submarines shortly after it left the Japanese home waters, and was intercepted by US carrier aircraft.

Under attack from more than 300 aircraft over a two-hour span, the world's largest battleship, *Yamato,* sank on **7 April, 1945**, after a one-sided battle, long before she could reach Okinawa. US torpedo bombers were instructed to aim for only one side to prevent effective counter flooding by the battleship's crew, and hitting preferably the bow or stern, where armor was believed to be the thinnest.

Of *Yamato's* screening force, the light cruiser *Yahagi* and 4 of the 8 destroyers were also sunk. The Imperial Japanese Navy lost some 3,700 sailors, including *Admiral Itō*, at the cost of 10 US aircraft and 12 airmen. Periodic heavy air attacks continued through April.

March 26 – April 30, twenty American ships were sunk and 157 damaged by enemy action. For their part, by April 30, the Japanese had lost more than 1,100 planes to Allied naval forces alone. Only four destroyers returned to Japan as its Navy was devastated.

The Japanese garrison on Okinawa was led by *GEN Mitsuru Ushijima* with a force of nearly 130,000 men (from his 32d Army) in addition to a 20,000-man home guard to supplement his forces. The defense force was battle hardened, well prepared, and willing to fight to the death.

The Japanese were able to create defensive lines that took away any good avenue of approach from the attacker by occupying every ridgeline on the southern portion of the island. The Japanese took advantage of all the island's natural obstacles and enhanced them through the utilization of tunnels and fortified defensive positions. The dense foliage and well-constructed defensive positions (particularly in the southern end of the island) provided as advantageous cover and concealment as a defender could ask for. *Ushijima* had concentrated the bulk of his defenders out of range of Allied naval guns off the beaches and behind the strong *Shuri* line at the southern end of the island, postulating that holding out as long as possible was the most honorable and beneficial death to give for the Emperor. He wanted to slow the American advance as much as possible to allow the mainland Japanese force to shore up its defenses and prepare its people for a bloody battle all across Japan.

The elaborate communications network under the *Shuri Castle* where *GEN Ushijima's* headquarters was located allowed him to make informed decisions as the castle was a highly defensible position at the center point of the middle *Shuri* defensive line. The decision as to when to withdraw to the next defensive line was made ultimately by *GEN Ushijima*, who received reports from his many officers along whichever one of the three defensive lines was being held at the time. *GEN Ushijima* held each line until its fate was sealed but there was still opportunity to tactically withdraw, set up in the defense, and start the process all over again.

The Japanese land campaign (mainly defensive) was conducted by the 67,000-strong (77,000 according to some sources) regular 32nd Army and some 9,000 Imperial Japanese Navy (IJN) troops at *Oroku naval base* (only a few hundred of whom had been trained and equipped for ground combat), supported by 39,000 drafted local Ryukyuan (Okinawan) people (including 24,000 hastily drafted rear militia called *Boeitai* and 15,000 non-uniformed laborers).

In Okinawa island, middle school boys were organized into front-line-service. The Japanese Imperial Army mobilized 1,780 middle school boys aged 14–17 years into front-line-service. About half of the middle schoolers were killed, including in suicide bomb attacks against tanks, and in guerrilla operations. After losing the Battle of Okinawa, the Japanese government enacted new laws in preparation for the decisive battles in the main islands. These laws made it possible for boys aged 15 or older and girls aged 17 or older to be drafted into front-line-service.

The prebattle intelligence gathering for the Americans was sparse in attaining valuable collections because of the isolation of the Ryukyu Island chain. There was limited intelligence gathered from old Japanese newspapers as well as from Japanese prisoners of war from other battles in the Pacific. Aerial photographs did not yield an accurate picture of the Japanese defensive strategy. The aerial reconnaissance was hampered by continual cloud cover over the majority of the island. The clever concealment of the *Shuri* line, in addition to most of it being underground, prevented its elaborate nature from being discovered.

The Americans knew there would be a heavy defensive force but the overall strength and where they came from was a mystery. Useful intelligence gathering and dissemination did not begin until contact with the *Shuri* line began. It was then that awareness of *GEN Ushijima's* plan for a war of attrition began to develop and the intricate nature of the Japanese defensive lines discovered.

The notable features of the island are the scattered hills which allowed the Japanese to create defensive lines at each ridge forcing a bloody fight for every inch taken. Every ridge had shooting lanes from multiple ridge locations.

The leadership in this battle was less dependent on tactical maneuvering and operational planning on a large scale and far more about small unit leaders facing utter chaos and destruction, leading from the front, and continuing to press on through hammering fire and mounting casualties. The objectives of the attacking Americans were relatively simple and always consisted of ***"take a hill and hold it".*** This was consistent with the operational goals of taking the entire island but first each defensive line had to be eliminated. This was done with precision force focusing on specific objectives but still having to fight inch by inch, taking the hills that anchored the edges of the defensive lines, forcing the Japanese to withdraw.

The torrential rains throughout the battle and the impact of the *Shuri* line defenses quickly took their toll. More mental health issues arose from the Battle of Okinawa than any other battle in the Pacific during World War II. The constant bombardment from artillery and mortars coupled with the high casualty rates led to a great deal of men coming down with combat fatigue. Additionally, the rains caused mud that prevented tanks from moving and tracks from pulling out the dead, forcing Marines (who pride themselves on burying their dead in a proper and honorable manner) to leave their comrades where they lay. This, coupled with thousands of bodies both friend and foe littering the entire island, created a scent you could nearly taste.

Morale was dangerously low by the month of May and the state of discipline on a moral basis had a new low barometer for acceptable behavior. The ruthless atrocities by the Japanese throughout the war had already brought on an altered behavior (deemed so by traditional standards) by many Americans resulting in the desecration of Japanese remains, but the Japanese tactic of using the Okinawan people as human shields brought about a new aspect of terror and torment to the psychological capacity of the Americans.

As noted by a Marine, *the environment that was lived and fought in was so atrocious, words could not accurately describe it. It required all of the senses to truly understand the horrors of the battle. There were piles of dead bodies at the bottom of every hill and if someone was to slip in the mud and fall down a hill, they were apt to reach the bottom vomiting.*

Said one Marine of the scene, *"I saw more than one man lose his footing and slip and slide all the way to the bottom only to stand up horror-stricken as he watched in disbelief while fat maggots tumbled out of his muddy dungaree pockets, cartridge belt, legging lacings, and the like."*

The 10th Army swept across the south-central part of the island capturing the Kadena and the Yomitan airbases within hours of the landing. In light of the weak opposition, General Buckner decided to proceed immediately with Phase II of his plan—the seizure of northern Okinawa. The 6th Marine Division headed up the Ishikawa Isthmus and by **7 April**, had sealed off the Motobu Peninsula.

The bulk of the Japanese forces in the north (codenamed *Udo Force*) were cornered on the Motobu Peninsula. Here, the terrain was mountainous and wooded, with the Japanese defenses concentrated on Yae-Dake, a twisted mass of rocky ridges and ravines on the center of the peninsula. There was heavy fighting before the Marines finally cleared Yae-Dake on **18 April**.

Assault on Ie Island (Ie Shima)

Ie Shima lies about three and one-half miles off the western tip of Motobu Peninsula and twenty miles north of the Hagushi beaches on Okinawa. It is oval in shape, about five miles long and two miles wide, the longer dimension lying east and west. Coral reefs fringe the entire island. Along the north and northwest coasts, the land rises abruptly in steep sea cliffs containing hundreds of caves, but along the southern shores are numerous beaches from which the terrain slopes gently upward. The best of these for landing heavy equipment, designated as Red 3 and 4 by the invading forces, lay on the southeast coast southwest of the town of Ie.

Engineers construct a causeway from the island to the sea to allow supplies to be trucked from ships to shore.

The island is spotted with small clumps of scrub trees, sparse areas of knee-high grass, and a few cultivated fields and patches of sugar cane. Almost its entire interior is occupied by a plateau approximately 165 feet in altitude, broken on the east by Iegusugu Mountain, which rises abruptly for about 600 feet above the level terrain and was appropriately called "the Pinnacle" by the soldiers. South of the Pinnacle lies the town of Ie, consisting of about 300 houses.

The Iegusugu Mountain was surrounded by clear fields of fire, and from it one could see the entire island. On the plateau the Japanese had established three landing strips, which together formed the pattern of the Roman numeral XI. No obstructions interfered with the approaches to these mile-long strips. Aircraft had unlimited expanses of open water over which to gain altitude.

Two battleships, four cruisers, and seven destroyers of the Fifth Fleet opened up a heavy bombardment of Ie Shima at dawn of **16 April**. LCI's swept the landing beaches with rockets and mortar shells. Thousands of rounds of 40-mm., 20-mm., and .50-caliber ammunition arched into the beaches from support craft and from guide boats escorting the first landing waves. Planes bombed and rocketed the island and dropped tanks of napalm on and behind the beaches. Billowing clouds of smoke and dust rose from the flaming napalm, exploding ammunition dumps, and burning gasoline stores. Within a few minutes Ie Shima was blacked out. Puffs of white smoke against the gray pall over the island showed where the rocket and mortar ships were preparing the beaches.

After advancing inland and wheeling to the east in the morning, the 305th RCT attacked east in a zone parallel to the coast, extending about 800 yards inland. Progress during the afternoon was slow. The enemy delivered rifle and machine-gun fire from coral emplacements west of the town of Ie and from caves and fortified tombs in the hillside below the plateau. It was mainly an infantry-engineer fight; armor and self-propelled guns were held up by mines, including many buried 500-pound aerial bombs. By nightfall the 1st Battalion had advanced only 800 yards from its beachhead; the 3d Battalion, which made the wide turn on the left of the regiment, had moved about 1,800 yards.

During the night of **16 April,** the enemy launched a coordinated attack on the 3d Battalion of the 305th. The attack came with suicidal recklessness. The Japanese were supported by mortars and 70-mm. guns, and were armed with small arms, sharpened stakes, bags of hand grenades, and literally hundreds of satchel charges, some of which had been improvised from mortar shells. Japanese worked up to the perimeters in small groups and either threw their satchel charges at close range or blew themselves up in an effort to take Americans with them. Some of the human bombs were successful, but most of the Japanese were killed before they came within effective range. One American had his arm broken by the flying leg of a Japanese soldier who had blown himself up. After hours of wild fighting in the dark the enemy withdrew, leaving 152 of his dead in and around the 3d Battalion's position. Meanwhile the 1st Battalion of the 305th RCT fought off a number of small harassing attacks, but the 306th had a relatively quiet night.

The next day, **17 April**, the 3d Battalion of the 305th quickly seized high ground in its sector, about 800 yards short of the town, after a brief fire fight during which Lt. Col. Edward Chalgren, Jr., the battalion commander, was wounded. The attack was slowed down by heavy machine-gun fire coming from caves in the coral slopes on the left (north) side of the regiment's zone of action as they reached the ioutskirts of Ie.

The 2d and 3d Battalions of the 307th landed on the beaches southwest of Ie during the morning of **17 April**, with the 3d Battalion on the east. The plan called for these two battalions to attack abreast northeast toward Ie. They were to pass through the 1st Battalion of the 305th Infantry, which was holding the ground inland to the west of the two beaches over which the 307th landed. The attack was to cut across the front of the 3d Battalion of the 305th, providing supporting fire from its flank position on the outskirts of Ie.

The 307th jumped off at 1300. Both battalions made about 400 yards in two hours against steadily increasing resistance. The troops had to move uphill over open ground. From his positions on the Pinnacle and on intervening high ground, the enemy had perfect observation of their movements. The strongest Japanese positions, aside from those in or around the Pinnacle, were along a prominent ridge and in a small rise on the ridge topped by a large concrete building, about 700 yards southwest of the Iegusugu Mountain. These positions came to be known as "Bloody Ridge" and "Government House Hill."

By late afternoon both battalions were receiving heavy mortar and small arms fire from dominating ground ahead of them. The numerous mine fields slowed the movement of self-propelled artillery, and since tanks had not yet been landed the foot soldiers and the engineers bore the brunt of the close-in action. Division artillery kept the rear enemy areas under attack. Elements of the 307th fought their way to a point 600 yards south of Government House Hill, but, being unable to consolidate their position for the night so close to Bloody Ridge, they withdrew to more favorable terrain about 400 yards inland from the beach. Casualties were mounting. Hopes for a quick victory were fading.

The plan for **18 April** called for continuation of the attack by the 307th, supported by the 305th, against the defense in depth established by the enemy in the town south of the Pinnacle. The 306th Infantry, pivoting on its right (south) flank, was to attack toward the Pinnacle from the west and north. Although this move would continue the encirclement of the enemy's main positions around Iegusugu, the main effort was to be the attack from the south and west. For two days the 305th and 307th were to batter in vain against Bloody Ridge south of the Pinnacle. In the fierce fighting south and west of the Pinnacle during **18 and 19 April**, the 77th Division was to meet the stiffest opposition in its experience and to sustain the bulk of its casualties on Ie Shima. From the rubble of Ie and from positions dug into Bloody Ridge the enemy fought back with heavy mortar, machine-gun, and rifle fire.

Infantrymen, closely backed by engineer blasting teams, often had to fight their way into the enemy positions and clean them out with grenades and bayonets.

After a heavy preparation by the artillery on Minna Shima, the 3d Battalion, 305th, attacked at 1130 on an 800-yard front. A house-to-house fight ensued amid the rubble of Ie. "Every street became a phase line," one observer reported. The necessity of forming a connecting link over the wide area between the 306th and the 307th made the fight harder.   Artillery was ineffective against many enemy positions and could not be used freely because other friendly units were so close by. Self-propelled guns were held up by mines and debris in the narrow streets. After working about halfway through the northwestern section of the town, the troops withdrew to a more secure position on the outskirts, their right (south) flank then being 500 yards west of Government House Hill, and their left (north) flank 100 yards west of the base of Iegusugu. They had made a net gain of only about 350 yards for the day.

When the attack of the 307th came almost to a standstill directly south of Government House Hill about midday of **18 April**, it was decided to send the 3d Battalion of the 307th around to the right, where it could attack toward the northeast in the eastern section of the town. The Americans hoped that resistance east of Government House Hill would be less severe than that encountered south of it, and such proved to be the case. The 3d Battalion made moderate progress and advanced to a point 300 yards north of the village Agarii-mae. Medium tanks and self-propelled guns covered the gap that developed between the two battalions of the 307th. These weapons put direct fire into caves, pillboxes, and enemy gun positions in the town of Ie and the Pinnacle. They could not be moved close to the enemy positions, however; deadly machine-gun and mortar fire held the infantry back and left the armor vulnerable to suicide attacks by Japanese armed with satchel charges, who hid in holes until the tanks and guns came within range.

In its advance north of Iegusugu the 306th made good progress during the day, despite almost continual mortar fire from positions on the Pinnacle from which the enemy had unlimited observation of all movements. In the center of the regimental zone the 1st Battalion encountered four pillboxes, which were finally reduced by hand-placed charges. The 3d Battalion, moving along the north coast, reduced enemy positions in caves in the bluffs after hours of fighting at close range.

From his positions in Ie, on Bloody Ridge, and on the Pinnacle, the enemy could put mortar fire on the beaches to the south and on the area directly behind them. During the night of **17-18 April** numerous enemy infiltration attempts supported by mortar and machine-gun fire had to be repulsed by shore party engineers. Not until **21 April** was the eastern exit free of Japanese fire.

On **19 April**, as on the two previous days, the plan called for the main effort to be directed against the strongest Japanese positions on Bloody Ridge in an attack by the 305th and 307th from the southwest.

The continuation of this attack after failure on the two preceding days was due largely to the critical situation at the beaches; American forces were attacking toward Bloody Ridge and the Pinnacle, with Red Beaches 3 and 4 a few hundred yards to the south. The protection of these beaches was the decisive element of the tactical plan. The rapid establishment of Ie airfield was highly important in the strategic concept of the Ryukyus campaign, and equipment for the airfield, as well as for a badly needed air warning service, was coming in over these exposed beaches.

After a half-hour artillery preparation, three battalions attacked at 0900 on **19 April**. The 3d Battalion, 305th Infantry, moved east against the northern part of Ie; the 2d and 3d Battalions, 307th, attacked north from their positions south of Bloody Ridge, moving abreast with the 3d Battalion on the east. By massing all the 81-mm. mortars and heavy machine guns of its ad and 3d Battalions and those of the 1st Battalion, 305th, the 307th built up a heavy base of fire for the advancing assault troops. The infantrymen along the line fought their way from one strong point to another in a series of bloody skirmishes marked by hand-to-hand combat.

From the high ground the enemy poured mortar and small-arms fire on the troops; there seemed to be more of it than ever. The controlling factors on the 19th were the same as on the 17th and 18th-heavy and accurate enemy fire from all the high ground and especially from Bloody Ridge; the ineffectiveness of artillery against many of the Japanese positions; and the restricted use of self-propelled artillery because of the rough terrain, the narrow roads, and numerous mines.

Companies F and G of the ad Battalion of the 307th, in the center, attacked at 0900 and slowly fought their way up the slopes of Government House Hill. After a frontal attack had failed because of heavy enemy fire, the two companies turned to the west, pushed into the edge of the town on the high ground, and then swung back to the nose of the ridge and proceeded to assault the large buildings there during the afternoon. Meanwhile the 1st Battalion, 305th, on the east flank of the ad Battalion, 307th, had attacked through heavy fire at 1330 and had reached high ground 300 yards east of Government House Hill.

Two battalions were now on Bloody Ridge, but they were not to stay for long. An enemy counterattack supported by mortar and automatic fire drove the men of the 1st Battalion, 305th, off the high ground and back to their original position near the beach. At this time the ad Battalion, 307th, was still fighting for Government House Hill 300 yards to the west. The Americans could not, however, consolidate their hold on the buildings. Their ammunition was running low; an amtrack started up the hill with resupply, but the drivers fled when a group of Japanese ran out of a small draw and flung a satchel charge into the vehicle. The troops on the hill were now receiving fire from the high ground just lost by the 305th as well as from the area to the north. Their commander was permitted to withdraw.

The Japanese on Ie Shima were using the defensive methods that had characterized their fighting on other Pacific islands: a house-to-house, cave-to-cave, yard-by-yard linear defense, supported by vicious counterattacks from platoon to company strength; ingeniously concealed detachments that harassed rear elements after the assault troops had passed by; and night infiltrators who even reactivated mines that had been collected by American troops during the day. Although they had few heavy weapons on Ie, the Japanese effectively used mortars, antitank guns, and light and heavy machine guns; when these were not available, they fought with satchel charges, grenades, and crude spears.   The soldiers on Ie, unlike those on Kerama, had the fanatical support of the civilians, including even women with babies, who took part in suicide raids and helped defend caves and tunnels.

On Ie Shima the Japanese sowed thousands of mines, most of them on the airfield, along the beaches and beach roads, and in the heavily defended area west of the town of Ie. Many mines were adapted from aerial bombs and set up in a crude manner: the bomb was fixed at the bottom of a hole, fuze up, and a rock was balanced on two poles at the top of the hole. A pull wire ran from one of the poles to a Japanese soldier concealed nearby who set off the contraption when an American vehicle approached. Such a bomb-mine could flip a 15-ton amtrack over on its back. Most of the mines, however, were of a more standard type.

General Bruce was determined to break the deadlock. On **19 April** he reconnoitered the eastern approaches to Iegusugu by sailing around the eastern end of Ie Shima in a Navy control boat. Aerial reconnaissance had failed to give an accurate picture of the terrain, but from his floating observation post General Bruce was able to study the terrain as it would appear to attacking infantrymen. He concluded that the most promising direction for the attack on Iegusugu would be across the favorable terrain north and east of the Pinnacle. His plan of attack for **20 April** shifted the main effort from the 307th Infantry, south of the Pinnacle, to the 306th, north of it, while the division as a whole tightened the ring around Iegusugu.

At 0850, **20 April**, artillery fired an intense preparation on enemy-held areas ahead of the troops. At 0900 the fires stopped. For ten minutes, as part of a stratagem to draw the Japanese out of their position, the infantry remained in place. Then at 0910 the artillery let loose an even heavier concentration, lasting fifteen minutes.

The three regiments attacked on the heels of the second bombardment. The 306th jumped off with the 1st Battalion in assault, supported by tanks and combat engineers. The 2d Battalion of the 306th remained in position on the north slopes of the Pinnacle, and the 3d Battalion followed the 1st, echeloned to the left (southeast) of the 1st to protect its flank. The 3d Battalion of the 307th, east of Iegusugu, pulled back to the south to give the attacking troops greater freedom of action. The 2d Battalion of the 307th, with the 1st Battalion of the 305th abreast of it on the east, again drove up the steep slopes toward the top of Bloody Ridge and the town and mountain beyond. The 3d Battalion, 305th, attacked east into Ie-for the fourth consecutive day.

All the assault units closing in on the Japanese came almost immediately under heavy fire. Enemy resistance seemed no less stubborn than on the previous days. The 305th and 307th, respectively south and west of the town of Ie, were soon involved in another bitter, yard-by-yard advance. Once again, the 3d Battalion, 305th, had to fight through a maze of rubble and narrow streets amid the ruins of Ie. Under intense mortar and small-arms fire, the 2d Battalion, 307th, and the 1st Battalion, 305th, pushed up once again toward the top of Bloody Ridge, the key to the enemy's defenses south of the Pinnacle. The two battalions moved out across open terrain dominated by the enemy, who had perfect observation of all their movements.

Leading elements of the 306th came under intense mortar and small-arms fire as they left the line of departure 600 yards northeast of the base of Iegusugu. The Pinnacle loomed above them, its slopes covered with masses of torn and twisted vegetation. Describing the Pinnacle on the morning of **20 April**, General Randle, assistant division commander of the 77th, stated: *"It is a damned highly fortified position with caves three stories deep, each house of concrete with machine guns in and under. Whole area of the village and circumference of mountain a maze of machine gun, mortar, and gun positions little affected by artillery fire we have poured on"*.

By early afternoon the attack of the 306th had secured all ground to within 200 yards of the base of the Pinnacle. The regiment halted to reorganize; in its 4-hour fight Company B, which had the hardest going on the right (northwest), had lost its commander and twenty-six men dead or wounded.

Company C of the 306th was passed through B to continue the attack. By a series of rushes through intense machine-gun and mortar fire, the troops gained the slopes of the Pinnacle. In twenty minutes the leading troops were halfway up the northeast side. Supported by direct gunfire from the area below, the infantry and engineers assaulted cave after cave. Higher up on the Pinnacle infantrymen trained in mountain climbing scaled sheer rock walls, hauling up flame throwers and charges to blast the enemy out of his holes.

General Bruce notified General Buckner at noon on **20 April**: *"Base of Pinnacle completely surrounded despite bitterest fight I have ever witnessed against a veritable fortress."*

While the 306th Infantry was assailing Iegusugu from the north on **20 April**, the 305th and 307th were attacking up the southern slopes of Bloody Ridge. After a bitter fight lasting several hours and resembling the yard-by-yard advances of previous days in this area, the 2d Battalion, 307th, again seized the buildings on Government House Hill, and the 1st Battalion, 305th, reoccupied the knob overlooking Government House Hill from the east. Knowing that it would be even harder to hold their positions than it had been to gain them, the Americans hastily fortified them against counterattack. Machine guns were mounted on the second floor of Government House, covering the area toward the Pinnacle, and the troops occupied the ground north of the buildings up to a shallow draw that led to the mountain. Company G was to the west, Company E to the east, and Company F in the center. Engineers and guns were brought up to strengthen the weakened units on Bloody Ridge, who were determined not to lose these positions again. Even as they consolidated their ground the Americans fought off two small but vigorous counterattacks and lost two tanks to Japanese carrying satchel charges.

The 3d Battalion of the 307th, east of Ie, and the 3d Battalion of the 305th on the west, attacked into the town during the day from opposite directions.

After fighting over difficult terrain covered with thick undergrowth and dotted with pillboxes and caves, the 3d Battalion, 307th, held a line at the base of Iegusugu running to newly won Bloody Ridge.

During the night of **20-21 April** small groups of Japanese probed the American lines around Government House Hill on Bloody Ridge, evidently looking for a weak spot in the defenses of the ad Battalion. At 0430 on **21 April** the enemy began an hour-long mortar concentration on the positions. At 0530, from 300 to 400 of the enemy stormed the American lines on the left (west) flank. Supported by intense mortar and small-arms fire, the Japanese advanced in columns-one from the north, another from the northwest, and a third from the west. Among them were women armed with spears. The enemy came through his own mortar fire in a last desperate attempt to knock the Americans off Bloody Ridge.

Here the command post personnel, attached engineers, and the remaining members of Company G fought for their lives. The battalion commander, staff officers, clerks, cooks, and drivers formed a line along the crest of the hill. In a suicide attack Japanese rushed into the line and exploded satchel charges. Some of them came within fifteen feet of the center of the command post area before they were shot down by the defending troops. The improvised line held. After an hour of struggle at close quarters, the Americans drove the enemy back and regained the lost position.

By dawn the counterattack had slackened off. Most of the attacking Japanese had been killed within the American lines. In the area of Company G there were 280 bodies; in front of F and E were 84 more. The American troops also suffered heavy casualties. Company G, already depleted by the previous fighting for Bloody Ridge, had only 36 effectives left on the morning of **21 April**. Company H had 49; Company E, 57. Of the two machine gun platoons of Company H, 19 men were available for duty, and two guns were left of the original eight. In the 2d Battalion, 307th, 30 officers had been killed or wounded by **21 April**-almost all its original officer complement.   However great the cost, Bloody Ridge was now won for good.

Fierce fighting continued on the sides of the Pinnacle as the infantrymen tightened their grip during the remainder of **21 April**. The battalions were now so close to one another that careful coordination was necessary to prevent troops from firing on friendly units. General Randle ordered successive attacks so that one battalion could attack while others took cover.

The southwest slopes of Iegusugu were still in enemy hands. At 1400 Company E on the right (south) flank of the 2d Battalion, 306th, made a coordinated attack with elements of the 3d Battalion, 305th, to push on to the southwest side. The attacking troops immediately came under fire from emplacements still occupied by the enemy. It was no longer possible to use artillery, the area still held by the Japanese being too small. Naval gunfire support had ceased on for the same reason. Even the use of self-propelled 75-mm. howitzers was limited. With small arms, grenades, flame throwers, and demolitions, the troops cleaned the Japanese from their positions on the steep slopes. Two tanks were brought up to help knock out a large fortified cave about halfway up the mountain. By 1445 the troops attacking from the west had seized their assigned area.

By midafternoon of **21 April** all units on the Pinnacle were engaged in mopping up. The exterior of the Pinnacle was secure, but Japanese still remained in subterranean passages and strongholds from which they made sallies against the troops. The openings were systematically blown out and sealed off.

At 1730 on **21 April,** Ie Shima was declared secure. *"The last three days of this fighting were the bitterest I ever witnessed,"* General Bruce stated when the operation was over.

For five days after Ie Shima was declared secure, elements of the 77th mopped up remaining groups of the enemy, sealed caves, destroyed pillboxes, marked or removed the thousands of mines that were still on the island, and buried the dead. During this period hundreds of Japanese were killed in and around the Pinnacle, in the town of Ie, and in caves along the coast line. Removal of mines on the airfield and on the roads feeding it was given priority in order to speed up airfield construction. The last noteworthy encounter on Ie Shima came during the night of **22-23 April**, when a group of Japanese soldiers and civilians, including women, all armed with rifles, grenades, and demolitions, rushed from caves on Iegusugu toward the lines of the 306th. They were all cut down without loss to American troops.

During the 6-day battle on Ie Shima the Americans killed 4,706 Japanese and took 149 prisoners. Many of the dead were civilians; it was extremely hard to distinguish between soldiers and civilians during the fighting or when inspecting the bodies afterwards. It was estimated that 1,500 civilians had been armed and supplied with Japanese Army uniforms. Some others were in American uniforms.

American casualties through 24 April were reported as 172 killed in action, 902 wounded, and 46 missing, a total of 1,120. According to the division surgeon, "casualties on Ie Shima were unusually severe, many of them compound fractures of the extremities and penetrating head wounds caused by small-arms fire."

Base development proceeded rapidly once the mopping up was completed. Although initially delayed by the large number of mines, the engineers quickly repaired the enemy airfield and began the construction of new strips. The coral foundation of the island and the rubble of the town of Ie facilitated the work.

✦ ✦ ✦ ✦

Ernie Pyle – War Correspondent and Roving Reporter

Ernie was a Pulitzer Prize–winning American journalist. For the last 10 years of his life, he wrote feature columns six time a week primarily for Scripps-Howard newspapers as a roving correspondent. He earned wide acclaim for his accounts of ordinary people in rural America, and later, of ordinary American soldiers during World War II. He spent time in Europe and Africa before coming to the Pacific after Germany's surrender. His syndicated column ran in more than 300 newspapers nationwide.

Ernie Pyle was not just any reporter. He was a household name during World War II and for years afterward. From 1941 until his death, Pyle riveted the nation with personal, straight-from-the-heart tales about hometown soldiers in history's greatest conflict. Pyle became a war correspondent and applied his intimate style to combat reporting. Instead of recounting the movements of armies or the activities of generals, Pyle generally wrote from the perspective of the common soldier. He won the Pulitzer Prize in 1944 for his spare, poignant accounts of "dogface" infantry soldiers from a first-person perspective. *"No man in this war has so well told the story of the American fighting man as American fighting men wanted it told"*, wrote Harry Truman. *"He deserves the gratitude of all his countrymen."*

This column below, published posthumously, describes Pyle's first direct contact with Japanese soldiers.

They Just Lay There, Blinking

*OKINAWA, **April 21, 1945** – Now I've seen my first Jap soldiers in their native state – that is, before capture. But not for long, because the boys of my company captured them quicker than a wink.*

It was mid-forenoon and we had just reached our new bivouac area after a march of an hour and a half. The boys threw off their packs, sat down on the ground, and took off their helmets to mop their perspiring foreheads.

We were in a small grassy spot at the foot of a hill. Most of these hillsides have caves with household stuff hidden in them. They are a rich field for souvenir hunters. And all Marines are souvenir hunters.

So immediately two of our boys, instead of resting, started up through the brush, looking for caves and souvenirs. They had gone about fifty yards when one of them yelled:

"There's a Jap soldier under this bush."

We didn't get too excited for most of us figured he meant a dead Jap. But three or four of the boys got up and went up the hill. A few moments later somebody yelled again:

"Hey, here's another one. They're alive and they've got rifles."

So, the boys went at them in earnest. The Japs were lying under two bushes. They had their hands up over their ears and were pretending to be asleep.

The Marines surrounded the bushes and, with guns pointing, they ordered the Japs out. But the Japs were too scared to move. They just lay there, blinking.

The average Jap soldier would have come out shooting. But, thank goodness, these were of a different stripe. They were so petrified the Marines had to go into the bushes, lift them by the shoulders, and throw them out in the open,

My contribution to the capture consisted of standing to one side and looking as mean as I could.

One Jap was small, and about thirty years old. The other was just a kid of sixteen or seventeen, but good-sized and well-built. The kid had the rank of superior private and the other was a corporal. They were real Japanese from Japan, not the Okinawan home guard.

They were both trembling all over. The kid's face turned a sickly white. Their hands shook. The muscles in the corporal's jaw were twitching. The kid was so paralyzed he couldn't even understand sign language.

We don't know why those two Japs didn't fight. They had good rifles and potato-masher hand grenades. They could have stood behind their bushes and heaved grenades into our tightly packed group and got themselves two dozen casualties, easily.

The Marines took their arms. One Marine tried to direct the corporal in handbook Japanese, but the fellow couldn't understand.

The scared kid just stood there, sweating like an ox. I guess he thought he was dead. Finally, we sent them back to the regiment.

The two Marines who flushed these Japs were Corp. Jack Ossege of Silver Grove, Kentucky, across the river from Cincinnati, and Pfc. Lawrence Bennett of Port Huron, Michigan.

Okinawa was the first blitz for Bennett and this was the first Jap soldier he'd ever seen. He is thirty years old, married, and has a baby girl. Back home he was a freight dispatcher.

The Jap corporal had a metal photo holder like a cigarette case. In it were photos which we took to be of three Japanese movie stars. They were good-looking, and everybody had to have a look.

Ossege had been through one Pacific blitz, but this was the first Jap he ever took alive. As an old hand at souvenir hunting he made sure to get the Jap's rifle.

That rifle was the envy of everybody. Later when we were sitting around, discussing the capture, the other boys tried to buy or trade him out of it. "Pop" Taylor, the black-whiskered corporal from Jackson, Michigan, offered Ossege a hundred dollars for the rifle.

The answer was no. Then Taylor offered four quarts of whiskey. The answer still was no. Then he offered eight quarts. Ossege weakened a little. He said, "Where would you get eight quarts of whiskey?" Pop said he had no idea. So Ossege kept the rifle.

So, there you have my first two Japs. And I hope my future Japs will all be as tame as these two. But I doubt it.

On **April 16**, the Army's 77th Infantry Division landed on Ie Shima, a small island off Okinawa, to capture an airfield. On the third morning, a jeep carrying Pyle and three officers came under fire from a hidden machine gun. All scrambled for cover in roadside ditches, but when Pyle raised his head, a .30 caliber bullet caught him in the left temple, killing him instantly, **18 April 1945**.

Roberts and two other photographers, including AP's Grant MacDonald, were at a command post 300 yards away when Col. Joseph Coolidge, who had been with Pyle in the jeep, reported what happened. Roberts went to the scene, and despite continuing enemy fire, crept forward – a "laborious, dirt-eating crawl," he later called it – to record the scene with his Speed Graphic camera. His risky act earned Roberts a Bronze Star medal for valor. **The Speed Graphic is commonly called the most famous press camera.**

"It's a striking and painful image, but Ernie Pyle wanted people to see and understand the sacrifices that soldiers had to make, so it's fitting, in a way, that this photo shows his own death … drives home the reality and the finality of that sacrifice," said James E. Tobin, a professor at Miami University of Ohio.

✦　✦　✦　✦

Back to Okinawa

While the 6th Marine Division cleared northern Okinawa, the US Army 96th and 7th Infantry Divisions wheeled south across the narrow waist of Okinawa. The 96th Infantry Division began to encounter fierce resistance in west-central Okinawa from Japanese troops holding fortified positions east of Highway No. 1 and about 5 mi (8 km) northwest of Shuri, from what came to be known as Cactus Ridge. The 7th Infantry Division encountered similarly fierce Japanese opposition from a rocky pinnacle located about 1,000 yd (910 m) southwest of Arakachi (later dubbed "The Pinnacle"). By the night of **8 April**, American troops had cleared these and several other strongly fortified positions. They suffered over 1,500 battle casualties in the process, while killing or capturing about 4,500 Japanese, yet the battle had only begun, for it was now realized they were merely outposts guarding the Shuri Line.

Cactus Ridge

Cactus Ridge was the name given to a rise of land approximately 600 yards southeast of Mashiki, Okinawa which commanded much of the ground between Uchitomari and Oyama, both of which lie along Highway No. 1. The defense of Cactus Ridge to the west, and The Pinnacle to the east, marked the start of iron resistance by Japanese land forces on Okinawa.

As the American 96th Infantry Division advanced south along Okinawa's Highway 1 on **4 April 1945**, it came under increasing fire from the south and from the ridges on their left (east). Three medium tanks from the 763d Tank Battalion were destroyed by a carefully sited and well-concealed 47 mm anti-tank gun. Firing twenty rounds, Japanese gunners set the three tanks afire. Japanese Army commanders later described this feat as an illustration of the effectiveness of 47 mm guns. *"Great results,"* Japanese combat instructions stated, *"can be obtained by concealing the guns and opening surprise fire on the tanks at close range."*

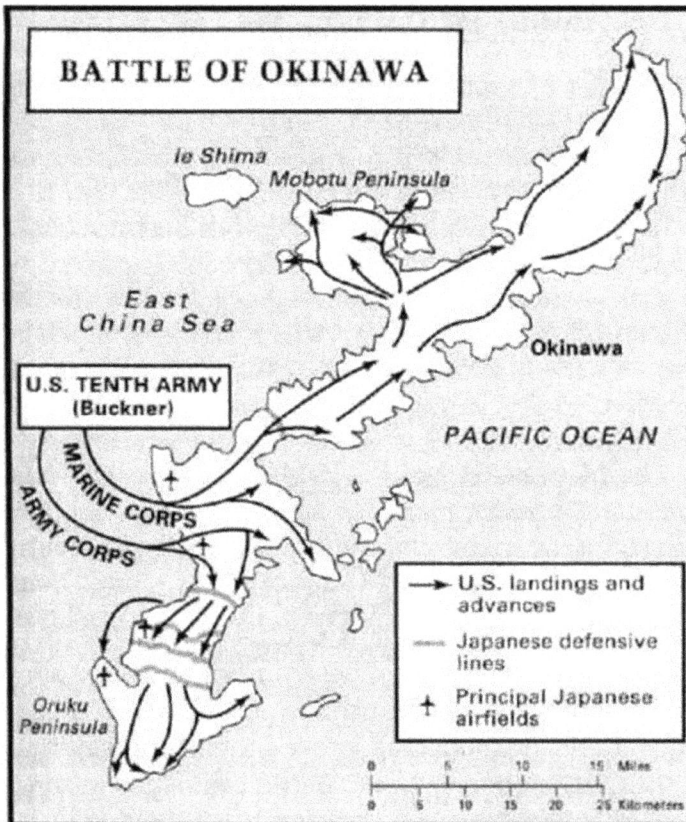

BATTLE OF OKINAWA

By **5 April**, the 383d regiment indicated that its forward elements were receiving fire from 20 machine guns and from 15 to 20 mortars, besides artillery pieces. As movement progressed, it encountered a series of fortified positions, the approaches to which were often covered by minefields. Dislodging the Japanese from these positions required coordinated enveloping movements and resulted in numerous American casualties.

On the following day, **6 April**, the fortified Japanese positions on Cactus Ridge continued to hold up the 383d. Attempts were made to dislodge the defenders with an airstrike early on that morning, but subsequent troops assaulting the targeted positions found defensive enemy fire as intense as ever. American forces continued to make direct frontal assaults, through heavy Japanese mortar fire, against the ridge. Such assaults ultimately resulted in charging and reducing Japanese positions with hand grenades and small arms fire.

By the end of **6 April**, these "Banzai" type charges by the 2d Battalion enabled the 383d to ultimately gain first the western half of Cactus Ridge. On **7 April**, similar tactics by the 2d Battalion allowed the 383d to capture the rest of Cactus Ridge.

As a result of the offensive actions of **4–7 April**, the 383d Infantry found itself assembled against the formidable Japanese positions on Kakazu Ridge.

The next American objective was Kakazu Ridge, two hills with a connecting saddle that formed part of Shuri's outer defenses. The Japanese had prepared their positions well and fought tenaciously. The Japanese soldiers hid in fortified caves. American forces often lost personnel before clearing the Japanese out from each cave or other hiding place. The Japanese sent Okinawans at gunpoint out to obtain water and supplies for them, which led to civilian casualties. The American advance was inexorable but resulted in a high number of casualties on both sides.

General John R. Hodge now had three divisions in the line, with the 96th in the middle, and the 7th to the east, with each division holding a front of only about 1.5 mi (2.4 km). Hodge launched a new offensive of **19 April** with a barrage of 324 guns, the largest ever in the Pacific Ocean Theater. Battleships, cruisers, and destroyers joined the bombardment, which was followed by 650 Navy and Marine planes attacking the enemy positions with napalm, rockets, bombs, and machine guns. The Japanese defenses were sited on reverse slopes, where the defenders waited out the artillery barrage and aerial attack in relative safety, emerging from the caves to rain mortar rounds and grenades upon the Americans advancing up the forward slope.

Kakazu Ridge

Kakazu Ridge, which faces the runways on the Marine Corp Air Station (MCAS) Futenma, is extremely steep and was the sight of some of the bloodiest fighting during the Battle of Okinawa from **April 8-24, 1945**. Located on the southern end of Okinawa.

Japanese troops staunchly defended the ridge to try to keep American forces from taking *Shuri*. It took Americans from several divisions, among them the Army's 27th Division, three weeks to get anywhere on the ridge. By **20 April**, American soldiers could crawl no more than 450 meters (492 yards) at a time due to the many advantages the Japanese soldiers had -- excellent look-outs, underground bunkers, mines strategically laid out, machine gun and mortar barrages, and reverse-slope defenses. The Americans finally overcame the Japanese on "that damned hill" with flame throwers and artillery fire, although they found that going cave by cave (man-made by the Japanese) gave the best results -- success. There were a high number of American casualties and injuries during this fighting. In fact, reports indicate that in one day of fighting alone there were over 700 men killed or wounded.

Hacksaw Ridge

Hacksaw Ridge, also known as Maeda Escarpment, or Hill 196, was the subject of a fierce 10-day fight between the Japanese 62nd and 24th Divisions and the US Army's 96th and 77th Infantry Divisions.

It was a 400-foot cliff that stretched across the island of Okinawa. It rose steeply for the first 360 feet and then there was a 50-60-foot sheer face to the top. The entire escarpment was tunneled through by the Japanese Army containing caves, pillboxes, machine gun and artillery emplacements, etc.

On April 25, 1945, the 96th Division spent the entire day conducting reconnaissance of Hacksaw Ridge while shelling and bombing it with high explosives and napalm. On the morning of April 26, the 96th launched an all-out attack to take the ridge in their drive for the 32nd Army's Headquarters at Shuri Castle.

Company G, 381st Regiment topped the ridge first but took 18 casualties within minutes. Similar to the fighting experienced on Kakazu Ridge to the south you can see Kakazu from the ridge as you look towards the Marine Corp Air Station located 5.8 miles northeast of Naha. The Japanese used "reverse slope" tactics, counter-attacking American forces as they crested the ridge from a complicated network of caves and tunnels on the southern slope.

Company F attacked the ridge from the eastern end at the large, monolithic rock formation dubbed Needle Rock. Company F used a human ladder to reach the top of the ridge but the first 3 soldiers to make the crest were killed by machine gun.

On **27 April**, Company G again crested the ridge and launched a concentrated attack on a huge pillbox that stood between their position and Needle Rock. For 3 days the 96th Division's forces attempted to take Hacksaw but eventually bypassed the ridge on **29 April**. Taking their place was the 307th Regiment of the 77th Division. By the time the 381st was relieved on **April 29** they were reduced to 40% of combat effectiveness and had sustained 536 casualties in 4 days on Hacksaw.

The 307th took over the fight for Hacksaw Ridge on **29 April** and noted that the Japanese were making very effective use of the tunnel network on the south side of the ridge. The tunnels were interlinked and had passages leading to the pillboxes and machine gun nests on top of the ridge.

It took 1st Battalion five days to conquer Needle Rock after being pushed back 9 times. On the night of **April 30,** 1st Battalion used four 50' ladders and five cargo nets to assist in their assault on the ridge. Company A mounted the ladders near Needle Rock but every soldier to stand on a rung was killed or wounded. Company B had more success with the cargo nets, which were used just below where the cache is placed. Two platoons of Company B had crested the ridge by nightfall but were driven off in a midnight counter-attack.

On **May 2**, a tank fired 6 phosphorus shells into one of the tunnels on the south side and within 15 minutes smoke poured from over 30 other openings across the ridge. To defeat the Japanese, the 307th launched an intense hand-to-hand demolition battle. Companies' A and B were back on the ridge on **2 May** and still experienced heavy Japanese resistance. One soldier was decapitated by machine gun fire that day. A substantial portion of the ridge was finally won by 1st Battalion after a grenade fight on **3 May**. Intense fighting continued on **4 May** with the 1st Battalion launching an immense demolition run against the large cave complex. Over 600 Japanese defenders were killed during the cave assault. On **May 5,** the southern slope was taken and most of the tunnels blasted shut.

In time, the heat, noise and stench of death was overpowering, according to Marine Maurice Vail. *"Guys who would get killed, if you went out the next day to get them, they were half eaten by maggots. It was total disaster."*

The First Conscientious Objector Medal of Honor Recipient

On 1 April 1942 Desmond Doss was inducted into the U.S. Army at Fort Jackson, South Carolina. As a conscientious objector he was immediately rejected by the officers and men of his unit. Several tried to have him discharged from the Army, but he explained he really wanted to serve his country, he just could not kill anyone. He remained in the service to the great displeasure of his unit's soldiers and officers.

Desmond and his unit, the 77th Infantry Division left San Francisco **24 March 1944** for Guam. He would prove himself as a medic with no fear during the battles at Guam and Leyte. Private Doss's next adventure was on the island of Okinawa and it was on the Maeda Escarpment **5 May 1945** that he would prove himself to the world by lowering 75 wounded soldiers down the cliff.

During the fight, a combat medic and contentious objector, PFC Desmond Doss, was instrumental in saving the lives of a large number of his fellow soldiers with no regard for his own life or safety. **His actions earned him the Congressional Medal of Honor. Mel Gibson directed the movie, Hacksaw Ridge, about PFC Doss and his bravery.**

✦ ✦ ✦ ✦

The Shuri Line and the Shuri Castle is on the southern end of Okinawa. The Final Line of Japanese defense is on the far southern end of the island.

By the end of May, monsoon rains which had turned contested hills and roads into a morass exacerbated both the tactical and medical situations. The ground advance began to resemble a World War I battlefield, as troops became mired in mud, and flooded roads greatly inhibited evacuation of wounded to the rear. Troops lived on a field sodden by rain, part garbage dump and part graveyard. Unburied Japanese and American bodies decayed, sank in the mud, and became part of a noxious stew. Anyone sliding down the greasy slopes could easily find their pockets full of maggots at the end of the journey.

The key to taking the second Shuri line was taking the anchoring positions on the west end at Sugar Loaf Hill. Sugar Loaf Hill was a small, insignificant-looking mound, barely 50 feet high and about 300 yards long, situated on the southern end of Okinawa. It was part of a triangle of strongpoints set up by the Japanese defenders designed to delay and damage the attacking American forces. The other two points of the triangle were the higher terrain of Shuri Heights and an irregular-shaped set of hills that Marines called the Half Moon.

The Sixth Marine Division was given the task of taking the mound called Sugar Loaf, and it would prove costly. By the time the area was considered secure, 1,656 Marines would be dead and another 7,429 wounded. Regiments were reduced to company strength, and companies to platoon size. Platoons and squads simply ceased to exist in some cases. It took 11 tries during a 12-day period and ate up most of three regiments before the hill was taken. The Japanese were so entrenched that many Marines fought the battles without ever sighting the enemy.

Each hill covering the other two, the Japanese had connected the three hills with hidden galleries and set up interlocking fields of fire by machine gun and various types of artillery. Counterattacks by the Japanese led to ownership of the hill changing many times with the Marines fully occupying and finally owning it on **18 May**. The killing ground leading up to Sugar Loaf was littered for days by the dead, and it was only after the battle that they could be recovered. The war ended shortly after Sugar Loaf and Okinawa was secured. For some of the survivors, it never ended.

By **22 May** the main Shuri line had been seemingly beaten and the Japanese began their withdrawal of the majority of its remaining 30,000 troops to the final defensive line on the southern tip of Okinawa. The defeat of this line forced GEN *Ushijima* to withdraw from his command post located more than 150 feet underneath the Shuri Castle.

The Japanese retreat, although harassed by artillery fire, was conducted with great skill at night and aided by the monsoon storms. The *32nd Army* was able to move nearly 30,000 personnel into its last defense line on the Kiyan Peninsula, which ultimately led to the greatest slaughter on Okinawa in the latter stages of the battle, including the deaths of thousands of civilians. In addition, there were 9,000 Imperial Japanese Naval troops supported by 1,100 militia, with approximately 4,000 holed up at the underground headquarters on the hillside overlooking the Okinawa Naval Base in the Oroku Peninsula, east of the airfield.

On **4 June**, elements of the 6th Marine Division launched an amphibious assault on the peninsula. The 4,000 Japanese sailors, including *Admiral Minoru Ōta*, all committed suicide within the hand-built tunnels of the underground naval headquarters around Shuri Castle on **13 June**. By **June 17**, the remnants of *Ushijima's* shattered *32nd Army* were pushed into a small pocket in the far south of the island to the southeast of Itoman.

In one instance a photo shows U.S. Marine Hart Spigal trying to have a conversation with two undersized, underaged Japanese soldiers. ***June 17, 1945***

On **21 June** the final contact for the Battle of Okinawa began. Instead of staying on the defensive, *GEN Ushijima* conducted one final offensive that, if successful, would have extended the battle further. Like most of the Japanese offensives on Okinawa, it was an utter failure. Though *Ushijima* made his troops aware of his respect for the honor they had given the Emperor by delaying the Americans for nearly three months, it was not enough.

Ushijima wrote the following in a letter before committing ritual suicide on **22 June**:

To my great regret we are no longer able to continue the fight. For this failure I tender deepest apologies to the Emperor and the people of the homeland. We will make one final charge to kill as many of the enemy as possible. I pray for the souls of men killed in battle and for the prosperity of the Imperial Family.

✦ ✦ ✦ ✦

The last remnants of Japanese resistance ended on **21 June**, although some Japanese continued hiding, including the future governor of Okinawa Prefecture, *Masahide Ōta*. *Ushijima* and *Chō* committed suicide by *seppuku* in their command headquarters on Hill 89 in the closing hours of the battle. Colonel *Yahara* had asked *Ushijima* for permission to commit suicide, but the general refused his request, saying: *"If you die there will be no one left who knows the truth about the battle of Okinawa. Bear the temporary shame but endure it. This is an order from your army Commander."* *Yahara* was the most senior officer to have survived the battle on the island, and he later authored a book titled *The Battle for Okinawa*.

The US military estimates that 110,071 Japanese soldiers were killed during the battle. This total includes conscripted (drafted) Okinawan civilians. A total of 7,401 Japanese regulars and 3,400 Okinawan conscripts (draftees) surrendered or were captured during the battle. Additional Japanese and renegade Okinawans were captured or surrendered over the next few months, bringing the total to 16,346.

The Japanese lost 16 combat vessels, including the super battleship *Yamato*. The number of conventional and *kamikaze* aircraft actually lost or expended combined with about 500 lost or expended by the Imperial Army at Okinawa, was roughly 1,430. The Allies destroyed 27 Japanese tanks and 743 artillery pieces (including mortars, anti-tank and anti-aircraft guns), some of them eliminated by the naval and air bombardments but most knocked out by American counter-battery fire.

The Americans suffered over 82,000 casualties, including non-battle casualties (psychiatric, injuries, illnesses), of whom over 12,500 were killed or missing. Battle deaths were 4,907 Navy, 4,675 Army, and 2,938 Marine Corps personnel.

Aircraft losses over the three-month period were 768 US planes, including those bombing the Kyushu airfields launching *kamikaze*s. Combat losses were 458, and the other 310 were operational accidents. On land, at least 225 tanks and many LVTs were lost. At sea, 368 Allied ships—including 120 amphibious craft—were damaged while another 36—including 15 amphibious ships and 12 destroyers—were sunk during the Okinawa campaign. The US Navy's dead exceeded its wounded, with 4,907 killed and 4,874 wounded, primarily from *kamikaze* attacks.

✦ ✦ ✦ ✦

American personnel casualties included thousands of cases of mental breakdown. According to the account of the battle presented in *Marine Corps Gazette*:

More mental health issues arose from the Battle of Okinawa than any other battle in the Pacific during World War II. The constant bombardment from artillery and mortars coupled with the high casualty rates led to a great deal of personnel coming down with combat fatigue. Additionally, the rains caused mud that prevented tanks from moving and tracks from pulling out the dead, forcing Marines (who pride themselves on burying their dead in a proper and honorable manner) to leave their comrades where they lay. This, coupled with thousands of bodies both friend and foe littering the entire island, created a scent you could nearly taste. Morale was dangerously low by the month of May and the state of discipline on a moral basis had a new low barometer for acceptable behavior. The ruthless atrocities by the Japanese throughout the war had already brought on an altered behavior (deemed so by traditional standards) by many Americans resulting in the desecration of Japanese remains, but the Japanese tactic of using the Okinawan people as human shields brought about a new aspect of terror and torment to the psychological capacity of the Americans.

✦ ✦ ✦ ✦

This was the first battle in the Pacific War in which thousands of Japanese soldiers surrendered or were captured. Many of the prisoners were native Okinawans who had been pressed into service shortly before the 82-day battle.

Ninety percent of the buildings on the island were destroyed, along with countless historical documents, artifacts, and cultural treasures, and the tropical landscape was turned into *"a vast field of mud, lead, decay and maggots"*.

On **23 June** all major combat operations ended on the island of Okinawa. **Over the three-month battle more than 8 million artillery and mortar rounds**

were fired, the equivalent of more than 1 round per second. For some, the silence after the battle was over was almost deafening.

The **Battle of Okinawa is the third-most lethal American battle by estimated number of Americans killed (20,195). Number one was the Battle of Normandy in WWII (29,204) and number two was the Battle of the Argonne Forest in WWI (26,277).**

After the battle, Okinawa provided a fleet anchorage, troop staging areas, and airfields in proximity to Japan in preparation for the planned invasion.

✦ ✦ ✦ ✦

B-29 Superfortress

The Boeing B-29 Superfortress is a four-engine propeller-driven heavy bomber designed by Boeing, which was flown primarily by the United States in the Pacific during World War II. Boeing submitted the proposal for the B-29 long-range heavy bomber to the Army in 1940, before the United States entered World War II.

Introduced: May 8, 1944
Top speed: 357 mph
Range: 5,592 mi
Ceiling 31,850 feet
Wingspan: 141 feet
Length: 99 feet
Armament: 12 – 50-caliber machine guns, 1 – 20mm cannon, 20.000lb bomb load.

Production of the B-29 was phased out after World War II with the last example completed by Boeing's Renton factory on **28 May 1946**

Four remote machine gun turrets with an analog computer-controlled fire-control system that could be operated by a single gunner and a fire-control officer for the nose, tail, and mid-fuselage. A manned tail gun installation was semi-remote. The analog computers helped operators aim, compensating for airspeed, gravity, temperature and humidity.

Boeing built a total of 2,766 B-29s at plants in Wichita, Kan., (previously the Stearman Aircraft Co., merged with Boeing in 1934) and in Renton, Wash. The Bell Aircraft Co. built 668 of the giant bombers in Georgia, and the Glenn L. Martin Co. built 536 in Nebraska. Production ended in 1946.

Facts about the B-29

1) The B-29 was the world's heaviest production plane because of increases in range, bomb load and defensive requirements.

2) The B-29 was one of the first military aircraft to have a pressurized cabin.

3) The nose and the cockpit were pressurized, but the designers were faced with deciding whether to have bomb bays that were not pressurized, between fore and aft pressurized sections, or a fully pressurized fuselage with the need to de-pressurize to drop their loads. The solution was a long tunnel over the two bomb bays so as not to interrupt pressurization during bombing. Crews could crawl back and forth between the fore and aft sections, with both areas and the tunnel pressurized. The bomb bays were not pressurized.

4) The Superfortress was initially designed as a high-altitude bomber, but after poor results, it was primarily used in night time low-altitude bombing missions. Accuracy at that altitude was limited.

5) The B-29 was capable of reaching 31,000 feet, which put it out of range of most Japanese fighter aircraft.

6) During WWII, B-29's dropped over 180,000 tons of bombs, and shot down 27 enemy aircraft.

7) During WWII, four B-29's made emergency landings in the Soviet Union after making bombing runs over Japan. The U.S. asked the Soviets to return the aircraft, but they refused.

8) Three of the B-29s, which were repairable, were flown to the Tupelov design bureau in Moscow. The bombers were then reverse-engineered and turned into the Tu-4. 847 Tu-4s were produced by the Soviet Union.

The B-29 was dedicated to the Pacific Theater. The first B-29 flight to airfields in China (over the Himalayas, or "The Hump") took place on **24 April 1944**. The first B-29 combat mission was flown on **5 June 1944**, with 77 out of 98 B-29s launched from India bombing the railroad shops in Bangkok and elsewhere in Thailand. Five B-29s were lost during the mission, none to hostile fire.

On 15 June 1944, 68 B-29s took off from bases around Chengdu, 47 B-29s bombed the Imperial Iron and Steel Works at Yawata, Kyoto Prefecture,

Japan. This was the first attack on Japanese islands since the Doolittle raid in April 1942.

The difficulty of strategic bombing had been seen on **June 15, 1944**, when a raid on Yawata's iron and steel works resulted in just 2% of the complex being damaged. On **August 20ᵗʰ**, a raid on the same plant led to 18 bombers being shot down out of 70 planes, an attrition rate of 25%. The target was barely touched. Such losses for so little reward convinced many crews that strategic bombing was untenable. Effective bombing raids on Japan would need a base for operations that was not just closer to Japan, but also easier to supply.

The tactic of using aircraft to ram American B-29s was first recorded on the second raid of **20 August 1944** on the steel factories at Yawata Japan. *Sergeant Shigeo Nobe* of the 4th *Sentai* intentionally flew his Kawasaki Ki-45 into a B-29; debris from the explosion following this attack severely damaged another B-29, which also went down. Several B-29s were destroyed in this way over the ensuing months. B-29s were withdrawn from airfields in China by the end of **January 1945**. The B-29 effort was gradually shifted to the new bases in the Mariana Islands in the Central Pacific, with the last B-29 combat mission from India flown on **29 March 1945**.

New bases became available in mid-1944 as US forces captured the Marianas; within months Tinian Island was home to the world's largest air base.

Naval construction battalions (Seabees) began at once to construct air bases suitable for the B-29, commencing even before the end of ground fighting. In all, five major air fields were built: two on the flat island of Tinian, one on Saipan, and two on Guam. Each was large enough to eventually accommodate a bomb wing consisting of four bomb groups, giving a total of 180 B-29s per airfield.

These bases, which could be supplied by ship, and unlike the bases in China, were not vulnerable to attacks by Japanese ground forces, became the launch sites for the large B-29 raids against Japan, in the final year of the war. The first B-29 arrived on Saipan on **12 October 1944**, and the first combat mission was launched from there on **28 October 1944**, with 14 B-29s attacking the Truk atoll. The 73rd Bomb Wing launched the first mission against Japan from bases in the Marianas, on **24 November 1944**, sending 111 B-29s to attack Tokyo.

The campaign of incendiary raids, started with the bombardment of Kobe on **February 4, 1945**. **It was from Tinian that General LeMay pioneered his strategy of low-altitude nighttime firebombing raids.** The first of these, called Operation Meetinghouse took place on **March 10, 1945**. More than 300 B-29's dropped a variety of incendiary bombs in a massive X pattern over several hours over Tokyo. They took off for a flight that would get them to Tokyo just before dawn, thus giving them the cover of darkness, but with daylight for the return journey to the Marianas. They flew at 7000 feet. This in itself may have baffled the city's defenders as they would have been used to the B-29's flying at 30,000 feet.

The raid had a massive impact on Tokyo. Photo-reconnaissance showed that 16 square miles of the city had been destroyed. Sixteen major factories were along with many cottage industries. In parts of the city, the fires joined up to create a firestorm.

The fires burned so fiercely and they consumed so much oxygen, that people in the locality suffocated. It is thought that 100,000 people were killed in the raid and another 100,000 injured. The Americans lost 14 B-29's; under the 5% rate of loss that was considered to be 'acceptable'.

General LeMay subsequently directed similar raids at every major industrial city in Japan: sixty-three cities lost significant areas to incendiary attacks and hundreds of thousands of civilians were burned by the war's end.

These were low-altitude nighttime incendiary bombing missions. In the Pacific War, during the last seven months of strategic bombing by B-29 Super fortresses in the air war against Japan, a change to firebombing tactics resulted in the death of over 330,000 Japanese and the homelessness of 5 million more.

✦ ✦ ✦ ✦

Fire Bombs

The **AN-*M69 incendiary* cluster bomb** was used in air raids on Japan during World War II. They were nicknamed *"Tokyo calling cards"*. The M-69 was a plain steel pipe with a hexagonal cross section 3 inches (7.6 cm) in diameter and 20 inches (51 cm) long. It weighed about 6 pounds (2.7 kg). The cluster-based bomb used napalm (jelled gasoline) as an incendiary filler.

Upon hitting a building or the ground, the timing fuse burned for three to five seconds and then a white phosphorus charge ignited and propelled the incendiary filling up to 100 feet (30 m) in several flaming globs, instantly starting intense fires. These bombs were then wired together in clusters of 6 or 25 with highly sensitive or proximity fuses. **Over 40,000 tons of AN-M69's were dropped on Japanese cities during the war.**

Standard Oil Development's creation of the AN-M69 started in early **October 1941**, almost two months before the attack on Pearl Harbor. The initial instigation was to find a way to make incendiary weapons that did not involve large amounts of magnesium, which was in short supply. The work was funded by the Office of Scientific Research and Development.

M-19's each contained 38 sticks of the AN-M69 incendiary bombs. These incendiary cluster bombs were dropped in a cluster of 38 within a container. One B-29 usually carried 37 of these containers, which equated to just over 1400 bombs per plane. The bombs were set free from the container at 5000 feet by a time fuse and then exploded on contact with the ground.

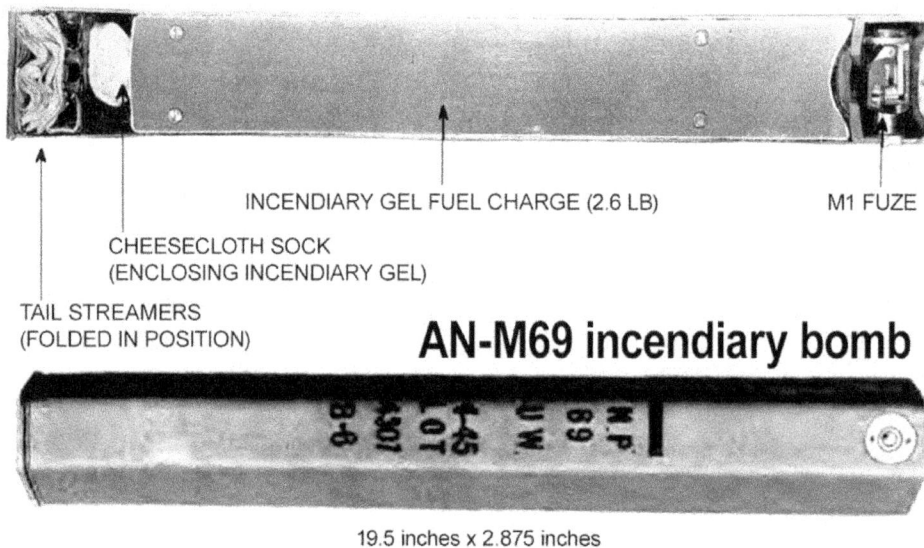

INCENDIARY GEL FUEL CHARGE (2.6 LB)   M1 FUZE

CHEESECLOTH SOCK
(ENCLOSING INCENDIARY GEL)

TAIL STREAMERS
(FOLDED IN POSITION)

AN-M69 incendiary bomb

19.5 inches x 2.875 inches

M-19

When they did this, they spread a jelly-petrol compound that was highly inflammable. They are not explosives but in fact are designed to slow the process of chemical reactions and use ignition rather than detonation to start and or maintain the reaction. Napalm is petroleum especially thickened with certain chemicals into a 'gel' to slow, but not stop, combustion, releasing energy over a longer time than an explosive device. In the case of napalm, the gel adheres to surfaces and resists suppression.

From January 1944 until August 1945, the U.S. dropped 157,000 tons of bombs on Japanese cities, according to the U.S. Strategic Bombing Survey. It estimated that 333,000 people were killed, including the 80,000 killed in the August 6 Hiroshima atomic bomb attack and 40,000 in Nagasaki three days later. Other estimates are significantly higher. Fifteen million of the 72 million Japanese were left homeless.

✦ ✦ ✦ ✦

From the Japan Times; March 10, 2015 excerpts

Where earlier raids targeted aircraft factories and military facilities, the Tokyo fire-bombing was aimed largely at civilians, in places including Tokyo's downtown area known as shitamachi, where people lived in traditional wood and paper homes at densities sometimes exceeding 100,000 people per square mile.

"There were plenty of small factories, but this area was chosen specifically because it was easy to burn," says historian Masahiko Yamabe, who was born just months after World War II ended.
Another departure from earlier raids: the bombers flew low.
"It was as if we could reach out and touch the planes, they looked so big," said Yoshitaka Kimura, whose family's toy store in downtown Tokyo's Asakusa district was destroyed. "The bombs were raining down on us. Red, and black, that's what I remember most."

Survivors speak of the hush as dawn broke over a wasteland of corpses and debris, studded by chimneys of bathhouses and small factories. Police photographer Koyo Ishikawa captured the carnage of charred bodies piled like blackened mannequins, tiny ones lying beside them.

XXIX   Beginning of the Atomic Age

In **1939**, Albert Einstein wrote a letter to President Roosevelt, warning him that a nuclear weapon was theoretically possible and that the Nazis may develop one first. FDR promptly ordered a feasibility study.

The Manhattan Project is kicked into high gear eleven days after the attack on Pearl Harbor. It employs 130,000 people and costs $2 billion.

Clinton Engineering Works

In **1943**, the town of Oakridge, Tennessee literally vanished from maps and became the production site known only as the **Clinton Engineering Works**. On 60,000 acres of farmland framed by the foothills of the Appalachian Mountains, it was one of the United States' three secret cities, remote sites chosen by Manhattan Project director Gen. Leslie Groves. The other two were Los Alamos, NM and Hanford WA. Civilian residents were evacuated, as the "Secret City" was repurposed for an urgent new mission: The production of the atomic bomb. Between 1942 and 1945, the population swelled from 3,000 to 75,000. Temporary housing was set-up for workers. Everyone was sworn to secrecy. Lie detectors were used to conduct security screenings. A major reason this spot was chosen for the Manhattan Project was the 17-mile long valley studded by parallel ridges. If a catastrophic explosion occurred, the ridges would act as buffers between the plants.

Hanford Project

Hanford Engineer Works, codenamed "Site W quickly acquired the land under its war powers authority and relocated some 1,500 residents of Hanford, White Bluffs, and nearby settlements, as well as the Wanapum people, Confederated Tribes and Bands of the Yakama Nation, the Confederated Tribes of the Umatilla Indian Reservation, and the Nez Perce Tribe.

The **Hanford Site** along the Columbia River in the state of Washington was established in **1943** as part of the Manhattan Project. The site was home to the B Reactor, the first full-scale plutonium production reactor in the world. Plutonium manufactured at the site was used in the first nuclear bomb, tested at the Trinity site, and in Fat Man, the bomb detonated over Nagasaki, Japan.

The Ames Project

The discovery of nuclear fission in **1939** necessitated advanced research on the chemical properties of uranium and other rare radioactive elements and isotopes that had only recently been discovered. In **1942**, Frank Spedding of **Iowa State College, Ames, Iowa,** an expert in the chemistry of rare earth elements, agreed to establish and direct a chemical research and development program to accompany the Manhattan Project's existing physics program.

The Ames Project, as it came to be known, was responsible for producing high purity uranium from uranium ores. The Ames' group, led by chemist Harley A. Wilhelm, developed a new method for reducing and casting uranium metal, making it possible to cast large ingots of the rare metal at a significantly lower cost.
The **Ames Project** provided about one-third, or around two tons, of the uranium used in the first-self-sustaining nuclear reaction at the University of Chicago in December 1942. **The Ames Project produced more than 1,000 tons of uranium for the Manhattan Project between 1942 and 1945.** The uranium production process developed at Ames is still used today.

On **October 12, 1945**, the Ames Project was awarded the Army/Navy E Flag for Excellence in Production of metallic uranium as a vital war material, an honor normally given to industry rather than educational institutions.

Los Alamos, New Mexico

Los Alamos, New Mexico, was the site of Project Y, or the top-secret atomic weapons laboratory directed by J. Robert Oppenheimer. The site was so secret that one mailbox, PO Box 1663, served as the mailing address for the entire town. By the end of the war, five thousand people were assigned P.O. Box 1663. they spent most of their time in laboratories, overcoming challenge after challenge to develop the Little Boy (gun-type) and Fat Man (implosion) atomic bombs. There was enough area available to ensure safe spacing of the various Project units. The nearest town was 16 miles away, which tended to isolate the site. Physicists, chemists, metallurgists, explosive experts and military personnel converged on the isolated plateau. At times, six Nobel Prize winners gathered with the other scientists and engineers in the weekly colloquia organized by Oppenheimer.

J. Robert Oppenheimer was an American theoretical physicist and professor of physics at the University of California, Berkeley. Oppenheimer was the wartime head of the Los Alamos Laboratory and is among those who are credited with being the "father of the atomic bomb" for their role

in the Manhattan Project, the World War II undertaking that developed the first nuclear weapons used in the atomic bombings of Hiroshima and Nagasaki.

✦ ✦ ✦ ✦

Mainline military historians believe that the Okinawa campaign led directly to the atomic bombings of Hiroshima and Nagasaki, as a means of avoiding the planned ground invasion of the Japanese mainland. This view is explained by Victor Davis Hanson in his book *Ripples of Battle*:

... because the Japanese on Okinawa ... were so fierce in their defense (even when cut off, and without supplies), and because casualties were so appalling, many American strategists looked for an alternative means to subdue mainland Japan, other than a direct invasion. This means presented itself, with the advent of atomic bombs, which worked admirably in convincing the Japanese to sue for peace [un-conditionally], without American casualties.

The Battle of Okinawa had a dramatic effect on the next step in the Pacific campaign. The battles in the Pacific made evident to America that they could defeat the Japanese in any fight. The painful realization from information gained from Okinawa was the high price that would be paid for every inch of Japanese land the Americans took. The Japanese mainland defense force was more than 1 million strong. In addition, the Japanese possessed 8,000 aircraft and kamikaze pilots who were being trained every day. Even the civilian population was trained for combat with the invading Americans; suicide attacks by civilians were expected. The greatest effect Okinawa had on the Pacific campaign was to convince the recently seated President Harry S. Truman to take any avenue to end the war outside of sending an invasion force onto mainland Japan as, unfortunately, firebombing the country was not adequate to convince the Japanese to surrender. The concept of conceding was one the Japanese simply could not fathom; admitting defeat without being completely subdued by their adversary was unconscionable to the Japanese.

This was all too apparent to President Truman who said, *"I do not want another Okinawa from one end of Japan to the other."*

This sentiment is what lead to the approval of the atomic bomb Little Boy being dropped on Hiroshima on **6 August 1945**. Even with the resulting vast destruction, the Japanese were still not willing to concede. The war cabinet was divided even after Fat Man was dropped at Nagasaki on **9 August 1945**. It still took negotiating to determine the status of Japan's surrender which unofficially took place on **14 August 1945** with a compromise that *Emperor Hirohito* could maintain his seat as emperor so long as he followed the orders and directions of the Supreme Allied

Commander. This was carried out by Gen. Douglas MacArthur who ostensibly ran Japan for the next 6 years after receiving the Japanese formal surrender from the Japanese Foreign Minister *Mamoru Shigemitsu* on the USS Missouri (BB63) on **2 September 1945**. The USS Missouri was also the last battleship commissioned by the United States.

The Trinity Explosion, which took place at New Mexico's White Sands Proving Ground on July 16, 1945, marked the beginning of the Atomic Age. Plutonium was used for this test. Uranium was used on Hiroshima and Plutonium was used on Nagasaki.

The test site at ground zero left a small crater. Instead, the blast traveled up and out from the ground. The extreme heat had melted the sand into green glass, a material soon to be known as **Trinitite**. **Trinitite is liquefied sand pulled into the blast that absorbed other vaporized droplets plus some fission products from the nuclear reaction.**

USS Indianapolis

The world's first operational atomic bomb was delivered by the Indianapolis, (CA-35) to the island of Tinian on **26 July 1945**. The components for two A-bombs were transported all the way across the Pacific, where they were assembled and prepared for detonation on the island of Tinian. Nor a single member of the crew, not even Captain Charles McVay III were told the truth about the mystery cargo. The plutonium core to arm the bombs was flown to Tinian.

The Indianapolis then reported to CINCPAC (Commander-In-Chief, Pacific) Headquarters at Guam for further orders. She was directed to join the battleship USS Idaho (BB-42) at Leyte Gulf in the Philippines to prepare for the invasion of Japan.

The Indianapolis, unescorted, departed Guam on a course of 262 degrees making about 17 knots. Captain McVay's request for a destroyer escort was denied despite the fact that no capital ship lacking anti-submarine detection equipment, such as the Indianapolis, had made this transit across the Philippine Sea without an escort during the entire war. Captain McVay was not told that shortly before his departure from Guam a Japanese submarine within range of his path had sunk a destroyer escort, the USS Underhill.

At 14 minutes past midnight, on **30 July 1945**, midway between Guam and Leyte Gulf, she was hit by two torpedoes out of six fired by the *I-58, a Japanese submarine*. The first blew away the bow, the second struck near midship on the starboard side adjacent to a fuel tank and a powder magazine. The resulting explosion split the ship to the keel, knocking out all electric power. Within 12 minutes she went down rapidly by the bow, rolling to starboard.

Shortly after 1100 of the fourth day, the survivors were accidentally discovered by LT. Wilbur C. Gwinn, piloting his PV-1 Ventura Bomber on routine antisubmarine patrol. Radioing his base at Peleiu, he alerted, "many men in the water". A PBY (seaplane) under the command of LT. R. Adrian Marks was dispatched to lend assistance and report.

Marks' crew began dropping rubber rafts and supplies. While so engaged, they observed men being attacked by sharks. Disregarding standing orders not to land at sea, Marks landed and began taxiing to pick up the stragglers and lone swimmers who were at greatest risk of shark attack. Learning the men were the crew of the Indianapolis, he radioed the news, requesting immediate assistance.

As complete darkness fell, Marks waited for help to arrive, all the while continuing to seek out and pull nearly dead men from the water. When the plane's fuselage was full, survivors were tied to the wing with parachute cord. Marks and his crew rescued 56 men that day. The Cecil Doyle was the first vessel on the scene. Homing on Marks' PBY in total darkness, the Doyle halted to avoid killing or further injuring survivors and began taking Marks' survivors aboard.

Doyle's captain pointed his largest searchlight into the night sky to serve as a beacon for other rescue vessels. This beacon was the first indication to most survivors, that their prayers had been answered. Help had at last arrived. Of the 900 who made it into the water, only 317 remained alive. After almost five days of constant shark attacks, starvation, terrible thirst, suffering from exposure and their wounds, the men of the Indianapolis were at last rescued from the sea on **4 August 1945**.

Potsdam Declaration

On **July 26, 1945** US President Harry Truman and Winston Churchill in concurrence with Jiang issued the Potsdam Declaration warning that the Japanese armed forces would be completely destroyed and the Japanese homeland devastated if Japan did not surrender unconditionally all its armed forces. Conditions included removing from authority those who had misled the people into attempting world conquest. The Declaration went on. Until this is accomplished and Japan's war-making capacity is destroyed, the Allies will occupy Japanese territory. Japan must fulfill the Cairo Declaration by returning Manchuria, Taiwan, the Pescadores and other territory to the Republic of China and by allowing Korea to be free and independent.

"Japanese sovereignty shall be limited to the islands of Honshu, Hokkaido, Kyushu, Shikoku and such minor islands as we determine." Japan's military forces must be completely disarmed. The Allies promised "stern justice" to all war criminals and democracy for Japan, which must establish freedom of speech, religion, thought, and human rights. Peaceful industries will be permitted to enable payment of reparations, and eventually trade relations will be allowed. Once the objectives are attained and after Japan has a responsible government, the occupying forces will withdraw. The concluding sentence warned, "The alternative for Japan is prompt and utter destruction."

On **July 28, 1945** at a press conference *Premier Suzuki* said that Japan would ignore the Potsdam offer and press forward with the war.

On the first two days of August <u>766 B-29s</u> bombed Nagaoka.

By then sixty Japanese cities had been devastated by <u>6,960 B-29</u>

<u>sorties dropping 41,592 tons of bombs</u>.

Half of Tokyo, Kobe, and Yokohama had been burned and destroyed along

with 40% of Osaka

And Nagoya

And 90% of Aomori.

The two atomic bombs that followed were just a mere expansion of the devastation being dropped on Japan with the incendiary bombs.

Through much of World War II, Allied bombers would sometimes drop leaflets warning of impending bombing of a city. The leaflets often told civilians to evacuate, and sometimes encouraged them to push their leaders to surrender. In **August 1945**, leaflets were dropped on several Japanese cities (including, supposedly, Hiroshima and Nagasaki). The first round, known as the **"LeMay leaflets"**, were distributed before the bombing of Hiroshima. These leaflets did not directly reference the atomic bomb and it is unclear whether they were used to warn citizens of Hiroshima and Nagasaki specifically. The second round features a picture of a mushroom cloud and a message about the Soviet invasion (which commenced on August 9). The historical record is unclear, but it seems as though these leaflets did not make it to Nagasaki until after it, too, had been hit by an atomic bomb. Later leaflets informed the Japanese populace about their government's surrender before the emperor's official announcement.

LeMay Leaflets reads as follows:

Read this carefully as it may save your life or the life of a relative or friend. In the next few days, some or all of the cities named on the reverse side will be destroyed by American bombs. These cities contain military installations and workshops or factories which produce military goods. We are determined to destroy all of the tools of the military clique which they are using to prolong this useless war. But, unfortunately, bombs have no eyes. So, in accordance with America's humanitarian policies, the American Air Force, which does not wish to injure innocent people, now gives you warning to evacuate the cities named and save your lives. America is not fighting the Japanese people but is fighting the military clique which has enslaved the Japanese people. The peace which America will bring will free the people from the oppression of the military clique and mean the emergence of a new and better Japan. You can restore peace by demanding new and good leaders who will end the war. We cannot promise that only these cities will be among those attacked but some or all of them will be so heed this warning and evacuate these cities immediately.

The cities named on the back of the LeMay Leaflet were: *Tokyo, Ujiyamada, Tsu, Koriyama, Hakodate, Nagaoka, Uwajima, Kurume, Ichinomiya, Ogaki, Nishinomiya and Aomori.* The next day half of these cities – *Aomori, Ichinomiya, Tsu, Ujiyamada, Ogaki and Uwajima* – were subjected to firebombing and thousands were killed.

Hiroshima

The Allies on **4 August 1945** dropped 720,000 leaflets warning that this city (Hiroshima) and others would be obliterated if Japan did not surrender at once.

6 & 8 August, 1945

What very few people in the world knew was that a new kind of bomb was being built in New Mexico, and a special B-29 Superfortress bomber was being built in Omaha, Nebraska to carry it. Col. Paul Tibbets had been chosen to lead the first atomic bomb mission and he came to the Martin Bomber Plant south of Omaha to pick out the plane he wanted. He named the plane the "Enola Gay," after his mother. Many of members of Tibbets' 11-man crew had been trained at the rural Fairmont, Nebraska, Army Air Field.

One of the most significant historical events of the 20th Century was initiated from the Island of Tinian at the North Airfield. It is the site where the atomic bomb, nicknamed "Fat Man" and "Little Boy" underwent final assembly and were then loaded onto the B-29 bombers that carried them to Hiroshima and Nagasaki. The atomic bomb pit is now a museum piece at Tinian Field.

Eventually, Tibbets, his crew, the Enola Gay and the bomb arrived at Tinian Island south of Japan (part of the Mariana Islands). In the early morning hours of **6 August 1945**, the Enola Gay dropped the atomic bomb over **Hiroshima**. At 0815 it exploded with the explosive power of 12500 tons of TNT, killing over 100,000 people.

The uranium atom bomb exploded 580 meters (1903 feet) above the city of Hiroshima with a blinding flash, creating a giant fireball reaching a diameter of 300 meters (1000 feet) and sending surface temperatures to 4,000 Celsius, 7,232 Fahrenheit. Fierce heat rays and radiation burst out in every direction, unleashing a high-pressure shockwave, vaporizing tens of thousands of people and animals, melting buildings and streetcars, reducing a 400-year-old city to dust.

The effects of the burns, disease, and radiation would cause about 20,000 to 50,000 more to die by the end of the year. Estimates of the total number who died as a result of the bomb have been estimated at 200,000. The industrial city of Hiroshima had 80% of its buildings destroyed by one bomb.

Nagasaki

8 & 9 August 1945

On **8 August** more leaflets were dropped over Nagasaki, and radio warnings were given.

9 August 1945 another Nebraska-built B-29 named "Bock's Car" dropped an atomic bomb on Nagasaki killing 70,000 with explosive force of 21000 tons of TNT.

Under the command of Maj. Charles W. Sweeney, the bomb was dropped at 11:02 a.m., 1,650 feet above the city. The explosion unleashed the equivalent force of 22,000 tons of TNT. The hills that surrounded the city did a better job of containing the destructive force, but the number killed is estimated at anywhere between 60,000 and 80,000 (exact figures are impossible, the blast having obliterated bodies and disintegrated records).

Hibakusha are people who fall into one or more of the following categories:

within a few kilometers of the hypocenters of the bombs;

within 2 km of the hypocenters;

within two weeks of the bombings;

exposed to radiation from fallout;

or not yet born but carried by pregnant women in any of these categories.

Many of them were fired from their jobs. Hibakusha women never got married, as many feared they would give birth to deformed children. Men suffered discrimination too. *"Nobody wanted to marry someone who might die in a couple of years."*

Radiation deaths were still occurring in large numbers in the following days. *"For no apparent reason their health began to fail. They lost appetite. Their hair fell out. Bluish spots appeared on their bodies. And then bleeding began from the ears, nose and mouth."*

XXX   VJ Day and the End of World War II

*E*mperor *Hirohito* announces that the Japanese are surrendering.

This is VJ Day   15 August, 1945

It still took from the **9th of August until the 15th** for the Japanese Emperor to go on the radio and announce to his people that Japan had been defeated. All across America the celebrations were loud and joyous.

After the Japanese conceded defeat, President Truman announced that **"Mighty Mo,"** the behemoth 58,000-ton flagship of the 3rd Fleet, would host the signatories of the instrument of surrender in Tokyo Bay.

2 September 1945:

Surrender ceremonies to end World War II take place aboard the US Navy battleship, USS Missouri.   Gen. Douglas MacArthur and *Japanese Foreign Minister Mamoru Shigemitsu* signed for the emperor Hirohito.

General Douglas MacArthur, a man sometimes referred to as an "American Caesar," emerged as one of the most powerful figures at the conclusion of World War II. As commander-in-chief of all forces in the Pacific area, MacArthur was the senior official in the conduct of the formal surrender of Japan aboard a United States warship in Tokyo Bay in September, 1945.

James L. Starnes, navigator of the battleship Missouri, was 24 years old when he learned he would play a key role in the ceremony to mark the end of World War II. *"My job was to make sure we did not screw up,"* said Starnes, who performed the role of officer of the deck the morning of Sept. 2, 1945.

This was MacArthur's opening paragraph to start the surrender ceremonies:

"We are gathered here, representatives of the major warring powers—to conclude a solemn agreement whereby peace may be restored. The issues involving divergent ideals and ideologies, have been determined on the battlefields of the world and hence are not for our discussion or debate. Nor is it for us here to meet, representing as we do a majority of the people of the earth, in a spirit of distrust, malice or hatred. But rather it is for us, both victors and vanquished, to rise to that higher dignity which alone befits the sacred purposes we are about to serve,

committing all our people unreservedly to faithful compliance with the obligation they are here formally to assume."

When the assembled representatives of the Allied Powers and of Japan had finished signing the agreements, General MacArthur, MacArthur stated:

"Let us pray that peace be now restored to the world and that God will preserve it always. These proceedings are closed."

The General then addressed the American people by radio as follows:

Opening Paragraph

"Today the guns are silent. A great tragedy has ended. A great victory has been won. The skies no longer rain death -- the seas bear only commerce men every-where walk upright in the sunlight. The entire world is quietly at peace. The holy mission has been completed. And in reporting this to you, the people, I speak for the thousands of silent lips, forever stilled among the jungles and the beaches and in the deep waters of the Pacific which marked the way. I speak for the unnamed brave millions homeward bound to take up the challenge of that future which they did so much to salvage from the brink of disaster."

Closing Paragraph

"And so, my fellow countrymen, today I report to you that your sons and daughters have served you well and faithfully with the calm, deliberated determined fighting spirit of the American soldier, based upon a tradition of historical truth as against the fanaticism of an enemy supported only by mythological fiction. Their spiritual strength and power has brought us through to victory. They are homeward bound— take care of them."

As the surrender ceremonies concluded, the Japanese were escorted off the deck. Suddenly, a swarm of U.S. aircraft roared overhead. 450 F4U and F6F carrier planes from the Third Fleet are flying in massed formation over the USS Missouri. A few minutes later, Army Air Forces B-29 bombers flew by which were part of the 20th Air Force Command, based in the Marianas. _"They were so low they made the sky black,"_ Starnes said. The noisily impressive demonstration underscored the power that had brought Japan and the Allies to this time and place.

✦ ✦ ✦ ✦

28 August, 1945 Dad Returned to USA

6 September 1945 Discharged as Staff Sergeant E-6 at Camp McCoy, Wisconsin. The following is a clipping from the Belgrade Tribune, Dad's hometown paper.

Staff Sergeant Elmer L. Madsen arrived home Saturday evening from Camp McCoy, Wis., where he had received his honorable discharge after three years and seven months service. He accompanied Mr. and Mrs. Chris Steffensen (Mom's parents) and Mrs. Madsen and daughter Faye, who had motored to Camp McCoy to meet him. He had been in the South Pacific for three years, with the 129th Infantry, 37th Division, in the Fiji Islands, New Hebrides, Guadalcanal, Bougainville and Luzon. The trip home from Luzon took him 33 days. Besides the good conduct medal, rifle marksmanship badge and infantryman's combat badge he had earned three campaign stars, the Philippine Liberation ribbon, Asiatic and Pacific theater ribbons, the Purple Heart Medal and an Oak Leaf Cluster, the latter two being for wounds in action.

37th Infantry Division

The 37th Infantry Division was a unit of the United States Army in WWI and WWII. It was a National Guard division from Ohio, nicknamed the **"Buckeye Division"**.

Activated: 15 October 1940 (National Guard Division from Ohio) Overseas: 26 May 1942.

Campaigns:

**Northern Solomons
Battle of Luzon**

Service Awards:

Distinguished Unit Citations: 9 Awards:
Congressional Medal of Honor – 7;
Distinguished Service Cross (United States) – 116;
Distinguished Service Medal (Army) – 4;
Silver Star – 1008;
Legion of Merit – 71;
Soldiers Medal – 101;
Bronze Star – 6807;
Air Medal – 84;

Commanders:

Maj. Gen. Robert S. Beightler commanded the Division during its entire period of Federal service in World War II. Beightler was the only National Guard commanding officer to have led his troops throughout the course of the entire war. They were demobilized in November 1945.

Beightler's philosophy was simple, the better trained the soldiers are, the fewer casualties there would be. He also had moral reasoning, having been quoted after World War II saying "... *I have never been able to completely harden myself to the sacrifice of American lives. I have always felt a deep-seated responsibility to the families of these men, many of whom might be called my neighbors.*"
Returned to U.S.: November 1945   Inactivated: 18 December 1945

Col. John D Frederick started at Espiritu Santo with the 37th Infantry Division and stayed their commander throughout the rest of the war. Promoted to Colonel, "Lil" was assigned to the 37th Division, moving to a combat area at Espiritu Santo in the Pacific Theater as Commanding Officer of the 129th Infantry Regimental Combat Team. Lil was seriously wounded in the battle for Baguio on Luzon but resolutely refused to be evacuated, carrying on and leading the advance of his outstanding combat team. His courageous leadership inspired the offensive spirit and combat aggressiveness of his regiment.

129th Infantry Drive in Joliet, Illinois is named in honor of the regiment.

Division Citation for Outstanding Performance on Bougainville

This Division Citation was earned on Bougainville. Reads as follows:

TO: THE BELGRADE TRIBUNE, Belgrade, Minnesota

WITH THE 37TH INFANTRY DIVISION SOMEWHERE IN THE SOUTHWEST PACIFIC AREA – Special – Member of an infantry heavy weapons company that has received a Division Citation for outstanding performance of duty in action against the Japanese is Staff Sergeant Elmer L. Madsen, 30, Belgrade, Minnesota, a mortar squad leader.

His company distinguished itself on Hill 129 Bougainville Island in helping repel four assaults by soldiers of the Japanese 6th Imperial Division, part of the 17th Army.

"Occupying crucial defense positions and manning weapons in excess of normal complement, (the men) valiantly served each crew weapon, and through their untiring efforts were able to furnish timely and accurate close-in supporting fires which disrupted the enemy's attack and inflicted heavy casualties," the citation by Major General Robert S. Beightler, division commander, states in part.

His parents, Mr. and Mrs. Christ Madsen; wife, the former Myrtle Steffensen, and their 2-year old daughter, Faye Myrtle, all live in Belgrade. He has two brothers in the service: Corporal Donald Madsen, 19, in the Air Force in England and Private First-Class Robert Madsen, 24, in the Air Force in Colorado.

Infantryman Madsen has been awarded the Purple Heart Medal, Soldiers' Good Conduct Medal, and Combat Infantryman Badge.

✦ ✦ ✦ ✦

In **February 1945** there are updates of the wellbeing of the three Madsen brothers from overseas. Each brother's status at that time is listed below taken from the Belgrade Tribune, their hometown paper.

THE MADSEN BROTHERS – ELMER (Mickey), ROBERT AND DONALD

Staff Sergeant Elmer L. Madsen, 30, who has been in the Southwest Pacific with the 129th Infantry since September, 1942, is now on the island of Luzon and took part in the action to regain Manila. He was inducted February 13, 1942 and received all his training at Camp Forrest, Tenn. Since embarking from San Francisco, he has seen service in the Fiji Islands and New Hebrides, Guadalcanal and Bougainville. He received the Purple Heart medal for shoulder wounds received at Bougainville, and also has earned the good conduct badge, infantryman's badge and rifle marksmanship medal.

Awaiting his return home are his wife, nee Myrtle Steffensen, and his 28-months-old, Faye Myrtle who was born after he left for overseas.

Corporal Robert H. Madsen, 25, now in training at Gulfport Field, Miss. Is a gunner on a B-17 Flying Fortress. He was inducted June 12, 1944, at Fort Snelling (St. Paul, MN.) and received his basic training at Buckley Field, Colo. Following that he attended aerial gunnery school at the Kingman, Ariz. Army air field, and was located for a short time at Drew Field, Tampa, Fla. He was promoted last month to the rank of Corporal.

Corporal Madsen was married November 13, 1944, to Lillian C. Iverson, Brooten, Minn. Prior to his induction, Corporal Madsen operated a gasoline service station in Belgrade for eight years. He is the third son on Mr. and Mrs. Christ Madsen.

Robert Madsen, son of Mr. and Mrs. Christ Madsen, was recently promoted from Corporal to the rank of Sergeant, according to a letter received from him on Monday.

Corporal Donald W. Madsen, 20, radio mechanic with a Ninth Air Force ground crew at a base in England, has charge of maintaining and servicing radio equipment on C47 air troop carriers. He enlisted in the air force and was inducted November 27, 1942, at Fort Snelling (St. Paul, MN.). He received his basic training at St. Petersburg, Fla. And then attended radio mechanics school at Truex field, Madison, Wis. He also received advanced training at Norfolk, Va. He embarked for England from an Atlantic coast embarkation port in March, 1944.

Prior to his enlistment, Corporal Madsen was a student at Belgrade High School where he took an active part in basketball.

Corporal Madsen has arrived safely overseas and is now at a camp somewhere in England, according to word received by his parents, Mr. and Mrs. Christ Madsen. He is a radio mechanic with a fighter squadron.

Authorized Army military campaigns for the Pacific Theater are as follows:

- 7 Dec 41 - 10 May 42
- Burma, 1942 7 Dec 41 - 26 May 42
- Central Pacific 7 Dec 41 - 6 Dec 43
- East Indies 1 Jan 42 - 22 Jul 42
- Philippine Island 2 Apr 42 - 28 Jan 45
- Air Offensive, Japan 17 Apr 42 - 2 Sep 45
- Aleutian Islands 3 Jun 42 - 24 Aug 43
- China Defensive 4 Jul 42 - 4 May 45
- Papua 23 Jul 42 - 23 Jan 43
- **Guadalcanal 7 Aug 42 - 21 Feb 43**
- New Guinea 24 Jan 43 - 31 Dec 44
- **Northern Solomons 22 Feb 43 - 21 Nov 44**
- Eastern Mandates 7 Dec 43 - 14 Jun 44
- Bismarck Archipelago 15 Dec 43 - 27 Nov 44
- Western Pacific 17 Apr 44 - 2 Sep 45
- Leyte 17 Oct 44 - 1 Jul 45
- **Luzon 15 Dec 44 - 4 Jul 45**
- Central Burma 29 Jan 45 - 15 Jul 45
- Southern Philippines 27 Feb 45 - 4 Jul 45
- Ryukyus 26 Mar 45 - 2 Jul 45
- China Offensive 5 May 45 - 2 Sep 45

Dad was involved with the campaigns above in bold print.

✦ ✦ ✦ ✦

For the first and only time in its history

Japan was occupied by foreign powers; this occupation lasted seven years. Allied occupation brought forth sweeping democratic reforms. It led to the end of the emperor's status as a living god and the transformation of Japan into a democracy with a constitutional monarch. In these ways, the pre-1945 and post-war periods regard completely different states: the pre-1945 Shōwa period (1926–1945) concerns the Empire of Japan, while post-1945 Shōwa period (1945–1989) was a part of the State of Japan.

461

A common theme throughout the Pacific campaign for the Japanese was *to engage in delaying action in the mountains, hills, or jungles to hold the island as long as possible*. The main reason for this comment made on every island battle was that there were preparations being made by their leaders to prepare for the invasion of the Japanese mainland. Also, that defeat to the Japanese was dishonorable and punishable by death or suicide. *"We Japanese soldiers were told to prefer death to the disgrace of getting captured alive."*

The war came to an end with the loudest man-made explosion the world had yet heard. It was in the Pacific, last to be settled by primitive man, last to be divided among the colonial powers, and last to witness the terrible ferocity and devastation of modern war; that the atom age opened.

Aristotle –

It is not enough to win a war;

It is more important to organize the peace.

It is the Soldier

It is the **Soldier**, not the reporter, who has given us freedom of the press.

It is the **Soldier**, not the poet, who has given us freedom of speech.

It is the **Soldier**, not the minister who has given us freedom of religion.

It is the **Soldier**, not the lawyer, who has given us the right to a fair trial.

It is the **Soldier**, not the politician, who has given us the right to vote.

It is the **Soldier**, not the campus organizer, who has given us the freedom to demonstrate.

It is the **Soldier**, who salutes the flag,

who serves beneath the flag

whose coffin is draped by the flag

who allows the protestor to burn the flag

XXXI   EPILOGUE

Post-War Economy

At the war's end the United States hoped to share with other countries its conception of liberty, equality and democracy. With the rest of the world in turmoil, struggling with civil wars and disintegrating empires, the nation hoped to provide the stability to make peaceful reconstruction possible. Unable to forget the specter of the Great Depression **(1929-1940),** America now fostered its familiar position of free trade, and sought to eliminate trade barriers both to create markets for American agricultural and industrial products, and to ensure the ability of West European nations to export as a means to generate economic growth and rebuild their economies. Reduced trade barriers, it was believed, would promote economic growth at home and abroad, and bolster stability with U.S. friends and allies.

The Soviet Union had its own agenda. The Russian historical tradition of centralized, autocratic government contrasted with the American emphasis on democracy. Marxist-Leninist ideology had been downplayed during the war but still guided Soviet policy. Devastated by the struggle in which 20 million Soviet citizens had died, the Soviet Union was intent on rebuilding and on protecting itself from another such terrible conflict. The Soviets were particularly concerned about another invasion of their territory from the west. Having repelled Hitler's thrust, they were determined to preclude another such attack. The Soviet Union now demanded "defensible" borders and regimes sympathetic to its aims in Eastern Europe.

Cold War

The Cold War was waged on political, economic and propaganda fronts and had only limited recourse to weapons. The term was first used by the English writer George Orwell in an article published in 1945 to refer to what he predicted would be a nuclear stalemate between "two or three monstrous super-states, each possessed of a weapon by which millions of people can be wiped out in a few seconds".

The aftermath of World War II was the beginning of an era defined by the decline of all great powers except for the Soviet Union and the United States, and the simultaneous rise of two superpowers: the Soviet Union (USSR) and the United States of America (USA). Allies during World War II, the USA and the USSR became competitors on the world stage and engaged in the Cold War, so called because it never re-

sulted in overt, declared hot war between the two powers but was instead characterized by espionage, political subversion and proxy wars.

Western Europe and Japan were rebuilt through the American Marshall Plan whereas Eastern Europe fell under the Soviet sphere of influence and eventually an "Iron
Curtain". Europe was divided into a US-led Western Bloc and a Soviet-led Eastern
Bloc that installed openly communist regimes. Internationally, alliances with the
two blocs gradually shifted, with some nations trying to stay out of the Cold War
through the Non-Aligned Movement. **The Cold War also saw a nuclear arms
race between the two superpowers with the Soviets exploding their first
atomic warhead in 1949**. Part of the reason that the Cold War never became a
"hot" war was that the Soviet Union and the United States had nuclear deterrents
against each other, leading to a mutually assured destruction standoff.

Soviet Union after World War II

The end of World War II saw the Soviet Union emerge as one of the world's two
great military powers. Its battle-tested forces occupied most of Eastern Europe. The
Soviet Union had won island holdings from Japan and further concessions from
Finland (which had joined Germany in invading the Soviet Union in 1941) in
addition to the territories seized as a consequence of the Nazi-Soviet Nonaggression
Pact. But these achievements came at a high cost. The war also inflicted severe
material losses throughout the vast territory that had been included in the war zone.
The suffering and losses resulting from the war made a lasting impression on the
Soviet people and leaders that influenced their behavior in the postwar era.

After World War II, the Soviet Union extended its control into Eastern Europe. It
took over the governments in Albania, Bulgaria, Czechoslovakia, Hungary, East
Germany, Poland, Romania and Yugoslavia. Only Greece and occupied Austria
remained free. The Baltic countries—Estonia, Latvia and Lithuania—were made into
republics. Even Finland was partly controlled by the Soviets. The Communist Party
was also strong in Italy and France. The Soviet Union also began exerting its
influence in Asia. Outer Mongolia became the first Communist regime outside of the
Soviet Union in 1945 when it taken over by a Soviet puppet government.

During the immediate postwar period, the Soviet Union first rebuilt and then
expanded its economy, with control always exerted exclusively from Moscow. The
Soviet Union consolidated its hold on Eastern Europe, supplied aid to the eventually
victorious communists in China, and sought to expand its influence elsewhere in the
world. This active foreign policy helped bring about the Cold War, which turned the
Soviet Union's wartime allies, Britain and the United States, into foes. Within the
Soviet Union, repressive measures continued in force; Stalin apparently was about

to launch a new purge when he died in 1953.

The war was followed by drought, famine, typhus epidemics and purges. In the famine after the war, people ate grass to keep themselves from starving. The postwar Five-Year plan of reconstruction focused on the arms industry and heavy industry at the expense of consumer goods and agriculture. the Soviet Union compelled Soviet-occupied Eastern Europe to supply machinery and raw materials. Germany and former Nazi satellites (including Finland) made reparations to the Soviet Union. The Soviet people bore much of the cost of rebuilding because the reconstruction program emphasized heavy industry while neglecting agriculture and consumer goods. By the time of Stalin's death in 1953, steel production was twice its 1940 level, but the production of many consumer goods and foodstuffs was lower than it had been in the late 1920s.

The Economic Commission for Europe and the Economic Commission for Asia and the Far East

Excerpts from **The Economic Survey of Asia and the Far East (AFE), 1947**.

For the first time a forum is provided by the United Nations at which the accredited representatives of the governments of the region can meet together to discuss common economic problems, establish agreed principles of action and carry out, if they choose, the policies determined by mutual agreement.

Communist infiltration into China and Korea, struggle for self- government in Indonesia and Indo-China, and communal conflicts in the newly founded dominions of India and Pakistan—all these combined to exert a hindering influence on post-war attempts at economic rehabilitation and development. The developments in Asia and the Far East were necessarily affected by the overall uncertainty prevailing in the world situation, which arose from the tense relation that existed between the two world powers, the United States and the Soviet Union. This was true in Asia and the Far East, as much as in other parts of the world, notably Europe.

Agriculture: *In an economy where agriculture played such a large part, fluctuations in agricultural production are bound to cause serious hardship to the people already on low margins of subsistence. Japan was the one country before the war in which the proportion of income derived from manufacture was appreciably higher than that contributed by agriculture. In every other country, the contribution made by agriculture to the national income is large, ranging from 52 per cent in India to about 76 per cent in Indonesia.*

Population: Before the war, this region afforded considerable scope for movements of population between the countries; thus, for instance, the migration of Chinese workers into various countries of the region, of Indians to Malaya, Singapore, Burma and Ceylon, opened outlets for the surplus population. But as each country in the region becomes politically free, there is an understandable desire to restrict the number of such immigrants. Thus Burma, Ceylon and other countries of South-east Asia are all imposing considerable restrictions, quantitatively and qualitatively, on the immigrants permitted to settle. The outlet for surplus population being closed, the only way by which the pressure of population may be reduced would be a reduction in the rate of the natural increase of population, but here the position is discouraging. Throughout this region, with only minor exceptions, although both the birth rate and death rate are high, the natural increase rate per annum varies from 0 • 8 to 2 • 5 per cent, and unless this rate decreases in the course of some years, it is doubtful whether even if improvements take place through industrialization and agricultural reorganization, they would not be lost through increases in population. The problem is so urgent and important that further studies seem to be indicated dealing more fully with the demographic features of the AFE countries.

Production: Some improvement in production, both in agriculture and in industry, is recorded in the year 1947, but the process of recovery is very slow. The recovery in production is considerable only as compared to 1946, but compared to pre-war, the production is still far behind. The decline in industrial and commercial crops, particularly in raw cotton, has led to the slower recovery of industrial production.

Economic: Slight improvements in industrial production are noticeable in some countries but everywhere on account of political and economic uncertainties, rehabilitation and recovery have been hampered. The deterioration in the clothing situation ranks only next to the food shortage as one of the major post-war difficulties facing the AFE countries.

Apart from political difficulties and unrest, and unsettlement caused by civil war and the fighting in some of the AFE countries, the economic causes arising from lack of essential materials and equipment are significant. If Asian recovery is to be speeded up, the removal of such bottlenecks and obstacles should occupy immediate attention.

Transportation: Transport was one of the things damaged in nearly all countries of the region and its restoration has been hampered by the same difficulties which militated against the speeding up of industrial and agricultural production. The railway lines that were displaced have not been opened to traffic and only about 53 per cent of the pre-war railways in six war-devastated countries of the region (Burma, China, Indo-China, Indonesia, Malaya and the Philippines) were open to traffic in 1946-7.

Import / Export: In most countries of the region, there has been a certain amount of planning of reconstruction and development but those plans have been held up on account of the difficulties of getting essential imports. The foreign trade position of most of the countries is unsatisfactory; many of the countries are struggling with deficits and however much they have tried to reduce imports, they have not succeeded in effecting a proper trade balance. The export capacity has also declined and hence the volume of foreign trade is on a lower level than what it was before the war. Some countries have sought to maintain equilibrium by drawing on foreign balances, others have had recourse to foreign loans; but once again it is clear that the fundamental factor that has operated to accentuate the difficulties all round is the fall in production and the difficulties in restoring it.

Standard of Living: The standard of living of the people of this region which at all times has been very low has become lower in the years during and after the war. Money wages in every country have gone up but except in one or two countries, real wages have lagged far behind on account of the inflationary conditions prevailing in the region as a whole. Contrary to the popular impression, the only country where wages have kept up with the cost of living is China, whose workers at least in the principal cities have been getting wages higher than before the war; in Burma and the Philippines real wages are about equal to pre-war levels but in India and Ceylon, in spite of increased production and less inflation, real wages are slightly lower than pre-war. One of the causes which have led to a fall in production has been industrial unrest in the countries of the region.

Unemployment: Apart from the failure of wages to keep pace with inflationary price levels, there has been a considerable degree of unemployment arising out of the failure to absorb workers who were demobilized after the war. Unemployment has increased in nearly all the countries of the region and this combined with general social factors militating against willingness to work has brought about a situation which calls for urgent action.

Living Standards: There is no easy way by which these countries can secure an improvement in their standards of living. Some of the factors that have depressed living standards in these countries are more fundamental; the relation between population and resources, the low level of economic and industrial organization, lack of technical knowledge, insufficient capital equipment, archaic methods of produc-tion, poverty, ignorance and insanitary conditions, all these are not amenable to immediate or short-term treatment. They require a continuous expenditure of re-

sources and time if they are to be treated adequately but it is a hopeful sign that the Asia and Far East countries have woke up and are all conscious of the need for bringing about rapid improvements all along the line. Much more fruitful results will follow if, instead of scattering available resources at all points, efforts are directed towards bringing about improvements in specific directions. The increase in food and agricultural production, increase in textiles and the restoration of transport offer immediate scope for useful action.

☆ ☆ ☆ ☆

Japan 1945 – 1952

Occupation and Reconstruction

After the defeat of Japan, the United States led the Allies in the occupation and rehabilitation of the Japanese state. Between 1945 and 1952, the U.S. occupying forces, led by General Douglas A. MacArthur, enacted widespread military, political, economic, and social reforms.

The groundwork for the Allied occupation of a defeated Japan was laid during the war. In a series of wartime conferences, the leaders of the Allied powers of Great Britain, the Soviet Union, the Republic of China, and the United States discussed how to disarm Japan, deal with its colonies (especially Korea and Taiwan), stabilize the Japanese economy, and prevent the remilitarization of the state in the future. The occupation of Japan can be divided into three phases: the initial effort to punish and reform Japan, the work to revive the Japanese economy, and the conclusion of a formal peace treaty and alliance.

The First Phase

Roughly from the end of the war in **1945 through 1947**, involved the most fundamental changes for the Japanese Government and society. The Allies punished Japan for its past militarism and expansion by convening war crimes trials in Tokyo. At the same time, SCAP dismantled the Japanese Army and banned former military officers from taking roles of political leadership in the new government.

The Second Phase

In the economic field, SCAP introduced land reform, designed to benefit the majority tenant farmers and reduce the power of rich landowners, many of whom had advocated for war and supported Japanese expansionism in the 1930s. MacArthur also tried to break up the large Japanese business conglomerates, or zaibatsu, as part of the effort to transform the economy into a free market capitalist system. In **1947**, Allied advisors essentially dictated a new constitution to Japan's leaders. Some of the most profound changes in the document included downgrading the emperor's status to that of a figurehead without political control and placing more power in the parliamentary system, promoting greater rights and privileges for women, and renouncing the right to wage war, which involved eliminating all non-defensive armed forces.

The Third Phase

Beginning in 1950, SCAP deemed the political and economic future of Japan firmly established and set about securing a formal peace treaty to end both the war and the occupation. The U.S. perception of international threats had changed so profoundly in the years between 1945 and 1950 that the idea of a re-armed and militant Japan no longer alarmed U.S. officials; instead, the real threat appeared to be the creep of communism, particularly in Asia.

The final agreement allowed the United States to maintain its bases in Okinawa and elsewhere in Japan, and the U.S. Government promised Japan a bilateral security pact. In September of 1951, fifty-two nations met in San Francisco to discuss the treaty, and ultimately, forty-nine of them signed it.

The aftermath of World War II also saw the rise of communist influence in Southeast Asia, with the People's Republic of China, as the Chinese Communists emerged victorious from the **Chinese Civil War in 1949.**

The Chinese Revolution

On October 1, 1949, Chinese Communist leader Mao Zedong declared the creation of the People's republic of China (PRC). The announcement ended the costly full-scale civil war between the Chinese Communist Party (CCP) and the Nationalist Party, or Kuomintang (KMT), which broke out immediately following World War II. The "fall" of mainland China to communism in 1949 led the United States to suspend diplomatic ties with the PRC for decades.

Division of Korea

The division of Korea between North and South Korea occurred after World War II, ending the Empire of Japan's 35-year rule over Korea in 1945. The United States and the Soviet Union each occupied a portion of the country, with the boundary between their zones of control along the 38th parallel.

With the onset of the Cold War, negotiations between the United States and the Soviet Union failed to lead to an Independent, Unified Korea. In **1948**, UN-supervised elections were held in the US-occupied south only. The anti-communist *Syngman Rhee* won the election while *Kim Il-sung* was appointed as the leader of North Korea by Joseph Stalin. This led to the establishment of the Republic of Korea in South Korea, which was promptly followed by the establishment of the Democratic People's Republic of Korea in North Korea. The United States supported the South, the Soviet Union supported the North, and each government claimed sovereignty over the whole Korean peninsula.

The subsequent Korean War, which lasted from 1950 to 1953, ended with a stalemate and has left the two Koreas separated by the Korean Demilitarized Zone (DMZ).

Great Britain

Although Britain achieved ultimate victory in the war, the economic costs were enormous. Six years of prolonged warfare and heavy losses of merchant shipping meant that Britain had lost two-thirds of her pre-war export trade by 1945. The loss of her export markets also caused a serious shortage of US dollars, which were crucial to servicing Britain's war debt and maintaining imports from the United States. When Lend Lease was terminated by the United States in August 1945, Britain was unable to pay for the import of essential supplies from America. Although the US agreed to cancel $20 million in Lend Lease debt, the UK was forced to obtain a $3.75 billion loan from the United States at 2% interest in December 1945.

In the 1945 general election, just after the end of the war in Europe, the Labor Party led by Clement Attlee was elected with a landslide majority (its first ever outright majority), introducing sweeping reforms of the British economy. Taxes were increased, industries were nationalized, and a welfare state with national health, pensions, and social security was created. Most rations were lifted during 1950, with a few of them remaining until 1954.

The next 15 years saw some of the most rapid growth Britain had ever experienced, recovering from the devastation of the Second World War and then expanding rapidly past the previous size of the economy. The economy went from strength to strength particularly after the Conservatives returned to government in 1951, still led by wartime leader Sir Winston Churchill until he retired to make way for Anthony Eden just before his party's re-election in 1955.

✦   ✦   ✦   ✦

United States Post War Economy

After soldiers returned home, in **1946 the "Baby Boom"** began and the construction of homes also boomed. The parents of the "baby-boomers" were frugal. Having lived through the Great Depression, these people distrusted banks and buying things on credit. Therefore, they saved and paid cash for whatever they wanted, unless absolutely necessary, as in the case of the purchase of a home. Their values and ethics were above reproach; "one's word is one's bond" was repeatedly spoken. People were decent with a respect for their neighbor's natural rights. There was little need for the police to patrol many neighborhoods. The majority of men worked for a living. Since inflation was so low, mothers could stay home and raise the children, even if they had worked during the war. Prevalent in this age was decency and the work ethic. Workers were dedicated to their jobs and their companies as evidenced with so many staying with the same employer until their retirement. Companies provided retirement benefits, the growth of unions protected the employees.

After **1945** the major corporations in America grew even larger. There had been earlier waves of mergers in the 1890s and in the 1920s; in the 1950s another wave occurred. New conglomerates -- firms with holdings in a variety of industries -- led the way. International Telephone and Telegraph, for example, bought Sheraton Hotels, Continental Baking, Hartford Fire Insurance, and Avis Rent-a-Car, among other companies. Smaller franchise operations like McDonald's fast-food restaurants provided still another pattern. Large corporations also developed holdings overseas, where labor costs were often lower.

A housing boom, stimulated in part by easily affordable mortgages for returning servicemen, fueled the expansion. The rise in defense spending as the Cold War escalated also played a part.

Below: from the Belgrade Tribune sometime **mid-1946.** This shows the housing demand even in the rural areas after the war. Belgrade MN population was just under 700 at this time.

Somebody remarked the other day that the housing shortage in Belgrade should be pretty well supplied by this fall when a dozen new houses will be completed and occupied. Unfortunately, that isn't true. The demand for houses seems to be as large as ever. There are still 18 houses accommodating two or more families, and 10 men employed in town are "commuting" from family homes on nearby farms or villages. Every house offered for sale brings a flock of a dozen to 15 inquiries from prospective buyers. We still need 20 to 25 more residences to satisfy the demand.

The war brought the return of prosperity, and in the postwar period the United States consolidated its position as the world's richest country. The growth had different sources. The automobile industry was partially responsible, as the number of automobiles produced annually quadrupled **between 1946 and 1955**.

General Motors purchased the **automatic transmission** protype and introduced the technology in the **1940 Oldsmobile model as a "Hydra-Matic" transmission.**

Chrysler introduced the first commercially available passenger car **power steering system** on the **1951 Chrysler Imperial under the name "Hydraguide".**

World War II produced important changes in American life; some trivial, others profound. One striking change involved fashion. To conserve wool and cotton, dresses became shorter; vests and cuffs disappeared, as did double-breasted suits, pleats, and ruffles.

More significant was a tremendous increase in mobility. This set families in motion, pulling them off farms, out of small towns, and packing them into large urban areas. Urbanization had virtually stopped during the depression, but the war saw the number of city dwellers leap from 46 to 53 percent.

War industries sparked the urban growth. Detroit's population exploded as the automotive industry switched to war vehicles. Washington, D.C., became another boomtown, as tens of thousands of new workers staffed the swelling ranks of the bureaucracy. The most dramatic growth occurred in California. Of the 15 million civilians who moved across state lines during the war, over 2 million went to California to work in defense industries.

The war had a dramatic impact on women. Easily the most visible change involved the sudden appearance of large numbers of women in uniform. The military organized women into auxiliary units with special uniforms, their own officers, and, amazingly, equal pay. By **1945** more than 250,000 women had joined the Women's Army Corps (WAC), the Army Nurses Corps, Women Accepted for Voluntary Emergency Service (WAVES), the Navy Nurses Corps, the Marines and the Coast Guard. Most women who joined the armed services either filled traditional women's roles, such as nursing, or replaced men in non-combat jobs.

Women also substituted for men on the home front. For the first time in history married working women outnumbered single working women as 6.3 million women entered the work force during the war. The war challenged the conventional image of female behavior, as **"Rosie the Riveter"** became the popular symbol of women who abandoned traditional female occupations to work in defense industries. Social critics had a field day attacking women. Social workers blamed working mothers for the rise in juvenile delinquency during the war.

Jobs - work in the 1950's

It was more a manufacturing and agricultural age, rather than the present-day information age. There were more blue-collar jobs and less white-collar occupations -

-more manufacturing and food processing; lot more smaller farms all over the country.

There was more need for secretaries, receptionist and support work. Typing pools in big offices mainly women typing letters, contracts, things that computers generate now.

Workers found their own lives changing as industrial America changed. Fewer workers produced goods; more provided services. By **1956** a majority held white-collar jobs, working as corporate managers, teachers, salespersons and office employees. Some firms granted a guaranteed annual wage, long-term employment contracts and other benefits. With such changes, labor militancy was undermined and some class distinctions began to fade. The average income of men in 1955, according to the Bureau of the Census, Department of Commerce was $3,400, a gain of about $160 over the previous year.

Farmers, on the other hand, faced tough times. Gains in productivity led to agricultural consolidation, as farming became a big business. Family farms, in turn, found it difficult to compete, and more and more farmers left the land. Other Americans moved too. In the postwar period the West and the Southwest continued to grow -- a trend that would continue through the end of the century.

Hi-Tech wartime advances in radar, aviation, antibiotics, electronics, and materials transformed everyday life.

The Culture of the 1950s

During the 1950s, a sense of uniformity pervaded American society. Conformity was common, as young and old alike followed group norms rather than striking out on their own. Though men and women had been forced into new employment patterns during World War II, once the war was over, traditional roles were reaffirmed. Men expected to be the breadwinners; women, even when they worked, assumed their proper place was at home. Television contributed to the homogenizing trend by providing young and old with a shared experience reflecting accepted social patterns.

As suburbs grew, businesses moved into the new areas. Large shopping centers containing a great variety of stores changed consumer patterns. The number of these centers rose from eight at the end of World War II to 3,840 in 1960. With easy parking and convenient evening hours, customers could avoid city shopping entirely.

The Federal-Aid **Highway Act of 1956**, popularly known as the National Interstate and Defense Highways Act (Public Law 84-627), was enacted on **June 29, 1956**, when President Dwight D. Eisenhower signed the bill into law. Eisenhower was president from 1953-1961 following President Harry S. Truman (1945-1953).

With an original authorization of 25 billion dollars for the construction of 41,000 miles (66,000 km) of the Interstate Highway System supposedly over a 10-year period, it was the largest public works project in American history through that time.

Eisenhower's observations of the German Autobahn network during World War II convinced him to support construction of the Interstate System when he became president. Germany had made him see the wisdom of broader ribbons across the land. His "Grand Plan" for highways, announced in 1954, led to the 1956 legislative breakthrough that created the Highway Trust Fund to accelerate construction of the Interstate System.

Eisenhower advocated for the highways for the purpose of national defense. In the event of a ground invasion by a foreign power, the U.S. Army would need good highways to be able to transport troops across the country efficiently. **Following completion of the highways the cross-country journey that took the convoy two months in 1919 was cut down to five days.**

City officials were eager for the new highways that would relieve congestion and restore economic vitality to central business districts. Right-of-way acquisition was another concern because so much of the Interstate System would be built on new locations. State highway agencies had rarely needed to acquire land or to do so by eminent domain. The States would need new legislation, standards, appraisers-and they needed them quickly.

As the economy grew, so did the demand for consumer goods. Life got easier with advancements in modern conveniences and automated machinery. Installment plans enabled people to get these appliances and conveniences (electric washers and dryers, televisions, etc.) into their homes like never before.

Transportation and communication got cheaper and more efficient, allowing more travel than ever before – as well as an increase in the need for gasoline and the advent of motels (motor hotels) for those on the road. Having free time to spend on a variety of pursuits was the major cause of all the pop culture elements of the late '40s and especially the '50s.

The biggest change in pop culture during that time was the rise of a teen culture. During this time, teens came to have more leisure time and more disposable income than had ever been the case before. This helped lead to the growth of such things as rock and roll music.

✦   ✦   ✦   ✦

Jackie Robinson

From **1942 to 1944**, Robinson served as a second lieutenant in the US Army. However, he never saw combat. During boot camp at Fort Hood, Texas, Robinson was arrested and court-martialed in **1944** for refusing to give up his seat and move to the bac k of a segregated bus. Robinson's excellent reputation, combined with the efforts of friends, the NAACP and various black newspapers, shed public light on the injustice. Ultimately, he was acquitted of the charges and received an honorable discharge. His courage and moral objection to segregation were precursors to the impact Robinson would have in Major League Baseball.

After Jackie's discharge from the Army in 1944, Robinson began to play baseball professionally. At the time, the sport was segregated, and African-Americans and whites played in separate leagues. Robinson began playing in the Negro Leagues, but he was soon chosen by Branch Rickey, president of the Brooklyn Dodgers, to help integrate Major League Baseball.

Jackie Robinson broke the color barrier when he became the first black athlete to play Major League Baseball in the 20th century. He joined the Brooklyn Dodgers in 1947 and was named Rookie of the Year that year, National League MVP in 1949 and a World Series champ in 1955.

✦ ✦ ✦ ✦

Television

Written by Claudia Reinhardt and Bill Ganzel, the Ganzel Group. Excerpts:

*Although television was invented in the **1920's**, it wasn't until the early 40's that the average person began adding a television to their home. In fact, television was so rare that in **1948**, only 10% of Americans claimed to have even seen a TV set with their own eyes, let alone own one. TV programming did not run all day and night. Most parts of rural America had to make do with a single television station. Due to World War II, many television programs and stations shut down, leaving options for TV watchers very limited. Since the television medium was only just beginning, there were only 4 networks, NBC, DuMont, ABC, and CBS. DuMont is the only one that no longer exists, although it was better known for manufacturing television sets.*

The DuMont network largely ignored the standard business model of 1950s TV, in which one advertiser sponsored an entire show, enabling it to have complete control over its content. Instead, DuMont sold commercials to many different advertisers, freeing producers of its shows from the veto power held by sole sponsors. This eventually became the standard model

for US television. Some commercial time was sold regionally on a co-op basis, while other spots were sold network-wide.

DuMont also holds another important place in American TV history. WDTV's sign-on made it possible for stations in the Midwest to receive live network programming from stations on the East Coast, and vice versa. Before then, the networks relied on separate regional networks in the two time zones for live programming, and the West Coast received network programming from kinescopes (films shot directly from live television screens) originating from the East Coast. **On January 11, 1949, the coaxial cable linking East and Midwest (known in television circles as "the Golden Spike," in reference to the Golden spike that united the First Transcontinental Railroad) was activated. This completed the East Coast-to-Midwest chain,** *allowing stations in both regions to air the same program simultaneously, which is still the standard for US TV. It was another two years (1951) before the West Coast got live programming from the East (and the East able to get live programming from the West), but this was the beginning of the modern era of network television.*

In the **1940s**, *television started, stopped, started again and then took off. In the process, the new medium turned on the lives of rural residents connecting them to the rest of the world even more than newspapers or radio.*

The first practical TV sets were demonstrated and sold to the public at the 1939 World's Fair in New York. The sets were very expensive and New York City had the only broadcast station.

When World War II started, all commercial production of television equipment was banned. Production of the cathode ray tubes that produced the pictures was redirected to radar and other high-tech war uses.

The **cathode ray tube** (**CRT**) is a vacuum tube that contains one or more electron guns and a phosphorescent screen, and is used to display images. It modulates, accelerates, and deflects electron beam(s) onto the screen to create the images. Cathode rays were discovered by Johann Hittorf in 1869 in primitive Crookes tubes. Discoveries made through later testing and modifications by individuals found cathode rays would be deflected by electric fields and later by magnetic fields. In 1897, J. J. Thomson succeeded in measuring the mass of cathode rays, showing that they consisted of negatively charged particles smaller than atoms, the first "subatomic particles", which were later named **electrons.**

In 1925, Kenjiro Takayanagi demonstrated a CRT television that received images with a 40-line resolution. By 1927, he improved the resolution to 100 lines, which was unrivaled until 1931. By 1928, he was the first to transmit human faces in half-tones on a CRT display. By 1935, he had invented an early all-electronic CRT television. RCA was granted a trademark for the term (for its cathode ray tube) in 1932; it voluntarily released the term to the public domain in 1950.

After the war television was something few had heard of. That changed quickly. In 1945, a poll asked Americans, *"Do you know what television is?"* Most didn't. But four years later, most Americans had heard of television and wanted one! According to one survey in 1950, before they got a TV, people listened to radio an average of nearly five hours a day. Within nine months after they bought a TV they listened to radio, but only for two hours a day. They watched TV for five hours a day.

Culture became much more dependent on mass media after WWII. The television programs were much more powerful than radio. There was also a large impact from movies and music. The war was over, and entertainment was very important.

In 1947, President Harry Truman's state of the union address and the baseball World Series were televised. A year later, CBS and NBC networks started 15-minute nightly newscasts. In the late 1940s there were 98 commercial television stations in 50 large cities.

By **1949**, prices of TV sets had gone down. Americans were buying 100,000 sets every week.

A test card, also known as a test pattern or start-up/closedown test, is a television test signal, typically broadcast at times when the transmitter is active but no program is being broadcast (often at sign-on and sign-off). 24-hour television was not available. Used since the earliest TV broadcasts, test cards were originally physical cards at which a television camera was pointed, used for calibration, alignment, and matching of cameras.

Farm families were not far behind their city brethren. Entrepreneurs hurried television stations to reach every part of the country. Even if there was only one, snowy, black and white station on the air, farmers and their children wanted that TV set. The first family in the neighborhood to get a TV would invite friends and neighbors to come over and watch.

The 1940s TVs didn't look like today's televisions. Most had picture screens between 10 and 15 inches wide diagonally, inside large, heavy cabinets. And, of course, color broadcasts and sets didn't arrive until much later, in 1954. There were knobs for horizontal, vertical, contrast and

477

brightness. Rabbit ears (antennas) were used mounting them on top of a television or using larger antennas to be placed on the roof of the house.

Shared Party Line

Party line systems were widely used to provide telephone service, starting with the first commercial switchboards in 1878. A party line (multiparty line, shared service line, party wire) is a local loop telephone circuit that is shared by multiple telephone service subscribers. Party lines provided no privacy in communication. They were frequently used as a source of entertainment and gossip, as well as a means of quickly alerting entire neighbourhoods of emergencies such as fires becoming a cultural fixture of rural areas for many decades.

The rapid growth of telephone service demand, especially after World War II, resulted in a large fraction of party line installations in the middle of the 20th century in the United States. This often led to traffic congestion in the telephone network, as the line to a destination telephone was often busy. Nearly three-quarters of Pennsylvania residential service in **1943** was party line, with users encouraged to limit calls to five minutes. Objections about one party monopolizing a multi-party line was a staple of complaints to telephone companies and letters to advice columnists for years and eavesdropping on calls remained an ongoing concern.

By the 1980s, party lines were displaced in most localities as they could not support subscriber-owned equipment such as answering machines and computer modems.

In 1971, Southern Bell had announced plans for phase-out of party lines in North Carolina. In 1989, the Chesapeake and Potomac Telephone Company replaced party lines with private lines in Talcott, West Virginia, a rural area which once had as many as sixteen subscribers on one line. In 1991, Southwestern Bell set out to replace all of its party lines in Texas with private lines by 1995.   Woodbury, Connecticut's independent telephone company abandoned its last party lines in 1991, the last in that state to do so.

Telephone Switchboard Operators

In the early days of telephony, through roughly the 1960s, companies used manual telephone switchboards, and switchboard operators connected calls by inserting a pair of phone plugs into the appropriate jacks.

Before the advent of automatic exchanges, an operator's assistance was required for anything other than calling telephones across a shared party line. Callers spoke to an operator at a Central Office who then connected a cord to the proper circuit in order to complete the call. Being in complete control of the call, the operator was in a position to listen to private conversations. Automatic, or Dial systems were developed in the 1920s to reduce labor costs as usage increased, and to ensure privacy to the customer. As phone systems became more sophisticated, less direct intervention by the telephone operator was necessary to complete calls.

Before the advent of operator distance dialing and customer Direct Dial (DDD) calling, switchboard operators would work with their counterparts in the distant central office to complete long distance calls.

With the development of computerized telephone dialing systems, many telephone calls which previously required a live operator can be placed automatically by the calling party without additional human intervention.

The Fair Deal

The Fair Deal was the name given to Harry Truman's domestic program in **January 1949**. Building on Roosevelt's New Deal, Truman believed that the federal government should guarantee economic opportunity and social stability, and he struggled to achieve those ends in the face of fierce political opposition from conservative legislators determined to reduce the role of government.

Truman's first priority in the immediate postwar period was to make the transition to a peacetime economy. Servicemen wanted to come home quickly, but once they arrived they faced competition for housing and employment. The G.I. Bill, passed before the end of the war, helped ease servicemen back into civilian life by providing such benefits as guaranteed loans for home-buying and financial aid for industrial training and university education.

More troubling was labor unrest. As war production ceased, many workers found themselves without jobs. Others wanted pay increases they felt were long overdue. In 1946, 4.6 million workers went on strike, more than ever before in American history. They challenged the automobile, steel and electrical industries. When they took on the railroads and soft-coal mines, Truman intervened, but in so doing he alienated millions of working-class Americans.

While dealing with immediately pressing issues, Truman also provided a broader agenda for action. Less than a week after the war ended, he presented Congress with a 21-point program, which provided for protection against unfair employment practices, a higher minimum wage, greater unemployment compensation and housing assistance. In the next several months, he added other proposals for health insurance and atomic energy legislation. But this scattershot approach often left Truman's priorities unclear.

Republicans were quick to attack. In the 1946 congressional elections they asked, "Had enough?" and voters responded that they had. Republicans, with majorities in both houses of Congress for the first time since 1928, were determined to reverse the liberal direction of the Roosevelt years.

Truman fought with the Congress as it cut spending and reduced taxes. In 1948 he sought reelection, despite polls indicating that he had no chance. After a vigorous campaign, Truman scored one of the great upsets in American politics, defeating the Republican nominee, Thomas Dewey, governor of New York. Reviving the old New Deal coalition, Truman held on to labor, farmers and black voters, and so won another term.

When Truman finally left office in 1953, his Fair Deal was but a mixed success. In July 1948 he banned racial discrimination in federal government hiring practices and ordered an end to segregation in the military. The minimum wage had risen, and social security programs had expanded. A housing program brought some gains but left many needs unmet. National health insurance and aid-to-education measures never made it through Congress. Truman's preoccupation with Cold War affairs hampered his effectiveness at home, particularly in the face of intense opposition.

Eisenhower's Approach

Dwight Eisenhower accepted the basic framework of government responsibility established by the New Deal, but sought to limit the presidential role. He termed his approach *"dynamic conservatism" or "modern Republicanism,"* which meant, he explained, *"conservative when it comes to money, liberal when it comes to human beings."* A critic countered that Eisenhower appeared to argue that he would *"strongly recommend the building of a great many schools...but not provide the money."*

Eisenhower's first priority was to balance the budget after years of deficits. He wanted to cut spending, cut taxes and maintain the value of the dollar. Republicans were willing to risk unemployment to keep inflation in check. Reluctant to stimulate the economy too much, they saw the country suffer three recessions in eight years.

In other areas, the administration transferred control of offshore oil lands from the federal government to the states. It also favored private development of energy sources rather than the public approach the Democrats had initiated. In everything the Eisenhower administration undertook, its orientation was sympathetic to business.

Eisenhower's inclination to play a modest role in public often led to legislative stalemate. Still, he was active behind the scenes pushing his favorite programs. And he was one of the few presidents who left office as popular as when he entered it.

✦ ✦ ✦ ✦

Dad and Mom bought a house with five acres sometime in **1946.** Two acres were for the two horses for grazing. My sister rode horses most every day. There was a barn for the horses. There was also room for the two pigs, roosting and hen laying chickens. Our house was two miles south of downtown Belgrade and the school was one mile from home. Dad would paint houses to earn extra money. I was told that he and Kenny Thompson painted the Crow Lake Lutheran Church.

After the war and until sometime in **1948** Dad & Mom, along with Uncle Archie & Aunt Evelyn, operated the Rite Spot Café in Belgrade for two years. Interesting to note that Dad & Archie were brothers and Mom & Evelyn were sisters. Our double cousins were Bonnie & Allen. I was told during that time Dad was a pretty good Pinochle card player and he played so much that he developed scraped knuckles from knocking on the table each time he was done playing his hand.

In **1948** when the VFW Club was organized, Dad became the first manager. The Saboe-Larsen Post 1825, Belgrade, MN. He was also a member of the Belgrade Lion's Club, Volunteer Fire Dept., Belgrade Sportsmen's Club, the Selective Service Board located in Melrose, MN and later on the Belgrade Centennial Publicity Committee (1985-88).

I came along in **1950.** From **1949 to 1953** Dad became a sub-clerk in the Belgrade post office. He attended the Dunwoody Institute (vocational college) in **1953** in Minneapolis and was offered a position as a railway distribution mail clerk in St. Paul, MN. He stayed with his Aunt Effie in St. Paul while working in the cities.

After two years in St. Paul a rural mail route opened up in Belgrade. Dad was appointed the position as a rural mail carrier in Belgrade in **1955** and he retired after almost thirty years of federal service on **October 8, 1976**. There were three rural mail routes out of Belgrade and Dad stayed on the same route the entire time. The farmers on Dad's route always knew what time it was when the mail came as Dad was always punctual.

Dad and Mom worked together in planting and harvesting a large garden. They canned everything out of the garden and stored it in our basement. I remember in the basement there were five shelves 24" deep and about twelve feet long full of canned goods. There was always something to do in the garden spring, summer and fall.

Dad loved to fish and hunt. Hunting that I remember included ducks, pheasant and deer. Fishing in the summer was going to northern Minnesota, two weeks in June and two weeks in August going to Little Boy Lake in northern Minnesota to the same resort fishing for walleye and northern pike. Dad had a Lund sixteen-foot aluminum boat with a five-horse boat motor and after several years purchased a fifteen horse Evinrude motor. They did this trip for many years.

Then there was ice fishing. Always had a fish house and an electric ice auger with jumper cables hooked to the car's battery. An ice fishing stick, bobber, tear drop hook and a wax worm. The fish house had a propane space heater that got real warm in the house and four holes in which to drop your line. Mom would always fish inside the fish house. We would come in to warm up as we enjoyed moving from hole to hole that Dad drilled outside of the fish house. The saying was dad was trolling on the ice as he would cut several holes following the school of panfish.

The years Dad had the rural mail route he started early and was home by 1PM six days a week. He traded cars every year. This was their only car and was traded in with about 70,000 miles on it. He bought Pontiacs the first few years until a Ford dealership opened up in Belgrade. Then he bought a Ford every year after. Four doors, no air conditioning and only an AM radio. Back then it was important to support the local merchants. I don't remember the number of rural mail boxes he serviced but his route was about 106 miles every day, six days a week. Sitting in the middle of a bench seat, left foot for the brake and gas, right arm to roll the window down. Most all the roads he drove on were gravel and he kept the right window down most of the time. Very dusty in & out.

In the fifties I also remember the oil burning stove in the kitchen. If there were chicken hatchlings during the bitter winter they would be brought into the house next to the oil burning stove with a heat lamp over them. We had a small barn for the two horses, two pigs, a couple of geese, and a small brooder area for the young chickens where the baby fuzzy yellow chicks were under the heat lamp. There was also an open walled shelter with a slate roof in a small grove of trees behind the garage. The three-foot wire chicken hooks with a wooden handle were used to hook onto the legs of roosting chickens that would later be butchered. I remember the egg store that Dad would take and sell the excess eggs. They would put the eggs individually under a light to make sure it wasn't fertile before buying them.

Dad deer hunted every year. If not around our town he would deer hunt in northern Minnesota.

As a member of the Sportsman's Club, Dad was always at the top of his game when it came to shooting and fishing. A **1956** picture in the Belgrade paper shows Dad, Kenny Thompson and Harold Norris with 9 pheasant, 9 blue geese and 9 snow geese which was their total limit for the day. The paper was always a good avenue for residents to show their skills.

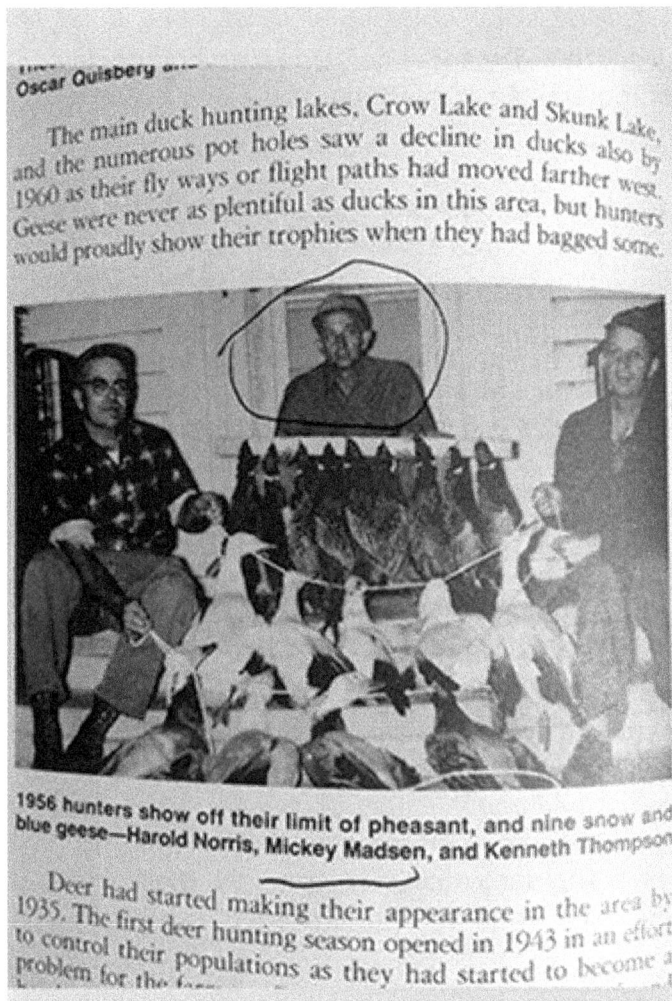

Oscar Quisberg...

The main duck hunting lakes, Crow Lake and Skunk Lake, and the numerous pot holes saw a decline in ducks also by 1960 as their fly ways or flight paths had moved farther west. Geese were never as plentiful as ducks in this area, but hunters would proudly show their trophies when they had bagged some.

1956 hunters show off their limit of pheasant, and nine snow and blue geese—Harold Norris, Mickey Madsen, and Kenneth Thompson

Deer had started making their appearance in the area by 1935. The first deer hunting season opened in 1943 in an effort to control their populations as they had started to become a problem for the f...

The Belgrade Tribune had this article. "Madsen Corners Contest Prizes" in the **1960** vermin hunting and fishing contests sponsored by the Belgrade Sportsman's Club winning the following categories; first prize in the gopher class and crow class of the hunting contest and first in largest northern, sunfish and crappie fishing. Donald Madsen won the largest walleye prize. The two other categories were fox and skunk won by Walter Lindner.

I got a hunting coat from Dad when I was about 12 years old (**1962**). The coat went to my knees and the sleeves were rolled half way up. I used that same coat until I moved away from home after college. The folded crease on the arms was very noticeable as I became older and grew into my hunting coat. My first gun was a 410-pump shotgun. The length of the gun was such that the stock had to fit under my armpit for the first few years.

483

I always will remember the hunting I got to enjoy with Dad, Uncle Archie, Uncle Donny, cousin Bruce, cousin Allen and others. Back then the pheasants and ducks around Belgrade were plentiful.

Duck season meant the wooden slatted ten-foot duck boat was my job to get ready. It was filled with water to expand the wooden joints against leakage. When the leaks stopped, it would be turned upside down and allowed to dry. When Dad deemed the boat dry enough, I would paint both the inside and outside with a dark green color.

Dad was known by everyone to be a great shot. He would always prove it whether duck or pheasant hunting. Doubles for him were not unusual. This is a fact from whoever hunted with Dad, including myself.

Crow Lake was about two miles long, east to west, and about a half mile wide. There was open water the length, a very muddy bottom, three feet of water and tall bulrushes surrounding the lake. Halfway the length of the lake was a point of bulrushes jutting out into the open water from the north side. We called this "Madsen Point". Every opening duck season cousin Bruce would be out there the night before to chase the other perspective hunters away. On opening day, the Madsen's had 4-5 boats around this point and about 150 duck decoys. The decoys were hollow, made of paper mache back then and painted. A string and weight were added to the loop on the bottom of the decoy to keep them from floating away. Uncle Donny was good at using his duck call when needed to bring the ducks to fly in over the decoys.

Uncle Archie kept his dog, a German Shorthair, in a dog house at our place. Brownie was great at pointing and holding the pheasants during our hunt for us to shoot and those birds were delicious to eat.

What a wonderful feeling I had growing up knowing how much I enjoyed all of my aunts, uncles, and cousins.

Brother Darrel was born in **1957**. Mom & Dad impressed upon their three children the belief in the advantages of hard work, thrift, a sense of responsibility, importance of saving and the love of the outdoors. Dad told Faye once, *"it is good to have to pay taxes because that means you are making money"*. Another important part of our upbringing was their desire to make sure we were baptized, attended church and were confirmed in the Lutheran faith all the while attending church. One of my most memorable trips was with the Luther League at age 15 to the Boundary Waters Canoe Area in northern Minnesota for ten days. Motorized boats were not allowed and there were no other humans during a five-day period. Several portages and a lot of wildlife.

✦ ✦ ✦ ✦

DD-214

DD Form 214 is a military service document and represents the complete, verified record of a service member's time in the military (Active and Reserve), awards and medals, and other pertinent service information, such as highest rank/rate and pay grade held on active duty, total military combat service and/or overseas service.

I submitted a DD-214 to the National Personnel Records Center in St. Louis, Missouri and this is the reply I received.

RE: *Veteran's Name:*   MADSEN, Elmer Leroy
       SSN/SN   *37162364*
       Request Number: *2-21176906094*

Dear Recipient:

Thank you for contacting the National Personnel Records Center. The Official Military Personnel File (OMPF) needed to answer your inquiry is not in our files. If the OMPF were here on July 12,1973, it would have been in the area that suffered the most damage in the fire on that date and may have been destroyed. The fire destroyed the major portion of records of Army military personnel for the period 1912 through 1959, and records of Air Force personnel with surnames Hubbard through Z for the period 1947 through 1963.

*An alternate record that is available for the veteran named in your request is a **Final Pay Voucher**. This particular document is an archival document belonging to the National Archives and is available to you for a fee. To help you decide if you would like to purchase the final pay voucher pertaining to the veteran named in your request, we are enclosing information about the document and a sample copy of an actual final pay voucher.*

*If you are interested in purchasing the final pay voucher, please complete the attached **Order for Archival Record Reproduction Services'** form. Please return this form with your payment within 30 days. Once payment is received, a photocopy of the final pay voucher will be mailed to you. If payment is not received within this period, we will assume that you do not wish to purchase the document and request will be closed automatically without further action.*

If you are interested in viewing available archival records in person, please contact the Archival Research Room at 314-801-0850 or stlarr.archives@nara.gov. An appointment to view the records must be made prior to your visit as at this time we cannot provide walk-in service. More information on the records available from the Archival Research Room can be found at http//www.archives.gov/st-louis/archivalprograms.

I was not interested in the Final Pay Voucher.

✦   ✦   ✦   ✦

I have been told my Dad was assertive and I am proud to have taken over that part of his personality. I learned a lot of life lessons from both my parents and will be forever grateful.

Mom & Dad always knew their children were special. They were always there for moral support while growing up and showering us with love from afar when we went our separate ways. My sister moved to Colorado and I ended up in Texas. My brother stayed in Minnesota. Our Dad continued to offer us advise and Mom used to say *"keep a stiff upper lip"* (meaning to show courage in the face of pain or adversity). Gosh, we sure loved our parents and we knew they loved us.

They enjoyed life and they enjoyed each other.

Mom & Dad

Dad Ice Fishing in Minnesota – January 1974

Compiled by - Merlin Madsen

Resources and Further Readings

-SOPACBACOM, The Bougainville Campaign, Chs. IV-IX, supplemented by rpts, jnls, and jnl files of XIV Corps, Americal Div, 37th Div, and the principal component units which participated;

-Maj Gen Oscar W. Griswold, Bougainville: An Experience in Jungle Warfare (type-script);

-ACofS G-2 XIV Corps, History of the "TA" Operation, Bougainville, March 1944 [21 Apr 44]; 8th Area Army Operations, Japanese Monogr No. 110 (OCMH), pp. 106-22;

-17th Army Operations, II, Japanese Monogr No. 40 (OCMH), 105-29;

-Capt. Francis D. Cronin, Under the Southern Cross:

-The Saga of the Americal Division (Washington: Combat Forces Press, 1951), pp. 143-68;

-Frankel, The 37th Infantry Division in World War II, pp. 141-70;

-Answers (27 Jul 49) of Gen Kanda [former CG, 6th Div] to questions by Hist Sec G-2 FEC, in

-Hist. Div MIS GHQ FEC, Statements of Japanese Officials on World War II

-OCMH. historyplace.com/unitedstates/pacificwar/timeline.htm

-M4 Sherman vs Type 97 CHI-HA. The Pacific 1945 by Steven J Zaloga.

-The War in the Pacific, Triumph in the Philippines by Robert Ross Smith

-U.S. Army Center of Military History by Stephen J. Lofgre;

-Japan's War and Defeat 1937-1949 by Sanderson Beck
       www.san.beck.org/21-9-japanswar1937-49.html

-The Belgrade Centennial book 1888-1988.

-Bill Ganzel of the Ganzel Group. First written and published in 2003

-John Miller, jr., CARTWHEEL: The Reduction of Rabaul, (1959)

-Ronald H. Spector, Eagle Against the Sun

-Eric Hammel, Munda Trail (1989)

-Harry A. Galley, Bougainville, 1943-1945: The Forgotten Campaign (1991)

-Louis Morton, Strategy and Command: The First Two Years, U.S. Army in World War II

-Samuel Eliot Morison, History of United States Naval Operations in World War 11, vol. 6,

-Breaking the Bismarcks Barrier: 22 July 1942 – 1 May 1944 (1950).

-Marines in World War II - Bougainville and The Northern Solomons ... by Major John N. Rentz USMR

-history.army.mil/brochures/northsol/northsol.htm

-The New York Times written by Nicholas D. Kristof Published: March 17, 1995

-Japan's War and Defeat 1937-1949 by Sanderson Beck

-The Second Battle of Bougainville by Captain John C. Guenther

-Minuteman: The Military Career of General Robert S. Beightler By John Kennedy Ohl

-Bougainville, 1943-1945: The Forgotten Campaign: By Harry A. Gailey

-Warfare History Network

-Graves Resignation Units by Mason B. Webb

-Scout.com/military/warrior/Article/33-Photos from the Battle for Okinawa

-Marine Corps Gazette Nov. 2012 Okinawa: The Final Great Battle of World War II. American triumph through bloodshed Vol 96, Issue 11: SSgt Rudy R. Frame, Jr.

-japantimes.co.jp/news/2015/03/10/national/deadly-wwii- - u-s-firebombing-raids-on-japanese-cities-largely-ignored

-https://donmooreswartales.com/2010/10/13/willard-chamberlin/

-patriotspoint.org/news-and-events/the-first-conscientious-objector-medal-of-honor-recipient/

-newenglandhistoricalsociety.com/u-boat-attacks-of-world-war-ii-6-months-of-secret-terror-in-the-atlantic/

-ww2-weapons.com/liberty-ship/#FtLDdMHIDrf6gRDh.99

-Eyewitness to History.com

-Sherrod, Robert, Tarawa: the Story of a Battle (1944)

-The Bloody Battle of Tarawa, 1943 Eye Witness to History, www.eyewitnesstohistory.com (2003)

-History WWII – Peleliu: The Forgotten Battle by Maj. Henry J. Donigan

-*Ernie's War: The Best of Ernie Pyle's World War II Dispatches,* edited by David Nichols, pp. 412-13. Pictures courtesy of The Lilly Library, Indiana University,

-The Office of Strategic Services America's First Intelligence Agency. Washington, D.C.: Public Affairs, Central Intelligence Agency, 2000

-CIA Library: Weapons & Spy Gear Archived February 21, 2014, at the Wayback Machine., *Historical Document*, March 15, 2007.

-Dogs at War: Caesar, One of the First Marine Dogs in the Pacific by Rebecca Frankel, for National Geographic

-Project Gutenberg's Leyte: The Return to the Philippines, by M. Hamlin Cannon

-pbs.org/thewar/at_home_communication_news_censorship.htm. With Katherine Phillips

-historynet.com/oak-ridge-the-town-the-atomic-bomb-built.htm

-defensemedianetwork.com/stories/torpedo-scandal-rear-adm-charles-lockwood-the-mark-14-and-the-bureau-of-ordnance/

-destroyerhistory.org

-nationalinterest.org/feature/japans-super-torpedo-was-the-hypersonic-missile-wwii/ by Michael Peck

-Japan's TA-Operation: A Blueprint for Disaster by Irwin J. Kappes

-Kerama Retto: Key to Victory at Okinawa by Pierre V. Comtois

-Banzai! The Compulsory Mass Suicide of Kerama Islanders in the Battle of Okinawa

-Kinjo Shigeaki interviewed by Michael Bradley Translation by Maehara Naoko

-markedbyteachers.com/gcse/sociology/social-and-cultural-change-after-ww2.html

-NY -NY Times, Unmasking Horror -- A special report.; Japan Confronting Gruesome War Atrocity. By Nicholas D. Kristof

-Louis Morton, Strategy and Command: The First Two Years, UNITED STATES ARMY IN WORLD WAR II

- Caltrap.org/history/bougainville

-Atomic Heritage.org

-The Battle of the Philippine Sea -- historylearningsite.co.uk. by C. N. Trueman

-Orlando Sentinel: Sept. 21, 2000: Rubber Tire Tracks Led to New Era in Farming by Joy Wallace Dickinson. Henry Swanson's book Countdown for Agriculture in Orange County, FL

Museums and Other Sources of interest to visit

National Museum of the Pacific War
                     Fredericksburg, TX.
the boyhood home of Fleet Admiral Chester W. Nimitz. I would spend a week here.

Smithsonian Museum and Monuments
                     Washington, DC.
I would spend a week+ here

Pearl Harbor historic sites:
                     Honolulu,   Hawaii
Pacific Historic Parks, WWII Valor in the Pacific National Monument, Battleship Missouri Memorial, USS Bowfin Submarine Museum & Park, Pacific Aviation Museum Pearl Harbor. I would spend a week+ here.

National World War II Museum
                     New Oleans, LA. I would
spend a week here

MacArthur Memorial
                     Norfolk, VA.
a memorial, museum and research center about the life of General Douglas MacArthur. It consists of three buildings on MacArthur Square.

National Guard Memorial Museum
                     Washington,   DC
Dedicated to telling the story of the citizen-soldier and the National Guard.

National Museum of the Marine Corps
                     Triangle, VA.

U.S. Army Aviation Museum
                     Fort Rucker, AL.

National Infantry Museum
                     Fort Benning, GA.

National Museum of the United States Air Force
                     Riverside, OH.
Wright-Patterson Air Force Base, Ohio

U.S. Naval Academy Museum
                     Annapolis, MD.

National Naval Aviation Museum
                     Pensacola, FL.

Home of the Blue Angels

Eldred World War II Museum
                     Eldred, PA.

Bradbury Science Museum
                     Los Alamos, NM.
artifacts and documents from the WWII Manhattan Project were displayed upon declassification. Other exhibits models of the Little Boy and Fat Man atomic bombs.

WWII Japanese American Internment Museum
                     McGehee, AR.

Heart Mountain War Relocation Center
                     Powell WY.

Rosie the Riveter/WWII Home Front Nat'l Historical Park, Richmond, CA.

The Scott Saewert War Museum   Prospect Heights, Ill.
Army Engineer Memorabilia Division is specific to the construction engineers in the Pacific Theater of Operations during World War II

You can visit military museums in every state of the union.

Google:

military and war museums in the U.S.

> **by state,**

> **by branch,**

> **by war.**

www.ingramcontent.com/pod-product-compliance
Lightning Source LLC
Chambersburg PA
CBHW061959090426
42811CB00006B/985